DEVELOPMENTAL PHYSICAL EDUCATION FOR TODAY'S ELEMENTARY SCHOOL CHILDREN

DEVELOPMENTAL PHYSICAL EDUCATION FOR TODAY'S ELEMENTARY SCHOOL CHILDREN

DAVID L. GALLAHUE

INDIANA UNIVERSITY

MACMILLAN PUBLISHING COMPANY
NEW YORK
COLLIER MACMILLAN PUBLISHERS
LONDON

Macmillan Publishing Company
866 Third Avenue, New York, New York 10022

Collier Macmillan Canada, Inc.

Library of Congress Cataloging-in-Publication Data

Gallahue, David L.
  Developmental physical education for today's elementary
school children.

  Includes index.
  1. Physical education for children.   2. Movement
education.   3. Motor learning.   4. Physical education
for children—Study and teaching.   I. Title.
GV443.G232   1987   372.8'6044   86-8599
ISBN 0-02-340380-2

Printing: 1 2 3 4 5 6 7 8   Year: 7 8 9 0 1 2 3 4 5

ISBN   0-02-340380-2

TO MARGIE HANSON
In Recognition of
a Lifetime of Dedication
to Children's Physical Education

PREFACE

Developmental Physical Education for Today's Elementary School Children has been written for undergraduate and graduate students taking a first course in elementary school physical education methods. The text is written from a developmental perspective and emphasizes the need to view children where they *are* in terms of their development rather than where they should be on the basis of chronological age or grade level. The text attempts to merge the more traditional activity orientation to elementary school physical education with the "newer" movement education perspective. This is done in a manner that is in harmony with the developmental nature of the child and congruent with a broad spectrum of educational philosophies.

The developmental approach advocated in Part I, "Background," focuses on movement skill development as the primary objective of the elementary physical education program. Fitness, perceptual–motor, and self-concept enhancement are other important outcomes of quality physical education, but the approach taken here stresses the importance of children learning to move with efficiency, control, and joy.

In order to teach developmentally, we must first understand the learner. Part II, "The Learner," emphasizes the process of movement skill acquisition in children. Skill learning is divided into the beginning, intermediate, and advanced levels in Chapter 6. These levels of movement skill learning are used throughout Part VI for grouping and presenting activities. Chapter 7, "Childhood Growth and Development," discusses several important factors affecting the processes of growth and development of children. "Children with Special Needs" is the topic of Chapter 8. A wide range of limiting conditions is discussed along with practical suggestions for including these children in the program. Part II concludes with Chapter 9, "Developmental Characteristics of Children." This chapter provides the reader with an overview of the psychomotor, cognitive, and affective characteristics of children during childhood. Implications for the developmental physical education program are included.

Part III is entitled "The Teacher." Chapter 10, "The Role of the Teacher," centers on the responsibilities, characteristics, and stages of concern of a teacher. Chapter 11, "Talking to Children," deals with verbal and nonverbal communication, improving communication skills, conveying enthusiasm, and listening to children. "Positive Discipline" is the topic of Chapter 12, which discusses a variety of techniques for maintaining class control and fostering self-control among children. Chapter 13, "Selecting and Using Appropriate Teaching Styles," deals with important factors that influence selection of various teaching approaches. Several styles are presented and analyzed in terms of their effectiveness with children at varying ability levels.

Part IV, "The Program," provides the reader with valuable practical information on how to develop the physical education program. Chapter 14, "The Developmental Physical Education Curriculum," carefully details the steps in the curricular process, using the developmental approach as an example. Chapter 15 outlines the steps in "Planning, Formatting, and Implementing the Lesson." Chapter 16, "Organizing the Learning Environment," provides helpful information on how to organize facilities and equipment. Preparing instructional aids and using student helpers are also discussed. "The Extended Curriculum" is the topic of Chapter 17. A variety of activities frequently the responsibility of the physical education teacher, in addition to the regular program, is discussed. This is followed by a chapter on "Legal Liability," Chapter 18. The conditions of liability and how to minimize one's exposure to liability are the central focus of this chapter. Chapter 19, "Assessing Progress," concludes this section. Both process and product assessment are presented, along with a discussion of the strengths and limitations of each. This chapter sets the stage for the skill theme chapters that follow in Part V.

Part V, "The Skill Themes," is in many ways the heart of the book. In Chapters 20 through 22 a variety of fundamental locomotor, manipulative, and stability skills are analyzed. Exploratory and guided discovery activity ideas are presented for each. Chapters 23 and 24 focus on "Stunts and Tumbling Skills" and "Apparatus Skills," respectively. Each skill is described, illustrated, and listed, from simple to complex. Suggestions are given for appropriate activities for children at various levels of movement skill learning. Chapters 25 through 29 ("Disc Sport," "Basketball," "Soccer," "Softball," and "Volleyball Skills") provide a sampling of appropriate sport skills to be included in the elementary program. Skills suitable for elementary school children in each of these sports are analyzed and a variety of warmup activities and skill drills are presented.

Parts VI, VII, and VIII are entitled "Games," "Rhythms," and "Self-Testing," respectively. Each part begins with a chapter on suggestions for teaching movement activities from that particular content area. These chapters are followed by several practical activity chapters. Each activity chapter provides the reader with a recommended sequence of progression for activity inclusion based on where children are developmentally. The objectives for each activity are listed along with the specific skills being developed or reinforced through participation.

As with any undertaking of this magnitude, there are numerous people to thank, for without their encouragement, support, and help, this effort would not have been possible. Therefore, I wish to thank my wife Ellie—for believing in me and giving me the "space." My children, David Lee and Jennifer—for being my inspiration. My typists, Laura Shipley and Debra Szemcsak—for their Olympian efforts. My dean, Tony Mobley—for giving me the time. My colleague and friend, Hal Morris—for being someone to talk with. My colleagues around the world—for their dedication to providing quality physical education programs for children. My graduate students—for their enthusiasm and quest for excellence. My editor, Lynne Greenberg—for her support and encouragement.

D. L. G.

CONTENTS

7 CHILDHOOD GROWTH AND MOTOR DEVELOPMENT 54

8 CHILDREN WITH SPECIAL NEEDS 61

9 DEVELOPMENTAL CHARACTERISTICS OF CHILDREN 77

PART III THE TEACHER 85

10 THE ROLE OF THE TEACHER 87

11 TALKING TO CHILDREN 95

12 POSITIVE DISCIPLINE 104

17 THE EXTENDED CURRICULUM 164

18 LEGAL LIABILITY 173

19 ASSESSING PROGRESS 183

PART V THE SKILL THEMES 191

20 FUNDAMENTAL LOCOMOTOR SKILLS 193

21 FUNDAMENTAL MANIPULATIVE SKILLS 236

22 FUNDAMENTAL STABILITY SKILLS 279

23 STUNTS AND TUMBLING SKILLS 299

24 APPARATUS SKILLS   319

25 DISC SPORT SKILLS   333

26 BASKETBALL SKILLS   344

27 SOCCER SKILLS 367

28 SOFTBALL SKILLS 388

29 VOLLEYBALL SKILLS 407

PART VI GAMES   423

30 TEACHING GAMES   425

31 LOW-LEVEL GAME ACTIVITIES   431

32 RELAY ACTIVITIES   443

33 LEAD-UP GAME ACTIVITIES   449

38 CREATIVE RHYTHMIC ACTIVITIES 498

39 FOLK AND SQUARE DANCE ACTIVITIES 507

PART VIII SELF-TESTING 525

40 TEACHING SELF-TESTING ACTIVITIES 527

41 PERCEPTUAL–MOTOR ACTIVITIES 531

42 HAND APPARATUS ACTIVITIES 559

43 FITNESS ACTIVITIES 570

PART I

BACKGROUND

CHAPTER 1

DEVELOPMENTAL PHYSICAL EDUCATION: WHY BOTHER?

Parents and teachers have become increasingly aware of the importance of providing children with meaningful movement experiences. There is a growing realization among educators that the vigorous physical activity engaged in by children plays an important role in their total development. For children, movement is at the very center of their life. It permeates all facets of their development, whether in the psychomotor, cognitive, or affective domains of human behavior. This chapter looks at the contributions that meaningful movement can make to each of these domains. This will set the stage for more extensive study of the potential outcomes of quality physical education for children in subsequent chapters. But first, a clear view on just what is meant by the terms *physical education* and *developmental education* is necessary.

WHAT IS PHYSICAL EDUCATION?

The aims of physical education have been stated by a variety of authors and leaders in the profession. Lofty ideals and flowery platitudes have often clouded the fact that the aims of physical education may be simply and succinctly stated as *learning to move* and *learning through movement*.

The learning-to-move aim of physical education is based on the recognition that the primary contributions of physical education lie in the area of movement skill and total fitness development. Physical education helps children learn to use their bodies more efficiently and knowledgeably in a wide variety of fundamental and sport-related movement skills. Furthermore, it makes positive contributions to children's physical fitness through promotion of an active lifestyle. Children's physical development is not simply a process of maturation; it relies heavily on both

WHAT IS DEVELOPMENTAL PHYSICAL EDUCATION?

Developmental physical education is that portion of the school day devoted to systematic instruction in the progressive acquisition of movement skills and physical abilities. It follows a progression of sequential skill acquisition and increased physical competency based on the developmental level of the individual. Developmental physical education recognizes that, although motor development is age-related, it is not age-dependent. Therefore, the movement activities engaged in by children in developmentally based physical education programs are geared to their stage of motor development and level of motor skill learning, rather than to their chronological age or grade level. Developmental physical education is not viewed as a frill or appendage that can easily be left out of the school program. The values of such programs that are well taught by dedicated teachers are seldom questioned by parents, colleagues, school boards, or taxpayers because the benefits of such programs are readily apparent.

Elementary school children are not miniature adults. Their needs, interests, and capabilities are considerably different from those of the adolescent and adult. Likewise, the developmental physical education program is not a recess or play period. It is a learning environment in which children are involved in the important task of learning to move and learning through movement. This learning is based on sound principles of child development and grounded in the needs, interests, and abilities of the individuals being served.

WHAT DOES DEVELOPMENTAL PHYSICAL EDUCATION CONSIST OF?

The unique contribution of physical education is in the realm of motor development. Physical education makes contributions to this area that no other type of education does, by enhancing

the quality and quantity of their movement experiences. Children must have abundant opportunities for practice, along with encouragement and quality instruction, if they are to learn to move with joy, efficiency, and control.

The learning-through-movement aim of physical education is based on the realization that the physical education program can make positive contributions to both the cognitive and the affective development of children. While children are learning to move, the understanding teacher is taking advantage of numerous opportunities to help them learn through movement. The cognitive and affective domains of human behavior are not separate and distinct from the psychomotor domain, as is often implied. They are closely related and complexly intertwined with the child's motor development and movement behavior.

both children's movement abilities and physical abilities. This does not, however, mean that physical education is limited to the motor domain alone. On the contrary, well-organized, well-taught, and developmentally appropriate movement experiences can make very real and positive contributions to cognitive and affective aspects of children's development.

More specifically, the primary objectives of developmental physical education are, first, in the area of movement skill acquisition and, second, in the area of fitness enhancement. Perceptual–motor, and social–emotional development are two other important objectives of the program.

Movement Skill Development

Movement skill development is at the very heart of the physical education program. With children, a movement skill refers to the development and refinement of a wide variety of fundamental movement skills and sport-related movement skills. These movement skills are developed and refined to a point that children are capable of operating with considerable ease and efficiency within their environment. As children mature, the fundamental movement abilities developed when they were younger are applied to a wide variety of games, sports,* and recreational activities that may be engaged in as a part of their daily life experiences. For example, the fundamental movement skill of striking an object in an underhand, sidearm, or overarm pattern is progressively developed and later utilized in numerous sports and recreational pursuits such as golf, tennis, and baseball.

Fundamental movement skills and sport skills may be categorized into broad and sometimes overlapping categories (Figure 1.1). These categories represent the primary focus of the developmental physical education program. Chapter 2, "Movement Skill Development," looks more

---

*The terms "sport" and "sport skills" are used throughout this text in the broadest sense and are not confined to athletics or athletic competition. Recreational and noncompetitive gross motor activities are viewed here as sport-related movement skills.

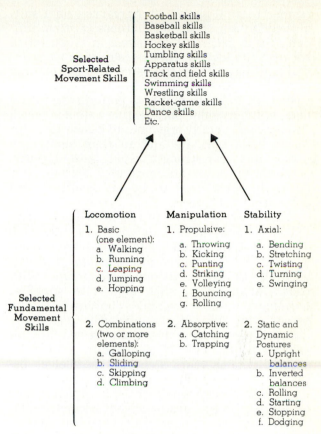

FIGURE 1.1 Fundamental movement skills must be developed and refined by the child prior to the introduction of sports skills by the teacher.

closely at the process by which children develop their fundamental and sport skill abilities. Development aspects of skill acquisition, as well as the influence of both heredity and experience, are discussed in relationship to developing and refining movement abilities.

Fitness Development

The fitness objective of developmental physical education deals with enhancing the ability of children to function within an environment that both requires and promotes the development of fitness. The term *fitness* may be viewed as possessing the elements of both physical fitness and motor fitness (Figure 1.2). Agreement on a suitable definition of physical fitness is often difficult and is generally described in broad terms because the level of fitness required of one individual may not be the same as that required of another. Hence, *physical fitness* is generally considered to be the ability to perform one's daily tasks without undue fatigue. It is a state in which ample reserves of energy should be available for recreational pursuits and to meet emergency needs. Muscular strength, muscular endurance, aerobic endurance, and muscular flexibility are generally considered to be the health-related components of fitness.

The concept of motor fitness is an elusive term that has been studied extensively over the past several years and is classified by some experts as an aspect of physical fitness. *Motor fitness* is generally thought of as one's performance abilities, influenced by such factors as speed of movement, agility, balance, coordination, and power. The generality and specificity of these abilities have been debated and researched for years, with the bulk of evidence in favor of its specificity. For years some let themselves believe that motor abilities were general in nature; as a result, the term *general motor ability* came into vogue. It was assumed that because an individual excelled in certain sports, corresponding ability would automatically be carried over to other activities. Although this often does occur, it is now considered to be a result of the individual's personal motivation, numerous activity experiences, and several specific sport aptitudes rather than direct carryover of skills from one activity to another. Simply stated, the notion of a "natural" athlete is not supported by the bulk of research on the topic.

Children's health-related and performance-related fitness play important roles in the development of total fitness. Chapter 3, "Fitness Development," deals with the potential fitness outcomes of the physical education program, as well as several other topics critical to helping children gain and maintain improved levels of fitness.

Perceptual–Motor Development

A variety of motor-training programs have been developed, claiming to enhance the cognitive functioning of children. The validity of these claims is speculative. To date, there has been little scientific support for the hypothesis that certain movement activities will have a *direct* affect on the cognitive functioning of children. This does not mean that the movement experiences engaged in by children during the physical education program cannot be effectively used as a medium for *learning through movement*. On the contrary, educators now recognize the importance of movement skill learning as a basic tool for enhancing the perceptual–motor abilities of children. In other words, movement can, through good teaching, be effectively used as a tool for enhancing children's awareness of themselves and the world around them. The proper use of the "teachable moment," along with emphasis on the development of the concepts of why, what, how, and when in relation to one's movement, play important roles in helping children learn by reinforcing information dealt with in the traditional setting of the classroom.

The development of perceptual–motor abilities is a process involving both maturation and experience. Not all children are at the same ability level upon entering school and, although little can be done about the maturational component of this process, parents and teachers can have an important influence on the experiential component.

FIGURE 1.2   The components of fitness dealt with in the Developmental Physical Education Program.

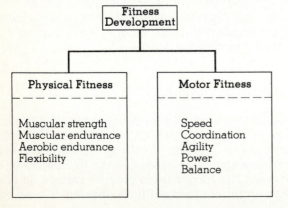

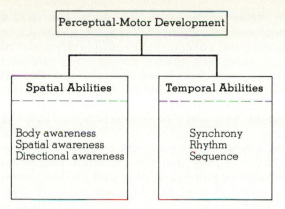

FIGURE 1.3 The components of perceptual-motor development dealt with in the Developmental Physical Education Program.

The development of perceptual–motor abilities involves the establishment and refinement of kinesthetic sensitivity to one's world through movement. This kinesthetic sensitivity involves the development and refinement of an adequate *spatial world* and *temporal world* (Figure 1.3). All movement occurs in space and involves an element of time. The development of these structures is basic to efficient functioning in a variety of other areas. For children's knowledge of their spatial world to be enhanced they need to be involved in movement activities designed to contribute to their body awareness, directional awareness, and spatial awareness. The temporal world of children may be correspondingly enhanced through activities that focus on synchrony, rhythm, and the sequencing of movements. Selected visual, auditory, and tactile abilities may be reinforced through movement in a variety of carefully selected activities. Chapter 4, "Perceptual-Motor Development," focuses more closely on the perceptual–motor objectives of the developmental physical education program.

Academic Concept Reinforcement

Movement activities can be used to enhance the understanding and application of academic concepts when they are integrated into the physical education program. Several authors have presented, in operational terms, how specific types of activities may be effectively used to enhance the acquisition of language arts competencies, basic mathematical operations, and social studies and science concepts (Figure 1.4). There are a variety of reasons why this occurs. Among them is the fact that active participation is fun. It is often a more natural approach that more closely approximates the needs and interests of children. Active participation in a game in which academic concepts are being dealt with makes it difficult for the child's attention to be diverted by extraneous stimuli. Also, a significant portion of today's children place high negative value on academic achievement but have a high positive regard for physical abilities. Using active games as a learning medium tends to pair pleasurable and highly regarded activity with that which may not be as highly valued, and thus tends to give more pleasure to the practice of the academic skill. Lastly, active learning through movement activities enables children to deal in concrete terms with their world rather than in the abstract.

Children generally regard movement as fun not to be equated with the routine "work" of the classroom. It should, however, be noted that not all children benefit best in the enrichment of their academic abilities through active participation in movement activities. On the contrary, there is an overwhelming amount of evidence indicating that the traditionally silent and relatively immobile form of thought and activity typical of the classroom is quite effective for many individuals. The point to be made here is that some

FIGURE 1.4 The components of academic concept reinforcement that may be dealt with in the Developmental Physical Education Program.

Academic Concept
Reinforcement

Science
Language arts
Mathematics
Social studies

children benefit greatly from a program that integrates movement activities with academic concept development and that most children will probably realize at least some improvement.

Social–Emotional Development

An important outcome of any quality physical education program is enhancement in the affective domain. Affective development involves dealing with children's increasing ability to act, interact, and react effectively with other people as well as with themselves. It is often referred to as "social–emotional development," and its successful attainment is of crucial importance to children. A good or poor parent, an affluent or culturally deprived environment, and the quality and quantity of stimulation given children will largely determine whether they view their world as one that they can control or as one that controls them.

The movement experiences engaged in by children play an important role in their view of themselves as individuals as well as how they are able to relate to their peers and utilize their free time. Astute parents and teachers recognize

the vital importance of balanced social–emotional development. They recognize the developmental characteristics of children and use these necessary understandings of behavior in enhancing children's *self-concept* and *play skill abilities* (Figure 1.5). This knowledge enables them to encourage and structure meaningful movement experiences that strengthen emotional and social development in accordance with children's needs, interests, and capabilities.

Children are active, energetic emerging beings. They are engrossed in play and utilize play experiences as a means of learning more about themselves and their bodies. The important beginnings of self-concept are formed during childhood. Children often view themselves on one end of two extremes—good or bad—in all that they do. Their egocentric nature does not permit them to view themselves objectively in light of their particular strengths and weaknesses. They are frequently unable to fully grasp the concept that one's abilities to do things lie somewhere between the self-limiting poles. Since their world is one of play and vigorous activity, the successes and failures they experience in this area are important in the establishment of their self-concept. Chapter 5, "Self-concept Development," further examines the nature of self-concept and the impact that teachers and movement activities can have on establishing a stable positive view of self.

FIGURE 1.5   The components of social-emotional development dealt with in the Developmental Physical Education Program.

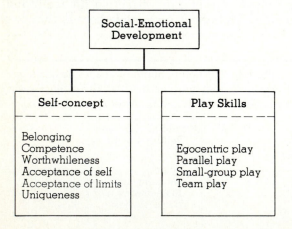

SUMMARY

The movement activities engaged in by children play an important role in their total development. Children are involved in the important and exciting task of learning to move effectively and efficiently through their world. They are developing a variety of fundamental movement and sport skill abilities and learning to move with joy, efficiency, and control. Children also learn through movement. Movement serves as a vehicle by which they explore all that is around

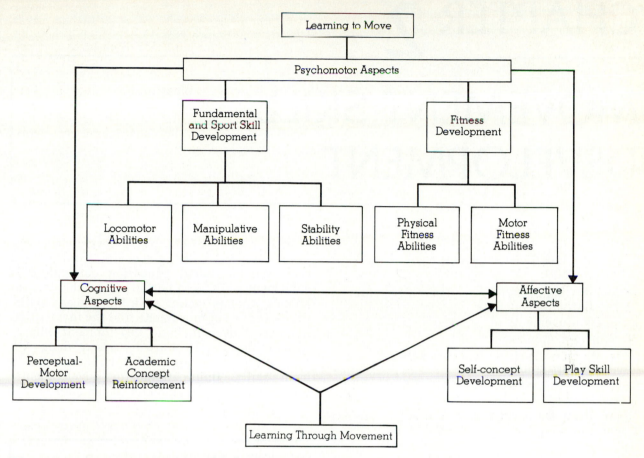

FIGURE 1.6 The aspects of the child's development dealt with in the Developmental Physical Education Program.

them. It aids in developing and reinforcing a variety of perceptual–motor abilities. Efficient movement contributes to social–emotional development by enhancing the self-concept and encouraging the worthy use of leisure time through constructive play. The interrelated nature of the psychomotor, affective, and cognitive aspects of development are readily apparent (Figure 1.6).

SUGGESTED READING

AAHPERD (1986). *Physical activity and well being.* Waldorf, MD: American Alliance Publications.

Bressan, Elizabeth S. (1986, February). Children's physical education: Designed to make a difference. *Journal of Physical Education, Recreation and Dance* 57:26–28.

Stull, G. Alan, and Eckert Helen, M. eds (1986). *Effects of physical activity on children.* Champaign, IL: Human Kinetics.

CHAPTER 2

MOVEMENT SKILL DEVELOPMENT

The unique and primary contribution of the elementary school physical education program is in the area of movement skill development. Although quality physical education contributes to other aspects of children's development, the primary objective of the developmentally based elementary physical education curriculum is movement skill acquisition. This chapter examines what is meant by a "movement skill," the categories of movement, and the factors that influence movement skill development. Phases of motor develolpment are discussed, along with the importance of developing children's movement skills. Implications for developmental physical education conclude the chapter.

WHAT IS A MOVEMENT SKILL?

Although used interchangeably, the terms *movement skill, fundamental movement skill, sport skill*, and *movement pattern* have important differences. A *movement skill* may be either a fundamental movement skill or a sport skill. It is a series of movements performed with accuracy and precision. In a movement skill, control of movement is stressed and extraneous movement is therefore limited.

A *fundamental movement skill* is an organized series of basic movements. Fundamental movement skills involve the combination of movement patterns of two or more body segments. Fundamental movement skills may be categorized as locomotor, manipulative, or stability movements. Running and jumping, striking and throwing, and twisting and turning are examples of fundamental movement skills from each of these categories. A *sport skill* is a fundamental movement skill or combination of fundamental movement skills that have been applied to the performance of a specific sport-related activity. Therefore, the fundamental movement skills of twisting the body and striking an object may be applied, in their horizontal form, to batting in the game of baseball or, in their vertical forms, to playing golf or serving a tennis ball.

A *movement pattern* is an organized series of related movements. More specifically, a movement pattern represents the performance of an isolated movement that in and of itself is too restricted to be classified as a fundamental movement skill or a sport skill. For example, the sidearm, underarm, or overarm patterns of movement alone do not constitute the fundamental movement skills of throwing or striking or the sport skills of pitching or batting in baseball. They merely represent an organized series of movements in which movement is stressed but accuracy, control, precision, and purpose are limited.

Developmental physical education recognizes the need to focus on the *process*, or mechanics, of movement skill acquisition prior to the *product*, or performance aspect of skill development. Physical educators who recognize the validity of developmental skill learning focus their teaching on the acquisition of fundamental movement skills and sport skills in a variety of locomotor, manipulative, and stability abilities.

WHAT ARE THE CATEGORIES OF MOVEMENT?

Movement skills may be subdivided into categories. A category of movement is a classificatory scheme based on common underlying components. As used here, the terms *locomotion, manipulation,* and *stability* represent these underlying components. These three categories, and their combinations, serve as the organizing centers of the developmentally based physical education curriculum.

Locomotor Movements

Locomotor movements are those in which the body is transported in a horizontal or vertical direction from one point in space to another. Such activities as running, jumping, hopping, leaping, and skipping are considered to be fundamental locomotor movements. Locomotor sport skill abilities represent an elaboration and further refinement of these fundamental skills at a higher level, as applied to specific sports. For example, the 50-yard dash, running the bases in softball, the triple jump in track, and running a pass pattern in football are all sport-related locomotor skills.

Manipulative Movements

Gross motor manipulative movements are those activities that involve giving force to objects or receiving force from objects. Throwing, catching, kicking, trapping, and striking are considered to be fundamental manipulative skills. Manipulative sport skills are an elaboration and further refinement of these basic skills. For example, hitting a tennis ball, throwing the javelin, catching a baseball, and playing the game of soccer all involve numerous manipulative skill abilities that are refinements of the fundamental tasks of striking, throwing, catching, and kicking, respectively.

Stability Movements

Stability movements are those in which the body remains in place but moves around its horizontal or vertical axes. In addition, they are also dynamic balance tasks in which a *premium* is placed on gaining or maintaining one's equilibrium in relationship to the force of gravity. For example, the forward roll in tumbling and dodging a ball are both considered to be stability abilities because of the strong emphasis placed on maintaining equilibrium throughout the task. Axial movements such as reaching, twisting, turning, bending, and stretching are fundamental stability abilities, along with lifting, carrying, pushing, and pulling. Other fundamental stability abilities involve a variety of positions involving inverted support, such as the tripod and headstand. Still others involve transitional postures, such as body rolling and springing movements. Stability abilities place emphasis on static (stationary) balance or dynamic (moving) balance. Sport skill abilities in tumbling and gymnastics, as well as in diving and figure skating, all focus on stability.

Movement Combinations

After children have mastered the basic elements of a fundamental movement, that movement is then combined with other skills. For example, rather than being content with jumping off the springboard and landing in a bent-knee position, children now want to jump off, land, and do a forward roll. Or they may want to jump with a half turn followed by a backward roll. As skill develops, these movement phrases become longer, more complex, and more refined.

Successful participation in most games and sports involves the combination of movements into sequences. For example, striking and running are combined into a phrase in baseball batting and base running, as are running, reaching, catching, and throwing in a typical baseball fielding sequence.

Movement skills, whether at the fundamental or sport skill phase of development, are generally learned best when first dealt with singularly. However, after the skill has been reasonably well mastered, it should be combined with others and used in dynamic gamelike situations. Purposeful movement is a series of coordinated phrases, not isolated, unconnected movements.

WHY BOTHER DEVELOPING CHILDREN'S MOVEMENT SKILLS?

Failure to develop and refine fundamental movement skills and sport skills during the crucial elementary years often leads to frustration and failure during adolescence and adulthood. Failure to develop mature patterns in throwing, catching, and striking, for example, makes it quite difficult to experience success and enjoyment in even a recreational game of softball. One can not take part, with success, in an activity if the essential movement skills contained within that activity have not been learned.

This does not mean that if the skills are not learned during childhood that they cannot be developed later in life. However, the individual is often beyond the critical period of childhood during which it is easiest to develop these skills, and as a result they too often remain unlearned. Several factors contribute to this situation. One is an accumulation of bad habits from improper learning. Learned behaviors, whether they take the form of correct or incorrect performances, are difficult to erase. It is much more difficult to "unlearn" faulty movements than to learn to do them correctly in the first place. Self-consciousness and embarrassment are a second factor. "I have two left feet," "I'm all thumbs," or "What a clutz" are all derogatory phrases frequently used to describe poor performance. A third factor causing many movement skills to remain unlearned is fear. Fear of being injured, or the fear of peer ridicule, are very real anxieties that often contribute markedly to difficulty in learning movement skills later in life. Therefore, it is crucial that children fully develop their fundamental movement abilities and a variety of basic sport skill abilities during the elementary school years.

FACTORS INFLUENCING MOVEMENT SKILL DEVELOPMENT

Historically, an erroneous assumption has been made by many educators that children somehow "automatically" develop their movement abilities as a result of maturation. Therefore, the physical education period, particularly during the primary grades, was often viewed as little more than a glorified recess period, in which an endless variety of games was played with little more reason than that they were fun or that they contributed to other social-emotional objectives. Little serious consideration was given to using the primary grades as a time for helping children master their fundamental movement abilities or using the upper grades to introduce children to a wide variety of sport skills. Elementary school physical education was instead viewed as a time to get away from the pressures of the classroom, have fun, and "blow off steam".

It is now widely recognized that experience does play a very important role in movement skill acquisition and that children need frequent *opportunities for practice, encouragement*, and *instruction* in order to develop and refine their movement abilities. The preschool and early elementary years are recognized as critical years for mastering fundamental movement abilities. Maturation alone will not account for this development. Children in the intermediate and upper elementary grades who have mastered these skills are then ready to begin the exciting process of developing sport skills and applying them to a wide variety of sport and recreational activities for a lifetime of vigorous movement.

Opportunity for Practice

Three factors play a crucial role in children's opportunities for practice in the development of their movement skills: *facilities*, *equipment*, and *time*. With regard to facilities, many children live in the congested atmosphere of the city. They live in high-rise apartments, cramped housing complexes, or sprawling suburbs, all of which frequently lack sufficient facilities to meet their need to move. There is often little space to play ball, fly a kite, or play a game of tennis. Frequently, facilities that have been set aside for public use are highly contested for by children, adolescents, and adults. All too often, the needs and interests of children are preempted by older individuals. As a result, children are left to fend for themselves in the pursuit of vigorous movement experiences.

Opportunities for practice are frequently limited by a lack of proper equipment. The cost of basketballs, baseball gloves, and hockey sticks, for example, is high. Parents and community centers often find it prohibitively expensive to purchase sufficient amounts and varieties of equipment for children to use.

PHOTO 2.1   Skillfull movement requires opportunity for practice, encouragement, and instruction.

A third factor, time, is frequently the most potent influence on opportunities for practice. Many children simply do not have the time to develop their movement skills. Their day is so highly programmed with school, television, and homework that little time is left for active movement.

If children do in fact need ample opportunities for practice in order to develop their movement abilities, we must then seek means of providing for appropriate facilities, equipment, and time. The elementary physical education program provides the best avenue of insuring opportunities for all children. The need for *daily* physical education has been endorsed by both the American Alliance for Health, Physical Education, Recreation and Dance (AAHPERD); the American Medical Association (AMA); and their Canadian counterparts. However, daily physical education is still not a reality in most North American schools. Continued efforts at providing daily physical education are necessary if we are to insure ample opportunities for all.

Encouragement

Many children do not receive sufficient encouragement to develop their movement abilities. The fast-paced society of today is often one in which both father and mother are employed. A frequent result is that neither parent has the time or the energy for active physical involvement with their children. Children learn by example and are quick to imitate Mom and Dad in their pursuit of the "good life"—the "workaholic" work ethic that leaves little time for family activities, leisure, and purposeful recreational pursuits. Children are frequently part of a family in which the cares of the workday are left behind, to be replaced by the mind-dulling escape of the television set or other passive activities. Failure to stimulate, encourage, and motivate children to active involvement in physical activity because of a lack of energy, interest, or personal example results in the failure of many children to develop their movement abilities.

Instruction

The instruction given to children is the third crucial factor influencing development of their movement skills. Opportunities for practice and encouragement alone will not account for the development of skillful movement in most children. Instruction is a key element. You, the teacher, are a *necessary* ingredient in movement skill acquisition. Without you, many children will never develop their fundamental movement or their sport skill abilities. The elementary school physical education program is the only place where it can be *guaranteed* that each child will receive the encouragement, opportunities for practice, and quality instruction so vital to movement skill development.

FUNDAMENTAL MOVEMENT SKILL PHASE*

The period ranging from about two to seven years of age is the ideal time for children to master fundamental locomotor, manipulative, and stability skills. These movement skills may be viewed as developing along a continuum of stages within this phase, progressing from the *initial* to the *elementary* and finally to the *mature stage* (Figure 2.1). A wide variety of fundamental locomotor, manipulative, and stability skills is described and pictured in Chapters 20 through 23.

Initial Stage

At the initial stage of developing a fundamental skill, children make their first observable and purposeful attempts at performing the task. This stage is characterized by relatively crude, uncoordinated movements. Valid attempts at throwing, catching, kicking, jumping, and so forth are made, but major components of the mature pattern are missing. Also, rhythmically coordinated execution of the movement is absent. Two- and three- year-olds are typically seen to function at the initial stage.

Elementary Stage

The elementary stage of fundamental movement skill development is typical of the performance of three- and four-year-olds. The elementary stage of development appears to be primarily dependent upon maturation. It is a transitional period between the initial and mature stages, in which coordination and rhythmical performance improve, and children gain greater control over their movements. However, movements at this stage still appear somewhat awkward and lacking in fluidity.

*The phases of motor development are classified as the reflexive phase, rudimentary phase, fundamental movement phase, and sport-related skill phase. For a detailed discussion of each of these phases, see Gallahue, D. L. (1982). *Understanding motor development in children.* New York: Wiley.

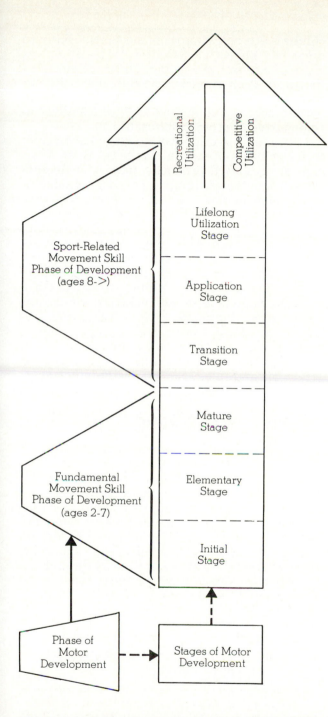

FIGURE 2.1   The fundamental and sport-related phases of motor development and their corresponding stages.

Many adults are only at the elementary stage in such basic activities as throwing, striking, and catching. They have progressed to this stage primarily through maturation but, because of insufficient encouragement, instruction, and practice, have failed to achieve the mature stage.

Mature Stage

A mature fundamental movement skill is characterized by integration of all the component parts of a pattern of movement into a well-coordinated, mechanically correct, efficient act. From this stage, performance improves rapidly. Children are, for example, able to throw farther, run faster, and jump higher after the mature stage has been attained. A mature fundamental skill may be continually refined, combined with other movement skills, and utilized in a variety of sport-related activities.

The mature stage can be attained in most fundamental movements by age six or seven. However, children reach this stage at varying rates. Some may be delayed, or they may fail to achieve the mature stage in various skills. Others may be advanced and reach this stage more rapidly. It is important to keep in mind that if development is delayed over a period of years, certain skills may never be attained in their mature form without considerable effort and outside influence.

SPORT-RELATED MOVEMENT SKILL PHASE

Around the seventh year, most children begin to develop a keen interest in sport. Boys and girls alike select their favorite sports heroes, don football jerseys and baseball caps, select their favorite running shoes, and frequently carry a basketball or a baseball glove to school. They are eager to learn new skills and apply them to a wide variety of sport activities. Efficient sports skill development is based on proper development of fundamental movement abilities. Although it begins in childhood, sport skill development frequently continues on through adolescence and into adulthood. The sport-related movement skill phase of development may be subdivided into the *transition, application* and *lifelong utilization stages* (Figure 2.1) A wide variety of sport-related movement skills is described and pictured in Chapter 23 through 29.

Transition Stage

The transition stage of sport skill development begins around seven years of age and extends to about the tenth year. Children at this stage generally have a high degree of expressed interest in many sports but little actual ability in any. If they have not developed mature skills during the fundamental movement phase, children *will* be hampered in sport skill acquisition. Children are eager to learn a variety of sports, and the physical education program should introduce sport skills and the basic elements of a wide variety of sport-related activities, but only after the mature stage has been reached in corresponding fundamental movement skills. Children should be given opportunities during the transition stage to further refine specific fundamental movements and to use them as sport skills in a variety of skill drills and lead-up activities. For example, the fundamental movement skill of kicking may be applied to the sport skill of using the instep kick in soccer. This skill may be practiced in drill situations and then applied to a lead-up activity such as line soccer, circle soccer, or six-a-side soccer. At the transition stage, children should not play the official sport as part of the instructional physical education program. Rather, they should be exposed to the basic skills, rules, and strategies of several sports through skill drills and a variety of lead-up activities.

Application Stage

The application stage is typified by the middle school or junior high school student, from about eleven to thirteen years of age. However, with the surge of participation throughout North America in youth sport programs, this stage may actually begin much earlier for many. Many children are applying their movement skills to organized sports participation as early as six years of age, or even sooner. The key element at the application stage is that sufficient skill and knowledge of the game have been developed to permit meaningful application of the activity to competitive or recreational settings.

Children at the application stage have begun to select types of sports that they prefer. Preferences are based primarily on previously successful experiences; body type; geographical location; and emotional, social, and cultural factors. Some may prefer individual sports, while others may prefer team sports. Some may enjoy contact sports, whereas others may prefer noncontact sports. Some may particularly enjoy water sports; others, court sports; and still others, dance activities. The narrowing of interests at this stage is accompanied with an increased desire for competence. Form, precision, accuracy, and standards of good performance are all important to the learner at the application stage. Therefore, more complex skills are practiced, and strategies and rules take on greater importance.

Lifelong Utilization Stage

The lifelong utilization stage is the final stage within the sport-related movement phase of development. This stage is based on previous sport and fundamental skill stages and continues throughout life. It is a period during which individuals select activities they particularly enjoy and utilize them as lifetime pursuits for fun, fitness, and fulfillment. At this stage, high interest in specific activities is evidenced through active participation on a regular basis, whether on a competitive or recreational level.

IMPLICATIONS FOR DEVELOPMENTAL PHYSICAL EDUCATION

Knowledge that fundamental and sport skill development is dependent upon environmental factors such as practice, encouragement, and quality instruction has vital implications for the physical education of children. For the vast majority of children, personalized, developmentally appropriate instruction is essential. This instruction must be coupled with sufficient time for practice in skill learning and the use of positive reinforcement techniques to continually encourage the learner.

As stated earlier, the process of movement skill development is age-related; it is *not* age-dependent. Skill acquisition is highly individualized because of the unique hereditary and experiential background of each child. Therefore, it is inappropriate to classify movement activities by age or by grade level; such a procedure violates the principle of individual differences. Care should be taken to select movement experiences based on the *ability level* of children, in terms of both their phase of movement skill development and their level of movement skill learning. (The levels of movement skill learning are discussed separately in Chapter 6). The use of approximate ages for the phases of motor development and their corresponding stages serves only as a guideline to the functioning of the majority of children. Some children may be significantly ahead of schedule, and others may be behind.

Frequently there are differences in movement skill development within the same child. For example, it is entirely possible for an eight-year-old to be highly skilled and functioning at the application stage in swimming or gymnastics, two popular age-group sports, and still be only at the initial or elementary stage in fundamental manipulative skills such as throwing, catching, and running. Although we should continue to encourage accelerated behavior in one area, we should be certain that the individual develops at least an acceptable level of proficiency in all aspects of movement. The developmentally based instructional physical education program provides for the *balanced* movement skill development of *all* children.

SUGGESTED READING

Gallahue, D. L. (1982). *Understanding motor development in children*. New York: Wiley.

Keogh, Jack, and Sugden, David (1985). *Movement skill development*. New York: Macmillian.

Mielke, Dan, and Morrison, Craig (1985, November/December). Motor development and skill analysis: connections to elementary physical education. *Journal of Physical Education, Recreation and Dance*.

Robertson, M. A., and Halverson, L. E. (1984). *Developing children—their changing movement: A guide for teachers*. Philadelphia: Lea & Febiger.

Thomas, J. R. (1984). *Motor development during childhood and adolescence*. Minneapolis: Burgess.

Wickstrom, Ralph L. (1983). *Fundamental motor patterns*. Philadelphia: Lea & Febiger.

CHAPTER 3

FITNESS DEVELOPMENT

lenged the validity of these studies and questioned the generalizations made from them, it is clear that much needs to be done to improve youth fitness and to heighten public awareness of the importance of fitness in children. The popular belief that children get plenty of regular, vigorous physical activity as a natural part of their everyday routine is little more than a myth for millions of youngsters. Although there is a heightened awareness among adults of the need for and benefits of vigorous physical activity, there has been only limited trickle-down of this fitness boom to the daily routines of children. Much needs to be done to eliminate this disgraceful situation. The improvement of youth fitness should be a national priority.

This chapter examines what is meant by the term *physical fitness* and its various components. The importance of fitness development in children, along with factors that influence the extent and degree of fitness, is discussed. A discussion of the role of fitness testing and the process of motivating children to an active way of life highlight this chapter, along with specific implications for the teacher.

Physical fitness is a topic of continuing interest throughout the world. In recent years professional as well as lay literature has devoted considerable coverage to the fitness status of youth. This was brought about largely by the results of studies comparing the physical fitness of youth over the past 30 years. These studies reveal that American boys and girls are in no better physical condition than their counterparts of 10, 20, and even 30 years ago. Although some have chal-

WHAT IS PHYSICAL FITNESS?

Physical fitness is a positive state of well-being influenced by (1) regular, vigorous physical activity; (2) genetic makeup; and (3) nutritional adequacy. The health status of the individual suggests the upper and the lower limits of physical fitness that can reasonably be expected. The in-

Muscular Strength

The ability to perform one maximum effort.

Muscular Endurance

The ability to perform a movement task over an extented period of time.

Aerobic Endurance

The ability of the heart, lungs, and vascular system to function efficiently at a high rate for an extended period of time.

Flexibility

The range of motion of the various joints of the body.

FIGURE 3.1   Health related components of fitness.

dividual's nutritional status will greatly inhibit or enhance the level of physical functioning. The genetic structure of the individual sets the upper limits of fitness that can be attained. All three factors should be considered in the development and maintenance of children's fitness.

Physical fitness has two aspects: health-related fitness, and performance-related fitness.

Health-related fitness is a relative state of being. It is *not* an ability, skill, or capacity. Health-related fitness is transient, genetically independent, and unrelated to athletic skill. The development and maintenance of health-related fitness is a function of physiological adaptation to increased overload. Therefore, it is readily alterable with use or disuse. On the other hand, the performance-related components of fitness *are* genetically dependent, relatively stable, and related to athletic skill. The performance-related components of fitness are generally referred to as one's motor fitness abilities, or simply as motor abilities.

WHAT ARE THE COMPONENTS OF FITNESS?

Muscular strength, muscular endurance, aerobic endurance, and *flexibility* are generally considered to be the health-related components of fitness. Each is briefly discussed in the following sections and summarized in Figure 3.1. The performance-related components of fitness, *coordination, agility, speed of movement, power,* and *balance* are summarized in Figure 3.2., and briefly discussed.

PHOTO 3.1   Muscular endurance is an important component of fitness.

Muscular Strength

Muscular strength may be defined as the ability of the body to exert a maximum force against an object external to the body. In its purest sense, it is the ability to exert one maximum effort. Children engaged in daily active play are doing much to enhance their leg strength by running and bicycling. Their arm strength is developed through such activities as lifting and carrying large objects, handling tools, and swinging on the monkey bars.

Muscular Endurance

Muscular endurance is the ability to exert force against an object external to the body for several repetitions. Muscular endurance is similar to muscular strength in the activities performed but differs in emphasis. Strength-building activities require overloading the muscle or group of muscles to a greater extent than endurance activities. Endurance-building activities require less of an overload on the muscles but require a greater number of repetitions. Boys and girls performing several situps, pullups, or pushups are performing muscular endurance activities.

When we speak of relative endurance, we are referring to the child's fitness level adjusted for body weight. It stands to reason that the adult's gross level of fitness is greater than that of children, but when one's body weight is divided into the total fitness score, the differences are much less pronounced.

Aerobic Endurance

Aerobic endurance, or circulatory–respiratory endurance as it is sometimes called, is specific to the heart, lungs, and vascular system. It refers to the ability to perform numerous repetitions of an activity requiring considerable use of the circulatory and respiratory systems. It is difficult to accurately measure the volume of oxygen utilized in aerobic activities with children without the use of sophisticated scientific equipment and considerable stress on the child. We do know, however, that children are *not* as

FIGURE 3.2   Performance related components of fitness.

Coordination

The rhythmical integration of motor and sensory systems into a harmonious working together of the body parts.

Speed

The ability to move from one point to another in the shortest time possible over a short distance.

Agility

The ability to move from point to point as rapidly as possible while making successive movements in different directions.

Power

The ability to perform one maximum explosive effort.

Balance

The ability to maintain one's equilibrium in relationship to the force of gravity in both static and dynamic movement situations.

active, on the whole, as they need to be in order to develop good aerobic endurance. Aerobic endurance is dependent, in large part, on the lifestyle of the individual child. The keys to developing aerobic endurance are frequency, duration, and intensity. The greater the frequency, the longer the duration, and the more intense the workout, the greater the impact will be on improving aerobic endurance. Activities such as running, peddling a bicycle, and swimming are all aerobic in nature and should be a part of the daily life experiences of children.

Flexibility

Joint flexibility is another aspect of physical fitness. It is the ability of the various joints of the body to move through their full range of motion. Flexibility is joint-specific and can be improved with practice. Most children are involved in numerous flexibility-developing activities. Their constant bending, twisting, turning, and stretching, along with the natural elasticity of their bodies, account for much of their flexibility. One needs only to look at the contorted positions that children sit in while watching television or listening to a story to realize that they have a good deal of flexibility in the hip and knee-joint areas. All too often, however, the range of motion diminishes in later childhood and adolescence due to lack of activity.

Motor Fitness Abilities

One's motor fitness abilities are an aspect of fitness and are considered to be related to the quality of one's movement performance. Children who display skill in several activities such as bicycling, swimming, throwing, catching, and climbing are said to possess good motor abilities. Motor abilities related to fitness include coordination, speed, agility, power, and balance (Fig. 3.2).

Coordination.   Coordination is the ability to integrate separate motor systems with varying sensory modalities into efficient movement. The harmonious working together of the synchrony,

rhythm, and sequencing aspects of one's movements is crucial to coordinated movement. Various parts of the body may be involved, such as eye–foot coordination, as in kicking a ball or walking upstairs. Eye–hand coordination is evident in fine motor activities such as bead stringing, tracing, and clay modeling or in gross motor activities such as catching, striking, or volleying a ball.

Speed.   Speed is the ability to move from one point to another in the shortest time possible. It is influenced by one's *reaction time* (the amount of time elapsed from the signal "go" to the first movement of the body) and *movement time* (the time elapsed from the initial movement to completion of the activity). Reaction time is generally considered to be innate, but movement time may be improved with practice. Children's speed of movement may be seen in activities such as running, climbing, and playing tag. Speed of movement may be improved by providing ample opportunities for practice and open spaces in which to run and play.

Agility.   Agility is the ability to change direction accurately while the body is moving from one point to another as fast as possible. This ability may be enhanced in children through participation in chasing and fleeing games and through certain dodging activities. Working through mazes and obstacle courses also aid agility development.

Power.   Power is the ability to perform one maximum effort in as short a period as possible. It is sometimes referred to as "explosive strength" and represents the product of strength times speed. This combination of strength and speed is exhibited by children when jumping, striking, or throwing for distance. The speed of contraction of the muscles involved, as well as the strength and coordinated use of these muscles, determines the degree of power.

Balance.   Balance is a complex aspect of one's motor abilities. It is influenced by vision, the inner ear, the cerebellum, the nerve endings around the joints (proprioceptors), and the skeletal muscles. Balance is the ability to maintain one's equilibrium in relation to the force of gravity. It is the ability to make minute alterations in one's body position when it is placed in various positions. Balance may be subdivided into static and dynamic balance. *Static balance* is the ability to maintain one's equilibrium in a fixed position, such as when standing on one foot or on a balance board. *Dynamic balance* is the ability to maintain one's equilibrium while the body is in motion, such as when walking on a balance beam and bouncing on a trampoline. In actuality, all movement involves an element of either static or dyamic balance, because balance is a basic aspect of all movement. As such, it is important for children to begin developing their balancing abilities at an early age.

WHY BOTHER DEVELOPING CHILDREN'S FITNESS?

Vigorous physical activity is necessary in childhood because exercise stimulates bone growth, develops lung capacity, aids in blood circulation, lowers blood pressure, and reduces cholesterol levels. Physical fitness contributes to a heightened self-concept, improved body image, sense of personal accomplishment, and self-discipline. It may also contribute indirectly to academic achievement. Children are more alert and tend to pay more attention to their classwork when they are physically fit. Furthermore, physical fitness helps prepare one for physical and emotional emergencies and aids in weight control.

Obesity and weight problems are found in children as well as in adults and should be of concern to parents and teachers. Inactivity is a more relevant factor than overeating in childhood obesity. Physical activity plays an important role in controlling one's weight. The obese child has less energy for vigorous activity and leads a more sedentary life. Although the total number of calories consumed by obese children may be no more, or may be even less, than non-obese children, because of the low level of physical activity, weight is actually gained.

FACTORS INFLUENCING FITNESS DEVELOPMENT

Certain factors play a major role in the improvement and maintenance of physical fitness. The following factors should be taken into consideration when determining the type of fitness program to establish and the amount of activity children should do.

Intensity

In order to increase fitness, a person must perform more work than he or she is generally accustomed to doing. This may be accomplished by either increasing the amount of work done or by reducing the time period in which the same amount of work is accomplished. An *overload* of the specific system enhances one's level of fitness. The amount of overload must be progressively increased in order to promote continual fitness improvement.

Specificity

Improvement in the various aspects of fitness is specific to the type of training engaged in and to the muscles being exercised. Even though the components of fitness and the various systems of the body are related, specific types of training result in developing specific qualities of fitness and produce greater amounts of change in the parts exercised. Strength activities, for example, will not have much influence on improving muscular or aerobic endurance. Coordination is not markedly improved through performance of pushups, and the shoulder-girdle muscles are not measurably strengthened by running or playing a game of soccer. Because of the needs of the total child, the fitness training program should contain several types of exercises.

Frequency of Exercise

Frequent use of a body part in various activities will either improve its efficiency or help it remain at about the same state. Failure to use the body part will cause it to diminish its efficiency. Muscles that are used regularly will hypertrophy, or increase in size, whereas muscles that are not used regularly will atrophy, or decrease in size. This can be aptly demonstrated by observing an arm or leg that has just been removed from a plaster cast. The limb is loose, flaccid, and smaller than its counterpart. Consistent use promotes improvement, while disuse leads to deterioration.

Individuality

Each person improves in level of fitness at his or her own rate. This is due to several factors, such as age, body type, nutritional status, body weight, health status, and level of motivation. There are no criteria for individual rates of improvement, and each child responds in a manner peculiar to his or her own particular environmental and hereditary characteristics.

FITNESS TESTING

Fitness testing is common in most schools. The results of these tests are used for (1) determining the physical status of students, (2) identifying those who are deficient in certain areas and need special help, (3) classifying students, (4) measuring progress, and (5) aiding in activity selection and program planning. The results of each child's performance on tests of fitness should be placed in the cumulative record and made available to parents. Parents should be encouraged to promote activities for their children that will help overcome deficiencies in fitness level. It is encouraging to note that many adults are eager to do whatever they can to help improve their child's physical functioning. Therefore, it is strongly urged that fitness test results and recommendations regarding each child be sent home for parent review.

When selecting a fitness test for inclusion in the program, you should be sure that it suits your purposes and meets certain criteria. Information concerning reliability, objectivity, validity, norms, and ease of administration should be readily available. A test that has *reliability* is one that measures whatever it is measuring consistently. A test with *objectivity* yields the same results even though it may be administered by different teachers. A test with *validity* is one that measures what it is supposed to measure and not something else. *Norms* are standards of performance that have been established in order that comparisons may be made within groups of children and between groups of children. Norms may be established on a school, city, state, or national basis, and they permit the teacher to judge pupils' performances in relation to other students' performances. A test that has *administrative feasibility* is one that can be given in a reasonable amount of time with a minimal amount of equipment.

Physical fitness tests can play an important role in the total program if the results of these tests are used to aid the teacher, pupil, and parent in improving children's level of fitness, their attitude toward the importance of physical fitness, and their knowledge of how to achieve improved levels of fitness.

The AAHPERD Youth Fitness Test and the AAHPERD Health-Related Physical Fitness Test are the most popular tests of fitness used in the United States today. Other measures, such as the Revised–AAU Physical Fitness Test and the Manitoba Physical Performance Test, are also popular across North America. A listing of popular tests of fitness and their components is located in Table 3.1. In addition to these widely used tests, there are several other worthwhile measures that have been developed by various agencies and school systems for local use.

MOTIVATING CHILDREN

During their early years, children are usually eager to participate in active play activities. Too often it is assumed that since young children do participate in play activities during their spare

TABLE 3.1 Popular Tests of Fitness

Fitness Test	Norms	Test Items	Fitness Components Measured
AAHPERD Youth Fitness Test American Alliance Publications P.O. Box 704 Waldorf, MD 20601	Ages 10–17	Distance Run Sprint Run Shuttle Run Standing Long Jump Situps Flexed-Arm Hang/Pullups	Aerobic Endurance Speed Agility Explosive Power Abdominal Endurance Arm/Shoulder Strength
AAHPERD Health-Related Physical Fitness Test American Alliance Publications P.O. Box 704 Waldorf, MD 20601	Ages 6–17	Distance Run Skinfold Measurement Situps Sit and Reach	Aerobic Endurance Body Composition Abdominal Endurance Flexibility
AAU Physical Fitness Test Indiana University 160 HPER Building Bloomington, IN 47405	Ages 6–17	Bent-knee Situps Pullups (boys) Flexed-Arm Hang (girls) Endurance Run Sit and Reach Optional Items are Also Included	Abdominal Endurance Arm/Shoulder Strength Arm/Shoulder Strength Aerobic Endurance Flexibility
Manitoba Physical Fitness Performance Test Manitoba Department of Education 411 Portage Avenue Winnipeg, Manitoba R36 OT3	Ages 5–18	Situps Sit and Reach Flexed-Arm Hang Agility Run Distance Run Skinfold Measurement	Abdominal Endurance Flexibility Upper-Body Endurance Agility Aerobic Endurance Body Composition

time, they do not need an instructional program of skill and fitness development. When this attitude is taken, the teacher often neglects to teach movement skills that are necessary for participation in vigorous physical activities. Children will participate in those activities in which they have developed sufficient skills to enjoy participation. By developing their movement skills, children can gain and maintain improved levels of fitness.

In addition to providing challenging experiences, teachers need to provide a great range of activities. By getting to know students and assessing their interests and abilities, you can plan activities that are appealing to children. This is important because it can help prevent experiences that are unsuccessful, frustrating, and not enjoyable. A positive attitude toward participation in vigorous physical activities is essential if children are to remain motivated toward an active way of life.

It is important to have a planned program and not leave physical activity to chance. Physical fitness is accomplished through regular, systematic, intense participation in vigorous activities. Some activities contribute more to one aspect of fitness than others. Therefore, a variety of activities is needed. It is important to provide many types of activities that interest children and motivate them to exercise on a regular basis. Activities that can be performed for a few minutes or for a long period of time, with others or alone, are important in the planning of fitness-building activities that children can do at home. It is helpful to give the children fitness challenges that they can practice or perform after school hours. Fitness "homework" consisting of several exercises to be performed while watching television can be used as a motivational tool.

Another area in which you can have an influence is that of parent education. Many parents are concerned when their child is not physically active, but they frequently do not know what to do to help. Also, many parents have lost or have never developed habits of regular, vigorous physical activity. Programs to help parents gain a better understanding of physical fitness, its importance to children, and how to make improvements can be conducted by the physical educator. Programs can be established in which interested parents attend sessions to learn more about various aspects of children's physical development, how to develop a family fitness program, and helpful fitness-building activities. Operating alone, the school can have only limited success. Fitness is a year-round, lifelong objective. Therefore, there must be cooperative efforts between the home and the school to develop and maintain the physical fitness of children.

Practical ideas for motivating children are presented in Chapter 43, "Fitness Activities." A wide variety of fitness activities enjoyed by children is also included.

Traditionally, schools have placed children in environments that demand rigid conformity to inactivity. The scheduled physical education class and recess period are frequently the only times children have an opportunity to be physically active during the school day. Although potentially helpful, the instructional physical education program generally is not capable of enhancing fitness levels to a significant degree because of insufficient duration and frequency. Similarly, recess is often a time of inactivity or relatively sedentary play. Because of these problems, many schools are incorporating daily "fitness breaks" of 15 to 20 minutes per day into the school program. The breaks are an all-school activity, engaged in by students, faculty, and staff *in addition* to the instructional physical education period. Emphasis is placed on continuous vigorous physical activity. Some schools use hallways, the gymnasium, the cafeteria, or outdoor facilities for mass participation. Other schools have self-contained breaks, led by the teacher in the classroom or on the play yard.

Improved fitness results from participation in vigorous activities that require skill and are interesting to children. Insuring that movement skills are developed so that avenues are opened for recreational pursuits is an important responsibility of the teacher. Schools must offer opportunities for children to develop and apply movement skills that are essential for self-direction in vigorous physical activities.

IMPLICATIONS FOR DEVELOPMENTAL PHYSICAL EDUCATION

Lifelong habits of activity, or inactivity, are established during childhood. Creating positive attitudes toward gaining and maintaining an acceptable level of physical fitness, as well as providing opportunities to develop the components of fitness, are important objectives of the physical education program.

SUGGESTED READING

AAHPERD (1986). *Physical activity and well-being.* Waldorf, MD: American Alliance Publications.

Corbin, Charles B. (1986 May/June). Fitness is for children. *Journal of Physical Education, Recreation and Dance.*

Getchell, Bud (1987). *Being fit: A personal guide.* Indianapolis, IN: Benchmark Press.

Kirshenbaum, J., and Sullivan, R. (1983, February). Hold on there, America. *Sports Illustrated,* pp. 60–74.

Lohman, T. G., and Massey, B. H. (1984, November/

December). A fit America in the coming decade 1985–1995. *Journal of Physical Education, Recreation and Dance* 55:24–60.

Pangrazi, Robert P., and Hastad, Douglas N. (1986) *Fitness in the elementary schools.* Waldorf, MD: American Alliance Publications.

Petray, Clayre K., and Blazer Sandra (1986). *Health related physical fitness: Concepts and activities for elementary school children.* Edina, MN: Bellwether Press.

CHAPTER 4

PERCEPTUAL–MOTOR DEVELOPMENT

Study of the perceptual process and perceptual–motor development attempts to answer the age-old question of how we come to know our world. The nature of the perceptual process and its impact on movement and cognition have been topics of considerable interest to researchers and educators for years. From the moment of birth, children begin to learn how to interact with their environment. This interaction is a perceptual as well as a motor process. This chapter focuses on what is meant by the term *perceptual–motor* and its component parts. The importance of devel-

oping perceptual–motor abilities is discussed, along with factors influencing perceptual–motor development and implications for physical education.

WHAT IS PERCEPTUAL–MOTOR DEVELOPMENT?

The hyphen in the term *perceptual–motor* is there for two specific reasons. First, it signifies the dependency of voluntary movement activity upon some forms of perceptual information. All voluntary movement involves an element of perceptual awareness, resulting from some sort of sensory stimulation. Second, the hyphen indicates that the development of one's perceptual abilities is dependent, in part, on motor activity. Perceptual abilities are learned abilities and, as such, use movement as an important medium for this learning to occur. The reciprocal relationship between sensory input and motor output enables both perceptual and motor abilities to develop in harmony.

It has long been recognized that the quality of one's movement performance depends on the accuracy of perception and the ability to interpret these perceptions into a series of coordinated movement acts. The terms *eye–hand coordination* and *eye–foot coordination* have been used for years as a means of expressing the dependency of efficient movement on the accuracy of one's sensory information. The individual in the process of shooting a basketball free throw has numerous forms of sensory input that must be sorted out and expressed in the final perceptual–motor act of shooting the ball. If the perceptions are accurate, and if they are put together into a coordinated sequence, the basket is made. If not, the shot misses. All voluntary movement involves the use of one or more sensory modalities to a greater or lesser degree, depending on the movement act to be performed. What has not been recognized until recently is the important contribution that movement experiences have on the development of the children's perceptual–motor abilities.

The term *perception* means "to know" or "to interpret information." Perception is the process of organizing incoming information with stored information, which leads to a modified response pattern. Therefore, perceptual–motor development may be described as a process of attaining increased skill and ability to function, involving:

1. *Sensory input:* receiving various forms of stimulation by way of specialized sensory receptors (visual, auditory, tactile, and kinesthetic) and transmitting this stimulation to the brain in the form of a pattern of neural energy.
2. *Sensory integration:* organizing incoming sensory stimuli and integrating it with past or stored information (memory).
3. *Motor interpretation:* making internal motor decisions (recalibration) based on the combinations of sensory (present) and long-term memory (past) information.
4. *Movement activation:* executing the actual movement (observable act) itself.
5. *Feedback:* evaluating the movement act by way of various sensory modalities (visual, auditory, tactile, and/or kinesthetic), which in turn feeds back information into the sensory input aspect of the process, thus beginning the cycle over again.

Figure 4.1 provides a pictorial representation of the perceptual–motor process. Take a few minutes to review this figure in order to fully appreciate the importance of perception in the process of movement.

WHAT ARE THE PERCEPTUAL–MOTOR COMPONENTS?

Although the movement experiences found in the regular physical education program are by definition perceptual–motor activities, there is a difference in emphasis in programs that focus on the perceptual–motor quality being reinforced rather than on the gross motor quality. In remedial and readiness programs, emphasis is placed on improving specific perceptual–motor components. Therefore, movement activities are grouped according to the perceptual–motor qualities they enhance, namely *body awareness, spatial awareness, directional awareness,* and *temporal awareness.* Activities designed to enhance these abilities are used in the regular instructional physical education program, but with the primary objective of movement skill acquisition rather than perceptual–motor skill acquisition.

Body Awareness

Body awareness activities are designed to help children gain a better understanding of the nature of their body and the functions of its parts. There are three aspects of body awareness: (1) knowledge of the body parts, (2) knowledge of what the parts can do, and (3) knowledge of how to make them do it. Movement experiences that draw attention to one or more of these components make positive contributions to the development of children's awareness of their bodies and movement capabilities.

Spatial Awareness

Spatial awareness activities are designed to enhance children's awareness of the orientation of their body in space and the amount of space that it occupies. Spatial awareness is developmentally based and progresses from egocentric localization to objective localization as a function of both maturation and experience. *Egocentric localization* refers to a period when children

FIGURE 4.1   The perceptual-motor process.

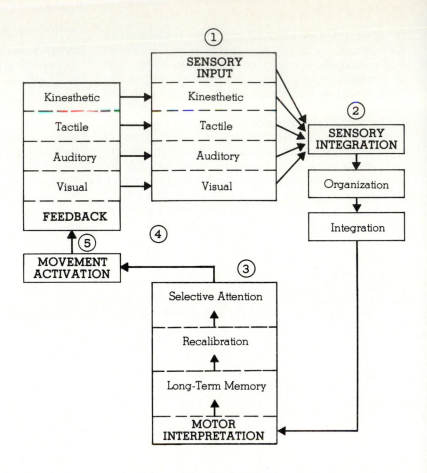

locate objects in space relative to themselves, frequently with an erroneous perception of the amount of space their body occupies. *Objective localization* refers to individuals being able to function independently of their body when making spatial and locational judgments. Movement experiences that focus on making spatial judgements in terms of body location and how much space it occupies make positive contributions to the child's awareness of space. Children need to understand that there are three types of space in which they can move. Their *self space,* or personal space as it is often called, is the area immediately surrounding their body. *General space* refers to the total available space in the room, gymnasium, or on the playground. *Restricted* space is a specifically prescribed or limited area in which they may move.

Directional Awareness

Directional awareness activities enhance awareness of the body as it is projected into external space. Directional awareness gives dimension to objects in space. The concepts of left, right, up, and down take on meaning when the child has established directional awareness. *Laterality* is the term used for an internal "feel" for direction. *Directionality* is the name given to the actual meaning of directions. Directionality usually develops prior to the internal sense of laterality. Movement activities that are linked to the verbal cues of forward, backward, up, down, over, under, left, right, and so forth help children develop a sense of directional awareness.

Temporal Awareness

Temporal awareness refers to the development of an internal time structure. Temporal awareness enables coordination of movements of the eyes and limbs in an efficient manner. The terms *eye–hand coordination* and *eye–foot coordination* refer to the end result of fully developed temporal awareness. Children who are developing their temporal awareness are in the process of learning how to synchronize movements in a rhythmical manner and to put them into the proper sequence. Rhythmical running, dancing, and juggling all require varying degrees of temporal awareness.

WHY BOTHER DEVELOPING CHILDREN'S PERCEPTUAL– MOTOR ABILITIES?

The study of the influence of perceptual–motor development falls into two broad categories: (1) the influence of perceptual–motor experiences on nonimpaired children *(readiness)* and (2) the influence of perceptual–motor training among groups containing some form of sensory, intellectual, physical, neurological, or emotional deficit *(remediation)*.

The primary concern of the physical educator interested in the study of perceptual–motor behavior is in the potential influence of planned programs of specific movement experiences on this behavior. Readiness programs are preventive and geared toward preschool and primary-grade children. Ample evidence exists to support the claim that practice in perceptual–motor activities will enhance children's abilities in this area.

Remedial training programs are directed at those children in the regular classroom who, for unexplained reasons, are failing to keep pace with their classmates. They do not have apparent physical, neurological, or intellectual disabilities, but they fail to reach their potential. Some of these children may have perceptually based learning difficulties. Limited evidence suggests that perceptual–motor training programs *may* make positive contributions to improved performance in the classroom by at least some of these children.

If there is indeed a relationship between the motor and the perceptual aspects of behavior, a program of directed movement experiences may play a part in both the prevention and remediation of some perceptually based difficulties. It would, however, be erroneous to conclude that these programs alone will overcome all the perceptual problems of the underachiever, or that participation in such a program will necessarily enhance or guarantee improved academic performance. There are no panaceas in remedial or readiness training. A physical education program that emphasizes perceptual–motor training must be viewed as only *one* avenue by which the perceptual abilities of children may be enhanced. We do not know if improved perceptual–motor abilities have a *direct* affect on improved academic performance in the classroom. A possible result of perceptual–motor-oriented physical education programs may be a positive effect on children's self-concept. It just may be that improved perceptions of oneself as being capable and worthwhile carry over to the classroom work of some children.

FACTORS INFLUENCING PERCEPTUAL–MOTOR DEVELOPMENT

The bodily senses by which we transmit sensory stimulation to the brain and interpret this stimulation into a perception may be classified as visual (seeing), auditory (hearing), tactile (touching), kinesthetic (feeling), olfactory (smelling), and gustatory (tasting). These senses, particularly vision, play important roles in perceptual–motor development, along with the important factor of experience.

The Sensory Modalities

The transmission of messages from various sensory end organs is made possible by special receptors in each sensory modality. A vast network of neurons forms a direct path from these sensors to the brain. The sensory impressions that are formed in the brain are organized, categorized, and combined with other sensory impressions and stored information. At this point, an interpretation of the sensory impressions is formed. As a result, the child sees, hears, touches, feels, smells, or tastes. These initial organizations and interpretations change and become more sophisticated through experience. Children gradually place more meaning on what the perceptual modalities tell them and begin to rely on one or two particular modes for most of the information received about their environment.

Vision is the core of our perceptual world. As children pass through the normal stages of development, their visual perceptual abilities become more acute and refined. This is due partly to the increasing complexity of the neuromuscular apparatus and sensory receptors and partly to their increasing ability to explore and act.

The newborn child receives all sorts of sensory stimulation through various sensory receptors. Responses are made to these stimuli, but they are limited in their utility and are more or less automatic. The infant is unable to combine these sensory impressions or to attach precise meaning to them, for the process of organizing incoming information and integrating it with stored information is a monumental task. Only when sensory stimuli can be combined with past experience do these sensations take on meaning and express themselves in the form of altered behavior that warrants being called a perception. For example, light rays impinge on the eyes, register on the retinas, and are transmitted to the appropriate nerve centers in the sensory area of the cortex (input). The newborn's reaction is simple (sensation): If the light is dim, the pupils dilate; if the light is bright, the pupils constrict and some of the stimulation is shut out. Soon the infant blinks at the stimulus. These simple reflex actions persist throughout life, but after a while, the infant begins to attach meaning to the visual stimulation received (organization and

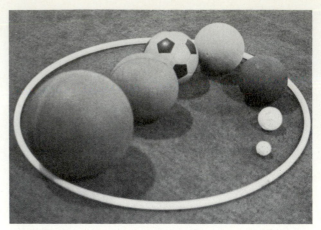

PHOTO 4.1   The visual perceptual maturity of the learner will determine the size, color, and texture of the balls that should be used.

integration). Soon a certain face becomes "mother"; a blob is identified as having three or four sides (perception). The child becomes increasingly able to attend to certain stimuli, organize them, and apply increasingly complex meaning to them.

Vision is basic for gaining accurate knowledge of the world around us. Our other senses are organized around vision and are generally not as highly developed, but they are no less important. For example, if you were deprived of all of your senses except vision, your tactile receptors would no longer provide you information concerning heat and cold or painful and pleasurable sensations. Your kinesthetic receptors would not be functioning, and, as a result, you would not know where your body was in space unless you could actually see it. You would even have to look at your feet as you walked in order to guide them in the right direction. If your auditory receptors were not functioning, you would no longer be aware of the numerous auditory cues that influence your movement. You would be unable to localize sounds and determine their origin. As a result, performance in numerous sports would be hindered, and your world would consist of only what you could see. You would be unable to distinguish the composition, size, or texture of objects by the sound that they made. Failure of your olfactory and gustatory receptors to function would prevent you from enjoying the varied smells and tastes of the food you eat. In short, failure of your sensory modalities to function would deprive you of a great deal of information necessary for effective interaction with your environment.

Experience

Perceptual–motor experiences are of importance to children because children rely heavily on motor input as a source of gaining information about the world in which they live. With age, children rely increasingly on the role of vision as an information-gathering process. As children's perceptual world develops, there is an effort to construct it with more stability in order to reduce variability as far as possible. As a result, children learn to differentiate between those things that can be ignored, those that are easily predictable, and those that are wholly unforeseen and must be observed and examined in order to be understood.

The majority of our perceptions, and visual perceptions in particular, result from the elaboration and modification of certain basic reactions that occurred spontaneously in childhood. Children's movement experiences serve as an important vehicle by which these capabilities are developed and refined. The physical education teacher plays an important role in the development of children's perceptual–motor abilities through the varied movement experiences that are incorporated into the developmentally sound physical education program.

IMPLICATIONS FOR DEVELOPMENTAL PHYSICAL EDUCATION

Developmental physical education makes contributions to perceptual–motor skill development through participation in gross motor activities that utilize the various sensory modalities. Furthermore:

1. Not all children are at the same perceptual ability level upon entering the first grade. Perceptual development is a process influenced by both maturation and experience and, as such, proceeds at the child's own individual rate.
2. Adequate perception is a prerequisite to success in school. Inaccurate perceptions may lead to difficulties in academic concept formation.
3. Perceptual readiness is an important aspect of total readiness for learning.
4. Perceptual–motor abilities can be improved through practice in perceptual–motor activities.
5. The percentage of perceptually based learning difficulties is great enough to initiate readiness programs for preschool and elementary school children even though the evidence is not conclusive that training has a direct effect on later learning.
6. Deprivation of experiences at an early age may hinder the development of the child's perceptual–motor abilities.
7. A well-planned physical education program that incorporates a variety of movement activities provides many of the perceptual–motor experiences that contribute to the development of children's perceptual–motor abilities.

Means must be devised to provide additional opportunities in a variety of movement experiences that are often absent in the life of children. Providing children with supplementary experiences that they are unable to create, receive, or fully utilize on their own will have a positive effect on the development of their perceptual–motor abilities. Physical education programs that are oriented toward the developmental approach provide many of the movement experiences that contribute to the development of children's perceptual–motor abilities.

SUGGESTED READING

Arnheim, Daniel D., and Sinclair, William A. (1979). *The clumsy child.* St. Louis: Mosby.

Karner, J. E. (1980). *The hidden handicap.* New York: Simon and Schuster.

Kavale, K., and Mattson, P. D. (1983). One jumped off the balance beam: meta-analysis of perceptual-motor training. *Journal of Learning Disabilities,* 16:165–173.

Nichols, D. B., Arsenault, D. R., and Giuffre, D. L. (1980). *Motor activities for the underachiever.* Springfield, IL: Charles C. Thomas.

Richels, M. A., List, L. K., and Lerner, J. W. (1983). *Reading problems: Diagnosis and remediation.* Englewood-Cliffs, NJ: Prentice-Hall.

Williams, H. (1983). *Perceptual and motor development.* Englewood Cliffs, NJ: Prentice-Hall.

CHAPTER 5

SELF-CONCEPT DEVELOPMENT

Our sense of personal worth or worthlessness is at the very core of our existence. Our self-concept is influenced by all aspects of our daily life and in turn affects how we approach our world. William James, one of the very early students of self-concept, considered the self-perceptions that an individual has to be an important variable in understanding human behavior. He once remarked that when two people meet, there are really six persons present. There is each person as they are, each as the other sees him or her, and each as seen by self. The view that we each have of ourself includes self-perceptions that may be quite accurate or quite different from reality. However, all self-perceptions are important because they comprise one's self-concept and determine if it is either positive or negative.

This chapter examines what we mean by the term *self-concept* as well as the components of a stable, positive self-concept. The importance of a positive self-concept is discussed, along with several factors that influence one's view of self. Specific implications for developmental physical education conclude the chapter.

WHAT IS SELF-CONCEPT?

Self-concept is a personal judgment of worthiness that is expressed in the attitudes one holds toward oneself. It refers to how we feel about ourselves and how we think others feel about us. It includes our awareness of our personal characteristics, abilities, limitations, and worthiness. The experiences in everyday life dictate whether we view ourselves as competent or incompetent, worthy or unworthy. These experiences help to form the self-concept, but our self-concept is also an active agent in shaping our experiences. How we act and react in various situations is determined in large part by our self-concept. Usually, we will not act in a way inconsistent with our self-concept. If we feel unable to do a task, then we are quite likely to act that way and quite literally be unable to perform. Our self-concept is also a determiner of our behavior because it shapes the way in which individual experiences are interpreted to the inner self.

Our self-concept determines what we expect to happen. People whose performances do not match their personal aspirations evaluate themselves as inferior, no matter how high their attainments may be. They are likely to have feelings of guilt, shame and depression. Conditions that threaten to expose personal inadequacies are a major cause of anxiety. Belief in oneself and the conviction that one can force or impose order upon a segment of the universe are basic prerequisites for a stable, positive self-concept. People with low esteem tend to be more conforming than those who have high esteem. In children, dominance, rejection, and severe punishment have a negative impact on self-esteem.

PHOTO 5.1   Cooperation and competence are important to self-concept enhancement.

WHAT ARE THE COMPONENTS OF A POSITIVE SELF-CONCEPT?

The components of a positive self-concept are *belonging, competence, worthwhileness, acceptance of self, acceptance of limits,* and *uniqueness.* Each plays an important role in children's feelings of personal worth. There are no definite pattern or specific conditions necessary to produce a positive view of self. Not all of the six components that follow must be present, but several should exist in order to provide a wholesome atmosphere for positive self-concept development.

Belonging

Belonging means that an individual is a part of the group and is accepted and valued by other members of that group. Not only is it necessary for the group to regard the individual as belonging, but also it is essential that the individual regard himself or herself as belonging.

Competence

Competence refers to self-evaluation on the basis of how efficiently we accomplish what we set out to do. Competence is often an inner feeling and not always observable. If feelings about the past are negative, it is possible that this can be changed. Potential for change is important for self-concept development. One of the steps teachers need to take in the process of improving children's self-concept is to reinterpret the past so that the meaning of past experiences is put into proper perspective, especially if these experiences were negative. Children need to see themselves as competent. Quality instruction in their attainment of movement skills and physical abilities contributes greatly to a sense of competence in children. Competence leads to confidence which in turn promotes an improved self-concept.

Worthwhileness

Worthwhileness develops out of seeing yourself as worthy because of the kind of person you are and because you see yourself as worthwhile in the estimation of others. Actions that are meant to express love and concern are not always pleasant (as in the case of a teacher disciplining a child). It is, therefore, crucial for children's sense of worth that the teacher's actions that are meant to express concern are perceived as such and are not viewed as an affront to their sense of worth as an individual.

Acceptance of Self

Accepting teachers are concerned about children and willing to exert themselves on their behalf. They are loyal sources of affection and support. They express their acceptance in a variety of ways, with expressions of interest and concern being perhaps the major underlying feature of their attitudes and behaviors. Their actions convey an attitude of unconditional acceptance of individuals for *who* they are and not *what* they are. This acceptance by others fosters acceptance of oneself.

Acceptance of Limits

Clearly defined and enforced limits are associated with a high self-concept. Concerned teachers permit greater rather than less deviation from conventional behavior, and there is freer individual expression. Teachers with clear limits generally use less drastic punishment. At first it may seem surprising that acceptance of well-defined limits is associated with high self-concept, but limits provide children with a basis for evaluating their performance and defining their social geography. When the boundaries are realistic, they serve as a guide to the expectations, demands, and taboos of that group. Limits clarify ambiguities and inconsistencies of social behavior. If clearly defined limits are provided early and accurately enough, and if they are upheld by behavioral and verbal reinforcement, children will gain the conviction that there is indeed a social reality that makes demands, provides rewards, and punishes violations. Children from environments where there are definite limits frequently tend to be more creative, less dependent, and more capable of expressing opinions and accepting criticism. In such environments, children can judge for themselves whether they have attained the goal, made progress, or deviated.

Uniqueness

Respect and latitude for individual differences within defined limits is a final contributor to a stable, positive self-concept. Teachers who are attentive to children recognize their unique qualities and structure their worlds along appropriate lines. They are then able to permit relatively great freedom within the structure they have established. It should be noted that the limits need to be reasonable and appropriate to the developmental level of children, that they are not inflexible and arbitrary limits, and that the uniqueness of the indiviudual is both respected and encouraged.

WHY BOTHER DEVELOPING CHILDREN'S SELF-CONCEPT?

It is almost universally agreed upon that the self-concept is learned. In the elementary school years, parents and teachers serve as the primary models for the developing behavior of children. They are children's primary feedback agents; through them children can know how their behavior is influencing others. Parents and teachers also serve as primary evaluators of behavior. They give "moral" or "worth" meanings to the activities of children. Therefore, the development of a stable, positive self-concept provides children with *security* and *status.*

Security

The security of children comes from identification with parents and teachers. This fact has several important implications for self-concept development. One is that identification provides a sense of belonging. Children begin to shape the self to become more like a revered adult. Another implication is that having a sense of security provides a place where children know they are safe; they can operate from this safe base without fear. Security gives children a measure of what they perceive to be power, since the wishes of parents and teachers now become the wishes that they adopt.

Status

Children are incompetent in most tasks in the early years of life, but considerable learning is going on during childhood, and a concept of status begins to emerge. The struggle throughout life is not so much between being competent or incompetent, but toward the goal of perceiving oneself in a positive way in spite of incompetencies that may be present. Children seek status and must look at incompetencies as learning tasks rather than as personal defects. The response of adults should be "You may not be able to do it now, but you will be able to do it!"

Just as children receive considerable feedback about their incompetence, they need to receive positive feedback about their newly developing competencies. As school-age children spend more time with their peers, competencies are evaluated by age mates. Their sense of competence or incompetence is likely to be enlarged or diminished by the peer group. This is a time when children must face harsh criticism from age mates because their peers have not reached the level of maturity required to temper criticism on the basis of other people's feelings. Competence begins to become enmeshed with competition during the elementary school period, and judgment begins to be made on the basis of how well children do in comparison with others rather than in comparison with past personal performances.

As children venture more into the world, it is possible for their sense of competence to grow.

They now have a larger set of evaluators and feedback agents, so there is the possibility of more positive and negative evaluations. Children become increasingly aware of themselves as members of a group. They enjoy their growing independence as they try to take care of their own needs in routine activities and in play. Their developing skills in gross motor activities help them play on equal terms with their peers. But with competition comes the increased possibility of failure. Failure may result in the lowering of one's status in the eyes of others and in one's self-evaluation. Success, on the other hand, tends to have the opposite effect and plays an important role in enhancing self-concept.

As the self-concept develops more completely, children act in ways consistent with that concept. Significant others in children's lives, such as parents, teachers, and coaches, who serve as models and mediators, play a crucial role in determining the results of learning. The self-concept develops only in the presence of others. One of our tasks as adults is to see to it that a profound sense of respect for the self is nurtured through our teaching, and that children develop security and status through quality, sensitive, caring teaching.

FACTORS INFLUENCING SELF-CONCEPT DEVELOPMENT

There are many factors that contribute to the development of a stable, positive self-concept in children. According to Felker (1974), the key ways that you the teacher can have an impact on children's self-concept are: *self-praise, encouraging children to praise themselves,* having *teachers and children praise others,* setting *realistic goals,* and fostering *realistic self-assessment.* Each is briefly discussed.

Self-Praise

It is often difficult for adults to praise themselves, but the children must know that it is all right to feel good about oneself. Children learn from models and from imitation. If you feel good but never verbalize the feeling, children have no way of knowing how you feel. Such feelings must be verbalized. In order to teach self-referent praise and reinforcement, teachers should reinforce and praise themselves verbally in front of students.

This is difficult to do because most of us have learned not to "brag" or to draw attention to ourselves for fear of being considered conceited or prideful. You can begin praising yourself by expressing praise and satisfaction in areas where objective criteria are absent. You might, for example, say how you feel about something you have done or made, like "I really felt good when I looked at the bulletin board I put up." If someone in the class responds with "I don't think it's so great," it is appropriate to say "I didn't say it was great, but things don't have to be perfect for us to feel good about them." Teachers should regard this self-reinforcement and positive self-referent language as a teaching activity. The purpose is not to enhance the teacher's self-concept but to teach children that it is okay to feel good about themselves. You can begin by praising your own work and then move to praising personal qualities. You can begin with things that are not highly personal. It is, however, important at some point to move into more personal qualities so that children begin to see that it is okay to say nice things about themselves as people, not only about what they have made or done. It may be helpful to tell your students what you are doing. This helps them to know it is all right to say nice things when they feel good about what they have done and that one of the joys of life is to share our good feelings with one another.

Children Praising Self

If children are to develop and maintain a positive self-concept, they need to become their own evaluators and reinforcers. Their behavior should be largely self-controlled. Teachers and parents should no longer be their total reinforcers. It may be easier to think of this as self-encouraging rather than self-praising. Also, it might be easier

to use group praise first, such as "The group did a tremendous job" or "Our class can do it" before using individual self-praise. Question asking is one of the tools that can be used to get children to praise themselves. A question such as "Don't you think you did well on that?" can give children a chance to praise themselves.

Teachers and Children Praising Others

Self-praise and praise of others are positively related. Learning to praise is a general skill that is applied to similar situations and is increasingly applied to self and others. When children and teachers learn the skill of praise giving, each individual becomes a reinforcer for other individuals. As a result, they are more likely to meet with positive responses, which will increase their praising behavior. Both children and teachers need to be taught how to give praise to others and how to receive praise from others.

Teachers should give positive reinforcement in specific small areas of good and poor performance. Children need to be given statements that cushion failure with success: "You will do better next time"; "You only got two right, but how unlike you"; "You were wrong this time, but you will probably be right the next time." This helps to connect the failure with hope for the future.

Setting Realistic Goals

Goals must be individual, must be made in relation to past performance, and must have an end in view. If students are to have a commitment to reach a goal, it is important that they have some part in setting the goal. The goal should be slightly higher than that reached by previous performance. This may be far below the eventual performance toward which the children are striving or toward which the teacher is aiming, but the lower level is reasonable, in the sense that it is attainable. This gives children reinforcement for the achievement of a near goal on the way to achieving a larger goal.

Realistic Self-assessment

Teaching children to evaluate themselves and others realistically is an important factor that is often ignored. Children do not naturally develop a basis for realistic evaluation and self-reward. They tend to be overly harsh with themselves and give themselves fewer rewards than adults would deem appropriate. To maintain a positive self-concept, the evaluation of self must be accurate and realistic. If you are dealing with true failure, look at it from the standpoint of learning. Improvement and learning extend the possibility of turning the experience of failure into one that can build up the individual's self-concept. Failure must be faced by children, but unrealistic evaluations only compound the problems of real failure. The purpose of realistic evaluation is not to have children completely avoid negative evaluations. Some realistic evaluations may be negative. However, a negative evaluation that is realistic provides a basis for change that will allow positive performance and, therefore, positive evaluation.

IMPLICATIONS FOR DEVELOPMENTAL PHYSICAL EDUCATION

Little research has been done that clearly reveals the unique contribution of human movement to the development of a positive self-concept in children. The number of variables influencing such research is formidable. This does not mean, however, that quality physical education programs cannot or do not have an impact on self-concept development. It simply means that at this time, precise measurement of the extent of the influence is not possible. Child development specialists, psychologists, and educators are quick to recognze that self-concept development is difficult to measure. However, it is relatively easy to observe positive changes in children who have been involved in a quality physical education program that is success-oriented, developmentally appropriate, oriented toward reasonable goals, challenging, individualized in instruction, and full of positive reinforcement.

The movement skill levels of children are often controlled by factors outside their influence. Such things as physical stature, health-related conditions, lack of experience, and lack of quality instruction make it impossible for many children to meet the standards of their peer group. Movement is not the only influence on self-concept, but it is an important one. If movement skills are poorly developed, chances are that this will have a negative effect on self-concept development. If children begin to feel they are not able to do things, they become less willing to participate. Also, if other children show that they do not hold a child in high regard because of lack of ability, the child is more apt to feel negatively, for the self-concept is to a large degree dependent on what we think others think of us.

It is important that children develop a proper perspective on success and failure. Children must be somewhat more exposed to success so that they can develop positive self-concepts. The use of a problem-solving approach in the teaching of movement skills is an excellent way in which to ensure a degree of success on the part of all children. The use of a problem-solving approach permits a variety of "correct" solutions by children.

The ratio of success to failure that children experience should emphasize success to the point that they are conditioned to expect further and greater success. Persons of low self-esteem wish just as much as others for success, but they do not believe they have the necessary qualities to achieve success. Children will gain little by repeating a task for which their responses are inappropriate, their ability inadequate, or their information insufficient. Children need to have some sense that eventually they will be able to master the condition; otherwise, they will not be willing to continue trying. This suggests the importance of analyzing the movement situations children are engaged in and the resources at their disposal for accomplishing movement tasks successfully.

Individualizing instruction is another way of programming for success. The activities are designed in accordance with the skill level at which the child is operating, so that there is some stretching and growing, but the step forward is small enough that the child can be assured of successful performance. Developmentally appropriate activities are necessary for the balanced and wholesome development of children.

Children respond often to scary or daring challenges, and so adventure activities will lure children to perform new and more challenging feats. There is a need to consider what is developmentally appropriate in the challenge. The task must be sequenced according to difficulty. This is of crucial importance in determining a child's sense of success or failure. Competition should be reserved for the time when children have developed a sufficient degree of skill in their movement abilities.

Another area in which movement can be an influence on children's developing self is in helping them establish reasonable expectations for themselves. Reaching the goal is an important boost to the self-concept. However, once a goal has been reached, a new one that is challenging needs to be set. Since self-concept is based in large part on what we think others think of us, it is important that adults working with children make their expectations known.

When praise and verbal and nonverbal encouragement are used, they must be sincere, for the child can soon detect if they are false. Nonverbal communication is just as important as verbal. The way children are treated tells them whether they are valued and whether they are living up to the teacher's expectations. Adults working with children need to be accepting and nurturing. There is no place for sarcasm or devastating criticism. Each of these can affect the self-concept drastically, and once the self-concept is firmly established, it is very difficult to change. The person who works with children in developing motor skills needs to be a warm, caring adults, for children need more than anything else the trust and endorsement of significant others. Caring teachers who are interested in helping children develop to their fullest potential should look seriously at the level of movement skills and the physical abilities children have attained. Although developmental physical education is not a panacea for all educational problems, it can make positive contributions to a stable, positive self-concept.

SUGGESTED READING

Bressan, E. S., and Weiss, M. R. (1982, Fall). A theory of instruction for developing competence, self-confidence and persistence in physical education. *Journal of Teaching Physical Education* 38–47.

Confield, J., and Wells, H. C. (1976). *100 ways to enhance self-concept in the classroom: A handbook for teachers and parents.* Englewood Cliffs, NJ: Prentice-Hall.

Felker, D. W. (1974). *Building positive-self-concepts.* Minneapolis: Burgess.

Pangrazi, R. (1982, November/December). Physical education, self-concept and achievement. *Journal of Physical Education, Recreation and Dance* 16–18.

Yawkey, D. L. (1980). *The self-concept of the child.* Provo, UT: Brigham Young University Press.

PART II

THE LEARNER

CHAPTER 6

MOVEMENT SKILL LEARNING

As a teacher, it is important to understand your students and to be able to translate this knowledge into action. People are complex, with many unique characteristics and differences that set them apart as individuals. There is, however, a surprising number of similarities in the way people learn movement skills. Because of this, it is possible for teachers to understand their students while at the same time being able to integrate common principles with unique individual differences.

Learning is a process of change brought about by both hereditary and environmental factors. It takes place in all aspects of the human experience, whether it be intellectual development, social–emotional development, or motor development. The processes of motor development and movement skill learning are orderly, sequential, and dependent in large part upon opportunities for practice, encouragement, and instruction. Without these three important ingredients, the vast majority of individuals will not reach their full potential in movement skill learning.

This chapter examines the types of movement skills that physical activities are composed of, the three stages of movement skill learning, the importance and use of feedback in the learning process, and the do's and don'ts of changing a well-learned technique. As this information is studied, care should be taken to apply it to the developmental level of your students and the specific movement skills being taught and to integrate this information with the unique individuality of each learner.

TYPES OF MOVEMENT SKILLS

Movement skills may be classified in a variety of ways. One popular classification scheme uses the words *dynamic* and *static* as descriptors of both the nature of the movement and the intent of the activity itself.

Dynamic Skills

Dynamic or "externally paced" movement activities involve making responses to constantly changing environmental cues. These dynamic environmental changes are usually rapid and unpredictable, as in bringing a soccer ball upfield or dribbling a basketball against a defensive player. As a result, rapidity and flexibility in decision making are required of the performer. The racquet sports, basketball, football, baseball, and soccer, are all examples of externally paced sports. Both the physical education teacher and the coach need to recognize the nature of dynamic activities and provide opportunities that promote rapid decision making and adaptive behaviors in a variety of gamelike situations.

Static Skills

Static or "internally paced" movement activities require a fixed performance in a given set of conditions. The performer is permitted the luxury of moving at his or her own pace through the activity and has time to recognize and respond to the static conditions of the environment. Internally paced activities generally place emphasis on accuracy, consistency, and repetition of performance. Bowling, golf, archery, and weight lifting are generally considered to be static activities, as are swimming and most track and field events. The teacher in these activities needs to provide ample opportunities for repetition of the activity under environmental conditions that duplicate, as nearly as possible, the actual performance environment.

For both static and dynamic movement activities, the teacher needs to:

1. Identify the type of activity (externally paced or internally paced).
2. Establish a learning and practice environment consistent with the dynamic or static nature of the activity.
3. Introduce dynamic activities under static conditions first (that is, control the environment and conditions of practice).
4. Introduce situations that require responses to sudden and unpredictable cues in dynamic activities as skill develops.
5. Strive for greater consistency, duplication, and reduction of environmental cues for static activities as skill develops.
6. Encourage the learner to "think through" the activity in the early stages of learning.
7. Encourage the learner to "screen" out unnecessary cues.

LEVELS OF MOVEMENT SKILL LEARNING

All movement skill learning, whether static or dynamic, involves a hierarchial sequence of learning. The sequential progression in learning a movement skill may be classified into broad levels (Fitts and Posner, 1967; Sage, 1984). The terms used here to represent these levels are *beginning, intermediate,* and *advanced.* Each level refers to a period during which both the learner and the teacher have specific, identifiable tasks and reponsibilities. The three levels in learning a movement skill are briefly discussed, with several suggestions for effective teaching at each level. Figure 6.1 provides a visual representation of these three levels and their interaction with the phases and stages of motor development.

Beginning Level

The beginning, or novice, level is the first level in learning a movement skill. At this level the movements of the learner are generally uncoordinated and jerky. Conscious attention is paid to every detail of the activity. At the beginning level the learner begins to construct a mental plan of the activity and is actively trying to understand the skill. Because of the conscious attention that is consistently given to the task itself, performance is poor. The early onset of fatigue, due more to the mental requirements of the task than to the task itself, is often apparent. At this level the learner tends to pay attention to *all* the information that is available but is unable to

FIGURE 6.1 The interrelationship between the phases and stages of motor development and the levels of movement skill learning.

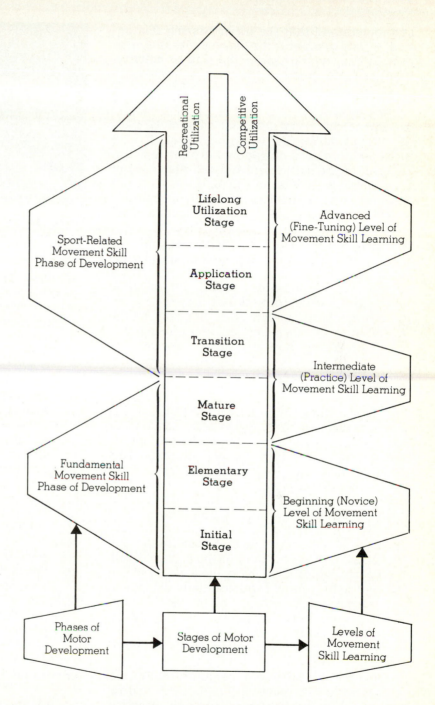

"screen" out the relevant from the irrelevant. The learner is attracted as much by what is not important as by what is important.

Teachers of students at the beginning level of learning a movement skill need to be aware of the conscious cognitive requirements of this level and understand that the intent, during this period, is only to provide the learner with the gross general framework idea of the skill or activity. In order to do this:

1. Introduce the major aspects of the skill only (be brief).
2. Provide for visual demonstrations of the skill.
3. Permit the learner to try out the skill.
4. Provide plenty of opportunity for exploration of the skill itself and self-discovery of general principles of the skill.
5. Recognize that this is primarily a cognitive phase and that the learner needs only to get the general idea.
6. Compare the new skill, when possible, to similar skills that the learner may be familiar with.
7. Provide *immediate, precise,* and *positive* feedback concerning the skill.
8. Avoid situations that place emphasis on the product of one's performance during this phase. Focus, however, on the process.

Intermediate Level

The intermediate, or practice, level of learning a new movement skill begins after the learner has obtained the general idea of the skill and is able to perform it in a manner approximating the final skill. The learner at this level has a better understanding of the skill, and a mental plan becomes more fully developed. The skill at this level has utility and is practiced repeatedly. Conscious attention to the elements of the task diminishes. More attention is devoted to the goal or product of the skill than to the process itself. The poorly coordinated, jerky movements so evident at the beginning level gradually disappear. The learner gains a "feel" for the skill as kinesthetic sensitivity becomes more highly attuned. As a result, there is less reliance on verbal and visual cues and greater reliance on muscle sense.

Teachers of students at the intermediate level recognize that the general idea is there and focus on skill enhancement through practice. Practice sessions are devised that promote skill refinement and maximize learner feedback. In order to do this:

PHOTO 6.1   Children are eager learners.

1. Provide numerous opportunities for practice and skill application.
2. Provide opportunities for skill refinement in a supportive, nonthreatening environment.
3. Devise practice situations that *progressively* focus on greater and greater skill refinement.
4. Provide short, fast-paced practice sessions with frequent breaks prior to longer sessions with few breaks.
5. Be able to analyze skills and provide constructive criticism.
6. Structure quality practice sessions that focus on quality performance ("perfect practice makes perfect").
7. Provide frequent, precise, immediate, and positive feedback.
8. Allow for individual differences in the rate of skill learning.
9. Focus attention on the *whole* skill whenever possible.
10. Practice at the rate and in the manner that the skill will be used during "real-life" performance of the skill.

Advanced Level

The advanced, or fine-tuning, level is the third and final level in learning a movement skill. The learner at this level has a complete understanding of the skill. The mental plan for the skill is highly developed, and very little attention is paid to the cognitive aspects of the task. In fact, individuals at this level often have difficulty describing how they perform the activity. They often resort to a "let me show you" or a "do it like this" statement, followed by actual performance of the skill. The learner at this level is refining and fine-tuning skills. In activities where movement is the key element, it is smooth, fluid, and highly coordinated. In activities where the absence of movement is most highly valued, there is a general appearance of ease, mastery, and total control. The performer is able to scan out irrelevant information and is not bothered by distractions. There is excellent timing and anticipation of movements, and the action *appears* to be automatic, although in reality it is a finely tuned skill requiring only minimum conscious control.

Performers at the advanced level of learning a movement skill are generally few at the elementary school level. However, with the increased tendency to specialize in sport skill development at an early age, this may change. Teachers at the advanced level have the responsibility of focusing on further refinement and maintenance of the skill and of providing selected feedback. In order to do this:

1. Structure practice sessions that promote intensity and enthusiasm.
2. Be available to provide encouragement, motivation, and positive support.
3. Offer suggestions and tips on strategy.
4. Structure practice sessions that duplicate gamelike situations.
5. Help the performer anticipate his or her actions in gamelike situations.
6. Know the performer as an individual and be able to adjust methods to meet individual needs.
7. Provide feedback that focuses on specific aspects of the skill.
8. Avoid requiring the performer to think about detailed execution of the skill, which might result in "analysis paralysis."

Each level in the process of learning a movement skill requires concerned, knowledgable, and sensitive guidance by the teacher. It is imperative that the characteristics of the learner at each level are understood, so that the physical education period may be structured most effectively for maximum learning and performance. The acquisition of skill in movement is a process that takes time. The instructor is in a position to guide and direct the learner in a manner that makes maximum effective use of that time. *Organized, quality instructional sessions geared to the skill level as well as the developmental level of the learner are crucial to realizing the student potential.*

PROVIDING FEEDBACK

Feedback is a term that refers to the information received from the senses during or after a movement. Feedback is necessary for efficient and effective learning. Teachers and coaches often rate their effectiveness, and that of others, based on the ability to provide the learner with meaningful forms of feedback during and upon completion of an activity. Although there are several factors that affect the efficiency of learning a movement skill, the type, quality, duration, and frequency of feedback are among the most critical.

Basically, feedback is the information that the performer receives as the result of some form of response. This information may (1) be provided through internal or external sources; (2) occur during performance (concurrent feedback) or after it has been completed (terminal feedback); (3) involve knowledge of performance or knowledge of results.

Internal feedback, or intrinsic feedback, as it is sometimes called, is obtained by the learner as a result of the task itself. For example, shooting an arrow at a target provides internal feedback concerning where the arrow lands in relationship to the bullseye. On the other hand, *external feedback,* or augmented feedback, as it is often called, takes the form of verbal cues from the instructor or from the use of some form of mechanical device. The internal feedback of hitting the target may be augmented with external feedback through comments about body alignment, aiming, and release of the arrow. Additional external feedback could be provided through the bursting of a balloon when the arrow hits the target or the use of a videotaped replay of the archer's performance.

Feedback that is supplied during performance of a task is called *concurrent feedback.* Athletes who say they are in the "groove" or have the "feel" of it are using internal cues about their body during the process of performing the activity. Feedback provided by the instructor during the activity may focus on the process. For example, one may caution the archer to concentrate, remain steady, or aim carefully as the performer prepares to release the arrow.

Feedback that is provided after performance of a task is called *terminal feedback.* Terminal feedback focuses on the product of one's actions. What occurs as a normal result of the performer's actions is called internal terminal feedback. For example, the arrow either hits or misses the bullseye, and the margin of error is evaluated and corrected for by the archer. Instructors can augment terminal feedback through comments to the performer or through use of videotaped replays of the activity.

Basically, feedback provides learners with information about the correctness of their actions. In doing this, it serves three basic functions. First, it provides the performer with *information* (knowledge of results and/or knowledge of performance) that leads to error correction and the desired response. Second, it serves to *reinforce* the performer in ways that may be either positive (praise) or negative (criticism). Positive reinforcement tends to preserve, augment, or enhance the desired behavior. Negative reinforcement tends to decrease or inhibit the behavior. Third, feedback serves to *motivate* the learner. Although it is not completely understood how feedback influences motivation, it is known that feedback of some sort is necessary to heighten the motivational level of the performer.

In physical education, feedback is one of the most important aspects of the teaching process. Because of this, it is important to:

1. Identify the *cause* of the learner's errors.
2. Use feedback during and immediately following performance.

3. Tell the learner the cause of the error (be precise).
4. Tell the learner how to correct the error (be concise).
5. Check to see that the learner *understands* the information given.
6. Focus on correcting one error at a time.
7. Use positive feedback techniques that encourage the performer.
8. Correct errors by beginning with a positive statement, following up with an instructional hint, and finishing with a compliment ("sandwich approach").
9. Be certain to reward approximations with praise.
10. Be frequent in the use of feedback in order to minimize practice errors.
11. Encourage the performer to improve through practice.
12. Be certain that praise is genuine, freely given, and rewards *individual* progress and improvement.
13. Provide ample opportunities for knowledge of results.
14. Encourage skill analysis during the beginning and intermediate stages of skill learning in order to make use of internal feedback.
15. Discourage verbal skill analysis during the advanced stage of skill learning.
16. Recognize the individuality of each learner and the need for varying types and degrees of feedback.

CHANGING WELL-LEARNED TECHNIQUES

Often, teachers encounter individuals who come to them with a well-learned but improper technique of performing a skill. The performer may be experiencing some success with the technique, but proper execution of the skill would be more efficient and would result in greater success. The instructor is now faced with the dilemma of determining whether to attempt to change the individual's habit or to leave it alone. A well-learned technique is difficult and time-consuming to change. Any new learning requires returning a learned behavior to a conscious level (that is, bringing it back to the beginning level). Under stress and in conditions where rapid decisions are required, the performer is likely to revert to the first or most well-learned response. It is only after considerable practice that the incorrect response will be replaced consistently by the correct action. In order to decide whether to make a change in the performer's technique:

1. Determine if there is sufficient time to make the change (think in terms of weeks and months, not hours or days).
2. Determine if the learner really wants to make the change.
3. Be certain that the learner understands why the change is being made.
4. Be certain that the learner realizes that performance will regress prior to improvement.
5. Provide a supportive, encouraging environment.
6. Structure practice sessions that will gradually bring the learner from the beginning to the intermediate and finally back to the advanced stage.

KNOWING THE LEARNER

It is vitally important that you as the teacher know your students and recognize that each comes to you with a different set of physical, mental, and social–emotional capabilities. An awesome list of individual differences confronts the teacher, all of which must be taken into consideration when planning the lesson. Table 6.1 provides examples. Some individual differences are easy to detect; others are not and may remain hidden. However, it is to the teacher's advantage to be aware of as many factors as possible. The teacher must recognize that:

1. Children learn at differing rates.
2. Children's potential level of performance excellence varies.
3. Requisite fundamental movement skills must be mastered prior to developing sport skills.
4. Response to instructional approaches vary among individuals.
5. The response to winning and losing varies among individuals.
6. The response to praise and criticism, reward and punishment varies among individuals.
7. The background of related experiences varies from child to child.
8. Differences in home life experiences influence children differently.
9. Deficiencies in certain areas can often be compensated for in other areas of performance.
10. Attention span and ability to concentrate vary among individuals.
11. The developmental level of children varies, resulting in dissimilar potentials for learning and performance.
12. The physical abilities of children vary (particularly during the preteen and early teenage years).

TABLE 6.1 Individual Differences to Be Taken Into Consideration When Planning the Lesson

Physical	Cognitive	Social–Emotional
Physical Fitness	Intelligence	Emotions
Motor Abilities	Concentration	Level of Aspiration
Movement Abilities	Analytic Abilities	Fears
Body Type	Conceptual Abilities	Personality
Body Size	Application Abilities	Attitude
Gender	Problem-Solving Abilities	Past Experience
Age		Peer Relations
Perceptual Abilities		Cultural Background

13.   Children will display greater or lesser degrees of movement skill, depending on their background of experiences and their heredity.
14.   The ability to analyze, conceptualize, and problem-solve varies among individuals.

KNOWING YOURSELF

Teachers, just like students, come in a variety of sizes, shapes, and colors. More importantly, however, they come from varying backgrounds and have varying expectations, interests, degrees of enthusiasm, teaching abilities, coaching skills, and organizational and leadership capabilities. It is just as important that students understand you as it is important for you to understand them. The following general guidelines may prove helpful.

Communication Skills

Recognize the developmental level of your students and talk to them at that level. Do not, however, try to use their jargon or popular slang. Maintain an image as the teacher and do not use language unnatural to your normal speech. Be sure to talk to students at a level they can understand. Don't talk over their heads, down to them, or at them. Talk, instead, *to* them (see Chapter 11, "Talking to Children"), being sure not to oververbalize. Remember, too much information can be confusing and just as harmful as too little information.

Communication is a two-way process. It implies listening as well as responding. Be sure to listen to what children have to say. If you expect students to listen to you, you will have to take the time and make the effort to listen to them.

Goal-Directed Behavior

It is important for the teacher to establish goals for the school year as well as to help students establish their own goals. When setting goals, it is wise to set them at a realistic level. Personal, individual, and group goals that are set too high and are unrealistic result in frustration, discouragement, and lack of motivation. On the other hand, goals that are set too low fail to challenge the individual or to promote improved performance. It is important that goals for yourself, the learners in the group, and the group as a whole be set realistically and at an individual level. Teachers need to promote the concept of obtaining personal standards of achievement, based on self-improvement.

Sequential Learning

In the quest for improved performance, it is often easy to overlook the fact that learning is an orderly, sequential process that proceeds in a logical progression, building skill upon skill. Be patient. Don't try to teach everything at once. Remember that each learner is unique and, because of that uniqueness, learning occurs at differing rates. Constantly attempt to structure instructional and practice sessions that account for differing levels of ability but are fun and challenging for all. Recognize the need for variety in practice sessions and the fact that what worked last year may not work this year. The "biological clocks" of children run at differing rates, even though the sequence of skill acquisition is generally the same. Therefore, you will need to have alternatives to the standard approaches that may have worked in the past. Be sensitive to the needs of students and creative in your approaches to meeting these needs.

SUMMARY

The learner progresses through characteristic phases and stages of motor development; these phases are orderly and sequential, but the rate is variable. Movement skills may be classified as internally paced or externally paced and are learned and refined in a series of advancing levels. The beginning or novice level precedes the intermediate level and the advanced level. As a teacher it is important for you to recognize the level at which the child is functioning. This knowledge will aid in structuring appropriate instructional and practice sessions. Practice sessions should make it possible to provide a variety of feedback concerning both the process and product of the learner's technique and performance.

Teachers often have to make important decisions concerning the advisability of changing well-learned techniques in favor of learning new ones. It is important to know the learner prior to making these decisions. Any decision should reflect what is known about the learning environment as well as what is known about the learner. Communication skills, goal-directed behaviors, and understanding of sequential learning will also have a major impact on your decisions in the learning environment.

SUGGESTED READING

Fitts, P. M., and Posner M. I. (1967). *Human performance.* Belmont, CA: Brooks/Cole.

Kerr, R. (1982). *Psychomotor learning.* Philadelphia: Saunders.

Magill, R. A. (1980). *Motor learning: Issues and applications.* Dubuque, IA: Wm. C. Brown.

Sage, G. H. (1984). *Motor learning and control: A neuropsychological approach.* Dubuque, IA: Wm. C. Brown.

Schmidt, R. A. (1982). *Motor control and learning.* Champaign, IL: Human Kinetics.

Singer, R. N. (1980). *Motor learning and human performance.* New York: Macmillan.

Stallings, L. M. (1982). *Motor learning: From theory to practice.* St. Louis: C. V. Mosby.

CHAPTER 7

CHILDHOOD GROWTH AND MOTOR DEVELOPMENT

In recent years there has been a surge of interest in the growth and motor development of children. No longer are educators content with the vague notion that children somehow magically increase their abilities to function as they advance in age. Physicians, physiologists, physical educators, and coaches have become more aware of the need for accurate information concerning the process of growth and motor development and its influence on the developing child.

Several questions must be answered before sound developmental physical education programs can be formulated. First, what is the normal, orderly process of growth? Second, what factors affect growth in children? Third, what are the influences of both maturation and experience on the process of motor development? Fourth, what factors affect the motor development and movement skill learning of children?

GROWTH

The growth period of childhood is marked by a steady increase in height, weight, and muscle mass. Growth is not as rapid during childhood as during infancy. It gradually decelerates throughout childhood until the preadolescent growth spurt. It is important to understand the process of physical growth throughout childhood and the factors that affect children's growth if physical educators are to be truly effective.

Early Childhood (2 to 6 years)

The annual height gain from the early childhood period to puberty is about 2 inches per year. Weight gains average 5 pounds per year. Differences may be seen between boys and girls in terms of height and weight, but they are minimal. The physiques of male and female preschoolers are remarkably similar when viewed from a posterior position, with boys being only slightly taller and heavier. Boys have more muscle and bone mass than girls, and both show a gradual decrease in fatty tissue as they progress through the early childhood period.

Body proportions change markedly during early childhood because of the various growth rates of the body. The chest gradually becomes larger than the abdomen, and the stomach gradually protrudes less. By the time children reach their sixth birthday, their body proportions more closely resemble those of older children in the elementary school.

Bone growth during early childhood is dynamic, and the skeletal system is particularly vulnerable to malnutrition, fatigue, and illness. The bones ossify at a rapid rate during early childhood unless there has been severe, prolonged nutritional deprivation.

Brain growth is about 75 percent complete by age 3 and nearly 90 percent by age 6.

The development of myelin around the neurons (myelination) permits the transmission of nerve impulses and is not complete at birth. At birth many nerves lack myelin, but with advancing age greater amounts of myelin are laid down along nerve fibers. Myelination is largely complete by the end of the early childhood period, thus allowing for efficient transference of nerve impulses throughout the nervous system. It is interesting to note that increased complexity in children's movement skills is possible following myelination. As the cortex matures and becomes progressively more organized, children are able to perform at higher levels, both motorically and cognitively.

The sensory apparatus is still growing during the preschool years. The eyeball does not reach its full size until about 12 years of age. The macula of the retina is not completely developed until the sixth year, and young children are generally farsighted.

Young children have more taste buds than adults. They are generously distributed throughout the insides of the throat and cheeks as well as on the tongue, causing greater sensitivity to taste.

Because of the shorter eustachian tube connecting the middle ear with the throat, young children are also more sensitive to infections of the ear.

Later Childhood (6 to 10 years)

The period of childhood from the sixth through the tenth year of life is typified by a slow but steady increase in height and weight and by progress toward greater organization of the sensory and motor systems. Changes in body build are slight during these years. Later childhood is more a time of lengthening out and filling out prior to the prepubescent growth spurt that occurs around the eleventh year for girls and the thirteenth year for boys. Children make rapid gains in learning and are capable of functioning at increasingly sophisticated levels in the performance of movement skills. This period of slow growth in height and weight gives children time to get used to their body. This is an important factor in the typically dramatic improvement seen in coordination and motor control during the later childhood years. The gradual change in size and the close relationship maintained between bone and tissue development are important factors in increased levels of functioning.

Differences between the growth patterns of boys and girls are minimal during the middle years. Both have greater limb growth than trunk growth, but boys tend to have longer legs, arms, and standing height during childhood. Likewise, girls tend to have greater hip width and thigh size during this period. There is relatively little difference in physique or weight exhibited until the onset of the preadolescent period. Therefore, in most cases, girls and boys should be able to participate together in activities.

During childhood there is very slow growth in brain size. The size of the skull remains nearly the same, although there is a broadening and a lengthening of the head toward the end of childhood.

Perceptual abilities during childhood become increasingly refined. The sensorimotor apparatus works in ever greater harmony so that by the end of this period, children can perform numerous sophisticated skills. Striking of a pitched ball, for example, improves with age and practice due to improved visual acuity, tracking abilities, reaction time, movement time, and sensorimotor integration. A key to maximum development of more mature growth patterns in children is utilization. In other words, if children have, through the normal process of maturation, improved perceptual abilities, they must be experimented with and integrated more completely with the motor structures through practice. Failure to have abundant opportunities for practice, instruction, and encouragement during this period prevents many individuals from acquiring the perceptual and motor information needed to perform skillfully.

FACTORS AFFECTING GROWTH

Growth is not an independent process. Although heredity sets the limits of growth, environmental factors play an important role in whether these limits are reached. The degree to which these factors affect motor development is not clear and needs further study. Nutrition, as well as exercise, illness, and lifestyle, play a significant role in the process of physical growth.

Nutrition

Numerous investigations have provided clear evidence that dietary deficiencies can have harmful effects on growth during childhood. The extent of growth retardation depends on the severity, duration, and time of onset of undernourishment. For example, if severe, chronic malnutrition occurs during the first four years of life, there is little hope of catching up to one's age mates in terms of mental development, because the critical brain growth period has passed.

The physical growth process can be interrupted through malnutrition at any time between infancy and adolescence. Malnutrition may serve as a mediating condition for certain diseases that affect physical growth. For example, lack of Vitamin D in the diet can result in rickets, Vitamin B-12 deficiencies may cause pellagra, and the chronic lack of Vitamin C results in scurvy. All are relatively rare in our society, but the effects of kwashiorkor, a debilitating disease, are seen in many parts of the world where there is a general lack of food and good nutrition. Children suffering from chronic malnutrition, particularly during infancy and early childhood, may

PHOTO 7.1 The joy of childhood.

never completely catch up to the growth norms for their age level. Evidence of this is shown in developing nations where adult height and weight norms are considerably lower than for industrialized nations.

Dietary excesses represent nutritional factors affecting the growth of children. Among affluent countries, obesity is a major problem. The causes of childhood obesity and its influences on motor development are of considerable concern. The constant barrage of television commercials loudly extolling one junk food or another, the "fast food" addiction of millions, and the use of edibles as a reinforcer for good behavior all may have an effect on the nutritional status of children. What is not known, however, is where the critical point between adequate and inadequate nutrition lies. The individual nature of children, with their own unique biochemical composition, makes it difficult to pinpoint where adequate nutrition ends and malnutrition begins.

Exercise

One of the principles of physical activity is the principle of use and disuse. Basically, this principle revolves around the notion that a muscle that is used will *hypertrophy* (increase in size) and a muscle that is not used will *atrophy* (decrease in size). In children, activity definitely promotes muscle development. Although the number of muscle fibers does not increase, the size of the fibers does increase. Muscles respond and adapt to increased amounts of stress. Maturation alone will not account for increases in muscle mass. An environment that promotes vigorous physical activity on the part of the child will do much to promote muscle development. Active children tend to have less body fat in proportion to lean body mass.

Although physical activity generally has positive effects on the growth of children, it may have some negative effects if carried to an extreme. The critical point separating harmful and beneficial activity is not clear. The rapid rise of youth sport and the intensity of training that often accompanies it leave many unanswered questions. It seems reasonable to assume, however, that strenuous activity carried out over an extended period of time may result in injury to children's muscle and bone tissue. "Swimmer's shoulder," "tennis elbow," and "runner's knees" are but a few of the ailments plaguing children who have exceeded their developmental limits. Care must be taken to supervise their exercise and activity programs. The potential benefits of exercise to the growth process are great, but the limits of the individual must be carefully considered.

Illness

The standard childhood illnesses (chicken pox, colds, measles, and mumps) do not have a marked effect on growth. The extent to which illnesses and diseases may retard growth is dependent on their duration, severity, and timing. Often, the interaction of malnutrition and illnesses in children makes it difficult to accurately determine the specific cause of growth retardation. The combination of conditions, however, puts the child at risk and greatly enhances the probability of measurable growth deficits.

Lifestyle

Lifestyle factors, or *secular trends,* as they are sometimes called, refers to the tendency for children to be both taller and heavier, age for age, and to mature at an earlier age than children several generations ago. The trend for secular increases is not universal. Increases in growth, maturation, and physical performance levels have been demonstrated in most developed countries. However, some developing nations have not demonstrated secular increases and in some cases have even shown secular decreases in stature. There may be many reasons for secular trends, but they are largely due to changes in lifestyle and nutritional habits from one generation to another.

Secular trends in size and maturation in North America and other developed nations appear to have stopped. There has been little indication of secular increases in height, weight, and maturation in these countries in the past several years. This may be due largely to the peaking of improved nutritional and health conditions.

FACTORS AFFECTING MOTOR DEVELOPMENT

The process of motor development is dependent on a variety of developmental factors, involving such things as the direction and rate of development, differentiation and integration of sensory and motor systems, readiness for learning, critical learning periods, and individual differences. Teachers must be aware of the tremendous complexity of the process of motor development and must objectively view their role as catalysts in this process.

Children need to learn more about their bodies. Gradual shifts or increments in the child's level of functioning occur in the stability, locomotor, and manipulative categories of movement behavior. During infancy, children gain the very simplest controls over their movements in order to survive at the lowest level of motoric functioning. Preschool and primary-grade children are involved in developing and refining fundamental movement skills. The many complex movements found in sport and dance are little more than highly elaborated forms of these fundamental movements.

The unique genetic inheritance that accounts for our individuality can account for our similarity in many areas. One of these similarities is the trend for human development to proceed in an orderly, predictable fashion. A number of factors that affect motor development tend to emerge from this predictable pattern.

Developmental Direction

Developmental direction refers to the orderly, predictable sequence of motor control. *Cephalocaudal development* refers specifically to the gradual progression of increased control over the musculature, moving from the head to the feet. Young children are often thought to be clumsy and to exhibit poor control over the lower extremities. This may be due to incomplete cephalocaudal development.

Proximodistal development refers specifically to progression in control of the musculature from the center of the body to its most distant parts. Young children, for example, are able to control the muscles of the trunk and shoulder girdle prior to gaining control over the muscles of their wrist, hand, and fingers. This principle is utilized by teachers of primary-grade children in the teaching of the less refined elements of manuscript writing prior to the introduction of the more complex and refined movements of cursive writing.

Rate of Growth

The rate of development for children follows a characteristic pattern that is universal for all children and resistant to external influence. Even interruption of the normal pace of growth is compensated for by a still unexplained self-regulatory process that comes into operation to help children catch up to their age mates. For example, a severe illness may retard a child's gain in height, weight, and movement ability, but on recovery from the illness there will be a tendency to catch up with age mates. This self-regulatory process is capable of compensating for *minor* deviations in the growth process, but it is unable to make up for major deviations. Restricted opportunities for movement and deprivation of experience have been shown to interfere with children's abilities to perform movement tasks that are characteristic of their age level. The extent to which children are able to catch up to their peers depends on the duration and severity of deprivation, the age of the child, and the level of motivation to make improvements.

Differentiation and Integration

The coordinated, progressive, and intricate interweaving of neural mechanisms of opposing muscle systems into an increasingly mature relationship is characteristic of the developing child's motor control. There are two different but related processes associated with this increase of functional complexity, known as differentiation and integration. *Differentiation* is associated with the gradual progression from the gross globular (overall) movement patterns of infants to the more refined and functional movements of children as they mature. *Integration* refers to bringing various opposing muscle and sensory systems into coordinated interaction with one another. For example, the young child gradually progresses from ill-defined corralling movements when attempting to grasp an object to more mature and visually guided reaching and grasping behavior. This differentiation of movements of the arms, hands, and fingers, followed by integration of the use of the eyes with the movements of the hand to perform rudimentary eye–hand coordination tasks, is crucial to normal development.

Readiness

Readiness refers to conditions within the individual and the environment that make a particular task appropriate for an individual to master. The concept of readiness, as used today, extends beyond biological maturation and includes consideration of environmental factors that can be modified or manipulated to encourage or promote learning. Influences include physical and mental maturation interacting with motivation, prerequisite learnings, and an enriched environment.

Sensitive Learning Periods

There are certain periods when an individual is more sensitive to certain kinds of stimulation. Normal development in later periods may be hindered if children fail to receive proper stimulation during a sensitive period. For example, inadequate nutrition, prolonged stress, inconsistent mothering, or lack of appropriate learning experiences may have a more negative impact on development if introduced early in life rather than at a later age.

The concept of sensitive periods has a positive side. It suggests that appropriate intervention during a sensitive period tends to facilitate more positive forms of subsequent development than if the same thing is introduced later. Current views on sensitive periods reject the notion that there are highly specific time frames in which one must develop movement skills. There are, however, broad periods during which development of certain skills is most easily accomplished.

Individual Differences

The tendency of children to exhibit individual differences is crucial. Each child is a unique individual with his or her own timetable for development. This timetable is a combination of a particular individual's heredity and environmental influences and, although the sequence of appearance of developmental characteristics is predictable, the rate of appearance may be quite variable.

The "average" ages for the acquisition of all sorts of developmental tasks have been bandied about in the professional literature and the daily conversation of parents and teachers for years. It must be remembered that these average ages are just that and nothing more. It is common to see deviations from the mean of as much as six months or more. The tendency to exhibit individual differences is closely linked to the concept of readiness and helps to explain why some children are ready to learn new skills when others are not.

SUMMARY

The motor development of children represents one aspect of the total developmental process. The importance of optimum motor development in children must not be minimized or thought of as secondary to other developmental processes. The unity of humankind clearly demonstrates the integrated development of the mind and the body and the many subtle interrelationships of each.

Factors of growth and motor development greatly influence the rate and level of skill acquisition. These factors are general and illustrate the gradual progression from relatively simple levels of functioning to more complex levels. Each factor is affected by the combined influences of maturation and experience.

Maturation and experience both influence the development of movement skills in children. Developing movement skills contributes to physical growth and motor development. The developmental physical education program must provide opportunities for large muscle activity and strive to increase the children's level of motivation for vigorous activity as well as their level of competence in movement skill acquisition.

SUGGESTED READING

Gallahue, D. L. (1982). *Understanding motor development in children.* New York: Wiley.

Keogh, J., and Sugden, D. (1985). *Movement skill development.* New York: Macmillan.

Krogman W. M. (1980). *Child growth.* Ann Arbor: The University of Michigan Press.

Haywood, Kathleen M. (1986). *Life Span Motor Development.* Champaign, IL: Human Kinetics.

Magill, R. A., Ash, M. J., and Smoll, F. L. (1982). *Children in sports.* Champaign, IL: Human Kinetics.

Robertson, M. A., and Halverson, L. E. (1984). *Developing children—their changing movement.* Philadelphia: Lea & Febiger.

Thomas, J. R. (1984). *Motor development during childhood and adolescence.* Minneapolis: Burgess.

CHAPTER 8

CHILDREN WITH SPECIAL NEEDS

Every school contains some children who are physically, mentally, emotionally, or learning-impaired. Their impairments may range from the mild to the severe, and they may be single or multiple, temporary or permanent. However, each of these children is limited in some measurable way in the ability to take part in, or benefit fully from, the physical activities characteristic of their peers. The Education for All Handicapped Children Act of 1975 (Public Law 94-142) insures that all exceptional children from 3 to 21 years of age are provided an "appropriate education."* This important federal law, which has dramatically influenced how individuals with limiting conditions are treated in the United States, is of particular importance to physical educators. Physical education is the only subject area specifically identified in the definition of an "appropriate education." The provisions of Public Law 94-142 mandate that all exceptional children must be provided with an appropriate physical education program and that this program must be offered in the *"least restrictive environment."* Therefore, children with special physical, mental, or emotional needs must be given the opportunity to take part in the *regular* physical education program *unless* their needs can only be met through a specially designed program as prescribed by their *Individualized Education Program*.

Physical education contributes to the growth and development of children with special needs through the medium of movement. This fact has been wisely recognized in Public Law 94-142, which mandates a policy of inclusion ("mainstreaming") whenever and wherever possible.

---

*Although Public Law 94-142 frequently uses the word *handicapped*, it is viewed as a degrading term by many. Use of terms such as *challenged, special needs, exceptional*, and *limiting condition* are generally viewed as more appropriate and are encouraged.

This chapter looks at several limiting conditions and examines the role of physical education in the education of children with special needs. The problems of social adjustment faced by the disabled and their special needs are also considered. Furthermore, several practical teaching strategies are included for the regular physical education program that includes children with special needs.

THE PHYSICAL EDUCATION PROGRAM

Children cannot be excluded from a physical education program because of a disability, whether temporary or permanent, mild or severe, single or multiple. Whenever possible, they must be mainstreamed into the regular physical education class. When the limiting condition prohibits participation in the regular physical education class, as determined by their Individualized Educational Program (IEP), a specialized program must, by law, be offered.

Children need to be included in the regular physical education program whenever possible in order to learn how to interact effectively with their environment, develop their movement and physical abilities, and learn how to use their leisure time wisely. Non-exceptional children are given an opportunity to learn tolerance, and acceptance and to be unencumbered by the notion that someone is "different."

At first, physical education teachers often feel overwhelmed by the fact that they must provide appropriate educational experiences for children with special needs. They often feel ill-prepared and frustrated by this requirement. Remember, however, that children with special needs are children first. Although they may have some unique needs, they are much more like nonimpaired children than they are unlike them. Avoid the trap of classifying your students as "handicapped" and "normal." There is actually no such thing as a "normal child." The normal child is a mythical average about which *all* children deviate to some degree. Some children deviate from this norm more than others. Because of this, they have special needs that must be met

somewhat differently than for their nonimpaired peers. These needs may be met through one or more of the following types of physical education programs: the adapted program, the corrective program, or the developmental program (Figure 8.1).

The Adapted Program

The adapted physical education program provides for physical activities that are modified according to the physical, mental, and emotional limitations of an atypical individual or group. The aim of the adapted physical education program is to permit each child to function within his or her range of abilities. In this sense, regular physical education programs that make real and constant efforts at individualizing instruction are in fact "adapting" their instruction to the needs of the children. These teachers are constantly modifying the learning goals and movement experiences based on the unique needs and current abilities of the children they teach.

The Remedial Program

The remedial physical education program differs from the adaptive program in that it is corrective in nature and includes specific exercises and physical activities designed to improve body mechanics. Improvement in such basic movement tasks as standing, sitting, and moving through space are important learning goals of the remedial program, as are improvement in perceptual–motor abilities.

The remedial physical education program should be conducted under the supervision of a physician and may incorporate suggestions from the physical therapist or school psychologist. Specialized training is required in the area of remedial or corrective physical education.

Unfortunately, most elementary schools do not have the physical facilities or specialized equipment often recommended for carrying out an effective remedial program. Consequently, teachers are often required to improvise and make use of what is available in the school and community. In any case, complete records must be kept for each child in the program. These records

FIGURE 8.1 The relationship between the adaptive, corrective, and developmental programs.

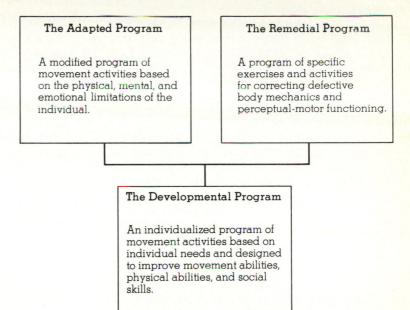

The Adapted Program

A modified program of movement activities based on the physical, mental, and emotional limitations of the individual.

The Remedial Program

A program of specific exercises and activities for correcting defective body mechanics and perceptual-motor functioning.

The Developmental Program

An individualized program of movement activities based on individual needs and designed to improve movement abilities, physical abilities, and social skills.

should include a health history, IEP, and an updated physician's report with a clear description of appropriate physical activities to be engaged in by the child. It should be reemphasized that specialized training is necessary to conduct an effective remedial physical education program and that these programs must be conducted under the supervision of a physician.

The Developmental Program

The developmental physical education program contains elements of both the adapted and remedial programs. It is concerned specifically with individual improvement in movement skill acquisition, physical fitness, and social adjustment. The developmental physical education program is concerned with all children, impaired and nonimpaired alike. Its primary goals are improvement in movement control, emotional control, and learning enjoyment. The developmental program is similar to the adapted program in that it strives to individualize learning and modify movement experience based on the unique physical, mental, and emotional abilities of each child. The developmental program

is similar to the remedial physical education program in that it shares the goals of improved body mechanics and perceptual-motor functioning.

The developmental physical education program can be implemented effectively with impaired and many nonimpaired children alike. It does, however, require the assessment of movement abilities *prior* to planning a specific program of activities. Assessment may take many forms. It may be subjective or objective, process-based, or product-based, individual or group. It *must*, however, be regular and systematic and occur *before* as well as *after* a program of activities is engaged in. Chapter 19 focuses on assessing progress.

CATEGORIES OF LIMITING CONDITIONS

Children with special needs are generally classified into four broad and sometimes overlapping categories: orthopedically impaired, mentally impaired, emotionally impaired, and learning-impaired. A brief look at several specific conditions that are frequently encountered in the public schools follow.

The Physicially Challenged

PL 94-142 defines a physical impairment as any physical condition the interferes with the child's educational performance and includes disabilities caused by disease, congenital factors, and other unspecified causes. About three percent of the school age population have physical impairments. Children with physical disabilities are characterized by faulty functioning of their sensory receptors or their musculature to a point where their ability to function is limited or restricted in some manner. Children with a physical impairment may suffer from one or more disabling conditions. These conditions restrict their movement and mandate modifications in the physical activities in which they engage. For purposes of discussion, physical disabilities have been subdivided here into sensory, cardiovascular, neurological, and musculoskeletal impairments (Figure 8.2)

Sensory Impairments. A sensory impairment is one in which the sensory receptors are unable to transmit or interpret stimuli in a manner conducive to educational performance. By far the most common sensory impairments are visual deficits and auditory deficits.

Visual Impairment. The child with a visual disability is defined as one whose educational performance is adversely affected even when corrective lenses are worn. PL 94-142 specifically states that the child does not have to be blind, or near blind, in order to qualify as being visually handicapped. The physical education program for visually impaired children may be modified to provide *additional* tactile, kinesthetic, and auditory stimulation for less severe impairments. Severe visual impairments may require *substitution* of other sensory modalities for sight. Verbal directional guidance, tactile stimulation, and the use of specialized sound-emitting devices can all be very helpful in the physical education program for the visually impaired.

Auditory Impairment. Children with an auditory impairment have difficulty processing verbal information, with or without amplification, and this interferes with their educational performance. Auditory impairments are one of the

FIGURE 8.2 Common types of disabilities encountered in the elementary school.

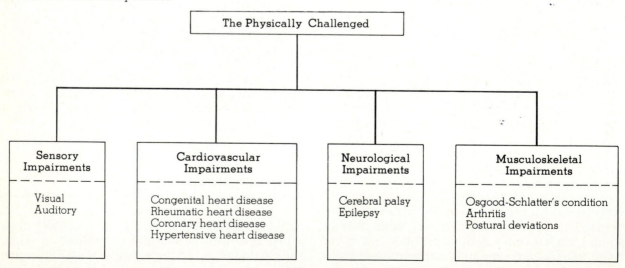

most common handicapping conditions found in children and adults. Hearing loss may range from partial to complete. Children with hearing impairments that have gone unattended are frequently mistaken for being mentally retarded, slow learners, or behavioral problems. The following is a list of possible signs of hearing impairment:

1. Faulty speech patterns; faulty pitch, tone, or volume.
2. Holding the head to one side, inattentiveness, excessive daydreaming, inability to follow directions.
3. Inability to detect who is speaking and what is being said.
4. Emotional instability; hostility or extreme withdrawal.
5. Failure in school.
6. Difficulty in maintaining balance.
7. Inability to join class discussions and group games.
8. Social inferiority.

Children with auditory impairments that can be corrected through the use of hearing aids should be able to take part in most of the activities of the regular physical education program. In those activities that necessitate removal of the aids (such as swimming and gymnastics) the student should be accompanied by a "buddy," and the teacher should be certain that he or she speaks clearly, distinctly, and directly toward the student. Children with severe auditory impairments that can not be corrected (deafness) will require special attention. Greater attention will need to be given to visual imput rather than verbal imput. Demonstrations, written descriptions, wall charts, and videotape replays are all effective teaching tools for use with the deaf child.

Cardiovascular Impairments. Cardiovascular disorders include congenital heart disease, rheumatic heart disease, coronary heart disease, and hypertensive heart disease. Although often thought of as a major health problem in adults, cardiovascular disorders are quite prevalent in children as well.

Depending on the specific nature of the disorder, children may be severely or only moderately restricted in the type, amount, and duration of physical activity in which they may take part. It is of utmost importance to work closely with the child's physician concerning the degree of involvement permitted and to observe for signs of stress. Most children with cardiovascular disorders can benefit from a modified physical education program that works within the limits of their abilities and is sensitive to their special needs.

Neurological Impairments. Children with neurological impairments are characterized by damage to the brain or spinal cord. There is a variety of neurological impairments, of which cerebral palsy and epilepsy are the most common.

Cerebral Palsy. Cerebral palsy is a nonprogressive, permanent condition caused by damage to the motor area of the cortex. It results in paralysis, weakness, tremor, or uncoordinated movement, depending upon the severity and location of the brain damage. Cerebral palsy is classified into five categories:

Spasticity is typified by limited voluntary control of movement as a result of hypertonus of the muscles. An exaggerated stretch reflex causes the arms and legs to contract rapidly when passively stretched and results in inability to perform precise movements. The legs are often rotated inward, the arms stiff and flexed at the elbows. Body movements are characteristically jerky and uncertain. Spasticity is the most common form of cerebral palsy, occurring in about 60 percent of all cases. Mental retardation, speech disorders, and perceptual problems are frequently associated with spastic cerebral palsy.

Athetosis accounts for approximately 25 percent of all cerebral palsy and is characterized by involuntary, jerky movements. Movement is uncontrollable, random, and almost constant. Facial grimaces are common, as are hearing, speech, and visual impairments.

Ataxia represents about 10 percent of all cerebral palsy and is typified by very poor balance and coordination. Movements are deliberate but awkward and wobbly. Perceptual abilities are generally diminished, especially in the proprioceptive and vestibular areas. Speech disorders are common.

Rigidity is characterized by extreme body stiffness and absence of the stretch reflex. Mental retardation is common with rigidity, as well as restricted movement and hyperextension. About 3 percent of all cases of cerebral palsy are classified as rigidity.

Tremor is the least frequent form of cerebral palsy, occurring in only about 2 percent of the cerebral palsy population. It is characterized by rhythmic, involuntary movements. When voluntary movement is attempted, the tremor tends to increase. Tremors are often mixed with muscle rigidity. Mental retardation is common.

The degree of involvement of cerebral palsy and other neurological impairments may be classified by location:

1. Monoplegia—involvement of only one limb (rare).
2. Paraplegia—involvement of both legs only.
3. Hemiplegia—involvement of one arm and one leg on the same side of the body.
5. Triplegia—involvement of three limbs (rare).
6. Quadriplegia—involvement of all four limbs.

In all cases of cerebral palsy, whether mild, moderate, or severe, the individual will benefit from a program of modified physical activities. The physical educator can do much, working in conjunction with the physician, to improve the child's level of physical functioning. Social integration with one's nonhandicapped peers is of special importance for the cerebral palsied child. The development of social skills and improved peer-group relationships is an important goal of the physical education program.

Epilepsy. Epilepsy is a condition caused by an electrochemical imbalance in the brain. It is typified by seizures that may be mild or severe. Seizures may, in many cases, be effectively controlled with a variety of drugs. Persons with epilepsy may exhibit one or more of the following seizures when uncontrolled by medication.

Grand mal seizures are accompanied by an *aura phase,* characterized by sinking feeling, or a vague feeling of uneasiness. This is followed by a *tonic phase,* in which there is a loss of consciousness and rapid, involuntary, writhing contraction of the muscles. The *clonic phase* follows, typified by intermittent contractions. This is followed by a deep, relaxed *sleep phase.*

Jacksonian seizures are similar to grand mal seizures but without the aura and tonic phases. There is intermittent contraction and relaxation of the muscles, beginning in one part of the body and spreading outward, accompanied by loss of consciousness.

Petit mal seizures are characterized by a momentary loss of consciousness. The child will suddenly stop all activity, appear dazed, and then resume regular activity.

Psychomotor seizures are characterized by short-term changes in normal behavior, in which there is no memory of the atypical behavior. Temper tantrums, incoherent speech, and aggressive behaviors are frequent.

Most children with epilepsy should be encouraged to take part in the regular physical education program. Excessive sensory stimulation or trauma to the head frequently trigger an epileptic seizure. Care should be taken to avoid both situations.

Musculoskeletal Impairments. A wide variety of musculoskeletal impairments, including Osgood–Schlatter's condition, arthritis, and postural deviations is frequently encountered in the physical education class. A musculoskeletal impairment is a disease or condition of the bones or muscles that affects the child's ability to move effectively and efficiently.

Osgood–Schlatter's condition. Osgood–Schlatter's condition is common in prepubescent boys and girls, typified by pain and swelling around the knee joint. It is completely curable with medical treatment and frequently disappears after a few years without medical intervention. Osgood–Schlatter's condition is caused by separation of the patellar ligament from the tibia. It is frequently the result of undue tendon strain, improper alignment of the leg, or direct injury to the knee. Repeated jarring activities, such as improper running technique or landing heavily, seem to contribute to this condition.

For treatment, some authorities recommend complete immobilization of the leg for a minimum of six weeks, followed by restricted physical activity for up to one year. Others recommend continuation with a program of regular physical activities, limited only by the individual's pain tolerance. Teachers at the upper elementary and junior high school level encounter frequent cases of Osgood–Schlatter's condition. Be prepared to modify or restrict activities as required by the child's physician.

Arthritis. Arthritis is frequently thought of as a disease of the aged. This is not so. A significant number of children are afflicted with this disease, for which a cure has not been found. Basically, arthritis is a painful condition caused by inflammation of the joints. *Rheumatoid arthritis* is the most common form of arthritis found in children. It attacks the entire skeletal system and results in inflammation, stiffness, and acute pain in the joints. Rheumatoid arthritis varies greatly in severity, but in all cases movement of the affected joints is recommended.

Children with arthritis should be included in the regular physical education program whenever possible. They should be encouraged to take part in sustained stretching activities in order to promote joint flexibility. Some activities may need to be modified during periods of time when the condition is particularly painful.

Postural Deviations. Postural deviations are common among elementary school-age children. They may be classified as either *functional* or *structural*. Functional postural deviations are the result of faulty muscular development. This is frequently caused by habitual postures and overdevelopment of certain muscle groups. Children who habitually carry their books on one side of the body, or who consistently assume a knees forward with feet behind while sitting on the floor are likely to develop functional postural deviations.

Structural postural deviations involve structural abnormalities of the skeletal system itself. These abnormalities may be due to congenital defects, functional deviations that have gone uncorrected, or skeletal injuries that have not healed properly. Structural impairments require surgery for correction, whereas functional impairments are correctable through a program of proper activities to strengthen identified muscle groups.

Postural problems are common among school-age children. Among these are scoliosis, lordosis, and kyphosis.

Scoliosis refers to lateral curvature of the spine. Scoliosis may be structural but is most often functional. If left untreated, the characteristic "C" curve of the spine may develop into an "S" curve. If scoliosis is detected in the young child, a program of corrective exercises should begin immediately. If it is not detected until late adolescence, little can be done, and the condition will probably not develop further. In order to modify the condition at this time a back brace must be worn for several years.

Lordosis, or swayback, as it is sometimes called, is typified by an exaggerated curve of the lower back. This exaggerated lumbar curve results in a forward tilt of the pelvis and weak abdominal muscles. Corrective activities at the early stages of lordosis include making the individual aware of his or her posture and helping the child to develop the habit of consciously tucking the hips under the spine. Activities designed to strengthen the abdominal muscles and to stretch the muscles of the lower back are helpful.

Kyphosis, or hunchback, as it is frequently called, is a condition characterized by an exaggerated curve in the thoracic region of the spine. Round shoulders, winged scapula, and a forward head tilt frequently are found in conjunction with kyphosis. A program of exercises designed to stretch the chest muscles and strengthen the back muscles will help alleviate this condition.

The Mentally Challenged

Mental impairments are typified by faulty development of intelligence to a point that it interferes with the ability to learn. The following classificatory scheme, adopted by the American Association on Mental Deficiency, is the most widely used and universally accepted categorization of levels of mental retardation:

1. Mildly retarded (55–69 IQ).
2. Moderately retarded (40–45 IQ).
3. Severely retarded (25–39 IQ).
4. Profoundly retarded (less than 25 IQ).

Both the mildly and moderately mentally retarded are considered to be in the *educable* range and may be expected to take part in the developmental physical education program. Educationally, the severely and profoundly retarded are considered to be at the *trainable* and *custodial* levels, respectively. They will benefit most from a special program of adapted physical activities geared to their particular needs.

It is generally assumed that roughly 3 percent, of the total population meets the criteria for being classified as mentally retarded. Of this 3 percent, approximately 95 percent are in the mildly to moderately retarded range. Only about 5 percent of the entire mentally retarded population is severely or profoundly retarded.

The causes of mental retardation are numerous and varied. The vast majority of retardation is due to brain damage that occurs prior to, during, or after birth; environmental factors caused by infections or intoxicants; and genetic factors caused by chromosomal abnormalities.

Brain damage is the primary cause of mental retardation. It is characterized by damage to the central nervous system. Organic conditions may arise before birth (prenatal), during birth (perinatal), or after birth (postnatal). Prenatal factors that have been linked with brain damage include maternal nutrition, the use of chemical agents (drugs, alcohol, and tobacco), and maternal illnesses. Perinatal factors include the use of drugs to aid in the birth process itself and the manner and type of delivery. Postnatal factors range from infant accidents and injuries to infant nutrition and chemical imbalances.

Environmental factors caused by infections and intoxicants to the expectant mother, the infant, or the young child are a secondary cause of mental retardation. For example, the expectant mother who contracts rubella (German measles) during the first trimester of her pregnancy runs the risk of damaging her unborn child. The syphilitic mother transmits her condition to her child, a frequent cause of retardation. Rh incompatibility, infant poisoning, and certain diseases during infancy also contribute to mental retardation.

Genetic retardation is the third and least frequent cause of mental retardation. Genetic retardation is brought about by chromosomal abnormalities. Deviations in the structure or number of chromosomes is related to gene mutations, certain drugs, viruses, and ionizing radiation. Downs syndrome is one of the most frequently encountered forms of genetic retardation. It is caused by chromosomal damage and results in mental retardation, cardiovascular impairments, and the characteristic mongoloid appearance.

The Emotionally Challenged

Emotionally disturbed children are characterized by behavior patterns that have a detrimental effect on their adjustment and interfere with the lives of others. The causes of emotional disabilities are not completely understood, nor is it clear why some individuals react in a negative fashion emotionally while others with equivalent backgrounds do not.

As defined by PL 94-142, the emotionally disturbed child is one who has an inability to learn that cannot be explained by sensory problems, health factors, or intellectual deficits; is unable to make and keep satisfactory interpersonal relationships with peers and adults; demonstrates inappropriate behaviors; is generally unhappy or depressed; or develops physical symptoms related to school or personal problems. Basically, the emotionally disturbed child is one who may be characterized by extremes in behavior, chronic unacceptable behavior, or persistent problems at home or school. It has been variously estimated that the number of emotionally disabled children ranges from only 2 to over 20 percent of the total population. Even using the conservative figure of 2 percent results in a school-aged population of over one million children who are considered to be seriously emotionally disturbed, a fact that warrants the attention of all educators.

Severe, prolonged emotional impairments have been shown to be linked to a variety of psychological, sociological, and physiological factors.

Psychological factors are the result of constant frustration. They arise from the child's inability to meet the requirements of his or her environment. The inability to cope with the real or imagined pressures of society results in feelings of anxiety, fear, hostility, or insecurity, which are manifested in inappropriate behavior patterns. Sociological factors include early home experiences and socioeconomic aspects of the home environment. Child abuse, ranging from physical and verbal abuse to sexual abuse and neglect, are important sociological contributors to severe emotional disturbances. Likewise, physiological factors such as heredity, neurological disorders, and chemical imbalances may contribute to emotional disabilities.

Emotionally disturbed children may exhibit unusual anxiety reactions, atypical frustrations, fears and phobias, and impulsive behaviors. The following signs and symptoms may aid in the detection of these children:

1. A tendency to have accidents.
2. Hyperactivity.
3. Imaginary fears and phobias.
4. Regressive, immature behavior.
5. Aggressive, hostile behavior.
6. Withdrawal into a fantasy world.
7. Abnormal fear of failure and criticism.
8. Unexplained poor school achievement.
9. Frequent disciplinary visits to the principal's office.
10. Inability to relate appropriately with the peer group.

The Learning Challenged

A fourth classification of children with special needs is the learning challenged. PL 94-142 defines the learning-disabled child as one who is restricted in the ability to read, write, think, speak, spell, or do mathematical operations due to the inability to fully utilize basic psychological processes involved in using spoken or written language. The term *learning-impaired* excludes problems in learning that may be traced to physical (visual, auditory, or motor) disabilities and mental (mildly, moderately, severely, or profoundly retarded disabilities. It also ex-

cludes learning disabilities brought about primarily by cultural, economic, or environmental conditions. Children with a specific learning disability are sometimes referred to as "ATLO" children, an acronym for "All Those Left Over."

Children with specific learning disabilities are frequently difficult to detect. They often appear quite normal in their physical, social, and mental development, but for some unexplained reason, they fail to achieve at an acceptable level in school. The discrepancy between potential and performance often results in peer-related problems and considerable emotional upheaval. The learning impairment itself may be relatively minor and specific to motor, perceptual, writing, or speaking difficulties; or it may be quite complex and involve the intricate interaction of these processes. Although perceptual–motor training programs have been advocated for years by a number of individuals as an effective means of remediating learning disabilities, the area is too diverse and too complex to merit such simple solutions. The effects of perceptual–motor programs on the academic achievement and cognitive processes of children with learning disabilities is highly speculative. The fact is that quality physical education programs do produce positive changes in the affective, social, and motivational response patterns of children. It may be that these factors have an *indirect* influence on the acquisition of skills and abilities necessary for academic success.

Other Challenges

The category of "other challenges" includes a variety of health restrictions that may not be as easily observed as those discussed earlier but that adversely affect the child's educational performance. PL 94-142 defines other health impairments as any condition that results in limited strength, vitality, or alertness. This may be due to health problems such as asthma, diabetes, obesity, hemophilia, anemia, tuberculosis, or leukemia. In each of these cases it is important for the physical education teacher to work closely with the physician, parents, rehabilitation specialists, and other school officials in order to provide appropriate educational opportunities in the least restrictive environment. Appropriate identification, assessment, programming, and evaluation of the child's health problem must be a team approach. *Identification* is the procedure by which children with special needs are located. *Assessment* is the means by which they are examined and their present status is determined. Once the child with special needs has been identified and his or her present level of abilities has been determined, it is possible to program appropriate learning activities. *Programming* involves development of the IEP. The IEP is individualized, need-based, and must be implemented in the least restrictive environment. The final aspect of the team process is evaluation. *Evaluation* refers to the procedures used to determine the degree to which the objectives have been met.

SPECIAL NEEDS OF CHALLENGED CHILDREN

The needs and interests of children with special physical, mental, or emotional challenges are essentially the same as nonhandicapped children. They generally profit most when mainstreamed into the regular physical education program. Children with limiting conditions need to be accepted for who they are and treated with respect as contributors to the group, class, and society as a whole. They need challenging movement experiences that are within the limits of their abilities. They need ample opportunities to solve problems for themselves and to develop a greater sense of independence rather than dependence. Children with physical, mental, or emotional impairments need to experience a wide variety of movement activities designed to break down the artificial limitations that are often built up around their disability. Like all children, they need ample opportunities for practice, sincere encouragement, and skilled instruction if they are to be expected to improve their movement and physical abilities. Children need especially to adjust socially to their handicapping condition and to establish a realistic body image.

Social Adjustment

A major problem encountered by children with limiting conditions is social adjustment. This problem is often the result of external or societal factors. Historical attitudes toward treatment of exceptional individuals have had an impact on our modern society and its attitude toward them. In the past, the physically, mentally, and emotionally impaired were treated as freaks, feared as being sent by Satan, cursed, given improper medical care and treatment, beaten, and even killed. It is only relatively recently that emphasis has shifted from a person's disabilities to his or her abilities. This more enlightened way of viewing the disabled has had a great effect on their education, as reflected in PL 94–142.

Great progress has been made in education, but unfortunately, many of the old fears and much of the social stigma of the past still exist. The past has influenced our present concept of disabled persons and hence has affected their concept of themselves. Our feelings about ourselves are greatly influenced by the views and reactions of others toward us. Acceptance by others is an important factor in promoting self-acceptance.

The physical education program in which children with limiting conditions are mainstreamed makes a profound positive impact on the social adjustment of impaired and nonimpaired children alike. The physical education program that is developmentally based, individualized, and personalized is geared to the needs and abilities of *all* children. As such, it influences future acceptance by society and hence the individual's acceptance of herself or himself. The nonimpaired population must understand that impaired persons are not looking for concessions or sympathy, but want to be like others within their individual limits. Inclusion leads to acceptance. Inclusion promotes understanding, encourages favorable attitudes, and leads to both public and self-acceptance.

Body Image Enhancement

We all possess some sort of awareness of our own body and its possibilities for movement and performance. This quality, or body images, as it is commonly called, is a learned concept that results from observation of the movements of parts of our body and the relationship of these different parts to each other and to external objects in space.

A well-developed body image is important because we do not deal in absolutes in our perceptions of ourselves or the world about us. If children fail to form a reasonably satisfactory body image, their self-concept is likely to be distorted, and they will be limited in their emotional and social development. The extent to which our body image is developed depends largely on movement experiences. Both the quality and the quantity of these movement activities are important. Movement experiences lead to a better orientation in space and provide information about the body that one would be unable to obtain otherwise. Movement enables us to gain sensory information concerning changes in tonus. The more information received, the better the quality of the information, and the more the body image is developed. The movement experiences and diverse gross motor activities inherent in a well-planned physical education program contribute a great deal to the development of a stable body image, which in turn influences self-concept.

Exceptional children who are either restricted from taking part in vigorous activities or whose performance is atypical fail to form a complete body image or may develop one that is distorted. This imperfect image further affects their perceptions of themselves and their external world. Distorted perceptions tend to undermine self-assurance, often leading to social and psychological difficulties.

Being able to perform a movement task in an acceptable manner contributes to one's confidence and self-assurance. When disabled children are given an opportunity to develop their movement abilities and to improve their body image, their confidence and self-assurance increase. Then the personality is reinforced and the likelihood of problems of social adjustment are diminished.

All children, including those who are physically, mentally, or emotionally challenged, must be given the opportunity to engage in vigorous physical activities. The adjustments that must be made by exceptional children may be modified by the environment in which they live. The physical educator is a part of that environment. Working as a team, parents, teachers, and rehabilitation workers can contribute to a child's physical and psychological development.

PRACTICAL TEACHING SUGGESTIONS

Children with limiting conditions who have been mainstreamed into a physical education program will frequently require modification of the physical activities in which they engage. PL 94–142 provides that handicapped children must receive physical education in the least restrictive environment. Therefore, they must be given the opportunity to participate in the regular program unless a specially designed physical education program is needed, as prescribed by the child's IEP. If a special program is required, the school is responsible for providing this service. If the school is unable to provide the necessary services, arrangements must be made through other public or private programs.

Several practical suggestions follow for incorporating children with special needs into the regular physical education program.

The Physically Challenged

Children with orthopedic conditions can frequently take part in and benefit from inclusion in the regular physical education. Appropriate modifications, specific to the particular handicapping condition, will need to be made. The following are practical suggestions used with the visually, auditorally, and cardiovascularly impaired. Other conditions include children with cerebral palsy, epilepsy, and various musculoskeletal disabilities.

The Visually Impaired. The visually impaired in the regular physical education program may range from the legally blind to the partially sighted. All will need significant modifications in their program of movement activities. Be certain to:

1. Use a whistle or verbal cue to signal the class to move or to stop.
2. Use a turning point for outdoor races that will guide the feet of the runners. Mats can be used for this purpose for indoor races or relays.
3. Clearly mark field dimensions and safety hazards in bright colors.
4. Use a "buddy" system for all activities.
5. Use many auditory cues to help the student gain a quicker understanding of space and distances.
6. Set definite goals and objectives to be reached.
7. Use music often, both for relaxation and for motivation.
8. Include strenuous big-muscle activities.
9. Modify activities that require quick directional changes.
10. Provide structure, routine, and consistency.

The Auditorially Impaired.   Children with auditory impairments in the public school will range from the hard of hearing to the totally deaf. Many will rely on hearing aids and may have speech problems in conjunction with their hearing loss. The physical education program will have to be modified to fit the individual needs of the child. It will be helpful to:

1. Establish and maintain good eye contact.
2. Place students where they can easily see the teacher.
3. Use visual cues in conjunction with auditory cues whenever possible.
4. Speak clearly and concisely.
5. Encourage working with a "buddy" in order to aid learning.
6. Make liberal use of visual aids.
7. Be aware that children with auditory impairments frequently have problems with balance and require extra spotting in many balance-based activities.
8. Do not yell in an attempt to make yourself heard. Instead, speak slowly and clearly, using visual prompts, demonstration, or signing when possible.
9. Be consistent, and patient, and be sure to follow through.
10. Do not take failure to respond or apparent disinterest as a personal affront.

The Cardiovascularly Impaired.   Children with cardiovascular impairments require special attention and careful monitoring of the amount of physical activity in which they take part. The regular physical education program will have to be modified to meet the needs and abilities of each child. Utilize the following guidelines:

1. Work within the guidelines clearly established by the child's physician.
2. Watch closely for signs of stress.
3. Provide frequent rest periods.
4. Incorporate nonvigorous physical activities into the program, including archery, golf, and bowling for older children.
5. Provide opportunities for less strenuous activities such as dance, simple games, and basic tumbling skills for younger children.
6. Work for increased fitness and skill levels at a slower, more relaxed pace than with nonimpaired children.
7. Require a periodic medical clearance for participation.
8. Listen to students, be sensitive to their requests to rest, and watch for signs of fatigue.
9. Use lighter-weight equipment when possible.
10. Require a physician's clearance after the student has been absent due to illness.

Cerebral Palsy Victims.   Children with cerebral palsy present a special dilemma to the physical education teacher because of the several types of cerebral palsy and the degree of involvement with the motor system. Be certain to:

1. Work in conjunction with the physical therapist in providing appropriate activities.
2. Stress socialization and acceptance by peers rather than skill perfection.

3. Focus on movement skills that have a high carryover value for later life and for present leisure-time activities.
4. Concentrate on throwing balls that may be easily gripped rather than hard balls, catching bounced balls rather than ones that are tossed, and kicking or striking stationary balls. These movements are easier and promote greater success.
5. Encourage rhythmic activities.
6. Encourage aquatic activities as an excellent medium in which to promote relaxation.
7. Initiate sustained, flowing-movement activities for spastic children.
8. Give athetoid students extra help with relaxation.
9. Avoid balance and fine motor-coordination activities with ataxic children..

Epileptics. The epileptic child may frequently take part in the regular physical education program with few restrictions or modifications. However, be certain to:

1. Work in conjunction with the child's physician in outlining a program of physical activities.
2. Remember that epileptic children are in all other ways like their peers except for occasional seizures, and these seizures are generally controlled effectively through medication.
3. Remain calm and administer appropriate first aid in the event of a seizure. Help the other children to understand what is happening and to be accepting of the condition.
4. Focus on activities requiring concentration, such as rhythmic activities.
5. Promote inclusion rather than exclusion.
6. Request that the classroom teacher give you an indication of the child's behavior, if abnormal, prior to the physical education class.
7. Avoid climbing activities when in doubt of the child's condition.

The Musculoskeletally Impaired. The wide range of possible musculoskeletal conditions makes it imperative that all physical activity be individually based and medically approved. As a general rule, it is wise to:

1. Conduct a program that is medically approved and within the guidelines established by the child's physician.
2. Provide activities that promote inclusion and maximuim participation.
3. Teach proper techniques of falling from wheelchairs, crutches, and standing postures.
4. Provide activities suited to the level of ambulation of the child.
5. With Osgood–Schlatter's condition, avoid jumping and landing and other activities that stress the knee.
6. Encourage and practice proper posture and body mechanics in the performance of activities.
7. Equalize teams so that all have an opportunity to win.
8. Promote aquatic activities for relaxation, control, and less muscular stress.
9. Encourage sustained stretching movements for children with arthritis.
10. Work closely with the physician and physical therapist in providing an individualized program of adapted physical activities.

The Mentally Challenged

Mentally retarded children, in addition to being below normal in their intellectual functioning, are generally below the performance level of their nonretarded counterparts on tests of motor ability, motor fitness, and physical fitness. This situation is due, in part, to the cognitive aspect that is part of all physical activity, as well as to a frequent lack of opportunity for activity on the part of retarded children. This statement should not be viewed simply as another means of demonstrating the vast differences between exceptional children and their chronological peers. It should, however, serve to point out that, to a large degree, this state of affairs is due to the gross neglect that the mentally retarded have suffered for years. What more can be expected if one's life is spent in endless hours of boredom brought about by constant inactivity? The human machine needs physical activity in order to continue functioning at its optimum level, no matter what its intellectual capabilities are. We cannot expect mentally retarded children to approach their chronological counterparts in terms of physical functioning if they do not have sufficient movement experiences and sound guidance in the development of their physical abilities. Although we must recognize that the ability of the retarded child's mind to function establishes outer limits on the potential functioning of his or her body, we must not let this distract us from striving for maximal performance.

Physical education and therepeutic recreation programs can aid greatly in reducing the "halo" of physical inadequacies that contributes to children being labeled as retarded. There is an ever-expanding circle of artificial disability that forms around the original and unalterable mental disability. This is evidenced by mentally retarded children's performances on numerous tests of physical status. A well-planned program of movement activities will help. This is not to say that physical education is a panacea for *curing* mental retardation. It is merely meant to say that the halo effect can be reduced through a quality physical education program and that the retarded can progress at a *rate* similar to that of nonretarded children, even though they may still be unable to perform at the same *level*.

Many of the mentally retarded do well in simple games and tumbling and such sports as track and field and football. The Special Olympics has aptly demonstrated that the retarded can find success, fitness, and fulfillment through physical activities. Physical educators can do much to help retarded children approach their chronological peers in terms of skill mastery by providing them with a well-planned, individualized program of activities that gradually increases in complexity and requires greater movement control. Thus, simple games and skills, when mastered, should be continually replaced by others that are more fun, challenging, and satisfying. The following are several suggestions for working with the mildly and moderately mentally retarded in a physical education setting.

The Mildly Retarded. Mildly retarded children frequently have motor and perceptual difficulties and often have poor motor coordination. They can develop an amazing amount of physical ability from teachers with great patience who constantly demonstrate loving care and understanding. In teaching the mildly retarded, it is suggested that you:

1. Stress gross motor movement activities focusing on fundamental locomotor, manipulative, and stability skills.
2. Work for higher levels of fitness in a consistent and progressive manner.
3. Be sure all instruction builds skill upon skill and is success-oriented.
4. "Show" more and explain less.
5. Include routine and structure in each session.
6. Keep rules simple.
7. Provide for many kinds of rhythmical activities.
8. Stress the "fun" element of physical activity.
9. Provide manual assistance in certain activities for the children as needed.
10. Reduce skills to their simplest components.
11. Name the movement or skill being taught to help develop a movement vocabulary.
12. Be sure that practice periods are short, with frequent changes in activities in order to reduce frustration.
13. Let children repeat their successes several times in order to enjoy the feeling of accomplishment.
14. Reward approximations of the skill with frequent verbal praise.
15. Avoid activities in which individuals are eliminated.
16. Set standards of acceptable behavior by praising good performance.

The Moderately Retarded. Each of the suggestions presented for the mildly retarded is valid for the moderately retarded with the following additions:

1. Permit more time for learning to occur.
2. Shorten sentences, using fewer verbal cues and more visual and tactile cues.
3. Teach only one skill at a time.
4. Be certain to reinforce all accomplishments, no matter how small, with praise.

5. Praise attempts as well as accomplishments.
6. Simplify instructions and repeat them frequently.
7. Use frequent demonstrations of the task to be learned and actual physical manipulation through the skill as necessary.
8. Use visual prompts and color coding as necessary.
9. Stress compliance with basic rules of safety.
10. Treat each individual with dignity, respect, and a sincere display of caring.

The Emotionally Challenged

The causes of emotional disorders are complex and not completely understood. Although the behaviors manifested by emotionally disturbed children range from prolonged withdrawal to extreme disruption, there are a number of basic suggestions that should be helpful:

1. You will do much better if you understand that disturbed children need someone stable and orderly to serve as an example of steadiness.
2. You should structure the learning environment in such a fashion that the child knows exactly what is expected. Use of a teacher-centered teaching approach often works best.
3. Learn to expect the unexpected. You can count on disturbed children to *overreact* to new or potentially threatening situations.
4. Limits should be set on what the child can and cannot do. A clear definition of what is acceptable and unacceptable behavior is essential. The process of limit-setting should be done in the spirit of helpful authority. Children feel safer when they know the boundaries in which they may operate.
5. Set limits in such a way that they arouse little resentment.
6. Limits should be phrased in language that does not challenge the child's self-respect. For example, say ''Time to put the balls away'' instead of ''Don't shoot another time, John. Put the ball away immediately!''
7. Accept the fact that there may be little

progress in the first month or two. This will depend on the severity of the disturbance. A sense of trust and rapport must develop between teacher and child.
8. Your nonverbal reactions and facial expressions often give away your thoughts. The disturbed child may depend a great deal on nonverbal clues of acceptance, resignation, disappointment, pride, and so forth. Learn to attend to the signs you communicate to the child as well as to the signs conveyed to you.
9. Help the child express feelings and vent hostilities through socially acceptable channels.
10. Be firm and consistent in your discipline, but discipline in a manner that conveys an attitude of helpfulness, not authority.
11. Learn each child's name and let them know yours. Refer to them by name.
12. Structure activities for success. Every child should be able to achieve an element of success in order to help overcome a sense of failure and lack of confidence.
13. Utilize immediate positive reinforcement for desired behavior.
14. Avoid imposing standards or limits that are not within the child's capabilities.
15. Be cognizant of individual differences and modify activities to meet these needs.
16. Avoid elimination activities.
17. Activities should be within the individual's capabilities but must be challenging. If they are too easy, the child will not perform. If they are too hard, the child will not perform or will quit.
18. Do not let small incidents ''snowball.'' The child must know who is the ''boss'' and respect that position.
19. Be thoroughly prepared, overplan, and try to anticipate problems before they occur.
20. Be patient, understanding, and quick to forgive.

The Learning Challenged

Children with learning impairments are generally included in the regular physical education program. They often benefit greatly from a well-planned and taught program of physical activities. Children with deficits in their perceptual–motor functioning have clearly been shown to be capable of improvement in their perceptual–motor abilities. Whether corresponding improvement in academic functioning can be expected as a *direct* result of active participation has not been demonstrated to the satisfaction of most. The fact is, however, that some children do show remarkable progress in their academic achievement after taking part in a specialized program for an extended period of time. With this in mind, be certain to

1. Know and understand the specific nature of the child's learning difficulty.
2. Structure personalized activities that work within the child's present level of abilities.
3. Help the child find an element of success during each lesson.
4. Progress from simple to more complex activities in small increments, being sure to utilize positive encouragement.
5. Provide numerous opportunities for reinforcing academic concepts through movements that are normally dealt with in a classroom setting.
6. Remember that children with specific learning disabilities have generally experienced a great deal of frustration and failure. Therefore, it is very important to create an atmosphere of challenge and success.
7. Promote a "yes I can" attitude.
8. Help the child gain a better understanding of his or her body, the space it occupies, and how it can move.
9. Help the child establish a sense or feel for direction through carefully sequenced movement activities.
10. Make frequent use of rhythmic activities and stress the rhythmical element to all coordinated movement.

SUMMARY

The aim of the special program of physical education is to help each individual child to obtain his or her potential physical, social, and emotional level of functioning in a well-planned, progressive program built around his or her special needs, interests, and abilities. Teachers of special children must realize that the objectives they set and the outcomes they seek are often quite different from those sought by the child. Avoid the pitfall of selecting activities to satisfy program objectives based on your own abilities, interests, and feelings.

Success in teaching special children lies in the ability to individualize and personalize instruction in order to meet unique needs and interests. It is the teacher's responsibility to establish a climate conducive to learning. This climate must be one in which children feel free to learn, to probe, and to explore. It should be one that establishes freedom within limits. These limits should act as guidelines rather than restraints and produce a nonthreatening environment that enables the teacher to start with children at whatever level they are on and take them forward as far as they can go.

SUGGESTED READING

Arnheim, D. D., and Sinclair, W. A. (1985). *Physical education for special populations: A developmental, adapted, and remedial approach.* Englewood Cliffs, NJ: Prentice-Hall.

Fait, H. F., and Duan, J. M. (1984). *Special physical education: Adapted, individualized development.* Philadelphia: Saunders.

Kalakian, L. H., and Eichstaedt, C. B. (1982). *Developmental adapted physical education.* Minneapolis: Burgess.

Miller, A. G., and Sullivan, J. V. (1982). *Teaching physical activities to impaired youth.* New York: Wiley.

Seaman, J. A., and DePauw, K. P. (1982). *The new adapted physical education.* Palo Alto, CA: Mayfield Publishing Company.

Sherrill, Claudine. (1986). Adapted physical education and recreation. Dubuque, IA: Wm. C. Brown.

CHAPTER 9

DEVELOPMENTAL CHARACTERISTICS OF CHILDREN

Growth and development are such complex processes with so many interrelated aspects that it is virtually impossible to deal with the child as a whole through the written word. Perhaps it would be best to stop and reflect at this point on the typical or "average" preschool and elementary school child. In this chapter the general growth and motor development, cognitive, and affective characteristics of the average child are considered. This is done in an effort to form a more complete picture of the whole child as he or she actually comes to you in the classroom or gymnasium. Although no two children are exactly alike, and the individuality of each learner should always be maintained, certain general characteristics do emerge.

EARLY CHILDHOOD (2 TO 6 YEARS)

Play is what young children do when they are not eating, sleeping, or complying with the wishes of adults. Play occupies most of their waking hours, and it may literally be viewed as the child's equivalent of work as performed by adults. Children's play serves as the primary mode by which they learn about their bodies and movement capabilities. It also serves as an important facilitator of cognitive and affective growth in the young child, as well as providing an important means of developing both fine and gross motor skills.

Preschool children are actively involved in enhancing their cognitive abilities in a variety of ways. These early years are a period of important cognitive development that have been termed *the preoperational thought phase* by Piaget. It is during this time that children develop cognitive functions that will eventually result in logical thinking and concept formulation. Young children are not capable of thinking from any point of view other than their own. Their perceptions dominate their thinking, and what is experienced at a given moment has great influence on them. During this preconceptual phase of cognitive development, seeing is, literally, believing. In the thinking and logic of preschool children, their conclusions need no justification. Even if they did, the children would be unable to reconstruct their thoughts and show others how they arrived at their conclusions. Play serves as a vital means by which higher cognitive structures are gradually developed. It provides a multitude of settings and variables for promoting cognitive growth.

Affective development is also dramatic during the preschool years. During this period children are involved in the two crucial social–emotional tasks of developing a sense of autonomy and a sense of initiative. Autonomy is expressed through a growing sense of independence, which may be seen in children's delight in the use of the word *no* to almost any direct question. The answer will often be "no" to a question such as "Do you want to play outside?" even though they clearly would like to. This may be viewed as an expression of a new-found sense of independence and an ability to manipulate some factors in the environment rather than always as an expression of sheer disobedience. A way in which to avoid this natural autonomous reaction to a question is to alter it to form a positive statement such as "Let's go play outdoors." In this way, the child is not confronted with a direct yes-or-no choice. Care must be taken, however, to give children abundant situations in which an expression of their autonomy is reasonable and proper.

Young children's expanding sense of initiative is seen through their curious exploring and their very active behavior. Children now engage in new experiences, such as climbing, jumping, running, and throwing objects, for their own sake and for the sheer joy of sensing and knowing what they are capable of doing. Failure to de-

PHOTO 9.1   Play is the world of the young child.

velop a sense of initiative as well as a sense of autonomy frequently leads to feelings of shame, worthlessness, and a sense of guilt. Establishment of stable self-concept is crucial to proper affective development in preschoolers because it has an effect on both cognitive and psychomotor functions.

Through the medium of play, preschoolers develop a wide variety of fundamental locomotor, manipulative, and stability abilities. If they have a stable and positive self-concept, the gain in control over their musculature is a smooth one. The timid, cautious, and measured movements of the 2- to 3-year-old gradually give way to the confident, eager, and often reckless abandon of the 4- and 5-year-old. Preschoolers' vivid imaginations make it possible for them to jump from "great heights," climb "high mountains," leap over "raging rivers," and run "faster" than an assorted variety of "wild beasts."

Children of preschool age are rapidly expanding their horizons. They are asserting their individuality, developing their abilities, and testing their limits as well as the limits of their family and others around them. In short, young children are pushing out into the world in many complex and wondrous ways. Care must be taken, however, to understand their developmental characteristics and their limitations as well as their potentials. Only in this way can we effectively structure movement experiences for them that truly reflect their needs and interests and are within their level of ability.

The following developmental characteristics represent a synthesis of findings from a wide variety of sources and are presented here to provide a more complete view of the "typical" child during the preschool years.

Growth and Motor Development Characteristics

1. Boys and girls range from about 33 to 47 inches in height and 25 to 53 pounds.
2. Perceptual–motor abilities are rapidly developing, but confusion often exists in body, directional, temporal, and spatial awareness.
3. Good bladder and bowel control are generally established by the end of this period, but accidents sometimes still occur.
4. Children during this period are rapidly developing fundamental movement abilities in a variety of motor skills. Bilateral movements such as skipping, however, often present more difficulty than unilateral movements.
5. Children are active and energetic and would often rather run than walk.
6. Motor abilities are developed to the point that the children know how to dress themselves, although they may need help straightening and fastening articles of clothing.
7. The body functions and processes become well regulated. A state of physiological homeostasis (stability) becomes well established.
8. The body builds of boys and girls are remarkably similar. A back view of boys and girls reveals no readily observable structural differences.
9. Fine motor control is not fully established, although gross motor control is developing rapidly.
10. The eyes are not generally ready for extended periods of close work, due to farsightedness, which is characteristic of both preschool and primary-grade children.

Cognitive Development Characteristics

1. There is constantly increasing ability to express thoughts and ideas verbally.
2. A fantastic imagination enables imitation of both actions and symbols with little concern for accuracy or the proper sequencing of events.
3. There is continuous investigation and discovery of new symbols that have a primarily personal reference.
4. The "how" and "why" of the child's actions are learned through almost constant play.
5. This is a preoperational thought phase of development, resulting in a period of transition from self-satisfying behavior to fundamental socialized behavior.

Affective Development Characteristics

1. During this period children are egocentric and assume that everyone thinks the way they do. As a result, they often seem to be quarrelsome and exhibit difficulty in sharing and getting along with others.
2. They are often fearful of new situations, shy, self-conscious, and unwilling to leave the security of what is familiar.
3. They are learning to distinguish right from wrong and are beginning to develop a conscience.
4. Two- and 4-year-old children are often seen to be unusual and irregular in their behavior, while those who are 3 and 5 are often viewed as stable and conforming in their behavior.
5. Their self-concept is rapidly developing. Wise guidance, success-oriented experiences, and positive reinforcement are especially important during these years.

Implications for Developmental Physical Education

1. Plenty of opportunity for gross motor play must be offered in both undirected and directed settings.

2. The movement experiences of the preschooler should involve primarily movement exploration and problem-solving activities in order to maximize the child's creativity and desire to explore.

3. The movement education program should include plenty of positive reinforcement in order to encourage the establishment of a positive self-concept and to reduce the fear of failure.

4. Stress should be placed on developing a variety of fundamental locomotor, manipulative, and stability abilities, progressing from the simple to the complex as the children become "ready" for them.

5. Interests and abilities of boys and girls are similar, with no need for separate activities during this period.

6. Plenty of activities designed specifically to enhance perceptual–motor functioning are necessary.

7. Advantage should be taken of the child's great imagination through the use of a variety of activities, including drama and imagery.

8. Because of their often awkward and inefficient movements, be sure to gear movement experiences to their maturity level.

9. Provide a wide variety of activities that require object handling and eye–hand coordination.

10. Begin to incorporate bilateral activities such as skipping, galloping, and hopping, with alternate foot leading, after unilateral movements have been fairly well established.

11. Encourage children to take an active part in the movement education program by "showing" and "telling" others what they can do in order to help overcome tendencies to be shy and self-conscious.

12. Activity should stress arm, shoulder, and upper-body movement.

13. Mechanically correct execution in a wide variety of fundamental movements is the primary goal, without emphasis on standards of performance.

14. Do not stress coordination in conjunction with speed and agility.

15. Poor habits of posture are beginning. Reinforce good posture with positive statements.

16. Provide convenient access to toilet facilities and encourage the children to accept this responsibility on their own.

17. Provide for individual differences and allow for children to progress at their own rate.

18. Establish standards for acceptable behavior and abide by them. Provide wise guidance in the establishment of a sense of doing what is right and proper instead of what is wrong and unacceptable.

19. The motor development program should be prescriptive and based on each individual's readiness level.

20. A multisensory approach should be utilized by the instructor, that is, one in which a wide variety of experiences is incorporated, using several sensory modalities.

LATER CHILDHOOD (6 TO 10 YEARS)

Children in the elementary grades are generally happy, stable, eager, and able to assume responsibilities. They are able to cope with new situations and are anxious to learn more about themselves and their expanding world. Primary-grade children take the first big step into their expanding world when they enter first grade. For many, first grade represents the first separation from the home for a regularly scheduled, extended block of time. It is the first step out of the secure play environment of the home and into the world of adults. Entering a school represents the first time that many children are placed in a group situation in which they are not the center of attention. It is a time when sharing, concern for others, and respect for the rights and responsibilities of others are established.

Kindergarten is a readiness time in which to begin making the gradual transition from an egocentric, home-centered play world to the group-oriented world of adult concepts and logic. In the first grade, the first formal demands for cognitive understanding are made. The major milestone of the first and second grader is learning how to read at a reasonable level. The 6-year-old is generally developmentally ready for the important task of "breaking the code" and learns to read. The child is involved in developing the first real understanding of time and money and numerous other cognitive concepts. By the second grade, children should be well on their way to meeting and surmounting the ever-broadening array of cognitive, affective, and psychomotor tasks that are placed before them.

The following is a listing of the general developmental characteristics of children from age 6 to 10.

Growth and Motor Development Characteristics

1. Boys and girls range from about 44 to 60 inches and 44 to 90 pounds.
2. Growth is slow, especially from age 8 to the end of this period. There is a slow but steady pace of increments, unlike the more rapid gains in height and weight during the preschool years.
3. The body begins to lengthen out with an annual gain of only 2 to 3 inches and an annual weight gain of only 3 to 6 pounds.
4. The cephalocaudal (head-to-toe) and proximodistal (center-to-periphery) principles of development are now quite evident, in which the larger muscles of the body are considerably better developed than the small muscles.
5. Girls are generally about a year ahead of boys in physiological development, and separate interests begin to develop toward the end of this period.
6. Hand preference is firmly established, with about 90 percent preferring the right hand and about 10 percent preferring the left.
7. Reaction time is quite slow, causing difficulty with eye–hand and eye–foot coordi-

nation at the beginning of this period. By the end of the period, it is generally well established.
8. Both boys and girls are full of energy but often possess a low endurance level and tire easily. Responsiveness to training, however, is great.
9. The visual–perceptual mechanisms are fully established. Such perceptual qualities as figure–ground perception, speed of vision, perceptual constancy, and spatial relationships are generally well established by the end of this period.
10. Children are often farsighted during this periods and are not ready for extended periods of close work.
11. Fundamental movement abilities should be well defined by the beginning of this period. Locomotor abilities are developed to the extent that children are able to gallop, skip, jump, and climb in a mature pattern.
12. Stability abilities are both static and dynamic. Balancing abilities are improved.
13. Basic skills necessary for successful play become well developed.
14. Activities involving the eyes and limbs develop slowly. Such activities as catching, kicking, striking, and volleying require considerable practice.
15. This period marks a transition from refining fundamental movement abilities to the establishment of a variety of sport skills in lead-up games and athletic skills.

Cognitive Development Characteristics

1. Attention span is generally short at the beginning of this period but gradually lengthens. However, boys and girls of this age will often spend hours on activities that are of great interest to them.
2. They are eager to learn and to please adults but need assistance and guidance in decision making.
3. Children have good imaginations and display extremely creative minds; however, self-consciousness seems to become a factor again toward the end of this period.
4. They are often interested in songs, tele-

PHOTO 9.2 Children will spend considerable time-on-task if they are interested in the learning activity.

vision, movies, computer games, and gymnastic activities.

5. They are not capable of abstract thinking and deal best with concrete examples and situations during the beginning of this period. More abstract cognitive abilities are evident by the end of this period.

6. Children are intellectually curious and anxious to know "why."

Affective Development Characteristics

1. Interests of boys and girls are similar at the beginning of this period but soon begin to diverge.

2. During the primary years, the child is self-centered and plays poorly in large groups for extended periods of time, although small-group situations are handled well.

3. During the intermediate and upper grades, the child becomes increasingly capable of playing in large groups. Effective group interaction techniques emerge.

4. The child is often aggressive, boastful, self-critical, and overreactive, accepting defeat and victory poorly. However, increased control develops with effective adult interaction.

5. There is an inconsistent level of maturity; the child is often less mature at home than in school, due to parental influence.

6. The child is responsive to authority, "fair" punishment, discipline, and reinforcement.

7. Children are adventurous and eager to be involved with a friend or group of friends in "dangerous" or "secret" activities.

8. The child's self-concept is becoming firmly established by age 8.

Implications for Developmental Physical Education

1. There should be opportunities for children to refine fundamental movement abilities in the areas of locomotion, manipulation, and stability to a point where they are fluid and efficient.

2. Children need to be helped in making the transition from the fundamental movement phase to the sport-related movement phase.

3. The assurance of being accepted and valued as a human being is important to children in order to know they have a stable and secure place in their school environment as well as in the home.

4. Abundant opportunities for encouragement and positive reinforcement from adults are necessary in order to promote continued development of a positive self-concept.

5. Opportunities and encouragement to ex-

plore and experiment through movement with their bodies and objects in their environment enhance perceptual–motor efficiency.

6. There should be exposure to experiences in which progressively greater amounts of responsibility are introduced to help promote self-reliance.

7. Adjustments to the rougher ways of the school playground and neighborhood without being rough or crude themselves is an important social skill to be learned.

8. Opportunities for gradual introduction to group and team activities should be provided at the proper time.

9. Storyplays and imaginary and mimetic activities may be effectively incorporated into the program during the primary years because of the child's vivid imagination.

10. Activities that incorporate the use of music and rhythmics are enjoyable at this level and are valuable in enhancing fundamental movement abilities, creativity, and a basic understanding of the components of music and rhythm.

11. Children at this level learn best through active participation. Integration of academic concepts with movement activities provides an effective avenue for reinforcing concepts in science, mathematics, social studies, and the language arts.

12. Activities that involve climbing and hanging are beneficial to development of the upper torso and should be included in the program.

13. Discuss play situations involving such topics as taking turns, fair play, cheating, and sportsmanship as a means of establishing a more complete sense of right or wrong.

14. Interest in sports is beginning to develop strongly during this period. Introduce basic athletic skills and simple lead-up games.

15. Begin to stress accuracy, form, and skill in the performance of movement skills.

16. Encourage children to "think" before engaging in an activity. Help them recognize potential hazards as a means of reducing their often reckless behavior.

17. Encourage small-group activities followed by larger-group activities and team sport experience.

18. Posture is important. Activities need to stress proper body alignment.

19. Specialized movement skills begin to be developed and refined toward the end of this period. Plenty of opportunity for practice, encouragement, and selective instruction is important.

20. Opportunities should be provided for participation in youth sport activities that are developmentally appropriate and geared to the needs and interests of children.

SUMMARY

Study of the many models of growth and development, along with careful observation and daily contact with children, enables one to compile a set of developmental characteristics in the psychomotor, affective, and cognitive domains that typifies the mythical "average" child. By no means should any of these characteristics be considered to be universal; one may easily call to mind a number of children who do not exhibit one or more of these characteristics at any given age. Careful study of the developmental characteristics typical of children at varying ages enables us to formulate programs that meet the needs, interests, and developmental capabilities of the greatest number of children. It does not guarantee that each child will exactly fit into a predescribed mold. This important fact is recognized by teachers who make room for individual differences through individualized instruction whenever possible.

SUGGESTED READING

Craig, G. J. (1983). *Human development*. Englewood Cliffs, NJ: Prentice-Hall.

Gibson, J. (1978). *Growing up: A study of children*. Reading, MA: Addison-Wesley.

Harris, J. R., and Libert, R. M. (1984). *The child*. Englewood Cliffs, NJ: Prentice-Hall.

Lawton, J. T. (1982). *Introduction to child development*. Dubuque, IA: Wm. C. Brown.

Smart, M. S., and Smart, R. C. (1982). *Children: Development and relationships*. New York: Macmillan.

Yussen, S. R., and Santrock, J. W. (1982). *Child development: An introduction*. Dubuque, IA: Wm. C. Brown.

PART III

THE TEACHER

CHAPTER 10

THE ROLE OF THE TEACHER

The ingredients of successful teaching in physical education are not unlike teaching in any other subject-matter area. To do a thorough job, the teacher must have specialized training, interest in and enthusiasm for the subject matter, a sound grasp of teaching techniques, the ability to communicate effectively with children, and a continuing desire to learn more. Teachers of physical education must be able to create a highly positive atmosphere between themselves and the children whom they teach. The atmosphere of the gymnasium should be one of informality, active involvement, instructional and behavioral feedback, and recognition of individual differences within the learning environment. It should be one of support, encouragement, and success-oriented experiences, skillfully guided by knowledgeable, caring teachers. This chapter focuses on the varied responsibilities of the physical education teacher, characteristics of the successful teacher, and the stages of concern for the teacher.

Teachers of elementary school physical education may be the regular classroom teacher or the specialized physical educator. In either case, the teacher has the responsibility for meeting the needs of students in terms of promoting increased movement skills, physical and motor fitness, perceptual–motor abilities, and an enhanced sensed of personal worth. Teachers of physical education, like all other educators, need to determine what they are trying to accomplish, how they intend to effect learning, and how they will assess the results of their efforts.

RESPONSIBILITIES OF THE TEACHER

Physical education teachers assume many responsibilities in carrying out their duties. They must take on the tasks of planning the curriculum, organizing the program, implementing the lesson, and assessing pupil progress. Additionally, teachers accept the seldom-mentioned responsibilities of counselor, community representative, and long-term professional growth.

Planning the Curriculum

The physical education teacher is frequently entirely responsible for developing the overall curriculum. This is an important task that must be taken seriously, and it is crucial to a successful program. Planning the curriculum takes time. It requires careful analysis of student needs and interests as well as a survey of available facilities, equipment, and time allotments. Successful curriculum planning requires input from many sources and coordination with fellow teachers and administrators. Refer to Chapter 14 for a complete discussion on the developmental physical education curriculum.

Organizing The Learning Environment

Along with planning the overall curriculum, the teacher is responsible for organizing the learning environment. Physical education teachers are generally responsible for ordering, inventorying, and maintaining gymnasium and playground equipment. They assume responsibility for periodic safety checks of gymnasium apparatus and outdoor play equipment. They are frequently responsible for escorting children to the gymnasium and back to the classroom. A great deal of organizational requirements will be placed upon you as the physical education teacher. You will have to work hard to carry out these obligations and make maximum effective use of your time and the time that you have with your students. Refer to Chapter 16 for a complete discussion on organizing the learning environment.

Planning and Implementing the Lesson

The very "heart" of the teacher's role is actual planning and implementation of the lesson. Developing the overall curriculum and organizing the learning environment are important, but they are basic to the manner in which the lesson itself will be planned and implemented. The teacher is first and foremost an instructor. The physical education teacher instructs primarily in the acquisition of movement skills, the attainment and maintenance of physical fitness, and the trans-

mission of knowledges and understandings of the games, sports, and rhythmic activities characteristic of the culture. The manner in which the lesson is implemented may take many forms, but it is of utmost importance that children develop an understanding of and appreciation for the *why* of physical activity and *how* to incorporate it into their daily routines. A variety of teaching approaches and motivational techniques may be utilized, which depend upon the philosophy, educational background, personality, and experience of the teacher, but all should lead to a physically educated individual. Refer to Chapter 15 for a complete discussion on planning, formatting, and implementing the lesson.

Assessing Pupil Progress

Coupled with implementing the lesson is assessment of student progress. Teachers serve as evaluators or assessors in order to determine if the objectives of their instruction have been met. Assessment may take many forms. It may be subjective or objective, formal or informal, process-oriented or product-oriented. Assessment of children should stress the positive aspects of their performance, focusing on *personal* improvement and the discovery of one's individual potential. Child-centered assessment should help promote an "I believe in you; you must believe in you" attitude between teacher and student. Assessment should serve as an important form of feedback to students, parents, and the teacher. Refer to Chapter 19 for a complete discussion on assessing progress.

Counseling Students

A frequent, although generally unwritten, role of the physical education teacher is that of counselor. For years physical educators and coaches have informally assumed this important but often overlooked role. Care must be taken when you are called upon to counsel students. Due to the very nature of physical activity and the rapport generated through sensitive, caring instruction, physical education teachers often have numerous informal opportunities to serve effectively as counselors on a wide range of matters. Counseling opportunities may range from adjusting to school, home, and peer situations to techniques for healthful living and understanding and coping with one's changing body. Your role as a counselor needs to be recognized and taken seriously. You need to recognize, however, that unless you have special training, your ability and effectiveness in dealing with major problems is limited. The impact that physical education teachers have as counselors is often as great as their impact as instructors.

TABLE 10.1   Selected Professional Journals of Interest to the Physical Educator

Journal Name	Mailing Address
Adapted Physical Activity Quarterly	Human Kinetics Publishers Box 5046 Champaign, IL 61820
Athletic Journal	1719 Howard Street Evanston, IL 60202
CAHPER Journal	333 Ch. River Road Vanier, Canada K1L 8B9
International Journal of Physical Education	c/o Verlag Karl Hofmann D-7060 Schorndorf, Postfach 1360 Federal Republic of Germany
Journal of Physical Education, Recreation and Dance	AAHPERD Circulation Department 1900 Association Drive Reston, VA 22091
Journal of Teaching in Physical Education	Human Kinetics Publishers Box 5076 Champaign, IL 61820
The Physician and Sports Medicine	McGraw-Hill Publishers 4530 W. 77th St. Minneapolis, MN 55435
The Physical Educator	9030 Log Run Drive North Indianapolis, IN 46234
The Physical Education Newsletter	Physical Education Publications Box 8 (20 Cedarwood Dr.) Old Saybrook, CT 06475
Quest	Human Kinetics Publishers Box 5076 Champaign, IL 61820
The Research Quarterly for Exercise and Sport	AAHPERD Circulation Department 1900 Association Drive Reston, VA 22091
Scholastic Coach	730 Broadway New York, NY 10003
Spotlight on Youth Sports	Youth Sports Institute Intramural Sports Circle Michigan State University East Lansing, MI 48824

Acting as Community Representative

Physical educators serve as representatives of the community for which they are employed. As a professional educator, your views in terms of the education of children will be sought. You will be expected to be knowledgeable about a variety of educational issues and to have formulated rational, intelligent positions. Your views on youth sport, weight training for children, diet, and exercise, among others, will be valued. Furthermore, your views will reflect on the school system or agency for which you are a representative.

The physical educator has a tremendous opportunity to serve as an effective community representative. You have training and knowledge about a variety of issues that are important to the public and the motor development of their children. This knowledge can be used to serve as an effective voice in the community.

Professional Growth

Continued professional growth is an important responsibility of the physical educator. This may take many forms, but it is generally accomplished through continuing education, professional reading, and involvement in professional organization and societies.

In order to continually develop as an effective teacher, the professional educator is committed to advanced education beyond the undergraduate degree. Most states require teachers to pursue a master's degree or some form of continuing education in order to maintain a valid teaching license. Continued professional growth may also be fostered through subscribing to and reading professional journals. The professional magazines listed in Table 10.1 are among the most popular and relevant to the professional physical educator.

Involvement in professional organizations or societies at the local, state, and/or national level is another long-term responsibility of the professional physical educator. This may take the form of attending professional workshops and special meeting, serving on committees and action groups, or even making professional presentations. The American Alliance for Health, Physical Education, Recreation and Dance (AAHPERD) is the professional association to which most physical educators in the USA belong. Local AAHPERD organizations are located in each state and region of the country. The Canadian Association for Health, Physical Education and Recreation (CAPHER) has affiliates in each province, and the International Congress for Health, Physical Education and Recreation (ICHPER) is the association to which many physical educators from around the world belong. Societies such as Delta Psi Kappa, Phi Delta Phi, and Phi Epsilon Kappa also provide a means for continual professional growth.

CHARACTERISTICS OF SUCCESSFUL TEACHERS

Successful teachers are those who, through planned means of instruction, are able to bring about positive change in the learner. Such change occurs in an environment that is meaningful and nonthreatening, one that aids in developing a thinking and acting individual. The following personal, classroom, and assessment traits contribute to successful teaching:

Personal Traits

Upon entering the classroom or gymnasium, the student sees the teacher. A variety of personal characteristics display the teacher's attitude toward the subject matter, individual students, and class itself (refer to Chapter 11 for a discussion on talking to children). The following are several personal traits chracteristic of successful teachers.

Interested. They display interest in students as individuals while refraining from being "buddy-buddy." This indicates to students that the teacher cares about them as people as well as students.

Honest. They are honest with themselves and their students. They are not condescending or

PHOTO 10.1 A smile is one of the teachers most important assets.

afraid to admit to a mistake or lack of knowledge. This shows students that they can be trusted.

Enthusiastic. They are alive with enthusiasm about the subject matter and are eager to share this knowledge. This tends to help students want to learn rather than making them feel that they have to learn.

Human. They smile. They have an aura of warmth and a sense of humor. Students want to believe that teachers are human; only by acting human can teachers display true concern for the class.

Good Speakers. They have a clear voice and a vocabulary geared to the students' level. They do not talk down to children or at them but talk *to* them by adjusting their vocabulary to the children they are teaching. It is a pleasure to listen to teachers who speak well and are easily understood.

Confident. They are confident in their abilities and do not find it necessary to enhance their egos through the students. They are able to be leaders and are sensitive to the needs of the group. This enables students to find comfort in the teacher's leadership without feeling threatened.

Properly Dressed. They recognize that, although it is superficial, personal appearance does have an effect on how students view them. They dress neatly and appropriately for their age. This helps create a positive image of the teacher and enhances enjoyment of the class.

Knowledgeable. They are in command of the subject matter. They are well read and remain up-to-date in their knowledge. This helps ensure that the students will receive high quality, current, and correct information.

Classroom Traits

As the teacher enters the classroom or gymnasium, the process of rigid scrutiny by students begins. There is a variety of factors involved in the teacher's actual conduct of the class that play an important role in the teacher's success (refer to Chapter 13 for a discussion on selecting and using appropriate teaching styles). Teachers who use up-to-date teaching methods, clearly state objectives, and strive for clarity and personalized instruction are often viewed as excellent by students. The following are several classroom or gymnasium traits characteristic of successful teachers.

Prompt. They are early or on time for classes. This illustrates enthusiasm and interest in the students. It also permits time for questions, comments, or informal conversation.

Prepared. They carefully plan each class period so that all of the time allotted is used wisely. Successful teachers do not drag out a period simply to fill in the time. This makes students feel that their time in class is well spent and worth the effort they make.

Resourceful. They use a variety of outside resources, when applicable, to enhance learning and vary the normal class routine. This serves to broaden the students' scope of knowledge and enhance interest in the class.

Review/Preview. They provide a brief verbal or visual review of the previous lesson and preview of the material to be covered during the current class period. This enables the students to link previous information with new information and to follow more closely the day's lesson.

Practical. They recognize the necessity for

practical application of ideas and concepts to everyday life. They illustrate the relevancy of the material for students and enable them to more accurately and personally apply the information.

Realistic.   They are consistent and realistic in their expectations of students. This provides them with clearly stated boundaries of acceptable behavior and standards of performance.

Open.   They remain open to student questions and comments and create a forum for idea exchange. This encourages thinking and synthesizing of knowledge on the part of students.

Clear.   Successful teachers clearly state the objectives of the lesson in language students understand. They do not overload them with verbiage. This helps students focus on what is important.

In Control.   They are objective, consistent, and constructive in the application of disciplinary measures, and they recognize the individuality of each student. This assures students that they will be dealt with fairly.

Assessment Traits

All teachers are faced with the responsibility of assessing students, but it is the student who must cope with the variety of techniques employed. Every student is an individual and, as such, prefers certain types of evaluative methods to others. The following is a list of several characteristics of successful teachers in terms of assessment.

Assess by Objectives.   They take the time to develop objectives for their students and for themselves. Students need to know what is expected of them and how they will be evaluated. Teachers must know what goals they want their students to reach and how they are going to help them achieve those goals.

Use Valid Instruments.   They employ valid instruments to measure students' mastery of the subject matter. Each assessment should be based on a testing situation relevant to that particular subject matter.

Vary Techniques.   They do not assess students by totally objective or subjective means. They combine objectivity and subjectivity in testing situations to help make the evaluation experience more meaningful.

Provide Feedback.   They use assessment as a consistent and positive form of feedback in terms of knowledge and performance. This helps students focus on their strengths and upgrade their weaknesses.

Timely.   They give meaningful feedback to their students as quickly as possible. They correct assignments and tests and return them as soon as possible with meaningful comments to give students an indication of their strong and weak points.

Understanding.   They realize and make concessions in view of the fact that people perceive things differently. This indicates that the teacher is interested enough in the students to listen to their interpretation of questions and the reasons for their answers.

Informed.   They recognize that there are external factors that may affect student performance. They take the time to learn about their students as individuals and to find out what they are involved in.

Fair.   They steadfastly refuse to let personal prejudice, bias, or preference interfere with fair and honest assessment. This assures students that they will be evaluated on what they know or can do, not on artificial criteria such as hair length, style of dress, or likeability.

STAGES OF CONCERN OF A TEACHER

Excellence in teaching is a worthy goal for which to strive. Only experience and a great deal of personal effort will help in this quest for excellence. There are worlds of difference separating the poor, the good, and the master teacher.

The process of becoming a master teacher does not occur overnight. Effective teaching is both an art and a science that takes considerable time, effort, and practice. Successful teachers are effective in both communicating with children and listening to children. They are good planners, organizers, and implementers of meaningful movement experiences. Successful teachers have a genuine concern for their students and manifest this concern in their teaching behavior.

It is interesting to note that on the road to becoming a successful teacher most people go through a series of predictable stages. The following are three stages of concern that you can expect to go through as you strive to become a master teacher.

Concern for Survival

No matter how well prepared you are at the completion of your education, or how many practice-teaching experiences you have had, your first concern as a new teacher is most likely to be that of survival—survival in the school itself, as well as survival in the gymnasium and on the playground.

Concern for survival in the school at large takes many forms. Adjusting to the policies and unwritten as well as written rules of your new place of employment is important to survival. Learning the names, roles, and expectations of your fellow teachers and supervisors is important to survival. Remember, you are "the new kid on the block," and you will have to make adjustments to what is already in place. Finding your way around the school, locating equipment and supplies, and becoming acquainted with the school custodian and secretary are important to survival. Often these individuals are crucial to the success of your program. They can be very helpful in maintaining facilities and equipment and ordering needed supplies and equipment. Both are often helpful in helping you adjust to the community mores and the character of the faculty, administration, and students.

Survival in the gymnasium and on the playground is often more immediate and crucial. What happens between you and your students during the early days, weeks, and months will do much to set the stage for their later behavior. All too frequently, new teachers enter a school totally unprepared for gaining and maintaining control of their classes. Too often, their teaching diminishes to a "tug-of-war" of who will be in control. In order to survive, you *must* win this battle. Survival as a teacher depends on your ability to command the respect of your students, gain and maintain their attention, and insure class control. See Chapter 12 for a discussion on positive discipline. The physical environment of the gymnasium and playground is quite different from that of the classroom. Children often exhibit a different set of behaviors in these environments. Therefore, it is of utmost importance to have a plan of action for your survival.

Concern for Self

Once teachers have mastered the basic elements of survival, concern is often focused inward. Teachers at this stage tend to ask questions such as "what's in it for me?," "How can I make this easier on me?,"or "Why me?"

At this stage of concern, there is a definite tendency to feel overworked and underpaid. As a result, you are likely to feel misunderstood and unappreciated by your peers as well as your students. Although this stage is self-centered and appears to violate the ideals of "dedicated" teaching, it is one that most go through. It does have its benefits. Teachers with an acute concern for self have done much to cause local school boards to reexamine pay scales, workloads, and extracurricular expectations. Therefore, this stage, when viewed in its proper perspective, has done much to make the teaching profession a more attractive place to seek employment in the past few years, and it does much to create a climate for the third and final stage of concern.

Concern for Students

Genuine concern for learning and the welfare of students is the essence of successful teaching. Teachers at this stage are not encumbered by the anxiety of survival—they have demonstrated their capability in this arena—nor are they preoccupied with a "what's in it for me" attitude. They recognize the benefits and liabilities inherent in their profession in general and their own situation in particular, and they have chosen to get on with the business of educating children to the best of their ability.

There is no timetable for each of the stages of concern that you are likely to encounter as a teacher. Some are early casualties and never get beyond the survival stage. Some never advance beyond the concern-for-self stage and look for little beyond a paycheck. Most successful teachers, however, have reached the third stage and demonstrate a genuine, lasting interest in their children, both as students and as individuals. It is hoped that you too will reach this third stage, because it is only in this way that the teaching profession will continue to be of real benefit to children and that the physical education profession, in particular, will be able to maintain a legitimate role in the total school curriculum.

SUGGESTED READING

Clayton, R., and Clayton, J. A. (1982). *Concepts and careers in physical education*. Minneapolis: Burgess.

Colfer, George C., et al. (1986). *Contemporary physical education*. Dubuque, IA: Wm. C. Brown.

Drowatzky, J. D., and Armstrong, C. W. (1984). *Physical education: Career perspectives and professional foundations*. Englewood Cliffs, NJ: Prentice-Hall.

Locke, Larry, and Griffin, Pat, Eds. (1986, April). Profiles of struggle. *Journal of Physical Education, Recreation and Dance*. 57:32–63.

Nelson, Jonathan E. (1986, April). Communication—The Key to Public Relations. *Journal of Physical Education, Recreation and Dance*. 57:64–67.

Pestolesi, R. A., and Baker, C. (1984). *Introduction to physical education: A contemporary careers approach*. Glenview, IL: Scott, Foresman.

CHAPTER 11

TALKING TO CHILDREN

Teaching is a learned behavior and, as such, is susceptible to change. Successful teachers recognize that if there is no learning on the part of the student, then there has been no real teaching. Good teaching requires much more than whistle blowing and the dissemination of information. It requires establishing an environment conducive to learning, with clear, open lines of communication between the teacher and the learner. Only when the lines of communication are open and the individual is receptive to what is being presented is there true learning, and hence, true teaching.

Talking to children is both a verbal and a nonverbal process. It is important to recognize that your communication skills have a tremendous impact on children and on the learning that takes place. This chapter will focus on specific techniques of verbal and nonverbal communication, how to convey enthusiasm to children, and specific techniques for improving your communication skills.

VERBAL COMMUNICATION

The spoken word is an important tool for the teacher, both in verbal explanations and in the presentation of movement challenges in a verbal format. No matter what teaching styles and techniques are used in the lesson, it is of crucial importance for you to be able to get and maintain the students' attention, and to provide clarity in your instruction.

Getting Attention

Getting the attention of a group of children requires a variety of communication skills. First, it is important to stand where you can be seen by all of the class. Standing at the edge of a circle formation or far enough back from a straight-line formation will insure that all students can see (see Chapter 16 "Organizing the Learning Environment," for more information on organizing groups of children). It is much easier to get the attention of the group if you can see, and make eye contact with, every child. One easy

PHOTO 11.1   Children need to be talked *to* not *at*.

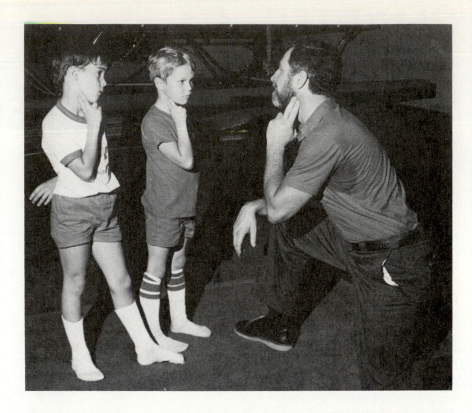

way to insure that you can see the entire class and maintain eye contact is to have the students seated when you talk to them as a group. In this way, children at the back of the group can be more easily seen and your line of sight will not be blocked by students in the front.

Getting the attention of a group of children can most easily be achieved through use of a predetermined signal. The cue you select should be used with consistency and only as a signal for the class to stop all activity, face toward you, and listen carefully for the next instructions. Traditionally, a whistle has been used by physical education teachers to get the attention of the class. This is most effective outdoors or when the class is spread out over a large area. However, the use of a whistle is not always practical, particularly when you are indoors with classrooms located nearby. Instead, some teachers use a drum or tamborine. Others merely clap their hands or silently raise a hand overhead. Still others use a verbal command, such as "Freeze," in order to stop all activity and get the attention

of the class. Whatever technique you select, the key is consistency. Be consistent in the use of cues and consistent in your expectation that *all* are to cease what they are doing and focus their attention on you.

Maintaining Attention

Once you have succeeded in getting the attention of the group, it is important to be able to maintain attention and concentration with a minimum of distractions. children, like adults, need to be talked *to*, not *at*. Therefore, it is of utmost importance not to treat them as "babies" by being condescending in your approach. The use of a monosyllabic, "sing-song" approach is not only condescending to most children, but is offensive as well. Children can be talked to in an effective manner without resorting to this type of verbal behavior. Your vocabulary may have to be modified to suit the level of understanding of the children you are dealing with, but remember, they are not babies and should not be treated as such.

The manner in which you project your voice is of special importance when trying to maintain children's attention in a physical education setting. Gymnasiums are large structures, often with poor acoustics, and playgrounds are open, so it is necessary to be able to project your voice in a manner that all can hear. In no case, however, should you attempt to shout over the din of noise characteristic of children. If you are unable to project your voice so that all can hear you clearly, then utilize your attention-getting command along with a second cue to rally the group to you.

Vocal intonation is worthy of mention because many a teacher has lulled students to sleep with a constant drone. Maintain a steady pitch in your speech, but alter it with inflections where appropriate. This creates a more interesting speech pattern and is easier to listen to. Avoid a speech pattern that starts off at an appropriate volume and gradually trails off to a whisper. This is very distracting to children and makes it difficult to maintain their attention.

Providing Clarity

Another important factor in effective verbal communication is clarity. As teachers, we are generally keenly interested in our subject matter and enthusiastic about conveying our interest to others. Therefore, there is frequently a tendency to oververbalize and to provide too much information. Keep verbalization to a minimum. Try to be concise in explanations, taking into account the maturity and skill level of the students. It is often more effective to give only a short explanation on the basic elements of skill or game, followed by immediate involvement in the activity. In this way, you can easily observe their level of understanding, as well as their ability, and you can adjust subsequent explanations to fit individual needs.

Verbalization should utilize good grammar. Classroom teachers are constantly concerned with children's grammar; therefore, it is important for the physical education teacher to set a good example for appropriate use of the English language. Improper use of tenses and terms and failing to put *ing* at the end of words, such as

going, doing, something, and *nothing,* are unacceptable. Avoid the use of slang and colloquialisms. It is unnecessary to demonstrate that you are "one of the group." Avoid distracting verbal hitches such as "Okay," "Listen up," and "Ah," as well as overuse of favorite words or phrases. The listener will soon focus in on these irregularities of speech and will tend to concentrate on them rather than on the message being conveyed.

In an effort to foster clarity, it is important to summarize, using key words or phrases. This helps children conceptualize the information and provides a brief review of the key points of your presentation. Providing frequent opportunities for questions about specific aspects of your verbal instruction is important. In the explanation of an activity, it is much better to stop from time to time to ask if there are any specific questions about that portion of the explanation. Avoid, at all costs, a complete, detailed explanation of an activity or task followed by the general statement "Are there any questions?" This will generally result in a rush of questions that could have been dealt with more easily earlier. Furthermore, when children have a question but must wait until the end for an answer, they tend to shut down all other thought processes and concentrate only on their question. As a result, much of your explanation is not absorbed, often forcing you to repeat yourself a second or even a third time. Much of this may be simply and easily avoided through the provision of frequent opportunities to ask questions about *specific* aspects of your explanation.

NONVERBAL COMMUNICATION

Nonverbal communication, or body language, as it is often termed, is another important mode of communication. It has been estimated that our verbal vocabulary ranges from about 28,000 to 40,000 words, but our nonverbal "vocabulary" is endless. It is important to learn the subtleties in our nonverbal communication and to recognize the messages that we tend to transmit.

We project a variety of messages to those around us, including our students, through subtle and often unconscious changes in our postures, gestures, and facial expressions. In fact, we are often more apt to convey these messages in their true form through body expression than through verbal expression. It is important that your body language convey to children that they matter and are valued and that you are pleased to be with them. The following discussion focuses on the use of various postures, gestures, and facial expressions and the messages that tend to convey.

Postures

The postures that you take when standing before a class will convey a variety of nonspoken messages. If you stand erect with your weight evenly distributed on both feet, you tend to convey confidence and assuredness. Standing with the body weight on on foot portrays an image of being relaxed, easygoing, and at ease. On the other hand, shifting your body weight from foot to foot is often an indication of uneasiness, nervousness, or restlessness.

The use of the arms represents an aspect of your posture and also conveys messages to students. For example, the arms folded tightly across the chest may convey a variety of messages. When this posture is assumed in conjunction with an erect body posture with the weight distributed evenly over both feet, the message is one of determination and steadfastness. On the other hand, if the arms are folded and the body weight is shifted from foot to foot, a need for comfort, security, and assurance tends to be conveyed. Placement of the hands on the hips or keeping them clasped behind the back are postures frequently assumed by teachers that convey a message of authority or of being in control.

Think for a moment of some of your frequent postures, or take time to observe the body postures of one or more of your instructors. What messages are your instructors giving you? It is important to note that one's postures may not provide *accurate* nonverbal messages. The point, however, is that they do provide *a* message, and it is this message, accurate or not, to which students react.

Gestures

Most of us use a variety of gestures in our daily communication with others. Teachers are often masters of the use of gestures that communicate meaning in very specific terms. In fact, it is often joked that many elementary school teachers would be unable to talk if their hands were tied to their sides. The gestures that they employ are often consciously used to supplement the spoken word. For example when using the words *big, small, high*, or *low*, teachers commonly make corresponding gestures. For young children this is often appropriate and provides visual reinforcement of basic verbal concepts. On the other hand, older children often find these descriptive mannerisms distracting and condescending when overused.

The use of pointing gestures often conveys a clear and undeniable message. Pointing the index finger forcefully at a student tends to be viewed as threatening. It singles the student out from the rest of the group and creates an uncomfortable feeling. Pointing the index finger forcefully downward conveys the message of reinforcing a point, while pointing it upward serves as a message of appeal from a high authority. Steepling the fingers often conveys the message of "I have the advantage," rubbing the hands together conveys a sense of expectation, and twiddling the thumbs is often viewed as a sign of boredom. Tapping the fingers, or playing with paper clips, rubber bands, or similar objects, conveys restlessness or nervousness. A variety of habitual gestures, such as persistent tugging on an ear, rubbing your chin, hiking up your pants, or clearing your throat, not only conveys a feeling of being ill at ease but also serves as distracting mannerisms upon which students tend to focus.

Take a few moments to analyze the gestures that you and others characteristically use. What messages are you conveying? What messages are being conveyed to you? Do any of your gestures convey the wrong message, or are any of them distracting mannerisms? If so, you will need to make a conscious effort to modify or eliminate these habitual forms of nonverbal communication.

Facial Expressions

It is said that a picture is worth a thousand words. Our facial expressions are often just that. Although we verbally say one thing, it frequently comes across to others as something else. This is due to the multitude of facial expressions that we use when communicating. Raising the eyebrows conveys a message of surprise. Squinting one eye tells others that we are suspicious. Wrinkling the brow provides a message of distaste. Standing with the mouth open displays awe or dumbfoundedness, and thrusting the jaw forward gives a message of defiance.

The eyes can be used as a very potent nonverbal form of communication. Staring out the window or glancing frequently at your watch convey boredom. Rolling the eyes gives a message of exasperation or "How could you be so stupid." An eye roll followed by mutual glances to another person convey the same message and indicate a desire for others to share in your nonverbal criticism of the offender. The tendency to focus on and talk to one segment of the class conveys to the others that they don't really count.

These are only a few of the facial expressions frequently used. Each of us has an almost limitless number of expressions that we use every day. It is important to remember and fully understand the messages that you are giving to others with these facial expressions. Often what is "heard" by others is in direct opposition to what was said, because what is said does not match the facial expressions, gestures, and postures. Our actions truly do speak louder than our words.

CONVEYING ENTHUSIASM

One of the most important but frequently overlooked aspects of successful interaction with children is the ability to convey enthusiasm for the subject matter and for the children themselves. Your verbal and nonverbal communication skills may be above reproach, but if you show little genuine enthusiasm in your teaching, you will have little success. Children are re-markably perceptive in their assessment of teachers. If they sense that you have little interest in them or in your subject matter, they will be quick to "turn you off." Let us take a brief look at what you can actively do to convey your enthusiasms.

Interest in Your Subject Matter

Children are quick to pick up on your interest or lack of interest in various aspects of the curriculum. If they see that you are hesitant to get involved in certain activities, it will have a correspondingly negative effect on their attitude. Trouble will manifest first in a series of groans and moans. It may advance to outright refusal to take part and other forms of belligerent behavior. On the other hand, a display of active, eager involvement by the teacher will do much to convey an atitude of acceptance and eagerness to participate.

Well-planned and executed lessons that move along quickly with a minimum of disruption also convey a sense of enthusiasm. Children do not look for a constant overflow of effervescent behavior on the part of teachers as a measure of enthusiasm. On the contrary, you may have a quiet and reserved manner and still be viewed by children as enthusiastic. The display of a genuine interest in their learning, as well as creating an environment that maximizes their potential for improvent, are more important to children than a surface show of energy.

Interest in Your Students

There are numerous ways in which successful teachers convey interest in their students. A fundamental way is by learning their names. This is often a difficult task, especially for the physical education teacher, who sees several different classes a day. The tendency is to learn only the names of those students who stand out in some way. As a result, the students who are persistent behavioral problems or are exceptionally good or poor in physical activities become known by name. Unfortunately, the majority of children often go nameless. One method to help learn names is to use group cards, with a Polaroid picture of the members of each group. Another is to use nametags (although this tends to interfere with certain activities) that the children make and decorate themselves during art class. Still another technique is to try to associate the child's name with some outstanding trait, characteristic, or ability. Once you have learned names, try to avoid the use of last names. The use of the child's given name is much more personal and conveys a message of warmth and interest in the child as a person.

Children judge teachers to be interested in them if they show a genuine interest in their learning and set high but realistic goals for achievement. Teachers show their interest in children by recognizing and respecting the individuality of the learner.

Successful teachers convey their interest in children by establishing acceptable standards for behavior and adhering to these standards in a consistent manner. It is difficult to display genuine interest in children and enthusiasm for teaching them if you are constantly reprimanding, scolding, and disciplining. Whether your boundaries are narrow or broad is not as crucial as your *consistent* adherence to whatever boundaries you have established and the impartial, fair manner in which unacceptable behavior is dealt with.

IMPROVING COMMUNICATION SKILLS

Understanding the various messages conveyed through physical distance, observing children in different settings, and self-study can do much to improve your ability to talk to children.

Respecting Physical Distance

Physical distance is an important factor in communication. How close you stand to those to whom you are talking has a marked effect on what they hear, attend to, and retain. The closer you are to the learner, the greater will be the attention given to you by the learner, up to a point. The greater the distance between you and the learner, the less you are able to attend to each other.

Generally speaking, distances from 4 to 10 feet are the most appropriate for effective teaching and learning. Distances of 1 to 3 feet tend to be too close and to invade one's "personal space." This space is generally reserved for special people or special occasions. Invasion of this space has the effect of making the individual feel ill at ease.

Distances greater than 10 feet tend to create an atmosphere in which the learner feels less involved in the learning situation. A distance between teacher and student of up to 15 feet is generally considered to be a formal distance, allowing the individual to psychologically move into or out of the learning environment at will. Distances over 15 feet are considered to be remote distances in which the individual has a feeling of being removed from contact with the learning environment.

Successful physical education teachers use physical distance as an effective teaching technique, constantly varying their distance from the students in order to achieve the desired effect. Table 11.1 provides a summary of approximate physical distances and the message they tend to communicate.

Observing Children

Another way to improve communication skills with children is to observe them in a variety of settings. Successful physical education teachers frequently visit the classroom or spent time with children during recess or at after-school activities. Occasional visits to the classroom serve two important functions. First, they enable you to observe children's behavior and interaction patterns with the classroom teacher, with whom they spend the bulk of the school day. This will provide valuable information that you can incorporate into your program, as well as specific techniques of class management and control. Second, it communicates to children that you are interested in them and in what they do when

TABLE 11.1 Physical Distances and Their Messages

Feet	Distance	Message
1 to 3	Intimate	"You are too close and threatening" (personal space, reserved for special people and occasions).
4 to 6	Near friendly	"I feel more comfortable and relaxed" (an informal, friendly distance).
7 to 10	Far friendly	"We can still communicate effectively but on less friendly terms" (a more formal friendly distance).
11 to 15	Formal	"I can move into or out of immediate contact with the situation at will" (a formal distance).
16 to 20	Remote	"I am removed and out of contact" (a remote distance).

they are not with you. Sitting in on and taking part in the activities of a reading circle or a science lesson will not only be enlightening but will help establish positive communication between you and the children as well as you and the classroom teacher.

Observing and interacting with children in a variety of settings is a positive step in improving your communication skills. It takes extra time, but it is well worth the effort.

Self-study

Effective means of getting feedback on your communication skills with children are through videotaping, audio taping, and peer assessment of your lessons. Each of these techniques can offer a great deal of useful information that will help maximize your effectiveness in talking to children.

Taking the time and effort to occasionally have one of your lessons videotaped will provide a wealth of useful information about the effectiveness of your nonverbal as well as verbal communication skills. Often teachers will respond, after viewing themselves, with comments such as "Did I *really* say that?" or "Is that how I look when I do that?" Videotaping enables you to chart the positive and negative aspects of your teaching and clearly document where you

have made improvements and where you need continued work.

The audio tape is also an effective tool in assessing communication skills. Although limited to providing feedback about your verbal behavior with children, the audio tape enables you to focus attention entirely on that mode of communication. The audio tape quickly reveals verbal hitches, redundancies of speech, lack of clarity, and problems in getting and maintaining attention.

Peer evaluations are a third technique of providing feedback about your verbal and nonverbal behavior. Peer evaluations are an excellent way to provide information about the organization and implementation of your lessons and whether the objectives of the lesson were achieved. Teachers should look forward to and request regular, systematic assessment of their teaching. The comments and helpful suggestions offered should be taken in a positive manner rather than defensively, as is sometimes the case.

Whether you choose to use videotapes or audio tapes, or peer evaluations of your teaching, it is important to continually look for objective means by which you can carefully analyze yourself as a communicator. Self-study is an ongoing process, which should not be limited to new teachers or nontenured teachers seeking substantiation of their abilities. Self-study is for everyone, whether new to teaching or a veteran.

LISTENING TO CHILDREN

An aspect of talking to children that is sometimes overlooked is listening to them. Teachers often are so busy with what they have to say and how they are saying it that they forget that the children are giving them messages. These messages take many forms and may be classified as verbal messages and nonverbal messages. The manner in which we pick up on and respond to these explicit and implicit messages will play a significant role in our success in effective, two-way communication with children.

Verbal Messages

Listen carefully to what children are saying to you and how they say it. Try to be alert to the meaning behind their words and the message they are giving you with their speech patterns. Children who speak loudly or tend to mumble may be giving you a message that they have a hearing problem. Boisterous children often convey an aggressive manner, whereas timid children tend to speak with a barely audible voice. Confident children will tend to give complete answers or explanations to inquiries and are not hesitant to acknowledge their failure to understand or comprehend. On the other hand, timid children are often slow to speak up if they do not understand or have questions. Furthermore, when forced to respond verbally, they tend to be shorter in their replies or explanations and to speak more softly. Children who tend to chatter almost constantly and need to be reminded to be silent are often displaying a need for acceptance or approval. The speech patterns of children can provide meaningful messages and help you to adjust your responses accordingly.

Nonverbal Messages

Alert teachers "listen" to children's nonverbal messages as well as the verbal ones. Often, their nonverbal messages provide clear insights to their many moods. For example, the child who is fidg-eting communicates a message of "Let's get moving." A child lying on the gym floor rather than sitting up in an attentive posture gives you an indication that the child is not interested in the lesson. Persistent head nodding is often used as an approval-seeking behavior.

The manner in which children raise their hands in response to a question is also revealing. Hesitant hand raising tends to communicate that "I think I know the answer, but I'm not quite sure." Wild hand waving communicates "Teacher, teacher, call on me!" Holding the hand high above the head gives a message of assurance and confidence in knowing the answer. Holding a raised hand in a propped-up position conveys a message of "Please take pity on me and let me answer your question."

Being sensitive to how children use their eyes and the messages they are trying to communicate is important. Avoiding eye contact conveys a message of "I'm not here; don't call on me." Staring out the window or off into space is often a sign of boredom. Rolling the eyes conveys the undeniable message of "Teacher, how could you be so dumb." Doing a double take after making an error or mistake in a game or sports activity serves as a common means of telling another that "It wasn't really my fault; some outside force caused me to do it" (drop the ball, miss the shot, and so on).

Children have numerous and unique ways to convey nonverbal messages. Remember, these messages may be actual indicators of things as they are, or they may be what the child *wants* you to think they are. In either case, it is important that you "listen" to these messages and respond to them accordingly.

SUGGESTED READING

Adler, Ron, and Towne, Neil. (1978). *Looking out/looking in: Interpersonal communication*. New York: Holt.

Buscaglia, L. (1982). *Living, loving and learning*. Thorofare, NJ: Slack.

Cullum, A. (1971). *The geranium on the window sill just died but teacher you went right on*. New York: Harlin Quist.

Gardner, M. Robert. (1983). *Self inquiry*. Boston: Little, Brown, and Company.

Patterson, G.R. (1980). *Living with children: New methods for parents and teachers*. Champaign, IL: Research Press.

Wagonseller, B. R., and McDowell, R. L. (1979). *You and your child*. Champaign, IL: Research Press.

Ziglar, Zig. (1985). *See you at the top*. Gretna, LA: Pelican Publishing Company.

CHAPTER 12

POSITIVE DISCIPLINE

Upon entering the gymnasium, the first concern of most new teachers is for personal survival—being able to take charge and be in control of their students. Without discipline in the gymnasium or classroom, there can be little effective learning. Therefore, one of the first responsibilities of the teacher becomes the creation and nurturing of an atmosphere of positive discipline.

This chapter focuses on what is meant by the word *discipline*. Techniques for imposing teacher control, delivering punishment, and promoting self-control are discussed. The conditions necessary for an environment conducive to positive discipline are also discussed.

WHAT IS DISCIPLINE?

The term *discipline* is often viewed as having many meanings. To some it is indicative of the level of *teacher control* existing in one's classroom: "I have good discipline." To others it signifies a form of *punishment*: "I had to discipline them." Still others interpret the word to mean a form of *self-control*: "She certainly is disciplined." The fact is that the word *discipline* can mean all three. It can be a method of external control imposed on students by teachers. It can take the form of punishment, and it can be a form of self-control imposed on students by themselves. Therefore, discipline is a means of enabling students to use their time in such a manner that their behavior is consistent with the learning objectives and does not inhibit others from attempting to achieve the goals of the lesson.

Teachers with good discipline are generally viewed as strong, confident adults, in charge of their classrooms or gymnasia. They are seen as leaders and as models for children. They are viewed as capable of and willing to assume authority in the matter of regulating and shaping children's behavior. Teachers with good discipline do not have to nag or, be mean, nasty, or frightening to children in order to make them behave. On the contrary, teachers who are considered to have good discipline generally take a series of *positive* steps in setting the boundaries for acceptable behavior and gaining the respect and trust of their students.

Good discipline does not depend solely on externally imposed standards for behavior. It requires an element of self-control and assumption of responsibility for one's actions. Good discipline does not require that every student be in rigid lines or formations, responding on command. On the contrary, such a setting does little to promote self-control or insure long-lasting positive behavior. Over-use of rigidity and structure, when not essential to the lesson, tends to stifle learning and provide little opportunity for children to become self-disciplined. In order for maximum learning to take place, children must be actively involved in the learning process, and the teacher must serve as a helpful guide and motivator of desirable responses. In the gymnasium and on the playground, learning is often a noisy process with plenty of activity and with children engaged in variety of related but often different tasks.

Discipline has not failed if children overtly express enthusiasm or excitement in exploring the movement potential of their bodies. It has not failed if the gymnasium is humming with task-related conversation or when eight eager youngsters simultaneously burst out with an idea, suggestion, or solution. Discipline, however, has failed if the rights of the class or individuals within the class are infringed upon by one or more disruptive children. It has failed if the specific objectives of the lesson cannot be effectively met because of the climate of the classroom, or if the interest, initiative, or individuality of any person is curbed by one or more disruptive individuals.

TECHNIQUES FOR IMPOSING TEACHER CONTROL

Most techniques of exerting control over students fail to get at the heart of persistent behavior problems. The best method of handling behavior problems is a program designed to *prevent* them from occurring. However, once they do occur, there are a number of remedial actions that can be taken. Each of the following techniques has been found successful in helping teachers establish and maintain class control through the use of nonverbal, verbal, and time-out responses.

Nonverbal Responses

There are a number of nonverbal responses that teachers can use in responding to children's misbehavior. Often these quiet forms of control can do much to improve individual behavior and the behavior of the class in general.

Your eyes are a valuable tool. Disapproving glances or a fixed gaze on the misbehaving child will frequently stop the misconduct. Stationing yourself close to the area where misbehaving students are located is also helpful. A *gentle* hand on the shoulder serves as a quiet reminder to the child who may be off task.

Verbal Responses

Your voice can be a powerful weapon. Use it wisely, because your choice of words, pitch, and tone can convey a very clear message of intent. Avoid, at all cost, yelling, screaming, sarcasm, and belittling children for their behavior. Instead, restore order immediately in the *least* disruptive manner possible. If the infraction is minor, treat it as such. All too often teachers overreact to every little bit of disruptive behavior find themselves exhausted and their children conditioned to their overreaction. As a result, the teacher has little emotion, or voice, to cope with the major problems that are sure to occur.

General comments to the class with a brief explanation of acceptable behavior is more appropriate.

Failure to gain control in this manner may require more severe techniques. Singling out those who are misbehaving by name with a brief comment of what *is* acceptable behavior is often effective. For example, "Mary and Billy, it's important for *everyone* to have their eyes focused up here and listening carefully to the lesson. Do you understand?" Be certain that you get a verbal response to the question at the end of your statement. This helps break the pattern of misbehavior and cause a refocusing of attention.

Time Out

If you are unable to bring disruptive students under control with your nonverbal and verbal techniques, it is appropriate to provide a "time-out" space. This should be a predesignated spot in the gymnasium or on the playground sufficiently removed from the class but in clear view of the teacher at all times. Removing a disruptive child from the class for a portion of the lesson provides both the student and the teacher with time to regroup and refocus. Be sure, however, not to exclude the child for too long a time. Exclusion for longer than five minutes tends to be less effective than shorter periods. Prior to inviting misbehaving children back into the lesson, be sure to talk quietly with them, establishing good eye contact, and out of the hearing range of the rest of the class. Ask if they know why they were required to take time out and explain your expectations in terms of acceptable behavior; then invite them to take part in the remainder of the class if they can behave.

Avoid, whenever possible, excluding students entirely from the class. Handle your own discipline problems whenever possible. This conveys a message of being in control to children. Teachers who constantly send disruptive students to the principal's office are actually inviting further difficulties. They are viewed by students and fellow teachers as ineffective leaders, unable to manage their own classrooms. You are less likely to have a behavioral problem solved by a neutral third party. There are, however, situations where delegating your authority to another is appropriate and useful, but, as a rule of thumb, avoid it whenever possible.

PUNISHMENT

If it becomes necessary to punish children, punishment should be for the behavior, not the individual. Punishment should be explicitly combined with a statement of what would have been the appropriate behavior in the situation. Punishment should occur immediately after the undesirable behavior to be effective in decreasing its frequency. Physical punishment, unless immediate, will be of little benefit other than for the reduction of frustration in the *punisher*.

The use of punishment for extended periods of time tends to reduce its effectiveness. When the punishment, or the threat of immediate punishment, is removed, the undesirable behavior often returns in extroverted children. On the other hand, introverted children often remain afraid too long and may actually develop phobias or neuroses as a result of prolonged punishment.

Although the threat of punishment is the most frequently used method of class control, it is often the least effective. Punishment merely represses undesirable behavior; it fails to get to the heart of the matter. It often creates harmful anxiety and escape and avoidance behaviors on the part of children. Corporal punishment (spanking) provides children with adult models of aggression; as a result of this example, they often view aggression as acceptable. Punishment should and can be used, but it must be immediate to be of real value. It should be accompanied by an explanation of the undesirable behavior so that the child can anticipate the same consequences in the future.

Although it is possible for punishment to be an effective management tool, it is often difficult to use it effectively in the typical gymnasium or playground setting. Because of large classes and the nature of the physical education lesson itself, the teacher cannot punish a particular behavior every time it occurs. There may be times when a teacher may use inappropriately severe punishment or relish giving punishment; in both cases, normal standards of ethics are violated. Because of these difficulties and the possible negative consequences of punishment, the appropriateness of punishment should be very carefully weighed for each situation.

Worry, fear, anxiety, hatred, guilt, shame, and avoidance may be instilled by punishment as a reaction not only to the undesirable behavior, but also to the teacher, the class period, or physical education itself. Students who are repeatedly punished or reprimanded may withdraw and try to avoid class or school by being "sick," tardy, or truant. Some students may genuinely fear school because of the emotional as well as physical pain incurred there. Withdrawal may be accomplished by daydreaming, doodling, or otherwise not paying attention, even though the student is physically present.

The more severe the punishment, the more it increases fear, anxiety, anger, and general emotionality in the punished person. Increases in emotion make it more difficult for children to change their behavior and learn new habits and may even increase the likelihood of future misbehavior.

Punishment often leads to aggression, but the amount of punishment necessary to cause aggression differs among individuals, as does the strength or kind of aggression. Almost any punished student is likely to make hostile remarks about the teacher or other punishing adult when out of that adult's immediate range of attention. The student is almost certain to like the teacher less.

Though other students may not immediately imitate either the act of punishment or the punished act, it has been found that both of these acts tend to increase in frequency in the absence of the teacher or other punishing adult. Children who witness shouting, shaking, sarcasm, and so on are more likely to do these things to other people who frustrate them than are children who witness calmer reactions. Much of human behavior is learned from models, and these should be models of fairness and temperance.

Children's behavior and self-concept are influenced strongly by how they think others perceive them. Punishment increases the chance that the child will come to believe that others have a negative view of him or her and increases the chances of developing a negative self-concept. If punishment is used, there should be acceptable alternatives made available that provide opportunities for praise, success, and positive reinforcement.

TECHNIQUES FOR DEVELOPING SELF-CONTROL

The highest form of discipline is self-discipline. Children are active, energetic beings in the process of developing self-control. The following are some guidelines that have proven helpful to teachers attempting to instill self-control in children.

Establish Routines and Rules

Children are generally more secure when they know what is expected of them and what comes next. A gymnasium with a regular sequence of activities and a limited number of clearly understood "house rules" will do much to provide children with a framework for acceptable behavior. It is important to remember that you must *teach* your students what the rules for acceptable behavior are. You cannot expect that they will know or willingly accept these rules unless you help them *learn* and understand. If children can expect that the routine of the lesson will follow a consistent format, then they tend to be more at ease and less disruptive. If the rules of the gymnasium have been clearly explained and posted where they can be easily seen by all, then children are less likely to overstep these boundaries. One technique in rule setting that works well is to request that the children help establish the rules and to *help* determine the consequences for violating them. Such a technique has the effect of involving the children in the decision-making process and promoting self-discipline.

PHOTO 12.1   Clearly defined rules for positive behavior are a must.

Reduce the "Don'ts"

When establishing guidelines for acceptable behavior, it is wise to limit the number of "don'ts" because the word reinforces unacceptable behavior by its mere mention. It is much better to state rules from a positive standpoint rather than a negative one. For example, rather than saying "Don't run," "Don't talk," or "Don't get out of line," it is generally better to say "Walk quietly," "Remain silent," or "Stay in line." Emphasis on the positive often has a correspondingly positive influence. You will, of course, need to make exceptions to this if the child's safety is at stake or for the protection of property. Avoid a long list of "don'ts" if the primary purpose is for your convenience or comfort.

Be Reasonable

Be reasonable; don't invariably demand the desirable or prohibit the undesirable. We have often heard adults complain, "Everything I want to do is either unhealthful, illegal, or fattening." If we, who have had years to reconcile ourselves to society's restraints and curbs on our basic, prim-

itive drives, still have these feelings, how much more do children resent the restrictions and taboos that are adult-conceived, and patterned, and at best are only vaguely understood by them? If a behavior problem exists or you are trying to improve on poor habits of compliance with instructions, try this method: (a) Start by asking the children to do the things you know they already like to do in order to change their negative attitude toward direction; (b) Ask them to do neutral things that are neither particularly pleasant or unpleasant to them; (c) finally, work up to the tasks or directions that were, in the past, disagreeable.

Follow Through

Immediate followup of an ignored important instruction (once you have established that it was heard or received) is essential for promptness in compliance and avoidance of "scenes." Don't wait until you are provoked, exasperated, or desperate. You cannot give an important instruction while attention is diverted elsewhere. Remember, you are helping to teach children good habits of listening, attending, and promptness—you do not teach these things by scolding or punishment. If you follow through, the child will know you mean business, and few warnings will be necessary.

Be Consistent

Perhaps only complete rejection disturbs children's security more than inconsistency. If you expect to get consistency in response to direction, you must provide a consistent stimulus and a consistent expectation of performance from day to day. A recent cartoon pinpointed the dilemma in which many children find themselves. The child says, "When *you* wanna do somethin' scary, you're a little tiny boy, but when *they* want you to do somethin' scary, you're a great big boy." A reward, or punishment that is consistent in frequency of occurrence, in kind, and in application, is essential, as is a united front by parents and teachers on policy matters. Always let the children know what they can expect from you, and expect the best of them.

Praise Others

Praise more than you punish. Praise effort as well as performance. Trying hard shows responsibility, even though the results may not be perfect. However, be sure that your praise is sincere. Children quickly sense lack of sincerity. Under no circumstances should you ever resort to bribes. They backfire and can cause great harm. They suggest the opposite behavior, encouraging deals and the placing of a price tag on being good and responsible. Avoid expecting perfection, and don't be afraid to admit that even you make mistakes.

Be Assertive

It is important to distinguish between the terms *assertive* and *aggressive* as applied to behavioral control. The aggressive teacher nags, accuses, argues, blows up in anger, gets into power struggles, and is a harsh punisher. The assertive teacher, on the other hand, makes clear, direct requests; reveals honest feelings; persists; listens to children's point of view; gives brief reasons; and carries out reasonable consequences. When children view you as assertive in your discipline, they will treat you with respect and will attempt to take responsibility for their actions. Teachers who are viewed as aggressive will establish class control out of fear and do little to help children develop self-control.

Demonstrate Trust

Show children that you have faith in them by the responsibility that you give them. If you believe in them and expect their best, you are more likely to *get* their best. Don't be afraid of losing their love. Children can understand that it is precisely because you do love them that you provide redirection, restraint, and punishment when warranted. On the other hand, don't be afraid of "spoiling" children through the generous use of kindness, affection, and consideration. These qualities don't spoil children, but lack of direction, inconsistency, and indecision do.

REQUIREMENTS FOR POSITIVE DISCIPLINE

Teachers with good discipline exhibit remarkable similarity in their authority style. Although there is not a universal formula or set of specific behaviors that will guarantee good discipline. teachers who are successful in this area tend to be positive role models, efficient planners, effective communicators, thorough assessors of behavior, and consistent in their expectations of children.

Effective Role Model

Teachers communicate a great deal about themselves and their expectations of children. Communicating genuine interest in your subject matter, enthusiasm for learning, and a willingness to participate with the class do much to create a positive atmosphere. Displaying interest in your pupils as people by establishing high but reasonable expectations for them and helping them reach these goals is a key to being an effective role model.

Teachers who are effective role models display confidence and willingness to accept their role of authority. They are personable and fair, and they react appropriately and consistently when children misbehave. They clearly communicate the boundaries of acceptable behavior and are impartial in the use of their authority when these boundaries are overstepped.

In order to be an effective role model for children, you must:

1. Be assertive rather than aggressive.
2. Act rather than react.
3. Act in proportion to the need rather than overreacting.
4. Be consistent rather than inconsistent.
5. Clearly communicate expectations rather than being vague.
6. Convey interest and enthusiasm rather than disinterest and boredom.
7. Set reasonable individual and group goals rather than unrealistic goals.

Teachers who set *positive* examples for children are doing much to provide a role model for self-discipline. Failure to establish a positive role model will inhibit your effectiveness in gaining and maintaining class control.

Efficient Planning

Teachers with good discipline are generally good planners. They take the time to plan their lessons carefully, are well organized, and make maximum effective use of their time.

Thorough planning enables you to be properly prepared. Physical education teachers need to pay particular attention to this because of the size of their teaching station, the necessity of moving groups of children from place to place, and the need for frequent changes in formation and the nature of the physical activity itself.

Teachers with good class control have taken the time to thoroughly plan their lessons in a manner that is responsive to the needs, interests, and ability levels of their students, and they are organized in their approach to learning.

Organization is important to the planning process and is a key element in maintaining good class control in the physical education setting. The consistent use of a variety of class management techniques contributes to class organization. Locker-room policies, squad formations, roll-call techniques, and methods of obtaining and securing equipment are all important organizational considerations. It is important that the lesson and the gymnasium environment itself be carefully organized in order to make maximum effective use of your time.

Lessons that make the best use of the allotted time are those that provide for a maximum of active involvement by all of the students. Poor lesson planning; failure to organize the class efficiently; and inactivity brought about by lack of equipment, waiting in line, or long, detailed explanations do little to create an atmosphere conducive to good discipline.

The physical appearance of the gymnasium is important. An atmosphere that is bright, cheery, and has a generally pleasant appearance is conducive to positive behavior. Bulletin boards, posters, and activity charts neatly displayed and frequently changed promote interest and give students a sense that you care.

In order to be efficient and effective in your planning, you must:

1. Carefully prepare each lesson.
2. Overplan for each lesson.
3. Develop lessons around the individual or group.
4. Take into consideration the space to be used.
5. Plan to minimize formation changes.
6. Establish and be consistent in the use of common class management techniques.
7. Have ample equipment available that is in good repair and is quickly obtainable for use.
8. Plan for a maximum of activity and a minimum of inactivity.
9. Strive to create a physical environment that is pleasant to be in and safe.

Effective Communication

Teachers effective in minimizing and dealing with behavioral problems tend to be good communicators. Those who recognize the power of the unspoken word as well as the spoken word and systematically work at interacting with children generally have fewer behavior problems. The use of positive reinforcement techniques rather than negative or criticizing behaviors has been shown to be effective in winning the respect and attention of children. Attempting to give attention to all students, not just the gifted or those that need extra attention, and to verbally or nonverbally reinforce their positive behaviors is a technique used by teachers with good class control.

The manner in which you respond to children's behavior is an aspect of communication that is sometimes overlooked. The formation of children's behavior is due largely to the manner in which teachers respond to their early attempts at behaving. Remember, good behavior is not suddenly or magically achieved by most children. It is a learned process and often takes time. This learning process is rooted in the teacher's responses to the student's attempts to improve their behavior. Responses that focus on the *positive* aspects of behavior rather than the negative aspects have repeatedly been shown to have a positive influence on shaping behavior. In *no* case should teasing, belittling, or condescending statements be used as a method of responding.

In order to communicate effectively with children, you must:

1. Develop effective verbal and nonverbal communication skills
2. Strive for meaningful interaction with children.
3. Work for maximum communication with children.
4. Use positive reinforcement techniques.
5. Work toward giving *each* child some form of positive reinforcement in *each* lesson.
6. Respond to children's attempts to behave in a positive manner.
7. Avoid nagging, teasing, shaming, belittling, and other aggressive forms of communication.
8. Be consistent in your meaning and use of verbal and nonverbal forms of communication.

Self-assessment

Teachers who periodically assess their own teaching behavior as well as the learning styles of their students generally have fewer behavior problems with their classes. The process of self-assessment enables teachers to stop for a moment, and look the situation over, and chart a new course, if necessary, for a more positive direction. Often minor changes in modeling, planning, or communication techniques will result in dramatically improved behavior on the part of the class. Self-assessment is most effective with the aid of videotaped replays of lessons and peer evaluations of your teaching.

It is a common mistake for physical education teachers to neglect assessing their students' behavior and to assume that they can use identical methods with each class they see during the course of the day. Remember, your job in maintaining class control and promoting self-control is considerably more complex than that of the classroom teacher. First of all, you deal not with one class for the entire day, but with several classes. Secondly, the physical environment of the gymnasium or playground itself tends to evoke a different set of behaviors than those found in the classroom. Lastly, and most importantly, each class that comes to your program tends to be a direct reflection of the standards for behavior established by the particular classroom teacher. Therefore, you may need to modify your methods for gaining and maintaining control for each class. Requesting constructive feedback from individual teachers and observation in the classroom will prove helpful in making the necessary adjustment. Do not make the assumption that because a certain set of techniques worked well the previous year with the third grade (or any other grade) that this year's third graders will respond in the same manner. You will be the one who must make the adjustments if you are going to be successful in your discipline.

In order to be a thorough assessor of student behavior, you must:

1. Focus on regular, systematic review of your teaching techniques.
2. Take stock of the direction your class-control techniques are leading and chart a new direction if warranted.
3. Observe children in a variety of settings.
4. Observe the classroom teacher's control techniques.
5. Modify your techniques as needed to fit the specific children you are dealing with.
6. Do not assume that teaching the same way as last year will be appropriate for this year.

Consistency

The positive characteristics of teachers successful in discipline are of little value without consistency. Consistency in the role model that you project, in planning and executing your lessons, in communicating your expectations, and in your self-assessment are all important. The following is a list of several reasons why consistency is important:

1. Children must learn to function in their environment in order to survive in society. Ignoring their environment or manipulating it does not help them cope with their environment.
2. Children must relate to a number of different people during the course of the day (parents, classroom teachers, physical education teacher, coach). Therefore, a single set of expectations tends to make life easier and increases the probability of acceptable behavior.
3. Children respond positively to the security of a consistent routine. It enables them to function more freely and puts them at ease by knowing what to expect.
4. Consistency in the form of specific statements and direction is much easier for the child to respond to than general comments. This helps reduce ambiguity. For example, it is better to say "Put the ball in the bag" than "don't play with the ball."
5. Life without limits is unrealistic. Life with inconsistent limits is scary. Clarifying acceptable limits of behavior and consistently applying the consequences of violating these limits promotes security and self-control.
6. Self-control develops gradually. The more consistent our treatment of children, the more consistent the development of acceptable self-control of behavior.
7. Children pattern their behavior after significant others. Teachers are significant others; therefore, the role model provided by the teacher enables children to act more consistently.

SUGGESTED READING

Canter, Lee, and Canter, Marlene. (1976). *Assertive discipline*. Santa Monica, CA: Canter and Associates Inc.

Canter, Lee, and Canter, Marlene. (1984). *Assertive discipline elementary resource materials workbook grades K–6*. Santa Monica, CA: Canter and Associates Inc.

Carter, R. (1972). *Help! These kids are driving me crazy*. Champaign, IL: Research Press.

Dobson, J. (1973). *Dare to discipline*. Wheaton, IL: Tyndale House.

Johnson, S. O. (1980). *Better discipline: A practical approach*. Springfield, IL: Charles C. Thomas.

Silberman, M. L., and Wheelan, S. A. (1980). *How to discipline without feeling guilty*. Champaign, IL: Research Press.

Weiner, E. L. (1980). *Discipline in the classroom*. Washington, D.C.: National Education Association.

CHAPTER 13

SELECTING AND USING APPROPRIATE TEACHING STYLES

There are a variety of teaching styles that may be effectively used in the elementary physical education program. Basically, a teaching style is a specific set of behaviors selected and used by the instructor to achieve the learning objectives of the lesson. In recent years a great deal has been written about various styles of teaching. Probably the best known work is by Muska Mosston, entitled *Teaching Physical Education* (1981). This text, in an earlier edition, was one of the first to present a spectrum of teaching styles ranging from the most direct, or command style, to the most indirect, or exploratory style.

As used here, the term *teaching style* refers to a specific set of behaviors used by the instructor during the lesson. Selecting an appropriate teaching style to use in a lesson should not be a matter left to chance. Instead, you should carefully examine a variety of factors concerning your students and the environment prior to using a particular style. This chapter focuses on these factors and outlines the structure, advantages, and disadvantages of several teaching styles that have gained popularity in the physical education profession.

FACTORS INFLUENCING SELECTION OF A TEACHING STYLE

In recent years there has been considerable discussion about the relative merits of various teaching styles. In fact, an undeclared war has been waging between some traditional physical educators, who tend to favor more direct, teacher-centered approaches, and some movement educators, who tend to favor more indirect, child-centered approaches. This war has polarized many professional physical educators and has resulted in them hardening their insistence on adopting and using one set of teaching styles to the exclusion of others. This is unfortunate because it is the children who lose the benefit of being exposed to a variety of methodologies geared to their developmental level.

The developmental approach to teaching physical education recognizes that movement skill learning factors and student comprehension factors must be considered prior to selecting direct or indirect teaching techniques for a particular activity. It also recognizes that there are factors within the environment itself that may dramatically influence the wisdom of selecting one style over another, and that there are several teacher-related factors worthy of consideration. It is not sufficient to declare that one style of teaching is superior to another. Teachers who are sensitive to the needs, interests, and developmental levels of their students and who have taken into account the environmental conditions under which instruction must take place carefully select from a variety of teaching styles and refrain from taking sides in the teaching style war.

Movement Skill Learning Factors

Whenever learning a new movement skill, children, and adults, tend to go through a series of learning levels. The three levels of learning a movement skill outlined earlier in Chapter 6 and reiterated here are based on two important developmental concepts: first, that the acquisition of movement abilities progresses from the simple to the complex, and second, that people proceed gradually from general to specific in the development and refinement of movement skills. Recognition of where the learner is in this skill-learning hierarchy is important because it has a direct impact on both the teaching styles and movement activities used.

Beginning Level.   Children at the beginning or novice level of acquiring a new movement skill first *explore* the skill itself. Exploration of the skill generally occurs as a single unit. That is, the task is broken down into its simplest elements and practiced rather than being combined with other skills. At this level the learner does not have good control of his or her movements but gets used to the task and forms a gross general framework idea of the skill. During this first level, the learner forms a mental image of the skill and attempts to bring it under conscious control.

As the learner proceeds with exploring the elements of the skill, the process of discovery begins. The learner *discovers* ways of performing the skill through problem-solving and other indirect means, such as observation of others, studying, photos, film, or textual information. The learner gains greater control and begins to coordinate the movements involved in executing the skill. During this period, basic performance of the skill tends to be under less conscious control than during the exploratory stage.

Individuals at the beginning level of learning a movement skill tend to benefit from indirect teaching styles that permit freedom of exploration and guided discovery (refer to Figure 13.1 for a visual representation of this concept). These styles permit the learner to explore the movement task in its many forms and to develop a conscious mental image of the task. These same individuals tend to be at the initial and elementary stages within the fundamental movement phase of motor development. They are typically children of the preschool and primary-grade age, but may be older children, adolescents, or adults. Remember that, although development is age influenced, it is not age-dependent. Therefore, individuals at the early stages of learning a new movement skill, be they children or adults, will benefit greatly from the use of indirect styles of teaching that help them get a general idea of how to execute the task.

Intermediate Level.   Once the learner has gotten a general idea of how to perform a skill, it is practiced and combined with other movement skills. At the intermediate level of learning a movement skill, the individual experiments with skill combinations. Skills are combined elaborated upon, and practiced in a variety of ways. Teaching styles may be indirect or direct, with emphasis placed on practice through *application* of the skill to a variety of game, rhythm, and self-testing situations (see Figure 13.1). The use of indirect teaching styles during the intermediate level is a logical extension of the same indirect teaching styles emphasized during the beginning stage of learning a skill. These expe-

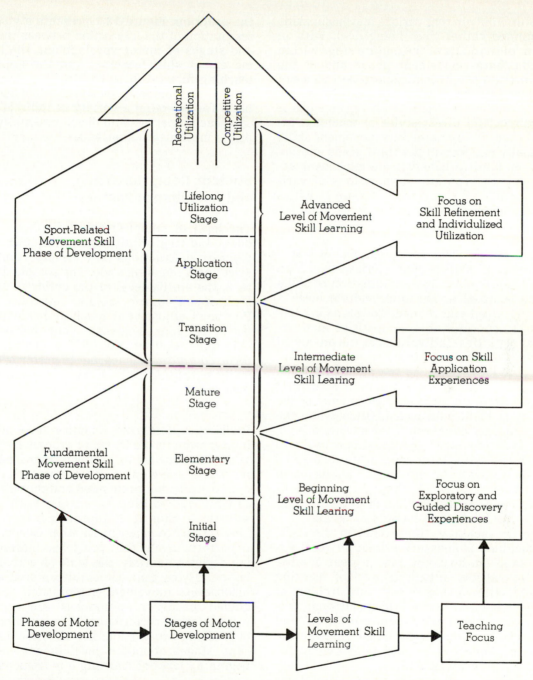

FIGURE 13.1 The interrelationship between the phases and stages of motor development, levels of movement skill learning, and teaching focus in movement skill acquisition.

riences differ only in that various movement skills are combined rather than being dealt with in isolation. Individuals at the mature stage within the fundamental movement phase and at the transitional stage within the sport-skill phase of motor development benefit from movement experiences that permit the interchangeable use of both indirect and direct styles of teaching. Individuals combining numerous movement skills are typically children in the third grade and beyond. They tend to benefit from movement activities that incorporate combinations of various skills, skill drills, and basic lead-up activities to the characteristic sports and recreational activities of their culture.

Advanced Level.   The advanced level of learning a movement skill is characterized by a high degree of *refinement*. The combination of skills that was selected at the intermediate level is further practiced and refined. The skills are frequently incorporated into competitive and recreational activities. Individuals at the advanced level focus on improved accuracy, precision, and economy of movement. At the advanced level, performance tends to be automatic, with little conscious attention given to the elements of the task as it is being performed. Often when the skilled performer has reached the advanced level, unique, *individualized* modifications begin to appear in the skill. These modifications may be subtle, or they may be blatantly obvious, as in high jumping, with Bill Fosbrury's invention of the now-famous Fosbrury Flop, or in tennis, with Chris Evert–Lloyd's two-handed backhand.

Generally speaking, the teacher in the regularly scheduled elementary school physical education program does not have a great number of children at the advanced level of learning movement skills. Although some children are at this level in some activities, the majority of children are at the beginning or intermediate level in the learning of movement skills. Appropriate experiences, however, should be provided for children at all levels of ability.

Where *your* students are in terms of their phase and stage of motor development, as well as their level of movement skill learning, are important determiners of the teaching styles you select and the movement activities included in the program. Figure 13.1 presents a visual representation of the interaction between the phases and stages of motor development, the levels of movement skill learning, and the appropriate teaching focus. Where children are in relationship to this model provides the teacher with a basis for selecting a variety of indirect and direct teaching styles and developmentally appropriate movement experiences.

Student Comprehension and Compliance Factors

The level of comprehension displayed by students and their ability and willingness to comply with instructions play an important role in selecting a teaching style. The complexity of the task, the ability level of the children, and their level of self-control are also important factors. You must adjust your teaching behavior to the needs of your students; your behavior will determine whether you *invite* the learner to perform, *command* the learner to perform, or physically *manipulate* the learner through the performance.

Inviting to Perform.   The first level of teacher intervention in the learning process involves inviting the learner to perform. If the movement tasks that make up the lesson are such that they can be easily comprehended and the children are capable and willing to comply with your instructions, then it is appropriate to extend an "invitation" to perform. In other words, inviting to perform means that you select indirect teaching styles to satisfy the skill objectives of the lesson. Styles that are child-centered and that incorporate movement exploration, as well as guided discovery approaches, are appropriate when inviting performance. These indirect styles of teaching are particularly effective during the early stages of motor development and at the beginning level of learning a movement skill.

Commanding to Perform.   As the individual progresses on to higher skill levels, or is required to combine two or more movement skills, experienced teachers frequently modify their instructional approach by "commanding" the individual to perform. The ability of the students to comprehend what the movement task entails or how to actually perform the task is often complicated by the complexity of the task itself. Safety factors involved in performance of the task, as well as available time, equipment, and facilities, all have to be considered. Students who are at the mature and transitional stage of motor development and at the intermediate level in learning a new skill tend to benefit from more directed styles of teaching as well as indirect styles. Using the command style or task style is effective for learners at this level.

Manipulating Through Performance. Sometimes, if a movement task is very complex, if the requirements are very exacting, or if safety is a major consideration, it becomes advisable to physically manipulate the learner through the task. For example, when teaching a back handspring, the gymnastics instructor generally assists the performer by physically manipulating her through the task several times at reduced speed. This is done in order to help form a conscious mental impression of the task or to "get the feel."

Physical manipulation is frequently used with severely impaired individuals. Actual patterning through a specific movement task is used as a means of reinforcing verbal commands. In this way the learner not only receives auditory and visual cues about the task, but also receives tactile and kinesthetic cues. The use of several sensory modalities tends to assist slow learners in grasping what is being requested.

Whether you invite, command, or physically manipulate children through performance of a movement skill depends on your students. It is important to be sensitive to their individual needs as well as the needs of the class as a whole so that you can incorporate appropriate teaching techniques at the appropriate time. It is altogether possible that within a single lesson you will do all three. You may *invite* performance by providing the class with movement challenges and other indirect forms of instruction. You may *command* performance by providing specific instructional cues, teacher and student demonstrations, and other direct forms of instruction.

You may even physically *manipulate* individual children by assisting them through various movement tasks. It is therefore important that you recognize where your students are in terms of their

1. Phase and stage of motor development.
2. Level of movement skill learning.
3. Level of cognitive comprehension.
4. Ability and willingness to comply with instruction.

Once you have taken these important factors into consideration, it becomes an easy matter to select suitable teaching styles.

STYLES OF TEACHING

Skilled teachers are thoroughly versed in the use of a variety of teaching styles. They refuse to be limited by the use of one or two favorites. Instead, they use a variety of styles, depending on the needs of the students they are teaching and the specific objectives of the lesson. Teaching is a learned behavior, and it is susceptible to modification and change. The manner in which we interact with children to help them learn is influenced by many factors. Important movement skill learning factors and student comprehension and compliance factors were discussed earlier. Factors such as the teacher's personality, expertise, values, and learning goals influence the choice of styles. The level of maturity, behavior, and interest in the lesson must also be taken into account, as well as available facilities, equipment, time, and safety considerations. Table 13.1 lists several of these determining factors.

Basically, teaching styles range from those that are *direct*, or teacher-centered, to those that are *indirect*, or child-centered. Few teachers use any one particular teaching style to the exclusion of all others. Instead, the tendency is to use a variety of direct and indirect styles based on the factors discussed earlier. Teachers who favor direct styles of teaching tend to use the command and task methods. Those who prefer more indirect styles often use the movement explo-

FIGURE 13.2 Visual representation of three different styles
of teaching.

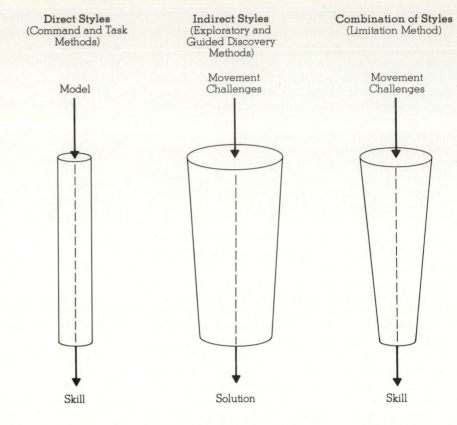

Direct Styles (Command and Task Methods)	Indirect Styles (Exploratory and Guided Discovery Methods)	Combination of Styles (Limitation Method)
Model	Movement Challenges	Movement Challenges
Skill	Solution	Skill

ration and guided discovery methods. Teachers who see the merit of both focus on a combination of styles (Figure 13.2).

Direct Styles

Direct styles of teaching movement skills are the traditional teaching approaches that have been used by physical educators and classroom teachers for years. These styles are teacher-centered, with the teacher making all or most of the decisions concerning what, how, and when the student is to perform. Direct teaching styles have many advantages. They are efficient, focused, and leave little chance for misunderstanding or misinterpretation. The structured learning environment of direct styles is conducive to good class control. Direct styles are easy to use with individuals or with large groups of children.

There are some disadvantages in using direct teaching styles of teaching. They often fail to allow for much individuality and inventiveness on the part of the learner. They tend to be more concerned with the goal or product of the learning experience than the process of learning involved. Direct styles make little allowance for individual differences. They are based on the false assumption that all children have reached about the same level of learning and progress at the same rate.

Although direct styles of teaching often have disadvantages, they can be modified in a variety of ways. Both verbal and nonverbal communication techniques may be altered significantly by the teacher. The manner in which the class is conducted need not be like a drill sergeant, but may rather be one in which duties, responsibilities, and privileges are shared, with the teacher still making the key decisions. The com-

Table 13.1   Factors Affecting Selection of an Appropriate Teaching Style

Student Factors	Environmental Factors	Teacher Factors
Stage of motor development	Facilities	Philosophy
Level of movement skill learning	Available equipment	Personality
	Time allotted	Lesson objectives
Cognitive comprehension	Safety considerations	Ability to adapt
Task complexity	Class size	Class control
Self-control		
Interest		

mand and the task methods are two of the most popular of the numerous direct styles of teaching.

Command Method.   Command teaching is the time-honored method of teaching movement skills. It consists of (1) a short explanation and demonstration of the skill to be performed, (2) student practice prior to giving further directions or pointing out specific errors, (3) general comments to the class about their performance, (4) further explanation and demonstration if necessary, (5) student practice with coaching hints to individuals or groups having difficulty, and (6) implementation of the skill in an appropriate activity. The command method makes all of the preperformance and performance decisions for the learner. The teacher controls what is to be practiced, how it is to be done, and when to begin and cease activity.

Task Method.   Task teaching is similar to the command method because the teacher still controls what is to be practiced and how it is to be performed. However, in using the task method, the teacher permits a greater degree of decision making on the part of the children. More freedom and flexibility are introduced into the learning environment. Children are given more responsibility for themselves but are not permitted to choose what to do or how to do the assigned task.

When using the task method, the teacher follows a sequence of (1) explanation and demonstration of different levels of the task to be performed by the class or individuals (task cards of varying difficulty in written or pictorial form are used), (2) practice of the designated task by stu-

dents at their own pace and at their particular level of ability, (3) help for individuals or groups having difficulty and challenges to advanced students to achieve higher levels of performance.

The task method permits children to work at their own personal level of ability. It may be undertaken on an individual, reciprocal, or small-group basis. Individuals may work alone at the task provided by the teacher and evaluate themselves, or they may work with partners who assess their performance. Students may work together in groups of three or four on specific tasks, with one performing, a second evaluating, and a third recording the students' performance of

PHOTO 13.1   Task cards can be used effectively with children.

the task. The task method provides more freedom for the learner than the command method. It is an effective approach to use with large groups, allows for individual standards of achievement, and maximizes active participation with limited resources.

Indirect Styles

Indirect styles of teaching movement skills came into vogue in North America during the early 1960's. Various indirect teaching styles had been advocated prior to that time, but it was not until the work of Rudolph Laban and Liselott Diem found their way to North America that educators began to look seriously at the potential for using indirect teaching styles in movement skill learning.

Indirect styles of teaching were initially rejected by many physical educators steeped in the direct methods of command and task teaching. Soon, however, a distinct division between those who have come to be known as "traditional physical educators" and those called "movement educators" developed. Each group claimed that its teaching methods were superior. Hence, the start of the undeclared teacher-behavior war.

There has been a mellowing of points of view, and many educators, rather than identifying with either direct or indirect styles, now recognize the tremendous value of both. There has been a shift in focus from the method to the learner. In trying to gear their methods of instruction to suit the learner rather than making the learner suit the methods, educators have become more developmentally oriented in their choice of teaching styles. As a result, indirect teaching styles have finally won their place in the spectrum of teaching styles used in physical education. They do not automatically insure optimal learning any more than direct styles do. They do, however, provide the learner with greater opportunity for freedom and assumption of responsibility within the educational setting.

Indirect teaching styles permit the student considerable freedom in setting goals and determining how these goals are to be accomplished. In other words, children become more involved in the learning process itself by being given opportunities and encouragement to explore and experiment with movement in a variety of ways. Another important advantage of indirect styles of teaching is that they allow for individual differences between learners. All students are able to find a degree of success at their particular level of ability.

The disadvantages of indirect teaching styles are mainly that they are time-consuming and that teachers unfamiliar with them frequently find them difficult to use productively. Indirect styles require practice and patience on the part of the teacher. Plenty of time must be permitted for experimentation, trial and error, and question asking. Because some teachers have not been trained in the techniques involved, they find indirect styles difficult to use. They often have trouble maintaining class control, structuring challenging movement problems, and providing for continuity both within lessons and between lessons. These disadvantages, however, do not mean that indirect styles are inferior to direct styles of teaching movement. On the contrary, indirect styles play a very important role in movement skill learning, particularly at the early levels. Indirect styles of teaching movement generally center on movement exploration and guided discovery methods.

Exploratory Method. The exploratory method to teaching movement requires the teacher to present broad-based movement challenges or questions without requiring a specific solution. Any *reasonable* solution of the task is considered acceptable. The teacher neither demonstrates how to perform the action nor presents a detailed verbal description. The students are given the opportunity to perform the movement task as they see fit. By focusing primarily on the learning process itself rather than on the product of learning, the exploratory method does not emphasize form or precision nor does it require each child to perform the task in the same manner. The teacher is interested, however, in providing meaningful movement tasks in which children are encouraged to explore the movement potential of their bodies, develop mature fundamental movement skills, find success, and express themself in a creative manner. Movement exploration may be totally free or guided by the teacher.

Guided Discovery Method. The guided discovery method permits the learner plenty of expression, creativity, and experimentation but somewhat restricts how the learner may respond to the movement tasks presented. A wide variety of responses is still encouraged, but the presentation of the task is modified. For example, the teacher may now say "Find three different ways to bounce the ball" or "Move from one end of the balance beam to the other, often changing your direction" (or level, speed, base of support, and so forth). The children experiment with several ways of accomplishing the tasks put to them.

It is the method employed by the learner in the solution of the movement challenges posed by the teacher that causes movement exploration and guided discovery to be considered separately here. The guided discovery method incorporates an *observation phase* into the total experience, instead of refraining from establishing a model of performance and accepting all solutions as correct, as with free exploration. The observation phase takes the form of observing the solutions of fellow students, the teacher, or individuals on film or videotape in relation to the movement challenges presented. Only after the students have had an opportunity to solve the problem within the limits of their own understanding and ability is the observation phase utilized.

Also, instead of movement problems being entirely open-ended, as with the exploratory method, there is a gradual funneling of questions in such a manner that they lead children to discovering for themselves how to perform the particular task under consideration. At the end of the process of attempting solutions to the problem at hand, the children have an opportunity to evaluate their interpretations in light of the solutions of others (Figure 13.3).

The key to effective use of any indirect teaching style is the thoughtful construction and use of movement challenges that allow for a variety

---

FIGURE 13.3 Differences between the exploratory and guided discovery methods, both of which utilize indirect approaches.

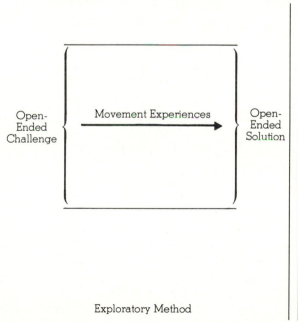

Exploratory Method

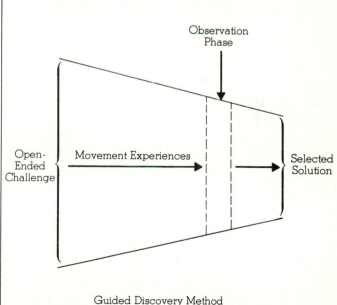

Guided Discovery Method

of interpretations but still remain within the confines of the stated objectives of the lesson. Although reasonable solutions to movement problems are considered correct, one should not infer that the lesson will take its own course simply by the instructor posing one or two questions to the class. The teacher must constantly rephrase and restructure questions in an effort to continually probe and challenge each student. The primary advantages of indirect styles are that they permit greater involvement on the part of the student in the learning process, and they account for individual differences among children by permitting them to solve movement problems presented to them. With no one "best" way to perform, all children work at their own level of ability and experience some degree of success. Indirect styles allow children to develop a movement vocabulary, to express themselves creatively, and to think and develop self-direction in their learning attempts.

Combining Direct and Indirect Styles

The limitation method of teaching movement skills uses both direct and indirect styles of teaching and attempts to include the best aspects of both (Figure 13.4). With the limitation method, children are permitted the opportunity to explore and discover but are also given specific skill instruction by way of the task or command methods. This combination of indirect and direct styles can be effectively used at all skill levels. The limitation method is advocated in the refinement of fundamental movement skills and the learning of new sport skills because it recognizes both the individuality of the learner and the necessity for developing a variety of movement skills during the critical elementary school years.

Limitation Method.   Briefly, the limitation method of teaching involves a sequence of (1) free exploration, (2) guided discovery, (3) progressive problem solving, and (4) specific skill instruction (Figure 13.5). The teacher first poses a general task to the students (free exploration). For example, the instructor may say, "Try to get the beanbag from one end of the room to the other any way you wish." Next, a few restrictions are added, and the problem may be modified: "See how many ways you can get the beanbag across the room while remaining in one spot." Guided discovery comments such as this are then followed by a series of questions or challenges posed to the student (progressive problem solving). Each movement problem is stated in such a way that the learner's response possibilities are limited and designed to lead directly to the desired skill. For example, "Using a throwing motion, see if you can get the beanbag across the room" may be followed by "Can you throw the beanbag overhand (underhand, and so on)?" and concluded with "How do we stand when we throw?" or "How do we make our bodies move when we want to throw as far as we can?" The

FIGURE 13.4   The scope of teaching styles and the link between direct and indirect teaching styles.

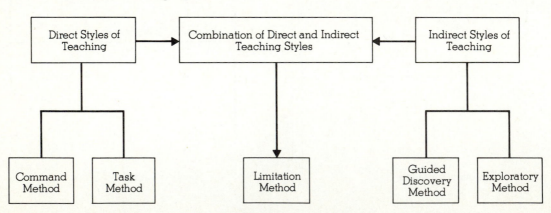

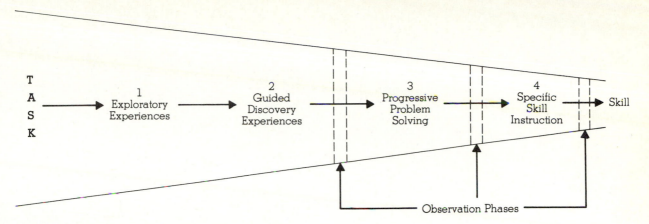

FIGURE 13.5 Elements of the limitation method, a progressive problem-solving approach to teaching movement skills.

teacher continually structures and restructures a variety of questions that are progressively more narrow in scope. Up to this point a specific explanation or demonstration of how to perform the overhand throwing pattern has not been given. After following the sequence of exploration, guided discovery, and progressive problem solving, the teacher now incorporates specific skill instruction into the lesson as needed. Many students will be able to perform the skill correctly at this point. They may be grouped with those who are experiencing difficulty and instructed to work on the overhand throw using small groups or peer tutoring (task teaching). Those having trouble may observe other students or the teacher perform the desired skill and then work on it under more direct supervision by the teacher (command teaching).

The limitation method possesses the advantages of both the direct and indirect styles but few of their disadvantages. The major disadvantages remaining are that it is time-consuming and takes practice on the part of the teacher to perfect. These may be outweighed, however, by the fact that each child is involved in the process of learning through exploration and guided discovery and is finding success while still working toward the goal of improved skill.

SUGGESTED READING

Anderson, W. G. (1980). *Analysis of teaching physical education*. St. Louis: C. V. Mosby.

Flanders, N. A. (1970). *Analyzing teaching behavior*. Reading, MA: Addison-Wesley.

Harrison, Joyce M. (1983). *Instructional strategies for physical education*. Dubuque, IA: Wm. C. Brown.

Mosston, M. (1981). *Teaching physical education*. Columbus, OH: Charles E. Merrill.

Schickedanz, Judith A. et al. (1983). *Strategies for teaching young children*. Englewood Cliffs, NJ: Prentice-Hall.

Sidentop, D. (1976). *Developing teaching skills in physical education*. Boston: Houghton Mifflin.

Singer, R. N., and Dick, W. (1980). *Teaching physical education: A systems approach*. Boston: Houghton Mifflin.

Templin, Thomas J., Olson, Janice K., Eds. (1983). *Teaching in physical education*. Champaign, IL: Human Kinetics.

PART IV

THE PROGRAM

CHAPTER 14

THE DEVELOPMENTAL PHYSICAL EDUCATION CURRICULUM

The elementary school physical education curriculum is an integral part of the total school program. As such, it incorporates a broad series of movement experiences that aid children in developing and refining their movement and physical abilities, along with promoting cognitive and affective development. The elementary school physical education curriculum that is well planned; well taught; and based on the needs, interests, and developmental level of children is not a frill or appendage to the school program. It is a positive force in the education of the total child.

In order to achieve the goals of physical education, a variety of movement activities is used that serves as the vehicle by which the objectives of the program are achieved. These activities are viewed as tools and not as an end in themselves in the elementary school. It is the role of the teacher to teach children through activities. The focal point must always be the child and not the activity.

If the goals of physical education are to have any real meaning, then curricular models congruent with these goals should be possible. Curricular models serve as a blueprint for action. In other words, they make up the basic structure around which the daily lesson is planned and carried out by the teacher in the gymnasium or on the playing field. What has been discussed in the preceding chapters is of little value if you cannot bring order to it and make practical application to the lives of children. The value of theory and research that fail to foster models for implementation is limited at best. Conversely, curricular models not based on sound research and theory are also of limited value. It is, therefore, the intent of this chapter to outline the steps in constructing a curriculum and to propose a developmentally based curricular model for implementing the physical education program during the preschool and elementary school years.

STEPS IN PLANNING THE CURRICULUM

There are five basic steps that must be followed in developing any curriculum. They are to *establish a value base for the program, develop a conceptual framework, determine the objectives of the program, design the program*, and *establish criteria for assessing the effectiveness of the program*. A discussion of each step follows.

Establish a Value Base

A necessary first step in all curricular planning is to establish the value base upon which the curriculum is to be built. The beliefs or philosophical position around which the curriculum is to be based should be clearly and concisely stated, along with a brief statement of goals.

Philosophy. The philosophy should be broadly based and should represent the best thinking of the curriculum committee. Hammering out a statement of philosophy, especially when it is a group effort, it often a difficult task. It is, however, the necessary first step simply because it will set the stage for all that follows and will serve as a cornerstone, outlining the reasons why physical education is important to the children you serve. The philosophy generally consists of several concise paragraphs. The first paragraph introduces the reader to the broad, general aim of the program. The next three or four paragraphs are terse statements about each of the general goals of the curriculum. These statements are sufficiently broad to cover the scope of the area being emphasized but are concise and to the point. The final paragraph generally summarizes what has been stated and reem-

TABLE 14.1 Sample Statement of Philosophy for the Elementary School

> Education is democracy's medium for the transmission of fundamental knowledge, skills, culture, values, and attitudes. The development of these qualities is essential in fulfilling the personal and social responsibilities that such a society and culture place on its members.
>
> The elementary school program must exert continuous effort to develop and refine pupils' academic skills through breadth and depth of learning in subject areas. This will enable pupils to acquire the critical skills of judgment, problem solving, and decision making required of participating citizens in contemporary society as well as in the society of the future.
>
> Social, physical, and emotional development must be emphasized to give pupils opportunities to gain experience and develop a positive sense of value concerning themselves and their place in the society to which they belong.
>
> The role of the teacher in facilitating, nurturing, and advancing learning changes as educators gain better understanding of learning and child development. As new methods and techniques of organization and instruction emerge, it is essential that the elementary school continually promote and implement needed innovations that reflect new knowledge.
>
> The ability of administrators, counselors, and instructional staff to be flexible and adaptable in the use of space, curricular change, scheduling, and innovation is an essential aspect of quality education. Staffing of the elementary school should reflect these characteristics.
>
> In achieving its goals, the elementary school must foster cooperative efforts and shared responsibility among all participants in the educational process—learners, parents, teachers, administrators, and the community.

phasizes the value of the program to the individual, community, and society. See Table 14.1 for a sample statement of philosophy as applied to the elementary school in general.

Goals.   A statement of the goals of the program follows the statement of philosophy. These general goals should be a direct reflection of the philosophy and may include statements such as the five that follow:

1. Movement skills will be developed and refined in a wide variety of fundamental and sport-related movement skills.
2. Fitness abilities, knowledges, and attitudes will be enhanced.
3. Perceptual–motor abilities will be enhanced through directed movement experiences.
4. Social and emotional behaviors that are valued by society will be fostered.
5. Leisure-time abilities will be increased through movement activities that are vigorous, challenging, and fun.

Establish a Conceptual Framework

A conceptual framework should undergird any curriculum. It is a basic but often overlooked aspect of curriculum building. The conceptual framework is the necessary link between your value base (philosophy and goals) and the actual design of the program. It provides for the definition and classification of terms and concepts as they are used in the curriculum. In a developmental physical education curriculum, the *categories of movement* (locomotion, manipulation, stability), traditional *content areas of physical education* (games, rhythms, self-testing), *movement concepts of movement education* (effort, space, relationships), *phases of motor development* (fundamental phase, sport-related phase), and *levels of movement skill learning* (beginning, intermediate, advanced) are all very important. A brief discussion of important aspects of the conceptual framework for the developmental curriculum follows.

Categories of Movement and Skill Themes.   The terms *locomotion, manipulation,* and *stability*

represent the three categories of movement. (Each was discussed earlier in Chapter 2, "Movement Skill Development".) These three categories serve as the organizing centers of the developmental physical education curriculum. In other words, they are the basis for the formation of units of instruction or developmental skill themes. A developmental skill theme is a group of related fundamental movements or sport skills around which one or more lessons are organized. In the developmental curriculum the categories of movement serve as the organizing center for each unit of the curriculum, while the skills to be stressed during each unit serve as the organizing centers, or themes, of the daily lesson.

Locomotion.   Locomotion refers to changes in the location of the body relative to fixed points on the ground. To run, jump, slide, or leap is to be involved in locomotion. Vertical jumping, hopping, rebounding, and high jumping are examples of skill themes that may be incorporated into the daily lesson plan at the fundamental or sport-skill phase of development. (See Chapter 20, "Fundamental Locomotor Skills".)

Manipulation.   Gross motor manipulation is that aspect of movement concerned with giving force to objects and absorbing force from objects by use of the hands or feet. The tasks of throwing, catching, kicking, trapping, and striking are included under the category of manipulation. Throwing a ball, passing a football, and pitching a baseball are examples of fundamental and sport skills within the manipulative category of movement. (See Chapter 21 and Chapters 25 through 29.)

Stability.   Stability refers to the ability to maintain one's balance in relationship to the force of gravity even though the nature of the application of the force may be altered or parts of the body may be placed in unusual positions. Stability is the most basic form of movement. It permeates all locomotor and manipulative movement. Body rolling, dodging, and static and dynamic balance skills are all examples of stability skill themes that may be incorporated into the lesson at the fundamental or sport skill phase of development. (See Chapters 22, 23, and 24.)

Content Areas of Physical Education.   Fundamental movements and sport skills within the categories of movement just outlined may be developed and refined through activities from the three traditional content areas of physical education: *games, rhythms*, and *self-testing*. The playing of particular games, rhythms, or self-testing activities is a *means* of reinforcing locomotor, manipulative, and stability skills appropriate to the developmental level of the child. Each activity used in the program should be selected with a conscious awareness of what it can contribute to developing and refining certain movement abilities. Children's primary objective may be fun, but serious teachers of movement have as their objectives learning to move and learning through movement. The possibility of fun as the motivation to learn is a byproduct of any good educational program and is an important objective. This point cannot be overemphasized. But when fun becomes the primary objective of the program for the teacher, then it ceases to be a physical education program and becomes a recreation period.

Games. Games are used as a means of enhancing movement abilities appropriate to children's developmental level (See Chapter 30, "Teaching Games".) They are often classified into various subcategories. The following is a frequently used system:

1. Low organized game activities (Chapter 31).
2. Relay activities (Chapter 32).
3. Lead-up game activities (Chapter 33).

Rhythms. Rhythmics are an important content area of the elementary school physical education program. (See Chapter 35, "Teaching Rhythmics.") They are frequently categorized as follows:

1. Fundamental rhythmic activities (Chapter 36).
2. Singing rhythmic activities (Chapter 37).
3. Creative rhythmic activities (Chapter 38).
4. Folk and square dance activities (Chapter 39).

Self-testing. Self-testing is the third major traditional content area of the elementary school

TABLE 14.2 The Movement Concepts of Movement Education

Effort (How the Body Moves)	Space (Where the Body Moves)	Relationships (Moving with Objects/People)
Body Movement with Varying:	**Body Movement at Varying:**	**Body Movement in Relation to:**
Force	Levels	Objects (or People)
strong	high/medium/low	over/under
light	Directions	in/out
Time	forward/backward	between/among
fast	diagonally/sideward	in front/behind
slow	up/down	lead/follow
medium	various pathways (curved,	above/below
sustained	straight, zigzag, etc.)	through/around
sudden	Ranges	People
Flow	body shapes (wide,	mirroring
free	narrow, curved, straight,	shadowing
bound	etc.)	in unison
	body spaces (self space	together/apart
	and general space)	alternating
	body extensions (near/far,	simultaneously
	large/small, with and	partner/group
	without implements)	

physical education program. This area represents a wide variety of activities in which children work at their own level and can improve their performance through their own individual efforts. (See Chapter 40, "Teaching Self-testing Activities.") Activities may be classified in a variety of ways. The following classification scheme is used here:

1. Perceptual–motor activities (Chapter 41).
2. Hand apparatus activities (Chapter 42).
3. Fitness activities (Chapter 43).

Movement Concepts of Movement Education. Abilities within the three categories of movement may be elaborated upon and dealt with in terms of movement elements or concepts. Development of abilities in these three content areas, namely, *effort, space*, and *relationships*, is a central focus of many movement education programs and is often omitted from more traditional physical education programs. In developmental physical education, the movement concepts are included and represent a content area of the program in addition to the three traditional content areas discussed earlier. A brief explanation of *effort, space*, and *relationships* follows and is displayed in Table 14.2.

Effort. The concept of effort deals with *how* the body moves. Children need to learn about the concept of effort. Effort may be subdivided into three aspects:

1. *Force*: The degree of muscular tension required to move the body or its parts from place to place or to maintain its equilibrium. Force may be heavy or light, or it may fall somewhere between those two extremes.
2. *Time*: The speed at which movement takes place. A movement may be fast or slow, gradual or sudden, erratic or sustained.
3. *Flow*: The continuity or coordination of movements. A movement may be smooth or jerky, free or restricted.

Space. The concept of space deals with *where* the body moves. Children need to understand where their body can move in space as well as how it can move. The following movement concepts of space can be directly related to all locomotive, manipulative, and stability movements.

1. *Level*: The height at which a movement is performed. A movement may be performed at a high, medium, or low level.
2. *Direction*: The path of movement. Movement may occur in a forward, backward, diagonal, up, down, left, or right direction, or it may be in a straight/curvy or zigzag pattern.
3. *Range*: The relative location of one's body (self space/general space) and how various extensions of the body (wide/narrow, far/near, long/short, large/small) are used in movement.

Relationships. The concept of relationships deals with both how and where the body moves in harmony with objects and other people. The concept of relationships is important for children to understand and experience through the medium of movement.

1. *Objects*: Stationing oneself in different positions relative to objects. Object relationships may be over/under, near/far, on/off, behind/in front, alongside, front/back, underneath/on top, in/out, between/among, and others.
2. *People*: Moving in various forms with people. People relationships include solo, partner, group, and mass movement.

Phases of Motor Development. The motor development of children follows a series of phases and stages that can be readily identified. These phases were discussed earlier in Chapter 2 and are briefly reiterated here.

Fundamental Movement Skill Phase. Developmentally normal children passes through the *initial, elementary*, and *mature* stages if proper instruction, adequate opportunities for practice, and sufficient encouragement are provided.

1. *Initial stage*: Characterized by the child's first observable attempts at the movement skill. Many of the components of the skill, such as the preparatory action and follow-through, are missing.
2. *Elementary stage*: Coordination and per-

formance improve, and the child gains more control. More components of the mature skill are integrated into the movement, although they are performed incorrectly.

3. *Mature stage*: The integration of all the components into a well-coordinated skill. However, it is lacking in terms of movement performance as measured quantitatively.

Sport-Related Skill Phase. After the child has attained a mature skill, it may be further refined or may be combined with other skills to form a sport-related movement skill at the *transitional, application*, and *utilization* stages.

1. *Transition stage*: Fundamental skills are applied in a general way to a variety of sport, dance, and recreational activities.

2. *Application stage*: Interests in sport activities narrow, and the child begins to pursue favorite activities. Sport selection is based on body type, motor abilities, available facilities, and group values. Form, accuracy, and strategy become more important to the individual.

3. *Lifelong utilization stage*: Individuals direct their attention to a few activities that they enjoy and desire to engage in as lifetime pursuits. They participate regularly and develop a degree of skill suitable for further enjoyment through recreational or competitive endeavors.

Levels of Movement Skill Learning. The traditional content areas and the movement concepts discussed earlier may be implemented in a variety of ways. The teacher must, however,

FIGURE 14.1 Levels and stages of learning a new movement skill.

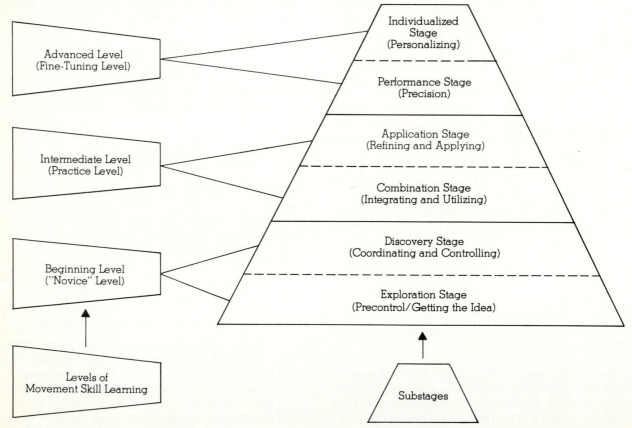

take into account that there are levels in the movement skill learning process. These levels were discussed earlier in Chapters 6 and 13 and are briefly reiterated and separated into stages here (Figure 14.1).

1. *Beginning Level (Novice Level)*
   a. *Exploration stage*: Experimenting with the movements involved in the task in relative isolation from one another. Movement control is lacking, but a conscious mental plan is being formed.
   b. *Discovery stage*: Finding ways and means of executing the movement tasks more efficiently. Movement control and coordination of the task improve and become less conscious.
2. *Intermediate Level (Practice Level)*
   a. *Combination stage*: The actions of one movement skill put together with those of other movement skills. This is a practice stage where separate tasks are integrated and practiced over and over.
   b. *Application stage*: Applying movement skills to a specific activity in the form of a game, sport or dance. More attention is given to smoothing out the task by further practice through utilization of the skill in an applied sense.
3. *Advanced Level (Fine Tuning)*
   a. *Refined performance stage*: Refining the elements of the skill to a high degree within one's particular level of ability. "Automatic" performance of the task is fully achieved.
   b. *Individualized stage*: Making fine-tuning adjustments and modifications in execution of the specific task according to the individual's needs. Creative application of means to achieve desired ends is possible.

Determine Objectives

Once the value base of the curriculum has been stated and the conceptual framework that will govern its structure has been described, it is possible to determine the *general objectives* of the curriculum. Once these have been determined, it is essential to describe *the conditions* under which the program will be conducted. This should be done *before* determining the *specific objectives* of the program.

State General Objectives. General objectives are broad, general outcomes that are established for the learner to achieve. These objectives might well be stated in terms of the psychomotor, cognitive, and affective areas of development, as follows:

Psychomotor Area
1. Movement Skill Objectives
   a. To enhance locomotor skill development (running, hopping, jumping, and so on).
   b. To improve manipulative skill acquisition (throwing, catching, kicking, and so on).
   c. To enhance stability skill development (dynamic and static balance, stunts and tumbling skills, and so on).
   d. To develop a variety of sport-skill abilities (soccer skills, softball skills, volleyball skills, and so on).
   e. To improve rhythmic abilities (folk, creative, square, and social dance skills.
2. Fitness Objectives
   a. To foster improved levels of physical fitness (muscular strength and endurance, aerobic endurance, and flexibility).
   b. To promote improved motor fitness (agility, speed, coordination, balance, and power).

Cognitive Area
1. Concept Development Objectives
   a. To improve perceptual–motor abilities (body, spatial, directional, and temporal awareness).
   b. To enhance perceptual abilities (visual, auditory, tactile, and kinesthetic).
2. Concept Reinforcement Objectives
   a. To develop knowledges and understandings in a variety of activities (rules, strategies, healthful living, decision making, and so on).
   b. To reinforce academic concepts dealt with in the classroom (math, science, social studies, and so on).

Affective Area

1. Emotional Skill Objectives
   a. To contribute to a positive self-concept (self-worth, fulfillment, competence, and so on).
   b. To encourage self-expression (creativity, appreciations, values clarification, and so on).
2. Social Skill Objectives
   a. To develop play-skill abilities (communication, teamwork, give and take, and so on).
   b. To enhance leisure-time abilities and interests (active and passive, group and single).

The physical education program that is developmentally based, properly planned, and carefully implemented can achieve the general objectives just listed. The degree to which each is achieved will depend upon the developmental level of the students, the philosophy and expertise of the teacher, and the teaching styles used.

Describe the Conditions.   Prior to establishing the specific objectives of the program, a thorough survey must be conducted of factors that may affect the actual content of the program. Those conditions that will impact on the specific design of the program should be concisely stated. This is done in order to provide a means of getting a picture of the boundaries within which the program must be conducted. Each of the following factors must be taken into account prior to determining the specific objectives of the program:

1. Facilities available (both school and community).
2. Equipment available.
3. Number of class periods per week.
4. Length of class periods.
5. Average number of pupils per class.
6. Pupils' assessed level of ability.
7. Geographic location.
8. Weather conditions.
9. Community mores.
10. Educational goals of the school system and community.

State Specific Objectives.   Once the general objectives have been established and the conditions under which the curriculum will be carried out have been stated, it is possible to determine the specific objectives of the program. The specific objectives that you establish may be stated in behavioral terms. *Behavioral objectives* have three important characteristics: (1) they are observable, (2) they are measurable, and (3) they establish the criterion for performance. The following are samples of behavioral objectives that may be appropriate for elementary school children.

The student will be able to:

1. Correctly perform two consecutive forward rolls from a squat to a squat position.
2. Demonstrate three types of soccer kicks in both drill and game situations.
3. Distinguish the difference between an even and an uneven beat in a musical composition and demonstrate it through appropriate movements.

Behavioral objectives are valuable, but they are time-consuming to write. Instead, many physical educators simply list the skills they want children to learn without establishing the criterion for performance. This method is acceptable; An example follows.

Skills will be taught in:

1. Stunts and Tumbling
   a. Log roll.
   b. Forward roll.
   c. Backward roll.
   d. Tripod.
   e. Headstand.
   f. Handstand.
2. Soccer
   a. Instep kick.
   b. Push pass.
   c. Punt.
3. Rhythmics
   a. Accent.
   b. Tempo.
   c. Intensity.
   d. Rhythmic pattern.

Design the Program

Once the objectives of the program have been determined, it is time to make a scope and sequence chart. Such a chart outlines the *scope, sequence*, and *balance* necessary to satisfy the specific objectives of the program from unit to unit and from year to year. Each of these aspects of the program design is discussed. Figure 14.2 provides a visual representation of a scope and sequence chart.

Scope.   The term *scope* as used in curriculum building refers to the content of the program in terms of its *breadth* or *range* throughout the academic year. The actual variety of units of work and skill through the year at any grade level represents the scope of the program for that grade level. In order for a curriculum to be effective, it must demonstrate sufficient scope. Its breadth should be enough to emcompass a multitude of skills, activities, and ability levels.

Sequence.   When using the term *sequence*, we are referring to progression in terms of the year-to-year ordering of skills taught in the curriculum. In other words, the sequence of the program is a reflection of the *timing* and *depth* of the program from grade to grade. In order for the curriculum to be effective, there must be clear

evidence of progressive skill development from year to year, building skill upon skill. This is reflected in the sequence of the curriculum.

Balance.   The term *balance* refers to the relative emphasis of the curriculum, in terms of time spent, on specific content areas and the *variety* inherent in the program. Figure 14.3 provides suggested approximate yearly time percentages for the various content areas of the elementary physical education program.

Any physical education curriculum that is to be of real value to children must endeavor to achieve harmony among scope, sequence, and balance. In doing so, it helps to insure that the activities engaged in by the children will be broad-based (scope), developmentally appropriate (sequence), and of continuing interest (balance).

Establish Assessment Procedures

Assessment is the final step in planning the curriculum. It is an important part of the total process, for only through assessment can it be determined if the students have achieved the objectives of the program. Evaluation serves as a method of determining the strong and weak points of your program and your teaching. It may

FIGURE 14.2   The scope and sequence chart.

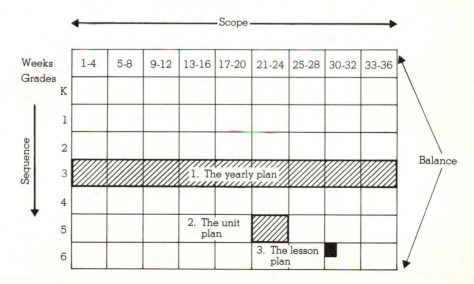

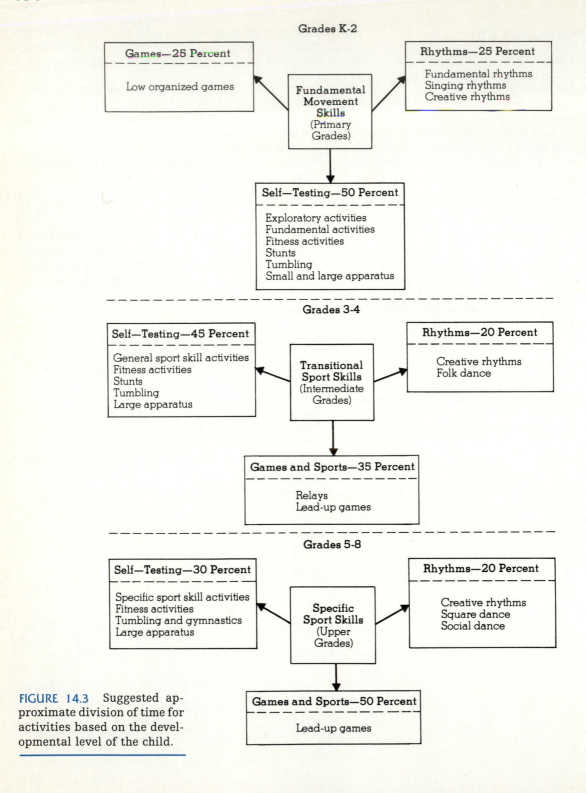

Grades K-2

Games—25 Percent

Low organized games

Fundamental Movement Skills
(Primary Grades)

Rhythms—25 Percent

Fundamental rhythms
Singing rhythms
Creative rhythms

Self—Testing—50 Percent

Exploratory activities
Fundamental activities
Fitness activities
Stunts
Tumbling
Small and large apparatus

Grades 3-4

Self—Testing—45 Percent

General sport skill activities
Fitness activities
Stunts
Tumbling
Large apparatus

Transitional Sport Skills
(Intermediate Grades)

Rhythms—20 Percent

Creative rhythms
Folk dance

Games and Sports—35 Percent

Relays
Lead-up games

Grades 5-8

Self—Testing—30 Percent

Specific sport skill activities
Fitness activities
Tumbling and gymnastics
Large apparatus

Specific Sport Skills
(Upper Grades)

Rhythms—20 Percent

Creative rhythms
Square dance
Social dance

Games and Sports—50 Percent

Lead-up games

FIGURE 14.3 Suggested approximate division of time for activities based on the developmental level of the child.

take many forms and be either subjective (process) or objective (product) in nature. Chapter 19, "Assessing Progress," discusses both process and product assessment. The important thing to remember in planning the curriculum is that each step is directly related to the preceding one and that curriculum building is a sequential process that proceeds in an orderly manner (Figure 14.4).

THE DEVELOPMENTAL CURRICULAR MODEL

The developmental physical education model is based on the concept that the development of children's movement abilities occurs in distinct but often overlapping phases of motor development in each of the categories of movement.

FIGURE 14.4 Steps to be followed in designing the developmental physical education curriculum.

This is achieved through participation in activities that are applied to the traditional content areas of physical education and the movement concepts of movement education. These activities are geared to the learner's appropriate level of movement skill learning and implemented through a variety of teaching styles. See Figure 14.5 for a visual representation of this conceptual framework.

Preschool and Primary Grades

Developmental teaching recognizes that preschool and primary-grade children are generally involved in developing and refining their fundamental movement skills. These skills serve as the themes of the curriculum and the basis for the formation of units of instruction at this level. More emphasis is placed during this period on indirect styles of teaching because children are at the beginning level of movement skill learning. Exploratory and guided discovery activities involving effort, space, and relationships, as well

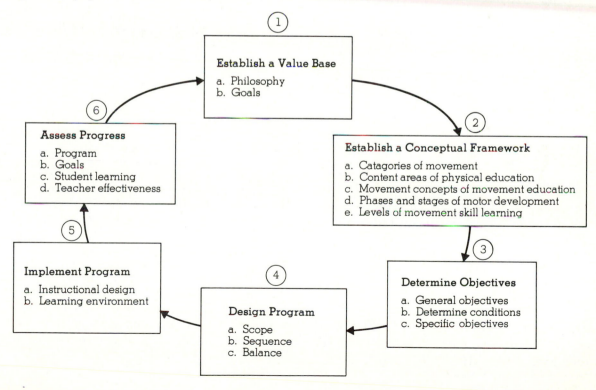

FIGURE 14.5   Outline of the conceptual framework for the developmental physical education program.

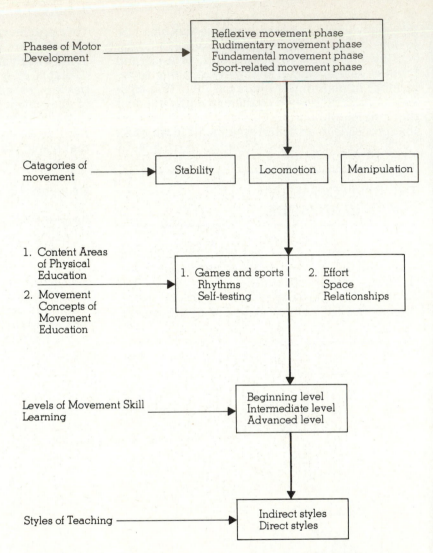

Phases of Motor Development → Reflexive movement phase / Rudimentary movement phase / Fundamental movement phase / Sport-related movement phase

Catagories of movement → Stability | Locomotion | Manipulation

1. Content Areas of Physical Education
2. Movement Concepts of Movement Education
→ 1. Games and sports / Rhythms / Self-testing | 2. Effort / Space / Relationships

Levels of Movement Skill Learning → Beginning level / Intermediate level / Advanced level

Styles of Teaching → Indirect styles / Direct styles

as games, rhythms, and self-testing activities facilitate the use, practice, and mature development of fundamental movement skills (Figure 14.6).

Intermediate and Upper Elementary Grades

When the developmental model is applied to the intermediate and upper elementary grades, the focus of the curriculum changes from the fundamental movement phase to the sport-related movement phase of development. During this phase, children are constantly combining and using various stability, locomotor, and manipulative skills in a wide variety of sport-related activities. At this phase, units of instruction are viewed in the context of the activity to which they are being applied. The game of softball, for example, becomes a sports skill unit and involves combinations and elaborations of fundamental manipulative skills (throwing, catching, striking), locomotor abilities (base running

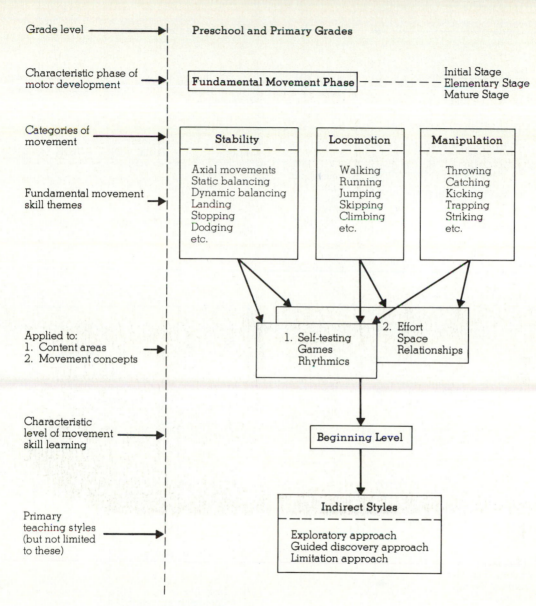

Grade level ⟶ Preschool and Primary Grades

Characteristic phase of motor development ⟶ **Fundamental Movement Phase** – – – – – – Initial Stage / Elementary Stage / Mature Stage

Categories of movement ⟶

Stability	Locomotion	Manipulation
Axial movements	Walking	Throwing
Static balancing	Running	Catching
Dynamic balancing	Jumping	Kicking
Landing	Skipping	Trapping
Stopping	Climbing	Striking
Dodging	etc.	etc.
etc.		

Fundamental movement skill themes ⟶

Applied to:
1. Content areas
2. Movement concepts ⟶

1. Self-testing Games Rhythmics   2. Effort Space Relationships

Characteristic level of movement skill learning ⟶ **Beginning Level**

Primary teaching styles (but not limited to these) ⟶ **Indirect Styles**

Exploratory approach
Guided discovery approach
Limitation approach

FIGURE 14.6   Implementing the developmental model at the preschool and primary grade level.

and sliding) and stability abilities (twisting, turning, and stretching). Teachers now focus their attention on developing the movement skills related to particular sport activities. These skills serve as the lesson themes within any given unit of instruction. These skills are applied to the various content areas and knowledge concepts (rules, strategies, understandings, and appreciations) of physical education. Children's characteristic level of movement skill learning at this

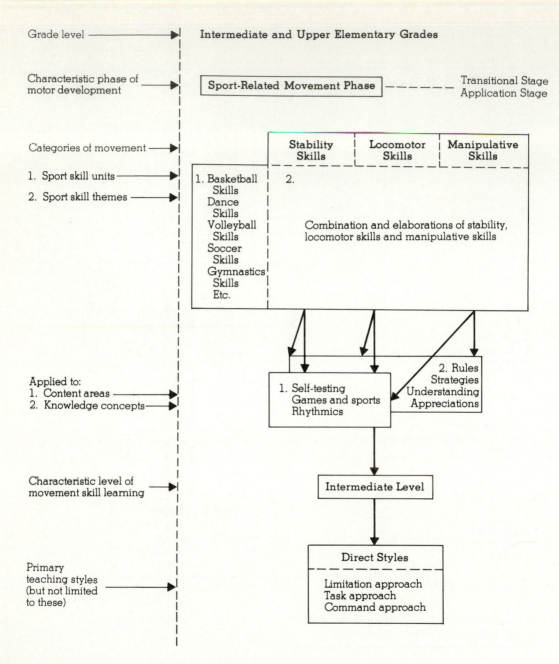

FIGURE 14.7 Implementing the developmental model in the intermediate and upper elementary grades.

phase is the intermediate level. Therefore, emphasis is placed on the combination of various skills and the practice of these skills in a variety of static drill situations and dynamic game situations. As a result, emphasis is generally placed on more direct teaching approaches (Figure 14.7).

SUGGESTED READING

Annarino, A. A., Cowell, C. C., and Hazelton, H. W. (1980). *Curriculum theory and design in physical education*. St. Louis: C. V. Mosby.

Laban, R., and Lawrence, F. (1947). *Effort*. London: Union Brothers.

Logsdon, B. J., and Barrett, K. R. (1984). Movement—the content of physical education, In Logsdon et al. *Physical education for children*. Philadelphia: Lea & Febiger.

Melograno, V. (1984, August). The balanced curriculum: Where is it? What is it? *Journal of Physical Education and Recreation* 55:21–24.

Melograno, Vincent. (1985). *Designing the physical education curriculum*. Dubuque, IA: Kendal/Hunt.

Siedentop, Daryl, Mand, Charles, and Taggart, Andrew. (1986). *Physical education: Teaching and curriculum strategies for grades 5–12*. Palo Alto, CA: Mayfield.

Ward, D., and Werner, P. (1981). Analysis of two curricular approaches in physical education. *Journal of Physical Education and Recreation* 52:60–63.

Willgoose, Carl E. (1984). *The curriculum in physical education*. Englewood Cliffs, NJ: Prentice-Hall.

CHAPTER 15

PLANNING, FORMATTING, AND IMPLEMENTING THE LESSON

The theme approach to teaching has become popular in recent years throughout education. Basically, a theme is a concept or skill center around which a specific lesson or group of lessons is organized. Therefore, a developmental movement skill theme is a movement skill or group of related movement skills on which a unit of study is based for the purpose of developing improved movement skills and knowledge concepts. Rather than centering on a particular content area (games, rhythmics, or self-testing activities) and specific activities within that content area, a developmental skill theme centers on specific movement skills (either fundamental or sport skills) that are to be developed and refined as the major focus on the physical education lesson. For example, children who are at the fundamental movement phase of development take part in a series of lessons designed to advance them to a more mature stage in running, jumping, throwing, or catching. Boys and girls at the sport-skill phase take part in units of work designed to refine specific movement abilities and to apply these skills to a number of sport-related skill activities. The developmental skills contained in Part V, "The Skill Themes," focus on several fundamental movement and sport-skill themes.

This chapter examines the actual steps involved in planning the physical education program at the grass-roots level. Planning the daily lesson, formatting the lesson itself, and evaluating its effectiveness are discussed, as well as when to move on to a new skill unit of instruction.

STEPS IN THE PLANNING PROCESS

A crucial element in the success of any educational program is planning. Without careful planning, the physical education class ends up being little more than a glorified recess period. Experience has shown that teachers who fail to plan are really in essence planning to fail. They delude themselves with the notion that they are too competent, too busy, or somehow above planning. As a result, they invariably run into difficulties and unwittingly encourage a series of disasters that are unnecessary, unfulfilling, and educationally unsound. The following represents a six-step approach to planning and implementing the physical education lesson. It is presented in detail here and again in outline form at the beginning of each chapter in Part V.

Preplanning

Once the basic parameters of the physical education curriculum have been established, you may begin the important and challenging process of planning the program for your unique teaching situation. A first step in the preplanning process is to inventory the actual facilities, equipment, and supplies that are available. The number of times classes meet per week, the length of each class period, and whether or not the children "dress" for gym will need to be determined. This important general information, along with other considerations, such as class size, alternative facilities during inclement weather, and community mores, provides facts necessary to get a *general* picture of the actual teaching–learning environment.

The exact amount of time to be spent on any one skill theme should remain somewhat flexible. With younger children, two to four class periods on some themes is appropriate, returning to them later on in the school year. With older children, you may wish to spend as long as four weeks on a specific unit of instruction. It is suggested that near-equal balance be given to skill themes during the course of the school year. The specific amount of time spent on particular skill themes will change as the abilities of individuals or the class change. For example, it may be helpful to children to focus more heavily on stability skill themes during the early periods of learning and gradually reduce this amount as they progress on to more mature stages of ability. Emphasis on some skill themes, particularly in the manipulative areas, should be increased from year to year. Others may remain constant.

Assessing Entry Levels

After the initial preplanning has been completed, it is necessary to observe your students and informally assess where they are at the present time in their movement abilities. The chapters in Part V, "The Skill Themes," provide descriptions of the characteristics of numerous fundamental movement and sport skills. It will be helpful to read these carefully and study the accompanying photos that visually portray each stage. Informally assess your students' present abilities in the movement skills on which you intend to focus. Based on this observational assessment, individuals or the group can be classified as to their level of movement skill learning (beginning, intermediate, advanced). With this information, *specific* plans for lessons can be made, taking care to utilize methods and techniques designed to move the class on to more skillful performance. The skill themes presented in the activity sections of this text contain Developmental Teaching Progression Charts. By referring to these charts, appropriate activities can be located and geared to the assessed level of ability.

It is crucial to the concept of diagnostic teaching that observation and assessment occur *before* beginning the specific planning and implementing phase. Teachers have often been guilty of planning and implementing lessons and entire programs on age-related criteria. Although it is true that the level of development of one's movement abilities is age-related, they are not age-dependent. Diagnostic teaching requires that we carefully observe and assess the entry level of the learner prior to formulating

FIGURE 15.1 Sample scope and sequence chart (K–5).

	PRIMARY GRADES				INTERMEDIATE GRADES		
Number of Lessons	Kindergarten	First Grade	Second Grade	Number of Lessons	Third Grade	Fourth Grade	Fifth Grade
5	Organization and Preassessment	Organization and Preassessment	Organization and Preassessment	5	Organization and Preassessment	Organization and Preassessment	Organization and Preassessment
10	Introduction to Body Awareness	Beginning Body Awareness	Intermediate Body Awareness	5	Fitness Testing	Fitness Testing	Fitness Testing
15	Introduction to Locomotor Skills I	Beginning Locomotor Skills I	Intermediate Locomotor Skills I	20	Beginning Ball Skills I	Beginning Soccer Skills	Intermediate Soccer Skills
15	Introduction to Upper Limb Manipulative Skills	Beginning Upper Limb Manipulative Skills	Intermediate Upper Limb Manipulative Skills	15	Beginning Strength Training	Intermediate Strength Training	Beginning Football Skills
10	Introduction to Body Handling Skills I	Beginning Body Handling Skills I	Intermediate Body Handling Skills I	20	Beginning Ball Skills II	Beginning Basketball Skills	Intermediate Basketball Skills
10	Introduction to Lower Limb Manipulative Skills I	Beginning Lower Limb Manipulative Skills I	Intermediate Lower Limb Manipulative Skills	15	Advanced Creative Rhythmic Skills	Beginning Folk and Square Dance	Intermediate Folk and Square Dance
15	Introduction to Rhythmics	Beginning Creative Rhythmic Skills	Intermediate Creative Rhythmic Skills	20	Beginning Ball Skills III	Beginning Volleyball Skills	Intermediate Volleyball Skills
10	Introduction to Flexibility and Body Control	Beginning Flexibility and Body Control Skills	Intermediate Flexibility and Body Control Skills	20	Upper and Lower Limb Striking Skills	Beginning Field Hockey Skills	Intermediate Field Hockey Skills
10	Introduction to Upper Body Propelling Skills	Beginning Upper Body Propelling Skills	Intermediate Upper Body Propelling Skills	15	Advanced Rhythmic Skills	Beginning Rhythmic Aerobics	Intermediate Rhythmic Aerobics
10	Introduction to Body Handling II	Beginning Body Handling Skills II	Intermediate Body Handling Skills II	15	Introduction to Lifetime Skills I	Beginning Disc Sport Skills	Intermediate Disc Sport Skills
10	Introduction to Locomotor Skills II	Beginning Locomotor Skills II	Intermediate Locomotor Skills II	15	Introduction to Lifetime Skills II	Beginning Softball Skills	Intermediate Softball Skills
15	Introduction to Upper Limb Manipulative Skills II	Beginning Upper Limb Manipulative Skills II	Intermediate Manipulative Skills II	15	Beginning Track Skills and Fitness Testing	Individual Track and Field Skills and Fitness Testing	Advanced Individual Track and Field Skills and Fitness Testing
15	Introductory Dance	Beginning Rhythmic Skills	Intermediate Rhythmic Skills				
15	Introduction to Upper Limb Striking Skills	Beginning Upper Limb Striking Skills	Beginning Track and Field Skills				
15	Introduction to Lower Limb Manipulative Skills II and Postassessment	Beginning Lower Limb Manipulative Skills II and Postassessment	Intermediate Lower Limb Manipulative Skills II and Postassessment				

FIGURE 15.2 Sample yearly plans for first grade and fifth grade.

Grade 1

Weeks	1-2	3-6	7-10	11-4	15-18	19-22	23-26	27-30	31-34	35-36
Unit	Class Preplanning and Assessment	Fundamental Locomotor Skills I	Fundamental Manipulative Skills I	Fundamental Stability Skills I	Fundamental Rhythmic Skills	Fundamental Locomotor Skills II	Fundamental Stability Skills II	Creative Dance Skills	Fundamental Manipulative Skills II	Review, Evaluation, and Summary
Specific Skill Themes to Be Stressed	Skill and fitness testing Review of skills from previous year	Running Starting Stopping Changing direction Tagging Dodging Pivoting	Overhand throw Underhand throw Catching Vertical toss Object manipulation	Static balance Dynamic balance Rolling	Movement to varying: Accents Tempos Intensities Rhythmic patterns Application of rhythmic fundamentals	Hopping Skipping Galloping Leaping Jumping	Static balance Dynamic balance Rolling Body supports Inverted supports	Singing dancer Simple dance forms	Kicking Bouncing Ball rolling Striking Dribbling	Skill and fitness testing Review of skills taught during the year

Grade 5

Weeks	1-2	3-6	7-10	11-4	15-18	19-22	23-26	27-30	31-34	35-36
Unit	Class Preplanning	Touch Football Skills	Soccer Skills	Rhythmic Skills	Gymnastics Skills	Basketball Skills	Volleyball Skills	Softball Skills	Track and Field Skills	Review, Evaluation, and Summary
Specific Skill Themes to Be Stressed	Skill and fitness testing Review of skills from previous year	Passing Catching Centering Blocking Defense Rules Strategy	Kicking Trapping Dribbling Passing Tackling Rules Strategy	Creative rhythmics Dances without partners Folk dance Square dance	Apparatus Tumbling Pyramids Free exercise	Dribbling Shooting Pivoting Passing Rules Strategy	Serving Bumping Setting Rotating Rules Strategy	Batting Pitching Throwing Fielding Catching Rules Strategy	Long jump High jump Dashes 600-yard run Hurdles Relays	Skill and fitness testing Review of skills taught during the year

and implementing specific strategies to advance the learner to the next stage of development.

Specific Planning

Once the preplanning and observational assessment of the entry level of ability has been completed, specific planning may begin. During this step, the teacher develops a total plan or scope and sequence chart (see Figure 15.1). Based on the outline of the scope and sequence chart, preplanning information, and the observed performance of the children, detailed yearly plans, unit plans, and daily lesson plans can be formulated.

The Yearly Plan. The yearly plan represents the scope of activities to be included in the curriculum at any one grade level for an entire school year. It is more detailed than the total curriculum outline and often reflects a seasonal influence that is based either on climatic conditions, which permit or prevent conducting classes outdoors, or the time of year for particular activities. The yearly plan should provide an outline of the skills to be engaged in by the class in each unit of instruction (Figure 15.2).

The Unit Plan. The unit plan is developed after the yearly plan. It represents the themes of instruction (such as touch football skills, gymnastic skills, or soccer skills) to be covered in a block of time. The unit plan is broken down into the specific skill themes that will be covered each week and the activities that will be used to develop these skills. Although the unit plan can be organized in numerous ways, each should contain the following information:

1. The title of the unit.
2. The specific objectives to be achieved by the learner.
3. The skills to be taught, in the appropriate sequence.
4. The specific activities to be used to develop these skills.
5. The equipment needed.

6. The methods of evaluating the students' achievement of the objectives.
7. Sources of information for teachers and students.

Figure 15.3 provides a sample unit plan outline.

The Daily Lesson Plan. Daily lesson plans enable teachers to make the best use of each class period, are energy and time savers, and assure progression in the program. Each lesson should be a meaningful experience through which the pupils learn something new as well as refine previously learned materials and skills. A well planned and conducted lesson will provide for:

1. Maximal participation in meaningful activities for all pupils in the group.
2. The development of each class member in accordance with the stated objectives.
3. Increased pupil interest in, appreciation of, and enthusiasm for vigorous physical activity.
4. A variety of well-selected activities that have educational value.
5. Opportunities to correlate and integrate physical education with other subject areas in the curriculum.
6. Opportunity for self-evaluation of daily accomplishments.

Lesson plans enable teachers to review and relate to the overall program objectives. They help in the preparation of the coming lesson, provide an organized and progressive procedure that aids in class interest and individual motivation, and often help prevent disciplinary problems from arising. Lesson plans help the teacher emphasize important points and skill elements. They aid in evaluating teacher as well as pupil progress. The lesson plan is more specific than the unit plan. It is simply a means of further clarifying exactly what you intend to do during each lesson. There are many formats for writing a lesson plan, ranging from highly detailed ones required by college professors in methods courses to "off-the-top-of-the-head"

FIGURE 15.3 Sample outline for a developmental skill theme unit.

GRADE _____ CLASS_____ ABILITY RANGE_____
LENGTH OF LESSON _____ MEETINGS PER WEEK _____ LENGTH OF UNIT_____
UNIT OBJECTIVES:_____
_____

	Day 1	Day 2	Day 3
SKILL THEME: INTRODUCTORY ACTIVITY: BODY: SUMMARY:			
	Day 4	Day 5	Day 6
SKILL THEME: INTRODUCTORY ACTIVITY: REVIEW ACTIVITY: BODY: SUMMARY:			
	Day 7	Day 8	Day 9
SKILL THEME: INTRODUCTORY ACTIVITY: REVIEW ACTIVITY: BODY: SUMMARY:			

Equipment Needed_____
Resources _____

lesson plans made by some teachers on their way to school each day.

Neither of these extremes is satisfactory, for obvious reasons. It must be remembered that the primary purpose of the lesson plan is to assist you in thinking through your lesson so that it is maximally efficient. Therefore, it is recommended that you consider writing a brief lesson plan for each day, based on your unit outline, on a 5-inch-by-8-inch index card. In this way, lesson plans may be kept in a card file for easy reference for the following year, when you may wish to utilize parts of the lesson again. You can make notations on the back of each card concerning the effectiveness of the lesson and suggestions for modifications. Figure 15.4 presents a sample daily lesson plan outline.

FORMATTING THE DAILY LESSON

Once the objectives of the lesson have been determined, it will be necessary to focus on the actual content of the lesson itself. The lesson generally consists of four parts: introduction, review, body, and summary (Figure 15.5).

Introduction

The introductory portion of the lesson is short, lasting about five minutes. It is designed to get the children organized and quickly involved in a vigorous activity. The introductory activity may

FIGURE 15.4 Sample format for a daily lesson plan on a 5″ × 8″ index card.

FRONT:

Lesson Objectives	Introductory Activity	Review Activity	Lesson Focus		Summary/ Dismissal
			Skill Development	Skill Application	

UNIT:_____ SKILL THEME:_____

GRADE:_____ CLASS:_____ DAY/WEEK/MONTH:_____

BACK:

EQUIPMENT NEEDED:

RESOURCES:

Class Evaluation	Self-evaluation

serve as a warmup or as a lead-in activity for the lesson to follow. The keys to successful introductory activities are total participation, vigorous activity, and ease of organization. The introductory activity often serves as an important way of burning off excess energy, thus enabling the children to focus their attention on the lesson to come.

Review

The review is the second part of the lesson. It generally lasts from five to ten minutes and provides a brief time to focus on the highlights of the previous lesson. Lengthy explanations and discussions of the previous lesson should be avoided. Rather, an appropriate activity, cou-

Introduction

Begin the lesson with an easy-to-organize, active, maximum-participation activity to be used as a warmup activity or as a lead-in to the body of the lesson.   5-7 minutes

Review

Briefly go over the main points of the previous lesson, using a specific activity and key teaching phrases.   5-10 minutes

Body

A. *Skill development:* Focus on new skill learning through practice in a variety of exploratory, guided discovery, or skill-drill activities that focus on improvement.   10-15 minutes

B. *Skill application:* Utilize new skills in appropriate game, sport, rhythmic, or self-testing activities.   5-10 minutes

Summary

A. *Review:* Briefly review the highlights of the day's lesson.   3 minutes

B. *Dismissal:* Rather than letting children run to the doors, provide a fun, novel, and challenging dismissal activity.   2 minutes

_____

30-50 minutes total

FIGURE 15.5 Suggested format and time frame for implementing the lesson.

pled with strategic teacher comments, should be the major aspect of this portion of the lesson. Remember, the reason for review is to help the child make the link between the material that was covered in the previous lesson and what will be presented as new material in the present lesson.

Body

The body is the central focus of the lesson, with the greatest amount of time devoted to it. The body of the lesson may range from fifteen to twenty-five minutes in length, depending upon the total time allotted. It contains the new material to be taught that day and the application of that material to appropriate activities. The body of the lesson centers on skill improvement through practice, using a variety of teaching approaches, depending on the developmental level of the class. Children at the fundamental movement skill phase benefit from a variety of exploratory, guided discovery, and basic skill development activities. Boys and girls at the sport skill phase benefit more from activities stressing skill application and improved performance abilities.

The body of the lesson also involves skill implementation through a variety of game, rhythmic, or self-testing activities. However, care should be taken to focus on the developmental aspect of the skill, with efforts concentrated on progressing to higher levels of ability rather than the playing of games for their own sake. Remember, only after the skill has been reasonably mastered should it be incorporated into game-type activities.

Summary

The summary, including the lesson review and class dismissal, is the last portion of the lesson. It is an important aspect of the lesson, even though it may last only two or three minutes. The summary provides the instructor with an opportunity to bring closure to the lesson by helping the children review what was stressed during the lesson and *why* they took part in certain activities. This permits time to highlight what will be presented in the next lesson and to arrange for orderly dismissal.

IMPLEMENTING THE DAILY LESSON

It is easy to read about a variety of teaching styles and to gain a textbook knowledge of how and when each method can be appropriately applied. Such textbook knowledge, however, is no substitute for experience. Therefore, it is the purpose of this section to offer practical suggestions in implementing the movement lesson. A variety of movement challenges is presented in the activity section of this text. The reader is cautioned to recognize that textbook knowledge will not make a good teacher. This knowledge must be coupled with frequent and regular practice with children to be of real and lasting benefit.

Putting It All Together

The primary objective of the developmental physical education lesson is the development and refinement of movement skills and fitness abilities. These objectives may be simply stated in terms of the learner's expected goal. Care should be taken to make sure that this goal is suitable for the child's stage of development. For example, the lesson objective may be "to improve jumping ability in the jump for distance" or "to be able to catch a small ball with greater efficiency."

Once the learning goal has been established, the teacher proceeds to formulate the movement tasks to be presented in the lesson. Initially, the tasks may be open-ended and exploratory, followed by guided discovery and then progressive problem solving. The progressive problem solving or limitation portion of the lesson should lead to refinement of the desired skill by insuring that each succeeding challenge or question given the learner is more narrowly defined. You should attempt to anticipate the broad range of possible responses before presenting the challenges in the lesson. It takes practice to structure meaningful challenges that lead to progressive skill refinement. Be prepared for solutions other than those anticipated and recognize the necessity for restructuring problems that initially are not clearly understood.

You will need to consider whether and at what point to intervene with more direct styles of teaching. Following the movement challenge portion of the lesson, you may decide to use the task or command approaches.

The teacher must next determine the specific game, rhythm, or self-testing activities to use. These activities should make use of the movement skills that earlier were incorporated into the lesson. You may decide, for example, to have the children play a circle or tag game to reinforce the running skills worked on in the lesson; or you may select a rhythmical activity with a fast tempo to permit rhythmical running.

The last part of lesson planning concerns the summary and review. It is important for you to sit down for a few minutes with your children at the end of the lesson to review the movement skills that were stressed. This summary reinforces the concepts dealt with and crystalizes them in the children's thinking and action.

Factors to Consider

When implementing the movement lesson, the teacher needs to be aware of several factors. First, it is important to have an understanding of the basic body mechanics of each skill. In order to foster efficient development of movement skills, the instructor must understand the principles of movement involved and how to apply them.

Second, the teacher must be certain that children are in fact making progress toward accomplishing the objectives of the lesson. It is not enough that each child is active. It must be activity designed for the purpose of achieving the lesson objectives.

A third factor to consider is safety. The teacher must be constantly concerned with whether safety precautions are being followed or ignored. Return to a more direct approach may be necessary during portions of the lesson in order to remedy an unsafe situation quickly and efficiently.

Fourth, the teacher should circulate throughout the class during the lesson and structure movement challenges in a variety of ways. Challenges may take the form of questions, problems, discussions, or verbal cues and should be varied so that none are used to the exclusion of the others. Phrases such as "Who can . . . ?," "How can you . . . ?," "Let's try . . . ," "Find a way . . . ," "Let's see if . . . ," and "Is there another way to . . . ?" are helpful. Care must be taken not to oververbalize at the expense of active involvement on the part of the children.

A fifth and final factor to consider in implementing the lesson is activity itself. Children have a great need to be active. Thus, the lesson should be one of *active* learning, not learning with little or no activity.

Success in combining teaching approaches depends on careful adherence to the factors discussed previously, as well as on the teacher's genuine interest, enthusiasm, experience, ingenuity, and imaginative approaches to teaching. To summarize, the five crucial factors in implementing the movement lesson are:

1. Knowing basic principles of movement.
2. Insuring that steady progress is being made.
3. Enforcing safety regulations.
4. Circulating throughout the class and using a variety of instructional formats.
5. Providing vigorous physical activity.

Helpful Hints

The following is a list of practical suggestions for implementing the daily lesson. Incorporating them into your lesson will help maximize its effectiveness:

1. Keep verbalization to a minimum.
2. Do not begin until everyone is listening.
3. Stand where everyone can see and hear you.
4. Do not "talk down" to students, but use a vocabulary that is understandable to them.
5. Do not attempt to emulate the pupils' height when talking to or working with them.

6. Summarize, using key words or phrases.
7. Analyze initial performance of the task. Comment on general problems; assist individually with specific problems.
8. When asking for questions from the class, be specific.
9. Place emphasis on the techniques employed during demonstrations rather than on the results.
10. Constantly observe and evaluate your pupils' performance.
11. Alter your approach and emphasis to meet their needs.
12. Encourage self-evaluation of progress by students.
13. Utilize the final few minutes for review, self-evaluation, and planning with the children for the next lesson.
14. Evaluate the lesson yourself in terms of achievement of the objectives.
15. Be thoroughly prepared. Overplan, and know exactly what you intend to do from minute to minute and how you plan to do it.
16. Be cheerful and show a genuine interest in your students, but do not become "buddy-buddy" with them or "one of the gang."
17. Have a thorough knowledge of the activity to be taught before introducing it.
18. Have on hand and readily available all necessary equipment and other required materials.
19. Keep all students actively participating throughout the period whenever possible.
20. Help students achieve proficiency in skills by devoting sufficient time to practice.
21. Provide equal opportunities for children with special needs to engage in and derive satisfaction from participation.
22. Modify rules and the size of activity areas according to student needs and abilities.
23. Develop a spirit of fun and pleasure during activities.
24. Treat all students fairly, recognize individual differences, and avoid embarrassing those who have made mistakes.
25. Offer as many varied activities as time, space, and equipment will allow.
26. Activities should be continued long enough for students to become skilled.

27. Develop necessary skills before trying them in an activity or game.
28. Build skill upon skill.
29. Warmup activities should pertain to the skills being used in the class.
30. Never let an activity drag. When the children begin to lose interest, use a variation or change the activity.
31. Avoid activities in which only a few can participate.
32. Use a variety of teaching approaches that help each child learn something new every day.
33. Analyze classes that did not go well; recognize that this is often your fault.
34. Arrange activities to provide continuous advancement throughout the entire school year, with definite objectives for each skill level.
35. Be observant of individual differences. Structure lessons so that all achieve a reasonable degree of success and feel challenged by the lesson.

EVALUATING THE DAILY LESSON

Each of the steps outlined in the prceeding paragraphs is important to successful teaching of the physical education lesson. Care should be taken to plan all aspects carefully in order to maximize the impact of each lesson. The effectiveness of your lessons should be periodically evaluated and adjustments made in the methods, techniques, and approaches used. Without periodic evaluation, it is impossible to know what has been achieved in terms of improved abilities and to plan effectively for subsequent lessons. Therefore, it is suggested that the teacher informally assess pupil progress on a regular basis. At the elementary school level, the key to successful evaluation is to keep it simple. There is little need for elaborate diagnostic procedures. As long as you are familiar with the developmental characteristics of both fundamental and sport skills, simple observational assessment (process assessment) will generally suffice. Based on your informal evaluation of progress or lack

of progress, you will need to make modifications in your lessons. Constant monitoring of pupil progress provides the teacher with information necessary for planning effective, challenging, and developmentally appropriate lessons. Chapter 19, "Assessing Progress," deals with both process assessment and product assessment of movement skill learning.

MOVING ON

Probably the most crucial but least scientific aspect of the entire planning process is to know when to move on to another unit. It is impossible to provide anything more than general guidelines on how much time should be spent on a particular skill theme. No two groups, classes, or individuals are exactly alike. Experienced teachers, however, sense when it is time to move on to another theme. Some of the cues that they use are

1. The percentage of children within the class who have achieved the objectives of the unit.
2. The percentage of children who have shown a reasonable degree of improvement beyond their entry level.
3. The interest that the children display in the lessons.
4. The amount of time the children spend on task.

Ideally, every teacher wants all children to achieve a 100 percent success rate throughout the entire curriculum. This, of course, is not possible, given the normal variation in natural abilities, learning styles, and other factors. Experienced teachers, however, continue to strive for 100 percent success, being fully aware that they will have to individualize their teaching in order to maximize this elusive goal. Do not be discouraged with less than perfection. It is important to adopt an attitude that success is equal to improvement and that improvement is relative to the individual's entry level and the movement challenges presented. For example, if the children are assessed at the onset of the unit to be at the initial stage in volleying and striking, and they have "only" achieved the elementary stage after several lessons, there has been improvement, even though the mature stage has not yet been reached. In order to maximize success, the movement challenges must be challenging but not overwhelming. Therefore, you need to carefully and continually observe and refocus the lesson in order to achieve a balance between success, challenge, and failure.

Subtle clues of frustration, boredom, inattention, and general off-task behavior are good indicators that it is time to refocus your lessons or move on to another skill theme. As a general rule of thumb, it is better to spend two or three lessons on a skill theme with children returning to it once or twice during the school year rather than focusing all your attention on it at one time. Older children tend to benefit from longer periods of time on a particular skill theme. It is suggested that you not spend beyond a maximum of eight to ten lessons on any one unit of instruction at one time. Remember, however, to be flexible and responsive to the needs of your students.

Successful teachers recognize the need for a scope and sequence chart that provides a blueprint for the physical education program. Successful teachers recognize the need for observational assessment and detailed planning but are never constrained by these plans. A constant process of evaluating and reassessing pupil progress, interest, and needs enables successful teachers to be flexible and able to refocus their lessons in order to create the most effective learning environment. Figure 15.6 provides an overview of the cyclic nature of the steps in planning and implementing the lesson.

FIGURE 15.6 Steps in planning and implementing the lesson.

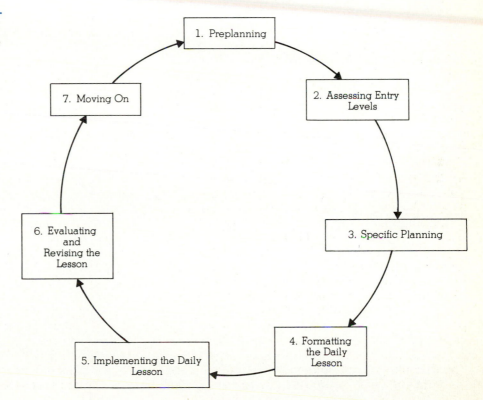

SUGGESTED READING

Evaul, T. (1980, September). Organizing centers for the 1980's. *Journal of Physical Education and Recreation* 51:51–54.

Heitnman, H. M. (1981, February). Integrating concepts into curricular modules. *Journal of Physical Education and Recreation* 52:42–45.

K-12 physical education (1981). Winnipeg, Canada: Manitoba Department of Education.

Siedentop, D., Herkowitz, J., and Rink, J. (1984). *Elementary physical education methods*. Englewood Cliffs, NJ: Prentice-Hall, Chapter 8.

CHAPTER 16

ORGANIZING THE LEARNING ENVIRONMENT

The most carefully designed curriculum and the (best-planned program will be of little benefit if the learning environment has not been properly organized and care has not been taken in planning and implementing the lesson. Teachers of physical education must possess a variety of organizational skills. They assume a great deal of responsibility in terms of the use of facilities, equipment, instructional aids, and student helpers. They conduct classes in large, nonconfined areas and must be able to organize and move large groups of children. The manner in which the learning environment is organized will have a dramatic effect on what takes place in the gymnasium or on the playground. Successful teachers pay close attention to the environment and make every effort to maximize its potential for creating an atmosphere conducive to learning. All the just-mentioned factors do much to create such an atmosphere. Each of these topics is discussed in this chapter.

ORGANIZING FACILITIES

Particular attention needs to be given to the actual indoor and outdoor facilities that serve as teaching stations. It is important that indoor facilities are free from safety hazards, have proper flooring, lighting, and acoustics; and are clean. Similarly, outdoor facilities need to be free from safety hazards, located away from occupied classrooms, and have clearly defined physical boundaries.

Indoor Facilities

The gymnasium is your classroom. It is a learning laboratory in which children use their entire bodies in the process of learning. Therefore, it is of utmost importance that the gymnasium be free from potential safety hazards. In many elementary schools the gymnasium serves as the school cafeteria or as a multipurpose room. Frequently lunch tables are stored against walls or shoved into a corner. Special care should be taken to store tables and other equipment elsewhere. If this is not possible, it is important that they be secured and that the boundaries of the gymnasium are clearly redefined to exclude the area in which tables or other equipment are stored. The space that is used by your students must be free of obstacles if it is to be safe.

The flooring used for the indoor learning environment is also important. Tiled, wooden, or carpeted floors all have important implications for the type of activities that can be safely included in the lesson and the type of footwear children should wear. The manner in which the floor is marked should receive your careful attention. Pressure-sensitive tape can easily be applied for temporary markings. Care, however, should be taken to be certain that this tape is removed when you are finished. If permitted to remain on the floor for several months, it often becomes very difficult to remove. In no case should masking tape be used for floor markings unless it is removed weekly. Masking tape dries out quickly and is extremely difficult to remove. A limited number of permanent markings is suggested for the gym floor in the elementary school. Too many lines tend to be confusing to children. Sample illustrations of appropriate floor markings for the elementary school gymnasium are located in the Appendixes.

The acoustics of many gymnasiums are difficult for some teachers to deal with. The large size of the gymnasium and the use of equipment, coupled with a lack of sound-baffling devices such as carpeting or ceiling tile often make for poor acoustics. Be certain that you are familiar with the acoustics of your indoor teaching station. Make provisions for adjusting your voice and the use of nonverbal cues accordingly. Failure to do so will result in considerable frustration and voice strain.

The gymnasium should be well lighted and free from shadows. All lights should be covered with protective grids to prevent breakage. The ceiling height and location of the lights will have a major impact on the inclusion or exclusion of certain activities. Volleyball, for example, should be prohibited if the lights are not covered or if the ceiling is too low to permit proper play.

The cleanliness of the gymnasium warrants constant attention. Gymnasium floors should be cleaned at least twice each day. Remember, much of the children's time is spent on the floor; therefore, it needs to be free from dirt and debris. A large push broom or mop should be kept close by for frequent use. Gymnasium mats should be neatly stored and periodically cleaned with a mild soap and water. Blindfolds, pinnies, and other cloth devices should be laundered frequently and stored properly.

Outdoor Facilities

The outdoor physical education facility should be inspected daily for potential safety hazards. Care should be taken to be certain that the area is free from obstacles, broken glass, and holes. Frequently, the outdoor facility is used after school hours by nonschool groups. It is important that the daily inspection of the outdoor facility be made immediately prior to conducting classes. This takes only a few minutes and helps reduce potential hazards.

The surface area on which outdoor physical education classes are conducted is important. The area should be level, dry, and free from stones and other debris. It should be far enough away from classrooms that it does not interfere with other classes. The outdoor facility should be located on school property as far from parking lots and city streets as possible. It should, however, be close enough to the school to permit easy access to equipment and shelter in case of a sudden change in the weather.

The boundaries of the outdoor instructional area must be clearly defined and enforced. The feeling of freedom that often comes with being outdoors must not hamper conduct of the class. It is important to be able to maintain visual and verbal contact with each member of the class at all times when outdoors. Defining, clearly marking, and enforcing boundaries will make your outdoor teaching job much easier.

ORGANIZING EQUIPMENT

The selection, placement, and use of equipment are important aspects of effective organization of the lesson. In order to encourage maximum class participation and to minimize disruptive behavior, *all* members of the class should be actively involved throughout the lesson. Waiting in long lines or sharing equipment among several children invites restlessness, boredom, and behavioral problems. On the other hand, if gymnasium equipment is properly selected, placed, and used, the learning objectives of the lesson can be maximized.

Equipment Selection

When purchasing equipment, it is wise to buy quality goods. Although quality equipment often costs more in the short run, it is generally less expensive in the long run. Purchasing quality equipment through reputable companies often affords longer, more effective use of the equipment and an opportunity for returns or exchanges when necessary. A list of appropriate equipment for use in the elementary school physical education program is located in the Appendixes, along with a list of reputable equipment companies.

It is helpful to keep a complete inventory of all gymnasium equipment available for use. A listing of all bats, balls, beanbags, and hoops, as well as mats and gymnastic apparatus, is a must. The condition of the equipment should be noted on the inventory checklist, and faulty or broken equipment should be immediately repaired or replaced. An equipment inventory should be conducted at least twice a year—once at the beginning of the school year and again at the end. This will provide a complete accounting of the equipment available for use and an indication of what is needed. A copy of the inventory and list of defective or missing equipment should be given to the building principal or other appropriate school officals.

Equipment Placement and Use

The actual placement and use of equipment has a dramatic effect on the lesson. Whenever possible, provide for maximum participation by all members of the class. When using small apparatus such as balls, hoops, beanbags, and wands, it will be helpful to have an implement for each child. The manner in which this equipment is distributed to the class and returned to its proper

PHOTO 16.1   Indoor facilities must be clean, well lighted, and free of safety hazards.

place is worthy of attention. Simply giving the command "get a ball" will not do. A predetermined system must be devised in order to minimize confusion, pushing, and other disruptive behavior. Equipment may be passed out to students by the teacher. Squad leaders may get and dole out equipment, or it may be obtained in small groups. Whatever methods you choose, be sure that they are quick and efficient and that they cause a minimum of disruption.

When using large apparatus, its actual placement in the gymnasium is important. The physical layout should be such that each piece of equipment is free from obstacles and can be easily viewed by the teacher from any part of the room. Care should be taken to insure that mats are placed under each piece of apparatus and that the equipment itself is safe for use. The equipment should be visually inspected and tested prior to its use. Safety hazards should be immediately corrected or repaired. In no case should you continue to use a piece of equipment that you know to be defective.

In order to make maximum effective use of the allotted time, it is important to have inspected all equipment and have it ready for distribution *prior* to class. Small equipment that is neatly stored on racks, in utility bags, or in containers can be quickly and easily put to use. Be certain, however, that after the equipment has been used, it is returned immediately to its proper location. This will insure easy access for the next class and a minimum of loss.

The use of large apparatus sometimes poses another problem. Setting up climbers, mats, balance beams, and the like is more time-consuming. Therefore, it is generally advisable to have as few large equipment changes as possible from class to class. Be certain, however, to have all of the equipment out in its proper place, inspected, and ready for use prior to the class entering the gymnasium. Failure to do so only wastes time and creates unnecessary confusion. If equipment changes are necessary, students can be taught how to move certain pieces of apparatus under direct supervision.

Remember, the balls, bats, hoops, mats, and other equipment available to you represent the "tools" of your profession. Considerable care should be given to this equipment, to be certain that it is in ample supply and good condition. There is little excuse for a physical education program with little or no equipment. Just as children cannot be expected to learn to read without books, they cannot be expected to develop their movement abilities without the proper equipment. The physical education program must have an annual budget that provides for equipment purchase, replacement, and repair. Insufficient funds can be supplemented, to a degree, through the use of homemade equipment. However, teachers cannot be expected to develop and implement first-rate programs using only homemade equipment. Money-raising projects sponsored by the PTA or other interested groups can *supplement* the equipment budget. Much of the gymnasium and playground equipment found in elementary schools is often there due to fund-raising projects and donations by parent and teacher organizations.

PREPARING INSTRUCTIONAL AIDS

Another aspect of organizing the learning environment is the preparation and use of instructional aids. Successful teachers make ample use of various devices in an attempt to enhance understanding and appreciation of the subject and to clarify instructions. The use of task cards, bulletin boards, and other visual aids can be an important aspect of the lesson.

Task Cards

A task card is a written description of what skill or movement activity should be performed. It clearly indicates acceptable individual levels of achievement and may provide the child with a verbal and or visual description of the task. Task cards are an effective visual technique to use with station teaching, individual pacing, and during open gym time. They provide students with information about what is to be done, how it is to be done, and standards of acceptable performance. The use of task cards enables the class to be working on one or more activities at the same time. They provide maximum participation and promote individual standards of achievement.

Bulletin Boards

The use of bulletin boards in the elementary school physical education program should not be overlooked. Bulletin boards can be used as a means of creating interest, imparting knowledge, and recording information. They may be located in the gymnasium or in the hallway. They should be neat and attractive and should reflect your creative talents. In order to be most effective, they should be changed frequently during the school year.

Bulletin boards featuring upcoming units of work can heighten interest. The use of magazine photos and drawings depicting outstanding performers executing the same skills that you will be focusing on tends to create an atmosphere of anticipation for the lessons to come.

Bulletin boards can be used effectively to impart knowledge. For example, the major muscle groups of the body may be depicted on a bulletin board throughout the school year. Their location

and appropriate activities for strengthening them may be highlighted. A nutrition bulletin board depicting the basic food groups may be displayed. Information may be imparted by posting a list of all those achieving a certain standard on a skills test. The various components and standards of the AAHPERD Health Related Physical Fitness Test may be the theme for an effective bulletin board.

Visual Aids

Film, videotape, and wall charts can be effectively used in the physical education program to provide children with a visual model of the skills or sports to be learned. A film or videotape of outstanding performers in gymnastics or soccer, for example, helps create a mental image of the level of skill that is possible. Care, however, must be taken when using this technique to be certain that the children are reminded that attaining such high levels of skills takes considerable time, effort, and practice. The approach should be "You may not be able to do this now, but if you work hard you will be able to do many of these skills later." The use of film or videotapes of skilled athletes helps to motivate students to learn and to do their best. It helps to provide them with a purpose for skill learning and practice.

Skill charts are another effective visual aid

PHOTOS 16.2 AND 16.3 Bulletin boards serve to create interest, convey knowledge, and record information.

used by many teachers. They may be purchased commercially from a variety of sources, or they may be homemade. The major advantage of a skill chart is that it provides students with a visual representation of the various elements of a particular skill. For example, the key elements in a soccer kick, an overhand throw, or a forward roll may be portrayed in photos, line drawings, or even stick figures. This is particularly important during the early stages of skill learning, when the learner is attempting to form a conscious mental image of the task.

ORGANIZING STUDENT HELPERS

The very nature of the physical education program lends itself to the use of helpers. Large classes, varying facilities, the use of many different types and amounts of equipment all highlight the importance of helpers in the physical education program. Also, the teacher is sometimes unable to demonstrate certain tasks or needs several extra hands to assist with spotting. Squad leaders and gym helpers can be of valuable assistance.

Squads and Squad Leaders

When organizing groups of children, you may find it helpful to divide the the class into squads. It is generally advisable to have an even number of squads so that they may be easily combined for various activities. The number of students per squad should be an even number and as small as possible to insure maximum participation. Small squad sizes of 6 or 8 are preferable to larger groups of 10 or more. The placement of students in squads should be teacher-directed in order to insure balance in ability levels. Squads should never be chosen in a manner that is embarrassing or humilating to children.

Once the class has been divided into squads, have them select an appropriate squad name.

Naming, numbering, or color-coding squads makes it easier for organization and regrouping throughout the lesson. It also helps create group identity and promotes group pride. A designated location for each squad to go upon entering the gymnasium is a helpful organizational technique.

Squad leaders should be selected for each group. The honor and responsibility of being a squad leader should be given to all children sometime during the course of the school year. Squad leaders should be changed frequently, generally at the beginning of a new unit of work. The composition of the squads themselves should be changed at least three or four times during the school year.

Squad leaders can perform many valuable functions. They may assist with taking roll, obtaining equipment, keeping records, moving their group, or leading exercises. Squad leaders should be praised for a job well done. Be sure to encourage them to have pride in the responsibilities of being a leader.

Gym Helpers

Physical education teachers are often permitted to incorporate gym helpers into their program. Gym helpers may be older students interested in working with youngsters. They may be high school students interested in a career in physical education. Some school systems provide funds for hiring adult paraprofessionals to serve as gym helpers. In any case, their presence in the program can be invaluable. Gym helpers can be assigned many of the routine chores of the physical education program. Organizing equipment, assisting with record keeping, officiating, leading activities, and helping with assessment can all be helpful duties. Remember, the use of gymnasium helpers is intended to provide you more time for personalized instruction; be sure to make maximum effective use of your time. Gym helpers should never be left in charge of the entire class. They should always to used in a professional manner to assist in providing the best program possible.

ORGANIZING GROUPS OF CHILDREN

A variety of activity formations is frequently used in the gymnasium and on the playground. Each formation is used for specific purposes. Proper use of activity formations can enhance the teacher's use of limited time. Avoid selecting activities that require frequent formation changes. Commonly used formations are diagrammed and described here.

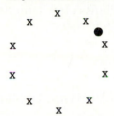

Single Circle Formation

1. Frequently used for circle games and dances
2. Often used for parachute activities.
3. Good formation for discussions.
4. Keep groups small for maximum participation (6 to 8 maximum).
5. Stand at the edge of the circle when talking, never in the center.

Double Circle Formation

1. Often used for circle partner activities.
2. Used for numerous circle dances and mixers.
3. Used for some circle games.
4. Use floor markings to designate places.
5. Change partners often.

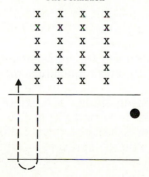

File Formation

1. Frequently used for locomotor and ball-dribbling activities.
2. Used for numerous sport-skill drills.
3. Keep groups small (no more than 8 to a group).
4. Be sure groups are even.
5. Clearly explain and enforce rules.

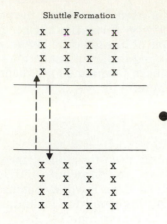

Shuttle Formation

1. Used for numerous locomotor, throwing, and catching activities.
2. Used for some sport-skill drills.
3. Explain and enforce a definite travel procedure.
4. Stand where all can see you.
5. Be sure students stay behind the restraining line until their turn.

Parallel Line Formation

1. Used for throwing, catching, and kicking skills.
2. Used for basketball sport-skill relays.
3. Provide a restraining line in order to keep lines straight.
4. Keep groups small with a maximum of 6 to 8 per line.
5. Be sure that lines are sufficiently apart in order to promote proper execution of the skill.

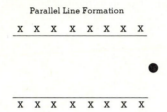

Scatter Formation

1. Used for movement exploration and problem-solving activities.
2. Great for creative expression activities.
3. Be sure to set geographical boundaries before scattering.
4. Be sure that each child has ample personal space for moving.
5. Do not stand in one place. Move throughout the class.

Half-Circle Formation

1. Frequently used for leader demonstrations.
2. Use existing circle markings whenever possible.
3. Avoid joining hands for extended periods when forming a half circle.
4. The leader stands slightly outside the half circle so that all can see.

Checkerboard Formation

```
X  X  X  X
 X  X  X  X
  X  X  X  X
   X  X  X  X
      ●
```

1. Excellent formation for structured activities and with large groups.
2. Provides maximum utilization of space.
3. Avoid standing at one end of the formation for long periods. Move around its perimeter.

SUGGESTED READING

Graham, G., et al. (1987). *Children moving: A reflexive approach to teaching physical education*. Palo Alto, CA: Mayfield.

Hoffman, H. A., et al. (1981). *Meaningful movement for children: A developmental theme approach to physical education*. Boston: Allyn and Bacon.

Kirchner, G. (1985). *Physical education for elementary school children*. Dubuque, IA: Wm. C. Brown.

Logsdon, B. J., et al. (1984). *Physical education for children: A focus on the teaching process*. Philadelphia: Lea & Febiger.

Morris, G. S. D. (1980). *Elementary physical education: Toward inclusion*. Salt Lake City: Brighton Publishing Company.

CHAPTER 17

THE EXTENDED CURRICULUM

The physical education teacher is frequently responsible for conducting several other programs as well as the basic instructional program. Recess and noon-hour programs, daily fitness programs, intramural and club sport programs, and interscholastic programs are all logical extensions of the physical education curriculum. Each type of program can make positive contributions to various aspects of children's development, but none should be viewed as a substitute or replacement for a quality instructional program in physical education.

RECESS AND NOON-HOUR PROGRAMS

Recess is a North American tradition. Practically every elementary school in North America has some form of daily recess. The recess period generally takes the form of a midmorning or midafternoon break from the normal academic routine. Recess generally lasts from 10 to 20 minutes and is held outdoors whenever possible. Children are given a time for free play and an opportunity to "let off steam" in acceptable ways. The theory behind the recess period is that this break from the relatively inactive routine of the classroom will enable children to refocus their energies and attention on their school work. There is sufficient empirical evidence to warrant continuation of *quality* recess programs.

The noon-hour program is an outgrowth of busing. In many school systems, children do not go home during the lunch hour. Instead, they remain at school. The noon-hour program follows the lunch period and allows children to take part in a variety of free-choice activities on the playground or in the gymnasium. Children should not be permitted to gulp down their lunch in an effort to get more time on the playground or in the gymnasium. Approximately 20 minutes should be set aside for eating lunch. Early finishers should be required to wait the full 20 minutes.

PHOTO 17.1   Recess and noon-hour programs require proper facilities, ample equipment, adequate supervision.

Both the recess and the noon-hour programs are, by tradition, loosely structured. Children are generally allowed free choice in their activity selection. Most children select vigorous play activities, but some choose more quiet and sedentary activities. The keys to a successful recess and noon-hour program are proper facilities, ample equipment, and adequate supervision. The physical education teacher is frequently assigned responsibility for insuring all three.

The facilities, whether indoors or out, are important to the success of the program. They should be free of safety hazards and regularly checked for unsafe conditions. The outdoor area should have ample space so that primary-grade children may play separate from older children. It should contain hanging and climbing apparatus when possible. Large grassy and asphalt areas for a variety of activities are ideal. Markings for line and circle games such as four-square, hopscotch, and so forth are helpful stimulators of purposeful, vigorous activity. Similarly, the indoor facility, whether it be the gymnasium or a multipurpose room, should be set up in a manner that allows for free choice and encourages vigorous activity.

The availability of equipment for the recess and noon-hour program is the second key to suc-cess. There should be ample equipment in the form of balls, frisbees, ropes, and so forth so that all who want to play may. In many schools, classroom teachers keep a "fun box" with equipment to be used for recess. Children check out the equipment and are responsible for returning it to the box.

Supervision is the third key to a successful recess or noon-hour program. Teachers frequently dread recess duty because of the mass chaos that often seems to accompany this responsibility. Such chaos is minimized if (1) one teacher is assigned to supervise no more than two classes at one time, (2) the supervisor can see all children at all times, (3) there is ample space and equipment for meaningful activity, and (4) the children are given instruction in appropriate playground activities.

The physical education teacher can play an important role in helping make the recess and noon-hour programs worthwhile to children and easy for classroom teachers to supervise. Taking the time to instruct children in how to get a game of kickball, soccer, or four-square organized works wonders. Insuring that the supervising teacher knows the basic rules of several appropriate games and has the proper equipment to help get them started is helpful. Finally, a be-

PHOTO 17.2   Daily fitness programs are frequently conducted in addition to the regular physical education program.

havior code for play on the playground or in the gymnasium will help reduce problems and maximize the educational potential of the recess and noon-hour programs.

DAILY FITNESS PROGRAMS

In recent years, many school districts in Canada and the United States have introduced daily fitness activities into the total school program. Daily fitness programs frequently replace a recess period or are conducted during the last fifteen minutes of the school day. Fitness programs are conducted in *addition* to the instructional physical education program and are frequently engaged in by the entire student body, faculty, and staff.

Due to the sedentary nature of our society, many children do not get sufficient regular, vigorous physical activity. The instructional physical education program generally does not have adequate amounts of time or the regularity of a daily program to positively influence fitness levels to a significant degree. The realization that children are not as physically active as they need to be, coupled with a wealth of recent research

linking the positive benefits of vigorous physical activity to human wellness, have caused many eductors to add daily fitness activities to the total school curriculum.

The daily fitness program is frequently conducted with the entire school population taking part during a specific 15- to 20-minute portion of the day. Hallways may be used for stationary jogging or aerobic exercise to music. The gymnasium or multipurpose room may serve as a station for rope-jumping activities, and the classroom may be used for flexibility and vigorous strength- and endurance-building exercises. Trained students as well as teachers can serve as fitness leaders. Daily fitness programs strive for total, active involvement for the entire time that has been set aside. People perform at their individual level of ability and are encouraged to do their best.

As the physical education teacher, you may be responsible for the daily fitness program. In schools where it does not yet exist, it will be your responsibility to develop a solid rationale to convince the administration, faculty, and students of the need for it. Once they are convinced, you will need to train fitness leaders. It will be important to keep interest in the program high and to demonstrate improved levels of fitness. Chapter 43, Fitness Activities, will be helpful in selecting appropriate activities for inclusion in the daily fitness program.

INTRAMURAL PROGRAMS

The intramural sports program is a logical extension of a quality physical education program. It should never be a substitute for physical education. Intramurals are generally conducted before school, during the noon hour, or after school. The intramural program should include all children who desire to participate, regardless of their skill level. In the elementary school, intramurals are special-interest programs for boys and girls who want to put the skills learned in the physical education class to further use. Intramurals are physical activity programs conducted between groups of students within the same school. Greater emphasis is placed on playing the game in the intramural program than on instruction, although there is frequently an instructional component in terms of rules and the application of strategies.

The physical education teacher is frequently responsible for conducting a varied intramural program throughout the school year. Activities may be seasonal and may last four to six weeks. Popular intramural activities with elementary students include floor hockey, basketball, touch football, kickball, soccer, dodgeball, and volleyball. Players may be grouped into teams in a variety of ways. No matter what procedure is selected, the teacher's primary consideration should be the equating of teams. All teams should have as near an equal chance to win as possible. Remember, emphasis in the intramural program should be on skill application and fun in a wholesome recreational setting.

In order for the intramural program to be successful, there should be written policies regarding parental approval, eligibility, first aid, medical care, and awards. The program should be evaluated on a regular basis in terms of the stated goals and objectives of the program. Because participation is voluntary, the number of participants is often a good barometer of the program's success in terms of student interest.

CLUB PROGRAMS

The club program is similar to the intramural program in that it is held before, during, or after school. However, it is different in terms of emphasis. The club program stresses further instruction in specific activities and is little concerned with competing against one's classmates. Elementary school children frequently enjoy being members of a gymnastics club, fitness club, bicycle club, or leaders club.

Club programs are an extension of the regular physical education class. They permit children with specific activity interests an opportunity to get additional practice and instruction. They are especially enjoyable for the teacher because they permit work with small groups of students who are highly motivated to learn more about the activity.

Club participants frequently make good gym helpers. With training, they can be given some special responsibilities in the regular physical education class. This not only provides leadership experiences for these students, but gives the teacher much needed assistance and freedom to work with others needing additional instruction.

INTERSCHOLASTIC PROGRAMS

The extramural or interscholastic program provides children an opportunity to compete against boys and girls from other schools. The interscholastic program can be of great value to the children it serves, but it should be included in the curriculum only *after* both quality physical education and intramural sports programs are in place. Interscholastic activities should never replace or disrupt these foundational programs.

Interscholastic athletic programs are intended for children as one of many avenues of providing them opportunities to develop into more complete and competent individuals. They are not intended to be an entertainment medium for parents, and they do not exist for the glorification of the coach. If athletic competition is to be of real value to children, it must (1) be developmentally appropriate, (2) include all who wish to take part, (3) avoid cutting players from the team, (4) give all who desire it an opportunity to play, (5) be conducted in a safe and healthful environment, (6) be led by competent, caring adults, and (7) be fun.

A win-at-all-costs attitude in any youth sport program should not be tolerated. Providing individuals the opportunity to pit their skills against others is the lifeblood of sport. Winning is important, but it must not be regarded as the primary reason for competition in the elementary school youth sport program.

SPECIAL PROGRAMS

The physical education teacher is frequently called upon to conduct various special programs. Unlike extended curricular activities, special programs generally last from less than an hour to a full day. Whether they are long or short, special programs generally involve extensive planning and preparation. Special activities in the form of play days, sports days, and field days, along with gym shows and public demonstrations, are frequently encountered at the elementary school level.

Special Days

At the elementary school level there are frequently three types of special-day activities: the play day, sports day, and field day.

The *play day* is a special day of activities involving children from the same school, or from two or more schools, playing together on the same team. Play days among schools are frequently held at a central location in the community. Activities might include softball, soccer, basketball, and volleyball games. Children are randomly assigned to teams. They do *not* compete as a class or as a school.

The *sports day* is similar to the play day except that classes or schools do compete against others as a team in a tournament-like atmosphere. More emphasis is placed on competition and awards. Sports days should emphasize participation by everyone. All children should have an opportunity to play on a team representing their class or school.

The *field day* generally focuses on one sport and may be held within a school or between two or more schools. Track and field days are popular in many elementary schools. The field day is generally held after school hours or on a Saturday. Children from each class or school compete in the field day. An important feature of the field day is that total scores are *not* kept. Emphasis is on pitting one's skills against children from other classes or schools, meeting new friends, and having fun.

Gym Shows and Public Demonstrations

An important tool used by many experienced physical education teachers to promote their program is the annual *gym show* or public demonstration. These special programs may be held after school, during the early evening hours, or on a weekend. They are frequently held in conjunction with a PTA meeting or a local service club program or as a special event at a shopping mall.

The gym show demonstrates the highlights of the year's program, but this should not be the goal. Guidelines for a successful gym show follow:

1. Involve all grades and every child in the show.
2. Keep the program short. Forty-five minutes to one hour should be sufficient.
3. Select activities that are part of the regular physical education program.
4. Select activities that can be easily learned and performed by all.
5. Do not worry about polished performances. Work for an acceptable standard.
6. Do not use physical education class time for extended practices.

7. Provide the audience with a printed program, outlining the sequence of performances and the objectives they achieve in the program.
8. Use scarfs, sashes, or hats as simple costumes to heighten the general appearance of the performances.
9. Use appropriate musical accompaniment whenever possible to add to the general effect.
10. Props such as parachutes, flashlights, streamers, and hoops add to the general effect.
11. Send an announcement home concerning the gym show along with a permission slip granting participation.
12. Allow for a complete runthrough of the program prior to the big night.
13. Take photos for use in a bulletin board display.
14. Enlist the help of classroom teachers for supervision on the night of the performance.

The *public demonstration* is different from the gym show in that it generally involves a smaller number of students. Local service organizations and shopping malls frequently provide opportunities for participation in a special event. The public demonstration might involve members from one or more of the club sport programs sponsored by the school. The gymnastics club, for example, may be asked to put on a demonstration of their skills. The public demonstration is generally more polished. Practice is provided *outside* of the physical education period, and those who participate have special interests and abilities in the activity. When planning for a public demonstration, the same guidelines may be followed as for the gym show. Be certain, however, to arrange for transportation to and from the demonstration site and to provide for ample adult supervision at all times.

Gym shows and public demonstrations are excellent promotional devices for the physical education program. Although they are time-consuming and often nervewracking, they are an important part of the extracurricular program. They serve to inform the public about physical education and to broaden the base of support for quality programs.

TOURNAMENTS

Tournaments are a common aspect of the extracurricular program. They may be conducted during recess or the noon hour, or they may be part of the intramural or club sport program.

FIGURE 17.1 Two forms of the single elimination tournament.

Tournaments can be beneficial to the physical education of children if the competitive element is not overemphasized and winning is not overly glorified. Tournaments permit the testing of one's skills against others. They may be held for individual or group activities. Single elimination, double elimination, round-robin, and ladder tournaments are frequently used in elementary schools.

Single Elimination Tournament

The single elimination tournament is the easiest tournament to arrange and the quickest to conduct. However, one loss automatically eliminates the individual or team from further competition; therefore, this tournament is generally not recommended for elementary school children. Figure 17.1 depicts two forms of the single elimination tournament. The first is for an even number of participants equaling any power of two. The second is for an odd number of teams or a total number of teams not equal to power of two. The number of games required to complete a single elimination tournament is one less than the total number of teams.

Double Elimination Tournament

The double elimination tournament is similar to the single elimination tournament except for the addition of a consolation bracket. The consolation bracket gives a team that loses one time another chance, thus assuring each participant of at least two games. Figure 17.2 depicts a typical double elimination tournament.

Round-Robin Tournament

The round-robin tournament permits every individual or team to play every other individual or team. This type of tournament takes the longest but is preferred if time permits. The player with the greatest number of wins is the winner in a round-robin tournament. Figure 17.3 depicts a double round-robin tournament for eight participants. By shading in the lower half of the score sheet, a single round-robin tournament is created.

FIGURE 17.2   Eight team double elimination tournament.

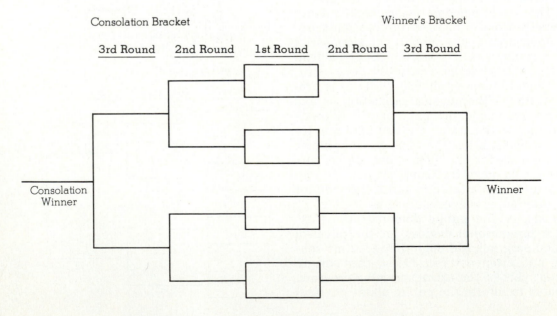

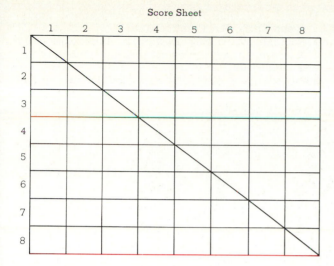

Score Sheet

	1	2	3	4	5	6	7	8
1								
2								
3								
4								
5								
6								
7								
8								

	Team Name	Wins	Losses	Place
1				
2				
3				
4				
5				
6				
7				
8				

FIGURE 17.3 Round robin tournament for eight teams.

Ladder Tournament

In the ladder tournament, players are arranged vertically. Any player may challenge another directly above. If that player wins, his or her name replaces the defeated player, who in turn moves down one rung on the ladder. A ladder tournament is a form of continuous competition limited only by time. The object is to climb to the top of the ladder and remain there until the tournament is over. Ladder tournaments work especially well for individual activities and can be conducted with a variety of skills for an ex-

tended period of time. They take little time to set up and can be easily run by the children themselves. Use of a grease pencil to record names or 3 x 5 cards placed in a slotted board works well, along with a simple set of rules placed next to the tournament board. Figure 17.4 depicts a typical ladder tournament. Guidelines for conducting a ladder tournament follow:

1. A player may challenge only the player one or two rungs above.
2. The winner of a game remains on the higher rung if he or she was already there or exchanges positions from a lower rung.
3. Once a challenge has been made, a deadline must be set by which the game must be played or canceled (within two or three days).
4. Set a completion date for the tournament.
5. Position players randomly to begin the tournament, or if skill abilities are known, place the most skilled on the bottom.

FIGURE 17.4 Format for a ladder tournament

Contest:
1
2
3
4
5
6
7
8
9
10
11
12

SUGGESTED READING

Annarino, A. A., Cowell, C. C., and Hazelton, H. W. (1980). *Curriculum theory design in physical education* (Chapters 22 and 23). St. Louis: C. V. Mosby.

Colgate, J. A. (1978). *Administration of intramural and recreational activities*. New York: Wiley.

Keller, I. A. (1982). *The interscholastic coach*. Englewood Cliffs, NJ: Prentice-Hall.

Melograno, V. (1985). *Designing curriculum and learning: A self-directed approach*. Dubuque, IA: Kendall/Hunt.

Willgoose, C. E. (1984). *The curriculum in physical education* (Chapter 11). Englewood Cliffs, NJ: Prentice-Hall.

CHAPTER 18

LEGAL LIABILITY

The very nature of physical education exposes the teacher in the gymnasium, swimming pool, or playground to greater liability for accidents and injuries than any other area of the school curriculum. This point should not go unheeded, nor should physical education teachers be unduly anxious over this fact. A clear understanding of what constitutes legal liability, as well as frequent conditions that lead to legal action, and how it may be minimized will do much to relieve anxiety and to promote a safe and healthful environment in which children can participate with reasonable assurance that proper precautions and care have been taken. This chapter provides a basis for understanding some of the legal responsibilities assumed by teachers. Care should be taken to become familiar with guidelines and statutes as they apply to local states, provinces, and school districts.

CONDITIONS OF LEGAL LIABILITY

Tort liability, or legal liability, as it is generally called, is a term applied to the concept that someone is at fault, that this fault has caused injury or loss to another, and that someone is legally responsible. Legal liability may be incurred by the physical education teacher through three means: *negligence, contributing to an attractive nuisance*, and *malpractice*. Each is briefly discussed.

Negligence

Legally, negligence is considered to be failure on the part of an individual to act in a manner judged to be reasonable, careful, and prudent. The physical education teacher who exposes children to unreasonable risks or who fails to supervise activities properly may be considered negligent.

Negligence may be claimed but must be proven in a court of law. There are four factors, all of which *must* be present in order to establish negligence: established duty, breach of duty, legal cause, and damage.

Established duty must be determined. It must first be established that the teacher has a duty to follow certain standards of behavior that protect the student from unreasonable risks.

Breach of duty must be proven. Once an established duty has been determined, it must be proven that the teacher actually failed to conform to these standards of behavior.

Legal cause must be established. If a breach of duty has been proven, it must then be determined if there is a reasonable relationship between the teacher's breach of duty and the injury received.

Damage must be determined. If legal cause is established, damage must be determined. Damage refers to actual injury or loss. At this point, proven injury or loss entitles the plaintiff to compensation for physical discomfort and financial loss and may place certain legal restraints on the defendant.

The best defense against being declared liable for an injury or loss due to negligence is to prove that at least one of the four aspects of negligence is *not* present. A key to establishing negligence is first determining if one acted in a manner to avoid foreseeable injury or harm. The law is clear in stating that the duty of the physical education teacher is to attempt to anticipate the dangers involved in the program and to guard against negligence. If, in fact, negligence is proven, it will be declared as negligence due to malfeasance, misfeasance, or nonfeasance.

Malfeasance. Malfeasance refers to committing an illegal act. For example, failure to comply with and implement the requirements of PL 94-142 (the Education for All Handicapped Children Act of 1975), or those of Title IX (the Educational Amendments Act of 1972) leaves a teacher liable for negligence due to malfeasance. Similarly, violations of student rights, ranging from students being denied the due process of law and unauthorized corporal punishment to discriminating against children for hair length and clothing choices, may expose teachers to negligence by malfeasance.

Misfeasance. Misfeasance is defined as improper performance of a lawful act. In other words, the teacher may operate within the law but not up to the standards deemed to be reasonable. For example, the use of improper first aid techniques in treatment of an injury that results in permanent disability or death falls under the category of misfeasance.

Nonfeasance. Nonfeasance is defined as failure to perform a required act deemed appropriate under the circumstances. For example, failure to administer emergency first aid when a student's life is in danger could result in liability due to negligence by nonfeasance.

Defenses Against Negligence

In the defense of a teacher charged with negligence, there may be several negating factors that may need to be considered. These are generally refered to as contributory negligence, assumption of risk, and acts of nature.

Contributory Negligence. Contributory negligence refers to the plaintiff being held partially or wholly at fault for the injury received. Before contributory negligence is determined, the child's age, capabilities (both physical and mental), and prior training are considered. If the plaintiff shares the fault, then he or she may *not* be compensated for damages. In some regions, however, the concept of *shared negligence* has been broadened to include comparative negligence. In these states the plaintiff may be compensated on a proportionally reduced basis that is prorated according to the actual percentage of shared negligence.

Assumption of Risk. Assumption of risk is a legal term indicating that in certain situations one assumes responsibility for his or her own safety. Individuals who participate in nonrequired intramural and athletic activities and are aware of the risks involved are generally considered by the court to have assumed the risk for their own safety and wellbeing. The same, however, is not so for students in the required phyiscal education class. A claim of negligence due to injury occurring through participation in required physical activities generally will not be considered to fall under the defense of assumption of risk. This is an important concept and has numerous legal implications for the incorporation of stress challenge and risk activities into the required physical education program. The age, experience, and maturity of the students, as well as their awareness of the risks involved and the degree to which they are required to take part in these activities or are given equal opportunity for participation in alternative activities all need to be carefully considered.

Acts of Nature.   An act of nature is considered to be something completely unexpected and unforeseen that is totally beyond the control of the defendent. If, for example, a tree is struck by lightning on a clear day and the children playing under that tree are injured or killed, this would be considered an act of nature.

Contributing to an Attractive Nuisance

A second manner in which legal liability may be incurred for injury or harm to students is through contributing to an attractive nuisance. An attractive nuisance is a place or thing. It may be a piece of equipment, supplies, or a facility. For example, a swimming pool or weight-training facility may be considered to be an attractive nuisance if left unattended or unsupervised. It is not enough to claim that students were told not to use these facilities or that warning signs were posted. If the facility permits easy, though uninvited or illegal, access, the defendent in a legal suit may be found guilty by reason of contributing to an attractive nuisance. Similarly, gymnastic equipment, boxing gloves, or fencing equipment may all be considered to be an attractive nuisance if they are used by students while unsupervised. Take, for example, a situation in which the gymnastics equipment is set up in the gymnasium and the teacher is enjoying a well-deserved planning period or lunch across the hall. A student peeking into the unattended gym, seeing the equipment, and subsequently sustaining an injury may have ample grounds for a lawsuit. The best way to avoid charges of contributing to an attractive nuisance is to properly store all equipment and supplies under lock and key, to arrange for proper supervision of facilities at all times, or to securely lock all facilities when they are not in use. Remember,

children love to explore and experiment with their ever-expanding world. It is perfectly natural for them to be attracted to the physical education facilities and equipment. Your duty as a teacher is to insure that the facilities and equipment are at all times properly supervised and secured.

Malpractice

Malpractice is a legal concept that has only relatively recently been applied to the teaching profession. Basically, malpractice is *negligent behavior, improper behavior*, or *unethical behavior* on the part of an individual, resulting in injury or damage to the student. Injury or damage may be mental, social, or emotional as well as physical. For example, in recent years entire school districts have been sued for malpractice by individuals who were passed on from grade to grade without the basic skills required and who obtained a school diploma without the minimal competencies expected for graduation. Physical education classes, intramurals, and athletic programs that use grossly improper teaching techniques, inappropriate activities, faulty or nonexistent spotting procedures, and archaic training methods may be liable for charges of malpractice. Also, physical education programs that base grades on nonrelevant criteria may be accused of malpractice.

Students have a right to assume that they will receive proper instruction, training, and care. If these rights are violated, they may have grounds for claiming liability on the part of the individual teacher, administrator, or school district. In any such lawsuit, negligence must be proven. The best way to prevent a lawsuit is at all times to exercise reasonable and proper care.

FREQUENT CONDITIONS LEADING TO LEGAL ACTION

A number of potential danger spots exist that may leave you, the physical education teacher, open to legal action. An awareness of these conditions and taking appropriate preventive measures will greatly reduce exposure to charges of legal liability. Among the most frequent conditions leading to charges of legal liability are ignoring mandated legislation, improper instruction, inadequate supervision, and failure to provide a safe environment.

Ignoring Mandated Legislation

Recent federal and state legislation has mandated certain procedures in the design and implementation of educational programs. Two pieces of mandated legislation that have had the greatest impact on physical education and athletic programs are the Educational Amendments Act of 1972 (Title IX) and the Education for All Handicapped Children Act of 1975 (PL 94-142).

Title IX makes it illegal to discriminate between students in matters of education based on gender. This law has had vast implications and ramifications within the physical education profession. Considerable progress has been made in the implementation of Title IX over the last several years, but educators still need to be reminded on occasion of their responsibility. The majority of accusations of discrimination have charged that female students were not given the same opportunities to participate as their male counterparts. The AAHPERD has published an excellent guide outlining the methods of implementing the mandates of Title IX in physical education and sport (AAHPERD 1978). Failure to comply with the requirements of Title IX has resulted in numerous lawsuits. Following the guidelines outlined in the AAHPERD publication will help avoid legal action.

P.L. 94-142 requires that all handicapped children be provided with a free and appropriate public education. It further mandates that school systems provide means to protect the rights of handicapped children. Most importantly, it provides that handicapped children be educated with nonhandicapped children (mainstreamed) as much as possible and that an individualized educational program (IEP) be prepared and implemented for each handicapped student. Furthermore, handicapped children must now be placed in the least restrictive environment, and their parents must be involved in the educational de-

cisions that affect their child. This sweeping legislation has dramatically changed how the handicapped child is educated in the public schools.

This law is of particular importance to the physical education profession because physical education was the only curricular area targeted as a specific focus of concern within this law. Physical education has been mandated as a direct service that *must* be provided to all handicapped children. The law does *not* permit the substitution of services or the use of related services in place of physical education. Failure to implement the provisions of PL 94-142 within the school district and within individual schools leaves both administrators and physical education teachers liable for legal action.

Improper Instruction

A frequent cause of legal action against physical education teachers is negligence due to inadequate or improper instruction. The very nature of many physical education activities involves an element of risk. Activities in the swimming pool, on the gymnastics apparatus, and on the athletic field all involve a certain amount risk. The job of the teacher is to reduce this risk through proper instructional techniques and supervision.

Frequent among lawsuits are those claiming that the instruction provided for an activity was inappropriate or nonexistent. It is crucial to have written lesson plans and an approved written curriculum in order to document the scope and sequence of your instruction. Progressive instruction that builds skill upon skill, follows established teaching procedures, emphasizes safety, and provides for the needs of the individual is clear evidence of adequate instruction. On the other hand, failure to follow an established curriculum; nonexistent lesson planning; use of outmoded instructional strategies and questionable activities such as bombardment, circle dodge ball, and certain combative activities; along with failure to follow reasonable safety precautions and spotting techniques all leave the teacher open for legal action.

PHOTO 18.1 Injury due to inadequate supervision is a frequent cause of legal action.

Inadequate Supervision

Claim of inadequate or improper supervision is another frequent cause of legal action brought against teachers. As a general rule, the teacher should never leave an individual or class unsupervised, even for a brief period of time. The very nature of most physical education activities and the equipment used makes it imperative that adequate supervision be provided at all times.

Supervision is an *active* process. It may be conducted by the teacher or other approved personnel. Supervision extends to the playground, lunchroom, after-school activities, and school-sponsored events. If an injury does occur, even while children are being supervised, a number of factors will need to be considered. Among them are the ratio of students to supervisors, whether a written supervisory policy was available and followed, and whether the injury was caused by improper supervision.

Proper supervision extends to conduct in the physical education class and on the athletic field. It is the teacher's responsibility to maintain good class control and to insure that all activities are carefully supervised. Supervision by adult volunteers or other students is not acceptable unless it is expressly permitted by the school district, as determined by state law.

Failure to Provide a Safe and Healthful Environment

Teachers are open to the possibility of legal action when they fail to insure a safe and healthful environment. A safe and healthful environment extends from insuring the proper condition of supplies, equipment, and facilities. It extends further to planning for safe use of locker-room and shower facilities.

It is the duty of the physical education teacher to routinely inventory the physical condition of the supplies, equipment, and facilities for which she or he is responsible and to keep an accurate record of the dates and results of these inspections. Any defects or potential safety hazards should be eliminated on the spot when possible or reported immediately in writing to the building principal. Continued use of defective equipment or participation in a hazardous environment is morally indefensible. All efforts should be made to bring existing facilities and equipment into compliance with acceptable standards of health and safety.

Locker rooms and shower areas are potential danger areas that present unusual hazards. They are frequently small, overcrowded, and slippery, presenting numerous opportunities for injury due to falls, bumps, and burns. A written policy for the use and supervision of locker-room and shower facilities should be developed. Traffic patterns, time limits, and a code of acceptable behaviors should be established and enforced.

MINIMIZING LIABILITY

An obvious way to avoid exposure to claims of legal liability and negligence is to eliminate the pitfalls discussed earlier. Implementing mandated legislation, requiring proper instruction and supervision, and providing for a safe and healthful environment are all basic to quality education. However, liability may be further reduced through good record keeping, written and enforced policies for emergency care and extra-curricular activities, heeding legitimate excuses, and liability insurance coverage.

Record Keeping

An excellent way to both avoid and minimize the effects of a lawsuit is through keeping accurate, up-to-date records. A written record should be kept of all accidents, no matter how minor, as well as a periodic inventory of the condition of all supplies, equipment, and facilities under your jurisdiction.

The Accident Report. If an injury does occur, it is essential that an accident report be filled out and filed with the principal's office no later than the close of the school day. Many school districts utilize a standard accident report form. A sample form is presented in Table 18.1 and may be used if one is not readily available.

Basically, the accident report should contain the name, address, phone number, age, and grade of the injured child. The location where the injury took place as well as the person responsible for supervision, the time of day, and a brief description of the activity leading up to the accident are essential. This should be followed by a detailed description of the emergency care given and the personnel involved. A brief description of the nature of the injury, including, if applicable, the name of the physician or school nurse providing treatment is important. How and when the student's parents were contacted should be included on the accident report form. Upon completion of the form, it should be signed and dated. The original should be retained in the principal's office and a copy kept for your files. At no time should the teacher discuss the injury with others unless directed to do so by a school official. No attempt should be made to diagnose the injury or to provide treatment beyond emergency first aid until qualified medical personnel can take over. The injured student should not be left alone while the teacher summons help. Help should be obtained, as a matter of written policy, by sending a trusted student to the central office of the school.

The Supply/Equipment Report. Some schools utilize a district-approved form for inventorying the condition and reporting the status of supplies and equipment. If one is not available, the sample form presented in Table 18.2 may be adopted or modified to suit your needs. The form should contain a complete inventory of all the supplies, equipment, and facilities under the teacher's jurisdiction. At the beginning and end of each semester, a complete accounting of all equipment and supplies should be made. The number and condition of all the balls, bats, bases, ropes, hoops, beanbags, and other supplies should be noted on the form. Defective materials, such as splintered bats, frayed climbing ropes, or broken playground equipment, should be specifically noted and immediately repaired or removed from use. Unsafe conditions should be brought immediately to the attention of the proper building official *in writing*. A copy of this correspondence should be retained in your files, along with your complete signed and dated supply/equipment report.

TABLE 18.1   Sample Accident Report Form

Student Accident Report

This form should be completed in triplicate and signed by the building principal, school nurse, and supervising teacher. The original will be forwarded to the superintendent's office. The second copy will be kept in the principal's office, and the third copy will be retained by the supervising teacher.

Name of Injured _____

Age _____ Grade _____ Home Room _____

Home Address _____ Phone _____

Date of Accident _____ Time of Accident _____

Specific Location of Accident _____

_____

Staff Person(s) Supervising _____

Address _____ Phone _____

Description of the Activity Leading to the Accident _____

_____

_____

Nature of the Injury _____

Description of Emergency Care Given _____

_____

_____

Emergency Care Given by _____

Address _____ Phone _____

Medical Treatment Recommended _____ Yes _____ No

Medical Official Providing Treatment _____

Address _____ Phone _____

Specify Where Taken After Accident

_____ First Aid Room _____ Home _____ Hospital _____ Other

Out-of-School Transportation Provided by _____

Address _____ Phone _____

Parent's Name _____

Parent's Contacted _____ Yes _____ No   When _____

Additional Comments _____

_____

Name of Person Filing Report _____

Date of Report _____ Time of Report _____

Signature of Supervising Teacher _____

Signature of School Nurse _____

Signature of School Principal _____

The Facility Report. The physical education teacher frequently has several facilities under his or her jurisdiction. Along with the gymnasium or multipurpose room, the physical education teacher is frequently responsible for supervising and reporting on the condition of the playground and athletic fields. A daily inspection of each of these facilities is recommended. This takes only a few minutes and may identify potential safety hazards such as improperly placed or stored equipment, dirty or unsafe floor condition, broken glass, potholes, and other un-

TABLE 18.2 Sample Supply/Equipment Report

SUPPLY/EQUIPMENT CONDITION REPORT					
		Condition		Recommendations	
Supplies/Equipment	Quantity	Satisfactory	Unsatisfactory	Repair	Destroy
_____	_____	_____	_____	_____	_____
_____	_____	_____	_____	_____	_____
_____	_____	_____	_____	_____	_____
_____	_____	_____	_____	_____	_____
_____	_____	_____	_____	_____	_____
_____	_____	_____	_____	_____	_____
_____	_____	_____	_____	_____	_____
_____	_____	_____	_____	_____	_____
_____	_____	_____	_____	_____	_____
_____	_____	_____	_____	_____	_____
_____	_____	_____	_____	_____	_____

The above supplies and equipment were inventoried by _____ on _____ . The items checked "unsatisfactory condition" have been removed from use. The items marked "repair" should be repaired at the earliest possible date, or destroyed.

I hearby acknowledge receipt of this Supply/Equipment Report:

Signature of report preparer	**Date**	**Principal's signature**	**Date**

safe conditions. Many of these potential hazards can be immediately rectified; others may require time. In any case, activity should not continue under unsafe conditions, and the appropriate school official should be notified, in writing, of unsafe conditions.

Written Policies

Written policies that are clearly stated and adhered to will do much to limit the extent of one's exposure to liability. Among the most important written policies are the emergency care policy and the extracurricular activity policy.

The Emergency Care Policy. Along with the accident report form, it is of utmost importance to have a written policy of what is to be done in the event of an emergency. A copy of this procedure should be made available to all teachers

and approved by appropriate school officials. The emergency care policy should clearly spell out each of the steps to be taken in the event of an injury. The following questions will need to be addressed in developing this policy:

1. Who should administer emergency first aid? Ideally, all teachers should be certified in first aid, but this is rarely the case.
2. How will help be summoned? The on-site teacher should not leave the injured child.
3. Who will determine if the injured student can be moved? When in doubt, this decision should be left to a physician or emergency medical technician.
4. Who will determine if the child needs additional medical attention? If emergency treatment is required, help should be summoned immediately.
5. Who will contact the child's parents, and what information will be given over the

phone? An updated file should be maintained in the central office, with the home and business phone numbers of all parents, as well as the family physician.

6. Who will fill out the accident report, and where and when is it to be filed? The supervising teacher should be responsible for filling out the accident report. The report should be filed by the end of the school day with the principal and other appropriate officials.

7. Who will take responsibility for followup on the injury, and what procedures will be used? The principal, school nurse, or other school official should be responsible for followup.

The Extracurricular Activity Policy. Participation in extracurricular activities frequently exposes teachers to increased liability. In order to reduce this exposure, it is important to have a written policy governing the conduct and supervision of these events. Parent permission slips that clearly spell out the nature of the activity, whether it be participation in a school-sponsored field trip or an athletic event at another school, are a must. Although the legal status of permission slips is questionable, they do provide a clear indication that the child's parents are aware and approve of participation. The parent permission slip does not remove or reduce the limits of liability, and the same requirements for proper supervision remain in effect.

Important points to consider in the formulation of an extracurricular activity policy are

1. Who is in charge of supervision? This person should be a teacher operating with the permission of the appropriate school official.

2. Who will be assisting in the supervisory duties? Adults, preferably parents of the children involved, should assist with supervision and have specific responsibilities in the performance of their duties.

3. What is the ratio of children to adult supervisors? Although no clear legal precedent has been established, it is assumed that the teacher will operate in a reasonable and prudent manner in determining the number of supervisors needed.

4. Who will arrange for transportation, and how will it be supplied? This is a critical point that must be determined in conjunction with the school attorney and insurance officials. It should not be assumed that children can be transported in private automobiles from the school to school-sponsored events in private automobiles without the school incurring additional liability. The law varies from state to state on this issue and should be clarified locally.

5. How will the nature of the activity and the quality of supervision be assessed? It is important to have some means of determining if the supervisory policies enacted are adequate and are being followed. In this way, difficulties can be rectified in the future.

Honoring Excuses

Frequently, children will request to be excused from participation in the physical education class for health reasons or because of religious beliefs. The law is clear in indicating that it is the teacher's duty to honor these requests if they have been written by parents or medical officials, requesting nonparticipation or modified participation. Failure to honor these written requests and insisting that the child take part is an open invitation to a lawsuit.

Even if you suspect that the reasons for the written excuse are not valid and that, based on your judgment, it would be in the best interests of the child to participate, you *must* honor the written request to be excused. It is perfectly appropriate to question the validity of the request, but even while you are doing so, the child should be excused from participation.

In many areas, children are forbidden to take part in certain activities because of religious beliefs. Often children are asked to be excused from all dancing, coeducational activities, or mass showering. These requests must be honored and carried out in such a manner as not to bring ridicule and attention to the child.

Requests from parents for their child to be excused from participation due to minor medical reasons should be carefully scrutinized. As a general rule, requests for nonparticipation for over one week should be accompanied by a physician's excuse. Frequently, children may need to be excused from physical education for only a day or two. A written excuse from a parent should be sufficient.

Insurance Coverage

Despite all the precautions advocated and all the professionally responsible efforts made by concerned, caring teachers, accidents and injuries still occasionally occur. Any time an injury occurs, the possibility of some form of legal action exists.Therefore, it is wise to be certain that you have adequate insurance coverage in the unlikely event that you should be found legally liable due to negligence, contributing to an attractive nuisance, or malpractice.

Insurance coverage may be provided in a variety of ways. First, in some states adequate liability insurance coverage is automatically provided for all teachers. Second, several local school districts carry liability insurance coverage on all their teachers. Third, professional teachers' organizations, including AAHPERD and the National Education Association (NEA) offer low-cost liability insurance policies to their members. A fourth source of liability insurance coverage is through commercial insurance companies. Many companies offer liability coverage as a rider to home insurance and health insurance policies for little additional cost.

Be certain to make yourself aware of the liability coverage available to you and the terms of the coverage. Today, due to astronomical settlement sums, many teachers are finding it prudent to take out additional liability coverage through their professional education association or through commercial insurance carriers, even though they may already be covered by their state or school district.

The likelihood of being sued and of the plaintiff recovering damages is still small, even though the actual number of lawsuits has been on the rise for several years. The cost of liability insurance is moderate, but the peace of mind provided makes it well worth the investment.

SUGGESTED READING

Arnold, Don E. (1983). *Legal considerations in the administration of public school physical education and athletic programs* Springfield, IL: Charles C. Thomas.

Blucker, Judy A., and Pell, Sarah W. (1986, January). Legal and Ethical Issues. *Journal of Physical Education, Recreation and Dance* 57:19–21.

Carpenter, Linda Jean, and Acosta, R. Vivian (1982, February). Negligence—What is it? How can it be avoided? *Journal of Physical Education, Recreation and Dance* 53:51.

Dougherty, N. J. (1983, June). Liability. *Journal of Physical Education and Recreation* 54:42–54.

Griffin, P. (1984, August). Coed physical education: Problems and promise. *Journal of Physical Education and Recreation* 55:36–37.

Kaiser, Ronald A. (1986). *Liability and law in recreation, parks and sports*. Englewood Cliffs, NJ: Prentice-Hall.

Kaiser, R. A. (1984, August). Program liability waivers. *Journal of Physical Education and Recreation* 55: 54–56.

Martin, C. (1982, May). Beginning teachers and school law. *The Physical Educator* 95–97.

Thomas, S. B., and Alberts, C. L. (1982, December). Negligence and the physical education teacher: Legal procedures and guiedlines. *The Physical Educator* 199–203.

CHAPTER 19

ASSESSING PROGRESS

An important aspect of any sound physical education program is assessment. Assessment provides teachers with a measure of students' current levels of ability, pupil progress, and their own teaching effectiveness. Motor assessment is the collection of relevant performance information for the purpose of making reliable discriminations among students.

By assessing the students' current level of ability, a baseline or yardstick by which to measure progress is obtained. This form of assessment is frequently termed formative or *entry-level assessment* and can be easily and quickly done at the very beginning of a unit of instruction. With this information in hand, the teacher can develop an instructional unit based on where students *are* rather than where they should be. Entry-level assessment permits the instructor to fit the program to the needs of the student rather than fitting the student to a predetermined program.

Assessment serves a second vital function, that of measuring pupils' progress over time. Evaluation of progress at the end of a unit of instruction is frequently called summative or *exit-level assessment*. If your operational philosphy centers around the goal of individual improvement, then you will want to combine exit-level assess-

ment ratings with entry-level assessment. For example, you could readminister a basketball skills test at the end of a unit of instruction to determine if there has been individual progress. This method of comparing individual entry and exit levels of achievement is frequently called criterion-referenced or *self-referenced assessment*. The self-referenced assessment approach differs from the normative or standards approach, in which students are compared against a previously established class standard or group norms.

Assessment serves the very practical function of measuring teacher effectiveness. By determining students' level of ability and rate of progress, teachers obtain an estimate of their effectiveness in terms of developing and refining movement skills. If, for example, you are able to show significant progress by your students in their level of basketball skill acquisition, then you can assume that learning has taken place and that you were instrumental in that progress. If, however, little or no progress is evident, then you may question your effectiveness in presenting that unit of instruction.

With regard to developing and refining children's fundamental movement, sport-skill, and fitness abilities, self-referenced assessment at *both* the beginning and the end of a unit of instruction is highly recommended. Part V, "The Skill Themes," which follows (Chapters 20–29), contains, specific information in each chapter for practical entry- and exit-level assessment.

Master teachers continually assess their students through both informal and formal means. They constantly make adjustments and revisions in their lessons in order to facilitate learning. At the elementary school level, two forms of

PHOTO 19.1 Self-referenced assessment of one's performance as an individual is more meaningful than group comparisons.

the act, such as how far the ball travels, how many baskets the child makes, or how fast the child runs the 50-yard dash. Instead, the teacher is concerned primarily with the body mechanics used to throw the ball, make the basket, or run the dash. Observational assessment is an effective *subjective* technique for knowledgeable teachers to use. It is an important technique when you consider that our primary goal is to teach people how to move. Concern for the proper mechanics, or the process of movement, must occur before focusing on the product, in the terms of, for example, how fast children can perform a certain movement skill.

The approach used throughout the skill theme chapters advocates that, for children at the fundamental movement phase of skill development, we assess whether they are at the *initial, elementary*, or *mature* stage. For those at the sport-skill phase of development, it must be determined if they are at the *transitional, application*, or *specialized* stage. It is *not* enough to assume that all first and second graders will be at one stage, third and fourth graders at another

PHOTO 19.2 Observational assessment takes into consideration form, style, and mechanics.

assessment are appropriate, *process assessment* and *product assessment*. Both may be used, depending on the level of student ability, the specific needs of the students and the teacher, and the amount of available time.

PROCESS (OBSERVATIONAL) ASSESSMENT

Process, or observational assessment, is concerned with the form, style, or mechanics used to perform a fundamental movement or sport skill. When focusing on the movement process, teachers are little concerned with the product of stage, and fifth and sixth graders at yet another stage. Remember, *skill development is age-influenced but not age-determined*. Due to the varying backgrounds of children, in terms of opportunities for practice, encouragement, and previous instruction, a rigidly graded or age-based approach to movement skill development is not acceptable as a valid means for curricular planning. Therefore, observational assessment of the process of children's movement becomes essential to effective use of the developmental approach.

FIGURE 19.1   Sample body segment group observational assessment chart for selected fundamental locomotor skills.

Fundamental Movement Skills — Body Segment/Class Observation Chart																				
Class _____ Grade _____ Observer _____																				
Mark the proper stage (I, E, M,S)* for each body segment. Then give an overall rating in the space provided. *I, initial stage / E, elementary stage / M, mature stage / S, sport-skill stage	Running				Jumping				Hopping				Skipping				Leaping			
Name	Leg Action	Trunk Action	Arm Action	Overall Rating	Leg Action	Trunk Action	Arm Action	Overall Rating	Leg Action	Trunk Action	Arm Action	Overall Rating	Leg Action	Trunk Action	Arm Action	Overall Rating	Leg Action	Trunk Action	Arm Action	Overall Rating

Guidelines

Observational or process assessment is subjective, and it therefore requires the teacher to have a clear knowledge of what actually constitutes the proper mechanics of a wide variety of movement skills. To this end, a verbal description and a visual description of children performing at the initial, elementary, and mature stages in over 20 fundamental movements is provided in the locomotor, manipulative, and stability skill-theme chapters that follow (Chapters 20–23). A verbal description and a visual description of a wide variety of sport skills is contained in the sport-skill-theme chapters (Chapters 24–29). The purpose of this information is to help you become familiar with the basic body mechanics and techniques used in executing the movement skills children should learn during their elementary school years.

When actually observing and assessing the

FIGURE 19.2 Sample total body group observational assessment chart for selected locomotor, manipulative, and stability skills.

Fundamental Movement Skills Total Body/Group Observation Chart																									
Class_____ Grade_____ Observer_____																									
Mark the proper overall stage rating (I, E, M,S)* for each skill in the space provided. *I, initial stage E, elementary stage M, mature stage S, sport-skill stage **Name**	Locomotor Skills										Manipulative Skills								Stability Skills							
	Running	Jump for Distance	Jump for Height	Jump from Height	Hopping	Skipping	Sliding	Galloping	Leaping	Climbing	Throwing	Catching	Kicking	Trapping	Dribbling	Volleying	Striking	Ball Rolling	Static Balance	Dynamic Balance	Body Rolling	Dodging	Springing/Landing	Axial Movements	Inverted Supports	Transitional Supports

process of children's movement, it is important to:

1. Be unobtrusive. This is especially important with young children, who will often alter their pattern of movement if they are aware that they are being observed.

2. Stress maximum effort. Instruct children to throw as far, run as fast, or jump as high as they can. This will encourage their best performance.

3. Stand where you can clearly view performance. Stand far enough away that you can observe the entire task.

FIGURE 19.3 Sample progress report for fundamental movement skills.

	Physical Education Progress Report																
Dear Parent: The skills checked have been assessed for this 9-week period. More then one check in a row indicates progress from one stage to another.	Child's Name _____ Grade _____ Class _____																
	1ST. 9Wks.				2ND 9Wks.				3RD. 9Wks.				4TH 9Wks.				Stages
	Initial Stage	Elementary Stage	Mature Stage	Sport-Skill Stage	Initial Stage	Elementary Stage	Mature Stage	Sport-Skill Stage	Initial Stage	Elementary Stage	Mature Stage	Sport-Skill Stage	Initial Stage	Elementary Stage	Mature Stage	Sport-Skill Stage	Initial: Poor Elementary: Fair Mature: Good Sport Skill: Excellent
Locomotor skills: Giving force to the body through space																	Comments
Running																	
Jumping																	
Hopping																	
Skipping																	
Leaping																	
Manipulative skills: Giving force to and receiving force from objects																	Comments
Throwing																	
Catching																	
Kicking																	
Dribbling																	
Striking																	
Stability skills: Maintaining balance in static and dynamic situations																	Comments
One-Foot Balance																	
Beam Walk																	
Body Rolling																	
Dodging																	
Landing																	
																	PARENT COMMENTS
PARENT SIGNATURE _____ DATE _____																	
PARENT SIGNATURE _____ DATE _____																	
PARENT SIGNATURE _____ DATE _____																	

4. Observe segmentally. Look at one part of the movement at a time. For example, first focus on the leg action, followed by the trunk action, then the arm action.
5. Compare. Occasionally ask another *trained* individual to observe and assess several children. Compare ratings for objectivity.
6. Be consistent. Strive for consistency in your observations in order to maximize the reliability of your process assessments.

Figures 19.1 and 19.2 provide both a segmental observational assessment instrument and a simplified version suitable for use with groups of children at the fundamental movement phase of development. An individual progress "report card" is depicted in Figure 19.3. The group assessment form is helpful for charting entry and exit levels of ability throughout the school year. The individual assessment form may be filled out from the group form and sent home periodically so parents may be kept abreast of their childrens' progress in the physical education program. The figures located at the end of each of the sport-skill chapters provide examples of observational assessment techniques for children at the sport-related movement phase.

PRODUCT (PERFORMANCE) ASSESSMENT

Product, or performance, assessment is concerned with the *how far, how fast, how high*, or *how many* of movement. In other words, it is concerned with the end product of one's movement, as measured by elapsed time, as in the 50- or 100-yard dash; distance covered, as with the standing long jump or shot put; accuracy, as in basketball goal shooting or target archery; or the number of repetitions, as with chinups or pushups. Performance assessment is an effective objective technique to use in skill assessment *after* the mechanics (process) of a task have

been mastered. After children have advanced to the mature stage of a skill, they are ready to begin applying the skill to specific sport-related activities. For example, the mature throwing pattern can now be further developed and applied to throwing a football or pitching a baseball. Remember, a sport skill, in terms of mechanics, is often little different from the fundamental movement skill. The goal has changed in terms of the speed, accuracy, or distance required for success in the sport activity, but the basic mechanics are essentially the same, adapted only to the specific demands of the task.

Guidelines

Product assessment is objective. It yields quantitative scores. The relationship between form (process) and performance (product) is yet unclear. Form does influence performance, but the extent to which performance is related to correct form is largely unknown. Therefore, in order to maximize the usefulness of performance scores, the following considerations are important:

1. Validity: Does the performance measure what it claims to measure?
2. Reliability: Does the performance measure assess whatever it is measuring consistently?
3. Objectivity: Does the performance measure yield highly similar results when administered by others?
4. Feasibility: Is the performance measure straightforward and easy to set up and administer? Can it be self- or partner-administered, or must it be teacher-administered?
5. Utility: Can the results be used for valid educational purposes such as self-appraisal, program planning, or reporting progress?

The figures located in the "Assessing Progress" section of each sport-skill chapter in Part V provide examples of performance measures for assessing a variety of sport skills. Each of these performance tests can be modified as needed.

SUGGESTED READING

Gallahue, D. L. (1982). *Understanding motor development in children*. New York: Wiley.

Herkowitz, J. (1978). Assessing the motor development of children: Presentation and critique of tests. In Ridenour (Ed.). *Motor development: Issues and application*. Princeton, NJ: Princeton University Press.

McClenaghan, B. A., and Gallahue, D. L. (1978). *Fundamental movement: A developmental and remedial approach*. Philadelphia: Saunders.

Roberton, M. A. (1981). Movement quality, not quantity. *Motor Development Academy Newsletter* 2:2–3.

Roberton, M. A., and Halverson, L. E. (1984). *Developing children: Their changing movement*. Philadelphia: Lea & Febiger.

Thomas, J. R. (Ed.) (1984). *Motor development during childhood and adolescence*. Minneapolis: Burgess.

Ulrich, Dale A. (1985). *Test of gross motor development*. Austin, TX: Pro-Ed.

PART V

THE SKILL THEMES

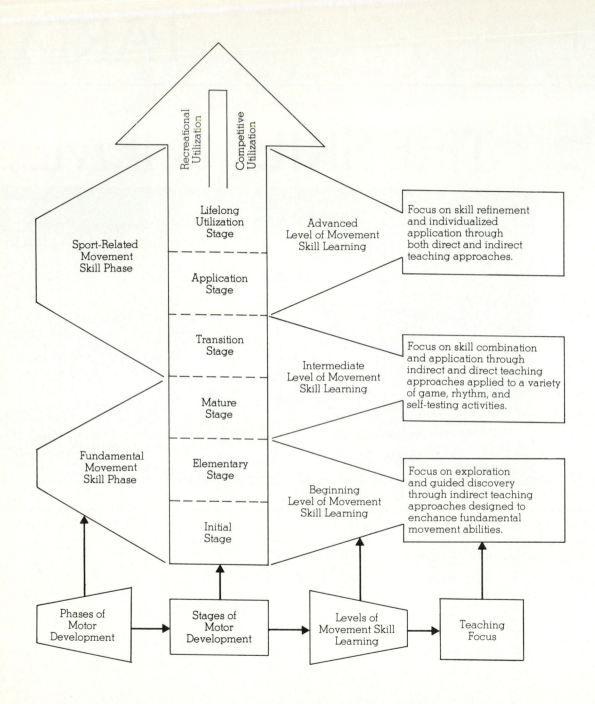

Developmental teaching progression chart for skill
theme utilization.

CHAPTER 20

FUNDAMENTAL LOCOMOTOR SKILLS

Locomotor skills are total body movements in which the body is propelled in an upright posture from one point to another in a roughly horizontal or vertical direction. Movements such as walking, running, leaping, jumping, hopping, skipping, galloping, and sliding are generally considered to be fundamental locomotor skills. These abilities are necessary for purposeful and controlled movement through our environment. They are basic to the numerous skills necessary for sports, dance, and recreational activities.

Locomotor skills do not develop automatically. Although there may be a phylogenetic (hereditary) basis for the appearance of the initial and even the elementary stage of several fundamental locomotor movements, attainment of the mature stage is dependent upon ontogenetic (environmental) factors. Factors within the environment, such as opportunities for practice, encouragement, and instruction, play a major role in the acquisition of mature patterns of locomotor movement. Failure to develop these mature skills will result in great difficulty in achieving acceptable levels of performance during the sport-related skill phase of locomotor skill development.

This chapter examines the importance of skill sequencing and the process of developing fundamental locomotor skill themes. Several locomotor skills are examined. A verbal description and visual description are provided, along with teaching tips and concepts children should know. This is followed by a sampling of appropriate skill-development activities.

DEVELOPING A LOCOMOTOR SKILL THEME

In order to make the most efficient use of your time when working on locomotor skill development, the following sequence of preplanning, observing and assessing, planning and implementing, and evaluation and revision is recommended.

1. *Preplan*
    - Determine what locomotor skills will be grouped together for each skill theme. The following works well:
    - Running and leaping
    - Jumping and hopping
    - Skipping, galloping, and sliding
    - Determine when to include each locomotor skill theme into the yearly curriculum. You will need to consider whether to space out lessons on each skill over the entire school year (distributed practice) or to group lessons together into concentrated units of instruction (massed practice).
    - Decide the total number of lessons that will be spent on locomotor skill development in relation to the entire curriculum.

2. *Observe and Assess*
    - Observe fundamental locomotor abilities of the children to be taught.
    - Assess whether they are at an initial, elementary, mature, or sport-skill stage in each of the skills to be included as a skill theme. Study the verbal description and visual descriptions for each locomotor skill on the pages that follow for help with this.

3. *Plan and Implement*
    - Plan appropriate movement activities geared to the needs, interests, and ability levels of the group. Study the teaching tips and concepts children should know in the pages that follow for guidance.
    - Implement a planned program of activities, stressing progression in skill development.

4. *Evaluate and Revise*
    - Informally evaluate progress in the locomotor skills being stressed in terms of improved mechanics (process) and performance (product). The questions found in Table 20.18 in the "Assessing Progress" section at the end of the chapter will be helpful.
    - Revise subsequent lessons as needed, based on student progress.

SKILL SEQUENCING

Although children are generally considered to have the developmental potential to perform most fundamental locomotor skills at the mature stage by age six or seven, this is often not the case. Because of many factors, elementary school children often exhibit immature fundamental movement patterns. As a general rule, children in the primary grades benefit most from a progressive program of fundamental locomotor skill development. However, numerous children in the upper grades can frequently be identified as exhibiting only an elementary stage of development in several locomotor skills.

It is important to know where your students are in terms of their locomotor skills, in order to plan effectively for all. Review of the Developmental Teaching Progression Chart at the beginning of Part V (see page 192) will be helpful in guiding your selection of appropriate developmental movement activities. Remember, skill sequencing is a process of building skill upon skill. This requires careful analysis of the complexity of the skill and the activities in which they are to be incorporated.

RUNNING AND LEAPING

The running and leaping patterns begin developing early in the child. Around the first birthday, the infant achieves an upright gait and begins to walk. Skill in walking develops rapidly until about age six, at which time it resembles the adult pattern in many ways. Care, however, must be taken to monitor the child's walking posture and to provide movement experiences that help him or her focus on the proper walking pattern. By 18 months, the child is attempting to run, but no flight phase in which the child is airborne is apparent. The initial attempts at running resemble a fast walk. A flight phase, marking the onset of true running, generally appears between the second and third birthday. With proper amounts of practice, encouragement, and instruction, the running pattern should continue to improve and be at the mature stage by age seven.

Leaping is a fundamental movement that may be viewed as an extension of the running pattern. The development of mature leaping is dependent somewhat on efficient running. The leap is similar to the run except that a longer flight phase is involved and it is generally performed as a single rather than a repeated skill. In other words, when one leaps, the act is either from a stationary position or preceded by a run. The performance of consecutive leaps is possible, but a momentary hesitation from one leap to the next is easily observable in all but the most skilled. Leaping is used in the play and recreational activities of children in hopscotch, hurdling, and crossing a brook; others use it in baseball, basketball, football, and track.

The movement patterns of leaping and running are basic to our everyday activities. It is essential that they be developed to the mature level. A variety of exploratory and guided discovery activities can aid in this process. Once the mature pattern has been obtained, these skills may be utilized in a variety of game, sport, and dance situations. Practice in running and leaping will enhance one's performance abilities. Speed and endurance will continue to improve with practice and will enable the individual to utilize these abilities in a variety of sport skills.

Running

Verbal Description
Initial Stage
- Leg swing is short, limited.
- Stiff, uneven stride.
- No observable flight phase.
- Incomplete extension of support leg.
- Stiff, short swing; varying degrees of elbow flexion.
- Legs tend to swing outward horizontally.
- Swinging leg rotates outward from the hip.
- Swinging foot keeps toes outward.
- Wide base of support.

Elementary Stage
- Stride length, swing, and speed increase.
- Limited but observable flight phase.
- Support leg extends more completely at take-off.
- Arm swing increases.
- Horizontal swing is reduced on backswing.
- Swinging foot crosses midline of the body at height of recovery to rear.

Mature Stage
- Length of stride is at its maximum; speed of stride is fast.
- Definite flight phase.
- Support leg extends completely.
- Recovery thigh is parallel to ground.
- Arms swings vertically in opposition to the legs.
- Arms are bent in approximate right angles.
- Little rotary action of recovery leg and foot.

Visual Description
Initial Stage

PHOTO 20.1   The initial run.

Elementary Stage

PHOTO 20.2   The elementary run.

Mature Stage

PHOTO 20.3   The mature run.

Teaching Tips
Common Problems
- Inhibited or exaggerated arm swing.
- Arms crossing the midline of the body.
- Improper foot placement.
- Exaggerated forward trunk lean.
- Arms flopping at the sides or held out for balance.
- Twisting of the trunk.
- Arrhythmical action.
- Landing flat-footed.
- Flipping the foot or lower leg either in or out.

Recommended Strategies
- Determine the characteristic stage in running ability.
- Plan activities designed to move the child to the next stage.
- Include plenty of activities involving movement exploration at the beginning level of skill learning.
- Work for good listening skills while running.
- Use the commands "freeze" and "melt" to develop listening skills.
- Stress not bumping into others.
- Stress stopping without sliding on the knees.
- When playing tagging games, teach proper tagging techniques.
- Incorporate activities that gradually increase aerobic capacity.
- Provide a wide variety of running activities.

Concepts Children Should Know
Skill Concepts
- Keep your head up when you run.
- Lean into your run slightly.
- Lift your knees.
- Bend your elbows and swing the arms freely.
- Contact the ground with your heels first.
- Push off from the balls of your feet.
- Run lightly.

- Running is basic to the successful playing of numerous games and sports.
- Running is good for your heart and lungs.

Movement Concepts
- You can run at many different speeds and levels.
- You can land heavily or lightly.
- Your run can be smooth or jerky.
- You can run in many different directions and paths.
- Your leg speed is influenced by your arm speed.
- Your stride length is determined by the force of your pushoff.

Leaping

Verbal Description
Initial Stage
- Child appears confused in attempts.
- Inability to push off and gain distance and elevation.

Visual Description
Initial Stage

- Each "attempt" looks merely like another running step.
- Inconsistent use of takeoff leg.
- Simultaneous landing on both feet.
- Arms ineffective.

Elementary Stage
- Child appears to be thinking through the action.
- Looks like an elongated run.
- Little elevation.
- Little forward trunk lean.
- Stiff appearance.
- Incomplete extension of legs during flight.
- Arms used for balance rather than for aiding in force production.

Mature Stage
- Relaxed, rhythmical action.
- Forceful extension of takeoff leg.
- Good summation of horizontal and vertical forces.
- Definite forward trunk lean.
- Definite arm opposition.
- Full extension of legs during flight.

PHOTO 20.4   The initial leap.

Elementary Stage

PHOTO 20.5   The elementary leap.

Mature Stage

PHOTO 20.6   The mature leap.

Teaching Tips
Common Problems
- Failure to use the arms in opposition to the legs.
- Restricted movement of the arms or legs.
- Lack of spring and elevation in the pushoff.
- Landing flat-footed.
- Failure to stretch and reach with the leading leg.
- Inability to lead with either leg.

Recommended Strategies
- Provide definite objects or barriers to leap over.
- Combine leaping with two or three running steps.
- Leap over very low objects followed by higher objects up to mid-thigh level.
- Encourage leading with either foot.
- Young children enjoy imagery when leaping "over deep canyons," or across "raging rivers."
- Use velcro straps or other devices that give way if the child comes in contact with the object that is leaped.

Concepts Children Should Know
Skill Concepts
- Push upward and forward with your rear foot.
- Stretch and reach with your forward foot.
- Keep your head up.
- Lean forward at the trunk as you leap.
- Alternate your arm action with your leg action.
- The leaping pattern is used in getting over obstacles and in track and field events.

Movement Concepts
- Your leap can be very forceful or it can be light.
- Your leap can be combined with running.
- Your leap can be high or low or in between.
- Your leap can only be in one direction—forward.
- Your leap can be long or short or in between.
- You can leap over objects or across objects or both.
- You can leap to rhythmical accompaniment.

- Your leap has a longer flight phase than your run and covers a greater distance.
- The distance and height of your leap are determined by the force of your pushoff.

JUMPING AND HOPPING

Jumping and hopping are fundamental movement skills that are used in a variety of sport, recreational, and daily living experiences. Jumping and hopping may take many forms, all of which involve a takeoff, a flight phase, and a landing. A jump differs from a hop in that a jump involves taking off on one or both feet and landing on both feet, while a hop involves taking off on one foot and landing on the same foot. Jumping may occur in a roughly horizontal plane, in a vertical plane, or from a height. Hopping may occur in place, or it may occur over a roughly horizontal plane.

The movement patterns of jumping and hopping are basic to numerous athletic, dance, and recreational activities. It is essential that the mature stage of each of these patterns is obtained at an early date. Once the mature stage has been achieved, the teacher and the child may begin to focus on improved performance scores and combining hopping and jumping with a variety of other locomotor and manipulative skills.

Horizontal Jumping

Verbal Description
Initial Stage
- Limited arm swing; the arms do not initiate the jumping action.
- During flight, the arms move in a sideways–downward or to the rear–upward action to maintain balance.
- The truck moves in a vertical direction; there is little emphasis upon the length of jump.
- Preparatory crouch is inconsistent in terms of leg flexion.

- Difficulty using both feet.
- Extension of the ankles, knees, and hips at takeoff is limited.
- Body weight falls backward at landing.

Elementary Stage
- Arms initiate jumping action.
- Arms remain toward the front of body during preparatory crouch.
- Arms move out to the side to maintain balance during flight.
- Preparatory crouch is deeper and more consistent.
- Extension of the knees and hips is more complete at takeoff.
- Hips are flexed during flight, and thighs are held in a flexed position.

Mature Stage
- The arms move high and to the rear during the preparatory crouch.
- During takeoff, the arms swing forward with force and reach high.
- Arms are held high throughout the jumping action.
- Trunk is propelled at approximately a forty-five-degree angle.
- Major emphasis is on horizontal distance.
- Preparatory crouch is deep and consistent.
- There is complete extension of ankles, knees, and hips at takeoff.
- Thighs are held parallel to the ground during flight; lower leg hangs vertically.
- Body weight at landing moves forward.

Visual Description
Initial Stage

PHOTO 20.7   The initial horizontal jump.

Elementary Stage

PHOTO 20.8   The elementary horizontal jump.

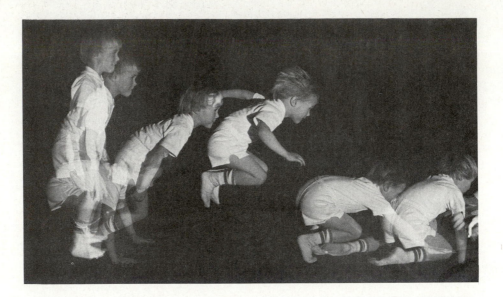

Mature Stage

PHOTO 20.9   The mature horizontal jump.

Teaching Tips

Common Problems

- Poor preliminary crouch.
- Inability to takeoff with both feet simultaneously.
- Restricted movements of the arms or legs.
- Poor angle of takeoff.
- Loss of balance in the air.
- Failure to extend fully upon takeoff.
- Landing on one foot at a time.
- Falling backward upon landing.

Recommended Strategies

- Start with exploratory activities and progress to more directed techniques as skill develops.
- Avoid jumping in socks or gym shoes with poor traction.
- Use carpet squares as a challenge to jump *over*.
- Place emphasis on coordinated use of the arms and legs.
- Children like to measure the length of their jump. This is a good time to reinforce measuring with a yardstick or meter stick.
- See if children can jump a distance equal to their height.
- Try jumping from different surfaces. Discuss differences.

Concepts Children Should Know

Skill Concepts

- Crouch halfway down.
- Swing your arms back, then forward forcefully.
- Explode forward from a coiled position.
- Push off with your toes leaving the ground last.
- Stretch and reach forward.
- Bring your knees to your chest as you prepare to land.
- Your heels contact first upon landing.
- "Give" with your landing and fall forward.

Movement Concepts

- You can land heavily or lightly, but it is best to land lightly.
- If you swing your arms fast, you will travel farther than if you swing them slowly.
- Your jump can be smooth or jerky, free or bound.
- You can jump in different directions and at different levels.
- You can combine your jump with other movements.
- You can jump in place, for height, for distance, or from a height.
- A jump requires taking off on one or two feet, but the landing must be on both feet.
- Jumping while holding an object will alter your pattern.

Vertical Jumping

Verbal Description

Initial Stage

- Inconsistent preparatory crouch.
- Difficulty taking off with both feet.
- Poor body extension upon takeoff.
- Little or no head lift.
- Arms tend to remain at side.
- Little height is achieved.

Elementary Stage

- Exceeds ninety-degree angle on preparatory crouch.
- Exaggerated forward lean during crouch.
- Takes off with both feet.
- Trunk does not fully extend during flight phase.
- Arms attempt to aid balance in flight, but often unequally.
- Noticeable horizontal displacement upon landing.

Mature Stage

- Preparatory crouch with knee flexed from sixty to ninety degrees.
- Forceful extension at the hips, knees, and ankles.

- Simultaneous, coordinated upward arm lift.
- Upward head tilt with eyes focused on the target.
- Full body extension.

- Elevation of reaching arm by shoulder girdle tilt combined with downward thrust of non-reaching arm at the peak of flight.

Visual Description
Initial Stage

Elementary Stage

PHOTO 20.10   The initial vertical jump.

PHOTO 20.11   The elementary vertical jump.

Mature Stage

PHOTO 20.12   The mature vertical jump.

Teaching Tips
Common Problems
- Inhibited or exaggerated crouch.
- Failure to extend the body, legs, and arms forcefully.
- Swinging the arms backward rather than upward.
- Flexion at the knees upon takeoff.
- Arms out to the side for balance.
- Failure to lift with the head and extend at the shoulder.
- Landing with insufficient crouch.

Recommended Strategies
- Some children may be "earthbound" and will require special assistance.
- Stress coordinated action of legs and arms.
- Require children to stretch and reach with the arms and head as they jump.
- Use plenty of exploratory activities at the initial stage, progressing to more directed techniques later on.
- Try jumping on different surfaces. Inner tubes, mattresses, and trampolines provide exciting experiences.
- Have children chalk their fingers to mark their jumps.
- Have children jump and place a piece of tape to mark their jump.
- Have children jump up and grab an object, keeping eye contact with the object.

Concepts Children Should Know
Skill Concepts
- Crouch about halfway down for your takeoff and landing.
- "Explode" upward.
- Forcefully swing and reach upward with your arms.
- Stretch, reach, and look upward.
- Extend at the shoulder of your reaching arm.
- This jumping pattern is used in rebounding and the layup shot in basketball, as well as the block and spike in volleyball.

Movement Concepts
- You must time your jump so that all body parts work together.
- You can jump high or low and with or without use of your arms.
- You jump higher if you use your arms.
- Your movements must be quick and forceful for the highest jumps.
- You can jump while holding objects, but your height will be less.
- You can jump only as high as the force of gravity will let you.
- Vertical jumping requires a two-footed takeoff in an upward direction and a landing on both feet.

Jumping from a Height

Verbal Description

Initial Stage
- One foot leads upon takeoff.
- No flight phase.
- Lead foot contacts lower surface prior to trailing foot leaving upper surface.
- Exaggerated use of arms for balance.
- Little flexion at knees upon landing.

Elementary Stage
- Two-foot takeoff with one-foot lead.
- Flight phase exists but is lacking in control.
- Arms used ineffectively for balance.

- One-foot landing followed by immediate landing of trailing foot.
- Inhibited or exaggerated flexion at knees and hip upon landing.

Mature Stage
- Two-foot takeoff.
- Controlled flight phase.
- Both arms used efficiently out to the sides to control balance as needed.
- Feet contact lower surface simultaneously with toes touching first.
- Feet land shoulder width apart.
- Flexion at the knees and hip is congruent with the height of the jump.

Visual Description

Initial Stage

PHOTO 20.13   The initial jump from a height.

Elementary Stage

PHOTO 20.14 The elementary jump from a height.

Mature Stage

PHOTO 20.15 The mature jump from a height.

Teaching Tips
Common Problems
- Inability to take off with both feet.
- Exaggerated or inhibited body lean.
- Loss of control while in the air.
- Failure to land at the same time on both feet.
- Landing flat-footed.
- Failure to "give" sufficiently upon impact.
- Loss of balance upon landing.

Recommended Strategies
- Start with a low height and gradually work up.
- Place a mat on the floor.
- Spot all jumping carefully.
- Encourage exploration, then gradually focus on the skill element.
- Begin with single-task skills, then combine two or three tasks (jump, clap your hands, land and roll forward).
- Stress proper landing techniques.
- Emphasize control while in the air.
- Provide different heights for different ability levels.
- Keep equipment well spaced for safety reasons.

Concepts Children Should Know
Skill Concepts
- Push off with both feet.
- Your toes are the last thing to leave the ground.
- Lean forward slightly.
- Move your arms forward or sideward in unison for balance.
- Keep your legs shoulder width apart in preparation for landing.
- Give at the ankles, knees, and hip joint upon landing.
- Jumping from a height and landing are used in your play activities and in numerous sports.

Movement Concepts
- You can land either heavily or lightly.
- Your jump can be from many different heights.

- The extent of your crouch upon landing is based on the height of your jump.
- You can jump in many different directions, going forward, backward, or to the side.
- Your jump should be smooth, but it can be jerky and awkward.
- Your jump can be far or near, high or low.
- You can jump and land while holding objects, but you must make adjustments.
- Jumping from a height requires taking off and landing on both feet.

Hopping

Verbal Description
Initial Stage
- Non-support leg flexed 90 degrees or less.
- Non-support thigh roughly parallel to the contact surface.
- Body upright.
- Arms flexed at elbows and held slightly to the side.
- Little height or distance generated in a single hop.
- Balance lost easily.
- Limited to one or two hops.

Elementary Stage
- Non-support leg flexed.
- Non-support thigh at 45-degree angle to contact surface.
- Slight forward lean with the trunk flexed at the hip.
- Non-support thigh flexes and extends at the hip to produce greater force.
- Force is absorbed upon landing by flexing at the hip and the supporting knee.
- Arms move vigorously up and down bilaterally.
- Balance poorly controlled.
- Generally limited in the number of consecutive hops that can be performed.

Mature Stage
- Non-support leg flexed at 90 degrees or less.
- Non-support thigh lifts with vertical thrust of support foot.
- Greater body lean.
- Rhythmical action of non-support leg (pendulum swing) aiding in force production.

- Arms move together in rhythmical fashion, lifting as the support foot leaves the contact surface.
- Arms not needed for balance but used for greater force production.

Visual Description
Initial Stage

PHOTO 20.16   The initial hop.

Elementary Stage

PHOTO 20.17   The elementary hop.

Mature Stage

PHOTO 20.18   The mature hop.

Teaching Tips
Common Problems
- Hopping flat-footed.
- Exaggerated movements with the arms.
- Exaggerated movement of the free leg.
- Exaggerated forward lean.
- Poor control of balance.
- Failure to synchronize leg and arm action.
- Inability to keep free leg from contacting floor (loss of balance).
- Inability to hop on either leg.

Recommended Strategies
- Provide activities that make use of hopping on the left foot and on the right foot.
- Begin with exploratory activities and progress to more directed experiences.
- Work for rhythmical flow in hopping.
- Stress rhythmical alteration of the feet.
- Do not emphasize hopping for speed or distance too early.
- Work for control, then gradually stress speed and distance.

Concepts Children Should Know
Skill Concepts
- Take off and land on the same foot.
- Lift your arms slightly as you spring up from your hop.
- Push off from your toes and land on the ball of your foot.
- Land softly.
- Hopping is used in combination with jumping in the triple jump and in the ballestra in fencing.
- Hopping is used in many dance steps, including the polka, mazurka, and schottische.

Movement Concepts
- You can land heavily or lightly when you hop.
- You can hop in place or move in different directions.
- You can hop at different speeds.
- You can hop at different heights and levels.
- You can hop over objects and in different pathways.
- You can hop smoothly and freely, or the movement can be bound and jerky.
- You can hop with either foot.
- You can alternate hopping feet.
- Hopping requires a takeoff and a landing on one foot.

SKIPPING, SLIDING, AND GALLOPING

Skipping, sliding, and galloping are fundamental movement abilities that begin developing during the preschool years and should be mastered by the first grade. Galloping occurs in a forward direction with one foot leading and the other trailing behind. Sliding is the same action but performed in a sideways direction. Generally speaking, children are able to gallop and slide prior to being able to skip. This may be explained by the fact that they are unilateral activities, requiring less differentiation and integration of neural mechanisms then the neurologically more complex bilateral action of skipping. It is recommended, therefore, that prior to introducing skipping, children be given opportunities to explore the many movement variations of galloping and sliding. Guided discovery activities should be incorporated with galloping and sliding in order that these patterns may be at the mature stage prior to introducing a teaching progression for skipping. In other words, if the child is not yet at the mature stage of galloping or sliding (with either foot leading), it is unwise to develop lessons that focus on skipping.

Sliding is similar in many ways to galloping, except that it is conducted in a sideward direction. Once again, it is generally more appropriate to introduce sliding after the child has experienced some success with galloping. The sliding pattern is utilized extensively in a variety of athletic and dance activities that require rapid lateral movement. Sliding is an integral part of many sport and dance activities. Lateral movements need to be smooth, and the child should be able to make rapid changes in direction. Be sure to point out specific instances where sliding is used in sports and to master sliding in relation to its specific use.

Skipping

Verbal Description

Initial Stage
- "One-footed skip."
- Deliberate step–hop action.
- Double hop or step sometimes occurs.
- Exaggerated stepping action.
- Arms of little use.
- Action appears segmented.

Elementary Stage
- Step and hop coordinated effectively.
- Rhythmical use of arms to aid momentum.
- Exaggerated vertical lift on the hop.
- Flat-footed landing.

Mature Stage
- Rhythmical weight transfer throughout.
- Rhythmical use of arms but reduced use during time of weight transfer.
- Low vertical lift on the hop.
- Toe landing.

Visual Description
Initial Stage

PHOTO 20.19   The initial skip.

Elementary Stage

PHOTO 20.20   The elementary skip.

Mature Stage

PHOTO 20.21   The mature skip.

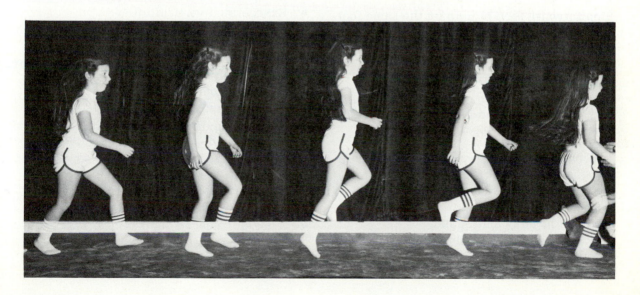

Teaching Tips
Common Problems
- Stepping on one foot and hopping on the other.
- Poor rhythmical flow.
- Failure to lift the forward leg sharply upward, causing too much gain in distance.
- Inability to use both sides of the body.
- Heavy stepping or landing.
- Extraneous movements of the arms.
- Inability to move in a straight line.
- Undue concentration on the pattern.

Recommended Strategies
- The child should be able to gallop with either leg leading before learning skipping.
- The child should be able to hop well on either leg before attempting to skip.
- Introduce skipping when child is ready.
- You may need to provide slow-motion demonstrations.
- Once the basic pattern is mastered, encourage exploration of variations of skipping.
- Utilize rhythmic activities that require skipping.
- Work for a rhythmical, flowing motion.

Concepts Children Should Know
Skill Concepts
- Step forward, then hop up on the same foot.
- Do the same with the other foot.
- Lift your knees sharply upward.
- Swing your arms upward in time with your legs.
- The skipping pattern is used in many folk and square dances and is basic to good footwork in numerous sports.

Movement Concepts
- You can skip in different directions, pathways, and floor patterns.
- You can skip at different speeds.
- You can skip in a smooth and free manner, or it can be jerky and bound.
- You can skip at different levels and land heavily or lightly.
- You can skip with a partner and while carrying objects.
- Skipping is a combination of two movements—stepping and hopping.
- Skipping requires you to use both sides of your body in a rhythmical fashion.

Sliding and Galloping

Verbal Description
Initial Stage
- Arrhythmical at a fast pace.
- Often reverts to a run.
- Trail leg fails to remain behind and often contacts in front of the lead leg.
- Forty-five degree flexion of trail leg during flight phase.
- Contact is in a heel–toe combination.
- Arms are of little use in balance or force production.

Elementary Stage
- Moderate tempo.
- Appears choppy and stiff.
- Trail leg may lead during flight but lands adjacent to or behind the lead leg upon contact.
- Exaggerated vertical lift.
- Feet contact in a heel–toe or toe–toe combination.
- Arms slightly out to the side to aid balance.

Mature Stage
- Moderate tempo.
- Smooth, rhythmical action.
- Trail leg lands adjacent to or behind lead leg upon contact.
- Both legs flexed at 45-degree angle during flight.
- Low flight pattern.
- Heel–toe contact combination.
- Arms not needed for balance; may be used for other purposes.

Visual Description
Initial Stage

PHOTO 20.22   The initial slide.

Elementary Stage

PHOTO 20.23   The elementary slide.

Mature Stage

PHOTO 20.24   The mature slide.

Teaching Tips

Common Problems

- Keeping the legs too straight.
- Exaggerated lean of the body.
- Jerky movements.
- Overstepping of the trailing leg.
- Too much elevation.
- Inability to move in different directions.

Recommended Strategies

- Work on sliding in both directions.
- Stress not crossing the feet.
- Begin with exploratory experiences, then progress to skill drills and other activities involving sliding.
- Stress keeping the knees slightly bent and the trunk forward, as well as staying on the balls of the feet ("ready position").
- Rhythmical accompaniment aids sliding.
- Work for ease of movement in both directions.

Concepts Children Should Know

Skill Concepts

- Step to the side and draw the other foot up quickly to the first foot.
- Repeat the action, landing with the same foot.
- Use your arms only as needed for balance.
- Move on the balls of your feet.
- Keep your knees bent slightly.
- Lean forward at the waist slightly.
- Sliding is used in a variety of sports such as tennis, baseball, basketball, and fencing. It is also used often in dance.

Movement Concepts

- You can slide to the left or right.
- When you slide forward or backward, it is called a gallop.
- Your movements can be fast or slow, smooth or jerky, free or bound.
- You can slide at different levels and for different distances.

- You can slide with a partner.
- You can dodge while sliding.
- When sliding sideways, remain on your feet and don't fall to your knees.

SKILL DEVELOPMENT ACTIVITIES

Mastery of fundamental locomotor skills requires environmental conditions that permit practice and provide instruction. Instruction may take many forms. However, when viewing children from a developmental perspective, it is necessary to first determine their phase of motor development (fundamental movement phase or sport-related movement phase). This will in turn provide cues to their level of movement skill learning (beginning, intermediate, advanced). With this information, it is then a simple matter to determine whether the lesson should focus on exploratory and guided discovery activities, skill application activities, or skill refinement activities.

TABLE 20.1   Exploratory Activity Ideas for Running

Can you run—

Effort	Space	Relationships
Force	*Level*	*Objects*
—like a pixie?	—very tall?	—on the line?
—like an elephant?	—very small?	—across the line?
—on your tiptoes?	—at a high level?	—under the bars?
—flat-footed?	—at a low level?	—behind the chair?
—as if you were floating?	—at a medium level?	—around the chair?
—as if you weighed a million pounds?	—fast or slow at a high level?	—over the hoop?
—as softly as you can?	—smoothly at a high level?	—through the hoop?
—as hard as you can?		—carrying a ball?
	Direction and Path	—carrying a suitcase?
Time	—forward?	—with boots on?
—as fast you can?	—backward?	
—as slowly as you can?	—to the left–right?	*People*
—starting slowly and showing form?	—diagonally?	—all by yourself?
—alternating fast and slow?	—and change direction once?	—in front of a partner?
	—and change direction three times?	—behind a partner?
Flow	—in a straight line?	—beside a partner?
—as smoothly as you can?	—in a curvy line?	—holding a partner's hand?
—with jerky movements?	—in a zigzag line?	—with the class?
—like a machine?	—in a pattern (show shapes)?	—without touching anyone?
—like a robot?		—with two others?
—like a deer?	*Range*	—in formation?
—like a football player?	—in your own space?	
—without using your arms?	—throughout the room?	**Combinations**
	—as far as you can?	An infinite variety of exploratory experiences can be devised simply by combining various effort, space, and relationship challenges.
	—and not bump anyone?	
	—with your feet wide?	
	—with big steps?	
	—with tiny steps?	

TABLE 20.2   Exploratory Activity Ideas for Leaping

Can you leap—

Effort	Space	Relationships
Force	*Level*	*Objects*
—and land lightly?	—as high as you can?	—over a rope?
—and land without a sound?	—as low as you can?	—over a hurdle?
—and land forcefully?	—at many different levels?	—over a partner?
—alternating hard and soft landings?	—alternating low and high leaps?	—across two outstretched ropes?
—and swing your arms forcefully?		—over two outstretched ropes?
—and keep your arms at your side?	*Direction*	—from one carpet square to the next?
—holding your arms in different positions?	—forward?	—from one footprint to a corresponding footprint?
	—backward?	
Time	—diagonally?	*People*
—and stay in the air as long as you can?	—with your left foot leading?	—the same distance as your partner?
—and land as quickly as you can?	—with your right foor leading?	—over your partner?
—and swing only one arm?	—alternating left and right foot lead?	—the length of your partner's body?
—in time to the accented beat of the drum?		—in unison with your partner?
—in time to the accented beat of the music?	*Range*	
	—as far as you can?	**Combinations**
Flow	—and keep one leg bent?	After several variations of leaping have been explored singularly, try combining various aspects of effort, space, and relationships. For example: Can you leap lightly as high as you can over a rope held by two partners?
—from a 3-step approach?	—and bend both legs in the air?	
—from a 2-step approach?	—and keep both legs straight?	
—from a 1-step approach?	—and twist your trunk in the air?	
—from a stationary position?	—and find different things to do with your arms while in the air?	
	—on different surfaces?	

Exploratory Activities

The primary purpose of incorporating exploratory activities into the movement lesson is to provide children who are at either the initial stage or the elementary stage an opportunity to get an idea of how and where their body can move when performing locomotor movements. Exploratory activities are intended to help children get in touch with their bodies and to lead them to

TABLE 20.3   Exploratory Activity Ideas for Horizontal Jumping

Can you jump——

Effort	Space	Relationships
Force	*Level*	*Objects*
—as quietly as possible?	—from as small a position as you can?	—over the box?
—as loudly as possible?		—across the rope?
—alternating loud and soft jumps?	—from as big a position as you can?	—through the hoop?
—like a pixie?	—and stay under my hand?	—like a frog or a rabbit?
—like a giant?		—while holding this ball?
	Direction	
Time	—forward/backward?	*People*
—very fast?	—sideways?	—with a partner?
—very slowly?	—in a straight line?	—as far as your partner?
—alternating fast and slow jumps?	—several times in a zigzag or circular pattern?	—over your partner?
—as if you were stuck in molasses?	—making various geometric shapes or letters of the alphabet?	—at the same time as your partner jumps?
—as if you were on ice?		**Combinations**
	Range	Numerous combinations of effort, space, and relationships are possible.
Flow	—as far as you can?	For example:
—with your arms and legs held stiffly?	—as near as you can?	—for distance and then for height?
—keeping your arms out?	—landing with your feet wide apart?	—as short and as low as possible?
—with your legs out?	—landing with your feet close together?	—as fast and as far as possible?
—in a relaxed manner?		—as quietly and as far as you can?
—like a wooden soldier?		—and toss a ball?
		—and catch a ball?
		—to my rhythm?
		—to the music?

experiment with the multitude of variations in effort, space, and relationships that can be experienced. Combinations of these can be successfully included in the lesson after the gross general framework idea has been established and children are progressing toward the mature stage in the movement skill. Tables 20.1 through 20.8 provide easy-to-use charts for presenting movement challenges that will permit children to explore their locomotor potential.

TABLE 20.4   Exploratory Activity Ideas for Vertical Jumping

Can you jump up—

Effort	Space	Relationships

Force
—and land lightly?
—and land heavily?
—like an elephant?
—like a robot?
 	
Time
—as fast as you can?
—as slowly as you can?
—like a rocket?
—like a growing flower?
 	
Flow
—without using your arms?
—and use only one arm?
—and keep your head down?
—and remain stiff?
—as relaxed as you can?
	Level
	—as high as you can?
	—as low as you can?
	—alternating high and low jumps?
	—and touch the same spot five times?
	—from a crouched position?
	—from an extended position?
	
	Direction
	—and land in the same spot?
	—and land in a different spot?
	—and land slightly forward/
	  backward/to the side?
	—and turn?
	
	Range
	—and land in your own space?
	—and land outside your space?
	—and land with your feet wide apart?
	—and land with your feet close
	  together?
		Objects
		—and strike the hanging ball?
		—with a weighted object?
		—with a ball?
		—on a trampoline?
		—on a bounding board?
		—over a jump rope?
		
		People
		—with a partner?
		—and alternate jumping up with
		  a partner?
		—while holding hands?
		—and touch your partner's
		  spot?
		
		Combinations
		Numerous combinations of effort, space, and relationships are possible.
		For example:
		—and toss a ball?
		—and shoot a basket?
		—and catch a ball?
		—and hop over a jump rope?
		—and turn?
		—and turn and catch?
		—as lightly, high, and as fast as you can?

TABLE 20.5   Exploratory Activity Ideas for Jumping from a Height

Can you jump—

Effort	Space	Relationships
Force	*Level*	*Objects*
—and land as lightly as you can?	—from a crouched position?	—over the wand?
—and land as forcefully as you can?	—from a tucked position?	—through the hoop?
	—as high as you can?	—and catch the ball in the air?
Time		—and throw the ball in the air?
—and land as quickly as possible?	*Direction*	—and catch a ball you toss while in the air?
—and stay in the air as long as possible?	—forward?	
—in slow motion?	—backward?	*People*
	—sideways?	—at the same time as a partner?
Flow	—and make a quarter turn?	—and land at the same time as your partner?
—with different arm actions?	—and make a half turn?	—and do what your partner does?
—without using your arms?	—and make a full turn?	—and do the opposite of your partner?
—while holding one arm to your side?	*Range*	
	—and land with your feet together?	**Combinations**
	—and land with your feet apart?	Numerous combinations of effort, space, and relationship activities involving exploration of jumping from a height are possible and should be used after the child has gained control of singular movements.
	—and land in this spot?	
	—and make yourself as big as you can?	

TABLE 20.6   Exploratory Activity Ideas for Hopping

Can you hop—

Effort	Space	Relationships
Force	*Level*	*Objects*
—as quietly as you can?	—in a small ball?	—over the rope?
—as noisily as you can?	—in a crouched position?	—on the carpet squares?
—alternating hard and soft landings?	—with little crouched hops?	—over the cones?
—hard four times on your left, then softly four times on your right?	—as high as you can?	—around the cones?
	—at a medium height?	—while bouncing a ball?
	—staying lower than my hand?	—while catching a tossed ball?
	—staying at the same level as my hand?	—while tossing and catching a self-tossed ball?
Time		
—as fast as possible?	*Direction*	*People*
—as slow as possible?	—in place?	—in rhythm with a partner?
—starting slowly and getting slower?	—forward?	—forward holding hands?
—in time to the music?	—backward?	—facing each other and hopping in unison to the wall?
	—sideways?	—imitating your partner's arm actions?
Flow	—and turn in the air?	
—without using your arms?	—and make a quarter (half, three-quarter, full) turn?	
—using only the arm opposite your hopping foot?		**Combinations**
—alternating feet every eight (four, two) beats?	*Range*	Numerous combinations of effort, space, and relationships can be explored while hopping after control has been gained in single-problem tasks. For example: Can you hop as quietly as you can over the rope?
	—in your own space?	
	—from spot to spot?	
	—and land on a different carpet square each time?	
	—and land on the same spot?	
	—and land in as small a spot as possible?	
	—and land in as large a spot as possible?	

TABLE 20.7 Exploratory Activity Ideas for Sliding and Galloping

Can you slide/gallop—

Effort	Space	Relationships
Force —landing flat-footed? —landing on your toes? —very quietly? —while pretending you are dragging an elephant? —while pretending you are trying to escape a charging elephant? *Time* —in either direction? —as fast as you can? —as slowly as you can? —to the beat of the drum? —in time to the music? *Flow* —keeping both legs stiff? —keeping one leg stiff? —keeping your trunk erect? —bending forward at your waist?	*Level* —sideways and get smaller? —sideways and get bigger? —somewhere in between big and small? —and change levels as I raise or lower my hand? *Direction* —sideways? —forward/backward (gallop)? —to the left/right? —to the left four steps then to the right four steps? —to the left two steps then to the right two steps? —alternating left and right? —in the direction I point? *Range* —to your right (or left) as far as you can until I say stop? —taking big steps? —taking small steps?	*Objects* —from one line to the other? —from one line to the other and return? —from one line to the other as many times as you can in thirty seconds? —in either direction while bouncing and catching a ball? —in either direction while dribbling a ball? —in either direction to catch a ball? *People* —facing a partner and travel in the same direction? —facing a partner and travel in an opposite direction? —facing a partner and travel four steps in the opposite direction, then four steps in the same direction? **Combinations** After exploring the many variations of sliding and/or galloping in isolation, you will want to combine various aspects of effort, space, and relationships. For example: Can you slide in either direction four steps and touch the line while bouncing and catching a ball?

TABLE 20.8　Exploratory Activity Ideas for Skipping

Can you skip—

Effort	Space	Relationships
Force —as quietly as you can? —as a giant would? —as loud as you can? —landing heavily on one foot and lightly on the other? —alternating loud/quiet, and hard/ soft skips?	*Level* —while making yourself very small? —and gradually get smaller? —as tall as you can? —with a high knee lift? —barely raising your feet off the ground?	*Objects* —without touching any of the lines on the floor? —without touching any cracks in the cement? —and try to step on each line or crack? —while carrying a heavy object?
Time —as fast as you can across the room? —as slowly as you can? —as if you were on a sandy beach? —downhill? —uphill? —to the beat of the drum?	*Direction* —forward/backward? —sideways (left/right)? —in a straight line? —in a curved or zigzag pattern? —in a circle?	*People* —with a partner? —going backward while your partner moves forward? —in unison with a partner? —while holding both of your partner's hands?
Flow —without using your arms? —swinging your arms outward/ inward/diagonally? —like a toy soldier? —in a relaxed manner?	*Range* —and see how many complete skips it takes to cross the room? —and measure how much space you cover in one complete skip? —with your legs wide apart?	**Combinations** Numerous ingenious combinations of effort, space, and relationships can be explored. For example: Can you skip as quietly as you can while making yourself very small and without touching any of the lines on the floor?

Guided Discovery Activities

The primary purpose for including guided discovery activities into the lesson is to provide children who are at the elementary stage of developing their fundamental locomotor abilities an opportunity to practice the skill. Practice, by using a problem-solving technique, permits

TABLE 20.9   Guided Discovery Activity Ideas for Running

	1. Have the children first explore the numerous variations of running.
	2. Then begin to put limitations on the possible responses to the movement challenges presented. For example:
General	• Run around the gym in a clockwise direction, then in a counterclockwise direction.
Arm action	• Run as fast as you can one time around the gym. What do your arms do? Do they move fast or slowly?
	• When you run slowly, do your arms move fast or slowly? Why?
	• How do you swing your arms when you run? Do they cross your chest, or do they stop before crossing?
	• Run with your arms crossing your chest. Now try it without crossing. Which is best? Why?
Leg action	• What part of your foot lands first when you are running as fast as you can? What about when you are jogging at a slower pace?
	• Run uphill. Run downhill. How does your stride change? Why does it change?
Trunk action	• Lean forward when you run. Now try to stay very straight. Now try something in between. Which feels the best for you? Why?
Total	• Show me how you would run a five-mile race. How would you run a mile race, a quarter mile, fifty yards?
	• Why is your run slightly different for each distance?
	• Can you run to the rhythm made by the drum?
	• What happens to your run when the beat speeds up or slows down?
	3. Now combine running with other activities in order to achieve a more automatic pattern.
	• Can you tag someone lightly while running?
	• Can you dodge someone who is trying to tag you?
	• Run barefooted. Now try it with your street shoes. Now with your gym shoes. How does it feel? Which way is most comfortable? Safest?
	• Run on different surfaces. How does it affect your running pattern? Why?

children to learn more about the skill and how their bodies should move. Emphasis at this level is placed on proper mechanics and the utility of various locomotor movements. Tables 20.9–20.17 present a sampling of guided discovery experiences.

TABLE 20.10   Guided Discovery Activity Ideas for Leaping

	1.	First explore the movement variations of leaping
	2.	Then begin to place limitations on the response possibilities to the movement challenges presented. For example:
Leg action	•	Try to leap as far as you can. What do you do when you want to go far? Can you show me? If you don't want to leap far, what do you do? Show me. Try pushing off forcefully with your trailing foot and stretching out with your lead foot. Does it make a difference?
	•	Try leaping and pushing off from different parts of your trailing foot. Try pushing off flat-footed and off the ball of your trailing foot. Which works best? See if there is any difference in the distance leaped trying both ways.
Trunk action	•	Try leaping and bending your trunk at different angles. Now try keeping your trunk erect. Which ways feel the most comfortable? Do you bend your trunk differently for different purposes? Watch your partner and see if he/she bends at the waist differently when trying to leap different heights and various distances.
	•	What do we know about bending at the waist? When is it best to bend far forward? When is it best to have very little bend at the waist? Experiment with a partner, then let me know your answer.
Arm action	•	Try leaping with your arms in many different positions. How does it feel? Which way helps you leap the farthest or the highest? Experiment and find out.
General	•	See if you can leap and coordinate the use of your arms, legs, and trunk. What are some important things we should remember when leaping?
	•	Try leaping from a standing position. Now try it from a running approach. Which way helps you go farther? Why?
	•	Try leaping off one foot. Now try the other. Is there a difference? Why? Practice both ways.
	3.	After a mature leaping pattern has been reasonably well mastered, combine it with other exploratory and guided discovery activities in order to reinforce the pattern and make it more automatic.
	•	Listen to the beat of the drum and leap on every hard note.
	•	Beginning at one end of the gym, perform three leaps in combination with running.
	•	Try to leap over the outstretched ropes placed on the floor.
	•	Let's try to run across the gym alternating leaping off our left and right foot.
	•	Can you leap and catch a tossed ball while in the air?
	•	Try leaping across the outstretched ropes and touching the balloon overhead (ringing a suspended bell is a real challenge).
	•	Using carpet squares or hoops, practice leaping from spaceship to spaceship, being sure that no other astronaut is in a spaceship that you leap to.

TABLE 20.11   Guided Discovery Activity Idea for Horizontal Jumping

	1. First explore several of the numerous variations of horizontal jumping.
	2. Now begin to place limitations on the responses to the movement challenges presented. For example:
General	• Try to jump over the unfolded newspaper. Can you get over the short part without touching? How about the long part?
Arm action	• What happens when you jump and don't use your hands? Why don't you go as far? What *should* we do with our arms when we jump? Show me.
	• Show me how you would use your arms. Several are doing this (demonstrate) with their arms. Why? Oh, I see. It helps you keep your balance.
Landing	• Can you show me several different ways to land? Try it now just doing different things with your feet. Now try landing with your feet way apart, close together, and in between. Which worked best for you? Why? What happens to your knees when you jump? Why? Would there be any difference if I jumped from a very high height or from a very low height?
Total	• When you put the entire jump together, what do you do with your head and eyes? Try three different things with your head (look up, down, straight ahead). Which works best? Now try jumping with your eyes closed. Scary, isn't it? Why? What should we remember about the use of our head and eyes when we jump from a height?
	3. When the mature pattern has been reasonably well mastered, combine jumping from a height with other activities in order to reinforce the pattern and make it more automatic. For example:
	• Jump and assume different postures in the air.
	• Jump and perform turns in the air.
	• Jump, land, and roll.
	• Jump, turn, land, and roll.

TABLE 20.12   Guided Discovery Activity Ideas for Vertical Jumping

	1. First explore several of the numerous variations of vertical jumping.
	2. Now begin to place limitations on the response possibilities to the movement challenges presented. For example:
Arm action	• What happens when you jump without using your arms? Does one arm help? When you use both arms, which way is best? Try three ways, then tell me which works best for you. Many of you thought that swinging your arms up as your legs uncoiled was best. Why is that so?
	• Try bending your knees at three different levels when you jump. Which is best? Why? Measure the height of your jumps from three different leg positions. Why is there a difference with each jump?
Trunk action	• Does your trunk stay bent forward when you jump or does it extend? Try both ways. Which is best? Why?
Head action	• Jump as high as you can with your head and eyes in three different positions. Which is best for you? Many thought looking up was best. You're right. Think of yourself as a puppet with a string attached to your nose. Every time you jump up, you stretch your entire body out and reach to the sky with your nose.
Landing	• Try landing in different ways. Which do you think is best? Why do you bend your knees when you land? How much should you bend them? Why? Did you land in the same spot you took off from? See if you can. Some people are landing in front of their takeoff spot. Do you get more height or less height when that happens? Why?
	3. When the mature pattern has been reasonably well mastered using these and other guided discovery challenges, combine vertical jumping with other activities in order to reinforce the pattern and make it more automatic. For example:

	• Try jumping on different surfaces:
	   bounding board
	   tires
	   trampoline

	• Try jumping with other objects:
	   jump ropes
	   high jumping
	   stretch ropes

	• Play jumping games.

TABLE 20.13   Guided Discovery Activity Ideas for Jumping from a Height

	1. First explore several of the variations of jumping from a height.
	2. Now begin to place limitations on the response possibilities to the movement challenges presented. For example:
Takeoff	• How do you takeoff when you jump? Do you do it with one foot leading or do both feet leave at the same time? Try it both ways. Which way gives you more control or balance? Why? Try turning in the air after you take off, or try a two-footed takeoff.
Flight	• What do you do while you are in the air? Try different things with your arms, your legs. To keep your balance best show me how you use your arms. What happens to your body when it is in the air? Can anyone show me what it looks like? Do you jump straight up? Do you just skim over the floor? Do you do something different?
	• What happens when you swing your arms forward very hard as you jump? Very softly? What happens when your arms swing all the way up to your head? Try it different ways and see which is best? Is it best to swing hard or soft, all the way up or only part way up when we jump as far as we can? Why? Show me.
Leg action	• When you jump, do you leave the ground with both feet at the same time or with one foot at a time? Try both. Why is it better to use both feet for a standing long jump? Try jumping as far as you can using both feet. Now put a beanbag on one foot and, while trying to keep it there, jump as far as you can. Which works better, one foot or both feet? Why?
Landing	• How do you land? Should you land and sit back or fall forward? What happens to your knees when you land? Are they stiff or do you bend them? Why?
Total	• Let's put it all together. Jump as far as you can. How does it feel? Can you get the legs and arms to work together? What happens when they do? Should you jump fast (explosively) or is it better to jump more slowly? Try both? Which works best? Why?
	3. When the mature pattern has been reasonably mastered, combine it with other activities in order to reinforce the pattern and make it more automatic.
	• Play jumping games.
	• Conduct cooperative jumping contests where partners try to jump the same distance. Two points are scored for jumping the same distance. One point is deducted for jumping different distances.
	• Jump from different surfaces. What happens to your distance when you jump from a very soft surface? Why?

TABLE 20.14   Guided Discovery Activity Ideas for Hopping

	1.	First explore several of the variations of hopping.
	2.	Now begin to place limitations and questions on the response possibilities present. For example:
General		• Hop in place on one foot. Can you do the same on the other foot? Can you hop to the wall on one foot and come back on the other?
Leg action		• Try hopping and putting your free leg in different positions. Which is easiest when you are hopping in place? For distance? Why? Try the same experiment with the other leg. Why do some people hop better on one leg than on the other? Do you have a better leg?
Arm action		• Try hopping as far as you can, using three different helps with your arms. Try it without using your arms at all. Which works best for you? Several seem to lift and swing the arms forward when they hop for distance. Try it. How does that feel?
		• Let's try that same arm action while hopping in place. What happened? Why? What do you want to do with your arms when hopping in place? Show me.
	3.	Once the mature hopping pattern has been reasonably well mastered for both the left and the right leg, move on to activities that utilize hopping in combination with other skills. Incorporation of hopping with other skills will reinforce the pattern and make it more automatic. For example:
		• Step-hops.
		• Various dance steps (schottische, step-hop, polka).
		• Jump-rope activities.
		• Track and field event activities.

TABLE 20.15   Guided Discovery Activity Ideas for Galloping

	1.	First explore several of the numerous variations of galloping.
	2.	Then begin to place limitations on the response possibilities to the movement challenges presented. For example:
General		• Put one foot forward and gallop around the room. Try it with the other foot leading. Which is easiest? Why?
Leg action		• Try galloping with your legs stiff. Try with them very bent. Now try different amounts of knee bend. What works best for you? Why do you think some knee bend is good?
Foot action		• What happens to your back foot when you gallop forward? Does it come up to meet your front foot or does it overtake it and move in front? Which do you think is best? Try both. Why is it best not to overtake your front foot with the rear foot?
Arm action		• Gallop across the room. What did you do with your arms? Now gallop back as fast as you can. Did your arms do anything that time?
		• How can your arms help you when you gallop? Let's time our partner going across the room, first using his or her arms and then without using them. Which was fastest? Which was most comfortable? Why?
	3.	After the mature pattern has been reasonably well mastered, combine it with other activities in order to reinforce the pattern and make it more automatic.
		• Experiment with the wide variety of combinations of effort, space, and relationships that are possible.
		• Conduct a story play or mimetic activities that utilizes imagery with galloping horses.
		• Practice galloping to the uneven beat of a drum or tamborine.
		• Gallop to some form of musical accompaniment. Can you gallop to an even beat or an uneven beat?

TABLE 20.16   Guided Discovery Activity Ideas for Sliding

	1. First explore the numerous movement variations of sliding.
	2. Then begin to place limitations on the response possibilities to the movement challenges presented. For example:
Leg and trunk action	• When you slide sideways, try doing it with your legs stiff. How does it feel? How do you think you could slide better? What happens when your knees are slightly bent and your trunk is bent forward slightly? Which is best: legs straight and back straight, or knees bent slightly and trunk bent slightly? Try both ways.
Foot action	• Do you cross your feet when you slide? Have a partner watch you and check. Now watch my finger and slide in the direction I point, changing direction as fast as you can when I point in the opposite direction.
	• It's best not to cross your feet, right? Why? When moving to your left, which foot should move first? What about to the right?
	3. After the mature pattern has been reasonably well mastered, combine it with other exploratory and guided discovery activities in order to reinforce the pattern and make it more automatic.
	• Watch my hand and slide in the direction I point.
	• Close your eyes and listen to my call of "left" or "right," then move in that direction.
	• Count for your partner and see how many times he or she can slide left and right between these two lines (indicate two parallel lines ten feet apart) in thirty seconds.
	• Slide left or right to catch the ball thrown to you in that direction. Why don't you cross your feet? What happens when you do?

TABLE 20.17   Guided Discovery Activity Ideas for Skipping

	1.	First explore several of the movement variations of skipping.
	2.	Then help the children discover how their body works when they skip. For example:
Leg action		• Try skipping around the room. Experiment with big steps, little steps, and in-between steps. When would you want to use each?
		• Be a detective and see if you can find out what two movements with your legs the skip is made up of. Who knows the answer? Good! Show me. Let's all take it apart.
Arm action		• What do you do with your arms when you skip? Try four or five different things. How does it feel when your arms swing as you skip?
		• Watch your partner. Do his or her arms swing with the same arm and leg leading alternately or with opposite arm and leg leading alternately?
		• What other locomotor skills do we do with alternating opposite arms and leg leading? Why do you think we do that? Try leading with the same arm as the leg that is leading. How does it feel? What do your friends look like? So you see it probably is best that we walk, run, and skip with leg and arm alteration because it is more comfortable and helps us move better.
	3.	When the mature pattern has been reasonably well mastered using the above and other guided discovery challenges, combine skipping with other activities to reinforce the pattern and make it more automatic. For example:
		• Play skip tag.
		• Skip to a drum beat.
		• Skip to selected musical accompaniment.
		• Modify chasing and fleeing games to incorporate skipping rather than running.
		• Teach the children folk dances that incorporate skipping.

TABLE 20.18   Self-Question Chart for Fundamental Locomotor Skill Development

Running		Yes	No	Comments

1. Are the children able to run from point to point with good postural control?
2. Are they able to make smooth transitions in direction, level, and speed?
3. Can they run about the gym or playyard without bumping into each other?
4. Can they utilize the running patterns in conjunction with other basic skills?
5. Do they run without undue attention focused on the process?
6. Are their movements relaxed, fluid, and rhythmical?
7. Is there observable improvement?

Leaping		Yes	No	Comments

1. Can they leap leading with either foot?
2. Can they make adjustments in height and distance with ease?
3. Is appropriate body lean used for the distance leaped?
4. Are the arms used properly in conjunction with the legs?
5. Is there observable improvement?

Jumping/Hopping		Yes	No	Comments

1. Can the children jump or hop with good control of their bodies?
2. Can the children take off simultaneously with both feet and land on both feet at the same time in all three jumping patterns?
3. Can the children take off on one or both feet and land on one foot when hopping?
4. Can they hop equally well on either foot?
5. Are the hopping and jumping actions smooth, fluid, and rhythmical?
6. Is there improved summation of force used to produce a hop or jump?
7. Is there an easy transition from one pattern to another?
8. Is there observable improvement?

Galloping		Yes	No	Comments

1. Can they gallop while leading with either the left or right foot?
2. Does the toe-trailing foot remain behind the heel of the leading foot?
3. Is the action smooth and rhythmical?
4. Is there observable improvement?

Sliding		Yes	No	Comments

1. Can the children slide equally well in both directions?
2. Do they slide without crossing the feet?
3. Is the action smooth and rhythmical?
4. Is there observable improvement?

Skipping		Yes	No	Comments

1. Is the skipping action smooth and rhythmical?
2. Is there rhythmical alteration of both sides of the body?
3. Is there sufficient knee lift?
4. Is the arm action appropriate for the purpose of the skip?

Skill Application Activities

After fundamental locomotor skills have been mastered and can be performed at the mature stage with reasonable consistency, it becomes appropriate to focus on skill application activities. Skill application activities permit practice and refinement of locomotor skills under dynamic conditions and are applied to a variety of game, rhythmic, and self-testing activities. Greater emphasis is placed on skill development in terms of improved performance abilities, as well as on combining single skills with others in a variety of sport, dance, and recreational activities.

Failure to achieve the mature stage in a fundamental locomotor skill prior to attempting to apply it at the sport-related movement phase of results is a "proficiency barrier." In other words, inability to perform the fundamental skill at the mature stage makes successful performance of the sport skill version unlikely. Therefore, locomotor skill application activities should be introduced into the program *after* the basic elements of these fundamental skills have been mastered.

The following chapters contain numerous locomotor skill application ideas that are appropriate for elementary school children:

Chapter 31   Low Organized Game Activities
Chapter 32   Relay Activities
Chapter 36   Fundamental Rhythmic Activities
Chapter 38   Creative Rhythmic Activities
Chapter 39   Folk and Square Dance Activities
Chapter 41   Perceptual–Motor Activities

ASSESSING PROGRESS

Assessment is necessary both at the entry level of a locomotor skill theme and at the exit level. Running, leaping, jumping, hopping, galloping, sliding, and skipping abilities should all be assessed. Once the entry level of a skill is known, it is an easy matter to determine what activities should actually be included in the lesson.

For children at the fundamental phase of developing their movement abilities, observational assessment works quite well. The sample assessment charts located in Chapter 19 (Figures 19.1 and 19.2) are a practical means of charting individual and group progress.

A second means of assessing progress in locomotor skill development is through answering a self-question survey similar to the one depicted in Table 20.18.

If you are unable to answer "yes" to each of the questions, you will need to make modifications in subsequent lessons to more closely fit the specific needs of the individual, group, or class.

SUGGESTED READING

Capon, J. (1981). *Successful movement challenges.* Byron, CA: Front Row Experiences.
Hacket, L. C., and Jennon, R. G. (1970). *A guide to movement exploration.* Palo Alto, CA: Peek Publications.
Riggs, M. L. (1980). *Jump to joy.* Englewood Cliffs, NJ: Prentice-Hall.
Wickstrom, R. L. (1983). *Fundamental motor patterns.* Philadelphia: Lea & Febiger.

CHAPTER 21

FUNDAMENTAL MANIPULATIVE SKILLS

Manipulative skills are gross body movements in which force is imparted to objects and/or received from objects. Manipulative movements such as throwing, catching, kicking, trapping, striking, volleying, dribbling, and rolling are generally considered to be fundamental manipulative skills. These skills are essential to purposeful and controlled interaction with objects in our environment. They are also necessary, in their refined form, for successful playing of many of the sports of our culture.

Manipulative skills do not develop automatically. Opportunities for practice, encouragement, and instruction are essential for most children in order to develop mature patterns of manipulative movement. Achievement of the mature stage in many fundamental manipulative skills generally occurs somewhat later than for most locomotor skills. This is due to the many complex visual-motor adjustments that are required for intercepting a moving object, as with catching, trapping, striking, and volleying. Therefore, the instructor should be alert to childrens' perceptual abilities as well as their motor abilities when focusing on manipulative skill development. Modification of the object to be intercepted through the use of balloons, beachballs, or foam balls frequently works well during the initial and elementary stages of the skill.

This chapter focuses on the importance of skill sequencing and how to develop a manipulative skill theme. Several manipulative skills are described. A verbal description and visual description are provided, along with teaching tips and concepts children should know. This is followed by a sampling of appropriate skill-development activities and suggestions for assessing progress.

DEVELOPING A MANIPULATIVE SKILL THEME

When planning a theme on fundamental manipulative skills, you will find it helpful to utilize the following sequence in order to make the most efficient use of your time.

1. Preplan
   - Determine which manipulative skills will be grouped together for each skill theme. The following grouping generally works well:
     - Throwing and catching.
     - Kicking and tapping.
     - Striking and volleying.
     - Dribbling and ball rolling.
   - Determine when in the yearly curriculum to include each manipulative skill theme. You will need to decide whether to space out lessons on each skill theme over the entire school year or group lessons into longer units of instruction. Distributed practice tends to work better than massed practice during the beginning level of movement skill learning.
   - Decide approximately how many lessons will be spent on fundamental manipulative skill development in relation to the total curriculum.
2. Observe and Assess
   - Observe the fundamental manipulative skills of the children to be taught.
   - Assess whether they are at the initial, elementary, mature, or sport-skill stage in each of the skills to be included as a skill theme. Study the verbal description and visual description of each manipulative skill for guidance.
3. Plan and Implement
   - Plan appropriate movement activities geared to the needs, interests, and ability level of the group. Study the teaching tips and concepts children should know in the pages that follow for help.
   - Implement a planned program of activities, stressing progression in skill development.
4. Evaluate and Revise
   - Informally evaluate progress in the manipulative skills being stressed in terms of improved mechanics and performance. The questions found in Table 21.18 at the end of the chapter will be helpful.
   - Revise subsequent lessons as needed, based on student progress.

SKILL SEQUENCING

Fundamental manipulative skills begin developing early in children. The interaction of young children with objects and their gross attempts at throwing, catching, and kicking are generally the first forms of gross motor manipulation. Simply by virtue of the maturation, most children progress to the elementary stage in their manipulative abilities. Progress to the mature stage is largely dependent upon environmental stimulation. Because of the sophisticated perceptual requirements of most fundamental manipulative skills, children often lag behind in the development of their ability to strike a pitched ball or to volley a ball repeatedly. Therefore, attainment of the mature stage in manipulative skills is dependent upon the combination of maturational readiness, environmental openness, and teacher sensitivity.

Although most children have the developmental *potential* to perform at the mature stage in their fundamental manipulative skills by seven years of age, many lag behind. In fact, it is not unusual to see numerous older children, and even college students, who are unable to throw, catch, volley, dribble, or strike a ball at the mature stage. It is important to know where your students are in terms of their manipulative skills in order to plan effectively for all. The Developmental Teaching Progression Chart that appears at the beginning of Part V (see page 192) will be helpful in guiding your selection of developmentally appropriate movement activities.

THROWING AND CATCHING

Throwing and catching are two fundamental movements that fit together especially well in the presentation of a skill theme. Throwing may take many forms. It may be performed in an overhand, underhand, or sidearm pattern and with either one or both hands, depending on the purpose of the throw. The overhand throwing pattern is dealt with here. It is probably the throwing pattern most frequently used by both children and adults. Throwing abilities begin developing early in life, and it is common to see individuals who have not received any formal instruction and have had only limited opportunity for practice functioning at the elementary level in the overhand throw. Most children progress to the elementary stage more as a function of maturation than experience. In most cases, however, they will continue to perform at this stage even as adolescents and adults unless there is sufficient practice and instruction.

Practice in catching can be facilitated with the use of objects of varying sizes, shapes, colors, and firmness. The child at the initial stage, for example, generally experiences greater success with catching a soft, brightly colored beanbag rather than a ball of comparable size. The child is able to grip the beanbag more securely than the ball. There is little fear of injury if the child is hit in the face or on a finger by the beanbag. The wise teacher provides opportunities for children to practice catching with a variety of objects. Care is taken to set up experiences that will not result in an avoidance reaction of the head or a closing of the eyes out of fear as the object approaches. During the early stages of learning, you should not require the individual to adapt to the equipment; rather, you should modify the equipment to the developmental needs of the child.

Throwing

Verbal Description

Initial Stage
- The action is mainly from the elbow.
- Elbow of the throwing arm remains in front of the body; action resembles a push.
- Fingers spread at release.
- Follow-through is forward and downward.
- Trunk remains perpendicular to the target.
- Little rotary action during throw.
- Body weight shifts slightly rearward.
- Feet remain stationary.
- There is often purposeless shifting of feet during preparation of throw.

Elementary Stage
- In preparation, arm is swung upward, sideways, and backward to position of elbow flexion.
- Ball is held behind head.
- Arm is swung forward, high over the shoulder.
- Trunk rotates toward the throwing side during preparatory action.
- Shoulders rotate toward throwing side.
- Trunk flexes forward with forward motion of arm.
- Definite forward shift of body weight.
- Forward step with leg on same side as throwing arm.

Mature Stage
- Arm is swung backward in preparation.
- Opposite elbow is raised to balance preparatory action in the throwing arm.
- Throwing elbow moves forward horizontally as it extends.
- Forearm rotates and thumb ends up pointing downward.
- Trunk markedly rotates to throwing side during preparatory action.
- Throwing shoulder drops slightly.
- A definite rotation through hips, legs, spine, and shoulders during throw.
- Weight during preparatory movement is on the rear foot.
- As weight is shifted, there is a step with the opposite foot.

Visual Description
Initial Stage

PHOTO 21.1   The initial throw.

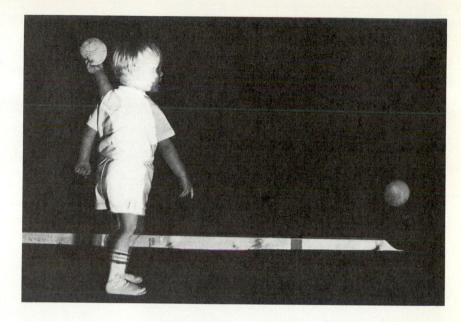

Elementary Stage

PHOTO 21.2   The elementary throw.

Mature Stage

PHOTO 21.3   The mature throw.

Teaching Tips
Common Problems
- Forward movement of the foot on the same side as the throwing arm.
- Inhibited back swing.
- Failure to rotate the hips as the throwing arm is brought forward.
- Failure to step out on the leg opposite the throwing arm.
- Poor rhythmical coordination of arm movement with body movement.
- Inability to release the ball in the desired trajectory.
- Loss of balance while throwing.

Recommended Strategies
- Provide numerous opportunities for practice. One or two sessions will not be enough to develop a consistent mature pattern.
- Focus first on throwing for distance, not accuracy.
- Work for speed of movement and good hip rotation.
- Use carpet squares, hoops, or tires as cues for stepping out on the opposite foot.
- Be sure to have an ample supply of balls or beanbags that can be easily gripped.
- Beanbags, newspaper balls, yarn balls, and stocking balls work well.
- Use beanbags for wall drills in order to emphasize the throwing action and not catching or retrieving.
- Speed, accuracy, and distance are the performance elements of throwing. Work first for distance, then speed, and finally accuracy.
- Follow a logical teaching progression, using the above recommendations as a guide.
- There should be 100 percent participation.

Concepts Children Should Know
Skill Concepts
- Stand with the leg that is on the other side of the throwing arm leading.
- Turn your shoulder toward the target.
- Raise your free arm and point toward the target.
- Raise your throwing arm and hold the ball close to your ear.
- Lead with your elbow on the forward swing.
- Bring your rear foot forward and follow through.
- The overhand throwing pattern is used in the sports of baseball, softball, and on the fast break in basketball. It is also similar to the overhand serves in volleyball and tennis and the smash shot in badminton.

Movement Concepts
- The effort that you give to your throw will influence how fast the ball will travel and the smoothness with which your throwing motion is performed.
- When you throw a ball, it can travel through space in a variety of directions and levels.
- A ball may be thrown using throwing patterns ranging from overhand and underhand to a variety of sidearm patterns.
- You can throw many different types of objects. The size, shape, and weight of the object will affect the distance it travels as well as the pattern you use.
- The coordinated use of your arms, trunk, and legs will affect the speed and distance of your throw.

Catching

Verbal Description
Initial Stage
- There is often a definite avoidance reaction of turning the face away or protecting the face with the arms (the avoidance reaction is learned and therefore may not be present).
- Arms are extended and held in front of the body.
- There is limited movement until contact.
- The catch resembles a scooping action.
- Body is used to trap ball.
- Palms are held upward.
- Fingers are extended and held tense.
- Hands are not utilized in the catching action

Elementary Stage
- Avoidance reaction is limited to the child's eyes closing at contact with ball.
- Elbows are held at sides with an approximately 90-degree bend.

- Since initial contact made with the child's hands is often unsuccessful, the arms trap the ball.
- Hands are held in opposition to each other; thumbs are held upward.
- At contact, the hands attempt to squeeze the ball in a poorly timed and uneven motion.

Mature Stage
- Any avoidance reaction is completely suppressed.

- Arms are held relaxed at sides and forearms are held in front of body.
- Arms give upon contact to absorb the force of the ball.
- Arms adjust to the flight of the ball.
- Thumbs are held in opposition to each other.
- Hands grasp the ball in a well-timed, simultaneous motion.
- Fingers make a more effective grasping motion.

Visual Description
Initial Stage

Elementary Stage

PHOTO 21.4   The initial catch.

PHOTO 21.5   The elementary catch.

Mature Stage

PHOTO 21.6   The mature catch.

Teaching Tips
Common Problems
- Failure to maintain control of the object.
- Failure to give with the catch.
- Keeping the fingers rigid and straight in the direction of the object, causing jamming.
- Failure to adjust the hand position to the height of the object.
- Inability to vary the catching pattern for objects of different weight and force.
- Taking the eyes off the object.
- Improper stance (that is, a straddle rather than a stride position in the direction of the oncoming object, causing loss of balance when catching a fast-moving ball.
- Closing the hands either too early or too late.
- Failure to keep the body in line with the ball (that is, reaching out to the side to catch).

Recommended Strategies
- Use soft objects for initial catching experiences. Yarn balls and beanbags work best.
- Give the child verbal cues such as "Ready—catch" in order to avoid surprises.
- Begin with large balls and progress to smaller sizes.
- Use brightly colored balls.
- Be aware of the background against which the ball is to be caught. Avoid figure–ground problems.
- Vary the speed, level, and trajectory of the ball as skill increases.

Concepts Children Should Know
Skill Concepts
- Get directly in the path of the ball.
- Place one foot ahead of the other.
- Adjust your hand position for the height of the ball—thumbs in for balls above the waist, thumbs out for balls below the waist.
- Curve your fingers and keep your eyes on the ball.
- Pull the ball in toward your body.

Movement Concepts
- You can catch an object in many different ways.
- You can catch with different body parts.
- You can catch from a variety of positions.
- The objects you catch may vary in size, shape, color, or texture.
- The objects you catch can come toward you at different levels and with varying degrees of speed.
- You can play a variety of games that involve catching.

KICKING AND TRAPPING

Kicking and trapping are two fundamental movement patterns that fit nicely together into a common skill theme. Basically, kicking involves imparting force to an object with use of the foot and leg. Kicking may take the form of kicking at a pebble, a can, or a ball. It may be part of a low-level game or part of the sports of soccer and football. In developing a mature pattern of kicking, emphasis should be on kicking for distance. Distance kicking (or kicking as forcefully as possible) will promote the mature pattern. More complete action of the kicking leg on the windup and follow-through, as well as the coordinated action of the trunk and arms, are necessary for a long kick. Kicking for accuracy should not be of concern until after the mature pattern has been mastered.

Trapping is a fundamental movement pattern that requires use of various parts of the body to stop the forward momentum of an oncoming object. With children, trapping a rolled ball should precede trapping a tossed object. The focus of the lessons on trapping should be on gaining control of the ball and being able to make appropriate adjustments relative to the speed of the ball and the level of contact.

Kicking

Verbal Description
Initial Stage
- Movements are restricted during the kicking action.

- Trunk remains erect.
- Arms are used to maintain balance.
- Kicking leg is limited in backswing.
- Forward swing is short: no follow-through.
- Child kicks ''at'' ball rather than kicking it squarely and following through.
- A pushing rather than a striking action is predominant.

Elementary Stage
- Preparatory backswing is centered at the knee.
- Kicking leg tends to remain bent throughout the kick.
- Follow-through is limited to forward movement of knee.
- One or more deliberate steps are taken toward the ball.

Mature Stage
- Arms swing in opposition to each other during kicking action.
- Trunk bends at waist during follow-through.
- Movement of kicking leg is initiated at hip.
- Support leg bends slightly at contact.
- Length of leg swing increases.
- Follow-through is high; support foot rises to its toes or leaves the surface entirely.
- The approach to the ball is from a run or a leap.

Visual Description
Initial Stage

PHOTO 21.7   The initial kick.

Elementary Stage

PHOTO 21.8   The elementary kick.

Mature Stage

PHOTO 21.9   The mature kick.

Teaching Tips
Common Problems
- Restricted or absent backswing.
- Failure to step forward with the non-kicking leg.
- Tendency to lose balance.
- Inability to kick with either foot.
- Inability to alter the speed of kicked balls.
- Jabbing at the ball without any follow-through.
- Poor opposition of the arms and legs.
- Failure to use a summation of forces by the body to contribute to the force of the kick.
- Failure to contact the ball squarely or missing it completely (eyes not focused on the ball).
- Failure to get adequate distance due to lack of follow-through and forceful kicking.

Recommended Strategies
- Focus on kicking for distance rather than accuracy. Accuracy kicking will not promote use of the mature pattern.
- If possible, have a ball for every other child.
- Begin with a variety of exploratory experiences, but progress to guided discovery experiences without too much delay.
- Encourage kicking with the non-preferred foot after the mature level has been reached with the preferred foot.
- Work jointly with kicking and trapping, using a peer teaching approach.
- Be sure to work for control of the height of the ball. This will make it necessary to teach the instep and inside-of-the-foot kick as well as the ever-popular toe kick.
- After the mature kicking pattern has been achieved, introduce accuracy kicking activities.
- Incorporate kicking into low-level games and lead-up games after the mature stage has been reached.
- Work for total body control when kicking.
- Practice kicking a stationary ball prior to a moving ball.
- Be sure to use balls about the same size as a standard soccer ball.

Concepts Children Should Know
Skill Concepts
- Stand behind the ball and slightly to one side.
- Step forward on the non-kicking foot.
- Keep your eyes on the ball.
- Swing your kicking leg back and then forcefully forward from the hip.
- The snap down from the knee gives the ball its speed.
- Contact the ball with the top portion of your foot (low ball), with your toe (high ball), or with the inside portion of your foot (ground ball).
- Follow through in the direction that the ball is to go.
- Use your arms for balance and force production.
- The kicking pattern is basic to the sport of soccer and is used in kicking games such as kickball.

Movement Concepts
- You can kick a ball at different levels (high, medium, low) by contacting it with different parts of your feet.
- You can kick either for distance or for accuracy, but the two processes will look different.
- The manner in which you coordinate the use of your entire body will influence the direction, distance, level, and pathway that the ball takes.
- You can kick the ball at objects and to people. Great precision is needed when kicking at or to something.
- It is important for you to keep your eyes on the ball when it is about to be kicked.
- Your kicks can be long or short, fast or slow, hard or soft and may travel in a variety of directions and at different levels.

Trapping

Verbal Description
Initial Stage
- Trunk remains rigid.
- No "give" with the ball as it makes contact.

- Inability to absorb the force of the ball.
- Difficulty getting in line with the object.

Elementary Stage
- Poor visual tracking.
- "Gives" with the ball but movements are poorly timed and sequenced.
- Can trap a rolled ball with relative ease but cannot trap a tossed ball.
- Appears uncertain as to what body part to use.

- Movements lack fluidity.

Mature Stage
- Tracks ball throughout.
- "Gives" with the body upon contact.
- Can trap both rolled and tossed balls.
- Can trap balls approaching at a high velocity.
- Movements are refined, fluid, and under control.
- Moves to intercept ball with base of the foot.

Visual Description
Initial Stage

PHOTO 21.10   The initial trap.

Elementary Stage

PHOTO 21.11   The elementary trap.

Mature Stage

PHOTO 21.12   The mature trap.

Teaching Tips
Common Problems
- Failure to position the body directly in the path of the ball.
- Failure to keep the eyes fixed on the ball.
- Failure to "give" as the ball contacts the body.
- Failure to let the ball meet the body but causing the body to meet the ball.
- Inability to maintain body balance when trapping in unusual or awkward positions.

Recommended Strategies
- Begin with trapping activities involving the feet and legs (foot trap and single- and double-knee trap).
- Teach how to trap a rolled ball prior to an elevated ball.
- Stress eye contact with the ball throughout.
- Introduce trapping a tossed ball only after the concepts involved in trapping a ground ball are mastered.

- Use a foam ball, beachball, or partially inflated ball in the beginning.
- Foam balls work nicely for the introduction of trapping an elevated object.
- Work for control with the stomach and chest traps by teaching how to deflect the ball downward.
- Emphasize the importance of getting in the path of the ball, giving with it, and absorbing its force over as much surface area as possible.
- Do not introduce kicking and trapping drills until both partners are at the mature stage.
- During partner practice, prohibit the use of the kick unless foam rubber balls are used. If soccer balls are used, they will travel too high and may hit the partner in the face.
- Work for control and a "feel" for the ball.
- Use a soccer ball only after the principles of trapping are understood and mastered.

Concepts Children Should Know

Skill Concepts

- Get directly in the path of the ball.
- Keep your eyes on the ball.
- "Give" with the ball as it touches the body part.
- Deflect an elevated ball downward.
- Let the ball meet your body.
- The trapping pattern is basic to the sport of soccer and any other activity in which the feet, legs, or trunk are used to stop an object.

Movement Concepts

- You can use any part of your body to trap a ball except your hands and arms.
- You can trap a ball at different levels.
- You can trap objects other than balls.
- You and your partner can practice trapping and kicking together.
- Your control of the ball will influence the success of your trapping.

DRIBBLING AND BALL ROLLING

The fundamental movement patterns of dribbling is applied primarily to the sport activities of basketball, soccer, and speedball. It is unique in that it is of only limited direct value to most recreational and daily living skills. Dribbling does, however, provide the individual with important experiences in interrupting an object and requires the sophisticated interaction of sensory and motor processes at a precise moment. Therefore, when we view dribbling as a fundamental movement, we may also view it as an ideal task for helping the individual learn how to coordinate the use of the eyes with the hands.

Dribbling is a fundamental movement that involves receiving force from an object and immediately imparting force from that object in a downward (hand dribble) or ground-level, horizontal (foot dribble) direction without the use of an implement. The developmental sequence for hand dribbling appears to be (1) bouncing and catching, (2) bouncing and ineffective slapping at the ball, (3) basic dribbling with the ball in control of the child, (4) basic dribbling with the child in control of the ball, and (5) controlled dribbling with advanced abilities.

The movement pattern of ball rolling has had limited scientific study. Little is known, through controlled experimentation, about the emergence of ball-rolling abilities. Ball rolling is, however, a fundamental movement pattern that is often applied to the sport and recreational activities of bowling, curling, boccie, and shuffleboard. The basic ball-rolling pattern may be observed in underhand tossing, softball pitching, and life-saving rope-tossing techniques.

Dribbling

Verbal Description

Initial Stage

- Ball held with both hands.
- Hands placed on sides of the ball with palms facing each other.
- Downward thrusting action with both arms.
- Ball contacts surface close to body, may contact the foot.
- Great variation in height of the bounce.
- Repeated bounce-and-catch pattern.

Elementary Stage

- Ball held with both hands, one on top and the other near the bottom.
- Slight forward lean wih the ball brought to chest level.
- Downward thrust with top hand and arm.
- Force of downward thrust inconsistent.
- Hand slaps at ball for subsequent bounces.
- Wrist flexes and extends and palm of hand contacts ball on each bounce.
- Visually monitors ball.
- Limited control of the ball while dribbling.

Mature Stage

- Feet placed in narrow stride position with foot opposite dribbling hand forward.
- Slight forward trunk lean.
- Ball held waist high.
- Ball pushed toward ground with follow-through of arm, wrist, and fingers.
- Controlled force of downward thrust.

- Repeated contact and pushing action initiated from the finger tips.

- Visual monitoring not necessary.
- Controlled directional dribbling.

Visual Description
Initial Stage

PHOTO 21.13   The initial dribble.

Elementary Stage

PHOTO 21.14   The elementary dribble.

Mature Stage

PHOTO 21.15   The mature dribble.

Teaching Tips
Common Problems
- Slapping at the ball rather than pushing the ball.
- Ball controlling the child rather than child controlling the ball.
- Inability to remain in one place while dribbling.
- Inability to move about under control while dribbling.
- Inability to dribble with either hand.
- Poor visual monitoring of the ball.
- Insufficient follow-through on the push, causing the ball to fail to return to desired height.
- Inconsistent or inappropriate force applied to the ball.

Recommended Strategies
- Utilize a playground ball or other ball that does not require as much force in dribbling as a basketball.
- Use different-colored or striped balls in order to avoid blending of figure and ground.
- Work first for controlled bouncing and catching.
- Provide plenty of opportunities for practice in an atmosphere of exploration and experimentation.
- As skill develops, challenge the children with a variety of guided discovery activities that focus on being more aware of the process.
- Do not introduce low-level games, relays, or lead-up games until the mature stage of dribbling has been reasonably well achieved.
- Practice dribbling with either hand.
- Stress eye contact at the initial and elementary stage, but work for kinesthetic control in the mature stage.
- Structure experiences that require making modifications in the dribbling pattern congruent with the situation.
- As a last resort, physically manipulative the occasional child who is unable to coordinate the bounce of the ball with the push of the hand. Do this only as long as needed to get a "feel" for the timing of the ball.

Concepts Children Should Know
Skill Concepts
- Push the ball down.
- Your wrist controls the bounce.

- Use your fingertips.
- Follow through.
- Push the ball slightly forward.
- Keep the ball below your waist.

Movement Concepts
- You can bounce the ball at different levels.
- You can bounce the ball with different amounts of force.
- You can control the amount of time between bounces by using different amounts of force and bouncing at different levels.
- The rhythmical flow of the bounced ball is important for controlled dribbling.
- You can bounce many kinds and sizes of balls.
- The density of the ball will influence its bouncing capabilities.

Ball Rolling

Verbal Description
Initial Stage
- Straddle stance.
- Ball held with hands on the sides of the ball with palms facing each other.

- Acute bend at the waist with backward pendulum motions of the arms.
- Eyes monitor the ball.
- Forward arm swing and trunk lift with release of the ball.

Elementary Stage
- Stride stance.
- Ball held with one hand on bottom, the other on top.
- Backward arm swing without weight transfer to rear.
- Limited knee bend.
- Forward swing with limited follow-through.
- Ball release between knee and waist level.
- Eyes alternately monitor target and ball.

Mature Stage
- Stride stance.
- Ball held in hand corresponding to trailing leg.
- Slight hip rotation and lean forward of trunk.
- Pronounced knee bend.
- Forward swing with weight transference from near to forward foot.
- Release at knee level or below.
- Eyes on target throughout.

Visual Description
Initial Stage

PHOTO 21.16   The initial ball roll.

Elementary Stage

PHOTO 21.17   The elementary ball roll.

Mature Stage

PHOTO 21.18   The mature ball roll.

Teaching Tips
Common Problems
- Failure to transfer the body weight to the rear foot prior to moving it to the front foot.
- Placing the hands improperly on the ball.
- Releasing the ball too high, causing it to bounce.
- Releasing the ball at the wrong angle, causing it to veer to one side.
- Failure to execute a perfectly vertical swing of the arm.
- Poor follow-through, resulting in a weak roll.
- Failure to keep the eyes on the target.

- Failure to step forward with the appropriate foot.

Recommended Strategies
- Begin practice with a large ball prior to using a small ball.
- Do not stress accuracy during the initial experiences.
- Focus on proper body mechanics. Have the children roll the ball at the wall from greater and greater distances.
- After the basic pattern has been mastered, begin working for greater accuracy. Begin with large targets in order to promote success.
- Gradually increase both distance and accuracy requirements.
- Do not use a bowling ball or other heavy object when working on the body mechanics.
- Practice rolling from a stationary position prior to adding an approach.

Concepts Children Should Know
Skill Concepts
- Stand with one foot leading.
- Swing your arm straight back as you rock back on your rear foot.
- Let go of the ball when it is six to twelve inches in front of your leading foot.
- Follow through with your swing in the direction of the target.
- Keep your eyes on the ball.
- The rolling pattern is basic to the sports of bowling, curling, and boccie. It is also used in games such as pin guard and guard the castle.

Movement Concepts
- You can roll a ball at different speeds.
- The force you apply to the ball will control its speed.
- The coordinated use of your muscles as you roll the ball will influence the force of the ball and its speed.
- You can place your body in many different positions when rolling an object.
- You can roll a ball in many different directions and cause it to travel in different pathways.

- You can roll different-sized balls.
- You can devise many challenging game activities that use ball rolling.

STRIKING AND VOLLEYING

Striking is a fundamental movement pattern that may be performed in several different planes, with or without the use of an implement. Striking may involve contact with a stationary or moving object. However, even though the plane, implement, and nature of the object to be struck may differ in a number of ways, they are all governed by the same mechanical principles of movement. First, the amount of momentum generated depends on the length of the backswing, the number of muscles involved, and the proper sequential use of the muscles. Second, the object to be struck must be contacted at the precise moment that maximum speed of the swing has been reached. The striking implement must follow through toward the intended target. Fourth, the striking implement should make contact at a right angle to the object. Fifth, the implement should be held out and away from the body in order to achieve maximum momentum.

The forms that striking takes are many, and its application to sports is varied. The horizontal striking pattern is found in baseball. The vertical striking pattern is found in tennis, golf, volleyball, badminton, handball, and racquetball. Only the horizontal striking pattern with an implement is described here. You should, however, be quick to recognize that the description, teaching tips, and concepts children should know apply equally well to striking an object in other planes or without an implement.

Volleying is a fundamental striking-pattern skill that involves receiving force from an object and immediately imparting force to that object in a roughly vertical direction, as with volleyball or with heading and juggling in soccer. Volleying is characterized by the fact that it can be repeated more than once in the same sequence with the same ball. The developmental sequence for effective volleying is much like striking, beginning with ineffective, uncontrolled efforts, followed by gradual control and increased proficiency. Volleying involves the complex interaction of visual and motor processes.

It will be helpful to initiate striking and volleying activities with the use of balloons, beach balls, or other light objects that enable the individual to have a longer visual tracking period. The size and color of the ball may influence volleying and striking activities. Care should be taken to be sensitive to these possible influencing factors. The teacher should be ready to make adjustments in ball type, size, or color in order to maximize the child's success potential.

Horizontal Striking

Verbal Description
Initial Stage
- Motion is from back to front.
- Feet are stationary.
- Trunk faces direction of tossed ball.
- Elbow(s) are fully flexed.
- No trunk rotation.

Visual Description
Initial Stage

PHOTO 21.19   The initial horizontal strike.

- Force comes from extension of flexed joints in a downward plane.

Elementary Stage
- Trunk turned to side in anticipation of the tossed ball.
- Weight shifts to forward foot prior to ball contact.
- Combined trunk and hip rotation.
- Elbow(s) flexed at less acute angle.
- Force comes from extension of flexed joints. Trunk rotation and forward movement are in an oblique plane.

Mature Stage
- Trunk turned to side in anticipation of the tossed ball.
- Weight shifts to back foot.
- Hips rotate.
- Transfer of weight is in a contralateral pattern.
- Weight shift to the forward foot occurs while the implement is still moving backward.
- Striking occurs in a long, full arc in a horizontal pattern.
- Weight shifts to forward foot at contact.

Elementary Stage

PHOTO 21.20 The elementary horizontal strike.

Mature Stage

PHOTO 21.21 The mature horizontal strike.

Teaching Tips
Common Problems
- Failure to keep the eyes on the ball.
- Improper grip of the striking implement.
- Failure to adjust properly for the intended flight of the ball.
- Inability to sequence the required movements together in rapid succession in a coordinated manner.
- Poor backswing.
- "Chopping" swing.
- Restricted body rotation.
- Keeping the elbow too close to the body.
- "Topping" the ball.

- Failure to get in line with a moving ball prior to contact.

Recommended Strategies
- Follow a sequence of teaching that progresses from striking with the hand and other body parts to using short-handled implements and then long-handled implements.
- Utilize balloons and beach balls at the initial stages.
- Practice hitting stationary objects prior to moving objects.
- Work with striking large objects and then progress gradually to striking smaller objects.

- Remember that the color of the ball and the background against which it is being struck may have an influence on figure–ground perception.
- Develop an efficient horizontal striking pattern before concentrating on the vertical plane.
- Check frequently to see that the proper grip is maintained and the eyes are on the ball.
- Work for effective weight shifting, summation of forces, and a level swing.
- Stress making a "big swing." Be sure that the ball is contacted with the elbows extended and at the maximum velocity of the swing.
- Stress follow-through in the direction of the target.

Concepts Children Should Know
Skill Concepts
- Be sure that your hands are touching when you grip a baseball bat and that your right hand is on top of your left (right-hand pattern).
- Keep your eyes on the ball at all times.
- Always contact the ball at the point of complete arm extension.
- Shift your weight back and forward as you swing.
- Swing in a level fashion.
- Follow through.
- The striking pattern is used in many sport activities. Some sports use striking with the hand as the implement, such as handball and volleyball. Others, such as baseball, hockey, golf, tennis, and racquetball, use an implement.

Movement Concepts
- You can strike a ball with different amounts of force.
- You can make the ball go fast or slow.
- The sequential and rhythmical use of your muscles will affect the force of your swing and the speed of the ball.
- The ball can be struck at many different levels.

- The ball may be contacted in a horizontal or vertical plane.
- You can hit a ball in many different directions.
- Objects other than balls can be struck.
- You don't always need to use an implement to strike something. You can use your hand, your head, or you feet effectively.
- Striking a moving object is a complex task, requiring very precise coordination of your eyes and muscles.
- The success of your striking will be influenced by many factors, including the size, shape, and color of the ball, as well as the size and shape of the implement and the speed of the object.

Volleying

Verbal Description
Initial Stage
- Inability to accurately judge the path of the ball or balloon.
- Inability to get under the ball.
- Inability to contact the ball simultaneously with both hands.

Elementary Stage
- Failure to visually track the ball.
- Gets in line with the path of the ball.
- Slaps at ball.
- Action mainly from the hands and arms.
- Little lift with the legs or follow-through.
- Unable to control the direction or intended flight of the ball.
- Wrists relax and ball often travels backward.

Mature Stage
- Gets under the ball.
- Good contact with both hands.
- Contact with fingertips.
- Wrists are stiff upon contact but extend as the arms follow through.

- Good summation of forces and utilization of the arms and legs.

- Able to control the direction and intended flight of the ball.

Visual Description
Initial Stage

PHOTO 21.22   The initial volley.

Elementary Stage

PHOTO 21.23   The elementary volley.

Mature Stage

PHOTO 21.24   The mature volley.

Teaching Tips
Common Problems
- Failure to keep the eyes on the ball.
- Inability to accurately judge the flight of the ball and to time the movements of the body properly.
- Failure to keep the fingers and wrists stiff.
- Failure to extend all of the joints upon contacting the ball (lack of follow-through).

- Inability to contact the ball simultaneously with both hands.
- Slapping at the ball.
- Poor positioning of the body under the ball.

Recommended Strategies
- Work for good positioning under the ball.
- Begin using balloons and progress to beachballs or foam balls prior to using a regulation volleyball.

- When using a volleyball, allow an intermediate bounce prior to contact if necessary.
- Teach the children to make a "window," with the thumbs and index fingers nearly touching.
- Emphasize looking through the window when contacting the ball.
- Work for good force production by stressing the importance of extending at the ankles, knees, hips, and shoulders upon contact.

Concepts Children Should Know
Skill Concepts
- Get into position directly beneath the ball.
- Watch the flight of the ball between the opening formed by your two hands.
- Extend the arms and legs as the ball touches your fingertips.
- Keep the fingers and wrists stiff throughout.
- Follow through in the direction that the ball is to go.
- Keep your eyes on the ball.
- Volleying is a striking pattern that is used in many games and in the sport of volleyball.

Movement Concepts
- You can vary your body position when you control the ball.
- You can alter the level of your body.
- You can make changes in the force that you apply to the ball.
- The coordinated contact of the ball will be influenced by how well all of your body works together.
- You can give direction to the ball.
- You can control the distance that the ball travels.
- You can volley many different objects.

- You can play volleying games with other people.

SKILL DEVELOPMENT ACTIVITIES

Prior to selecting movement activities for inclusion in the lesson, it is necessary to determine the typical stage of motor development displayed by the class. Knowing the stage of motor development will in turn provide cues to their level of movement skill learning. With this important information, it is now possible to determine whether the lesson should focus on exploratory, guided discovery, skill application, or skill refinement activities.

Exploratory Activities

Exploratory activities provide children at the initial or elementary stage an opportunity to get an idea of how their body can move, where it can move, and how it moves in relation to other objects. The movement elements of effort, space, and relationships should be explored in order to develop a more complete idea of one's manipulative movement potential. Tables 21.1 through 21.8 provide a sampling of exploratory activities that can be used as movement challenges for children at the beginning level of manipulative skills learned. These challenges should first be presented separately. They may, however, be combined into an infinite variety of challenges after the basic elements of the skill have been mastered.

TABLE 21.1   Exploratory Activity Ideas for Throwing

Can your throw—

Effort	Space	Relationships
Force —as soft as you can? —as hard as you can? —so that the ball makes a loud noise when it hits the wall? —alternating hard and soft throws? —stepping forward with a loud noise? *Time* —as slowly as you can? —as fast as you can? —moving your throwing arms as fast as you can? —and twist your body (hips) as fast as possible? *Flow* —using as little movement as possible? —using as much of your body as possible? —like a robot? —like plastic person? —without using your legs? —without using your trunk? —using only one other part of your body besides your throwing arm? —as smoothly as you can?	*Level* —up high? —down low? —as low as you can? —at the wall as high as you can? —at high-, low-, and medium-height targets? —alternating high and low throws? *Direction* —forward? —backward? —to the side? —at an angle? *Range* —as far as you can? —as near as you can? —with your right hand? —with your left hand? —with both hands? —overhand? —underhand? —sidearm? —with your arm going through short and long ranges of motion?	*Objects* —a wiffle ball? —a fluff ball? —a softball? —a baseball? —a football? —a newspaper ball? —a playground ball? —at a target? —into the bucket? —over the rope? —from inside a hoop or inner tube? *People* —to a partner? —as far as your partner? —as hard/soft as your partner? —the same way as your partner? **Combinations** Initial experiences should focus on exploring the various aspects of effort, space, and relationships in isolation prior to structuring experiences involving combinations such as: Can you and your partner find three different ways to throw at the target from a far distance?

TABLE 21.2   Exploratory Activity Ideas for Catching

Can you catch—

Effort	Space	Relationships
Force	*Level*	*Objects*
—with your arms in different positions?	—a ball tossed at a low level?	—a playground ball?
—without making a sound with your hands?	—a ball tossed at waist level?	—a small ball?
—as loudly as you can?	—a ball tossed at a high level?	—a large ball?
—keeping your arms straight?	—at many different levels?	—a beanbag?
—keeping your arms bent?	—from a sitting position?	—five different objects?
	—from a lying-down position?	—five different types of balls?
Time	—in many different positions?	
—and go with the ball?		*People*
—without going with the ball?	*Direction*	—a ball while holding both hands with a partner?
—the ball as quickly as you can?	—a ball tossed from in front of you?	—while holding one hand with a partner?
—after waiting for he ball as long as you can?	—a ball tossed from an angle?	
Flow	—a ball tossed from the side?	**Combinations**
—a ball as smoothly as you can?	—a ball coming down from above?	Exploratory experiences should begin with these and other
—with varying degrees of smoothness?	—a tossed ball coming at you from different directions?	activities, first in isolation. Later, combinations of effort, space, and
	Range	relationships should be added. For example: Can you catch a self-
	—using different body parts?	tossed ball at waist level while
	—from different positions?	jumping in the air?
	—with one eye closed?	
	—with both eyes closed?	

TABLE 21.3   Exploratory Activity Ideas for Kicking

Can you kick the ball—

Effort	Space	Relationships
Force —as hard as you can? —as soft as you can? —with a forceful leg swing but a light hit? —with a lazy leg swing but a forceful hit?	*Level* —high? —low? —as high as you can? —so it stays on the ground? —so it doesn't go higher than your waist?	*Objects* —and hit the wall? —and hit a big target? —and hit a small target? —over the goal? —into the goal? —under the stretched rope? —through the chair legs? —around the cones using several controlled kicks?
Time —so it goes fast? —so it goes very slowly? —from here so it hits the wall in five seconds? —from here so it hits the wall in two seconds? —from here and turn around before it hits the wall? —and touch the floor before it hits the wall?	*Direction* —forward? —backward? —sideways? —diagonally? —alternating left and right feet (dribbling)?	*People* —to a partner? —to a partner while walking (passing)? —at different levels to a partner? —in different directions to a partner? —with different amounts of force to a partner? —at different speeds to a partner?
Flow —with a big leg swing? —with no knee bend? —without using your arms? —while swinging *both* arms back? —while swinging both arms forward? —with no follow-through? —with no backswing?	*Range* —as far as you can? —as near as you can? —with your feet wide apart? —with your body in different positions? —with your opposite foot?	**Combinations** Numerous exploratory activities that combine elements of effort, space, and relationships can be explored after first trying them in isolation. For example: Can you find ways to kick the ball with different amounts of force, at different levels, with your partner?

TABLE 21.4 Exploratory Activity Ideas for Trapping

Can you trap—		
Effort	**Space**	**Relationships**
Force	*Level*	*Objects*
—a ball that is rolled slowly toward you?	—a ball that is rolling toward you?	—a beanbag?
—a ball that is tossed lightly at you?	—a ball that is rolling off to one side?	—a beachball?
—a ball that is rolled rapidly toward you?	—a ball at waist level?	—a fleeceball?
—a ball that is tossed forcefully at you (use a fleeceball)?	—a ball at stomach level?	—a playground ball?
	—a ball at chest level?	—different size balls?
Time		—a soccer ball?
—in slow motion?	*Direction*	
—a fast-moving ball?	—a ball moving toward you?	*People*
—a slow-moving ball?	—a ball moving away from you?	—a ball and kick it back to your partner?
	—a ball moving in front of you?	—a ball and have your partner count the number of different ways you can do it?
Flow	—a ball moving to one side?	
—a ball and "give" with the ball?	*Range*	
—a ball without "giving" with the ball?	—a ball with your foot?	**Combinations**
	—a ball with your shin?	Combinations of effort, space, and relationships can be devised and explored after a variety of isolated activities are explored. For example: Experiment with how much you must "give" with your body when trapping five different types of balls.
	—a ball with your stomach?	
	—a ball with your chest?	
	—a ball with either foot?	
	—a ball with a large body part?	
	—a ball with a small body part?	

TABLE 21.5   Exploratory Activity Ideas for Dribbling

Can you bounce (or dribble) the ball—

Effort	Space	Relationships
Force —as hard as you can? —as soft as you can? —changing from hard to soft? *Flow* —and catch it? —repeatedly after catching it repeatedly? —without catching it? (dribbling) *Time* —as fast as you can? —as slow as you can? —alternating fast and slow? —and allow as much time as you can between bounces? —as many times as you can until I say "stop"?	*Level* —at knee level? —at waist level? —at leg level? —higher than your head? —lower than your knees? —and change levels with each bounce? *Direction* —in front of you? —to one side? —behind you? —in different pathways? —in a straight line? —in a circle? —in a curved line? —in a zigzag line? *Range* —in your space? —hitting the same spot each time? —while moving around the room? —as far away from you as you can? —as close to you as you can? —with other body parts? —with your other hand?	*Objects* —around the chairs? —under the outstretched rope? —over the outstretched rope? —while walking close to the wall? —if it is a basketball? —if it is a playground ball? —and notice any difference with different types of balls? *People* —to your partner? —alternating with a partner? —in time to your partner's bounce? —and each move away and back together with the same number of bounces? **Combinations** As the individual gradually gains control of the ball rather than the ball controlling him or her, add various combinations of effort, space, and/or relationships. For example: Can you dribble the ball at waist level but to one side of your body as you go around the field?

TABLE 21.6 Exploratory Activity Ideas for Ball Rolling

Can you roll the ball—

Effort	Space	Relationships
Force	*Level*	*Objects*
—softly?	—while lying on the floor?	—no matter what size it is?
—as hard as you can?	—from your knees?	—on the balance beam?
	—from a sitting position?	—on a line?
Time		—between the boxes?
—as slowly as possible?	*Direction*	—into the can?
—as fast as you can?	—in a straight line?	—through the tube?
	—so that it curves?	—under a wicket?
Flow		—at the pins?
—using your arms only?	*Range*	
—using only one side of	—around yourself?	*People*
your body?	—with your other hand?	—to a partner?
—smoothly?	—as far as you can?	—alternating back and forth?
—like a robot?	—as accurately as you can?	—mirroring your partner?
—like a champion bowler?	—without moving off the line?	—shadowing your partner?
	—with an approach?	

Combinations

Numerous combinations of effort, space, and relationships related to rolling are possible as well as combinations with other fundamental movements. For example: Can you roll the ball with differing amounts of force? Can you roll the ball at a low level with a partner?

TABLE 21.7   Exploratory Activity Ideas for Striking the Ball

Can you strike the ball (balloon, beachball)—

Effort	Space	Relationships
Force —as hard as you can? —as soft as you can? —so it makes a loud noise? —like a strong monster? —squarely?	*Level* —so it travels at different levels? —with your body at different levels? —from a high level to a low level? —from a low level to a high level?	*Objects* —over the rope? —under the rope? —through the chairs? —around the chair? —into the bucket? —using different-sized objects? —using objects with different shapes? —with different implements?
Flow —limply? —with jerky movements? —with smooth movements?	*Direction* —in a straight line? —with a level swing? —up? —down? —forward? —backward? —in different pathways?	*People* —to a partner? —as your partner does?
Time —slowly? —quickly? —firmly?	*Range* —using different body parts? —and keep it in your space? —with your other hand? —from the other side? —with a wide base? —with a narrow base?	**Combinations** After exploring the many variations of striking in isolation, it will be helpful to combine various aspects of effort, space, and relationships. For example: Can you hit the balloon as hard as you can so that it travels at a low level to a partner?

TABLE 21.8 Exploratory Activity Ideas for Volleying the Ball

Can you volley the ball—

Effort	Space	Relationships
Force —very hard? —very softly? —high? —low? *Flow* —alternating hard and soft volleys? —but relax your fingers? —but tense your fingers? —and give with the ball? —without giving with the ball? *Time* —as many times as you can until I say "stop"? —as few times as you can in 30 seconds?	*Level* —when you are in different positions? —from a seated position? —from a kneeling position? —without it going above your head? —with it going as high as possible? *Direction* —forward? —backward? —to the side? —in a circle? *Range* —and have it drop in your personal space? —and have it drop outside your space? —from a position directly under it? —from a position off to one side?	*Objects* —if it is a beach ball? —if it is a balloon? —if it is a large ball? —if it is a small ball? —if it is a volleyball? —over the rope? —over the net? —with different body parts? —with your head (heading)? —with your knees (juggling)? *People* —to a partner? —tossed by a partner? —back and forth to a partner? **Combinations** Simple exploratory activities with light objects (balloons and beachballs) are essential prior to using volleyballs. Combine activities only after reasonable control has developed. For example: Can you find different ways to volley the ball to your partner so that he or she can volley it back at different levels?

Guided Discovery Activities

The sampling of guided discovery activities presented in Tables 21.9 through 21.16 is intended to provide children with a variety of activities designed to lead them to mature manipulative patterns of movement. This guided approach permits children to learn more about the skill and how their body should move. Guided discovery activities permit children at the beginning level of skill-learning opportunities to practice the skill and to focus on its use in a wide variety of movement situations.

TABLE 21.9 Guided Discovery Activity Ideas for Throwing

Throwing		
	1.	First explore the movement variations of throwing.
	2.	Now begin to place limitations on the response possibilities to the movement challenges that you present. (You may want to use a beanbag rather than a ball for these activities in order to promote a minimum of confusion when retrieving the thrown objects.) For example:
General		• Stand about a body length from the wall and throw your beanbag at it. Now try the same thing from here (15–20 feet). Try it again from here (30–50 feet). Do you have to do anything different in order to hit the wall each time? Why?
Leg action		• Experiment with different ways of using your legs as you throw. Try throwing with your feet together (initial stage). Now try it by stepping out on the foot on the same side as your throwing arm (elementary). Try it this time by stepping out on the opposite foot (mature). Did you notice any difference in how far the ball went? Which way does a baseball player use? Why?
Trunk action		• Try throwing without twisting your trunk. Now try it with twisting. Experiment with different combinations of twisting your trunk and using your legs. Now show me the best combination. Can you stand facing this wall but throw the ball at the wall to your left? Try it first without bringing your hips around. Now try it bringing your hips around to the left (for right-hand throw). Now try it with stepping out on your left foot and turning to your left.
Arm action		• Experiment with different ways of using your arms when you throw. Can you find three different arm patterns you can use when throwing? Let's work on the overhand throw. Throw the ball overhand without rotating your hips. Try it while rotating your hips. Which way caused the ball to go the farthest? Throw the ball so that it hits high on the wall. Throw it now so that it hits the wall as hard as possible. Now throw the ball as far as you can. Now throw far but over the outstretched rope (6–8 feet high).
Total		• Let's see if we can put it all together. Try throwing while stepping forward on the opposite foot and turning your trunk while your arm moves forward. Practice throwing with a partner. Now pretend that it is a hot potato that you must throw back as fast as you can. What happens when you try to get rid of the ball fast? Some of you went back to the elementary level instead of throwing at the mature level. Why? Will it help to practice?
	3.	After the mature throwing pattern has been reasonably well mastered in practice sessions, begin to combine it with other activities. Apply it to numerous situations in order to make it more automatic.
		• Introduce basic throwing and catching games that will provide plenty of opportunities for practice.
		• Throw different objects.
		• Throw distances that encourage mature use of the pattern.
		• Throw for distance.
		• Throw at a stationary target.
		• Throw at a moving target.
		• Combine distance and accuracy throwing.

TABLE 21.10   Guided Discovery Activity Ideas for Catching

Catching	
	1. First explore the movement variations of catching.
	2. Then begin to place limitations on the response possibilities to the movement challenges you present. You may find it helpful to experiment with brightly colored balls and different backgrounds. Also, it will be helpful to catch nonthreatening objects such as a fleeceball or beachball. Practice with catching different-sized objects is also important. The following are a few examples of movement challenges that will help lead children to the mature stage of catching:
General	• Experiment with catching a lightly tossed ball. How many ways can you catch the ball? Try experimenting with different arm positions. Now try catching the ball without it touching your body. Can you catch the ball in your hands only?
Arm action	• What should your arms do when they catch a ball? Do they stay straight? Do they stay bent as if you were making a basket, or are they first straight and then do they bend as you catch the ball? Why do they give (bend) when you catch the ball? Try catching a softly thrown ball and a ball thrown hard. Is there any difference in how much your arms give as you catch? Why?
Hand action	• Experiment with different ways of holding your hands when you catch. Is there a difference in how you place them for a high ball and for a low ball? Can you catch a low ball with your little fingers together, side by side? Now try it with your hands facing each other. Are there times when you want to use one ball-catching method and times when you use another? Let's try the same experiment while catching a ball that is above the waist.
Eyes	• We all know it's best to catch a ball with our eyes open and looking at the ball, but sometimes we close our eyes or turn our head away. Why do you think some people do that? What are some things we can do to help people look at the ball and not turn away? Let's play catch with a partner and see if we can find some ways to help our partner if he or she has this problem. Should we use a large ball or small ball? Why? Should we tell them we are going to toss the ball or not? Why? Let's try each and see what works best. Find what works best for your partner and practice until he or she feels comfortable. Then begin to try out different size balls, speeds, and heights.
	3. After the mature catching pattern has been mastered in a structured environment, you will want to provide experiences that permit further practice and use of catching in various situations. The attempt now should be to help make the mature pattern more automatic and adaptable to a variety of backgrounds, ball sizes, colors, objects, speeds, and positions in relationship to the body. • Introduce basic catching and throwing games. • Stress variations in ball size and hardness. • Try fielding grounders, fly balls, and balls not directly in line with the body.

TABLE 21.11   Guided Discovery Activity Ideas for Kicking

Kicking	
	1. First explore the movement variations of kicking.
	2. Then begin to place limitations on the response possibilities to the movement challenges you present. For example:
Leg action	• Try kicking the ball without bending your leg. Now bend first at your kicking knee, then kick the ball. Which way caused the ball to go farther? Which felt best?
	• Try kicking the ball as far as you can, using different amounts of knee bend but no follow-through (that is, stopping your leg as soon as you contact the ball). Now try the same thing, but follow all the way through. Which amount of knee bend works best? Does a follow-through on your kick help the ball go farther?
	• Try different ways of approaching the ball before you kick it, using a full bend at the knee of your kicking leg and extending at the hip. Does the ball go farther after a kick from standing still, or does it help to take a step or two? Why? Let's practice kicking as far as we can, using a step to the ball.
Trunk action	• Do you think it will help if you move your trunk backward when you kick the ball? Try it. Now keep your body straight and then try leaning far forward. Do you notice any differences? Let's try to kick the ball as far as we can and practice leaning back a little as we make contact with the ball.
Arm action	• What do you do with your arms when you kick the ball? Watch your partner. What does she or he do? Experiment with different arm positions as you kick. Which way works best? Let's practice kicking as hard as we can and swing our arms so the arm opposite our kicking leg is swung forward while the other moves backward.
Total	• Try kicking the ball as far as you can and as hard as you can. Now try kicking at the target (a suspended hula hoop works fine). Did you notice any changes in how you kick when you kick for accuracy rather than distance?
	• Try kicking a rolling ball. Try kicking while on the run. Experiment with kicking the ball, but first tell your partner if it will be a high, medium, low, or ground kick. Can you control the level of your kick? What must you do to control the level? Show me. Try using different parts of your foot when you kick. Use your toe, your instep, the inside of your foot. What differences do you notice in level, in speed, in accuracy, in distance?
	3. After a mature kicking pattern has been reasonably well mastered, it is important to combine it with other activities in order to reinforce the pattern and make it more automatic.
	• Make quick kicks.
	• Kick at a stationary target.
	• Kick at a moving target.
	• Kick at a target from a run.
	• Kick for control in high, low, and ground-level kicks.
	• Kick back and forth to a partner while moving in the same direction (passing).
	• Maneuver and kick at a target against a defense.
	• Play kicking relays.
	• Play kicking games.

TABLE 21.12 Guided Discovery Activity Ideas for Trapping

Trapping		

General		
	1.	First explore several of the movement variations of trapping. Remember that a primary purpose of these exploratory activities is to lead the child to a better understanding of the movement concepts of effort, space, and relationships as applied to trapping an object.
	2.	Then begin to place limitations on the response possibilities to the movement challenges that you present. Remember that your reason for doing this is so that you may lead the individual to the mature pattern of movement through his or her own discovery of the solution to the movement problems that you structure. Trapping, for example, may be performed in a variety of ways. There are the foot trap, knee trap, stomach trap, and chest trap. Although each utilizes a different part of the body to intercept and stop the oncoming object, all incorporate the same principles of movement, namely (1) absorbing the force of the ball over the greatest surface area possible and (2) absorbing the force of the ball over the greatest distance required for successful trapping. The following are examples of several movement challenges to present that help bring out these movement principles.

- Try to stop a rolling ball with your feet. What happens to the ball when you let it hit your feet without "giving" when it hits? Why does this happen? How can you cause the ball to stop right after it hits your feet? What do you have to do?

- Let's try the same thing with the ball being tossed at your legs (stomach, chest, etc.). What must you do each time in order to get the ball to drop and stop in front of you? Try different ideas, then show me the one that works best for you. Did you notice how you had to "give" with the ball to get it to stop?

- Do you have to give with the ball as much if the ball is traveling slowly as when it is traveling fast? Why? Show me how you give with the ball when it is coming fast and then when it is coming slowly.

- Is it best to try trapping the ball with a small body part or a large body part? Try both ways. Which works best? Why?

- If a ball is traveling fast, would you want to give with the ball over a longer distance or a shorter distance? How about over a large part of your body or over a small part? Experiment with the different ways of trapping and let me know which is best.

3. After trapping has been reasonably well mastered in controlled guided discovery lessons, you will find it helpful to structure experiences that demand greater control and rapid decision making. For example:

- Trap a ball kicked by a partner, then kick it back.
- Trap a ball coming from different directions and levels and at different speeds.
- Play games and take part in relay races involving kicking and trapping.

TABLE 21.13   Guided Discovery Activity Ideas for Dribbling

Dribbling	
General	1. First explore several of the movement variations of dribbling. 2. Then begin to place limitations on the response possibilities to the movement challenges you present. For example: • Try dribbling your ball in your own space with your feet together, legs straight, and standing straight. How does it feel? Now try it several different ways. Which way feels best? Why?
Trunk action	• When you dribble the ball in place, what do you do with your feet? Your trunk? Is it easier to control the ball in one place standing straight or bent slightly forward at the waist? Try both. Which was best? Why?
Leg action	• Experiment with different foot positions when you dribble in place. Are there any differences? Why? • Try moving about the room while dribbling the ball. Is it easier or harder than when you are standing in your space? Why is it harder? • Listen to my commands and move only in the direction I call out. Can you do it? Why is this hard for some people and easier for others? All those who are "experts" try the same thing but use your opposite hand to dribble the ball. Did you "experts" notice any difference in how well you did? Why?
Arm and hand action	• Experiment with using your hand and arm in different ways as you dribble the ball. What do we do with our fingers, our wrist, and our arms when we dribble the ball? Show me. Why do we push the ball down rather than slapping at it? Can you keep your wrist stiff and dribble the ball off your fingertips? Try it. • Try to stay in your own space, dribbling the ball off your fingertips with a stiff wrist and good follow-through. Now try it with slapping at the ball. Which way gives you the most control? Show me. Why?
Eyes	• Look at the ball as you dribble. Now try the same thing looking up here at me. Try it now with your eyes closed. Which was easiest? Which was hardest? When you are playing basketball, is it best to look at the ball as you dribble or is it better to be looking where you are going? Let's try to dribble without looking at the ball.
General	• Let's practice dribbling with the opposite hand. Now let's alternate dribbling first with one hand, then the other. Is it harder with one hand than the other? Why? • See if you can dribble around an object changing hands each time around. Now change hands each time you change direction. 3. After the mature dribbling pattern has been fairly well mastered, it should be combined with other activities in order to reinforce the pattern and make it more automatic. • Dribble around obstacles. • Dribble the ball while touching and changing hands, level, and/or the direction of the dribble. • Keep the ball away from an opponent while dribbling.

TABLE 21.14   Guided Discovery Activity Ideas for Ball Rolling

Ball Rolling		
	1.	First explore several of the numerous variations of rolling.
	2.	Then begin to place limitations on the responsibilities to the movement challenges you present. Focus on how the body should move and why when rolling an object. For example:
General		• Let's experiment with different ways of rolling the ball. How many ways can you find? Show me.
		• What should we do if we want the ball to go as fast as possible? Show me. Why?
		• What can you do to make the ball go as straight as possible?
		• If you want the ball to go both fast and straight, how would you roll it? Why?
Arm action		• Try rolling the ball from between your legs. Now try placing it by your side and rolling. Which way allows the ball to go the fastest? Which is the most accurate? Why?
		• What happens when you use a small ball and then a large ball? Which ball will go fastest? Which ball travels more accurately? Try both, then tell me.
Leg action		• Why do you think bowlers bowl like this (demonstrate)? Try doing different things with your legs as you roll the ball. Try standing with your feet together and your knees locked. Does it work well? What happened to the ball? Why did it bounce before it began to roll?
		• See what you can do to prevent the ball from bouncing as it is rolled. Can you do anything with your trunk? Can you do anything with your legs that will help? Show me. Why does it help to bend forward and step out on the leg opposite the ball? Let's all try it and see how straight we can roll our ball.
	3.	After a mature ball-rolling pattern has been reasonably well mastered, it is time to begin focusing on accuracy and increasing the distance to the target. A variety of low-level games and lead-up activities to bowling can be incorporated at this point. You will also want, however, to combine rolling with a variety of other movements in order to reinforce the proper pattern and make it more automatic. For example:
		• Roll different-sized balls.
		• Roll the balls on different surfaces.
		• Try to control the direction of a rolled ball.

TABLE 21.15   Guided Discovery Activity Ideas for Striking

Striking	
	1. First explore several of the numerous variations of striking. Emphasis here should be on getting used to the idea of striking in terms of effort, space, and the ball's relationship to objects and people.
	2. Then begin to place limitations on the response possibilities to the movement challenges you present. For example:
Arm action	• Try hitting the ball off the tee using your hand, a paddle, a bat. Which way caused the ball to go the farthest? Why?
	• Now try using a bat, but keep your arms bent. Then try it with your arms straight when the bat hits the ball. Did you notice a difference? Which works best and why?
	• See if you can find different ways to swing your bat. Experiment with different ways of holding the bat. Can anyone tell me the best way to hold the bat and the best way to swing it if I want what I'm hitting to go as far as possible?
	• Now we want to have our right hand on top (right-handed batter) and our left on the bottom, and we want our swing to be level. Let's try it.
Leg action	• Let's try standing in different ways when we strike the ball. Try to find five ways to stand as you hit the ball off the tee. Which helps the ball go the farthest? Show me.
	• Now let's see what we can do with our feet when we hit the ball. Try standing with your feet together, wide apart, and less apart. Which feels best?
	• Will it help to step out as we swing at the ball? Try it. Why do you think that it helps?
General	• Try hitting the balloon with your hand, a ping pong paddle, a wiffle ball bat. Which was easiest? Hardest? Why?
	• Now try to hit the beachball the same way—first with your hand, then a ping pong paddle, then a bat. Which was easiest? Hardest? Why?
	• Let's practice hitting a suspended ball. Can you hit it as it is swung to you? Can you tell me what you need to do with your arms, your trunk, and your legs when you strike the ball? Do we do each separately, or do we try to put them together smoothly? Why?
	3. After a mature striking pattern has been reasonably well mastered, you will want to begin practicing hitting a tossed ball. In order to maximize skill development, you may want to:
	• Use a large ball, then gradually work down to a small ball.
	• Use an oversized bat prior to using a regulation bat.
	• Use a bat that is slightly shorter or have the child "choke up" on the bat.
	• Toss the ball slowly, then gradually increase its speed.
	• Experiment with different pitching distances.
	• Experiment with different ball colors and backgrounds.
	• Incorporate the striking pattern into a variety of low-level and lead-up games.

TABLE 21.16   Guided Discovery Activity Ideas for Volleying

Volleying		
General	1.	First explore several of the movement variations of volleying, taking care to use an object appropriate to the ability of the individual.
	2.	Then begin to place limitations on the response possibilities to the questions you ask. Focus on eliciting the mature volleying pattern, first using a balloon, then a beachball, and finally a volleyball. In order to aid children with tracking and accurately interrupting the ball, you may permit an intermediate bounce of the ball before it is actually volleyed in the following activities: • Can you hit the balloon, beachball, etc. into the air so that it comes right back to you? Try hitting it several times in a row, staying in your own space. What must you do to be sure that the ball comes back to you? What about your hands? Do you have more control with one or both hands?
Hand and arm action		• Try volleying your balloon with both hands as many times as you can. What must you do to keep the ball up over your head? Show me. What do you do with your hands and fingers and wrists when you volley the ball? • Try volleying a beachball or volleyball. Is it easier or harder than the balloon? Why? • Use your volleyball to volley with, but let it bounce once before you try hitting it again. Is that easier than before? Why? • Let's try volleying different-sized balls. Is there any difference? Can you use two hands as easily with a small ball?
Foot and leg action		• Experiment with different foot positions as you volley. Now try it with your knees locked, with them apart, with them bent slightly. Which works best?
	3.	Considerable time will need to be spent with discovery activities in order to help the children focus on control of the object. Intercepting a ball and volleying or striking it are extremely complicated tasks requiring sophisticated interaction of visual and motor processes and exact timing. Be patient in your approach and be sure to utilize objects and activities that permit the beginner ample opportunity to track the ball visually prior to intercepting it. Once the volleying pattern has been mastered to a reasonable degree and the individual is exhibiting mature control of the ball, it will be wise to focus on a combination of activities that reinforce the correct pattern and make it more automatic. • Volley the ball to different heights. • Volley from different body levels. • Volley continuously without an intermediate bounce. • Volley against a wall. • Volley with a partner. • Volley with a group. • Volley the ball in a direction different than that from which it came.

Chapter 42

Skill Application Activities

Once the mature stage has been attained in a manipulative skill, it is appropriate to begin focusing on skill application activities. The application of manipulative skills to a variety of game, rhythm, and self-testing activities permits practice and refinement of manipulative skills under dynamic conditions in a constantly changing environment. Overlearning of manipulative skills and practice in a variety of situations are important in order to insure that the mature patterns of movement can be performed consistently.

The following chapters contain several manipulative skill application ideas that are appropriate for elementary school children:

Chapter 31   Low Level Game Activities
Chapter 32   Relay Activities
Chapter 33   Lead-Up Game Activities
Chapter 37   Singing Rhythmic Activities
Chapter 41   Perceptual–Motor Activities
Chapter 42   Hand Apparatus Activities

ASSESSING PROGRESS

It is important to informally assess children at the beginning of a manipulative skill theme and again at the end. Once the childrens' entry level of ability is known, it is a relatively easy matter to determine the types of activities to include in the lesson. The sample assessment charts located in Chapter 19 (Tables 19.1 and 19.2) can be applied to manipulative skills. These charts are a practical means for recording individual and group progress.

Fundamental manipulative skills may also be informally assessed through a self-question chart similar to the one depicted in Table 21.17. You should be able to answer ''yes'' to each of the questions. If you cannot, modification in your lessons is in order. Subsequent lessons will need to be modified to more closely fit the specific needs of the individual, group, or class.

TABLE 21.17   Self-question Chart for Fundamental Manipulative Skill Development

Throwing	Yes	No	Comments
1. Does the child throw consistently with a preferred hand?			
2. Is the child able to control the trajectory of the ball?			
3. Does the child utilize arm and leg opposition?			
4. Is there definite hip rotation?			
5. Is there efficient summation of forces in use of the arms, trunk, and legs?			
6. Is there noticeable improvement in throwing ability?			

Catching	Yes	No	Comments
1. Does the child maintain eye contact with the ball throughout?			
2. Is the child able to adjust easily to a ball thrown at different levels?			
3. Is the child able to adjust easily to a ball thrown at different speeds?			
4. Are proper adjustments made in the arm and hand action for large and small balls?			
5. Is the catching action smooth, coordinated, and in good control?			
6. Is there observable improvement in catching abilities?			

TABLE 21.17   (*continued*)

Kicking	Yes	No	Comments
1. Does the child make consistent contact with a stationary ball?			
2. Can the child make good contact with the ball from an approach?			
3. Can the child control the direction, level, and distance of his or her kick?			
4. Is there an acute bend at the knee and backward extension at the hip when the child is kicking for distance?			
5. Is the entire trunk and the arms brought into play for a forceful kick?			
6. Can the child consistently kick a moving ball?			
7. Is there noticeable improvement in the kicking pattern?			

Trapping	Yes	No	Comments
1. Can the child trap a rolled ball?			
2. Can the child trap a tossed ball?			
3. Does the child make easy adjustments for trapping balls traveling at different speeds?			
4. Does the child make adjustments for the surface area used to trap the ball based on the speed of the ball?			
5. Are the movements of the child fluid and in control?			
6. Is there observable improvement in trapping abilities?			

Striking	Yes	No	Comments
1. Can the child strike a balloon with good control (does the child control the balloon or does the balloon control the child)?			
2. Can the child strike a ball off a batting tee?			
3. Does the child use a level horizontal swing?			
4. Does the child grip the implement properly?			
5. Is the stance appropriate for the task?			
6. Does the child show evidence of proper summation of forces?			
7. Is there observable improvement?			

Volleying	Yes	No	Comments
1. Can the child volley a balloon repeatedly with good control?			
2. Can the child volley a beachball with good control?			
3. Can the child volley and remain in his or her own space?			
4. Can the child control the direction of the volley?			
5. Can the child volley a ball that has been permitted to bounce one time?			
6. Does the child exhibit controlled use of the fingers, hands, and arms?			
7. Does the child utilize an efficient summation of forces upon contact?			
8. Does the child maintain eye contact throughout?			
9. Is there observable improvement?			

(*continued*)

TABLE 21.17   *(continued)*

Dribbling	Yes	No	Comments
1. Is the child in control of the ball?			
2. Is the child able to dribble in her or his own space?			
3. Can the child dribble while moving about the room?			
4. Can the child dribble the ball without stopping to catch it?			
5. Does the child exhibit proper use of the fingers, wrist, and arm while dribbling?			
6. Is the trunk bent forward slightly while dribbling?			
7. Is the action smooth and rhythmical?			
8. Can the child vary the height and direction of the ball at will?			
9. Can the child dribble with either hand?			
10. Is there observable improvement in the ability to dribble with control?			

Ball Rolling	Yes	No	Comments
1. Does the child use a rolling pattern to one side of the body?			
2. Can the child make adjustments for different size balls?			
3. Does the child adjust to the distance and accuracy required?			
4. Does the child exhibit a good backswing?			
5. Is there sufficient follow-through?			
6. Can the child control the pathway of the ball?			
7. Is there observable improvement?			

SUGGESTED READING

Capon, J. (1975). *Ball, rope, hoop activities.* Belmont, CA: Fearon–Pitman.

Capon, J. (1975). *Bean bag, rhythm stick activities.* Belmont, CA: Fearon–Pitman.

Gallahue, D. L. (1982). *Understanding motor development in children.* New York: Wiley.

Roberton, M. A., and Halverson, L. E. (1984). *Developing children—their changing movement.* Philadelphia: Lea & Febiger.

Wickstrom, R. L. (1983). *Fundamental motor patterns.* Philadelphia: Lea & Febiger.

CHAPTER 22

FUNDAMENTAL STABILITY SKILLS

Stability represents the most basic of the three categories of movement. In fact, there is an element of stability in all locomotor and manipulative movements. Children who are exposed to a variety of movement situations generally have little difficulty in developing fundamental stability abilities. On the other hand, children who do not have a varied background of movement experiences frequently lag behind in the development of basic stability abilities.

Use of the term *stability* goes beyond the notion of nonlocomotor movements and static and dynamic balance. Stability is the ability to sense a shift in the relationship of the body parts that alter one's balance, along with the ability to adjust rapidly and accurately for these changes with appropriate compensating movements. Therefore, the concept of stability encompasses *axial movements, springing movements, upright support*, and *inverted supports*, all of which involve both static or dynamic balance.

Axial movements are nonlocomotor stability movements in which the axis of the body revolves around a fixed point. Movements such as bending, stretching, twisting, turning, reaching, lifting, and falling are generally considered to be axial movements that place emphasis on maintaining one's balance. Springing movements involve forceful projection of the body into space in either an upright or an inverted position. Movement skills such as the straddle jump, headspring, and handspring are considered to be springing movements. Emphasis in these tasks is placed on the sudden loss and regaining of contact with one's base of support.

Upright supports are static or dynamic balance skills where emphasis is placed on maintaining one's equilibrium when the body is placed in unusual positions. Individual stunts, such as the coffee grinder, bear dance, V-seat, and front scale, are upright postures. Partner stunts, such as the wheelbarrow, swan balance, and shoulder stand, are upright postures.

Inverted supports involve supporting the body momentarily or for a sustained period in an inverted position. The tripod, headstand, and handstand are all sustained inverted supports. Momentary inverted supports include forward and backward rolls, cartwheels, and the round-off.

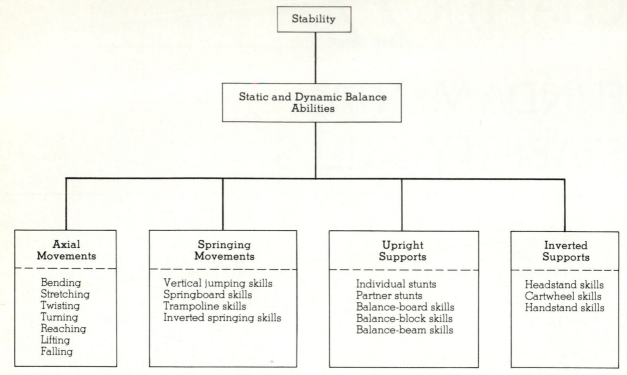

FIGURE 22.1   Components of the fundamental movement category of stability.

The concept of stability is broad. As used here, the movement category of stability includes any movement in which a *premium* is placed on gaining or maintaining one's equilibrium. Figure 22.1 provides a partial list of stability skills.

Due to the interactive nature of stability, this chapter is presented somewhat differently than the previous two. The beam walk and the one-foot balance have been selected as representative samples of the many dynamic and static balance skills, along with body rolling and dodging. A verbal description and visual description are provided for each, along with teaching tips and concepts children should know. This is followed by a sampling of appropriate skill development activities for body rolling and dodging only. Chapters 23 and 24 are filled with a wide variety of appropriate stability enhance-

ment activities in the form of stunts and tumbling skills and apparatus skills.

DEVELOPING A STABILITY SKILL THEME

When planning a theme on fundamental stability skills, you will find it helpful to utilize the following sequence in order to make maximum efficient use of your time.

1. Preplan
    *   Determine what fundamental stability skills will be grouped together for each skill theme. The following grouping may be considered:
        *   Axial movements and springing movements.

- Stunts and tumbling skills.
- Small apparatus skills.
- Large apparatus skills.
- Determine when to include each stability skill theme in your yearly curriculum.
- Decide approximately how many total lessons will be spent on fundamental stability skill development in relation to the total curriculum.

2. Observe and Assess
- Observe the static and dynamic balance skills of the group to be taught.
- Assess whether they are at the initial, elementary, or mature stage in their static and dynamic balance abilities. Study the verbal description and visual description for stability skills on the pages that follow for help.

3. Plan and Implement
- Plan appropriate movement activities geared to the needs, interests, and ability level of the group. Study the teaching tips and concepts children should know in the pages that follow for assistance.
- Implement a planned program of activities stressing progressive skill development.

4. Evaluate and Revise
- Informally evaluate progress in the stability skills being stressed in terms of improved mechanics. The questions found in Table 22.5 at the end of the chapter will be helpful.
- Revise subsequent lessons as needed, based on student progress.

SKILL SEQUENCING

Because stability is basic to all that we do, fundamental stability abilities begin developing early in life. However, the extent to which these abilities are developed and refined depends largely upon environmental factors.

When working on stability skill development, it is important to follow a logical progression of activities from simple to complex, building skill upon skill. Axial movements are a good place to start. Experimenting with how the body can bend, stretch, twist, and turn places children in new and unusual positions. Upright supports are good activities to include next. They provide practice in supporting the body in progressively more difficult ways on the floor, on the mat, or on various pieces of large and small apparatus. Springing activities, in which the body is projected into the air in an *upright* posture, should be the third level of stability skill sequencing. These activities permit the body to be projected into the air for a short time, and they require progressively more sophisticated coordination as well as dynamic balance abilities. Inverted supports and inverted springing activities should be the last skills incorporated into the skill progression. These skills require considerable coordination and kinesthetic sensitivity to where the body is in space. All stability skill development activities should follow a logical sequence of progression from beginning to intermediate to advanced-level activities. Failure to do so will only lead to frustration and failure on the part of children and the development of splinter skills that have little utility.

STATIC AND DYNAMIC BALANCE

Balance is generally defined as the ability to maintain one's equilibrium in relation to the force of gravity, whether in a static posture or when performing a dynamic activity. In order for a person to be in balance, the line of gravity that passes through the individual's center of gravity must also lie within the base of support. If the line of gravity falls outside the base of support the person cannot remain in balance and will fall unless compensating movements are made. A *static balance* activity may be defined as any stationary posture, upright or inverted, in which the center of gravity remains stationary and the line of gravity falls within the base of support. Standing in place, balancing on a board, or standing on one foot are all examples of static balance from an upright posture. Examples of inverted postures include performing a tripod, tip-up, headstand, or handstand. The essential factor in any static balance activity is that the body is maintained in a stationary position for a specified period of time.

Dynamic balance involves controlled movement while moving through space. In a dynamic balance activity, the center of gravity is constantly shifting. Locomotor and manipulative movements involve an element of dynamic balance. Virtually all movement involves an element of static balance. Therefore, we may look upon balance as the basis from which all controlled movement emanates. As a result, the balance experiences engaged in by children play an important role in the development of total body control.

Because of the unique relationship of dynamic and static balance to movement skill development of the individual in both locomotor and manipulative movements, the format of this chapter has been altered somewhat to focus on those activities that clearly place a premuim on the gaining and maintaining of one's equilibrium. The beam walk and the one-foot balance have been selected as representative fundamental dynamic and static balance movement patterns, respectively.

Beam Walk

Verbal Description
Initial Stage
- Balances with support.
- Walks with assistance.
- Uses follow step with dominant foot leading.
- Eyes focus on feet.
- Body rigid.
- No compensation movements.

Elementary Stage
- Can walk a two-inch beam but not a one-inch beam.
- Uses follow step with dominant foot leading.
- Visual focus is on beam.
- May "tie" one arm to the side of the body.
- Loses balance easily.
- Limited compensating movements.
- Forward movement only.

Mature Stage
- Can walk a one-inch beam.
- Uses alternate stepping action.
- Visual focus is beyond the beam.
- Both arms used at will to aid balance.
- Can move forward, backward, and sideways.
- Movements are fluid, relaxed, and in control.
- May lose balance occasionally.

Visual Description
Initial Stage

PHOTO 22.1   The initial beam walk.

Elementary Stage

PHOTO 22.2   The elementary beam walk.

Mature Stage

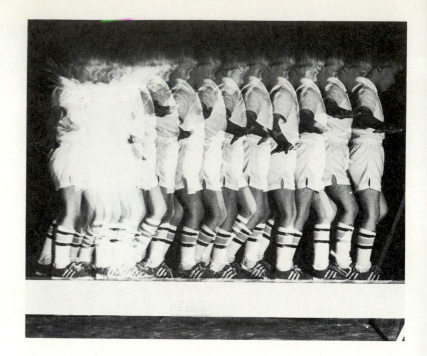

PHOTO 22.3   The mature beam walk.

One-Foot Balance

Verbal Description
Initial Stage
- Raises nonsupport leg several inches so that thigh is nearly parallel with contact surface.
- Is either in or out of balance (no in between).
- Overcompensates ("windmill" arms).
- Inconsistent leg preference.
- Balances with outside support.
- Only momentary balance without support.
- Eyes directed at feet.

Elementary Stage
- May lift nonsupport leg to a "tied-in" position on support leg.
- Cannot balance with eyes closed.
- Uses arms for balance but may "tie" one arm to the side of the body.
- Performs better on dominate leg to a free position by bending at the knee.

Mature Stage
- Can balance with the arms or trunk as needed to maintain balance.
- Uses both arms or the trunk as needed to maintain balance.
- Lifts nonsupport leg.
- Focuses on external object while balancing.
- Changes to nondominant leg without loss of balance.

Visual Description
Initial Stage

PHOTO 22.4   The initial one foot balance.

Elementary Stage

PHOTO 22.5   The elementary one foot balance.

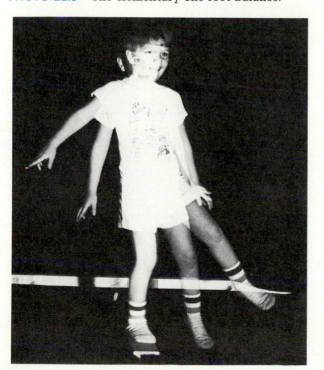

Mature Stage

PHOTO 22.6   The mature one foot balance.

Teaching Tips (Static and Dynamic Balance)
Common Problem
- Inabililty to maintain balance.
- Inability to balance unaided.
- Leading with one foot only.
- ''Tying'' one arm to the side while balancing with the other.
- Failure to use the arms to compensate for changes in balance.
- Looking down at the feet.
- Inability to alter level or direction.

Recommended Strategies
- Spot activities carefully, but only as needed.
- Offer your hand for assistance, encouraging the child to grasp it less securely as balance is gained.
- Use a long pole to aid in balancing with the use of both sides of the body.
- Encourage proper focusing of attention by having child identify numbers that are held up.
- Work for good body control in different directions and at different levels.
- Have child try to pick up objects while balancing in order to alter the balance problem and to change level.
- Provide plenty of variety and opportunity for experimentation, remembering that the primary objective is to enhance balance and not just to walk a balance beam or balance on a board.
- Provide numerous balance experiences, utilizing various forms of equipment and relationships of the body.
- Begin with low-level activities prior to introducing high-level activities.
- Practice on a low bench and low balance beam is helpful prior to using a regulation beam.

**Concepts Children Should Know
(Static and Dynamic Balance)**
Skill Concepts
- Holding your arms out to the side will help you balance.
- Focusing on an object will help you balance.

- When walking on the beam, you should try to use an alternate stepping pattern.
- Be sure to have a spotter at your side.
- Do not rely on your spotter too much.
- The lower your center of gravity, the greater your stability.
- The wider your base of support, the greater your stability.
- Your line of gravity must stay within your base of support in order to balance.
- Balancing on one body part is usually more difficult because of a narrower base of support.

Movement Concepts
- You can balance your body at many different levels.
- You can balance on many different objects.
- You can balance while holding many different objects.
- You can move in different directions while balancing.
- You can balance while moving with others.
- You can widen your base when you balance for greater stability.
- You can lower your body when you balance for greater stability.

BODY ROLLING

Body rolling is a fundamental movement that requires the individual's body to move through space around its own axis while momentarily inverted. Rolling may be either forward, sideways, or backward. Children love to roll. The thrill of being upside down, along with the uncertainty of where they are in space and the dizziness, combine to make rolling an enjoyable activity for most children. Body rolling is a fundamental movement pattern that is integral to the sports of gymnastics and diving. It is found in various forms in the martial arts, wrestling, and acrobatic skiing. The body awareness and spatial awareness demanded of the individual in any activity that involves rotating the body around its own axis is tremendous. Therefore, it is important that children have many and varied opportunities to develop their body-rolling abilities.

Forward Roll

Verbal Description
Initial Stage
- Head definitely contacts surface.
- Body curled in loose "C" position.
- Inability to coordinate use of the arms.
- Cannot get over backward or sideways.
- Uncurls to "L" position after rolling forward.

Elementary Stage
- After rolling forward, actions appear segmented.

- Head leads action rather than inhibiting it.
- Head still touches surface.
- Body curled in tight "C" position at onset of roll.
- Body uncurls at completion of roll.
- Hands and arms aid rolling action somewhat but supply little pushoff.
- Can perform only one roll at a time.
- Back of head lightly touches surface.

Mature Stage
- Head leads the action.
- Head only lightly touches the surface.
- Body remains in tight "C" throughout.
- Arms aid in force production.
- Momentum returns child to starting position.
- Performs consecutive rolls with control.

Visual Description
Initial Stage

PHOTO 22.7 The initial forward roll.

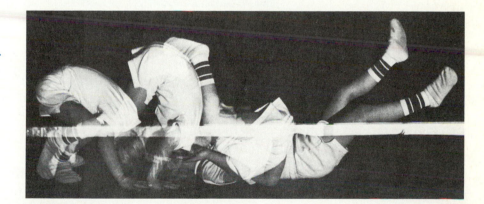

Elementary Stage

PHOTO 22.8 The elementary forward roll.

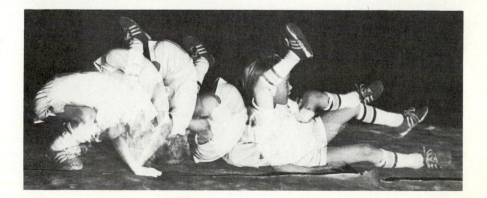

Mature Stage

PHOTO 22.9   The mature forward roll.

Teaching Tips
Common Problems
- Failure to move in a straight line.
- Failure to keep tucked into a small ball.
- Failure to keep the limbs close to the body.
- Failure to use the hands to absorb body weight and to aid in pushing the body over.
- Placing the front or top of the head on the mat.
- Uneven pushoff with the hands or legs, causing a lopsided roll.
- Inability to utilize the forces of the body in a coordinated manner.
- Inability to perform consecutive rolls.
- Dizziness.

Recommended Strategies
- A grassy area or carpet is adequate if mats are not available.
- Provide careful spotting wherever needed.
- It is not necessary to spot every child individually. If individual spotting is desired, instruct the children in how it is done.
- Insist on good spotting when it is used.
- Work crossways on the mats to permit maximum practice.
- Use a block of wood and a tennis ball to demonstrate the difference between a round object (our curled body) and a nonrounded object (our uncurled body) when rolling.
- Set up four or five mat stations (forward-roll mat, backward-roll mat, combination mat, advanced mat, and trouble mat), stationing yourself wherever children need specific instruction.
- Begin with an exploratory approach, but be sure the movement challenges that you present are within the ability level of your children.
- Use a guided discovery approach to facilitate an understanding of why the body moves as it does and how it moves when rolling.
- Children will often be at diverse levels of ability within a class. Be sure to provide experiences that meet the individual needs of

each child. This will require diversity and creativity in teaching.

Concepts Children Should Know
Skill Concepts
- Stay tucked in a small ball throughout your roll.
- Use your hands to support or push off so as little of your head touches the floor as possible.
- Keep your chin against your chest.
- Push off evenly with both hands.
- If you stay tucked during your roll, you can come all the way back to your starting position.
- Focus your eyes on an object in front of or behind you to help you roll in a straight line.
- Rolling is basic to the sports of gymnastics and diving and plays an important part in wrestling and the martial arts.

Movement Concepts
- You can roll in many directions.
- You can roll from different levels.
- You can roll using a variety of body positions.
- You can roll with objects and with people.
- You can roll at different speeds and with different amounts of force.
- Your roll can be smooth and coordinated, or it can be disjointed and jerky.
- You can combine rolling with a variety of other activities.

DODGING

Dodging is a fundamental movement ability common to the game, sport, and play activities of children and adults. Dodging is often accompanied by running and involves quick, deceptive changes in direction. In the running dodge, the knees bend, the center of gravity moves lower, and the body weight is shifted rapidly in a sideways direction. Dodging may occur from a stationary position and may involve a number of axial movements, including bending, twisting, stretching, or falling.

Dodging is an important element in chasing and fleeing games and the dodgeball games of childhood. It is and important element in the sports of wrestling, football, hockey, soccer, baseball, rugby, and lacrosse. Because of the natural combination of running with dodging, you may wish to group these two movement patterns into a common skill theme.

Verbal Description
Initial Stage
- Definite segmented movements.
- Body appears stiff.
- Little knee bend.
- Weight is on total foot.
- Feet generally cross.
- No deception.

Elementary Stage
- Movements coordinated but little deception.
- Performs better to one side than the other.
- Too much vertical lift.
- Feet may occasionally cross.
- Little spring in movement.
- Sometimes "outsmarts" self and becomes confused.

Mature Stage
- Knees bent, trunk leans slightly forward (ready position).
- Fluid directional changes.
- Performs equally well in all directions.
- Head and shoulder fake.
- Good lateral movement.

Visual Description
Initial Stage

PHOTO 22.10   The initial dodge.

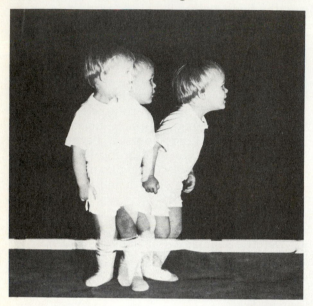

Elementary Stage

PHOTO 22.11   The elementary dodge.

Mature Stage

PHOTO 22.12   The mature dodge.

Teaching Tips

Common Problems

- Inability to smoothly shift the body weight in the intended direction of movement.
- Slow to react.
- Lack of deceptive movements.
- Failure to bend at the knees.
- Failure to shift the body weight back over the base of support during the initial change in direction.
- Failure to bend at the knees in preparation for changing direction.

Recommended Strategies

- Stress bending at the knees in anticipation of dodging.
- Begin with activities that require changing direction on a cue or verbal command.
- Explore various aspects of dodging in conjunction with effort, space, and relationships.
- Avoid dodgeball activities as a central focus of the lesson.
- Utilize a limited amount of dodgeball-type activities, only after the child has reached the mature level. Always use a foam ball or a partially deflated ball.
- Stress the necessity for quickness and deception.
- Work on dodging in all directions. Avoid activities in which only one direction is stressed.
- May be effectively combined as a skill theme with running and leaping or with throwing and catching.

Concepts Children Should Know

Skill Concepts

- Stop your movement suddenly and shift your body weight rapidly to one side.
- Keep your center of gravity low for better balance.
- You keep your center of gravity over your base of support for balance, but you must put your body weight outside your base momentarily in order to dodge with quickness and deception.
- Use your head, shoulders, eyes, or trunk to face the new direction of your intended movement.
- Dodging is an important element in tagging and dodgeball games, as well as in sports such as football, basketball, lacrosse, soccer, and hockey.

Movement Concepts

- You can alter the effort that you use in your dodging to fit the demands of the situation.
- Your dodge can be altered in the amount of force applied, speed of performance, and flow.
- You can alter the space which you dodge from place to place.
- You can dodge in different directions and at different levels.

SKILL DEVELOPMENT ACTIVITIES

Prior to selecting specific stability activities for inclusion in the lesson, it is necessary to determine the typical stage of motor development displayed by the class. This will in turn provide important cues to their level of movement skill learning. With this information, it is now possible to determine whether the lesson should focus on exploratory and guided discovery activities, skill application activities, or skill refinement activities.

Exploratory Activities

Exploratory activities provide children at the initial or elementary stage of developing their stability abilities an opportunity to get an idea of how their bodies can balance alone and in relation to other objects or people. The movement elements of effort, space, and relationships are explored in order to help children develop a more complete idea of their stability potentials. Tables 22.1 and 22.2 provide a sampling of exploratory ideas for body rolling and for dodging. The same type of exploratory experiences may be used with a wide range of static and dynamic balance skills.

TABLE 22.1   Exploratory Activity Ideas for Body Rolling

Can you roll—		
Effort	**Space**	**Relationships**
Force	*Level*	*Objects*
—as quietly as you can?	—from as low as you can go?	—on the mat?
—as loudly as you can?	—from as high as you can go?	—between the blue panels?
—so I cannot hear you?	—in a medium position?	—through the hoop?
—(rock) back and forth very hard?		—down the mat?
—(rock) very softly?	*Direction*	—over the rolled mat?
	—forward?	—on the bench?
Time	—sideways?	—while holding on to a ball?
—very fast?	—backward?	
—very slowly?	—in a straight line?	*People*
—in slow motion?		—with a partner?
—at your regular speed?	*Range*	—at the same time as your partner?
—(rock) fast?	—from a wide base?	—together?
—(rock) slowly?	—from a narrow base?	—and move apart?
	—in your own space?	—like twins?
Flow	—with your head touching the ground?	
—in a tight ball?	—without your head touching the mat?	**Combinations**
—in four separate steps?		After ample opportunity has been provided for exploration of the various elements of rolling, you may want to combine them. For example: Can you roll forward with a wide base from a high level?
—in one smooth motion?		
—in a jerky motion?		
—(rock) to my beat?		

TABLE 22.2   Exploratory Activity Ideas for Dodging

Can you dodge—

Effort	Space	Relationships
Force	*Level*	*Objects*
—with great force?	—from a high level?	—a fleece ball?
—with no force?	—from a low level?	—a playground ball?
—with some force?	—from a high to a low level?	—a tossed ball?
Time	—from a low to a high level?	—a rolled ball?
—as fast as you can?	—keeping yourself at a	
—as slow as you can?	medium level?	*People*
—alternating fast and		—a person chasing you from
slow dodges?	*Direction*	behind?
—at a medium speed?	—in different directions?	—a person in front of you?
—with a burst of energy?	—sideways?	—in the same direction as your
Flow	—to your left?	partner?
—smoothly?	—to your right?	—in the opposite direction as your
—roughly?	—backward?	partner?
	—forward?	
		Combinations
	Range	After ample opportunities have
	—and concentrate on making	been provided for exploration of
	different body shapes?	the various elements of dodging,
	—while staying in your own	you may want to combine them. For
	space?	example: Can you dodge a rolled
	—assessing all the space you	ball as fast as you can from a low
	need?	level to a high level?
	—while on one foot?	
	—without using your arms?	

Guided Discovery Activities

The sampling of guided discovery activities in Tables 22.3 and 22.4 are intended to provide you with a variety of problem solving activities designed to lead the learner to mature rolling and dodging abilities. Guided discovery activities permit children who are at the intermediate level of learning a new stability skill with the opportunity to practice the skill, learn more about it, and focus on it in a variety of movement situations. An infinite variety of guided discovery activity ideas can easily be devised for all types of static and dynamic balance skills.

TABLE 22.3   Guided Discovery Activity Ideas for Body Rolling

General	1. First explore several of the movement variations and combinations of rolling.
	2. Then begin to place limitations on the response possibilities to the movement challenges presented. For example:
	• Try rocking back and forth from many different positions. How many ways can you find? Did you notice anything special when you were rocking on your front, or your back, or your side? Did you keep your body straight or did you curve your body? Why?
Trunk	• Does your head do anything special when you rock? Why do you think you tuck your chin in when you rock on your back or from side to side? Try it with your head up. Does it work as well? Why not?
	• When we do a forward roll, do we keep our body curved or straight? Can anyone show me how curved they make their body when getting ready for a forward roll?
Head	• What do you do with your head? Do you keep it up or curve it way down to your chest? Show me how your body and your head look when you do your forward roll. Practice rolling.
Arms	• What do we do with our hands and arms when we roll forward? Try it, then tell me. So our hands help us? How? See if you can use your hands more as you roll. Try it.
Feet	• Can our feet help us when we roll? What can they do? Why does a good pushoff help? Show me.
Combination	• Let's put it all together. Make a good, tight ball with your body and head, push off with your feet, and use your hands to catch your weight as you come over.
Finish	• If we want to come right back to our feet, what should we do? Try it. Can you get to your feet without using your hands to push you off?

3. After the mature rolling pattern comes under the child's control, provide numerous opportunities for varying the pattern and combining it with other activities. For example:
   • Consecutive forward rolls.
   • Wide-base forward rolls.
   • One-handed rolls.
   • No-handed rolls.
   • Rolls along a bench.
   • Partner rolls (eskimo rolls).
   You will also find it helpful to introduce the sideways and backward rolls, using many of the same activities used for the forward roll. Variations and combinations of these body-rolling patterns can be elaborated upon also, once the mature stage has been obtained. For example:
   • Backward roll to a squat.
   • Backward roll to a stand.
   • Backward straddle roll.
   • Backward roll to a momentary handstand.
   • Combination forward and backward rolls.

TABLE 22.4   Guided Discovery Activity Ideas for Dodging

General	1. First have the children explore several variations of dodging. 2. Then begin to place limitations on the response possibilities to the movement challenges presented. For example: • Can you run forward and change direction quickly? Try it while running backward and sideways. What do you do when you change directions quickly? Do you do the same thing when moving in different directions? Why?
Leg action	• Try to tag your partner who is facing you. What does your partner do to try to avoid your touch? What does she or he do with the feet and legs? Why are the knees bent and the feet apart? Now you try it, but try dodging your partner's touch from a position with your legs straight and starting with your feet together. Which way do you think works best? Try both ways. You're right, but why is it better to dodge from a standing position with your feet apart and your knees bent? • Now try dodging your partner while being chased. What do you do to avoid being tagged? When you dodge to the right, what do you do with your legs? Why does your right leg step out to one side as you pivot? Show me how you can do it to the opposite side. • Do you find it easier to dodge from a run in one direction than the other? Why? Let's practice dodging to our weak side.
Faking	• From a position facing your partner, try to avoid his or her tags while using deceptive (feinting) movements of your head, eyes, or trunk. Does it work? What do you do with these body parts when you want to fake out your partner? Look at your starting position. Are your feet apart and your knees slightly bent? Don't forget to use that as your ready position and then use other body parts to give the impression that you are going one way when you actually are going the other. 3. When the mature dodging action has been reasonably well mastered, combine dodging with other activities. Often children can dodge satisfactorily in an isolated experience. However, when placed in a situation requiring dodging an oncoming object or in a complicated game that utilizes dodging as only one of many elements of the game, children often become confused and unable to dodge with proficiency. Activities such as those that follow will help develop more integrated utilization of dodging. • Dodge one or more persons while running across the playfield. • Dodge oncoming objects. Be sure to use foam balls. • Use dodging maneuvers to advance a ball downfield or down court. You can run, dribble, or kick a ball while dodging.

TABLE 22.5   Self-Question Chart for Fundamental Stability Skill Development

One-Foot Balance	Yes	No	Comments
1. Can the child balance for 30 seconds on one foot?			
2. Does the child make adjustments with the arms as needed to maintain balance?			
3. Can the child balance for 10 seconds with both eyes closed?			
4. Does the child keep the nonsupport leg free?			
5. Does the child focus forward rather than downward?			
6. Can the child balance on either foot?			
7. Is there observable improvement?			

Beam Walk	Yes	No	Comments
1. Can the child walk a 10-foot-long beam, 4 inches wide, unaided?			
2. Does the child use an alternating step?			
3. Can the child travel backward and sideways as well as forward?			
4. Does the child focus forward rather than downward?			
5. Can the child use both arms to compensate for changes in balance?			
6. Can the child change levels and directions with ease?			
7. Can the child walk independent of a spotter?			
8. Is there observable improvement?			

Body Rolling (forward, backward, and/or sideways)	Yes	No	Comments
1. Does the child curve the body adequately?			
2. Does the child tuck the head?			
3. Does the child push off evenly with both feet?			
4. Does the child take the body weight on the hands and arms?			
5. Do the head and body stay tucked in throughout the roll?			
6. Is the child able to keep the front and top of the head from touching the mat?			
7. Can the child come to his or her feet unaided immediately after the roll?			
8. Is the child able to travel in a straight line?			
9. Can the child perform consecutive rolls?			
10. Is there observable improvement?			

Dodging	Yes	No	Comments
1. Can the child dodge a partner from a facing position?			
2. Can the child effectively dodge a partner from a fleeing position?			
3. Does the child dodge well in all direction?			
4. Is the child able to combine dodging with other game skills?			
5. Does the child use deceptive movements when dodging?			
6. Is the action quick, fluid, and in control?			
7. Is there observable improvement?			

Skill Application Activities

Once children have developed basic abilities to balance their bodies in static and dynamic situations, it is appropriate to begin focusing on skill application activities. Static and dynamic balance abilities can be developed through practice in a variety of stunts and tumbling skills, large apparatus skills, and small apparatus skills. Stability abilities may be applied to a number of game, rhythm, and self-testing activities.

The following chapters contain several stability skill development and application ideas that are appropriate for elementary school children:

Chapter 23 Stunts and Tumbling Skills
Chapter 24 Apparatus Skills
Chapter 31 Low Level Game Activities
Chapter 32 Relay Activities
Chapter 38 Creative Rhythmic Activities

ASSESSING PROGRESS

Children can easily be evaluated at the beginning and at the end of a fundamental stability skill theme. Select and evaluate four or five stability skills that are representative of the particular skill theme. Once their entry level of ability has been determined, it is an easy matter to determine the types of activities to be included in the lesson. The sample assessment charts located in Chapter 19 (Figures 19.1 and 19.2) can be adapted to stability skills. These charts are a practical tool for recording individual and group progress.

Fundamental stability abilities may also be informally assessed through a self-question chart similar to the one depicted in Table 22.5. You should be able to answer "yes" to each of the questions. If you cannot, modifications will need to be made in subsequent lessons. These modifications will be made in order to more closely fit the specific needs of the individual, group, or class being taught.

SUGGESTED READING

Block, S. D. (1977). *Me I'm great: Physical education for children three through eight.* Minneapolis: Burgess.

Capon, J. (1975). *Balance activities.* Belmont, CA: Fearon–Pitman.

Morrison, R. (1969). *A movement approach to educational gymnastics.* London: J. M. Dent and Sons Limited.

Torbert, M. (1980). *Follow me.* Englewood Cliffs, NJ: Prentice-Hall.

Wall, J. (1981). *Beginnings: Movement education for kindergarten and primary children.* Montreal: McGill University Printing Service.

Williams, J. (1979). *Themes for educational gymnastics.* London: Lepus.

CHAPTER 23

STUNTS AND TUMBLING SKILLS

Stunts and tumbling skills are performed on the floor or on a mat. Stunts are generally considered to be movement activities in which the body maintains a static center of gravity. Skills such as the tip-up, tripod, and headstand are considered to be stunts. Tumbling skills, on the other hand, are generally considered to be activities in which the body moves down a mat in which the center of gravity is constantly shifted.

A forward roll, headspring, handspring, and walkover are all considered here to be tumbling skills.

Stunts and tumbling skills place considerable emphasis on static and dynamic balancing abilities. The concepts children should know concerning static and dynamic balance (refer to Chapter 22) can all be learned through a progressive program of stunts and tumbling skill development. This chapter focuses on body rolling, springing, upright supports, and inverted support skills. Each skill is described and sequenced in a logical progression from simple to complex as a *beginning*, *intermediate*, or *advanced*-level skill.

SKILL SEQUENCING

The skills contained in this chapter and the next (Apparatus Skills) are sequenced in progression from simple to complex for children at the beginning, intermediate, and advanced levels of learning a skill. Children without previous experience in stunts and tumbling, and apparatus activity will benefit most from beginning-level skills *regardless* of their grade level. These activities have been carefully selected and sequenced to provide novice gymnasts with success and the necessary background of experiences to progress on to intermediate-level skills. Most children in the primary grades will be at the beginning level unless they have had previous training.

Intermediate-level skills are suitable for children who have successfully completed the beginning level. Children in the third or fourth grade are often at the intermediate level *if* they have completed the beginning level. Fifth and sixth graders are frequently ready for advanced-level skills *if* they have been in a progressive program of skill development throughout the earlier grades. The teaching progression charts found in this chapter and the next are listed in a progressive order of difficulty within each of the three movement skill learning levels. The progressive presentation of gymnastic type skills is essential in order to maximize skill development and learning enjoyment.

DEVELOPING A GYMNASTICS SKILL THEME

When planning a series of lessons that focus on stability skill development through stunts and tumbling activities or apparatus, the following sequence will be helpful: preplanning, observing and assessing, planning and implementing, and evaluation and revision.

1. *Preplan.* Determine when and approximately how many lessons will focus on gymnastic skills. Locate a sufficient number of mats, being certain that they are clean and in good repair.
2. *Observe and assess.* Select a few basic skills, such as the forward roll, star jump, V-seat, and headstand, for observation. Informally assess the group to determine if they are at the beginning, intermediate, or advanced level of gymnastics skill learning.
3. *Plan and implement.* Based on your observational assessment, plan a progressive program of activities using the suggested progressions found in Tables 23.1-23.4, and 24.1-24.6.
4. *Evaluate and revise.* Informally assess the gymnastic skills of the class through the use

of aim charts similar to the ones found at the end of this chapter (Figure 23.1), and Chapter 24 (Figure 24.1).

SAFETY CONSIDERATIONS

The following safety considerations should be rigidly adhered to in order to minimize safety hazards and to maximize learning enjoyment.

1. Use several tumbling mats.
2. Keep the mats clean (use mild soap and water) and neatly stored when not in use.
3. Never drag the mats. Always carry them from place to place.
4. Stress the importance of a thorough warm-up before attempting activities.
5. Stress individual responsibility.
6. Follow a definite progression of activities.
7. *Do not* permit students to attempt tasks beyond their ability level.
8. Stress the need for mastery of the foundational skills before more advanced skills are attempted.
9. Do *not* include backbends, back walkovers, or front walkovers in the regular instructional program. (Recent research has uncovered a number of low-back injuries due to these activities being taught too soon). Reserve these and other advanced skills for a special-interest group of gymnasts.
10. Spot skills as necessary.

SPOTTING

Spotting is an important aspect of any successful gymnastics program. It is a form of assisting the performer through a skill in order to assure safety or to aid in teaching the skill. Correct spotting is an art. The following are suggestions for spotting.

1. Protecting the performer is the primary goal of spotting. Therefore, don't hesitate.

2. Be alert at all times. Don't permit your attention to be diverted.

3. Be in the proper position, ready to move instantly.

4. Be close enough to the performer to be able to assist as needed, but not so close to interfere with performance (don't overspot).

5. Know the skill and what movements the performer must make.

6. Coach the performer through the skill, using key words.

7. By being confident in your spotting techniques, you will instill confidence in the performer.

8. If there is a need to catch the performer, it is generally only necessary to check the fall.

9. Use mature students as spotters after they have been sufficiently trained.

10. Don't assume that a spotter is no longer needed just because nothing has happened for a long period of time. Use good judgment in selecting skills or individuals that continue to need to be spotted.

TEACHING TIPS

The following are some important teaching suggestions to consider when teaching stunts and tumbling skills.

1. Provide a wide variety of activities.
2. Consider the body build, strength, and flexibility of students before presenting new skills.
3. Follow a logical progression from simple to complex, thus insuring success.
4. Develop an attitude among the students that practice is important and that instant success is rare.
5. Use proper spotting techniques both as a teaching medium and as a safety precaution.
6. Provide for individual differences and wide ranges in ability.
7. Give students an opportunity to demonstrate their new skills to others.

8. Devise simple free-exercise and tumbling routines that combine several skills.

9. Give students an opportunity to pursue their interests in an early-morning, noon-time, or after-school gymnastics program.

10. The program should be fun and full of action. It should stress learning something new each day.

BODY-ROLLING SKILLS

Body-rolling activities are enjoyed by most children. The thrill of turning oneself over and the sense of vertigo make rolling an enjoyable activity. Be certain, however, to recognize that some children are totally unfamiliar with this sensation and lack sufficient body and spatial awareness to feel comfortable. Therefore, it is necessary when working with a group of inexperienced tumblers to be certain to follow a logical progression of activities, building skill upon skill. Table 23.1 provides such a progression.

Objectives

Practice in body rolling skills will enable children to:

1. Perform a variety of sideways, forward, and backward rolling skills.
2. Develop stability abilities in unusual rotational balance situations.
3. Improve body awareness and spatial awareness abilities.
4. Enhance the motor fitness abilities of agility and coordination.
5. Enhance the health-related fitness abilities of strength and flexibility.

Movement Experiences

Sideways Rolling. Sideways rolling is quite easy for most children. Stress should, however, be placed on improved body control and directional awareness.

TABLE 23.1 Selected Body-Rolling Skills

Body-Rolling Skills	Suggested Progression for Children			
	Beginning Level	Intermediate Level	Advanced Level	Page
Sideways Rolling				301
Soldier log roll	X			302
Rocket log roll	X			302
Sideways roll		X		302
Forward Rolling				
Look back	X			303
Tip over	X			303
Back rocker	X			303
Roll-up	X			303
Forward roll		X		303
Consecutive forward rolls		X		303
Step-roll		X		303
Reach-over roll		X		303
Dive roll			X	303
Partner dive roll			X	304
Straddle roll			X	304
Eskimo roll			X	304
Backward Rolling				304
Back rocker	X			304
Back tucker	X			304
Rabbit ears	X			304
Snail balance	X			304
Back shoulder roll	X			304
Rock-back shoulder roll	X			304
Forearm sit and roll		X		304
Forearm rock and roll		X		304
Backward roll		X		304
Consecutive back rolls		X		304
Forward–backward roll combination			X	305
Back straddle roll			X	305
Back extension roll			X	305

Soldier Log Roll. From an "attention" lying position with the legs straight and the arms held rigid at the sides, roll from one end of the mat to the other.

Rocket Log Roll. From a lying position with the arms extended overhead and the fingers clasped, roll from one end of the mat to the other.

Sideways Roll. From a hands-and-knees kneeling position, drop one shoulder and roll over, back to the starting position.

PHOTO 23.1   The rocket log roll.

Forward Rolling.   The forward roll can be easily learned if a proper teaching progression is followed. Numerous variations of the forward roll are possible.

Look Back.   From a position with the hands on the floor, raise the hips by straightening the legs and look back between the legs.

Tip Over.   From a squat position with the hands on the mat and the knees between the arms, raise the hips and look back, placing the back of the head on the mat. Tip over onto the back and finish in a sitting position.

Back Rocker.   From a sitting position on the mat with the knees tucked and the hands clasping the shins, sit and rock back onto the back and shoulders. Rock forward and back to a sitting position. Repeat.

Roll Up.   From a sitting position with the legs tucked, the arms outstretched forward, and the chin tucked, rock backward, then forward to a *squat* position. Be sure to lean the head out over the feet and lift the buttocks when rolling forward.

Forward Roll.   From a standing position at the edge of the mat, squat down, placing the hands on the mat close to the feet so that the knees are between the arms. Raise the hips and tip over, being sure to stay in a tucked position. Continue the roll back to a squat position by keeping the head tucked, knees bent, and arms forward.

Consecutive Forward Rolls.   After completion of one forward roll back to a squat position, continue down the mat with three or four more rolls.

Step-Roll.   From a standing position one foot from the edge of the mat, step forward and execute a forward roll back to a standing position.

Reach-Over Roll.   From the edge of the mat with a partner or a low object in front (no higher than knee height), bend over the object and do a forward roll.

Dive Roll.   From a standing position two steps from the edge of the mat, take one step forward and a short jump onto both feet on the second step (hurdle step). Spring into the air and do a dive roll in which the feet leave the ground before the hands contact the floor.

PHOTO 23.2   Forward roll.

Partner Dive Roll.   With a partner curled up at the edge of the mat, perform a dive roll over the partner. Be sure to spot carefully from a kneeling position at the far side of the curled partner.

Straddle Roll.   From a standing position with the legs spread wide apart, bend forward at the waist and contact the floor with the hands in the area between the legs. Execute a forward roll, keeping the legs spread. Continue forward, by pushing with the hands, back to a straddle position.

Eskimo Roll.   Lie on your back and grasp the ankles of your partner, who is standing overhead. Raise your legs so that your ankles may be grasped by your partner. Your partner leans forward and places your feet on the floor, while executing a forward roll. Your partner continues forward and back to a stand, while you repeat the same action. The process continues the length of the mat.

Backward Rolling.   The backward roll is difficult for some children to master. Follow a definite progression and employ proper spotting techniques.

Back Rocker.   From a sitting position at the edge of the mat with the knees bent and the arms at the side, sit and rock back onto the shoulders, then back to a sitting position. Repeat.

Back Tucker.   From a squatting position at the edge of the mat with the hands grasping the shins, rock back and forth.

Rabbit Ears.   From a squatting position at the edge of the mat and the hands by the ears, facing forward, sit and rock back, keeping the chin tucked, so that the palms of both hands touch the floor and the elbows point toward the ceiling.

Snail Balance.   From the same position as for rabbit ears, rock backward and touch the toes to the mat behind. Explore the area behind with the feet.

Back Shoulder Roll.   From a sitting position, rock backward and execute a shoulder roll by rolling toward the right or left shoulder. Repeat to both sides.

Rock-Back Shoulder Roll.   Do a back shoulder roll from a squat to a squat position.

Forearm Sit and Roll.   From a sitting position with the knees tucked, the fingers clasped behind the head, and the elbows bent, rock back and over to a kneeling position. Be sure to stay tucked and that the forearms contact the floor.

Forearm Rock and Roll.   Same as the forearm sit and roll except from a squat to a squat position. Tuck the chin, use momentum, and curl the toes to get back to a squat position.

Backward Roll.   From a squat position at the edge of the mat, sit back and roll over in a tuck position, pushing off with both hands back to a squat position.

Consecutive Back Rolls.   After completion of one backward roll, continue down the mat with three or four more rolls.

PHOTO 23.3   Backward roll.

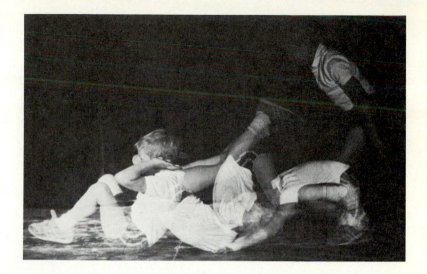

Forward–Backward Roll Combination.   Beginning at one end of the mat, perform a forward roll, crossing the legs at the end of the roll, turning, and doing a backward roll. Repeat, beginning with a backward roll.

Back Straddle Roll.   From a standing position with the legs spread wide apart, bend forward at the waist and place both hands on the mat between the thighs, while assuming a sitting position. Continue to roll backward, pushing with the hands and keeping the legs straight and spread, back to a straddle position.

Back Extension Roll.   From an inverted backward roll position, extend the legs and push them forcefully upward, while at the same time pushing with the hands. When correctly done, the performer will go through handstand position.

SPRINGING SKILLS

Children love to jump and leap. They enjoy the sensation of springing into the air. Springing can be done from an upright position or an inverted position. Upright springs can be done off the floor or off a springboard. Table 23.2 provides a teaching progression chart for springing, with a suggested progression of springing activities for children at beginning, intermediate, and advanced skill levels.

Objectives

Practice in springing skills contribute to:

1. Dynamic balance abilities.
2. Jumping and landing skill development.
3. Improved body and spatial awareness.
4. Enhancing the health-related fitness components of strength and flexibility.
5. Improving the performance-related fitness components of speed, coordination, and power.

Movement Experiences

Upright Springing.   Upright springing may be performed off the floor or off a springboard. Stress keeping the head up and the eyes focused forward in order to aid balance.

Rocket Ship.   From a standing position with the arms overhead and the fingers touching, gradually squat down on the count "5, 4, 3, 2, 1." On the command "blast off," jump high into the air.

TABLE 23.2 Selected
Springing Skills

Springing Skills	Suggested Progression for Children			
	Beginning Level	Intermediate Level	Advanced Level	Page
Upright Springing				305
Rocket ship	X			305
Knee lifter	X			306
Jump and tuck	X			306
Ankle slapper	X			306
Butt kicker	X			306
Toe toucher		X		306
Half-turn		X		306
Three-quarter turn		X		306
Full turn		X		306
Straddle jump		X		306
Star jumps		X		306
Knee straddle		X		306
Ankle straddle			X	307
Toe straddle			X	307
Inverted Springing				307
Low mat roll		X		307
Mat headspring		X		307
Headspring			X	307
Neck spring			X	307
Knee–neck spring			X	307
Partner handspring			X	308
Front handspring			X	308

Knee Lifter. From a standing position, jump straight upward, lifting the knees so that the upper leg is parallel with the floor. Keep the head up and slap the thighs with the hands.

Jump and Tuck. From a standing position, jump straight upward, lifting both knees toward the chest. Keep the head up and bring the arms momentarily to the shins.

Ankle Slapper. From a standing position, jump straight upward, bringing the feet behind and upward. Slap the ankles at the height of the jump.

Butt Kicker. From a standing position, jump straight upward, bringing the heels to the buttocks at the height of the jump.

Toe Toucher. From a standing position, jump straight up, piking at the waist. Keep the head up and try to touch the knees. Repeat, trying to touch the ankles and then the toes.

Half-Turn. From a standing position, jump up-

ward and execute a half-turn to the right or the left.

Three-Quarter Turn. From a standing position, jump forcefully upward and execute a three-quarter turn to either the right or the left. There should be rapid head, shoulder, and arm rotation.

Full Turn. Same as the three-quarter turn. There should be a forceful takeoff, rapid rotation, and controlled landing.

Straddle Jump. From a standing position, jump upward, spreading the legs wide apart and returning them to shoulder-width apart upon landing. Try it also from a squat position.

Star Jump. From a squat position, forcefully jump upward, spreading the legs and arms wide apart at the height of the jump. Return to a squat position after each jump.

Knee Straddle. From a standing or a squatting

PHOTO 23.4   The star jump.

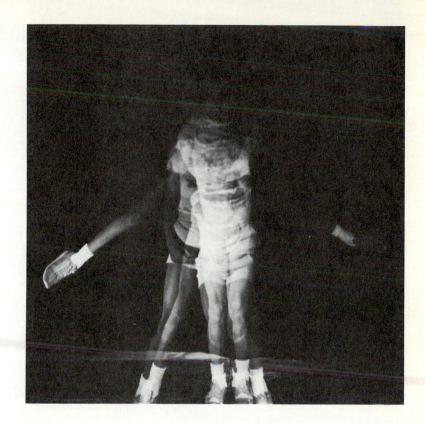

position, jump forcefully upward, piking at the waist while the legs straddle outward. Touch both knees at the height of the jump.

Ankle Straddle.   From a standing or a squatting position, jump forcefully upward. Spread the legs wide apart and pike at the waist. Touch both ankles at the height of the jump.

Toe Straddle.   Same as the ankle straddle except that the toes are pointed and touched at the height of the jump.

Inverted Springing.   Inverted springs should be done on a mat and under the watchful eye of a competent spotter. Gym helpers and teacher aids, with prior training, can be good spotters.

Low Mat Roll.   From a standing position two steps away from a rolled mat, take a step forward, placing the hands at the base of the mat and the back of the neck on the rolled mat. Continue to roll forward to a stand.

Mat Headspring.   From a standing position one step away from a rolled mat, take a step, placing both hands and the head on the mat. Roll forward, unfolding at the waist, pushing with the hands, and snapping the head forward, to a squat position.

Headspring.   From a squat position, place the head close to the mat with the arms in a bent-arm position. Roll forward with the legs straight and the hips leading. Snap (unfold) the hips and legs forward while forcefully pushing with the arms. Finish in a standing position with the arms extended overhead. Be certain to spot carefully, not allowing the head to contact the mat.

Neck Spring.   From a squat position, roll back as if doing a backward roll. When the hands contact the mat, forcefully push off while at the same time extending at the waist and snapping the head forward. The return is to a squat position. Spot carefully.

Knee–Neck Spring.   Similar to a neck spring except the arms are placed on the knees. The ac-

PHOTO 23.5   The front handspring.

tion comes from the forceful pushing on the knees, unfolding at the waist, and the forward head snap.

Partner Handspring.   One person assumes a back lying position with the knees bent and the arms outstretched forward. The top person faces the down person and takes one step forward, placing her hands on his knees and her shoulders in his hands. Keeping the head up and kicking through a handstand, the top person continues over to a stand. It is important that the bottom person be strong enough to control the action and that spotters are present.

Front Handspring.   From a short run and a one-foot takeoff, the arms are swung forcefully downward and the legs kicked up into hand-stand position. Momentum carries the body over, landing in an upright position with the hands extended overhead. Spotters are required.

UPRIGHT SUPPORT SKILLS

The upright support skills found here are sub-divided into *individual supports* and *partner supports*. Some of them may be performed with-out a mat. Most, however, should be practiced on a mat to insure safety. Table 23.3 provides a teaching progression chart for upright support skills. It provides a logical progression of stunts for children at the beginning, intermediate, and advanced levels of stunt skill learning.

Objectives

The primary objectives of upright body support skills are:

1.   To enhance static and dynamic balance abilities.

TABLE 23.3 Selected Upright Support Skills

Upright Support Skills	Suggested Progression for Children			
	Beginning Level	Intermediate Level	Advanced Level	Page
Individual Supports				310
Rocker	X			310
Thread the needle	X			310
Coffee grinder	X			310
Corkscrew	X			310
Turk stand	X			310
Egg seat	X			310
Egg roll	X			310
Seal crawl	X			310
Nose dive	X			310
Fishhawk dive		X		310
Wicket walk		X		310
Stump walk		X		310
Bear dance		X		310
V-seat		X		310
Candle stand		X		311
Heel click		X		311
Greet the toe		X		311
Human ball		X		311
Inchworm		X		311
Knee dip		X		311
Knee spring			X	311
Hitch kick			X	311
Pirouette			X	311
Straight fall			X	311
Shoot through			X	311
Front scale			X	311
Side scale			X	311
Partner Supports				311
Butter churn	X			311
Partner walk	X			311
Two-person rocker	X			312
Wheelbarrow	X			312
Wring the dishrag	X			312
Chinese get up	X			312
Leapfrog	X			312
Chest balance		X		312
Thigh stand-in		X		312
Front swan		X		312
Back swan			X	312
Hand–knee shoulder stand			X	312
Hand–foot, foot–hand stand			X	312
Hand-to-foot stand			X	312
Thigh stand			X	312
Shoulder stand-out			X	312

2. To improve body awareness and spatial awareness abilities.
3. To enhance the health-related fitness components of flexibility and strength.
4. To enhance the performance-related fitness components of coordination and agility.

Movement Experiences

Individual Supports. Children enjoy individual stunts that permit them to balance their bodies in a variety of postures. Stunts that require supporting the body in various upright configurations contribute to improved stability abilities as well as coordination, strength, and endurance.

Rocker. From a front lying position, arch the back and grasp the ankles with the hands. Rock back and forth, simulating a rocking chair.

Thread the Needle. Clasp the fingers and form a circle close to the floor in front of the body with the arms. Step through the arms without releasing. Repeat in the opposite direction.

Coffee Grinder. From a side lying position with the bottom hand contacting the floor and the arm straight, walk around the pivot hand, keeping the legs straight.

Corkscrew. From a standing position with the feet shoulder width apart, bring the left arm across the back of the legs and touch the right toe. Repeat with the right arm.

Turk Stand. Cross the legs and the arms, sit down, and return to a stand without uncrossing the feet.

Egg Seat. Sit with the knees bent. Grasp the toes and extend the legs. Hold a balanced position for 10 seconds.

Egg Roll. From a squatting position with the arms around the knees and the head tucked, roll around the mat.

Seal Crawl. From a front support with the legs straight and the toes pointed behind, drag the body forward with the arms and hip action but no leg action.

Nose Dive. From a kneeling position with the hands behind the back, bend forward to pick up a clean tissue with the teeth.

Fishhawk Dive. Same as the nose dive, but done from one knee and using the arms for balance.

Wicket Walk. Grasp the ankles and walk forward without bending the legs.

Stump Walk. From a kneeling position on a mat, grasp the toes or ankles with both hands. Walk on the knees. Lean forward slightly to maintain balance.

Bear Dance. From a squat position with the arms folded, extend one leg forward. Repeat with the opposite leg while bringing the outstretched leg back to position. Repeat in rhythmical alternation.

V-Seat. From a seat on the floor with the legs straight and both hands on the floor, assume a "V" shape by lifting both legs high.

PHOTO 23.6   The "V" seat. An upright support skill.

Candle Stand. From a lying position on the floor with the arms out from the sides, raise the legs straight up over the head and maintain this extended position.

Heel Click. Hop on the right foot and extend the left leg to the side. Click the heels together. Try for two, then three clicks.

Greet the Toe. From a standing postition, grasp one foot and bring it upward to touch the nose while balancing on one foot. Repeat with the opposite foot.

Human Ball. From a sitting position with the knees bent and each arm intertwined around the corresponding leg and grasping the toes, roll in a clockwise direction. Repeat in the opposite direction.

Inchworm. From a front support position on the hands, walk the feet up to the hands without moving the hands. Then walk the hands away from the feet back to a prone support position. Repeat.

Knee Dip. From a standing position with one knee bent and held from behind the back by the opposite hand, squat until the knee touches the mat and return to a stand. Repeat with the opposite leg.

Knee Spring. From a kneeling position with the toes extended behind, come to a stand by swinging the arms vigorously upward while extending from a bent position at the hips. Try also with the arms folded.

Hitch Kick. From a stand or a short run and one-foot takeoff, kick both legs high into the air and land on the opposite foot.

Pirouette. From a standing position, leap into the air, turn the head and shoulders sharply to the left, and pull the right arm across the chest, executing a full turn of the body.

Straight Fall. Fall toward the mat with one leg elevated. The body is caught and the force absorbed by the arms.

Shoot Through. From a front support position with the arms straight, the legs extended backward, and the weight on the toes and hands, raise the legs and hips quickly and shoot the legs between the arms, finishing in a sitting position.

Front Scale. Bend forward at the waist, balancing on one foot with the supporting leg straight. Extend the other leg fully to the rear and raise to shoulder level. The arms are extended out from the side and raised above shoulder level.

Side Scale. While balancing on the left leg, lean to the left, lifting the right leg. The left arm is extended overhead. The right arm is held alongside the body. The body is parallel to the floor. Repeat to the opposite side.

Partner Supports. Partner support skills should be introduced after children have sufficient strength and body balance to support a person for five seconds or more. Partner supports may be performed in a variety of configurations by two or more people, to form a variety of pyramids.

Butter Churn. Partners stand back to back with elbows hooked. Take turns bending forward and lifting partner's feet off the ground. Do *not* pull over.

Partner Walk. Partners face each other, grasping upper arms. One partner stands on the other partner's toes while he walks forward.

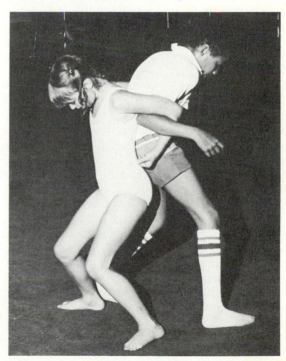

PHOTO 23.7 The Chinese get-up.

Two-Person Rocker. Partners sit, with knees bent, on each other's feet, with upper arms clasped. They alternate rocking back and forth.

Wheelbarrow. One person assumes a front support position on the hands with the legs extended behind. Partner stands between the down partner's legs, grasps at the *knees*, and lifts her legs. Partners walk forward a *short* distance on a *mat*.

Wring the Dishrag. Partners face each other, join hands, and raise their arms high. One person turns clockwise and the other counterclockwise, without releasing their grasp, until they are again facing each other. Repeat in the opposite direction.

Chinese Get Up. From a position with partners standing back to back with elbows hooked, sit all the way down and come back to a stand without releasing arms.

Leapfrog. The down partner bends forward at the waist and places his hands on his knees. The up partner runs up from behind and, from a two-foot takeoff, pushes off from the base of the down partners shoulders and straddle vaults her partner. Alternate.

Chest Balance. One partner kneels on all fours. The top partner places her arms under the bottom partner's chest and places her chest on the kneeling partner's back. Then she kicks upward into a chest balance on the partner's back. Spot carefully.

Thigh Stand-In. The top person is in a half-squat position, facing a partner. The top person places her hands behind the bottom person's neck, while the bottom person places his hands behind the top person's hips. The top person steps onto the bottom person's thighs. When a solid position is reached they join hands and both lean backward. Spot carefully.

Front Swan. The support partner assumes a back lying position. He grasps the hands of his partner and places his feet on his partner's stomach. The partner being supported rocks forward until she is in a prone position, supported by her partner's feet. Spot carefully.

Back Swan. The support partner assumes a back lying position and grasps the hands of his partner. He then places his feet on his partner's buttocks and lower back. The partner being supported rocks backward until she is in a back lying position above the floor, supported by her partner's feet. Spot carefully.

Hand–Knee Shoulder Stand. The support person lies on his back with knees bent, heels close to buttocks, and arms extended in a catch position perpendicular to the floor. The top partner, from a position behind the support partner's head, places her hands on the support partner's knees and her shoulders in his hands. She then kicks up into an inverted support position. Spot carefully.

Hand–Foot and Foot–Hand Stand. The support partner assumes a back lying position with his legs and arms extended above his body and perpendicular to the floor. The partner on top stands at the head of the support partner and places her hands on the feet of the support partner and her feet in her partner's hands, assuming a support position above the floor. Spot carefully.

Hand-to-Foot Stand. The support partner takes a back lying position with the legs extended above the body and perpendicular to the floor. His hands are placed palm-up beside his ears. The partner on top straddles the support's head, places her feet in her partner's hands, and grasps her partner's ankles. On a signal, the person on top jumps into the air, pushing on the ankles of her partner, who in turn pushes her above his head. Once they are balanced, the person on top releases the support person's ankles and stands erect with her arms out to the side for balance. The person supporting locks his elbows and returns his legs to the floor. Spot carefully.

Thigh Stand. One partner assumes a quarter-squat position with the body weight concentrated on the heels and both arms extended forward at shoulder level. The other partner, standing with her back to her partner, places one foot on his thigh and her hands on his arms. She places the other foot on the thigh and steps upward, leaning forward to a standing position on her partner's thighs. The support partner grasps her thighs and leans backward to offer additional support. Spot carefully.

Shoulder Stand-Out. Partners stand facing one another, grasping right hand to hand and left to left (right hands are on top). The support partner assumes a quarter-squat position. The top partner steps with her left foot to the left thigh of her partner (the heel is placed on the inside of the leg) and steps up and around with her right foot to the right shoulder of her partner. She now steps with her left foot to the left shoulder and releases her hands as she gains her balance. The support partner provides additional support by holding his partner's ankles close to his head. Spot carefully.

INVERTED SUPPORT SKILLS

Inverted supports are classified here as *headstand skills, transitional supports,* and *handstand skills.* It is absolutely essential that children be exposed to a progressive program of inverted supports that builds skill upon skill. Neglecting to do so will only lead to failure and frustration on the part of the students. The static and dynamic balance requirements of inverted support skills are too great to be left to chance. The teaching progression chart for inverted supports that follows in Table 23.4 presents a logical teaching progression.

Objectives

Practice in inverted support skill activities will contribute to the following:

1. Static balance abilities.
2. Dynamic balance abilities (transitional supports).
3. Body awareness.
4. Spatial awareness.
5. Strength development.
6. Coordination.

Movement Experiences

Headstand Skills.   Children enjoy learning how to balance themselves in various inverted positions. Care, however, should be taken to insure that the muscles of the neck are sufficiently strong before engaging children in headstand-type ac-

PHOTO 23.8   The tripod is a headstand lead-up skill.

tivities. Children are generally sufficiently strong in this region of the body by age six.

Head Balance.   From a front kneeling position with all four limbs on the mat, put the head down on the mat so that the top of the forehead touches. Raise hips and straighten the legs for a five-point balance. Now raise the hands off the mat for a three-point balance. Finally, try balancing on only two points, using one foot and the head.

Greet the Elbows.   From a squat position with the hands on the mat outside the knees, place the forehead on the mat, forming a triangle with the head and the hands. Do not move the hands or head. Bring one knee up to touch the elbow and hold in a 4-point balance. Return and repeat with the other knee. After good balance is achieved, repeat, but this time balance *one knee on the elbow of a support* arm while the other leg extends with the toes touching the mat.

Tripod.   The tripod is similar to the preceding skill except both knees are placed on the elbows, forming a three-point balance. See who can balance for three, five, seven, and ten seconds.

One-Knee Tripod.   Same as the tripod, except only one knee is balanced on an elbow while the other leg is outstretched and free from support.

TABLE 23.4   Selected
Inverted Support Skills

Inverted Support Skills	Suggested Progression for Children			
	Beginning Level	Intermediate Level	Advanced Level	Page
Headstand Skills				313
Head balance	X			313
Greet the elbows	X			313
Tripod	X			313
One-knee tripod	X			313
Half headstand		X		314
Three-quarter headstand		X		314
Headstand		X		314
Kick-up headstand		X		314
Headstand to a roll		X		314
Drag headstand			X	315
Forearm stand			X	315
Transitional Supports				315
One leg up	X			315
Side switch	X			315
Half cartwheel	X			315
Cartwheel		X		315
Consecutive cartwheels		X		315
Olympic cartwheel			X	316
Heel-click cartwheel			X	316
One-hand cartwheel			X	316
Round-off			X	316
Running round-off			X	316
Handstand Skills				316
Swing-up		X		316
Mule kick		X		316
Wall stand			X	316
Partner-aided handstand			X	317
Handstand			X	317

Half Headstand.   From a tripod position, bring the knees together to the chest and hold.

Three-Quarter Headstand.   Same as the half headstand except that the hips straighten, leaving only the knees bent.

Headstand.   From a tripod position, the knees are brought together at the chest, the hips unfold, and the legs straighten overhead. The body is supported by the hands and the head. The legs are together, with the toes pointed and the back slightly arched. Hold and return in the same manner.

Kick-Up Headstand.   From a three-point triangle position with the legs extended behind, walk the feet close to the head, being certain not to move the hands or head. Raise one leg, straighten overhead, and kick up with the other to a headstand position. Hold and return in the same manner.

Headstand to a Roll.   From a full headstand po-

sition, bend at the waist, tuck the head, and roll forward to a squat position.

Drag Headstand.   From a front lying position with the toes pointed, hands on the mat at chest level, and forehead on the mat, slowly raise the hips upward and drag the toes, keeping the legs straight, to a headstand position.

Forearm Stand.   From a heads-up kneeling position with the forearms on the mat, the elbows pointed out, and the thumbs and index fingers touching, kick up to an inverted support. The head is raised and the body is supported by only the forearms.

Transitional Supports.   Transitional supports include skills such as the cartwheel and the round-off. These skills require a great deal of dynamic balance and directional awareness. Considerable stress is placed on the coordinated actions of the limbs, sometimes operating in harmony with one another and sometimes in synchronous opposition.

One Leg Up.   From a standing postion at the edge of the mat with one foot slightly ahead of the other, bend forward, placing both hands on the mat. Keeping the head up, take the body weight on the hands and kick the back leg up behind.

Side Switch.   From a standing position at the edge of the mat with one leg slightly ahead of the other, bend forward, placing the hands down in front of the feet. Lean forward onto the arms, kick the trailing foot into the air, and swing the hips to the *prefered* side. Both legs will come off the floor and the forceful turn will bring the body around to the other side of the mat.

Half Cartwheel.   From a standing position with one leg slightly forward and the hands placed in front of the chest, lean forward and turn slightly to face the leading foot. The hand opposite the lead foot contacts the mat, followed immediately by the other hand. The legs are brought around roughly parallel to the floor.

Cartwheel.   From a standing position with one

leg slightly forward, extend the arms overhead and rock back onto the back foot. The arm and shoulder corresponding to the lead foot should be slightly forward. Swing forcefully downward, bending at the hips and kicking the trailing foot into the air. The hands contact the mat (trailing hand first) parallel to each other and shoulder width apart as the legs are brought overhead. The lead leg continues and comes down first opposite the takeoff spot. The trailing leg follows, and the body returns to a standing position facing the direction of takeoff.

Consecutive Cartwheels.   After the completion of one cartwheel back to a stand, try three or four cartwheels in succession.

Olympic Cartwheel.   From a straddle position with the arms outstretched at the sides, and standing on a line, perform a cartwheel action to the preferred side, trying to land back on the line.

Heel-Click Cartwheel.   Heels are clicked together when the legs are overhead in the cartwheel position.

One-Hand Cartwheel.   The one-hand cartwheel is similar to the cartwheel, except a more forceful downswing is required, in order to increase momentum.

Round-Off.   From a standing position with one leg slightly forward and the arms outstretched overhead, rock back onto the back foot and swing forward at the waist. The hands are brought to the mat simultaneously toward the side that the performer is facing. The legs swing overhead and the hips are rotated so that upon landing, both feet contact the mat at the same time and the performer faces the opposite direction from the takeoff. A forceful snap down of the legs, simultaneous contact, and facing the opposite direction are the key differences between the cartwheel and round-off. The round-off is an important preparatory move for numerous backward tumbling activities.

Running Round-Off.   Same as the round-off but done from a running start, with a one-foot takeoff and more forceful execution of the entire action, resulting in considerable backward momentum in preparation for additional stunts.

Handstand Skills.   The handstand is an exciting and difficult stunt to master. Because of the

PHOTO 23.10   The handstand takes considerable practice.

inverted posture, high center of gravity, and two-point stance, the handstand usually takes considerable practice to master.

Swing-Up.   From a standing position with one leg slightly forward, bend at the waist and swing both arms down. The hands contact the mat slightly ahead of the lead foot. The trailing leg is kicked first into the air followed by the lead leg. Practice keeping the arms straight, the head up, and getting the legs and hips up over the head.

Mule Kick.   Same as the swing-up except that from a half-inverted position, both legs are bent, then forcefully extended backward while the hands push off the mat.

Wall Stand.   From a stride position about two

feet from the wall, the hands are placed shoulder width apart, on the floor with the fingers spread and arms locked. The head is up and the body weight is over the shoulders. The trailing leg kicks up and is followed by the lead leg. The heels contact the wall. The performer balances herself and lightly pushes away from the wall as the balance position is found.

Partner-Aided Handstand.   From a stride standing position with the arms overhead, rock back onto the rear foot and swing forward, bending at the waist. The hands contact the mat

shoulder width apart with the fingers spread and facing forward, slightly in front of the lead foot. The trailing leg is brought overhead, followed by the other. The body is balanced in this inverted position with the line of gravity drawn from the center of the base of support. The partner lightly grasps the lead leg at the ankle as needed to help locate the proper balance position (Note: *never* hold both legs).

Handstand.   Same as the partner-aided handstand except without the aid of a spotter.

FIGURE 23.1   Sample aim chart for selected stunts and tumbling skills.

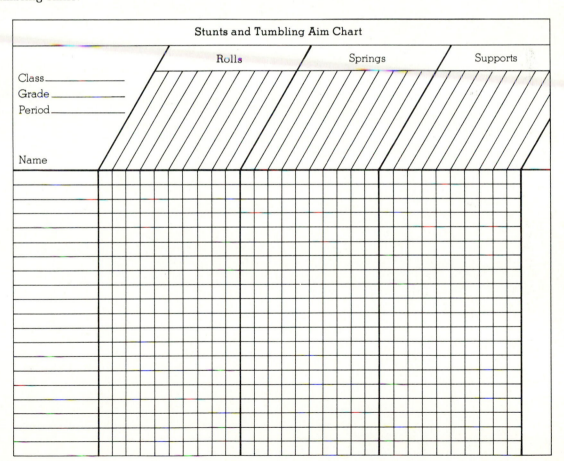

ASSESSING PROGRESS

Stunts and tumbling skills can be a fun and exciting part of the developmental physical education program *if* they are properly taught and if they are presented in a logical developmental sequence. Within any class, children will frequently be at the beginning, intermediate, or advanced level of skill learning. It is therefore essential that teaching be sufficiently personalized to allow for individual differences and various rates of progress.

Adaptation of the sample stunts and tumbling aim chart, depicted in Figure 23.1, to suit your program of skills can be a helpful motivational device for students and an assessment tool for the instructor. Aim charts enable children to chart their progress. They also provide an informal means of skill assessment.

SUGGESTED READING

Brown, J. R., and Wardell, D. B. (1980). *Teaching and coaching gymnastics for men and women*. New York: Wiley.

Gillom, B. C. (1970). *Basic movement education for children*. Reading, MA: Addison–Wesley.

O'Quinn, G. (1978). *Developmental gymnastics*. Austin: University of Texas Press.

CHAPTER 24

APPARATUS SKILLS

The use of traditional gymnastics apparatus is frequently limited at the elementary school level. The cost of commercial equipment, its size, and storage problems often make it prohibitive to purchase gymnastics apparatus. However, apparatus of a nontraditional nature can often be included in the elementary program. The climbing, hanging, and swinging skills developed on horizontal ladders, turning bars, and climbing ropes are especially helpful in developing the muscles of the upper trunk and shoulder girdle. The balancing and springing skills practiced on balance beams, large innertubes, and vaulting boxes are also important to the motor development of children.

This chapter contains a recommended sequence of skill progression for several pieces of large apparatus frequently available in elementary schools. The apparatus included here, *balance beam, climbing ropes, horizontal ladder, innertubes and springboard, vaulting box*, and *turning bar* have been selected for their potential contributions to the child, their versatility, and their general availability.

SAFETY CONSIDERATIONS

There are a number of important safety factors to take into consideration when using large apparatus. Adherence to the following suggestions will minimize unnecessary safety hazards.

1. Place mats under the apparatus whenever it is being used.
2. Know your group, and be sure to spot activities carefully.

3. Teach responsible children proper spotting techniques and use them as spotters in nonweight-bearing activities.
4. Stress thinking the skill through before attempting it.
5. Stress not attempting a skill unless a spotter is present.
6. Emphasize building skill upon skill.
7. Provide suitable warmup activities prior to using the apparatus.
8. Do not tolerate horseplay on the apparatus.
9. Do not overspot. Permit the performer to get the feel of the skill.
10. Caution children to stop and rest when tired.

TEACHING TIPS

Following are a number of teaching suggestions for various pieces of apparatus.

1. Build skill upon skill in small increments, recognizing differences in strength, coordination, and agility.
2. Use pieces of apparatus as a station within a circuit. Place task cards nearby for both performers and spotters.
3. Begin with low-level skills and progress to higher level skills.
4. Lines and ropes stretched out on the floor make an excellent practice medium for practicing balance-beam skills.
5. Do *not* knot the bottom of the climbing ropes; this will prevent children from relying on the knot for support.
6. Stress a thumbs-around grasp for all climbing and hanging skills.
7. Do not permit sliding down the climbing rope. Use a hand-under-hand method.
8. Be certain that the area for swinging activities is clear.
9. Turning-bar activities should be done using a low horizontal bar first, then a higher bar as skill develops.
10. When using the innertube or springboard,

stress keeping the head up and maintaining body control in the air.

BALANCE-BEAM SKILLS

The low balance beam is a very useful piece of apparatus. It is used primarily for developing static and dynamic balance abilities. Balance beams may be purchased commercially, or they may be easily made for a fraction of the price. Stress focusing the eyes forward and performing all movements slowly, in good control. Beam activities should be spotted, being careful not to overspot in order that the child may get the full benefit from negotiating the balance problem. Table 24.1 provides a suggested progression chart for balance-beam skills.

Objectives

Movement activities on the balance beam contribute to:

1. Improved static balance abilities.
2. Improved dynamic balance abilities.
3. Better coordination and agility.
4. Body and directional awareness.
5. Increased endurance and flexibility in the legs.

Movement Experiences

Beam Stand. Step up onto the beam and hold a balanced position without falling.
Balance and Touch. Balancing on the beam, touch body parts called out by the teacher.
Beam Walk. Walk forward, backward, and sideways the length of the beam. First use a follow step, then use an alternating step.
Walk–Turn–Walk. Walk forward on the beam to the middle, make a halfturn, and finish by walking backward.
Double-Turn Walk. Walk forward on the beam

TABLE 24.1 Selected
Balance-Beam Skills

Balance-Beam Skills	Suggested Progression for Children			
	Beginning Level	Intermediate Level	Advanced Level	Page
Beam stand	X			320
Balance and touch	X			320
Beam walk	X			320
Walk–turn–walk	X			320
Double-turn walk	X			320
Walk and touch	X			321
Toe walk	X			321
Dip walk	X			321
Crouch walk	X			321
Cat walk		X		321
Knee touch		X		321
Full turn		X		321
Step over		X		321
Go through		X		321
Over and through		X		321
Beanbag pickup		X		321
Beanbag balance		X		321
Knee scale			X	322
Front scale			X	322
V-seat			X	322
V-seat to knee scale			X	322
Partner pass			X	322
Partner scale			X	322
Toss and catch			X	322

to the middle, make a halfturn, and walk to the end backward. Return to the middle by walking forward, make a quarter turn, and finish by walking sideways to the end.

Walk and Touch. While traveling from one end of the beam to the other, touch three body parts with the hand (one above the waist, one above the knees, one below the knees).

Toe Walk. Walk from one end of the beam to the other without the heels touching.

Dip Walk. Walk the beam using alternate dipping steps.

Crouch Walk. Walk the beam at a low level.

Cat Walk. Walk the beam with the hands in contact with the beam, the hips up, and the legs straight.

Knee Touch. Walk to the middle of the beam, squat down so that one knee touches the beam, and return to a stand.

Full Turn. Walk to the center of the beam, make a full turn on the toes, and continue to the end.

Step Over. Step over objects placed on the beam.

Go Through. Step through two or three hoops held on the beam.

Over and Through. Alternate stepping over and going through objects on the beam.

Beanbag Pickup. Place several beanbags on the beam. Pick up each bag while walking from one end to the other. The next person puts the beanbags back on the beam while walking from one end to the other.

Beanbag Balance. With a beanbag or eraser balanced on the head, practice all of the preceding activities.

PHOTO 24.1   A knee scale on the balance beam.

Knee Scale.   From a single-knee kneeling position, grasp the beam with the hands and raise the nonsupport leg high behind.

Front Scale.   From a standing position on one foot at the center of the beam, bend forward at the waist and raise the nonsupport leg high in back.

V-Seat.   From a sitting position straddling the beam, with the hands grasping the beam from behind, raise both legs to a V-seat position and hold.

V-Seat to Knee Scale.   From a V-seat, bring the legs down as the body moves forward. Regrasp the beam in front, place one knee on the beam, and execute a knee scale.

Partner Pass.   With a partner at the opposite end of the beam, walk to the center and pass each other without losing balance.

Partner Scale.   At the center of the beam, clasp hands with a partner and both execute a front scale.

Toss and Catch.   With a partner at the other end of the beam, play catch with a soft ball.

CLIMBING ROPE SKILLS

Many gymnasiums throughout North America are equipped with climbing ropes. This piece of apparatus can be both fun and challenging if a few basic safety rules are followed. First, spot activities carefully. Second, never require children to attempt an activity beyond their ability level. Third, permit only the most skilled children to climb to the top. Fourth, do not permit sliding down the rope; instead, teach the use of a hand-under-hand grip. Table 24.2 provides a suggested sequence of progression for selected climbing rope skills. See Figure 24.1 for a description of the foot positions for rope climbing.

Objectives

Practice in activities on climbing ropes will contribute to:

PHOTO 24.2   Proper positioning for the rope climb.

1. Improved upper-arm and shoulder girdle strength.
2. Better climbing abilities.
3. Improved coordinated use of the hands, arms, and legs.

Movement Experiences

Head Touch.   From a sitting position, grasping the rope in both hands, lie back until the head touches the mat.

Back Lift.   From a sitting position, gripping the rope, extend at the hips and arch back so that the body is straight and only the heels touch the mat.

Heel Pivot.   From the back-lift position just described, pivot in a circle around the heels.

Straight Pull.   From a sitting position, grasping the rope, pull to a stand, keeping the legs straight.

Nose Touch.   From a stand, grasping the rope overhead with both hands, jump up and touch the nose to the hands and return.

Nose-to-Rope Touch.   From a stand, grasping the rope with the arms straight overhead, jump up and touch the nose to the rope *above* the hands and return.

Jump and Grasp.   From a stand, with the arms grasping the rope overhead, jump up to a mounting support, wrapping the legs around the rope. Hold for three counts and return.

Jump and Hold.   Jump to a hands-and-legs support and hold for up to ten seconds.

Swing and Hold.   Run forward, pull up onto the rope, and hold. Swing forward and drop off at the end of the backswing.

Tarzan and Jane.   From a support position, swing forward and back twice, dropping off at the end of the second backspring.

Rope Pull-Ups.   From a support position, with the hands above the head, pull up and touch the nose to the rope above the hands. Return to a straight-arm hang. Repeat.

Leg Hold.   Jump to a proper arm-and-leg grasp position, release the hands, and hold for three counts with only the legs.

Rope Climb.   The rope is gripped between the shin and the calves, with one foot pressing on the rope. The hips are fully flexed and the arms are extended overhead. As the legs are straightened, the arms pull up and the elbows bend. The bottom hand releases, reaches up over the other hand, and regrasps. The process is repeated halfway up the rope. The process is then reversed when climbing down. Do not slide down the rope. Use a hand-under-hand.

Bell Ringer.   Only after individual students have demonstrated sufficient control should they be permitted to climb to the top of the rope. Secure a small bell at the top that can be rung for positive reinforcement.

Double-Rope Hold.   Grasping two ropes, jump up and hold in a bent-arm position with the aid of the legs.

Double-Rope Swing.   Grasping two ropes, run

TABLE 24.2 Selected
Climbing Rope Skills

Climbing Rope Skills	Suggested Progression for Children			
	Beginning Level	Intermediate Level	Advanced Level	Page
Head touch	X			323
Back lift	X			323
Heel pivot	X			323
Straight pull	X			323
Nose touch	X			323
Nose-to-rope touch		X		323
Jump and grasp		X		323
Jump and hold		X		323
Swing and hold		X		323
Tarzan and Jane		X		323
Rope pull-ups		X		323
Leg hold			X	323
Rope climb			X	323
Bell ringer			X	323
Double-rope hold			X	323
Double-rope swing			X	323
Double-rope candle stand			X	324
Double-rope pullover			X	324

FIGURE 24.1 Feet positions for rope climbing.

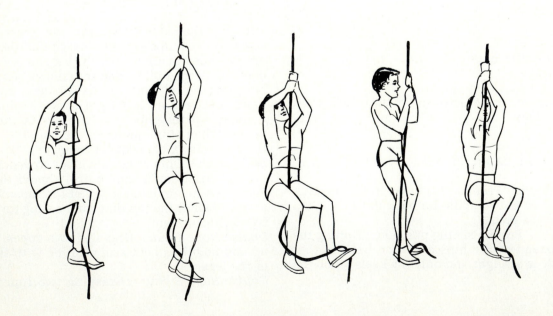

forward and pull up to a bent-arm support, swing forward, and drop off at the end of the back-swing.

Double-Rope Candle Stand.   Grasping two ropes in a straight-arm support position, pull up and turn over to an inverted support position. Spot carefully.

Double-Rope Pullover.   Grasping two ropes, jump to a bent-arm hold. Bend the knees to the chest and drop the head back. Pull over to an inverted position and release to a standing position on the mat. Spot carefully.

HORIZONTAL LADDER SKILLS

Many playgrounds and some gymnasiums are equipped with a horizontal ladder. The horizontal ladder should be positioned high enough to permit the feet to dangle freely, and mats should be placed underneath for inverted skills. Activities on the ladder should be spotted whenever the body is inverted. Also, stress should be placed on a thumbs-around-the-bar grasp in order to minimize the chance of losing one's grip. Table 24.3 provides a recommended progression for selected horizontal ladder skills.

PHOTO 24.3   Rail travel on the horizontal ladder.

Objectives

Practice in activities on the horizontal ladder will contribute to:

1. Increased muscular strength in the arms and upper trunk muscles.
2. Improved muscular endurance.
3. Improved dynamic balance abilities.
4. Increased body and spatial awareness.

Movement Experiences

Straight Hang.   Grasp a single rung with both hands and hang for up to 10 seconds.

Single-Knee Lift.   From a straight hang, raise one leg, then the other.

Double-Knee Lift.   From a straight hang, raise both knees to the chest and return. Repeat.

Leg Lift.   From a straight hang, raise both legs to a position parallel with the floor and hold.

Trunk Twister.   From a straight hang, twist the trunk from side to side.

Bicycle Hang.   From a straight hang, make a continuous bicycle peddling action.

Hang and Swing.   From a straight hang, swing forward and back, dropping off at the end of the backswing. Try dropping at the end of the forward swing also. Discover which is safer.

Half Chin.   From a straight hang, pull to a position in which the arms are flexed at a 90-degree angle. Hold for three or more seconds.

TABLE 24.3 Selected Horizontal Ladder Skills

Horizontal Ladder Skills	Suggested Progression for Children			
	Beginning Level	Intermediate Level	Advanced Level	Page
Straight hang	X			325
Single-knee lift	X			325
Double-knee lift	X			325
Leg lift	X			325
Trunk twister	X			325
Bicycle hang	X			325
Hang and swing	X			325
Half chin		X		325
Flexed-arm hang		X		326
Chinups		X		326
Side-rail travel		X		326
Single rail travel		X		326
Single-rung travel		X		326
Monkey rung travel		X		326
Super monkey travel		X		326
Inverted pushups		X		326
Inverted hang			X	326
Inverted swing			X	326
Pull through			X	326
Skin the cat			X	326
Pull to top			X	326

Flexed-Arm Hang. Pull to a fully flexed-arm hang with the chin parallel to the bar. Hold.

Chinups. From a straight hang with a palms-facing grip, perform chinups or pullups.

Side-Rail Travel. Grasp the outer portion of the side rails with the palms facing in. Travel from one end of the ladder to the other.

Single-Rail Travel. Grasp one rail and travel sideways from one end to the other.

Single-Rung Travel. From a straight hang, travel as far as possible with a follow grasp from one rung to the next.

Monkey Rung Travel. From a straight hang, travel with an alternating grasp, with only one hand touching *each* rung.

Super Monkey Travel. From a straight hang, travel from one end of the ladder to the other, skipping rungs.

Inverted Pushups. From a straight hang, swing the legs upward and hook the knees over the bar. Perform repeated "pushups" by bringing the nose up to the bar and then returning.

Inverted Hang. From a straight hang, pull the legs up and hook the knees around one rung. Let go of the hands and hang by the knees. Spot carefully.

Inverted Swing. From a knee-hanging position, swing back and forth with the arms dangling overhead.

Pull Through. From a straight hang with the arms slightly more than shoulder width apart, drop the head back as the knees are brought to the chest, turn over backward, and drop to standing position.

Skin the Cat. From a straight hang with the arms slightly more than shoulder width apart, drop the head back as the knees are brought up to the chest. Turn over backward and hang. Return to a straight hang.

Pull to Top. From a straight hang, pull the body

to a knee-hang position. With aid of the arms, pull the body through a rung and finish sitting on top of the ladder. Spot carefully.

INNERTUBE AND SPRINGBOARD SKILLS

Innertubes may be obtained from tire-salvage store. Several large *truck* tubes may be tied together and placed on tumbling mats. Be certain to secure the valve and stem of each innertube prior to use and to use proper spotting techniques. Many of the same skills may be performed with the springboard. Table 24.4 provides a suggested progression of skills.

Objectives

Innertube activities contribute to:

1. Enhancing dynamic balance abilities.
2. Improving basic jumping skills.
3. Improving body and spatial awareness.
4. Developing leg strength.
5. Improving total body coordination.

PHOTO 24.4   The ankle slapper off the springboard.

Movement Experiences

Sit and Bounce.   From a sitting position on the tube, bounce up and down.
Walk Around.   From a standing position on the tube, walk all the way around without losing balance.
Stand and Bounce.   From a standing position on the tube, bounce up and down. Spot carefully.
Center Jump.   From a standing position on the tube, jump into the center and back up on the other side.
Ins and Outs.   From a standing position on the floor, jump up onto the tube, jump into the center, jump back up on the other side, and jump off.
Half-Turn Bounce.   From a standing position on the tube, bounce and turn halfway around in two bounces. Try one bounce.

Bounce and Touch.   From a standing position on the tube, bounce and touch with your hand body parts named by the instructor.
Bounce and Squat.   From a standing position on the tube, spring upward and land in a squat position on the mat.
Bouncing Bunny.   From a standing position on the tube, facing out, spring upward, landing in a squat position on the mat with the hands also on the mat. Immediately do a bunny hop forward.
Bounce and Roll.   From a standing position on the tube facing out, spring upward, landing in a full squat position on the mat. Immediately do a forward roll.
Tuck Jump.   From a standing position on the tube, facing out, bounce and tuck knees to the chest before landing back on your feet.

TABLE 24.4 Selected Innertube and Springboard Skills

Innertube and Springboard Skills	Suggested Progression for Children			
	Beginning Level	Intermediate Level	Advanced Level	Page
Sit and bounce	X			327
Walk around	X			327
Stand and bounce	X			327
Center jump	X			327
Ins and outs	X			327
Half-turn bounce	X			327
Bounce and touch	X			327
Bounce and squat	X			327
Bouncing bunny	X			327
Bounce and roll		X		327
Tuck jump		X		327
Toe jump		X		328
Knee bounce		X		328
Full-turn bounce		X		328
Partner bounce		X		328
Around the world		X		328
Feet to seat		X		328
Bounce and kick		X		328
Jump and half turn		X		329
Star bounce			X	329
Jump and full turn			X	329
Bounce and knee straddle			X	329
Bounce and ankle straddle			X	329
Bounce and jackknife			X	329
Bounce and toe straddle			X	329
Double spin			X	329
Double reverse spin			X	329
Double spin plus			X	329

Toe Jump. From a standing position on the tube, facing out, jump up and touch the toes prior to landing back on your feet.

Knee Bounce. From a standing position facing the tube, bounce the knees on the tube and return to a controlled stand. Repeat.

Full-Turn Bounce. From a standing position on the tube, bounce and do a full turn in three bounces; then try for two.

Partner Bounce. From a standing position on the tube, facing in, partners hold hands and bounce together. Try alternate bouncing also.

Around the World. From a standing position on the tube, facing in with partners holding hands, bounce in a clockwise direction around the tube. Repeat in the opposite direction.

Feet to Seat. From a standing position on the tube, facing in, bounce and land on your seat with feet in the center of the tube.

Bounce and Kick. From a standing position on

the tube, bounce up and hit the buttocks with the heels prior to landing on the mat.

Jump and Half Turn. From a standing position on the tube facing out, jump and do a half turn, landing on the mat.

Star Bounce. From a standing position on the tube, facing out, bounce off the tube, spreading both the arms and legs wide apart and landing in a controlled squat position on the mat.

Jump and Full Turn. From a standing position on the tube, facing out, jump and do a full turn, landing on the mat.

Bounce and Knee Straddle. From a standing position on the tube, facing out, bounce and bend the knees backward and touch them prior to landing on the mat in a controlled upright position.

Bounce and Ankle Straddle. From a standing position on the tube, facing out, bounce and do a straddle jump, touching the ankles.

Jackknife. From a standing position on the tube, facing out, bounce and lift the legs forward and upward, keeping the feet close together. Touch the ankles or toes with the hands and land on the mat.

Bounce and Toe Straddle. Do a straddle jump, touching pointed toes at the height of the jump. Land in a controlled upright position on the mat.

Double Spin. From a standing position on the tube, facing out, jump and make a full turn in the air, land on the mat, and immediately rebound off the mat with another full turn.

Double Reverse Spin. Same as the double spin except the second full turn is in the opposite direction from the first.

Double Spin Plus. After executing a double spin or a double reverse spin, finish with a forward roll, cartwheel, or round-off.

SPRINGBOARD VAULTING SKILLS

Springboards and vaulting boxes may be purchased commercially or made by a skilled carpenter. Vaulting apparatus should be adjusted to the average height of the group. Mats should always be used in the landing area, and proper spotting techniques should be employed. The

PHOTO 24.5 Straddle mount.

springboard should be 8 to 12 inches from the base of the vaulting box. Springboard vaulting is not recommended for children at the beginning level because of the combination of springing and vaulting skills required. Table 24.5 provides a recommended progression of skills.

Objectives

Springboard vaulting activities promote:

1. Improved eye–body coordination.
2. Better dynamic balance abilities.
3. Strength development.
4. Improved coordination and agility.
5. Improved muscular power.

Movement Experiences

Squat Mount. From a standing position on the springboard with both hands on the apparatus, jump up with a two-foot takeoff to a squat position.

TABLE 24.5 Selected Springboard Vaulting Skills

Springboard Vaulting Skills	Suggested Progression for Children			
	Beginning Level	Intermediate Level	Advanced Level	Page
Squat mount	X			329
Free mount	X			330
Running squat mount	X			330
Running free mount	X			330
Jump and land	X			330
Jump and turn	X			330
Upright springs	X			330
Jump and roll	X			330
Jump, turn, and roll	X			330
Squat vault			X	330
Flank vault			X	330
Straddle mount			X	330
Straddle vault			X	330
Shoot squat vault			X	330

Free Mount. From a standing position on the springboard, jump up to a stand on the box.

Running Squat Mount. From a run and a two-foot takeoff, place the hands on the box and do a squat mount.

Running Free Mount. Execute a free mount from a run and a two-foot takeoff.

Jump and Land. Spring to a position on the box, jump off, and land with good control.

Jump and Turn. Spring to a position on the box, making a half, three-quarter, or full turn in the air before landing in good control.

Upright Springs. Spring to a position on the box, then spring off the box, executing any one of several upright springs.

Jump and Roll. Spring to a position on the box, then jump off, land, and do a forward roll. Spot carefully.

Jump, Turn, and Roll. Spring to a partner on the box, jump off, making a half turn in the air, land, and do a backward roll. Spot carefully.

Squat Vault. From a run with a two-foot take-off, place both hands on the box, spring upward, and squat through the arms to a position on the floor on the opposite side.

Flank Vault. From a run with a two-foot take-off, place both hands on the box, swing the legs to the side, release the hand to the swinging side, and land on the opposite side of the box. Spot carefully.

Straddle Mount. From a run with a two-foot takeoff, place both hands on the box and spring upward, raising the hips and keeping the legs straight. Spread the legs wide and mount the box in a straddle position. Spot carefully.

Straddle Vault. Follow the same procedures as the mount, but push forcefully with the hands, landing on the opposite side. Spot carefully.

Shoot Squat Vault. Perform as a squat vault, but extend the hips as the legs are pulled through, landing in a box-out position. Spot carefully.

TURNING BAR SKILLS

North American children are often weak in the upper arms and shoulder girdle. Activities on the turning bar or the low horizontal bar are excellent for developing these muscle groups. Place mats under the bar for all inverted activities. Stress a thumbs-around grip and spot carefully. The following are suggested activities that children may perform on a turning bar, starting with beginning-level activities and pro-

PHOTO 24.6   A bird's nest on the turning bar.

gressing to advanced activities. Table 24.6 provides a recommended progression of elementary turning bar skills. Spot all carefully.

Objectives

Turning bar activities promote:

1. Increased strength in the muscles of the upper arms and shoulder girdle area.
2. Improve inverted balance abilities.
3. Increased body awareness and spatial awareness.

Movement Experiences

Straight Hang.   Grasp the bar in both hands and hang for up to 10 seconds.
Single Toe Point.   From a straight hang position, point the toes of one foot at designated objects.
Double Toe Point.   From a straight hang, point the toes of both feet at designated objects below waist level.

Double Knee Raise.   From a straight hang, bring both knees up as high as possible and return. Repeat.
Hanging Walk.   From a straight hang, pretend to walk forward with the legs.
Bicycle Hang.   From a straight hang, pretend to peddle a bicycle forward. Repeat, peddling backward.
Hang and Swing.   From a straight hang, swing forward and backward.
Pivot Swing.   From a straight hang, swing the legs forward, sideways, and backward in a circle.
Change Grips.   From a straight hang, change hand grips while performing any of the preceding activities.
L-Seat.   From a straight hang, raise both legs and hold in an "L" position for three counts.
Straight Swing.   Swing forward and backward from the hips, keeping the legs straight.
Toe Toucher.   From a straight hang, bring the toe up to touch the fingers and return. Spot carefully.
Swing and Drop.   Swing forward and drop off at the end of the backswing.
Swing and Clap.   Swing forward and backward, clapping the hands once before landing at the end of the backswing.
Swing and Turn.   Swing forward and backward, dropping off at the end of the backswing with a quarter, half, or full turn.
Bar Travel.   Starting at one end of the bar, travel to the other using an alternate grip.
Monkey Travel.   Starting at one end with the legs wrapped around the bar and both hands grasping, travel to the opposite end and return. Spot carefully.
Knee Hang.   From a straight hang, bring the knees to the chest and drop the head back. Hook the legs around the bar at the knees and release the hands. Hang by the knees for three counts. Return to a straight hang. Spot carefully.
Knee Swing.   From a knee-hanging position, swing forward and back with the instructor spotting with the hand lightly supporting the ankles.
Pull Through and Drop.   From a straight hang, lift the knees to the chest and drop the head back. Pull through to an inverted position, then to a reverse straight hang and drop.

TABLE 24.6 Selected
Turning Bar Skills

	Suggested Progression for Children			
Turning Bar Skills	Beginning Level	Intermediate Level	Advanced Level	Page
Straight hang	X			331
Single toe point	X			331
Double toe point	X			331
Double knee raise	X			331
Hanging walk	X			331
Bicycle hang	X			331
Hang and swing	X			331
Pivot swing		X		331
Change grips		X		331
L-seat		X		331
Straight swing		X		331
Toe toucher		X		331
Swing and drop		X		331
Swing and clap		X		331
Swing and turn		X		331
Bar travel		X		331
Monkey travel		X		331
Knee hang			X	331
Knee swing			X	331
Pull through and drop			X	331
Skin the cat			X	332
Birds nest			X	332

Skin the Cat. Same as preceding movement, but return to a straight hang.

Bird's Nest. From a straight hang, lift the knees to the chest and place the backs of the toes on top of the bar. Arch by raising the head up. Spot carefully.

ASSESSING PROGRESS

Progress in skill development on the large apparatus may easily be assessed with the use of aim charts. Charts can be placed on the wall or kept in the teacher's possession. When students are able to perform a new skill, they can check it off themselves or have the instructor record their accomplishments. For self-checked items, you may want to periodically spot check to be certain that individuals can actually perform the skills that they have checked.

SUGGESTED READING

Capon, J. (1981). *Successful movement challenges.* Byron, CA: Front Row Experience.

Kirchner, G., Cunningham, J., and Warrell, E. (1978). *Introduction to movement education.* Dubuque, IA: Wm. C. Brown.

Ryser, O. E., and Brown, J. R. (1980). *A manual for tumbling and apparatus stunts.* Dubuque, IA: Wm. C. Brown.

Stanley, S. (1980). *Physical education: A movement orientation.* Toronto: McGraw-Hill.

CHAPTER 25

DISC SPORT SKILLS

The Frisbee disc was invented in the 1950s. Discs were originally marketed in Southern California. Since that time their growth in popularity has been phenomenal. In fact, it is reported that each year more discs are sold than baseballs, basketballs, and footballs combined. Standard discs are excellent for outdoor use. Mini discs and cloth discs work well in more confined areas.

Children and adults can be found tossing a disc on the playground, at the beach, or in the backyard. It has developed into a popular recreational pastime for millions and is enjoyed as a sport by many. The game of Ultimate is the team-sport version of disc playing. The rules of Ultimate are presented later in this chapter. This chapter provides information on how to develop a skill theme for disc activities and the importance of skill sequencing.

DEVELOPING A DISC SPORT SKILLS THEME

In order to make the best use of your time and to maximize learning, you will find it helpful to utilize the following sequence.

1. *Preplan*. Determine approximately how long and when you will include disc skills in the program as a skill theme. Secure a sufficient number of discs so that at least every other child has one.
2. *Observe and Assess*. Observe the class or group in terms of their skill levels after studying the verbal descriptions and visual

descriptions on the pages that follow. Assess ability levels in terms of their level of movement skill learning, determining if they are at the beginning, intermediate, or advanced level of developing their disc throwing and catching skills.

3. *Plan and Implement.* Plan a program of skill development activities. Use the teaching tips and concepts children should know for help. Implement a developmentally appropriate program of sequential skill development activities.

4. *Evaluate and Revise.* Evaluate progress through informal observational assessment techniques or through formal skill testing procedures. Revise subsequent lessons based on student progress.

SKILL SEQUENCING

From the third grade on, children are generally at the sport skill phase of development. They should have mastered their fundamental manipulative abilities and be ready to begin developing the basics of disc throwing and catching. The disc skills program should be based on the present level of ability of the class or group. In terms of disc skill learning, second- and third-grade children are typically at the beginning level, while fourth and fifth graders are often at the intermediate level of skill learning. Children in the sixth grade and beyond are sometimes at the advanced level. Remember, however, that this does not guarantee that all are at the level *typical* for their age. Some may be ahead. Many others may be behind. It is important to know where your students are, in order to be able to plan more effectively for all.

A suggested progression for teaching disc skills and a developmental activities chart are located in Tables 25.1 and 25.2, respectively. These will be helpful in identifying appropriate disc sport skills to teach and skill drills to incorporate into your lessons. A brief description of each of these drills is found in the skill development activities section of this chapter, along with a list of several recommended warmup activities.

DISC THROWING

There are three basic ways to throw the disc: backhand, forehand, and overhand. The backhand is generally the easiest to master and is usually taught first. The keys to successful disc throwing are smoothness, control, and good wrist snap. Most children can learn to throw a disc well with a few basic teaching hints. Once this is learned, a whole new world of recreational and competitive play opens to children.

Teaching Tips

Common Problems
- Gripping the disc improperly.
- Failure to lead with the shoulder.
- Trying too hard, causing too much body rotation and arm action.
- Failure to follow through in the intended direction of flight.
- Inability to keep the disc from wobbling due to poor release technique.
- Failure to snap at the waist, resulting in short and poorly controlled throws.

Recommended Strategies
- Have one disc for every two children.
- Send a note home asking children to bring in extra discs that they may have at home.
- Work for smoothness and control prior to working for distance and speed.
- Work for a good flat spin first.
- Begin with partners about 10 meters apart.
- Concentrate on short, flat flights, gradually working back as skill increases.

Concepts Children Should Know

Skill Concepts
- You can move the fingers in close to the rim of the disc for greater power.
- Power comes from your wrist snap.
- Control comes from a smooth delivery.

TABLE 25.1
Selected Disc Skills

Disc Skills	Suggested Progression for Children			Page
	Beginning Level	Intermediate Level	Advanced Level	
Throwing				334
Backhand throw	Introduce	Refine		336
Forehand throw		Introduce	Refine	336
Overhand throw			Introduce	337
Catching				337
Sandwich catch	Introduce	Refine		338
Clap catch	Introduce	Refine		339
One-hand catch		Introduce	Refine	339
Associated Skills				341
Curve	Introduce	Refine		341
Hover	Introduce	Refine		341
"Trick" catches			Introduce	342
Tipping			Introduce	341
Finger delay			Introduce	341
Skipping			Introduce	341
Understanding the Game				
Rules		Introduce	Refine	340
Strategy		Introduce	Refine	340

TABLE 25.2
Developmental Activities
Chart for Disc Sport Drills

Disc Sport Skill Drills	Throwing Skills	Catching Skills	Associated Skills	Page
Flat throw	X			341
Bullseye	X			341
Hoop throw	X			341
Throw for distance	X			341
Disc bowl	X			341
Bird shoot	X			341
Distance/accuracy throw	X			341
Hover	X		X	341
Curve	X		X	341
Throw around	X			341
Throw and catch	X	X		341
Mobile throw and catch	X	X		341
Keep away	X	X		341
Gunner	X	X		341
Self-throw and catch	X	X		341
Self-throw, run, and catch	X	X		341
Partner guts	X	X		341
Team guts	X	X		341
Skip it	X	X	X	341
Freestyle	X	X	X	342

- Keeping the disc parallel to the ground will result in long, flat throws.
- Raising the front rim of the disc will result in high, arching throws.
- The greater the lift on the front rim, the higher and shorter the throw will be.
- Your disc will spin in different directions in the backhand and forehand throws.

Movement Concepts

- You can throw the disc from many different body positions.
- You can throw the disc at different speeds.
- You can throw the disc in different directions.
- You can throw the disc with varying amounts of force.
- You can throw the disc in different trajectories.
- You can throw the disc over, under, around, and through objects.
- You can throw the disc in a variety of ways to a partner, who can catch it in a variety of ways.

Backhand Throw

The cross-body backhand toss is generally the first disc toss learned by children and adults alike.

Verbal Description

- Hold lightly with the thumb on top, index finger on the rim, and the remaining fingers spread under the disc.
- Stand with the lead shoulder facing the target and the feet slightly spread.
- The throwing arm is brought back across the body and the trunk twists at the waist.
- The throwing arm moves forward with a straight-arm action, and the body weight is shifted forward.
- The disc is released flat with a snap of the wrist.
- The throwing arm follows through, ending with the index fingers pointing at the target.

Visual Description

PHOTO 25.1   Backhand throw.

Forehand Throw

The forehand throw is generally the second disc throw learned by children. It is usually best to teach this skill after the backhand has been reasonably well mastered.

Verbal Description

- Disc is gripped between the thumb and forefinger with rim at the base of the thumb.
- Thumb firmly grips the top edge.
- Forefinger is extended and grips from the bottom.
- Nonthrowing shoulder leads, facing toward the target.
- Nonthrowing arm points in the intended direction of flight.

- Throwing arm is swung back as trunk twists and weight shifts to the rear foot.
- Arm swings low across the front of the body as weight shifts forward.
- Disc is released flat in a smooth, controlled motion.
- Throwing arm follows through in the direction of flight.

Visual Description

PHOTO 25.2   Forehand throw.

Overhand Throw

The overhand throw is more difficult to master than either the backhand or forehand throws. It should be reserved for students at the advanced level of disc throwing.

Verbal Description
- Disc is gripped with the same two-finger grip used for the forehand throw.

- Face the target, legs in a slight stride, with the leg opposite the throwing arm leading.
- Disc is brought above and behind the throwing shoulder to a near-vertical position as the weight shifts back.
- Arm is brought forcefully forward, the wrist snaps, and the body shifts forward.
- Disc is released and the arm follows through in the intended direction of flight.

Visual Description

PHOTO 25.3   Overhand throw.

DISC CATCHING

Catching a disc is easy to master with a little practice. Because of the tendency of the disc to float in the air, children have more time to get into position and to track the oncoming object. It does, however, take a while to judge where to best intercept the disc.

Teaching Tips

Common Problems
- Failure to get in the proper ready position.
- Failure to get behind the disc.
- Failure to track the disc to the hands.
- Closing the eyes or looking away as the disc approaches.
- Keeping the catching arm stiff.
- Clamping too late.

Recommemded Strategies
- Work with catching skills in conjunction with throwing skills.
- Stress tracking the disc all the way to the hands.
- Use a cloth disc for those who close their eyes or look away.
- Practice catching soft, flat throws directly in front of the body prior to harder-thrown discs coming from varying trajectories.

Concepts Children Should Know

Skill Concepts
- The direction of spin is different for right- and left-handed players and for forehand and backhand throws, which affects the preparation for your catch.
- Get in the ready position and be prepared to react to unexpected placements of the disc.
- Keep your eyes on the disc all the way to your hands.
- Give with the disc as it is caught.

Movement Concepts
- You can catch the disc in various body positions.
- You can catch a disc from different directions.
- You can catch discs traveling at different speeds.
- You can alter your catching in many ways.

Two-Handed Sandwich Catch

The sandwich catch is the most basic pattern used to catch a disc. The two-hand sandwich catch is sometimes called a pancake catch.

Verbal Description
- Feet are in a narrow stride postition with either leg forward and both knees bent.
- The eyes track the path of the oncoming disc directly to the hands.
- The arms are held slightly bent in front of the body with one hand facing up and the other down.
- As the disc approaches, the hands are "sandwiched" together, trapping the disc between the palms at its center.

Visual Description

PHOTO 25.4   Two-hand sandwich catch.

Two-Hand Clap Catch

The clap catch is two-handed and is usually the second catching pattern learned by children.

Verbal Description
- Stand facing the disc, feet parallel and shoulder width apart, knees slightly bent.
- Track the disc directly to the hands.
- The arms are held slightly bent in front of the body with the fingers spread and elbows out.
- The hands clamp onto opposite sides, with the thumbs on top and the fingers beneath the disc.

Visual Description

PHOTO 25.5   Two-hand clap catch.

One-Hand Catch

The one-hand catch is the most popular and most used catching technique. The exact nature of the one-hand catch will be affected by the height of the disc, the speed, and the direction of spin. The one-hand catch is made with the thumb on top for above-the-waist catches and with the thumb on the bottom for below-the-waist catches.

Verbal Description
- Assume the ready position.
- Track the disc to the hand.
- Place the catching arm comfortably in front of the body.
- The hand is open, with the thumb and fingers forming a "C" shape.
- As the disc approaches, it is clamped between the thumb and the fingers.
- As contact is made, the arm and body gives slightly.

Visual Description

PHOTO 25.6   One-hand catch.

BASIC RULES

Ultimate is a team sport that incorporates running, pinpoint passing, and often spectacular catching. It is a fast-paced, noncontact game played on a rectangular field up to 130 yards long and 40 yards wide.

The game is played with as few as two and as many as seven players per team. The object of the game is to score goals. The disc is moved by passing it to a team member. Once the disc is caught, the player with the disc may not take any forward steps toward the goal. Any time a pass is incomplete, interrupted, knocked down, or contacts and out-of-bounds area, a turnover occurs. A turnover results in an immediate change of possession at the point where the disc is recovered. A goal is scored when a player successfully passes the disc to a teammate in the opposing team's end zone.

The game is played in two 24-minute periods. Overtime periods, in case of a tie, are 5 minutes long. Each team is permitted three time outs per half.

Play is started with a flip of the disc. The team winning the flip may choose the goal they wish to defend, or they may choose to begin the game with the initial *throw-off*. A throw-off occurs at the beginning of each half and after each goal from anywhere in the players' end zone. The disc may not be touched by an opposing player until after it has first been touched by a teammate of the person making the throw-off.

Fouls and violations occur when:

1. More than one defensive player guards a player at a time.
2. There is physical contact between the thrower and the defender.
3. There is contact between opposing players *before* the disc is caught.
4. A player travels with the disc.
5. A player strips the disc from an opposing player's hands.

*For a complete set of rules to Ultimate, write Ultimate Players Association, P.O. Box 4844, Santa Barbara, California 93103.

6. A team called for a foul or violation turns the disc over to the opposing team and play continues in the opposite direction.

SKILL DEVELOPMENT ACTIVITIES

In order for children to master the skills of Ultimate, it will be necessary for them to first practice the skills individually in static drill situations. After the basic elements of a skill have been mastered, it can be practiced under controlled dynamic drill situations in which the conditions of the environment change based on the nature of the drill. Drills that combine the use of two or more skills should then be added, and finally lead-up games should be played. The skill drills presented in this section proceed from simple to complex, in that they range from static to dynamic practice drills and from single-skill to multiple-skill activities. A list of suggested warmup activities to be performed prior to engaging in skill drills is also included.

Warmup Activities

Warmup activities are essential prior to vigorous play. The activities that follow involve stretching and suppeling. They may be performed in the gymnasium or on the playing field. A variety of other stretching and suppeling exercises may be performed. Variation in the warmup activities and rapid movement from one exercise to another are keys to a successful warmup session.

Door Opener.   From a stand with bent arms parallel to the floor and hands at chest height, pull the arms forcefully back and hold for four counts. Repeat.

Arm Circles.   From a stand with the arms extended out from the sides, make small arm circles forward. Repeat in the opposite direction.

Trunk Twister.   From a stand with the feet parallel and shoulder width apart and the arms extended out from the sides, twist left and right from the hips without moving the feet.

Knee Lifter.   From a stand, bring one knee up

to the chest, pull tight, and hold for three counts. Repeat with other leg.

Leg Stretching.   From a seat with the legs spread, bend forward and grasp one ankle. Pull down and hold. Repeat to other side.

Skill Drills

A wide range of disc skill drills can be successfully practiced by children at all levels of ability. The primary emphasis of disc skill drills should be on improving the skills of throwing and catching under a variety of conditions. A game can be made out of any drill simply by giving it a name, making a few modifications in the procedures, and modifying the objectives. The following is a sampling of disc skill drills appropriate for elementary school children.

Objectives

Practice in the following skill drills will contribute to:

1. Improved disc-throwing skills (backhand, forehand, overhand throws).
2. Improved disc-catching skills (sandwich, clap, and one-hand catch).
3. Aerobic endurance.
4. Improved agility and coordination.

Movement Experiences

Flat Throw (backhand, forehand throwing). Practice controlled flat throws at a wall from a distance of 10 meters. Gradually increase the distance.

Bullseye (throwing).   Practice throwing at a large bullseye target taped to the wall from a distance of 5 meters.

Hoop Throw (throwing).   Practice throwing through a suspended hoop from 8.5 meters back. Gradually increase distance.

Throw for Distance (throwing).   Practice throwing the disc as far as possible.

Disc Bowl (throwing).   Set up several empty po-tato-chip cans in a group. Players try to knock the cans over.

Bird Shoot (throwing).   Players move around the gym, taking one "shot" at each potato-chip can, placed at varying levels. Partner retrieves disc.

Distance/Accuracy Throw (throwing).   Throw the disc as far as possible along a straight line. Total distance is the distance thrown minus the distance off the center line.

Hover (throwing).   Using a backhand throw, release the disc at a 45-degree angle, banking the back edge down. Try different angles.

Curve (throwing).   Using a backhand throw, bank the edge down in the intended direction of the curve.

Throw Around (throwing).   Set up an obstacle course with objects to be thrown over, under, around, and through. The disc may be advanced only with successful throws.

Throw and Catch (throwing, catching).   Practice throwing and catching with a partner. Begin 5 meters apart, gradually increasing the distance.

Mobile Throw and Catch (throwing, catching). Partners move about the field while passing the disc back and forth.

Keep Away (throwing, catching).   With two partners and a person in the middle, the middle person tries to intercept a passed disc in the air.

Gunner (throwing, catching).   Played the same as Keep Away, except the person in the middle is armed with a disc. She may use it to knock down a pass in anyway possible.

Self-throw and Catch (throwing, catching). Throw the disc in the air and catch your own throw. Knowledge of trajectory and wind factors is necessary.

Self-throw, Run, and Catch (throwing, catching).   Throw the disc as far as possible while still being able to catch it yourself.

Partner Guts (throwing and catching).   Player throws the disc as fast as possible to a partner, who tries to catch it. She in turn returns it as forcefully as possible.

Team Guts (throwing, catching).   Three players per team, 15 meters apart. Teams try to throw the disc so that it lands behind the opposing team's goal line. Hard, fast throws and one-handed catches are stressed.

Skip It (throwing, catching, bouncing).   Using a

backhand throw and a hard surface, throw the disc forcefully so that it hits the floor halfway to a partner. Disc should contact the floor on its edge and rebound upward.

Freestyle (throwing, catching, tipping, "trick" catches, finger delay).   With a partner and popular music playing, players are given three to five minutes to do their thing with their own variations of throwing and catching.

ASSESSING PROGRESS

Periodically during a disc sport skill theme you will want to evaluate the progress of individuals and the group. Your assessment can be informal and process-based. It can be conducted during partner practice activities. Table 25.3 gives an example of a simple observational instrument that may be helpful. You should be able to answer "yes" to each of the questions. If you are unable to do so, modifications will need to be made in subsequent lessons in order to more closely meet the specific needs of students.

Assessments may also be product-oriented and include more objective criteria, such as (1) total distances thrown; (2) maximum time aloft; (3) throw, run, and catch for distance; and (4) accuracy throws. If you choose to use product measures such as these, it is a simple matter of standardizing your assessment items, gathering your information, and interpreting scores. Saving scores over a period of a few years is a good idea if you intend to develop norms.

Another form of product assessment is the self-referenced method. In this method, the children evaluate their own abilities, both at the beginning and at the end of a skill theme. Individual improvement in terms of distance, accuracy, and so forth is noted and becomes the focus of concern rather than how one compares to the entire group. Examples of self-referenced assessment are located in Chapters 26 through 29. All three forms of assessing progress are acceptable. The methods chosen will depend on your objectives and philosophy of assessment.

TABLE 25.3 Self-Question Chart for Disc Throwing and Catching

Disc Throwing	Yes	No	Comments
1. Does the child use a preferred hand?			
2. Is the child able to control the trajectory of the disc?			
3. Does the child use proper body mechanics?			
4. Is there good wrist snap?			
5. Is there noticeable improvement?			

Disc Catching	Yes	No	Comments
1. Does the child maintain eye contact with the disc throughout?			
2. Does the child adjust easily to a disc throw at different levels?			
3. Does the child adjust easily to a disc throw at different speeds?			
4. Does the child catch the disc successfully on a consistent basis?			
5. Is the catching action smooth, coordinated, and in good control?			
6. Is there observable improvement?			

SUGGESTED READING

Donna, M., and Poynter, D. (1978). *Frisbee player's handbook.* Santa Barbara, CA: Parachuting Publications.

Kalb, I., and Kennedy, T. (1982). *Ultimate: Fundamentals of the sport.* Santa Barbara, CA: Revolutionary Publications.

Roddick, D. (1980). *Frisbee disc basics.* Englewood Cliffs,NJ: Prentice-Hall.

The rules of Ultimate. Ultimate Players Association, P.O. Box 4844, Santa Barbara, CA 93103.

Tips, C. (1977). *Frisbee by the masters.* Millbrae, CA: Celestial Arts.

Tips, C., and Roddick, D. (1979). *Frisbee sports and games.* Millbrae, CA: Celestial Arts.

CHAPTER 26

BASKETBALL SKILLS

Basketball is a very popular game in North American culture and throughout the world. Basketball is truly an American game, invented by Dr. James Naismith in 1892 in Springfield, Massachusetts. Its original intent was to provide a vigorous activity that could be played indoors during the cold New England winters. The original game invented by Dr. Naismith has undergone many changes and has become an international sport enjoyed by both females and males at all levels of ability.

The game of basketball combines and refines numerous fundamental movement skills. Successful basketball sport skill development is dependent upon attainment of mature patterns of fundamental movement. At the elementary school level, basketball instruction should focus on skill development and *not* on playing the game. This point cannot be overemphasized. Too often teachers skip the skill development phase of the basketball lesson and go directly to playing the game. This may be fine for the more skilled youngsters or those who have had previous instruction in the basic skills of the game. However, the less fortunate and less talented are ignored by such an approach. The developmental physical education program that stresses skill development will have little or no time for playing the regulation game of basketball during the regularly scheduled physical education program. Children with a desire to play the regulation game should be encouraged to take part in the intramural, interscholastic, or agency-sponsored youth basketball programs found in most communities.

With this in mind, the chapter focuses on the

procedures to follow in developing a basketball skills theme or unit and the importance of proper skill sequencing.

DEVELOPING A BASKETBALL SKILLS THEME

The primary difficulty encountered in a basketball skills theme with children in the upper elementary grades is the diversity of skill levels. Some children have taken part in youth basketball programs and are relatively proficient in a number of skills. Others have spent hour upon hour shooting baskets or playing playground basketball. And still others have had virtually no experience in any aspect of the game of basketball. The diversity of skill levels in basketball is probably greater than for any other single sport. This presents a unique challenge to the physical educator, namely, to design and implement an instructional unit that will be beneficial to children at all skill levels. In order to maximize learning and make the best use of your time, it will be helpful to implement the steps of: (1) preplanning, (2) observing and assessing, (3) Planning and implementing, and (4) Evaluating and revising, as discussed on page 333 in the preceding chapter.

SKILL SEQUENCING

Because of the immense popularity of the game of basketball throughout North America, there will be little difficulty in generating interest among the children. Care, however, must be taken to recognize the wide range of abilities among children in basketball. As a rule of thumb, third- and fourth-grade students are generally at the beginning level of developing their basketball skills, while fifth and sixth graders are typically at the intermediate level.

The suggested teaching progression depicted in Table 26.1 should help you select appropriate basketball skills to focus on as a developmental skill theme. When you have done this, you will need to select appropriate skill drills. The developmental activities chart for basketball (Table 26.2) lists several skill drills, progressing from simple to complex. A brief description of each of these drills is located in the "Skill Development Activities" section of the chapter, along with several recommended warmup activities. Appropriate basketball lead-up games may be found in Chapter 33.

PASSING AND CATCHING

Passing and catching are the basic ways in which the ball is transferred from one player to another. There are several types of passes used in basketball. The type of pass used will depend on the distance the ball must travel and the location of opposing players. The manner in which the ball is caught will depend on the location of the passed ball in terms of height and trajectory.

The chest pass, bounce pass, one-hand overarm pass, and two-hand overarm pass are important basketball passing skills to be learned. Teaching tips for passing and catching skills, including a list of common problems and recommended teaching strategies, follow, along with a list of concepts children should know. A brief verbal description and a visual description are also included for study.

Teaching Tips

Common Problems
- Poor control.
- Insufficient force.
- Lack of accuracy.
- Poor summation of forces.
- Insufficient follow through.
- Failure to transfer weight forward.
- Trapping a caught ball against the trunk.
- Failure to track a passed ball into the hands.

TABLE 26.1   Selected
Basketball Skills

| Basketball Skills | Suggested Progression for Children | | Page |
	Beginning Level	Intermediate Level	
Passing and Catching			345
Chest pass	Introduce	Refine	348
Bounce pass	Introduce	Refine	348
One-hand pass		Introduce	349
Two-hand overarm pass	Introduce	Refine	350
Catching	Introduce	Refine	350
Dribbling and Pivoting			351
Stationary dribble	Introduce	Refine	352
Moving dribble	Introduce	Refine	352
Crossover dribble		Introduce	353
Pivoting	Introduce	Refine	354
Goal Shooting			355
One-hand push shot	Introduce	Refine	356
Jump shot		Introduce	357
Layup shot		Introduce	358
Free-throw shooting	Introduce	Refine	359
Associated Skills			
Stopping	Introduce	Refine	362
Guarding	Introduce	Refine	362
Rebounding		Introduce	363
Understanding the Game			
Rules	Introduce	Refine	360
Strategy		Introduce	

Recommended Strategies

- Stress control prior to accuracy.
- Stress force after reasonable control is mastered.
- Stress accuracy only after control has been gained and force is sufficient.
- Use a smaller ball in order to assist with gaining control.
- If possible, have a ball for every other child.
- Stress following through by having the child point at the target after the ball is passed.
- Use floor markings (line, carpet square) as a visual reminder to step forward.
- Practice against a wall prior to working with a partner.
- Use a nerf-type ball for children who appear to be afraid of catching the ball.
- Emphasize visual tracking of the ball when catching.
- Attempt to get directly in the path of the ball when catching.

Concepts Children Should Know

Skill Concepts

- Step toward your target as you release the ball.
- Keep your eyes on your target.
- For two-hand passes, keep your elbows in and close to your body.

TABLE 26.2 Developmental Activities Chart for Basketball

Basketball Skill Drills	Passing/Catching Skills	Dribble/Pivoting Skills	Goal-Shooting Skills	Associated Skills	Page
Wall pass	X				361
Partner pass	X				361
Over–under	X				361
Keep away	X				361
Overhead pass	X				361
Line passing	X				362
Star passing	X				362
Stationary dribble		X			362
Dribble and look		X			362
Line dribble		X			362
Line-dribble pass		X			362
Wander dribble		X			362
Directional dribble		X			362
Chair dribble		X			362
Dribble and weave		X			362
Pivot drill		X			362
Pivot wall pass	X	X			362
Partner pivot	X	X			362
Four-point pivot	X	X			362
Pivot keep away		X			362
Center guard	X	X		X	362
Spot shot			X		362
Two-column free-throw shooting			X		362
Pass and shoot	X		X		363
Dribble and shoot		X	X		363
Pass, pivot, and shoot	X	X	X		363
Block that shot	X		X	X	363
Rebound ball	X		X	X	363

- For two-hand passes, apply equal amounts of force to each hand.
- Snap your wrists and follow through with your fingers pointing toward the target.
- Lead your teammate with a pass to where she will be when the ball arrives.
- Pass to the opening, not to the player.
- Catch a passed ball before moving toward the basket.
- Passing and catching should first be practiced under static conditions, then in progressively more complex, dynamic game situations.

Movement Concepts

- The speed at which a passed ball travels to a teammate is determined by the summation of forces applied.
- The ball will respond to all of the forces applied to it. Conflicting forces will result in an inaccurate pass.
- The speed of your passes can be and must be adjusted to meet the demands of the situation.
- Your passes will require greater coordinated summation of forces as the distance increases.
- In a dynamic game situation, your passes and your catching will needed to be varied as the immediate conditions dictate.
- Catching will occur at unexpected levels and from varying directions during dynamic game situations.
- Balls traveling at different rates of speed require varying amounts of force absorption.

Chest Pass

The chest pass is the most frequently used form of passing in basketball. It is effective for short passes and when an opposing player is not in the intended path of the ball.

Verbal Description

- Ball held chest-high.
- Hands grip ball from the side, toward the back.
- Fingers are spread with thumbs close together.
- Elbows are close to the body.
- Step forcefully forward into a stride stance.
- At the same time, extend arms forcefully.
- Push ball off the fingertips.
- Ball is caught at chest level.

Visual Description

PHOTO 26.1   Chest pass.

Bounce Pass

The bounce pass may be executed three different ways. The two-handed bounce pass should be learned first. Only after this has been mastered should the one and two handed overhand bounce pass be taught. The bounce pass is an effective passing skill used to cover a short distance, when an opposing player prevents use of the chest pass. It is also an effective pass to use to penetrate the defense. Children will need to experiment with the bounce pass at different distances in order to become familiar with the proper trajectory. The two-handed bounce pass is described here.

Verbal Description

- Ball held chest-high.
- Hands, arms, and legs positioned in same way as chest pass.
- Ball is pushed forward and downward.
- Ball contacts floor about three-quarters of the distance from the passer to the catcher.
- Ball rebounds at waist level to catcher.

Visual Description

PHOTO 26.2   Bounce pass.

One-Hand Overarm Pass

The one-hand overarm, or baseball pass, as it is frequently called, is used for long throws. This pass is difficult to control and should be taught only with a smaller than regulation ball at the elementary school level.

Verbal Description

- Assume stride position.
- Ball held with fingers spread in throwing hand.
- Nonthrowing hand steadies ball as it is brought to shoulder level.
- Body weight shifts to the rear foot, then onto the forward foot.
- As body weight is shifted forward, hips and shoulders forcefully rotate.
- Ball is released with a downward snap of wrist and fingers.
- The arm is extended at the point of aim.

Visual Description

PHOTO 26.3   One-hand overarm pass.

Two-Hand Overarm Pass

The two-hand overarm pass is used for shorter passes than the baseball pass and when one player wants to pass to a teammate above the reach of an opponent. It is also effective as an inbound passing technique.

Verbal Description

- Ball is held overhead with arms slightly bent.
- Hands grip the sides of the ball.
- Fingers are spread.
- Step forcefully into a stride position.
- Weight is transferred to forward foot as ball is brought forward.
- Arms follow through with extension at the elbows.
- Wrists and fingers turn downward and snap forward.

Visual Description

PHOTO 26.4   Two-hand overarm pass.

Catching

The manner in which the basketball is caught will depend on the height of the ball and the trajectory at which it is intercepted. The chest pass should be caught at chest level, the bounce pass at waist level, and the two overarm passes over the head. The baseball pass is frequently caught using a two-handed underhand pattern. A description common to all forms of catching a basketball follows.

Verbal Description

- Ball is visually tracked into the hands.
- Both hands contact ball at the same time.
- Hands make contact on the sides or behind the ball.
- Arms give upon contact to absorb force.
- Legs are positioned in stride position with knees bent slightly.
- Legs give slightly upon contact to absorb force.

Visual Description

PHOTO 26.5   Catching.

DRIBBLING AND PIVOTING

Dribbling is repeated one-hand bouncing of the ball, the way in which the ball is advanced by a player from one point to another. It is an integral part of the game of basketball and must be reasonably mastered under static practice situations prior to being used in skill drills and lead-up games, in which the conditions of the environment (an opposing player) are ever-changing. Stationary dribbling should be introduced first, followed by the moving dribble and finally crossover dribbling. While dribbling skills are being mastered, pivoting may be included in the lesson. Pivoting is the primary way in which the player with the ball avoids attempts by an opponent to take the ball away. Teaching tips and concepts children should know common to all forms of dribbling and pivoting follow, as well as a verbal description and visual description of each.

Teaching Tips

Common Problems
- Visually monitoring the ball.
- Slapping at the ball.
- Momentarily palming the ball while dribbling (double dribble).
- Inability to dribble well with either hand.
- Failure to protect the ball from an opponent.
- Insufficient follow-through.
- Poor rhythmical coordination of movements.
- Changing pivot feet.
- Dragging the pivot foot.
- Failure to crouch properly when pivoting.
- Failure to protect the ball when pivoting.

Recommended Strategies
- Work first for control of the ball.
- Practice stationary dribbling prior to any other form.
- Practice under static environmental conditions prior to dynamic drill and game situations.
- Stress keeping the ball low and close to the body while dribbling.
- Use wall markings to encourage students not to visually monitor the ball.
- Practice dribbling first with the preferred hand, then, after reasonable mastery, the nonpreferred hand.
- If possible, have a ball for each student in the class.
- Teach pivoting in conjunction with dribbling and catching.
- Use appropriate background music for children having difficulty hearing the rhythm of the movement.

Concepts Children Should Know

Skill Concepts
- Dribble the ball off to the side of the body.
- To be skillful in dribbling, you must not visually monitor the ball.
- Control the downward thrust of the ball with your fingertips.
- Dribble low in order to minimize the chances of losing the ball.
- Keep your body between the ball and your opponent.
- Once dribbling has been reasonably mastered with the preferred hand, it should be practiced with the other hand.
- Do not get your hand too far under or behind the ball. You will be called for a double dribble.
- Pivot on the ball of the established pivot foot.
- Learn to pivot with both feet and/or either foot.
- Be in the "ready position" when pivoting, prepared to pass or receive the ball.

Movement Concepts
- You can dribble the ball with varying amounts of force.

- The speed of your dribbling will be determined by the distance the ball must travel.
- The height of your dribble will be determined by the amount of force applied.
- You can dribble at different levels and in different directions.
- Your follow-through will strongly influence return of the ball.
- Dribbling should be rhythmical and controlled.
- The speed of your pivot will be determined by the pushoff foot.
- You can pivot forward or backward.
- You can adjust your level while pivoting.

Stationary Dribble

The stationary dribble should first be mastered with the preferred hand, then the nonpreferred hand.

Verbal Description
- Feet assume narrow stride position.
- Legs are bent slightly.
- Ball is held in hand opposite forward foot.
- Trunk leans forward slightly.
- Ball is pushed downward off the fingertips with follow-through from the arm, wrist, and fingers.
- Downward thrust is controlled.
- Ball returns no higher than waist level and action is repeated.
- Eyes do *not* monitor the ball.

Visual Description

PHOTO 26.6   Stationary dribble.

Moving Dribble

Once the stationary dribble has been reasonably mastered, the moving dribble should be introduced. The same action is employed, with the addition of the following.

Verbal Description
- Body is held low with bend at the knees and a slight forward lean.
- Ball is pushed slightly forward with each downward thrust.
- Ball is kept to the side of the body as player advances forward.

Visual Description

PHOTO 26.7   Moving dribble.

Crossover Dribble

The crossover dribble is often difficult for elementary students to master. It requires considerable coordination and use of the nonpreferred hand. All elements of the stationary dribble are the same, with the addition of the following.

Verbal Description
- Ball is pushed from one side of body to the other.
- Slight sideward thrust as the ball is projected downward.
- Body is kept low.
- Action is fluid and relaxed.
- Directional changes are made as needed.

Visual Description

PHOTO 26.8   Cross-over dribble.

Pivoting

Pivoting is a basic element of footwork in the game of basketball. It involves changing direction of movement by rotating around a fixed point. Practice in pivoting should stress movement control with emphasis on maintaining one's declared pivot foot.

Verbal Description
- Feet are parallel and shoulder width apart.
- Knees are slightly bent and weight is evenly distributed.
- Trunk is bent forward slightly.
- Hands are held in front of the body (with or without the ball).

- Eyes focus forward.
- Weight transfers to ball of pivot foot.
- Nonpivot foot pushes off and body makes a one-quarter turn (forward or backward) around the pivot foot.
- Pivot foot remains stationary around a fixed point at all times.

GOAL SHOOTING

Basketball goal shooting is an essential skill. Successful shooting demands considerable co-

Visual Description

PHOTO 26.9   Jump stop pivot.

PHOTO 26.10   Stride stop pivot.

ordination and sufficient power to be able to get the ball up to the level of the goal. With elementary-age children, it is recommended that the basketball goals be lowered to eight feet and the size of the ball be reduced. These modifications will permit practice with the proper techniques of goal shooting and will promote success. Basketball goal shooting is a very popular recreational activity. Emphasis should, however, be placed on the proper techniques of shooting. At the elementary school level, the one-handed push shot, the jump shot, the layup shot, and the free-throw shot should be taught. Teaching tips and concepts children should know common to all forms of basketball goal shooting follow, along with a verbal description and a visual description of each shot.

Teaching Tips

Common Problems
- Elbows out from the body.
- Lowering the arms toward the waist when preparing to shoot.
- Placing the wrong foot forward.
- Failure to visually monitor the goal throughout the entire shot.
- Lack of follow-through.
- Failure to extend the wrist and fingers.
- Unequal application of force to both hands (for the two-hand set shot and the underhand free-throw shot).

- Insufficient force to get the ball up to the basket without altering the correct pattern of movement.
- Limited accuracy.

Recommended Strategies

- Lower the basket.
- Use a smaller ball.
- Emphasize proper mechanics.
- Provide numerous opportunities for practice in a static drill situation prior to dynamic situations.
- Stress visually monitoring the ball until it touches the basket.
- Practice following through on all shots by pointing toward the basket after each shot.
- Modify scoring with less skilled children (score 1 point for hitting the backboard, 2 points for hitting the rim, and 3 points for making a basket).
- Tape a target on the blackboard to indicate where ball should strike.
- Focus on the process (mechanics) prior to the product (ball going through the hoop).
- Structure activities for success, particularly at the early stages of skill learning.
- Do not deal in absolutes during the early stages of learning (i.e., reward approximations).
- Remember a smaller ball and/or a lower basket will reduce many of the problems in mechanics and force production.
- For free-throw shooting, stress exact repetition of the entire sequence from the moment you step to the line until the ball arrives at the basket.
- Stress total concentration on all shots.

Concepts Children Should Know

Skill Concepts

- Keep your elbows in close to your body.
- Work for coordinated summation of the forces of the legs, trunk, and arms.
- The angles made by the wrists and elbows form a square prior to extension.

- Look at the basket throughout the shot.
- Follow through with your shots.
- Extend at the wrist and fingers at the end of your shot.
- Work for a high arc on the ball.
- On angle shots, make the ball hit the backboard before it goes through the hoop.
- Remember that the angle of reflection is exactly opposite the angle of incidence.
- With the layup shot, you take off on the foot opposite your shooting hand.
- With the one-handed set shot, you assume a narrow stride position with the same foot forward as your shooting hand.
- For the jump shot, release the ball at the height of your jump.
- When shooting free throws, repeat the same exact process each time.
- Practice, practice, practice.

Movement Concepts

- You can shoot the ball from varying levels.
- You can shoot the ball at varying angles from the basket.
- You can shoot the ball from varying distances from the basket.
- Your field-goal percentage will increase as you attempt shots closer to the basket.
- You can cause the ball to travel in varying pathways toward the basket (high arc, low arc, flat).

One-Hand Push Shot

The one-hand push shot, or set shot, as it is frequently called, is generally easier to master and much more frequently used than the two-hand push shot. It is therefore recommended that the one-hand shot be taught rather than the two-hand shot. It is generally used when shooting from a fairly long distance without an opposing player directly in the line of the shot.

Verbal Description

- Feet are in a narrow stride position, knees slightly bent.

- Shooting hand corresponds to forward foot.
- Ball held with both hands opposite the chin and in line with the lead foot.
- Back is straight, eyes are focused on the rim of the basket.
- Ball is tipped back onto the spread fingers of the shooting hand with the wrist cocked.
- Elbows are kept in.
- Knees and arms extend simultaneously and nonshooting hand releases ball.
- Shooting arm extends forward and upward in a high arc.
- Ball is released from fingertips with a slight snap of the wrist.

Visual Description

PHOTO 26.11 One-hand shot.

Jump Shot

The jump shot is similar to the one-hand set shot, but it has the addition of the release of the ball at the height of a vertical jump. The jump shot is generally used for shots closer to the basket than the set shot, and when an opposing player is in direct line with the shot. It is probably the most difficult shot for children to learn because of the summation of forces required.

Verbal Description
- Same upper-body action as the one-hand push shot.
- Jump is from both feet.
- Jump is straight up.
- Ball is released at height of jump.

Visual Description

PHOTO 26.12 Jump shot.

Layup Shot

The layup shot involves driving toward the basket by means of dribbling or receiving a pass, leaping into the air, and releasing the ball off one hand. If the basket is approached from the left, the ball will be rolled off the left hand; if from the right, it will be rolled off the right hand. The layup shot has the highest scoring percentage in basketball and is frequently easier for children to master than either the one-hand set shot or the jump shot.

Verbal Description
- Approach basket from either the left or right.
- Takeoff is from the foot *opposite* shooting arm.
- Execute a one-foot leaping takeoff, moving up toward the basket.
- Ball is brought up as far as possible with both hands.
- Nonshooting hand releases ball.
- Shooting hand is under ball with fingers spread.
- Ball is pushed with shooting hand gently against backboard.
- Ball contacts backboard slightly above the hoop.

Visual Description

PHOTO 26.13   Lay-up shot.

Free-Throw Shooting

The key to successful free-throw shooting is consistency. Whatever technique is adopted, and there are many, complete concentration, rhythmic execution, and exact repetition of all actions from the moment the player steps to the free-throw line to the moment that the ball reaches the basket are a must. The one-handed set shot is the most popular form of free-throw shooting. The mechanics are the same as described earlier. The two-handed underhand free-throw shot is also often used by elementary-age children and is described here.

Verbal Description
- Feet are parallel or in a short stride position with weight evenly distributed.

- Knees are slightly bent and back is straight.
- Both hands are on the sides and slightly under the ball.
- Fingers are spread and ball is gripped by the fingertips.
- Ball is held down and in front of the body with the arms straight.
- Eyes focus on the basket rim.
- The arms swing forward and upward as the legs straighten.
- Ball is released at chest level in a high arc.
- Ball is released simultaneously from fingertips of both hands.
- Back remains straight and arms follow through.

Visual Description

PHOTO 26.14   Underhand free throw shot.

BASIC RULES

Basketball is played on a court up to 94 feet long and 50 feet wide. The game is played by two opposing teams of five players each. The object is to gain possession of the ball, advance it into a scoring position by passing or dribbling, and get it through the opponents' basket. The team that does not have the ball tries to stop the other team from scoring by trying to get possession of the ball, in order to score at the other end of the court. A field goal counts two points. Free throws, given for an infringement of a playing rule, count one point each.

A team is made up of two forwards, two guards, and a center. A jump ball at the center circle starts the game at the beginning of each half. After a field goal, the ball is put back into play by the team scored upon through a throw-in from out of bounds behind their basket.

Free throws from the free-throw line are awarded to a player who had a foul committed against her by an opposing team member. For less serious violations of the playing rules, a team loses possession of the ball.

SKILL DEVELOPMENT ACTIVITIES

Mastering of basketball skills involves progressing from the simple to the more complex and progressing from practice with single skills to practice with multiple skills. It is crucial that the foundational skills of the game be mastered prior to incorporating them into basketball game activities. The reason for this is simple. Practice in skills under static conditions (conditions where the environment remains the same, as in a stationary passing drill or a zigzag dribbling drill) at the beginning level of skill development fosters learning. It helps the player form a conscious mental picture of the skill and get the idea of how it is to be performed. After this has been accomplished, it is then wise to practice the same skills under dynamic conditions (con-

ditions where the environment is constantly changing, as in a two-on-one passing drill or a one-on-one dribbling drill). Players at the intermediate level of movement skill learning benefit from dynamic skill drills. The following sequence of skill drills and lead-up game activities is recommended in order to maximize basketball skill learning:

1. Introduce single skills under static conditions ("walk-through").
2. Practice single skills in a controlled dynamic environment (drill).
3. Introduce multiple-skill drills in a static environment.
4. Practice multiple-skill drills in a controlled, dynamic environment.
5. Implement multiple skills in simple lead-up game activities.
6. Practice multiple skills in increasingly complex lead-up game activities.

The sampling of skill drills that is presented in this section proceeds from simple to complex and may be practiced under static or dynamic conditions. A suggested list of basketball warm-up activities is also included.

Warmup Activities

The warmup activities that follow should be engaged in for 20 to 30 seconds each, for 5 to 7 minutes. Select several and move quickly from one to the next. Variety and proper execution are important in order to get maximum enjoyment and benefit from the warmup session.

Each of the following activities involves the use of a ball. If a basketball is not available for every child, volleyballs, soccer balls and playground balls will do.

Stand and Stretch. Holding the ball overhead, stretch forward and hold, sideways and hold, backward and hold, sideways and hold. Repeat in the opposite direction.

Sit and Stretch. From a sitting position with the legs spread and holding the ball overhead, bend forward and touch the ball to the toes of one foot and hold. Keep the arms straight. Try to touch the floor and hold, then move to the other foot and hold.

Stretch and Roll. From a sitting position with the legs together, roll the ball around the body, first in one direction then in the other. Repeat with the legs spread wide apart.

Push and Catch. From a back lying position, push the ball up with both hands (4 to 6 feet) and catch it. Repeat with a one-hand push shot.

Stretch and Dribble. From a sitting position with the legs spread, dribble the ball around the body, first in one direction, then in the other.

Arch. From a front lying position with the ball overhead, raise the ball off the ground as the head and chest lift off. Repeat several times.

Rocker. Same as preceding exercise, but raise the legs also. Repeat several times.

Half Pushups. From a pushup position (use modified pushup position if necessary) lower the body until the nose touches the ball and return. Repeat several times.

Situps. From a back lying position with the legs straight and arms extended overhead, sit up, bringing the knees to the chest and swinging the arms forward.

Chest Curl. From a back lying position with the knees bent and ball held at the chest, curl the trunk around the ball until the shoulders and upper back are off the ground. Hold. Repeat several times.

Dribble and Run. Dribble the ball several times around the perimeter of the gymnasium.

Around the Body. From a standing position, circle the ball rhythmically around the body several times, starting high and working low and returning to high (head, chest, waist, thighs, knees, ankles).

Body Weave. Same as preceding exercise, but weave the ball between the legs while stretching forward.

Human Dribble. With a partner, one player acts like a ball being dribbled as the other pushes down on her head. Change positions.

Skill Drills

A wide variety of skill drills can be introduced and practiced with elementary school children. Each of the skill drills that follow can be modified to fit the varying skill levels of the children in a class. By giving the drill a name and introducing an element of competition, you can easily turn it into a game. Be careful, however, not to emphasize the game aspect (product) until the basic mechanics (process) have been reasonably mastered.

Objectives

1. To improve passing and catching skills (chest, bounce, one-hand and two-hand passes).
2. To improve dribbling and pivoting skills (stationary, moving, crossover dribbles).
3. To improve basketball goal-shooting abilities (one-hand push, jump, layup shots).
4. To introduce the associated skills of stopping and rebounding.
5. To improve endurance levels (aerobic, muscular endurance).
6. To develop group cooperation and teamwork.

Movement Experiences

Wall Pass (chest pass and catch). From a position 2 to 3 feet from the wall, the player executes a chest pass against the wall and catches it on the rebound. Work for control, then speed. As skill progresses move back from the wall.

Partner Pass (passing and catching). With a partner, practice passing and catching. Being about 6 feet apart and gradually increase distance as skill increases.

Over–Under (chest pass, bounce pass). One partner performs a chest pass, while the other executes a bounce pass at the same time. This forces the players to react quickly to an oncoming ball and to release their ball quickly.

Keep Away (passing). With three people, practice chest, bounce, and overhead passes between two players while the third tries to intercept the passed ball.

Overhead Pass (overhead passing). With a partner, practice overhead passing to a partner 10 feet away. As skill develops, increase the distance to 20 feet and play keep away.

Line Passing (passing, catching).   With six to eight in a line, practice passing in a zigzag manner from one end of the line to the other. Work for control prior to speed.

Star Passing (passing, catching).   With five players in a star formation, each player passes to a second person to the left. Add a second ball as skill increases. Practice passing back and forth. As skill develops call the player's name to be passed to. Then pivot and pass suddenly without notice. This will help improve reaction time and reinforce the need to be ready to receive a pass at all times.

Stationary Dribble (dribbling).   Players practice dribbling in their own space, first from a double-knee kneeling position, then from a single-knee position, and finally from a standing position. Skilled players may practice crossover dribbles and dribbling between the feet.

Dribble and Look (dribbling).   Players practice dribbling while looking forward at the instructor. The instructor may hold up letters, numbers, or simple math facts to be answered to encourage dribbling without visually monitoring the ball.

Line Dribble (dribbling).   Players each find a line of the floor and dribble while walking forward on the line. Each time a new line intersects players change direction and follow the new line.

Line-Dribble Pass (dribbling).   Same as preceding exercise, except that each time two players meet coming from opposite directions, they must pass while continuing to dribble the ball *and* remaining on the line.

Wander Dribble (dribbling).   Players dribble informally about the room, taking care not to interfere with each other. This will promote kinesthetic awareness of the player's surroundings and reduce visual monitoring. As skill increases, reduce the area.

Directional Dribble (dribbling).   Players face the instructor and, while dribbling, move in the direction to which instructor points. May be performed with a whistle for less skilled players who visually monitor the ball (one blast = forward, two blasts = backward, three blasts = sideways).

Chair Dribble (dribbling).   Players dribble around a chair, being sure to keep their bodies between the ball and the chair.

Dribble and Weave (dribbling).   With four to six chairs in a straight line, the player dribbles from one end to another, weaving in and out of the chairs and back. Stress switching hands and keeping the body between the ball and the chair.

Pivot Drill (pivoting).   Players face instructor, holding a ball in both hands in the ready position. Instructor points to the left or right, and players pivot in that direction. As skill develops, have the players fake a pass in the direction pivoted. Practice first with quarter turns, then half turns.

Pivot Wall Pass (pivoting, passing).   From a position three to five feet from the wall, player stands with his back to the wall, pivots, and chest-passes the ball against the wall. Repeat in both directions.

Partner Pivot (pivoting, passing).   With a partner, practice pivoting first with the partner stationary, then moving to one side, then to the other.

Four-Point Pivot (pivoting, passing).   Player in center of square formed by four players pivots and passes from one player to the next. Practice first with small pivots, then larger.

Pivot Keep Away (pivoting, passing, guarding). One player practices pivoting and passing to a second player, while a third player tries to tie up the ball. Change positions so all have a chance at each position.

Center Guard (pivoting, passing, guarding). With six to eight players in a circle and two in the center, one player attempts to pivot and pass the ball to the outer circle, while a second attempts to block the pass. When ball is at the outside of the circle, players attempt to pass to the center player, who is being guarded.

Spot Shot (goal shooting).   With six to eight players per basket, players stand in an arc and practice shooting from that spot. When a shot is made from that spot, move along to another.

Two-Column Free-Throw Shooting (goal shooting).   With six to eight players per basket, stand in two columns at the free-throw line. First player in column A shoots at the basket and goes to the end of column B. The first player in column B retrieves the ball and passes it to the next player in column A, while going to the back of column A.

Pass and Shoot (goal shooting, passing). One player passes to a partner, who takes a shot at the basket. Practice first from close range; then gradually increase the distance. Practice from several spots on the floor.

Dribble and Shoot (goal shooting, passing). With two columns of six to eight players per column, players in column A dribble forward and attempt a layup shot, while players in colmn B retrieve the ball and pass to the next person in column A. Players go to end of the opposite column.

Pass, Pivot, and Shoot (passing, pivoting, goal shooting). One player passes to another who has his or her back to the basket. Player pivots and shoots.

Block That Shot (passing, stopping, goal shooting, guarding). One player passes to a partner, who stops, sets and shoots the ball, while a third player attempts to block the shot.

Rebound Ball (shooting, rebounding, passing). One player shoots at the basket, while a partner rebounds the ball and passes it back. As skill develops, work for rebounding the ball while in the air.

ASSESSING PROGRESS

It will be necessary to assess both the entry and exit level of children's basketball skills. Because of the vast difference in the amount of experience children have had in practicing the skills and playing the game, there will be a wide range of ability levels. Determining ability levels and measuring progress can be done rather quickly and reliably. Although a number of objective basketball skills tests exist, it is recommended that teachers at the elementary school level be concerned with subjective assessment of mechanics or techniques (process assessment) and self-referenced assessment of performance abilities (product assessment).

Process Assessment

Process assessment of children's basketball skills is based on the teacher's judgment of their level of ability in terms of proper mechanics. The instructor is concerned primarily that the proper techniques are being used to pass, dribble, and shoot the ball. Children can be informally assessed during a skill drill or lead-up game activity. By charting their abilities at the beginning of an instructional unit and again at the end, you can determine what skills need to be emphasized and the amount of progress made. The rating chart depicted in Figure 26.1 will help determine where students are in terms of their basketball skills.

Product Assessment

A number of basketball skills tests have been reported in the professional literature. However, their validity for use with elementary school-age children is questionable, along with their administrative feasibility. It is therefore recommended that you develop your own "teacher-made" test of basketball skills, save your yearly results, and develop your own norms. Also, it is appropriate at the elementary school level to develop your own self-referenced assessment instrument. A self-referenced test of basketball skills is one that is self-administered, or administered with the help of a partner, and simply compares the student's present performance with previous performances. The student compares his or her entry-level assessment information with exit-level information. This technique works quite well with children, particularly when the operational philosophy of the physical education program is one of *individual improvement* and the teacher is not pressed into assigning letter grades. The sample self-referenced basketball skills test depicted in Figure 26.2 will help students determine where they are in terms of their basketball abilities. It will help the teacher objectively measure skill learning and may serve as a useful report to parents of student progress.

Basketball Skills Rating Chart															
Class _____ Grade _____															
Entry Assessment Date _____ Exit Assessment Date _____															

Directions	Passing/Catching Skills				Dribbling/Pivoting Skills				Goal-Shooting Skills				Associated Skills		Key
Observe during drill or play situations. Mark entry rating in upper left corner and exit ratings in lower right corner of each square.	Chest Pass	Bounce Pass	Two-hand Pass	Baseball Pass	Stationary Dribble	Moving Dribble	Cross-over Dribble	Pivoting	Push Shot	Jump Shot	Lay-up Shot	Free Throw	Guarding	Rebounding	**A: Advanced—** Correct technique plus good control and force production.
															I: Intermediate— Correct technique but lacking in control or force production.
															B: Beginning— inconsistent use of correct technique.
															Comments

FIGURE 26.1   Sample form rating chart for basketball.

Basketball Skills Rating Chart

Student's
Name _____ Grade _____ Class _____ Year _____

See Reverse for Description		Skills	Entry Rating	Comments	Exit Rating	Comments
Thirty-Second Chest Pass	Thirty-Second Bounce Pass	Passing	D a t e		D a t e	
B <10 I 10-15 A 16>	<5 6-10 11>	Chest Pass				
		Bounce Pass				
Down and Back	Zigzag Dribble	Dribbling	D a t e		D a t e	
B 25>sec. I 15-25 sec. A <15 sec.	30>sec. 20-30 sec. <20 sec.	Moving Dribble				
		Crossover Dribble				
30-Second Layups	10 Free Throws	Shooting	D a t e		D a t e	
B <5 I 6-10 A 11>	3 for 10 4-7 for 10 8 for 10	Goal Shooting				
		Free-Throw Shooting				

Parent's Signature _____ Date _____

Comments:

FIGURE 26.2 Sample self-referenced performance rating card for basketball, with *approximate* sample standards.

FIGURE 26.2 *(continued)* Reverse side of self-referenced performance rating card for basketball.

KEY: B = Beginning Level of Skill   I = Intermediate Level of Skill   A = Advanced Level of Skill

Description of Tests:

30-Second Chest Pass: With a partner, player stands behind a line 3 feet from the wall. On the signal "go" player does chest pass against the wall as many times as possible in 30 seconds. Must stay behind line.

30-Second Bounce Pass: Same as above, but from a line 5 feet from the wall, player executes bounce and catch against wall for 30 seconds.

Down and Back: With a partner timing, player dribbles the ball in a straight line from the starting line to a line 45 feet away and back as fast as possible.

Zigzag Dribbble: With a partner timing, player weaves in and out of 4 chairs placed in a line 5 feet apart, beginning 15 feet from the starting line, touches the 45-foot line, and returns.

30-Second Wall Pass: With a partner timing, player shoots the ball at the basket as many times as possible in 30 seconds on the sound of "go." Score number of baskets made in 30 seconds.

10 Free Throws: From behind the free-throw line, player takes 10 shots. Score the number of baskets made.

SUGGESTED READING

Coaching young league basketball. (1978). AAHPERD, Athletic Institute, N. Palm Beach, FL: The Athletic Institute.

Ferrell (Ed.) (1979). *Youth basketball association leaders' manual*. Colorado Springs, CO: National Board of YMCAs.

Ferrell (Ed.) (1985). *Youth basketball association manual for players in grades 3–6*. Colorado Springs, CO: National Board of YMCAs.

Humphrey, J. H., and Humphrey, J. N. (1980). *Sport skills for boys and girls*. Springfield, IL: Charles C. Thomas.

Jeffries, Stephen, and Levin Robert (Eds). (1984). *Y basketball coaches manual*. Champaign, IL: Human Kinetics.

Johnson, Connie (1986). *Coaching basketball effectively*. Champaign, IL: American Coaching Effectiveness Program.

Krause, Jerry (1984). *Better basketball basics: Before the X's and O's*. Champaign, IL: Human Kinetics.

Levin, Robert (1984). *Y basketball passes manual. Y basketball dribblers manual*. Champaign, IL: American Coaching Effectiveness Program.

CHAPTER 27

SOCCER SKILLS

The game of soccer is undoubtedly the most international of all sports. It is played in practically every country and enjoyed by millions worldwide. Historically, the game has been called "football" throughout most of the world. The derivation of this word comes from the London Football Association, which formalized the game and developed the rules in 1863. They called the game "Association Football." The word association was later shortened to assoc, which later became soccer. Due to the rise in popularity of "American football" in North America, the game finally became known as soccer in North America, but it remains football throughout the rest of the world.

Soccer is a great game for the elementary physical education program. It can be played equally by both boys and girls. Specialized equipment other than a ball is not required. Children of all sizes and skill levels can take part and find enjoyment. Its continuous action and vigorous nature promote many aspects of physical fitness and improved coordination. The rules are simple, the objectives clear, and the variations limitless. For these reasons, soccer has been selected for inclusion in this text rather than the game of football. Although football is an important game in North American culture, it lacks many of the benefits of soccer and may be more appropriately introduced in the physical education programs at the middle school or junior high school level. Furthermore, the popularity of soccer in North America has grown tremendously among children in the last several years and will continue to grow for years to come.

DEVELOPING A SOCCER SKILLS THEME

In order to make the best use of your time and to maximize learning when focusing on the development of soccer skills, it will be helpful to utilize the sequence of : (1) preplanning, (2) observing and assessing, (3) planning and implementing, and (4) evaluating and revising outlined in Chapter 25 (page 333), refer to Chapter 33 "Lead-up Game Activities" for a list of soccer lead-up games and how they are played.

SKILL SEQUENCING

The soccer skills program should be based on the present level of ability of the class or group. In terms of soccer skill learning, third- and fourth-grade children are typically at the beginning level, while fifth and sixth graders are typically at the intermediate level of skill learning. Remember, however, that this does not guarantee that all are at the level typical for their age. Some may be ahead, and others may be behind. It is important, however, for you to know where your students are in order to be able to plan more effectively for all. The Selected Soccer Skill Chart (Table 27.1) and the Development Activities Chart for Soccer (Table 27.2) that follow will help you in selecting appropriate soccer skills to teach and movement activities to include in the lesson. A brief description of each drill is located in the "Skill Development Activities" section of this chapter, along with recommended warmup activities for soccer. Appropriate soccer lead-up games are located in Chapter 33.

KICKING SKILLS

Kicking is the primary method of advancing the ball in soccer. There are several types of kicks that are used. Frequently children unfamiliar with the skills of soccer will want to use a toe kick. This form of kicking is seldom if ever used in soccer because of poor control. The instep kick, inside-of-foot kick (push pass), outside-of-foot kick, dribble, and punt are all important kicking skills that can be developed with elementary school children.

Teaching Tips

Common Problems
- Kicking with the toes. The toe kick is rarely used in soccer.
- Failure to get in line behind the ball.
- Taking the eyes off the ball.
- Contacting a moving ball too soon or too late.
- Lack of accuracy and control.
- Contacting the ball too low or too high.
- Inappropriate amount of backswing.
- Improper placement of the nonkicking foot.
- Failure to use the arms in rhythmical alternation to the legs.
- Poor summation of the forces of the arms, trunk, and leg.
- Lack of follow-through.
- Failure to lead teammate.

Recommended Strategies
- When indoors, use partially deflated balls, foam balls, or indoor soccer balls.
- Provide a ball for at least every other child.
- Do not teach the toe kick; it will only inhibit learning of other kicking skills.
- Do not permit toe kicks. They lift the ball too high, are difficult to control, and may cause injury.
- Allow children to protect their faces and chests with their arms for high kicked balls.
- Emphasize keeping the ball low and under control.

TABLE 27.1 Selected
Soccer Skills

Soccer Skills	Suggested Progression for Children		
	Beginning Level	Intermediate Level	Page
Kicking			368
Instep kick	Introduce	Refine	370
Push pass	Introduce	Refine	371
Outside of foot		Introduce	372
Punting		Introduce	372
Trapping			373
Shin trap		Introduce	374
Sole trap	Introduce		375
Inside of foot	Introduce	Refine	375
Inside of thigh	Introduce	Refine	376
Chest trap		Introduce	376
Dribbling			377
Inside of foot	Introduce	Refine	378
Outside of foot		Introduce	378
Volleying			379
Juggling		Introduce	380
Heading		Introduce	380
Associated Skills			
Basic goalkeeping	Introduce	Refine	384
Screening/blocking	Introduce	Refine	384
Tackling		Introduce	384
Understanding the Game			
Rules	Introduce	Refine	381
Strategy		Introduce	

- Paint or tape a spot on the ball in order to demonstrate where contact should be made.
- Stress keeping the eyes on the ball.
- Stress the chest being positioned over the ball at the point of contact.
- Emphasize getting behind the ball and following through.
- Practice kicking with both feet.
- Practice first in static, then dynamic drill situations. Then move to increasingly complex lead-up games as skill develops.

Concepts Children Should Know

Skill Concepts
- Get behind the ball.
- Keep your eyes on the ball.

- Step into your kick with the nonkicking leg.
- The placement of your nonkicking foot will determine the direction of flight.
- Use your arms for balance and to aid in force production.
- A toe kick is of little use in soccer.
- It is important to be able to control your kick.
- Follow through.

Movement Concepts
- You can control the speed of the ball by the force of your kick.
- The force of your kick is determined by the coordinated action of your arms, trunk, and leg.
- Snap at the knee.
- You can control the range of your kick through

TABLE 27.2   Developmental Activities Chart for Soccer

Soccer Skill Drills	Kicking Skills	Trapping Skills	Dribbling Skills	Volleying Skills	Associated Skills	Page
Wall kick	X	X				383
Target kick	X	X				383
Partner pass	X	X				383
Circle pass	X	X				383
Criss-cross passing	X	X				383
Distance kick	X					383
Accuracy kick	X					383
Partner punting	X					383
Partner trapping		X				383
Toss and trap		X				383
Circle trap		X				383
Follow the leader			X			383
Shadow			X			383
One-on-one dribble kick			X			383
Dribble shuttle			X			384
Obstacle dribble relay			X			384
Push-pass relay	X	X	X			384
Volley drill				X		384
Circle volley				X		384
Keep-it-up				X		384
Partner keep-it-up				X		384
One-on-one	X		X	X	X	384
Three-on-three	X	X	X	X	X	384
Three-on-three change	X	X	X	X	X	384

the amount of force applied by the forcefulness of your knee snap.

- You can control the height of the ball by the point of contact.
- You can influence the height of the ball by the portion of your foot that makes contact.
- You can control the direction of your kick by the placement of your nonkicking foot, the portion of your foot that makes contact with the ball, and the angle at which contact is made.
- The greater the surface area contacting the ball, the greater the control you will have.
- You can pass the ball to a partner through controlled kicking.

Instep Kick

The instep kick is probably the most frequently used kicking pattern in soccer. The instep is that portion of the foot directly behind the toes, where the laces of your shoes are located. Children will frequently want to kick with the toe, but with practice, skill will develop with the instep kick. The instep kick is used for passing and goal shooting.

Verbal Description
- The ball is approached from behind and slightly to one side.
- The nonkicking foot is in line with the ball, pointing in the direction desired.

- The head and trunk lean forward slightly.
- The eyes focus on the ball.
- The kicking leg is brought backward with an acute bend at the knee and hip.
- The kicking leg is swung forcefully forward and the arms move in opposition.

- Contact is made low on the ball for a high pass and at the center for a low pass.
- The kicking leg follows through in the direction of the intended path of the ball, and the support foot raises to the toes or loses contact with the ground.

Visual Description

PHOTO 27.1   Instep kick.

Push Pass

The push pass, or inside-of-foot kick, as it is sometimes called, is an effective kick for short, accurate passes to a teammate and for dribbling. It should be practiced equally with both feet so that it may be performed in either direction. The push pass can be likened to using the inside of the foot as a "daisy-cutter."

Verbal Description
- The head and trunk lean forward slightly to a position directly over the ball.
- The eyes focus on the ball.

- The support foot is placed parrallel to the ball, 6 to 12 inches to the side, with the knee bent slightly.
- The kicking leg is drawn backward from the hip in a straight line.
- The knee is bent, with the inside of the foot cocked and facing the ground.
- The leg is swung forcefully forward with the ankle cocked and stiff.
- Contact is made with the inside of the foot, toward the arch and ankle bone.
- The kicking leg follows through in front of the support leg in the intended direction of the ball.

Visual Description

PHOTO 27.2   Push pass.

Outside-of-Foot Kick

The outside-of-foot kick is a type of push pass used for short passes, when dribbling, and in order to avoid an opponent. It is not a forceful pass and should be practiced with both feet in order to develop skill in either direction.

Verbal Description
- The head and trunk lean forward slightly to a position directly over the ball.
- The eyes focus on the ball.
- The support leg is parallel to and about the length of one's foot from the ball.
- The kicking foot is lifted with the toes pointed down and rotated inward.
- The ankle joint is locked.

- The leg is swung forward and downward, with contact made on the outside of the foot.
- The leg follows through in the intended path of the ball.

Visual Description

PHOTO 27.3   Outside-of-foot kick.

Punting

Punting is a kick frequently used by the goalkeeper. In fact, the goalkeeper is the only player permitted to punt the ball because it requires contacting the ball with the hands. It is used for lifting the ball high and kicking long distances.

Verbal Description
- The body is in a stride position with the trunk bent slightly forward and the ball held waist-high with both hands.

- The body weight is transferred to the non-kicking leg and the eyes focus on the ball.
- The kicking leg is drawn backward with an acute bend at the knee and the arms are extended forward.
- The leg extends forcefully forward as the ball is dropped.

- Contact is made with the instep and the leg follows through in the intended path of the ball.
- The closer to the ground that the ball is contacted, the lower the trajectory will be.

Visual Description

PHOTO 27.4   Punting.

TRAPPING SKILLS

Trapping in the method used to stop and control an approaching ball that is rolling on the ground or traveling in the air. The arms and hands are the only portions of the body not permitted to contact the ball when executing a trap. The type of trap used will depend on the height, trajectory, and speed of the ball. Trapping requires precise movements. Several forms of trapping can be mastered by children in the elementary grades. The sole, shin, foot, body, and chest traps are discussed in this section.

Teaching Tips

Common Problems
- Failure to visually monitor the ball.
- Failure to get behind the ball.
- Closing the eyes or turning the head on aerial balls.
- Failure to give with the ball upon contact.
- Losing balance.

Recommended Strategies
- Provide a ball for at least every other child.
- Stress keeping the eyes on the ball until it touches the body.
- Emphasize getting in line behind the ball.
- Emphasize giving with the ball.
- Practice maintaining a wide base of support while trapping.
- Use foam balls when introducing aerial trapping.
- Strive for control of the ball within six inches of the body.
- Work for control in static drill situations, then add performing a pass or dribbling immediately after trapping the ball.

Concepts Children Should Know

Skill Concepts
- Get behind the ball.
- Keep your eyes on the ball.
- Maintain a wide base of support.
- Give with the ball as it contacts you.

Movement Concepts
- You can trap the ball with different body parts.
- The body part used to trap the ball will depend on the height of the ball.
- The amount of give to your trap will be directly proportioned to the speed of the ball.
- The trapping surface generally applies downward force to the ball.
- The timing of your trapping action is very important.

- The faster the ball is traveling, the faster your giving action must move.
- Trapping is followed by immediate performance of another skill, usually passing or dribbling.

Shin Trap

The shin trap is used for controlling a rolling or low-bouncing ball. It is an excellent skill to learn as an introduction to trapping.

Verbal Description
- The body is brought into position directly behind the ball.
- The eyes track the ball to the point of contact.
- The feet are parallel, about four inches apart.
- As the ball approaches, the knees are flexed and the trunk bends slightly forward.
- The arms move out from the side for balance.
- The ball is wedged downward by the shins as contact is made.

Visual Description

PHOTO 27.5 Shin trap.

Sole Trap

The sole-of-the-foot trap is used for completely stopping a rolling ball. It is often difficult for younger children to master, especially in a game situation, because of the precise eye–foot coordination required.

Verbal Description
- The body is placed directly behind and in line with the ball.

- The eyes track the ball to the point of contact.
- One foot is raised about eight inches off the ground with the ankle cocked, forming a 45-degree angle between the ground and the ankle.
- The ball is contacted by the sole of the foot, at the back and toward the top, and squeezed toward the ground.
- The contact leg and foot give slightly upon impact.

Visual Description

PHOTO 27.6   Sole trap.

Inside-of-Foot Trap

The inside-of-foot trap is used extensively for stopping a rolling, bouncing, or low aerial ball. It is most frequently used trap in soccer and should be practiced with balls coming from different angles, at different heights, and at various speeds. It should be practiced with both the left foot and the right.

Verbal Description

- The body is placed in as near a direct line with the ball as possible.
- The eyes track the ball to the point of contact.
- The body weight is supported on the non-trapping leg.
- The trapping leg is brought back slightly.
- The ankle is rotated so that the inside of the foot is in direct line with the ball.
- The inside of the foot contacts the back and top portion of the ball.
- The contact foot gives slightly as the ball is wedged down toward the ground.

Visual Description

PHOTO 27.7   Inside-of-foot trap.

Inside-of-Thigh Trap

The thigh trap is used for controlling a ball that approaches at a level above the knees but below the chest. The force of the ball is absorbed by the inner of upper thigh. This is not a difficult trap for children to master, but it should be practiced first with a foam or partially deflated ball.

Verbal Description

- The body is placed in line behind the ball.
- The eyes track the ball to the point of contact.
- The arms move out from the side of the body as needed to aid balance.
- The trapping leg is lifted forward and upward, with the knee rotated outward.
- Upon contact midway along the inner thigh, the leg gives quickly to absorb the impact.
- The ball is deflected downward to a point just in front of the support foot.

Visual Description

PHOTO 27.8   Inside-of-thigh trap.

Chest Trap

The chest trap should be used by elementary-age children only after the other forms of trapping have been mastered. The chest trap takes time to learn and is used for an aerial ball approaching above waist level but below the shoulders. Practice should first be with a partially inflated or foam ball.

Verbal Description
- The body is brought directly in line with the path of the ball.
- The eyes track the ball to the point of contact.
- The feet are placed in a stride position, with the knees bent and the hips thrust forward.
- The shoulders are behind the hips, with the chest thrust forward.
- The arms are held out from the sides of the body.
- As the ball makes contact with the chest, the knees flex deeper and the chest gives with the impact of the ball.
- The ball drops beside the forward foot and is controlled with a sole trap.

Visual Description

PHOTO 27.9   Chest trap.

DRIBBLING SKILLS

Dribbling is the method by which the ball is moved, under control by the feet, down the field of play. It involves making short pushes of the ball forward or sideways with either foot. Controlled dribbling takes considerable practice, first without an opponent and then with an opponent, who attempts to steal the ball. There are two primary forms of dribbling, the inside-of-foot dribble and the outside-of-foot dribble. Both are presented here, along with teaching tips and a list of concepts children should know.

Teaching Tips

Common Problems
- Kicking the ball with the toe.
- Kicking the ball too far in front of the body.
- Visually monitoring the ball.
- Inability to alter direction.
- Inability to use both feet equally well.

Recommended Strategies
- Use a partially deflated ball when learning the skill indoors.
- Stress control prior to speed.
- Stress control while moving forward prior to making directional changes.
- Practice making short *pushing* actions, alternating left and right foot.
- Push the ball diagonally forward and not to the side, unless you are avoiding an opponent.
- Permit visual monitoring only during the early phase of learning.
- After control is gained, work for speed and controlled directional changes.
- Practice static drill situations prior to dynamic game situations.

Concepts Children Should Know

Skill Concepts

- Push the ball; don't kick it.
- Keep the ball under your control.
- Don't use your toes; stay behind the ball.
- Dribble without looking down at the ball.
- Contact the ball as often as possible as you advance it forward.

Movement Concepts

- You can contact the ball with varying amounts of force.
- You can dribble the ball with different amounts of speed.
- You can dribble either forward or sideways.
- You can change direction while dribbling.
- You can dribble with the ball close to you.
- You will not be able to control the ball if you dribble it too far in front of you.
- You can alter the flow of your dribbling.
- Your dribble is a rhythmical step–step–kick action under static conditions, but it alters under dynamic conditions.
- You can use your body to screen an opponent while dribbling.
- You will need to continually alter the direction of your dribble in order to evade opponents.

Inside-of-Foot Dribble

The inside-of-foot dribble is the most basic form of foot dribbling. It is the one used most frequently by beginners and skilled players alike.

Verbal Description

- The body is directly behind the ball in a controlled running action.
- The ball is contacted and pushed diagonally forward with the inside of the forward foot.
- The distance of the push depends on the degree of control desired.
- The ball travels diagonally forward and is contacted by the opposite foot on the next or subsequent forward action of that leg.

- Although visual monitoring is common, effort should be made to look in the direction of travel.

Visual Description

PHOTO 27.10   Inside-of-foot dribble.

Outside-of-Foot Dribble

The outside-of-foot dribble is used in conjunction with the inside-of-foot dribble and is especially useful when making sudden changes in direction. It should be introduced after the basic inside-of-foot dribble has been reasonably mastered.

Verbal Description

- Body is aligned with the ball in the same way as with the inside-of-foot dribble.
- Contact is made with the outside of the foot against the ball.

- The ball is pushed in the same direction as the kicking foot. The exact direction depends on the angle of contact.

- The body realigns itself behind the ball, and forward progress continues with the inside-of-foot dribble.

Visual Description

PHOTO 27.11   Outside-of-foot dribble.

VOLLEYING SKILLS

Juggling and heading are the two primary ways in which the path of an aerial ball may be altered without first trapping the ball. The ball may be juggled off the instep, knee, or thigh. Heading is a specialized form of volleying in which the direction of the ball is altered by contact with the head. Juggling and heading should be introduced along with the other basic skills of soccer. Heading should generally wait until the other skills have been reasonably mastered. Heading should be introduced only to the most skillful players and generally not before the fifth grade. Controlled heading and juggling require practice first in controlled drill situations with the use of a foam or partially deflated ball. A regulation soccer ball should be introduced only after the basic mechanics have been mastered.

Teaching Tips

Common Problems
- Failure to get directly behind the ball.
- Failure to visually monitor the ball until contact.
- Failure to stiffen the body properly to cause the ball to rebound.
- Relaxing the body part upon contact.

Recommended Strategies
- Work first with balloons and foam balls, then with a partially deflated ball.
- Color-code the ball and have the student call out the color that is making contact.
- Practice first with lightly tossed balls.
- Stress keeping the eyes on the ball.
- Emphasize following through with the body part in the intended direction of the ball.

- Practice under static drill conditions prior to dynamic game situations.

Concepts Children Should Know

Skill Concepts
- Keep your eyes on the ball.
- Get in direct line with the path of the ball.
- Keep the body part still upon contact.
- Follow through after contact.

Movement Concepts
- You can volley the ball with different body parts.
- Repeated volleying to oneself is called juggling.
- Volleying with the head is called heading.
- The body part used to volley the ball will depend on its height at the point of interruption.
- The trajectory (arc) of the ball will be determined by the point of the ball contacted.
- The distance the ball travels after contact will depend on the amount of force applied.
- The direction the ball travels after impact will depend on the angle at which it was contacted.

Juggling

Juggling may be done off the inside or outside of the foot or off the thigh. Repeated juggling of the ball to oneself is an excellent drill for mastering control of the ball.

Verbal Description
- The body part (inside or outside of the foot, thigh) is brought into direct line with the ball.
- The body part selected will be determined by the path of the approaching ball.
- The eyes visually track the ball to the point of contact.
- The body weight is shifted to the support foot and the contact leg is lifted to the desired position.

- The arms are held out to the side to aid balance.
- The body part stiffens upon contact and the leg follows through in the intended new direction of the ball.

Visual Description

PHOTO 27.12   Juggling.

Heading

Heading, when taught at the elementary school level, should be done from a standing position. Jumping or power heading is too dangerous to be a regular part of the program.

Verbal Description
- The legs are placed in a stride position with the knees slightly bent.
- The hips are thrust forward and the shoulders line up with the rear foot.
- Body weight is on the rear foot.

- The arms are held out from the sides.
- The head and chin are raised and the eyes follow the path of the ball to the point of contact.
- Contact is made at the hairline.
- The neck is kept stiff.
- As contact is made, the body weight is shifted forward and upward and the knees straighten.
- Rock into the ball from the hips.

Visual Description

PHOTO 27.13   Heading.

BASIC RULES

The regulation game of soccer is played by two teams, each with eleven players that include one goalie, two fullbacks, three halfbacks, and five forwards. The ball may not be touched with the hands or arms. It is advanced toward the opponents' goal with the feet, body, or head.

At the start of the game, the center forward of the offensive team kicks the ball from the center circle toward a teammate. The ball must travel forward its own full circumference. The defensive team must remain outside the circle until the ball is touched. Then the players on both teams may cross the center line and play the ball wherever it goes. The object of the game is to move the ball down the field and into the opponents' goal for a score. The ball is moved by dribbling, passing, or volleying to another teammate. A defending player may intercept the ball and reverse the action of play.

When unnecessary roughness takes place, the offending team is penalized by a penalty kick or a free kick. A *penalty kick* is awarded when a foul is committed in the penalty area by the defensive team. The offensive team takes a penalty kick from the penalty mark with all the players, except the goalie, staying outside the penalty area. A *free kick* is awarded for fouls committed outside the penalty area. The ball is kicked from the spot of the foul. The opponents must be at least 10 yards away until the ball is kicked.

If the ball is kicked over the sideline, it is put into play by the opposite team. A halfback usually puts the ball into play from the sideline by a two-handed overhead throw-in. When the ball is kicked over the goal line but not through the goal by the offensive team, the goalie of the defensive team punts the ball back into the game. The other team must remain 10 yards away until the ball is punted. A *corner kick* is awarded the opposite team when the defensive team causes the ball to go over its own goal line. This kick is taken by a member of the offensive team from the corner of the field closest to the ball when it went out of bounds. One point is awarded for each goal. After a goal is scored, the team scored against kicks off from the center of the field.

Fouls include *carrying, handling, trapping,* and *pushing.* Carrying occurs when the goalie takes more than two steps with the ball in his hands. Handling is touching the ball with the hand or any part of the arm between the wrist and shoulder. Pushing involves moving an opponent away with the hands, arms, or body.

The goalie may pick up the ball with the hands, punt the ball away from the goal line, and throw the ball away from the goal. He may take only four steps with the ball. The other players may dribble, pass, trap, or volley the ball. They may kick the ball to a teammate when trapped by an opponent and stop the ball by blocking with any part of the body except the hands or arms.

SKILL DEVELOPMENT ACTIVITIES

In order for children to master the skills of soccer, it will be necessary for them to first practice the skills individually in static drill situations. After the basic elements of the skill have been mastered, it should be practiced under controlled dynamic drill situations in which the conditions of the environment change based on the nature of the drill. Drills that combine the use of two or more skills should then be added, and finally lead-up games should be performed in an open environment. The skill drills presented in this section proceed from simple to complex, in that they range from static practice drills to dynamic practice drills and from single-skill to multiple-skill activities. A list of suggested warmup activities to be performed prior to engaging in skill drills is also included.

Warmup Activities

Warmup activities are essential prior to vigorous play in the game of soccer. The activities that follow may be performed in the gymnasium or on the playing field. Each child should have a ball. A volleyball or playground ball will do. Each of the activities that follow should last only 20 to 30 seconds, proceeding from simple to complex. Variation in the warmup drills and rapid movement from one to another are the keys to a successful warmup session.

Dribble Around.   From a standing position, dribble the ball with the hands around the body, moving clockwise, then counterclockwise.

Roll Around.   From a sitting position with the legs straight, roll the ball with the hands around the legs and body, clockwise, then counterclockwise.

Sit and Stretch.   From a sitting position with the legs straight, lift the ball with both hands back behind the head, stretching back. Then relax forward so the ball touches the toes.

Rocking.   From a front lying position with the arms overhead holding the ball, lift the toes and rock.

Jump and Catch.   From a standing position with the ball between the feet, jump up and catch the ball. Work for higher and faster jumps.

Ball Pushups.   Do pushups while holding the ball. Spread the legs to aid balance.

Ball Situps.   Do situps, starting with the ball overhead and the legs straight. Sit up, swinging the ball overhead while bending the knees toward the chest.

Prone Dribble.   From a front lying position with the arms overhead, bounce the ball with the hands.

Ball Jump.   From a standing position, jump forward, sideways, and backward over the ball.

Body–Ball Roll.   From a sitting position with the legs straight and the ball resting between the legs, roll the ball back and forth from the ankles to the chest without using the hands.

Body–Ball Catch.   From a standing position, toss the ball upward, catching it without using the hands or arms. Repeat several times, using several variations.

Twister.   From a sitting position with the legs straight and the ball between the feet, twist from side to side with the legs elevated.

Twist and Roll.   Same as preceding exercise, but roll over without losing control of the ball.

Jump and Touch.   Jump off the left foot and touch the top of the ball with the right foot. Repeat with opposite feet. Practice in rhythmical cadence.

Sole Dribble.   Dribble the ball with the soles of the feet.

Keep It Up.   Juggle or lead the ball off the instep or thighs.

Aerobic Dribble.   Dribble the ball with the feet from one end of the field to the other, alternating fast and slow dribbles.

Wall Kick.   From five feet away from a wall, kick the ball against the wall as often as possible. Use both feet.

Agility Dribble.   Dribble and trap the ball down the field with direction changes or speed changes every time whistle is blown.

Skill Drills

There is a wide range of skill drills that can be successfully practiced by children at all levels of ability. The primary emphasis of soccer skill drills should be on improving the skills of kicking, trapping, dribbling, and volleying. You can, however, make a game out of the drill simply by giving it a name, making a few modifications in the procedures, and modifying the objectives. The following is a sampling of soccer drills appropriate for elementary school children.

Objectives

1.   To improve soccer kicking skills (instep kicks, push pass, outside-of-foot kick, punting).
2.   To improve trapping skills (sole trap, shin trap, foot trap, thigh trap, chest trap).
3.   To enhance dribbling abilities (inside-of-foot dribble, outside-of-foot dribble).
4.   To develop basic skills in volleying (juggling heading).
5.   To introduce basic tackling skills (shoulder tackling, leg tackling),
6.   To improve overall fitness (aerobic endurance, coordination, agility, muscular endurance).
7.   To develop group cooperation and teamwork.

Movement Experiences

Wall Kick (push pass).   From varying distances, practice kicking the inside-of-foot kick against a hard, flat surface. Stress working with both feet. Practice rhythmical alteration of the feet.

Practice along with the outside-of-foot kick. First trap the ball on each rebound. Then volley the ball back on each rebound.

Target Kick (instep kick, trapping).   Using an instep kick, practice kicking at a designated target against a hard surface. Stress work with both feet. Trap the ball on each rebound.

Partner Pass (kicking, trapping).   With a partner, practice passing, first from a stationary position, then to a moving partner (be certain to teach players how to lead their partner), then from a moving position.

Circle Pass (kicking, trapping).   With six to eight players in a circle, practice passing the ball around the circle. Work for control first, speed later. Then add two or three balls.

Criss-Cross Passing (kicking and trapping).   With six to eight players in a circle, practice passing the ball across the circle. Call out the name of the player being kicked to.

Distance Kick (instep kicking).   Practice the instep kick for distance with a partner at the opposite end of the field.

Accuracy Kick (kicking).   Player stands with legs spread while partner attempts to kick ball between the legs, using an appropriate kick.

Partner Punting (punting).   Practice punting for distance with partner at the opposite end of the field.

Partner Trapping (trapping).   Ball is tossed by a partner at varying heights, angles, and speeds. Player attempts to control the ball, using appropriate trapping actions.

Toss and Trap (chest trap).   Player tosses the ball up and attempts to control it with a chest trap.

Circle Trap (trapping).   With six to eight players in a circle and a leader in the center, the ball is tossed at varying heights without warning to anyone in the circle.

Follow the Leader (dribbling).   Leader dribbles ball in various directions; class follows, each with his own ball, in the same direction.

Shadow (dribbling).   One player leads *without* a ball, partner follows, dribbling *with* a ball. Emphasis is placed on looking ahead.

One-on-One Dribble Kick (dribbling, tackling). Partners each have ball. Each dribbles his or her own ball in a defined area while attempting to kick the partner's ball away.

Dribble Shuttle (dribbling). From a shuttle relay formation with lines 40 to 60 feet apart, player A dribbles ball to opposite end. Player B controls ball and returns. Process is repeated. The drill may also be used with players at one end only, passing the ball back to the head of the line.

Obstacle Dribble Relay (dribbling). Cones or chairs are placed 10 to 15 feet apart. Player A dribbles around the markers and back. Player B controls the ball and repeats the process. The drill may be varied by using shuttle formations with players at each end. Stress control prior to speed.

Push-Pass Relay (push pass, trapping). Players are in a shuttle relay formation 10 to 15 feet apart. Each player, in turn, passes the ball to the opposite player, who controls the ball and push passes it back. The drill may be varied by having the player run to the back of the opposite line after passing the ball or run to the opposite line and back to the rear of her own line.

Volley Drill (volleying, heading). Ball is tossed by a partner at varying heights. Ball is volleyed back to the partner with foot, knee, thigh, or head. Use foam ball or partially deflated ball until skill develops.

Circle Volley (volleying, heading). Players form a circle with a leader in the center. Leader tosses the ball to members of the circle with no warning. Player volleys ball back to leader. Use a foam ball or partially deflated ball until skill develops.

Keep-It-Up (juggling). Ball is self-tossed and kept in the air by means of repeated volleying with the foot, knee, thigh, or head. Use a foam ball or partially deflated ball until skill develops.

Partner Keep-It-Up (juggling). Same as preceding exercise but partners alternate control of the ball. May also be practiced in a circle with four to six players.

One on One (dribbling, kicking, tackling). Use half of the field only, with two players per side. One player acts as goal, standing astride goal line. Other player tries to put the ball through the opponents' goal (area between the legs). Positions change after one minute. Stress continuous play and use of dribbling, trapping, and tackling skills.

Three on Three (dribbling, passing, trapping, volleying, tackling). Same as preceding exer-cise but with an additional player. Stress passing at least twice before taking a shot. Rotate positions frequently. The objective of this drill is for the players to learn to keep a triangle formation as they move around the field.

Three-on-Three Change (dribbling, passing, trapping, volleying, tackling). Same as preceding exercise, but on a given command by the instructor, players rotate positions within their triangle. They attempt to use as much space in the half field as possible and keep a triangle position throughout. Vary the drill by requiring players to change positions by dribbling, passing.

ASSESSING PROGRESS

Assessment of soccer skills should include evaluating kicking, trapping, dribbling, and volleying proficiency. Assessment may focus on the process, which is the techniques employed in performing each skill, or on the product, which is the level of performance, or both. Whatever way is chosen, it is important to assess both entry and exit levels of skill. In this way, the teacher can more effectively plan appropriate movement experiences to maximize the effectiveness of the instructional unit in promoting learning.

Process Assessment

The teacher's subjective judgment of the technique used for each skill forms the basis for process assessment. This should be an ongoing process, but it is particularly beneficial at the beginning of a skill theme. The instructor is concerned primarily with the body mechanics used to perform the various skills of soccer. Children may be observed in an appropriate skill drill or lead-up game activity. By charting their abilities at the beginning and again at the end of an instructional unit, you can determine both what needs to be emphasized and how much progress has been made. The sample soccer skills rating chart depicted in Figure 27.1 will help determine where children are in terms of their soccer skill.

Soccer Skills Rating Chart

Class _____ Grade _____

Entry Assessment Date_____ Exit Assessment Date_____

Directions	Kicking Skills				Trapping Skills					Dribbling Skills		Volleying Skills		Associated Skills			Key
	Instep Kick	Push Pass	Outside-of-Foot Kick	Punting	Sole Trap	Shin Trap	Foot Trap	Thigh Trap	Chest Trap	Inside-of-Foot Dribble	Outside-of-Foot Dribble	Juggling	Heading	Goal Keeping	Screening/Blocking	Tackling	

Directions: Observe during drill and play situations. Mark entry rating in upper left corner, and exit ratings in lower right corner of each square.

Key:
A: Advanced—Correct technique plus good control and force production/absorption.
I: Intermediate—Correct technique but lacking in control or force production/absorption.
B: Beginning—inconsistent use of correct technique.

FIGURE 27.1   Sample form rating chart for soccer.

Product Assessment

Soccer skill tests that assess the performance abilities of children on selected skills can easily be devised. It is a relatively simple matter of selecting the skill tests you wish to use, standardizing their procedures, and collecting and compiling scores from year to year. After a few years, you can establish your own performance norms.

Because of the time involved in mass skill testing, it is recommemded that self-referenced partner testing be adopted. Self-referenced partner testing encourages children to view improvement on an individual basis and also intermittently involves them in a process that is both fun and educational. The sample soccer skills test presented in Figure 27.2 is and example of a self-referenced assessment tool.

Soccer Skills Progress Report						
Student's Name _____ Grade _____ Class _____ Year _____						

See Reverse for Description of Tests		Skills	Entry Rating	Comments	Exit Rating	Comments
10 Wall-Goal Kicks	Punt for Distance	Kicking	D a t e		D a t e	
B < 3	< 40'	Instep Kick				
I 4-7	40-90'					
A 8 >	90' >	Punting				
10 Traps		Trapping	D a t e		D a t e	
B < 4						
I 4-7		All Traps				
A 8 >						
Figure 8 Dribble		Dribbling	D a t e		D a t e	
B 60 sec. >						
I 45-59 sec.		All Dribbling				
A < 45 sec.						
Keep It Up		Volleying	D a t e		D a t e	
B < 4						
I 4-7		Heading				
A 8 >		Juggling				

Parent's Signature _____ Date _____

Comments:

FIGURE 27.2   Sample self-referenced performance rating card for soccer with *approximate* sample standards.

FIGURE 27.2 *(continued)*   Reverse side of self-referenced performance rating card for soccer.

KEY: B = Beginning Level of Skill   I = Intermediate Level of Skill   A = Advanced Level of Skill

Description of Tests:

10 Wall-Goal Kicks: With a partner, player stands 20 feet from the wall and takes 10 forceful kicks, trying to place the ball in a 6-foot-high by 12-foot-wide goal area taped on the wall one yard above the floor. One point is scored for each "goal."

Punt for Distance: With a partner, player stands behind a restraining line and punts the ball as far as possible. Two lines mark the 0-40-foot area (B) and the 40-90-foot area (I). Over 90 feet is an advanced kick (A).

10 Traps: With a partner tossing the ball so players must execute 5 different traps two times each, player attempts to stop or control ball while standing inside a 3-foot circle.

Figure-8 Dribble: Two restraining lines are placed 40 feet apart, with cones or chairs 10 feet apart. Partner says "go," player dribbles the ball with the feet in and out of the chairs to the opposite lne and back. Total elapsed time is the score.

Keep It Up: Player tosses ball up to self and attempts to keep it in the air by juggling it. Process is repeated with heading, but only for the most advanced.

SUGGESTED READING

Coaching youth soccer. (1979). AAHPERD Athletic Institute, N. Palm Beach, FL: Athletic Institute.

Handbook for youth soccer. (1985) New York: U.S. Soccer Federation, 350 Fifth Avenue, N.Y., N.Y. 10010

Hopper, Chris, and Davis, Mike (1986). *Coaching soccer effectively.* Champaign, IL: American Coaching Effectiveness Program.

Houseworth, Steven (Ed.) (1985) *Soccer kickers manual.* Champaign, IL: Human Kinetics.

Mazzei, J. (1982). *Pélé soccer training program.* W. Orange, NJ: Soccer Marketing Associates.

Simon, Malcolm, and Reeves, John A. (Eds.) (1982). *The soccer games book.* Champaign, IL: American Coaching Effectiveness Program.

Thomson, W. (1980). *Teaching soccer.* Minneapolis: Burgess.

CHAPTER 28

SOFTBALL SKILLS

The game of baseball is deeply imbedded in North American culture. Softball is closely related to baseball in that it is played under the same basic rule structure, uses a similar field of play, and involves many of the same skills. Children at the elementary school level have often had at least minimal exposure to the game of baseball through their own participation or through observing it being played by others. However, the skill level within any grade or class will vary widely. Some children will be quite skilled and may take part in summer league play. Many others will be quite unskilled, with little or no idea how to execute the basic skills or play the game. Therefore, at the elementary school level the primary focus should be on instruction and practice in the skills and rules of the game.

Slow-pitch softball is generally considered to be better suited than baseball for the instructional program for several reasons. Success can be achieved at lower skill levels because softball skills are somewhat less complex and less demanding than baseball. Softball requires less space and equipment and can be learned earlier and played later in life than baseball.

The game of softball combines and refines several fundamental movement skills. Successful development of the skills required to play softball is dependent upon attaining mature fundamental movement patterns. If one is unable to throw, catch, or strike a ball in a mature pattern, then it will not be possible to acquire the sport skills of throwing and pitching, catching and fielding, and batting and bunting that are an integral part of softball. Therefore, at the elementary school level, softball instruction should focus on skill development and *not* on playing the regulation game. A wide variety of skill drills and lead-up games of increasing complexity should be included in the program and should be used as a means of improving skill and knowledge about the game. However, little time should be spent on actually playing the regulation game of softball during the instructional physical education lesson. Play of the regulation game should be reserved for the intramural, interscholastic, or agency-sponsored program.

DEVELOPING A SOFTBALL SKILLS THEME

In order to maximize learning and make the best use of your time when focusing on the development of softball skills, it will be helpful to follow the recommended sequence of: (1) preplanning, (2) observing and assessing, (3) planning and implementing, and (4) evaluating and revising. In terms of movement skill learning, determine if students are at the beginning level, intermediate level, or advanced level of developing their softball skills. Based on this information and your assessment information, sequentially list the skills that will be stressed in the unit. Then select appropriate drills, geared to the particular skill levels of the class. Several skill drill activity ideas are located at the end of this chapter. After the skill drill portion of your lesson, you will find it beneficial to incorporate lead-up game activities that focus on implementing the skills. Refer to Chapter 33, "Lead-Up Game Activities," for a list of softball lead-up games and how they are played.

Assess the exit level of softball skills through either informal or formal assessment. You may wish to use the suggestions found in the "Assessing Progress" section at the end of this chapter. Modify subsequent lessons to more closely suit specific individual and group needs.

SKILL SEQUENCING

In terms of softball skill learning, third and fourth graders are typically at the beginning level. Fifth and sixth graders are typically at the intermediate level of softball skill learning. Some will be at the advanced level. This does not, however, mean that all are at the same level. With the popularity of softball/baseball activities in youth sport programs, several children in each class can be expected to be at a relatively high level of skill. Therefore, it is important that you know where your students are in terms of their softball skills in order to be able to plan more effectively for all. Table 28.1, "Selected Softball Skills," and Table 28.2 "Developmental Activities Chart for Softball," should help you select appropriate softball skills to teach and skill drills to use. A brief description of each drill is located in the "Skill Development Activities" section, along with recommended warmup activities. Appropriate softball lead-up games are located in Chapter 33.

THROWING

Skilled throwing and pitching are two essential aspects of the game of softball. There are basically three types of throws used in softball: overhand, sidearm, and underhand. The throw used depends on the position in which the ball is fielded, the distance it must travel, and the speed at which it must arrive at its destination. Pitching is a specialized underhand throwing pattern. Teaching tips for softball throwing and pitching, including a list of common problems and recommended teaching strategies, follow, along with a list of concepts children should know. Brief verbal and visual descriptions are also included for study.

TABLE 28.1   Selected
Softball Skills

Softball Skills	Suggested Progression for Children		
	Beginning Level	Intermediate Level	Page
Throwing			389
Overhand Throw	Introduce	Refine	392
Sidearm Throw		Introduce	392
Underhand Throw	Introduce	Refine	393
Pitching		Introduce	393
Fielding			394
High Fly Ball	Introduce	Refine	395
Low Fly Ball	Introduce	Refine	396
Ground Ball	Introduce	Refine	396
Hitting			397
Batting	Introduce	Refine	398
Bunting		Introduce	399
Associated Skills			
Base Running	Introduce	Refine	402
Base Playing	Introduce	Refine	402
Base Stealing		Introduce	402
Understanding the Game			
Rules	Introduce	Refine	400
Strategy		Introduce	

Teaching Tips

Common Problems

- Failure to grip the ball properly.
- Failure to lead at the elbow for overhand and sidearm throws.
- Insufficient shoulder and hip rotation for forceful throws.
- Poor rhythm of movement.
- Leading with the wrong foot.
- Lack of follow-through.
- Inability to get desired distance.
- Poor control.

Recommended Strategies

- Practice basic mechanics of throwing to insure that all are at mature stage.
- Stress proper mechanics before accuracy or control.
- Practice throwing for distance in both overhand and sidearm patterns.
- Provide infield practice situations for the underhand toss.
- Provide plenty of opportunities for practice with the correct throwing techniques in gamelike situations.
- After technique has been mastered, work for accuracy.
- Partner throwing and catching drills will promote control and accuracy.
- Target throwing drills will promote control and accuracy.
- Do not introduce pitching until reasonable control has been mastered with underhand tossing.
- Use smaller and softer balls as needed.
- Stress accuracy in pitching prior to speed.
- Stress gripping the ball with the thumb and fingertips.
- Combine fielding and throwing drills after reasonable skill has been separately attained for each.
- Select skill drills and lead-up games that emphasize increasingly complex skill development.

TABLE 28.2 Developmental Activities Chart for Softball

Softball Skill Drills	Throwing Skills	Fielding Skills	Base-Running Skills	Batting Skills	Page
Wall toss		X			401
Vertical toss and catch		X			401
Partner toss and catch	X	X			401
Exchange throwing	X	X			401
Over/under exchange throwing	X	X			402
Alternate over/under	X	X			402
Stretch and catch	X	X			402
One-bounce drill	X	X			402
Fly ball drill	X	X			402
Fly ball/pick-off drill	X	X			402
Around the horn	X	X			402
Throwing/catching shuttle	X	X			402
Run, throw, catch	X	X	X		402
Fielding grounders		X			402
Grounder exchange		X			402
Grounder/fly ball exchange		X			402
Partner throw-out	X	X			402
Strong-side throw-out	X	X			402
Weak-side throw-out	X	X			402
Grounder shuttle		X	X		402
Speed base running			X		402
Around the bases			X		402
Base-runner pick-off			X		402
Base reverse			X		403
Suspended-ball batting				X	403
Swinging ball batting				X	403
Tee batting				X	403
Batting practice		X		X	403
Pepper		X		X	403
Pepper pick		X		X	403
Fungo batting		X		X	403

- Practice moving toward ground balls, picking it up, pivoting, and throwing.
- Stress the importance of the ready position and being alert at all times.

Concepts Children Should Know

Skill Concepts
- Grip the ball with your thumb and fingertips.
- Don't let your palm touch the ball.

- Use plenty of shoulder and hip rotation when you throw the ball.
- Lead with your elbow as you release the ball in the overhand and sidearm throws.
- Step forward on the nonthrowing foot as you release the ball.
- Release the ball at about waist level for the underhand throw.
- Follow through in the direction of your target.

Movement Concepts

- The speed at which the ball travels is dependent upon the proper summation of forces.
- Forceful hip and shoulder rotation will add speed to the ball.
- The distance the ball travels is dependent upon the force applied and the trajectory at which it is released.
- The accuracy with which you can throw a ball overhand is dependent upon the distance to be covered, constant visual monitoring of the target, and complete follow-through.
- In a dynamic game situation, your throwing pattern will vary between overhand, sidearm, and underhand, depending on the immediate conditions.
- You may have to throw from awkward positions dictated by how and where you caught the ball.
- Pitching is a specialized skill requiring considerable practice to gain accuracy and control.

Overhand Throw

The overhand throw is the basic throwing skill used by all players except the pitcher. The mechanics of the overhand throw in softball are the same as the mature fundamental overhand throwing pattern. The difference lies in the specialized nature of the throw, requiring improved performance in terms of the distance thrown, the accuracy and control of the throw, and the speed at which the ball travels.

Verbal Description

- See Chapter 20 (page 238) for a description of the mechanics of the mature overhand throwing pattern.
- Grip the ball with the thumb and three or four fingers.
- Fingertips and thumb grip ball; palm does not touch.
- Greater speed is imparted to ball through rapid hip rotation while forcefully bringing

the arm around and stepping out on the leg opposite the throwing arm.

- Greater distance is achieved by executing the preceding steps and releasing the ball in a high arc.
- Greater accuracy is achieved by concentrating on the target and by complete follow-through.
- Greater control and consistency are achieved through practice in a variety of drill and gamelike situations.

Visual Description

PHOTO 28.1   Overhand throw.

Sidearm Throw

The sidearm throw is used if the ball is caught when the player is off balance or if the ball is caught to one side of the player's body. It is used frequently by players in the infield to cover a short distance and get there in a hurry. The same basic mechanics are used for the sidearm throw as are used for the overhand throw except for the following:

Verbal Description

- Throwing arm is extended diagonally from the shoulder.
- Forearm is extended straight from the elbow.
- Arm angle may vary from diagonal to just above the horizontal.
- Arm follows through across the body.

Visual Description

PHOTO 28.2   Sidearm throw.

Verbal Description

- Grip the ball with the thumb and fingertips.
- From a closed stance, transfer the weight to the foot that corresponds to the throwing arm (right arm, right foot).
- At the same time, swing the throwing arm down and backward in a pendular motion.
- Step forward on the foot opposite the throwing arm (right arm, left foot).
- At the same time, swing the throwing arm forward and transfer weight to the forward foot.
- Release the ball off the fingertips in the desired trajectory.
- Follow through in the direction of the target.

Visual Description

PHOTO 28.3   Underhand throw.

Underhand Throw

The underhand throw is used in softball to cover a shorter distance than the sidearm throw. It is frequently used when the ball is caught low or scooped up from the ground by an infield player and tossed to another person. The underhand toss is basic to the pattern used in softball pitching.

Pitching

Pitching should be introduced only after reasonable mastery has been attained in underhand throwing. Accuracy should be stressed prior to speed.

Verbal Description

- Stand with feet parallel in a closed position, facing the batter.

- Both hands hold the ball as it is presented forward to the batter.

- The nonthrowing hand is released as the ball is brought down backward and then forward in a pendular motion.

- The shoulder of the throwing arm rotates slightly down and backward at the height of the backswing, and the body weight is transferred to the rear foot.

- The throwing arm swings forward in a pendular action close to the trunk and leg, and the shoulder rotates forward.

- At the same time, the body weight is transferred to the opposite foot as it steps forcefully forward.

- The ball is released off the fingertips at about waist height.

- Follow-through is made in the direction of the batter.

Visual Description

PHOTO 28.4   Pitching

FIELDING

Fielding is an important element of the game of softball. Proficiency in fielding a ball is often difficult for elementary-age children to acquire because of the speed at which the ball approaches, the varying trajectories in which the ball may approach, and the uncertainty of where the ball should be intercepted. The primary fielding skills to be learned by elementary school-age children involve catching a fly ball, catching a line drive, and fielding ground balls. Teaching tips, including a list of common problems and recommended strategies, follow, along with a list of the skill concepts and movement concepts children should know. A verbal description and a visual description of fielding skills are also included for study.

Teaching Tips

Common Problems
- Failure to get behind the ball.
- Failure to visually track the ball into the hands.
- Looking away as the ball approaches.
- Failure to reach out to catch the ball.
- Failure to give with the ball as it is caught.
- Failure to adjust the hands properly to the height of the ball.
- Failure to catch the ball in the "pocket" of the glove.

Recommended Strategies
- Work for proper mechanics of the basic elements of catching first.
- Stress tracking the ball into the hands.
- Use yarnballs or beanbags when players are first learning to catch a fly ball or a line drive.
- Use super-soft softballs or whiffle-type balls if gloves are not available.
- Incorporate drills that work on one catching skill at a time in a static manner prior to introducing more complex activities.
- As skill develops, practice in dynamic, game-like situations that require various forms of catching.
- Gradually increase the speed of ground balls to be fielded.
- Work for control prior to speed in fielding grounders.
- Stress controlling ground balls and keeping them in front of the body.
- Incorporate throwing drills with catching drills.
- Stress getting rid of the ball (throwing to a teammate) immediately after the catch.
- Stress attacking the ball with a quick but balanced release.

Concepts Children Should Know

Skill Concepts
- Get directly in line with the path of the ball.
- Keep your eyes on the ball at all times.
- Adjust your hand position to the height of the ball.
- Intercept the ball away from your body.
- Bring the ball toward your body (give with the ball) as it is caught.

Movement Concepts
- The ball can be caught at different levels.
- The ball can be caught coming from different directions.
- You can catch balls traveling at different speeds.
- You will need to make adjustments in your body position and catching pattern, depending on the height and speed of the ball.
- The greater the speed of the ball, the more you will have to give with its force.
- If you intercept the ball away from your body, you will have more distancce to absorb the force.
- It is easier to catch and control the ball if you get directly in line with its path.

High Fly Ball

Catching a high fly ball is exciting to watch and thrilling to perform. The major task in catching a high fly ball is getting into the proper position. This is a complex skill in itself, requiring sophisticated perceptual judgments from both visual and auditory cues. Based on this information, the fielder moves to the spot where the ball is anticipated to land and prepares to catch the ball.

Verbal Description
- body is placed in direct line with the path of the ball, in a narrow stride stance.
- Head is raised and eyes track the ball throughout its approach.
- Arms and hands are raised upward, the arms are slightly bent, and in line with the chin.
- Thumbs are close together, with the fingers spread, and the gloved hand is slightly forward.
- Eyes track the ball into the glove.
- As the ball is caught in the pocket, the glove

is squeezed together slightly and the non-gloved hand covers the ball.

- The knees flex slightly and the arms bend toward the body to absorb the force of the ball.

Verbal Description

- Body is placed in direct line with the ball, the feet are spread, and the knees are slightly bent.
- Hands are brought in line with the ball.
- Fingers are spread and the hands are close together.
- Ball is contacted out from the body.
- Ball is visually tracked into the glove.
- Nongloved hand covers the ball.
- Arms give upon impact.

Visual Description

PHOTO 28.5   Fielding a high fly ball.

PHOTO 28.6   Fielding a low fly ball.

Low Fly Ball

Catching a low fly ball often poses problems to children, especially when the flight of the ball is interrupted just above waist level. Indecision about the proper hand position frequently results in a dropped ball. Any ball intercepted below the waist should be caught with a thumbs-out position.

Ground Ball

Fielding is an important softball skill that is often made more difficult by rough terrain, which causes the ball to bounce wildly. This, coupled with the limited skill level of many children, frequently makes fielding a grounder in the classic manner difficult to master. The "sure-stop" method of fielding a grounder that follows is generally more appropriate for elementary school children. If the ball is missed by the hands, it will generally be stopped by the body.

Verbal Description
- Body is placed in direct line with the path of the approaching ball.

- The knees bend, with one knee brought to the ground.
- The waist is bent forward and the hands and arms are extended downward.
- The eyes visually track the ball into the glove.
- The nongloved hand covers the ball as it is brought up to the body in preparation for the throw.
- Both hands work together.

Visual Description

PHOTO 28.7   Fielding a ground ball.

HITTING

Striking a pitched ball is a very complex task. In fact, it is thought by many to be the single most difficult sports skill in terms of perceptual–motor complexity. Therefore, it is important to proceed slowly in developing children's batting and bunting abilities. Modification must frequently be made for all but the most skilled, especially with younger children.

Teaching Tips

Common Problems
- Grasping the bat cross-handed.
- Grasping the bat with the hands apart.

- Gripping the bat too high or too low.
- Indecision over where to stand.
- Bending forward at the waist.
- Laying the bat on the shoulder.
- Standing with the legs straight and feet together.
- Failure to assume the proper ready position.
- Pulling the elbows in close to the body.
- Swinging down on the ball in a chopping action.
- Swinging up on the ball.
- Swinging too late.
- Inability to visually track the ball.
- Shying away from the ball as it approaches.
- Poor summation of forces.
- Lack of follow-through after contact.
- Failure to step toward the ball.

Recommended Strategies
- Practice batting off a tee prior to hitting pitched balls.
- Use larger balls. A beachball or utility ball is frequently helpful.
- Vary the color of the ball to promote better tracking.
- Use a large-headed bat in order to increase success.
- Work just for contact and control.
- Use floor markings to indicate proper foot position.
- Practice striking slowly moving balls, prior to more rapid pitches.
- Provide plenty of opportunities for practice and structure the activity for success.
- As success develops, increase the complexity of the task.

Concepts Children Should Know

Skill Concepts
- Keep your eyes on the ball.
- Grip the bat with your hands together and your right hand on top (right-handed batter).
- Extend at your elbows.
- Keep your swing level

- Step into your swing.
- Contact the ball at the point of complete extension of your arms.
- Snap the wrists as the ball is contacted.

Movement Concepts
- The distance the ball travels will depend on the amount of force applied.
- The direction the ball travels will depend on the point of contact and the direction of your follow-through.
- Contact with the ball depends on successfully converting what you see (perceptual input) into what you do (motor output).
- Choking up on the bat will give you greater control of your swing.
- Taking a long grip will enable you to impart more force to the ball.
- Moving toward the ball as you swing will increase body balance and force production.

Batting

Developing skill in batting takes time and plenty of practice. Its complexity in terms of the precise skill required frequently makes it difficult for children to learn without initial modification.

Verbal Description
- Stand at the side of the plate with the side of the body facing the pitcher.
- The feet are spread slightly more than shoulder width apart.
- The knees are slightly bent and the body weight is evenly distributed.
- The bat is gripped with the hands touching each other and the right hand above the left (right-handed batter).
- Bat is brought back to a position over the shoulder, pointing up and back.
- Elbows are held away from the body.
- As the ball approaches, the swing begins and the eyes track the ball.
- As the movement progresses, there is a shift in weight from the back to the front leg.

- The hips rotate toward the pitcher and the forward leg takes a short step forward.
- The bat is brought around parallel to the ground in line with the ball.
- The bat contacts the ball when the arms are fully extended and the weight is transferred to the forward foot. The back foot remains grounded.

Visual Description

PHOTO 28.8   Batting.

Bunting

Bunting should be introduced only after reasonable skill has been attained in batting. Bunting is frequently used in softball as a sacrifice move to advance a teammate already on base.

Verbal Description (Right-Handed Batter)
- As the ball is released, the batter turns to face the pitcher.
- The right foot is by the plate; feet are slightly spread with weight evenly distributed.
- The right hand slides halfway up the bat and holds loosely.
- Be careful of the fingers. Keep the hand that has moved up behind the bat.
- The bat is brought in front of the body, parallel to the ground.
- The ball is contacted along the top half of the bat in a downward motion.
- The ball is directed along the ground toward the first-base or third-base line.

Visual Description

PHOTO 28.9   Bunting.

BASIC RULES

The regulation game of slow-pitch softball is played by two teams, each with 10 players, which include a pitcher, catcher, three basepersons, a shortstop, and four outfielders. The object of the game is for the team at bat to hit balls delivered underhand by the pitcher into the field in fair territory and score runs. One run is scored for each player who successfully circles the bases and returns to home plate. The team in the field attempts to prevent the batting team from scoring by catching the ball on the fly or by touching the base runner with the ball while off base. The base runner must run consecutively from first to second to third base and then home. He may stop at any base after hitting a ball into fair territory, and he may continue to the next and subsequent bases on the next fairly hit ball. After three persons have been put out on the batting team, the teams exchange positions.

The pitcher must present the ball to the batter and may take one step forward on the delivery, keeping the rear foot on the pitcher's plate. The ball must be thrown underhand at a moderate speed in an upward arc from 6 to 12 feet above the ground. The ball should cross home plate between the shoulders and knees of the batter.

The batter may swing at a pitched ball or let it go by. It is a *strike* if the batter swings and misses. It is a *foul ball* if the ball does not land in fair territory. A foul ball is counted as a strike unless the batter already has two strikes. The batter is also out in slow-pitch softball if the ball is bunted, hit downward in a chopping motion, or hit foul after the second strike.

After a ball has been hit into fair territory, the batter becomes a *base runner*. The batter also becomes a base runner if she is hit by the ball on the pitch or if the catcher interferes with the batter. The base runner must touch the bases in regular order. Only one base runner may occupy a base at a time. The base runner is out if he is tagged by the ball while off base, if he runs more than three feet out of the base path, if he passes a preceding runner, if he leaves the base before a fly ball has been caught, or if he leaves the base before a pitched ball reaches home plate.

SKILL DEVELOPMENT ACTIVITIES

In order for children to master the skills of softball, they will need to practice them first individually in static drill situations. After the basic elements of throwing, pitching, fielding, and batting have been mastered under these situations, it will be profitable to practice under controlled dynamic drill situations in which the environment changes during the drill based on the nature of the activity itself. Then it will be helpful to add skill requirements to the drill and finally to take part in lead-up games that are performed in a dynamically changing environment. The following sequence of skill drills and lead-up game activities is recommended in order to maximize skill learning:

1. Introduce single skills in a static environment ("walk through").
2. Practice single skills in a controlled dynamic environment (drill).
3. Introduce multiple-skill drills in a static environment.
4. Practice multiple-skill drills in a controlled, dynamic environment.
5. Implement multiple skills in simple lead-up game activities.
6. Practice increasingly complex lead-up game activities.

The skills drills presented in this section proceed from simple to complex, in that they range from static skill drills to dynamic skill drills and from single-skill to multiple-skill activities. A list of suggested warmup activities to be performed prior to engaging in softball skill drills is also included.

Warmup Activities

Warmup activities are highly recommended prior to engaging in skill drills and lead-up activities. Each of the activities that follow should last 20 to 30 seconds. Keep varying the warmup drills and move rapidly from one activity to the next in order to maintain interest and obtain maximum benefit. See Chapter 43, "Fitness Activities," for a description of each of these exercises.

Stretching
a. Trunk twisting.
b. Static toe touch.
c. Static hurdler's stretch.
d. Toes to the ground from overhead.

Suppling
a. Arm circles.
b. Arm flings.
c. Over-the-shoulder hand pull.
d. Behind-the-back hand pull.

Strengthening
a. Bent-knee situps.
b. Pushups/modified pushups.
c. Front rocker.
d. Half squats.
e. Toe raisers.

Running
a. Wind sprints.
b. Base running.
c. Shadow tag.
d. Stops and starts.
e. Agility running.

Tossing and Catching
a. Repeated vertical tossing and catching from a stand.
b. Repeated vertical tossing and catching from a sitting position.
c. Repeated vertical tossing and catching from a lying position.
d. Tossing and catching at different levels.

Batting
a. Swinging practice.
b. Bat stretching activities.
c. Shadow batting.
d. Fungo hitting.

Skill Drills

Numerous skill drills can be devised to practice the essential elements of softball. The primary emphasis of softball skill drills at the elementary school level should be on improving *throw-*

ing, fielding, and *batting* skills. By giving a skill drill a name and introducing as element of competition, you can easily turn what may be to children a rather dull drill into a lively game. Be careful, however, not to emphasize the game before the mechanics of the movement have been reasonably mastered and practiced under static conditions. Failure to remember this basic point will result in many children regressing in their performance rather than progressing. The following is a sampling of softball skill drills appropriate for elementary school children.

Objectives

1. To improve throwing skills (overhand, side-arm, underhand).
2. To improve fielding skills (high fly ball, low fly ball, ground ball).
3. To improve striking skills (batting, bunting).
4. To introduce the associated skills of base running, base playing, and sliding.
5. To improve overall fitness (strength, endurance, coordination, flexibility).
6. To enhance group cooperation and teamwork.

Movement Experiences

Wall Toss (catching). Player tosses ball against a wall from a postition 5 to 10 feet from the wall and moves into position to catch it. May be done with alternating partner wall tosses and catches.
Vertical Toss and Catch (catching). Player tosses ball vertically into the air and catches it, using high fly ball catching position. Work for height on the throw and proper catching action.
Partner Toss and Catch (throwing, catching). With a partner, practice throwing and catching. Begin 10 to 15 feet apart and gradually increase distance. Stress maximum effort prior to accuracy.
Exchange Throwing (catching, throwing). With a partner, each with a ball, throw to each other at the same time. This forces the players to catch the ball, transfer it to the throwing hand, and

release it while getting ready to receive another ball.

Over/Under Exchange Throwing (catching, throwing). Same as preceding exercise, except one partner throws overhand while the other throws underhand.

Alternating Over/Under (catching, throwing). Same as preceding exercise, but partners alternate in their overhand and underhand throws.

Stretch and Catch (catching, throwing). The player keeps a foot anchored on an imaginary base and stretches as far forward or sideways as possible while catching balls thrown by a partner.

One-Bounce Drill (fielding, distance throwing). One player throws the ball and a partner retrieves it after one bounce. Work for distance on the throws and for immediate release after the catch.

Fly Ball Drill (high fly ball catching). The player tosses the ball high into the air while a partner moves under it and makes the catch.

Fly Ball/Pick-Off Drill (high fly ball catching, throwing). Same as preceding exercise, but add an immediate throw to a base to pick off a base runner.

Around the Horn (throwing, catching). Take all infield positions except the pitcher's. The catcher throws to the shortstop, who throws to first, who throws to second, who throws to third, who throws back to the catcher again. Work for control, then speed. Rotate positions so that each player gets to play each position.

Throwing/Catching Shuttle (throwing, catching). Form two columns, 20 to 60 feet apart, of four players per column. Player at the head of column A throws to player at the head of column B, then runs to the back of the line. The process is repeated over and over, working first for control, then speed.

Run, Throw, Catch (throwing, catching, running). Form two columns, 20 to 40 feet apart, with four players per column. Ball rests on the floor between the two groups. First player in column A runs to retrieve the ball, picks it up, throws (underhand toss for short distance, overhead for longer) to the first player in column B, and goes to the back of that line. First player in column B catches the ball, returns it to the resting spot, and goes to the rear of column A. Practice at varying distances, first stressing control, then speed, then accuracy.

Fielding Grounders (fielding grounders). One player throws ground balls to a second player. Alternate throwing ground balls between players, gradually adding speed to the throws.

Grounder Exchange (fielding grounders). Two partners, each with a ball, practice throwing grounders to each other at the same time. This will encourage getting the ball away quickly before the other ball arrives.

Grounder/Fly Ball Exchange (fielding fly balls and grounders). Same as preceding, except one player throws grounders and the other throws fly balls.

Partner Throw-Out (fielding sidearm throwing). One player throws a grounder, a low fly ball, or a high fly ball. The partner fields the ball and throws immediately back, as if trying to throw the other player out at first base. Practice the sidearm throw with this drill to decrease time.

Strong-Side Throw-Out (fielding, sidearm throwing). Same as preceding exercise, but throw to a third person, who is off at an angle to the same side as the throwing arm.

Weak-Side Throw-Out (fielding, sidearm throwing, pivoting). Same as preceding exercise, but throw is to a third person standing off at an angle on the *opposite* side of the throwing arm. This will force the fielder to pivot prior to throwing.

Grounder Shuttle (fielding grounders, running). Form two columns of four players each, about 20 to 40 feet apart. Lead-off player in column A throws a grounder to lead player in column B, who throws it to the next player in column A. After throwing the ball, the player runs to the end of the opposite column.

Speed Base Running (base running). Players individually practice running the bases, trying to improve their time each trial.

Around the Bases (base running). There are four players per group, each standing on a base. They run the bases, trying to overtake the player in front of them. Stress touching each base and running in a slight arc so that they are not at right angles to each other when going from base to base.

Base-Runner Pick-Off (stealing). Class faces the teacher with knees bent, feet shoulder width apart, weight evenly distributed. Teacher points; players react either to the left or right, as if trying to steal second base. If teacher points to their right, they run full out. If the point is to the left, they dive back for the imaginary base.

Base Reverse (base running).   Same as preceding activity, but reverse directions at the sound of a whistle.

Suspended-Ball Batting (batting).   Player practices striking a stationary suspended ball that has been adjusted to the proper height.

Swinging-Ball Batting (batting).   Same as preceding activity, but the ball swings through a wide arc prior to contact.

Tee Batting (batting).   Using a road cone with a golf tube through the top and a softball balanced on the tube, practice batting. Partner at opposite end retrieves the ball and *rolls* it back to the batter.

Batting Practice (batting, fielding).   Form groups of six (batter, pitcher, catcher, and three fielders), with four to six balls per group. Players rotate positions after a set number of batted balls. The pitcher throws the ball easily so it can be hit.

Pepper (bunting, fielding grounders).   Form groups of six (batter, pitcher, four fielders), with four to six balls per group. Pitcher tosses the ball so it can be easily hit. Batter bunts the ball back. Fielders recover the ball. Rotate after a set number of bunts.

Pepper Pick (controlled bunting, fielding grounders).   Same as preceding activity, but batter calls out the player that is being bunted too.

Fungo Batting (batting, fielding).   Four to five players form a group (one batter, remainder fielders). Batter self-tosses the ball into the air and hits it to the fielders, who throw it back. Rotate after a set number of hits or after a player has made a set number of catches.

ASSESSING PROGRESS

Assessment of softball skills is important at both the beginning and the end of an instructional unit. Assessment need not take up large segments of time. Process assessments are subjec-

tive and can be informally conducted by the teacher. Product assessments can be self-referenced and student-led. At the elementary school level, little attention need be given to comparing children through the use of standardized softball skills tests. The range of skill will vary markedly, depending on the extent of previous experiences the children have had. It is more important at this level for you to know where they are in terms of the ability to execute basic softball skills, and for them to be able to see improvement in their level of performance.

Process Assessment

Process assessment is based on the subjective judgment of the instructor with regard to the demonstrated level of ability in the basic skills of softball. With process ratings, the instructor is primarily concerned with the body mechanics or technique used to perform the various throwing, fielding, and batting skills of softball. The form rating chart depicted in Figure 28.1 is an example of a process assessment instrument that can be used to quickly and accurately chart the manner in which these skills are performed. Charting students at the beginning of an instructional module will help determine where they have improved.

Product Assessment

Students can determine their own level of skill in the various elements of softball by working with a partner and using a self-referenced performance rating card similar to the sample depicted in Figure 28.2. The limited amount of time allotted to the physical education period plus large numbers of students often make it impractical for the instructor to administer a softball skills test. Students working in small groups of four to six can, with a minimum amount of training, easily and accurately determine their own levels of performance. If the primary reason for skill assessment is to chart individual progress and is not the awarding of grades, then there is little danger of children inflating their scores. The softball skills performance rating may

Softball Skill Rating Chart													
Class _____ Grade _____													
Entry Assessment Date _____ Exit Assessment Date _____													
Directions	Throwing Skills				Fielding Skills			Batting Skills		Associated Skills			Key
Observe during drill or play situations. Mark entry rating in upper left corner and exit rating in lower right corner of square.	Overhand	Sidearm	Underhand	Pitching	High Fly	Low Fly	Grounder	Batting	Bunting	Base Running	Base Playing	Base Stealing	A: Advanced—Correct technique plus good control and force production. I: Intermediate—Correct technique but lacking in control or force production. B: Beginning—inconsistent use of correct technique.
													Comments

FIGURE 28.1 Sample form rating chart for softball.

Softball Skills Progress Report						

Student's Name _____ Grade _____ Class_____ Year_____

See Reverse for Description		Skills	Entry Rating	Comments	Exit Rating	Comments
Distance Throw	Hoop Pitch	Throwing Skills	Date		Date	
B 0-30 ft. I 30-90 ft. A 90 ft.>	0-1 for 5 2-3 for 5 4-5 for 5	Distance Throw				
		Accuracy Pitch				
Flies and Grounder Drills		Fielding Skills	Date		Date	
B 0-3 for 10 tries I 4-8 for 10 tries A 9-10 for 10 tries		Flies				
		Grounders				
Batting	Bunting	Batting Skills	Date		Date	
B 0-1 for 5 I 2-3 for 5 A 4-5 for 5	0-1 for 5 2-3 for 5 4-5 for 5	Batting				
		Bunting				

Parent's Signature_____ Date _____

Comments:

FIGURE 28.2 Self-referenced performance rating card for softball, with *approximate* sample standards.

FIGURE 28.2 *(continued)* Reverse side of self-referenced performance rating card for softball.

KEY: B = Beginning Level of Skill   I = Intermediate Level of Skill   A = Advanced Level of Skill

Description of Tests:

Distance Throw: With a partner, player throws the ball as far as possible from behind a restraining line. Field is marked off with three line. The first line is 30 feet from the restraining line (B area), the second is 60 feet (I area), and the third is 90 feet (A area). Each player takes 3 throws. Longest throw counts.

Hoop Pitch: With a partner and a hoop suspended at strike-zone height, player stands 40 feet away and pitches the ball underhand through the hoop. Each player makes 5 pitches.

Flies and Grounders: With a partner 30 feet distant, player alternates throwing 5 high balls and 5 grounders. Partner attempts to catch each ball.

Batting: With a partner who pitches the ball so it can be easily hit, player bats the ball 5 times as far as possible. Balls that are hit or that roll into the outfield in fair territory count one point each.

Bunting: Same as above, but ball must stay in fair territory in the infield.

be placed on a card, have comments added to it, and be sent home to parents as a progress report.

SUGGESTED READING

ASA youth coaches' handbook. (1985). Oklahoma City, OK: Amateur Softball Associates, 2801 NE 50th Street.

Coaching youth softball. (1984). AAHPERD, Athletic Institute, N. Palm Beach, FL: Athletic Institute.

Softball Coaching Manual. (1984). Coaching Association of Canada. Vanier, Ontario: 333 River Road.

Houseworth, Steven, and Kivkin, Fran (1985). *Coaching softball effectively.* Champaign, IL: American Coaching Effectiveness Program.

Stockton, Bragg (1984). *Coaching baseball.* Champaign, IL: American Coaching Effectiveness Program.

CHAPTER 29

VOLLEYBALL SKILLS

The game of volleyball was invented by William Morgan, a YMCA physical director in Holyoke, Massachusetts, in 1895. Since then the game has steadily gained in popularity, both as a recreational activity and a competitive sport. Power volleyball has become very popular throughout North America. It was given a big boost by the extensive coverage of the sport in the Olympic games and the superb showing of both the men's and women's teams representing the United States and Canada.

Basic volleyball skills can be developed at the elementary school level *only* if significant modifications are made. First, the net should be lowered to a height of about six feet for beginning players. Second, the ball should be modified for all but the most skillful players. The use of beachballs and foam balls works well during the skill development phase. Third, the size of the court should be modified and a maximum of six players per side should be permitted. Simply dividing the class in half and playing with 15 to 20 children per side is ridiculous. Such a procedure only promotes inactivity and encourages the more skillful to dominate play. Fourth, the foundational skills of the game must be learned and eye–hand coordination must be sufficiently developed before attempting to play regulation volleyball. Care must be taken to adhere to each of these requirements in order to maximize successful learning.

DEVELOPING A VOLLEYBALL SKILLS THEME

Unlike basketball and softball, the vast majority of children will have had little or no prior volleyball playing experience. Therefore, most will be at the beginning level of skill development. This, coupled with the complexity of the task of volleying itself, makes it generally advisable to wait until at least the third grade before developing children's volleyball skills. When a volleyball skills theme is planned and implemented, it will be helpful to utilize the sequence of : (1) preplanning, (2) observing and assessing, (3) planning and implementing, and (4) evaluating and revising. Then select appropriate drills geared to the skill levels of the class. Several skill drill activities are located at the end of this chapter. After the skill drill portion of the lesson, you will find it helpful to incorporate lead-up game activities. Lead-up activities that focus on further skill refinement should be chosen. Refer to Chapter 33 "Lead-Up Game Activities," for a list of appropriate activities and how they are played.

SKILL SEQUENCING

Children's visual-motor capabilities are sufficiently developed by the third grade for most to benefit from practice in the various modified volleyball skills. There are relatively few skills involved in volleyball, in comparison with most other team sports. These skills are, however, quite precise and require sophisticated, coordinated interaction between the visual and motor systems. Third, fourth, and fifth graders are generally at the beginning level of developing their volleyball skills. Therefore, particular attention should be given to modifying the type of ball used, the height of the net, and the number of players involved. By the sixth grade most children have the potential to perform at the intermediate level, given ample opportunities for learning in the previous grades.

The teaching progression for selected volleyball skills depicted in Table 29.1 will help you select appropriate volleyball skills to focus on as a developmental skill theme. Once this is accomplished, it will be necessary to select appropriate skill drills. The Developmental Activities Chart for Volleyball (Table 29.2) lists several skill drills, progressing from relatively simple single-skill drills to more complex multiskill drills. A brief description of each drill is located in the "Skill Development Activities," section, along with recommended warmup activities. Appropriate lead-up games to volleyball may be found in Chapter 33.

VOLLEYING

Volleying, or passing, as it is sometimes called, requires considerable eye–hand coordination for successful performance. The development of volleying skills will require initial modification in the ball used. As skill develops, a regulation volleyball should be introduced. The primary volleying skills used in volleyball are the overhead pass, bump pass, dig pass, and setup. This section examines common problems encountered by children and recommends strategies for developing volleying skills. The skill concepts and movement concepts that children should know are presented, along with a verbal description and visual description of each type of volley.

Teaching Tips

Common Problems
- Failure to get under or behind the ball.
- Insufficient use of the legs in conjunction with the arm action.
- Failure to visually track the ball.
- Relaxing the wrists, causing the ball to travel backward with the overhead pass or set.

TABLE 29.1
Selected Volleyball Skills

Volleyball Skills	Beginning Level	Intermediate Level	Page
	Suggested Progression for Children		
Volleying			408
Overhead Pass	Introduce	Refine	410
Set	Introduce	Refine	411
Bump		Introduce	412
Dig		Introduce	412
Serving			
Underhand Serve	Introduce	Refine	413
Overhead Serve		Introduce	414
Understanding the Game			415
Rules	Introduce	Refine	416
Strategy		Introduce	

TABLE 29.2
Developmental Skills Chart for Volleyball

Volleyball Skill Drill	Volleying Skills	Serving Skills	Associated Skills	Page
Volley and catch	X			417
Self-volley	X			417
Bump and catch	X			417
Bump it up	X			417
Over–under	X			417
High wall volley	X			417
Low wall volley	X			417
Partner toss	X			417
Partner volley	X			417
Spot	X			417
Partner set	X			417
Three-person set	X			417
One-two-three over	X			417
Circle volley	X			417
Bounce volley	X			417
Partner wall volley	X			418
Bump and run	X			418
Wall serve		X		418
Over-net serve		X		418
Alley serve		X		418
Serve and set	X	X		418
Net dig			X	418

- Contacting the ball with the palms of the hand.
- Slapping at the ball.
- Failure to assume ready position.
- Poor summation of forces.
- Excessive arm swing (bump).
- Ball contacting the upper portion of the arm rather than the forearms (bump).
- Contact made with only one arm, rather than simultaneous contact with both arms (bump).

Recommended Strategies
- Stress control of the ball.
- Use balloons, beachballs, foam balls, and volleyballs in a progressive sequence.
- Practice volleying a tossed ball first, then self-volley, and finally wall volleys.
- Practice volleying to oneself.
- Practice volleying with a partner and finally in a small group of four to six.
- Emphasize getting under the ball or behind the ball.
- Practice under static drill conditions, using modified balls, prior to dynamic game situations using regulation balls.
- Stress keeping the eyes on the ball.
- Work with the bump pass prior to other passing skills.
- Introduce the overhead pass and set only after the bump pass has been reasonably mastered.

Concepts Children Should Know

Skill Concepts
- Get directly in line with the path of the ball.
- Keep your eyes on the ball.
- For overhead volleying, make a "window" with your hands (thumbs and index fingers nearly touch); look through the window as you contact the ball.
- Bend your knees prior to contacting the ball.
- Straighten your legs and your arms as you make contact with the ball.
- Don't slap at the ball.

- Don't contact the ball with your palms.
- A ball will rebound off a flat surface in a more predictable direction than off an angular surface.
- Keep your wrists stiff throughout.
- Follow through in the desired path of the ball.

Movement Concepts
- You can contact the ball at many different heights.
- You can contact the ball from many different levels.
- You can contact the ball with varying amounts of force.
- You may not contact the ball more than once in succession (unless contact is made off a block).
- You can control the direction of the ball.
- You can make contact from underneath the ball, behind the ball, or to the side of the ball.
- You can volley many different types of balls.
- Light balls are easier to volley than heavy balls.

Overhead Pass

The overhead pass is generally used to pass the ball from the back row to the front row or to clear the ball over the net. It is used for a ball that approaches at chest level or above and is a frequently used pass.

Verbal Description
- Feet are in a stride position, with the knees bent slightly and the back relatively straight.
- Arms are raised upward, with the elbows slightly flexed.
- Fingers are spread, with the thumbs and index fingers closed, forming a "window."
- Eyes track the ball through the "window" as contact is made.
- Fingertips contact ball and wrists are stiff as contact is made and the arms extend.
- Knees straighten as arms extend.

- Wrists extend as arms follow through in the direction of intended flight.

Visual Description

PHOTO 29.1   Overhead pass.

Set

The set is usually the second hit in the series of three permitted. The ball is volleyed high and positioned so the next person can direct it over the net with a spike. Controlled setting takes considerable time and practice to master.

Verbal Description
- Feet are in an exaggerated stride position with plenty of bend at the knees, and the back is straight.

- Arms are raised forward and upward, with the elbows flexed.
- The fingers are spread, with the thumbs and index fingers nearly touching, framing a "window."
- Eyes track the ball through the "window" as contact is made.
- Legs and arms extend as the ball is volleyed off the fingertips.
- Contact is made at the level of the forehead and the arms follow through in an upward direction.

Visual Description

PHOTO 29.2   The set.

Bump Pass

The bump pass, or forearm pass, as it is frequently called, is used when a ball must be contacted below waist level. It is important that the bump pass be learned properly from the very beginning and that contacting the ball with open hands not be permitted. Once an open-hand bump pass is learned, it becomes difficult to change, and it is an illegal pass in the regulation game of volleyball. The bump pass is used to receive the serve and is used to initiate the set and finally the spike or overhead pass over the net. In addition, as play becomes refined, the bump is used to retrieve a spike.

Verbal Description
- Method 1. One hand is placed in the palm of the other with the thumbs together and on top. Be certain that both arms are level.
- Method 2. Form a fist with one hand and wrap the other hand around it, making sure not to cross the thumbs.
- Method 3. Interlock the fingers and place the thumbs on the index fingers. By pressing downward the wrists and elbows extend, thus allowing a very flat, even surface.
- The arms are straight, with the forearms held close together.
- The body is brought in line behind the ball, with one foot in front of the other.
- The knees are bent deeply, but the back remains erect.
- The eyes track the ball to contact with the flat area formed by the forearms.
- The ball should rebound high off the forearms with little follow-through or leg extension.
- The angle at which the ball is contacted will determine the path of its flight.

Visual Description

PHOTO 29.3 Bump pass.

Dig Pass

The dig is a one-handed pass used only when a player cannot get directly behind the ball or as a last attempt at contact before the ball touches the floor. The dig should only be taught after all other forms of passing have been mastered. It should never be taught as a standard method of passing a ball.

Verbal Description
- The arm is extended and a tight fist is made.
- The ball is visually tracked to the point of contact.

- Upon contact, the ball should rebound off the area of the hand and the wrist.
- Little attempt should be made at following through.

Visual Description

PHOTO 29.4   Dig pass.

skill concepts and movement concepts children should know are presented, along with a verbal description and a visual description of both the underhand and overhead serves.

Teaching Tips

Common Problems
- Taking the eyes off the ball.
- Holding the ball too high or too low.
- In the underhand serve, tossing the ball in the air before hitting it.
- Holding the ball too far to one side of the body.
- Making contact with the palm of the hand rather than with the heel of the hand.
- Making contact with the elbow bent.
- Insufficient backswing.
- Poor summation of forces, causing the ball to fall short of the net.
- Lack of follow-through.

Recommended Strategies
- Practice first with lighter balls.
- Practice without a net prior to using a net.
- Practice at a shorter distance from the net prior to full-court distance.
- Measure where the ball should be held by swinging the contact arm back and forth one time.
- Stress proper positioning.
- Emphasize maintaining visual contact with the ball.
- Use a carpet square to stress weight transference to the front foot as the ball is hit.
- Let students experiment with various hand positions.
- Practice the preferred technique repeatedly.
- Master the underhand serve before teaching the overhead serve.
- Practice throwing the ball across the net using the underhand and overhand throwing patterns before practicing the actual serve. This allows students to warm up and to get the feel of the action.

SERVING

Serving is a basic element of the game of volleyball. With practice, children can develop a reasonable degree of proficiency in serving. The underhand serve should be taught prior to the overhead serve. This section focuses on common problems in learning how to serve and recommended strategies for teaching serving skills. The

Concepts Children Should Know

Skill Concepts
- Keep your eyes on the ball.
- Make contact with the heel of your hand or with your fist, not with your knuckles.
- Keep your wrist stiff.
- Follow through in the direction you want the ball to go.

Movement Concepts
- You can contact the ball with varying amounts of force.
- You can make the ball travel faster by putting greater force behind the ball.
- Good summation of forces will put more force behind the ball.
- You can make contact with the ball at different heights.
- The level of your body can be varied when you serve the ball.
- You can make contact on different parts of the ball.
- You cause the ball to travel in different areas based on your follow-through.
- You control the direction of the ball through your point of contact.

Underhand Serve

The underhand serve is generally the first serve learned by children in elementary grades. With practice, it can be mastered by most children in the intermediate grades with a regulation volleyball.

Verbal Description (Right-Hand Serve)
- Feet are in a narrow stride position with the left foot slightly ahead of the right.
- Knees are bent slightly.
- Ball is held in the palm of the left hand just below waist level.
- Eyes focus on the ball until contact is made.
- The right arm is swinging downward and backward in a pendulum motion and weight is transferred to the rear foot.
- The right arm swings forward in a pendular action and the weight is transferred to the front foot as contact is made and the knees straighten.
- Contact is made with the heel of the hand from a half-fist position.
- The wrist remains stiff throughout and the arm follows through in the intended direction of the ball.

Visual Description

PHOTO 29.5 Underhand serve.

Overhead Serve

The overhead serve is somewhat more difficult to master than the underhand serve. However, it should be introduced when the skill level of individuals or the class permits, because it is virtually the only serve used in the regulation game of power volleyball. The overhead serve may eventually be developed into a "floater" or a top-spin serve, both of which are more difficult to return than the underhand serve.

Verbal Description (Right-Hand Serve)
- Feet are in a stride position with the left foot forward and pointing toward the opposite court.
- The body rotates partially to the right as the right arm begins its backswing.
- The ball is raised up in the left hand and tossed lightly upward to a position slightly in front of the head and over the right shoulder.
- The weight shifts to the rear foot as the toss is made.
- As the ball descends, the weight is shifted forward as contact is made with the right hand.
- The right arm is straight and makes contact with the ball at the peak of its arc.
- Contact is made with stiff heel of the hand, or with a fist, at midcenter of the ball and slightly forward of the head and right shoulder.
- The hips and shoulders rotate to face forward and the legs straighten as the arm follows through.

Visual Description

PHOTO 29.6   Overhead serve.

BASIC RULES

The regulation game of volleyball is played with six players per team, which includes three forward players and three back players. The object of the game is to keep the ball in the air on your side and cause it to contact the floor on the opposing team's side.

The ball is put into play with a *serve* from behind the rear line within 10 feet of either sideline. The player in the right back position must serve the ball. The ball may be hit in any manner with the hand. Only one attempt is permitted. The ball must go over the net in the opponents' court for it to be played.

If the ball lands out of bounds or touches the net, it is *side-out*; otherwise, the ball is played by the opposing team. A side-out is also called if one team fails to get the ball over the net into the opponents' court after a maximum of three hits. After a side-out, the nonserving team rotates, and the right back from that team serves the ball and play continues. Teams rotate by moving one player to the right in a clockwise direction.

If a *violation* is committed by the nonserving team, the serving team is awarded a point. If a foul is committed by the serving team, it is side-out and the opposing team is given the ball to serve. Violations are committed when a player touches the net or steps over the center line, a player lifts or throws the ball (hand ball) rather than making a distinct hit of the ball, a player touches the ball more than once in succession, (unless off a block) four or more hits are made before the ball goes over the net, a back-court player blocks or spikes in front of the 10-foot spiking line.

Fifteen points constitute a game. Teams must win by at least two points. The best three out of five games constitute a *match*. Teams change courts after each game. Balls landing on a boundary line are in bounds.

SKILL DEVELOPMENT ACTIVITIES

Mastery of the skills of volleyball involves careful sequencing and progression of activities from simple to complex. Simply by changing the ball from a balloon, to a beachball and then to a foam ball, and finally to a volleyball will dramatically affect the success of any skill drill activity. Each of the activities that follow can be significantly altered in terms of difficulty merely by altering the object to be volleyed or served.

Warmup Activities

The warmup activities suggested for basketball (page 360), soccer (page 382), and softball (page 400) are all appropriate for volleyball. Warmup activities should emphasize the muscles of the upper trunk as well as the leg muscles.

Skill Drills

Each of the skill drills that follows may be practiced with different types of balls. Many of them may be practiced alone and others with a partner or in a small group. It is of critical importance that the ball used by any child be geared to his or her present level of ability. As skill develops, heavier balls should be used, progressing to a regulation leather volleyball.

Objectives

1. To improve volleying skills (overhand, set, bump, and dig passes).
2. To improve serving skills (underhand and overhand serves).
3. To improve various aspects of motor fitness (eye–hand coordination, eye–body coordination, agility).
4. To introduce the associated skills of blocking and spiking.

Movement Experiences

Volley and Catch (overhead volley set).   Player tosses the ball into the air, volleys it upward, and catches it as it comes back down. Process is repeated several times, with player trying to remain in the same spot. As skill develops, vary the height of the toss and the height of the volley.

Self-Volley (overhead volley).   Player tosses the ball overhead and tries to keep it in the air with repeated overhead volleys. Progress from two to three to four or more volleys. Work for height and control.

Bump and Catch (bump pass).   Player tosses the ball upward and contacts it below the waist with a bump pass. Bump it up and catch it. Work for greater control and height.

Bump It Up (bump pass).   Same as preceding activity, but work for two, three, four, or more consecutive bump volleys.

Over–Under (overhead volley, bump pass). Player tosses the ball overhead and tries to keep it in the air by alternating overhand and bump passes.

High Wall Volley (overhead volley).   Player stands three to five feet from the wall and volleys the ball upward repeatedly against the wall. Work for clean, crisp volleys and increasing the height of each volley.

Low Wall Volley (bump pass).   Same as preceding exercise, but the ball is contacted below the waist. Work for high bump passes and good control.

Partner Toss (overhead volley).   Player tosses the ball up and returns it with an overhand volley. Partner catches ball and repeats. Partners work for height and control.

Partner Volley (overhead volley).   Partners volley repeatedly back and forth, working for control and height on each volley.

Spot (set).   Player tosses ball up and volleys it high, so that it lands within a designated spot. Start with the free-throw circle and work down to setting into a hoop or box lying on the floor.

Partner Set (set pass).   Player tosses the ball upward and sets it up to a partner, who sets under the ball but catches it.

Three-Person Set (set).   One player executes a self-tossed overhand pass to a second player, who in turn executes a setup to a third player. Third player catches the ball.

One-Two-Three Over (overhead pass, setup). Same as preceding exercise, except that on the third hit, the ball is volleyed over the net.

Circle Volley (setup).   With six to eight per circle, teacher (or a child) tosses the ball to a player, who sets the ball back to the teacher. As skill develops, toss the ball high or low or off to one side. The teacher (child) may also set the ball back.

Bounce Volley (overhead volley, bump pass). Player volleys the ball high into the air with an overhand pass, lets it bounce, then volleys it again with a bump pass. Repeat.

Partner Wall Volley (overhead volley or bump pass). With a partner, and with both players standing 5 to 10 feet from the wall, one player throws ball high against the wall, while partner moves to intercept, sets, and volleys the ball upward. Partners change positions.

Bump and Run (bump pass). With partner about 10 feet apart, the first player tosses ball to either side, partner runs to that spot, and attempts to bump pass the ball upward before it hits the ground. For beginners, point to where the ball will be tossed. Later toss it to either side without warning.

Wall Serve. Player stands 30 feet from the wall and serves the ball underhand to a spot 6 to 8 feet up on the wall. As skill develops, introduce the overhead serve.

Over-Net Serve (serving). With partners at opposite ends of the gymnasium, practice serving back and forth. Work for distance, then control. As both develop, introduce the overhead serve. Start at a shorter distance (spiking line) and gradually move back.

Alley Serve (serving). With four players per group, one player serves the ball three times, trying to get it to drop into one of three allys that have been drawn on the floor on the opposite side of the net.

Serve and Set (serving, setting). Player stands 20 feet from the wall, serves the ball against the wall, moves to position on its rebound, and sets it back against the wall.

Net Dig (dig, bump pass). One player throws the ball forcefully into the net; partner uses a dig to pass the ball upward.

ASSESSING PROGRESS

Throughout the volleyball unit, you will want to make periodic checks on the progress of individuals and the group. Assessment can be quick, informal, and instructive. It need *not* take up large segments of time and should be focused on the operational goal of individual improvement. Both process and product assessments can be made at the beginning of the unit and again at the end.

Process Assessment

Process assessments are based on the instructor's subjective judgment of the student's level of ability in each of the basic skills of volleyball. The instructor is primarily concerned with the body mechanics or techniques used to execute the various volleying and serving skills of volleyball. Developing and using a rating chart like the one depicted in Figure 29.1 will help determine where students are in terms of their volleyball skills and where to focus instruction. It will also help to determine the extent of progress that has been made at the end of the volleyball unit.

Volleyball Skills Rating Chart

Class _____ Grade _____

Entry Assessment Date _____ Exit Assessment Date _____

Directions	Volleyball Skills				Serving Skills		Associated Skills		Key
Observe during drill or play situations. Mark rating in upper left corner of box for entry assessments, and lower right corner for exit assessments.	Overhead	Setup	Bump	Dig	Underhand	Overhead	Blocking	Spiking	A: **Advanced**—Correct technique plus good control and force production. I: **Intermediate**—Correct technique but lacking in control or force production. B: **Beginning**—Inconsistent use of correct technique.
									Comments

FIGURE 29.1   Sample form rating chart for volleyball.

Product Assessment

Numerous tests of volleyball skills have been reported in the literature. Their validity, however, for use with elementary school children is questionable. Also, the feasibility of administering these tests as part of the instructional program is questionable. Therefore, it is recommended that you devise your own "teacher-made" test, collect information over several years, and establish your own norms. Also, you may wish to develop your own self-referenced assessment of volleyball skills, in which the children themselves determine their level of proficiency. A self-administered volleyball performance test is depicted in Figure 29.2. The performance rating card can be filled out by students, and comments can be added by the teacher. If desired, it may be sent home to parents as a progress report.

Volleyball Skills Report

Student's Name _____ Grade _____ Class _____ Year _____

See Reverse for Description		Skills	Entry Rating	Comments	Exit Rating	Comments
Self-volley Drill		Volleying Skills	Date		Date	
B	0-3 times	Overhead				
I	4-7 times					
A	8-10 times	Bump				
Over Net Serving Drill		Serving Skills	Date		Date	
B	0-2 for 5 tries	Underhand				
I	3 for 5 tries					
A	5 for 5 tries	Overhead				
Blocking/Spiking Drill		Associated Skills	Date		Date	
B	2 for 5 tries	Blocking				
I	2 for 5 tries					
A	3 for 5 tries	Spiking				

Parent's Signature _____ Date _____

Comments:

FIGURE 29.2 Sample self-referenced performance rating card for volleyball, with *approximate* sample standards.

FIGURE 29.2 *(continued)* Reverse side of self-referenced performance rating card for volleyball.

KEY: B = Beginning Level of Skill **I = Intermediate Level** of Skill **A = Advanced Level** of Skill

Description of Tests:

Self-Volley: Player tosses the ball overhead and attempts to volley it repeatedly upward for up to 10 times (overhead and bump volley are done separately).

Over net Serve: With a partner at the opposite end of the court, player serves the ball five times from behind the serving line (underhand and overhand are done separately).

Blocking/Spiking Drills: With a partner, player attempts to block or spike a ball set in position up to 5 times each. The net is 6' high.

SUGGESTED READING

Cox, R. H. (1980). *Teaching volleyball.* Minneapolis: Burgess.

Sawula, L., and Valeriote, T. (1984). *Volleyball development model.* Coaching Association of Canada/Canadian Volleyball Association. Vanier, Ontario: 333 River Road.

Slaymaker, T., and Brown, V. H. (1983). *Power volleyball.* Philadelphia: Saunders.

PART VI

GAMES

CHAPTER 30

TEACHING GAMES

Active games are part of the cultural heritage of all children. Although environmental conditions and standards of living change, the urge to play games remains a dominant characteristic of every culture. Geographic location does not alter the original theme or idea, for games are built upon the age-old urges to run, jump, hop, chase and flee, hide and seek, hunt, guess, and dodge. One may find hundreds of variations of these themes, with as many different names, but the original theme remains the same.

Games can be of value in elementary school physical education if they are used properly and for the right reasons. However, some physical education programs have become little more than glorified recess periods, in which games are endlessly played for their own sake and because they are fun. Fun is a worthy byproduct of any good educational program. It is not, however, the primary purpose of the developmental physical education program. Games are a means to an end, rather than an end in themselves.

TYPES OF GAMES

Games may be classified in a variety of ways, depending on their purpose and nature. The developmental approach to teaching children's physical education views games primarily as a tool for enhancing, reinforcing, and implementing the use of a variety of fundamental movement and sport skills. They are *not* viewed as a primary means of developing movement skills. Although movement skill acquisition is the primary objective of the developmental approach, other important objectives can still be achieved through proper game selection and good teaching.

Games are generally classified as low-level type games, relays, lead-up games, and official sports. Each of these classifications is briefly discussed.

Low-Level Games

The term *low-level games* is used to denote activities that are easy to play, have few and simple rules, require little or no equipment, and may be varied in many ways. Low-level game activities may be easily modified to suit the objectives of the lesson, the size of the room, and the number of participants. They are easy to learn and can be enjoyed by both children and adults but are used as an educational tool primarily during grades one through three. When viewed from a developmental perspective, games of low organization are classified as fundamental locomotor, manipulative, or stability games (see Chapter 31). That is, low-level games are classified according to the category of movement skill that they reinforce and promote. Games are sometimes classified according to their (1) theme (tag, holiday and seasonal games), (2) formation (mass, circle, and line games), (3) special space requirements (limited-space and classroom games), and (4) activity level (active and passive games). Chapter 34, "Games for Limited Spaces and Special Places," presents a variety of low-level games appropriate for situations where movement skill development cannot be the primary objective of the activity.

Relays

Relays are popular among children from the primary grades and beyond. As the team concept begins to develop, children become better able to work in small groups toward a common goal. Relay-type activities can be used to *practice* a variety of fundamental and sport skills. Care, however, must be taken not to stress the competitive aspect of relays during the early stages of learning a new skill. Emphasis on winning and being first will only cause the developing skill to deteriorate. Only after the basic elements of the skill have been mastered under static conditions should the dynamic competitive element be introduced. At that time, relays become a valuable tool for further refining the movement skill and improving performance abilities. Relays can be an effective learning tool if they are not overused. Competitive relays should be used to *im-*prove skill levels, not to *prove* skill levels. Chapter 32 presents a variety of relay activities designed to improve locomotor, manipulative, and stability abilities.

Lead-Up Games

The term *lead-up games* is generally used to denote active games that involve use of two or more of the sport skills, rules, or procedures used in playing the official sport. Lead-up games may be relatively simple, or quite complex. Lead-up games should be viewed as a means to an end or as an end in themselves. As a means to an end, they are preparatory to playing the official sport and are used as a way of further developing one's ability to cope with the skills, rules, and strategies of the official sport. As an end in themselves, they may represent a less complex version of the official sport, which is more suited to one's skill level and to the available facilities and equipment.

Lead-up games play an important role among upper elementary and junior high school students. They serve as a means in which sport skills can be practiced and perfected in a modified environment. Most youngsters are not thrilled with the repetitive practice of skill drills. They are, however, interested when these same skills are used in gamelike situations. Therefore, it is recommended that, after the skill has been reasonably mastered, skill drills be modified to take on game form. As proficiency is gained, lead-up games should become more complex by the incorporation of a greater number of skill elements, more involved strategies, and a closer approximation of the regulations of the official sport. Chapter 33 contains several progressively more demanding lead-up games for the sports of basketball, soccer, softball, and volleyball.

Official Sports

Official sports are many and varied. They are most frequently classified as team sports, dual sports, and individual sports. They are sometimes classified according to the (1) facilities used (court sports, aquatic sports), (2) type of team interaction (contact sports, noncontact sports, combative sports), and (3) equipment used (racket sports, ball sports). An *official sport* is a game governed by a set of rules and regulations that are recognized and interpreted by an official governing body as the standard for performance and play. Official sports have no place in the elementary school physical education program. They may, however, be engaged in during the intramural program or the interscholastic sports program. The physical education period is a learning laboratory for practicing new skills and putting them to use in a variety of movement situations.

SELECTING APPROPRIATE GAMES

The inclusion of games in the physical education lesson generally begins in the first three grades. The often independent nature of preschool children is generally not conducive to game activities. Games are used by the astute teacher as an educational tool. Every game that is played should be chosen for specific reasons. These specific reasons may vary, depending upon the nature of the lesson, and may range from practicing specific movement skills and enhancing various components of physical fitness to promoting social learnings and academic concept development. If the teacher has clearly defined objectives for the use of a particular game or games in a lesson, and these objectives are articulated in a variety of ways, then we may be sure that games will serve an educational purpose. If, however, our objective is primarily fun with only remote consideration given to skill, fitness, social, or academic objectives, then we have "missed the boat" entirely and are making little or no contribution to the physical *education* of children.

When choosing a game for inclusion in the lesson, one must not limit selection to the "appropriate" grade level placement so often seen in textbooks and card files of games. Children with a sound movement background can easily play and master games graded one or two levels above the one generally expected of their age.

The process recommended for selecting appropriate game activities for inclusion in the lesson is:

1. *Determine the specific objectives* of your lesson and select games that will help satisfy these objectives.
2. *Determine the ability level* of your students in terms of skill, comprehension, and interest.
3. *Modify the game* to fit the specific objectives of the lesson, the ability of the class, and the movement skills used.

The list of active games is almost endless. Textbooks and card files are filled with thousands of different activities. It is not, however, necessary to be familiar with all or even most of these games if the principles of game selection and modification just listed are adhered to. Remember, a game is only a vehicle used to achieve an end. It is not, or should not be, an end in itself in the developmentally based physical education program.

Determining Objectives

Games are fun. They add a dimension of group interaction to the lesson and may be used to promote skill development. The selection of a game for inclusion in a lesson may be made for one or more of the following reasons:

1. Movement Skill Development
   a. To enhance fundamental movement abilities (basic locomotor, manipulative, and stability skills).
   b. To enhance recreational and competitive sport skill abilities (individual, dual, and team sports).
2. Fitness Development
   a. To promote inproved physical fitness (strength, endurance, flexibility, aerobic endurance).
   b. To promote improved motor fitness (speed, agility, coordination).
3. Social–Emotional Development
   a. To promote positive interaction with

others (group spirit, group cooperation, sportsmanship, competition, fun).
   b. To promote positive self-growth (tension release, self-discipline, self-acceptance).
4. Cognitive Development
   a. To promote readiness skills (learning to listen, following directions).
   b. To reinforce academic concepts taught in the classroom (science, mathematics, language arts, social studies).
   c. To stimulate thinking (strategy, knowledge, and application of rules).

Determining Ability Levels

Once the objectives of your lesson have been clearly determined, you must assess the general ability level of the class. You will also need to know your students ability to understand and comply with the rules of the game. Finally, you will need a feel for the potential level and duration of interest in the activity.

If the skill requirements of the game are beyond the children, they will soon lose interest and quit. If the complexity of the game is such that few are able to comply with the rules, there will be mass confusion and little benefit derived from the activity. If the game involves long waiting for a turn, is of an elimination type, or provides little chance for meaningful participation by all, then all but the most highly skilled will soon lose interest.

By simply knowing your children, it is relatively easy to determine their ability levels. Games *can* be changed. Their rules are not chiseled in granite. It is important that they be modified to suit the ability of *your* students and not the mythical students addressed in this or any other text.

Modifying Games

The game activities selected for inclusion in your lesson may be modified to better suit the objectives of the lesson, the ability of your students, and the specific movement skills involved. This may be done simply by carefully reading the de-

scription of the game and then modifying it as needed.

The game itself may be modified in a variety of ways. The following is a sampling:

1. Modify or add to the movement skills used to play the game.
2. Modify the equipment used.
3. Modify the duration of the game.
4. Modify the number playing in a group.
5. Modify the formations or boundaries used.
6. Modify the game by stepping up the intensity or pace of the game.
7. Modify the game by changing the rules or the scoring.
8. Modify the game to encourage problem solving.
9. Modify the game to stimulate creativity in making up new games.
10. Modify the game to promote maximum active participation of all students.
11. Modify the game to reinforce specific academic concepts.
12. Redistribute teams *during* the game.
13. Modify the game to represent a special holiday or event.
14. Change the medium in which the game is played (in the snow, pool, classroom, and so on).

Once you know how to modify games, it is possible, from a limited number of resources, to devise an endless variety of meaningful and educationally sound games. A solid grasp of the lesson objectives, a good imagination, and willingness to experiment will aid greatly in successfully incorporating games into the lesson.

PRACTICAL SUGGESTIONS

The methods used to teach low-level games, relays, and lead-up games will depend on several factors. The objectives of the lesson, as well as the ability of your students, the size of the class, available time, equipment, and facilities will all influence the activities selected and how they are presented. The following are general suggestions to consider when utilizing games in the lesson.

Selecting and Presenting Activities

When selecting a game and when presenting it for the first time, a number of practices should be adopted.

1. Choose games appropriate to time, space, class size, and available equipment, as well as the specific objectives of the lesson.
2. Use a variety of formations (circle games, line games, and relays).
3. Choose games that are varied in amount of activity.
4. Have plans made in advance. Think through the games and have lines drawn, equipment ready, and other preplanning procedures completed.
5. Stand so the entire group can see and hear you. When talking to a line of children, ask those on the ends to move in and form a semicircle around you so all will be the same distance away and be able to hear equally well.
6. Avoid technical terms. Speak in the language of the grade level, but do not talk down to the children.
7. Make explanations clear, brief, simple, and to the point.
8. Limit the number of questions.
9. Demonstrate when possible instead of talking, or combine demonstrations with explanation.
10. When outdoors, have children face away from the sun during explanations and when watching demonstrations.
11. Make eye contact with everyone in the group during explanations rather than just those immediately in front.
12. Place the class in the game formation when explaining how it is played.
13. Correct outstanding faults, but avoid fine details in the beginning in order to get the game going.
14. Avoid stopping the game too frequently to make corrections.
15. Make suggestions in a positive way.
16. Plan special ways for disabled children to take part.
17. Demonstrate interest by occasionally taking part.
18. Do *not* overplay the game. Stop at the height of interest in order to maintain enthusiasm for the activity at a later date.

Supervising Games

The following suggestions for supervising game activities should be given careful consideration.

1. Have a definite signal for starting and stopping the game. A hand signal is often better than a whistle. Have a second signal for the class to gather near you for explanations and discussions. Insist on instant attention to signals.
2. Circulate among all groups. Do not allow a few children to take up all your teaching time.
3. Do not allow aggressive children to monopolize play.
4. Watch for fatigue. Guard against overexertion of children who have just returned to school after an illness.
5. Avoid too much excitement. Children should have fun, but this does not necessitate undue yelling and screeching.
6. Keep your voice low and controlled. Be enthusiastic and radiate the spirit of fun.
7. Give children a chance for discussion, but do not permit any talking while you are talking.
8. Anticipate potential safety hazards so that accidents may be avoided.
9. Make up special rules to guard against certain hazards.
10. Stress safety rules and see that they are obeyed.
11. Do not permit undue roughness or other undesirable behavior.
12. Impress on children that, once decisions have been made, they are final and are to be accepted cheerfully and courteously.
13. Comment on improvement. Encourage poor players as well as the skillful.

14. Stop the game from time to time to reinforce specific teaching points.

General Suggestions

1. Select lead-up games that do not violate the rules or skills of the sport itself.
2. Increase complexity gradually as skill increases.
3. Encourage children to decide for themselves what they need to practice.
4. Frequent, short periods of practice are generally better than long, extended ones at the early stages of skill learning.
5. Make skill drills into games that are fun and challenging.
6. Simply—give it a name and make it a game.
7. In teaching a new skill, try to relate it to something already familiar.
8. When using a new game formation, have a few players demonstrate and the rest watch until all understand. Some game formations and rotations can be taught by walking through the procedure until it is understood.
9. Avoid long explanations of rules before beginning to play. Provide just enough of the essential rules to get started, and explain other rules as the need for them comes up in actual play.
10. Move about in such a way that all groups are within your field of vision.
11. Stress the importance of teamwork and the fact that participants must play their own positions in order not to interfere with others.

Games are, when used properly, an important educational tool of the physical education program. Games may be static or dynamic. They may be predesigned, teacher-designed, or student-designed. The predesigned games found in the following chapters are merely sample activities to help get you started. These activities can easily be modified to suit your needs. Designing your own games is also a worthwhile task. After all, who knows your children's needs and interests better than you? Furthermore, games designed by the children themselves can be of significant value, although this generally takes additional time and a gymnasium atmosphere conducive to creative problem solving.

SUGGESTED READINGS

Mauldon, E., and Redfern, H. B. (1981). *Games teaching.* Great Britain: Macdonald and Erans.

Morris, G. S. D. (1980). *How to change the games children play.* Minneapolis: Burgess.

Orleck, T. (1978). *The cooperation sports and games book.* New York: Pantheon.

Poppen, Jerry D. (1986). *Games that come alive: Book II.* Puyallup, WA: Action Productions.

Riley, M. (Ed.) (1977, September). Games teaching. *Journal of Physical Education and Recreation* 48: 17–35.

Werner, P. H. (1979). *A movement approach to games for children.* St. Louis: C. V. Mosby.

CHAPTER 31

LOW-LEVEL GAME ACTIVITIES

A small sampling of locomotor, manipulative, and stability games is presented in this chapter. Many have been used for generations and may be found in numerous textbooks. They have been selected for inclusion here because they (1) provide for maximum activity, (2) promote inclusion rather than exclusion, (3) are easily modified and varied, (4) aid in the development of a variety of movement abilities, and (5) are fun for children to play. A format is used in which each game is first viewed from the perspective of the particular *movement skills* that it incorporates, followed by the *formation, equipment,* and *procedures* to be followed.

LOCOMOTOR GAMES

There is an almost endless variety of locomotor games that children enjoy playing. The vast majority of locomotor games, however, are designed around running as the primary mode of movement. The alert teacher will feel free to substitute other locomotor movements as they suit the nature of the lesson and the skills being stressed. Each of the games that follow may be modified in a variety of ways (see Table 31.1).

Objectives

The primary objectives of locomotor game activities are:

1. To enhance fundamental locomotor movement abilities.
2. To enhance agility and general body coordination.
3. To enhance rhythmic performance of locomotor movements.
4. To enhance ability to participate in a team effort.
5. To develop listening skills.
6. To enhance the ability to follow directions and obey rules.

TABLE 31.1 Selected Locomotor Games

Locomotor Games	Movement Skills Stressed				Page
	Walking/ Running	Jumping/ Hopping	Skipping/ Sliding/ Galloping	Leaping	
Crowns and Cranes	X	X	X		432
Squirrels in the Trees	X	X	X		432
Colors	X	X	X		433
Magic Carpet	X	X	X	X	433
Back-to-Back	X	X	X	X	433
Hunter	X	X	X		433
Spaceship	X		X		433
Touch and Follow	X		X		434
Where's My Partner?	X	X	X		434
Whistle Stop	X		X	X	434
Frog in the Sea	X	X			434
Crossing the Brook		X		X	434
Jump the Shot		X			434
Jack Be Nimble		X		X	435

Movement Experiences

CROWS AND CRANES

Movement Skills: Running, dodging, pivoting, starting, and stopping.
Formation: Two lines of children facing each other about 10 feet apart.
Equipment: None.
Procedures: The class is divided into two groups. One group is called the crows and the other, the cranes. The groups line up at each end of the playing area facing each other. On a signal, they will advance toward one another. The instructor either calls "crows" or "cranes." If crows are called, the crows chase the cranes back to their goal and all persons caught join the crows. If cranes are called, they become the chasers. The instructor calls various names, beginning with cra . . . before calling crows or cranes (for example, cra . . . ckers, cra . . . yfish, cra . . . yons).

SQUIRRELS IN THE TREES

Movement Skills: Running.
Formation: Groups of three. Two children stand with hands joined, third is in between.
Equipment: None.
Procedures: One player is designated as a fox, the others as squirrels. The remaining players scatter around in groups of three. Two of the players stand and hold hands above their head (tree); the others squat between them (squirrel). The game begins with the fox chasing the squirrel. To avoid being caught, the squirrel may run under a tree, and the squirrel originally under the tree must flee from the fox. When tagged by the fox, the squirrel becomes the fox and the fox becomes a squirrel.

COLORS

Movement Skills: Running.
Formation: Two lines of players facing one
                   another.
Equipment: None.
Procedures: The groups stand on opposite
goals with the teacher in the middle. Each group
chooses a color and then moves toward the center
of the playing area until the two groups are about
5 to 10 feet apart. The teacher calls out a color.
When the color selected by either side is called, the
players on that side run to their goal and the other
group chases them. Those tagged before they reach
their goal must join the other side. The teacher may
call several colors before he calls one of the colors
selected. The side having the most players at the
end of the playing time wins the game.

MAGIC CARPET

Movement Skills: Skipping, running, and walking.
Formation: Scatter formation with lines, cir-
                   cles, and spots drawn on the floor.
Equipment: None.
Procedures: The entire play area is considered to be the "carpet." Spots, circles, and other
markings on it represent the "magic spot." The class
follows the leader in single file around the play
area. When the leader stops, the children run to a
magic spot and stand. Those that do not reach a
spot are eliminated. The game ends when there are
only as many magic spots as there are children.
You may designate specific shapes or colors to go
to.

BACK-TO-BACK

Movement Skills: Running, skipping, hopping,
                   jumping, and sliding.
Formation: Partners standing back-to-back
                   with one extra child.
Equipment: None.
Procedures: The number of children should
be uneven. On signal, each child stands back-to-

back with another child. One child will be without
a partner. This child can clap his or her hands and
call out the next position to be taken, such as face-
to-face or side-to-side, and all children change
partners, with the extra player seeking a partner.
Other commands can be given, such as "Everybody
run [hop, skip, jump, slide]" or "Walk like an elephant." When the whistle is blown, they immediately find a partner and stand back-to-back.

HUNTER

Movement Skills: Running.
Formation: Scatter.
Equipment: None.
Procedures: One player is the hunter and says
to the other children, "Come with me to hunt ti-
gers." The other children fall into line behind the
hunter and follow in the hunter's footsteps as he
or she leads them away from the goal. The hunter
tries to tag as many players as possible before all
reach safety. As each child is tagged, the hunter
calls out the child's name. The hunter chooses a
new hunter from the players who reached the base
safely. Since the setting of this game is believed to
be jungle, imitations of animal movements (bear-
walk, kangaroo hop, elephant drag) may be used
instead of running.

SPACESHIP

Movement Skills: Running, starting, and stopping.
Formation: Scatter.
Equipment: An object to represent the Earth
                   (beanbag, tree, or the like).
Procedures: Children and teacher decide upon
an object that will represent the earth, such as a
tree, beanbag, circle, base, and so on. Children are
spaceships, and on the countdown "Five, four, three,
two, ONE!" the rockets blast the spaceships off the
ground; they quickly pick up speed and go into
orbit around the earth. After one or more orbits,
spaceships return and "splash down." The game
may be repeated any number of times, with spaceships flying any number of orbits. To improve endurance, children run longer and faster each time.

TOUCH AND FOLLOW

Movement Skills: Walking, skipping, and galloping.
Formation: Single circle facing in.
Equipment: None.
Procedures: The children stand in a large circle with their hands held out toward the center, palms upward. One child is chosen to be in the center of the circle. That child moves about and then lightly touches the outstretched hand of some child. The child who is touched must follow the first child around the circle, imitating any activity chosen. They may skip, gallop, trot, or perform any other appropriate activity. They go once around the circle and then the follower becomes the one in the center. The game can also be played so that the entire circle imitates someone rather then involving just one other child.

WHERE'S MY PARTNER?

Movement Skills: Skipping, galloping, walking, running, and hopping.
Formation: Double circle of couples facing each other.
Equipment: None.
Procedures: The children are arranged in a double circle by couples, with partners facing each other. The inside circle has one more player than the outside. When the signal is given, the children in the circles skip to the players' right. When the command "Halt" is given, the children in the circles face each other to find partners. The player left without a partner is in the "mush pot." The game can also be played with music. When the music stops, the players seek partners. The game can also be altered to a gallop, run, walk, or hop, rather than a skip.

WHISTLE STOP

Movement Skills: Running, stopping, and chasing.
Formation: Scatter formation.
Equipment: Whistle.
Procedures: Children are scattered around the playing area. On the signal "Run!" the children run in any direction until the whistle blows', then they stop immediately. They start again on the signal "Run!" Children must be able to run and stop on appropriate signals, staying within the boundaries and avoiding other runners. The game may be varied to explore directions, time, and movement.

FROG IN THE SEA

Movement Skills: Running.
Equipment: None.
Procedures: One child is the frog and sits in the center of a circle. Other children dare the frog by running in close to him and saying, "Frog in the sea, can't catch me!" If a child is tagged by the frog, he or she also becomes a frog and sits in the circle beside the first frog. Frogs must tag from a sitting position. The game continues until four players are tagged. Then the first frog chooses a new frog from the players who were not tagged. Jumping like a frog can be performed rather than running.

CROSSING THE BROOK

Movement Skills: Jumping and leaping.
Formation: File.
Equipment: Chalk or tape.
Procedures: Two lines are drawn to represent a brook. The children try to jump over. If they fall in, they must return home and pretend to change shoes and socks. The width of the brook should vary from narrow to wide in order that all will find a degree of success. You may try placing an object in the brook to be jumped on, such as a stepping stone.

JUMP THE SHOT

Movement Skills: Jumping and hopping.
Formation: Single circle facing in.
Equipment: Beanbag on the end of 10-foot line.
Procedures: The teacher squats down in the

center of the circle and swings the rope about three to six inches off the ground. The end of the rope should be beyond the outside of the circle. The children jump to avoid being hit. Be sure to warn the children of the dangers of tripping, and do not turn the rope too fast. The children can also gallop, side hop, or perform tricks over the rope.

JACK BE NIMBLE

Movement Skills: Jumping, leaping.
Formation: Lines of four or more.
Equipment: Indian clubs to represent candles. One for each team.
Procedures: The following rhyme is recited by the children:

Jack (Jane) be nimble,
Jack be quick.
And Jack jump over the candlestick.

As the rhyme is repeated, the first player in each line runs forward and jumps over the candle. The other follow. Anyone knocking down the candle must set it up again. Caution the children to wait for the signal to "jump over the candlestick."

MANIPULATIVE GAMES

There are several game activities that may be used to reinforce fundamental manipulative abilities. Manipulative games can serve as an effective reinforcer of the particular skills being stressed. The teacher must keep in mind the desired outcomes of the game and feel free to modify the activity whenever necessary to ensure maximum participation and practice of the skills being stressed. Table 31.2 lists the manipulative games included in this chapter and the movement skills stressed.

Objectives

The basic objectives of manipulative game activities are:

1. To enhance fundamental manipulative abilities in throwing, catching, kicking, trapping, volleying, striking, bouncing, and rolling.
2. To enhance eye–hand and eye–foot coordination.
3. To encourage working together in a group effort.
4. To enhance listening abilities.
5. To encourage following directions and obeying rules.

Movement Experiences

HOT POTATO

Movement Skills: Tossing and catching.
Formation: Single circle facing in, with six to ten per circle.
Equipment: One playground ball.
Procedures: The children sit in the circle an arm's length apart. On the command "Go" the ball is passed around the circle until the signal "Stop" is given. The child left holding the ball drops out of the circle. The game continues until only two players remain. To avoid the exclusion element of this and many other games, set up a point system. If a person gets caught with the ball twice, for example, they have to sit in the "mush pot" in the center of the circle for one turn or perform a stunt for the class.

TEACHER BALL

Movement Skills: Throwing and catching/kicking and trapping/dribbling and volleying.
Formation: Several circles containing six to eight children each with the "teacher" in the center.
Equipment: One playground ball or foam ball for each group.
Procedures: One child stands in the center of the circle ("teacher") and tosses the ball to each member of the circle. A new "teacher" then goes into the center. This game may be used as a prac-

TABLE 31.2   Selected
Manipulative Games

Manipulative Games	Movement Skills Stressed				
	Throwing/ Catching	Kicking/ Trapping	Dribbling/ Volleying	Striking/ Rolling	Page
Hot Potato	X				435
Teacher Ball	X	X	X		435
Moon Shot	X				436
Spud	X	X			436
Keep Away	X	X			437
Tunnel Ball				X	437
Roll It Out				X	437
Kick-Away		X			437
Cross the Line		X			437
Balloon Volleying			X	X	437
Kick the Can		X			438
Corner Kickball		X	X	X	438
Guard the Castle	X	X		X	438
Target Bombardment	X	X		X	438

tice drill or be developed into a race between circles as the children's skill level increases. Various sizes and types of balls may be used. Also various throwing, catching, kicking, trapping, and volleying skills may be developed this way.

MOON SHOT

Movement Skills: Throwing and catching.
Formation: Single circle facing in with an outer circle also drawn on the floor, one child in the center.
Equipment: Beanbags.
Procedures: Each child stands on the inner circle and in turn tries to "shoot the moon" with the beanbag. The "moon" is a small circle placed inside two larger circles. If the child is successful, he or she moves to the outer circle and shoots from there when a turn comes again. When a child makes a successful throw, that person moves to, or remains on, the outer circle. When unsuccessful, the player remains on, or returns to, the inner circle. Each successful throw from the inner circle counts one point, and from the outer circle, two points. The center player is retriever and throws the beanbag to each player in turn, or each player may re-

trieve his or her own beanbag and pass it to the next player. After the beanbag has gone around the circle once, the retriever (if one is used) chooses a player from the outer circle to be the new retriever and exchanges places with him.

SPUD

Movement Skills: Throwing, and catching.
Formation: Single circle facing in with the leader in the center.
Equipment: One playground ball for each circle of eight to ten players.
Procedures: The leader stands in the center of the circle, tosses the ball into the air, and calls another player's name. The player called runs to the center of the circle and tries to catch the ball. At the same time, the remaining players scatter. "It" catches the ball and says "Stop" as soon as it is caught. The fleeing players freeze. "It" is permitted to take three giant steps in any direction and then can throw the ball at one of the players. If that person, who is not permitted to move, is hit, he or she then becomes "it." If the ball misses, the same player remains "it" and begins the game again with a toss from the center of the circle.

KEEP AWAY

Movement Skills: Throwing and catching/kicking and trapping.
Formation: Single circle of eight to ten participants facing in, one child in center.
Equipment: Playground balls.
Procedures: The children form a circle and one child is placed in the center. The remaining children attempt to pass the ball, keeping it away from the child in the center. If the child in the center catches the ball, the child who threw it takes the place in the center.

TUNNEL BALL

Movement Skills: Rolling.
Formation: Single circle of eight to ten players facing in, one child in center.
Equipment: Playground balls.
Procedures: Ten players form a circle with one player in the center of the circle. The players in the circle spread their feet apart, and the player in the center tries to roll the ball through their legs or between the players. If successful in the attempt, the player in the center takes the place of the player in the circle. The player in the circle can block the ball with his hands, but he cannot move his feet.

ROLL IT OUT

Movement Skills: Rolling.
Formation: Single circle facing in, either seated or kneeling, with eight to ten per circle.
Equipment: One playground ball per circle.
Procedures: A ball is rolled into the circle. When it comes near a child, the player tries to roll it between two of the circle players by batting it with a hand. The player may stop it first and then roll the ball. If the player succeeds, she or he changes places with the circle player on whose right side the ball goes out.

KICK-AWAY

Movement Skills: Kicking and trapping.
Formation: Several circles with eight to ten children per group.
Equipment: One 8-inch playground ball or foam ball per group.
Procedures: One player has the ball on the ground in front of him or her with a foot resting on it. The ball is kicked across the circle, using the inside of the foot to avoid lofting. The child receiving the ball traps it and kicks it quickly away to another child. Children continue to kick the ball until it goes outside the circle. The player who retrieves the ball brings it back to the circle and starts again.

CROSS THE LINE

Movement Skills: Kicking and trapping.
Formation: Five to eight players per group facing a kicker.
Equipment: One 8-inch playground ball per group.
Procedures: The "line" is a 25-foot line drawn a distance of 20 to 40 feet from the kicking circle. Other players scatter in playing field in front of the wall. Kicker places the ball on the ground inside the kicking circle. The player calls, "Cross the line" and kicks the ball toward the line. Any fielder who can trap the ball before it goes over the line is the new kicker. If the ball crosses the line, the original kicker kicks again. If no one stops the ball after she has kicked three times, she chooses a new kicker.

BALLOON VOLLEYING

Movement Skills: Striking and volleying.
Formation: Scatter.
Equipment: Enough round balloons for each child to have one.
Procedures: The player who can keep a balloon up the longest is the winner.

KICK THE CAN (OR PINBALL SOCCER)

Movement Skills: Kicking and trapping.
Formation: Two parallel lines 30 feet apart with eight to ten players per group.
Equipment: Nerf soccer ball, five large cans, Indian clubs or cartons.
Procedures: Divide players into two teams, each team standing on its own kicking line. Kicking lines are 30 to 60 feet from center line, depending upon skill of players. Give soccer ball to player on one team, who kicks the ball at a can that has been placed in the center of the playing area from her own kicking line. Opponents trap ball with their feet as it rolls to them and kick from their line. Game continues until all the cans are down. A team makes one point for each can it knocks down. When all cans are down, the team with higher score is the winner. A player may block the ball with his or her body but may not touch it with the hands unless it goes out of bounds, in which case it is carried to the kicking line and the game started again. If the ball is touched with the hands, it is a foul, and opponents win one point.

CORNER KICKBALL

Movement Skills: Kicking, trapping/dribbling.
Formation: Two parallel lines 30 feet apart with eight to ten players per group.
Equipment: One soccer-type ball per group.
Procedures: Players divide into two teams, each team standing behind its own restraining line. The ball is placed in circle in center of field. On the signal "Go!" the two end players from each team run to the center and try to kick the ball to a teammate behind them or to the side. (The ball may not be kicked forward on the initial kick). Teammates try to pass the ball to the center person on their team, who now attempts to kick the ball to the opponents' goal line. The successful team wins two points. After a score, the kicking players all return to center positions in their own line, and four new

ends run out. Line players try to block ball from going over the goal line, and kick or throw it back to their centers. Line players may not cross their own restraining line. Center players may not use hands, but line players may use hands or body to block the ball. Out-of-bounds balls are played in from the point where they went out.

GUARD THE CASTLE

Movement Skills: Throwing, kicking, and trapping.
Formation: Circle with an empty milk carton in the center. Eight to ten players per group.
Equipment: Utility ball.
Procedures: The circle players throw the ball at the carton, attempting to knock it down. The guard tries to prevent it from being knocked down, stopping the ball in any manner. Whoever knocks the carton down becomes the guard. If the guard accidently knocks down the carton, the circle player who last threw becomes the new guard. Don't allow circle players to move within the designated area and don't allow the guard to stand over the carton.

TARGET BOMBARDMENT

Movement Skills: Throwing/kicking.
Formation: Two teams of eight to ten spread out on their respective sides of a half-court line.
Equipment: Ten to fifteen empty milk cartons lined up on the two ends of the playing area and two utility balls.
Procedure: Each team tries to knock down the cartons of the other team with thrown balls. The team knocking down all the other team's cartons is the winner. Players may not cross the center line. If a carton is knocked down, it must stay down; this includes cartons knocked down by players on the defending team. Players may not stand over the cartons in order to guard them.

TABLE 31.3   Selected Stability Games

Stability Games	Movement Skills Stressed				
	Dynamic Balance	Dodging/ Feinting	Axial Movements	Static Balance	Page
Beanbag Balance Tag	X	X			440
Super Beanbag Balance Tag	X	X			440
Circle Freeze Tag		X	X		440
Mirror Touch Tag	X	X			440
Animal Tag		X	X		440
Amoeba Tag		X			440
Fly Trap			X		440
Opposites			X	X	441
Circle Tug-of-War	X	X			441
Silly Simon			X	X	441
Circle-Point Dodgeball		X			441
Team-Point Dodgeball		X			441
Engineer and Caboose Dodgeball	X	X			442

STABILITY GAMES

Although most games of low organization are thought of as locomotor or manipulative games, there are several activities that can make specific contributions to developing and reinforcing fundamental stability abilities. Many of the stability games that follow use locomotor or manipulative tasks, but their primary feature is that they stress one or more aspects of stability (see Table 31.3). Several tag games are included. Tag is a great activity for reinforcing dodging and feinting skills. Most tag games can be adapted to the particular skill and interest level of the group. Additional tag games are located in Chapter 43, "Fitness Activities."

Included in this section also are several dodgeball-type activities. Although dodgeball utilizes throwing and catching skills, the primary focus is on dodging and feinting. Dodgeball is a very popular activity with many children. It should, however, be used *only* to achieve

educational purposes and in such a manner to insure the maximum safety and participation of all students. Therefore, it is strongly recommended that only foam balls or partially deflated balls be used, that elimination games be modified to stress maximum continual participation, and that cooperative teamwork be stressed.

Objectives

The primary objectives of stability game activities are:

1. To enhance fundamental stability abilities.
2. To enhance dodging and feinting abilities.
3. To improve dynamic and static balance abilities.
4. To improve body, spatial, and directional awareness.
5. To enhance cooperative group efforts.
6. To encourage following directions and obeying rules.

Movement Experiences

BEANBAG BALANCE TAG

Movement Skills: Dynamic balance, dodging, and feinting.

Formation: Scatter formation.

Equipment: One beanbag or other suitable object for balancing.

Procedures: One player is "it." This player places the beanbag on top of his head. "It" chases the other players and tries to tag someone. A tagged player must take the beanbag and become "it."

SUPER BEANBAG BALANCE TAG

Movement Skills: Dynamic balance, dodging, and feinting.

Formation: Scatter formation, each player balancing a beanbag on the head.

Equipment: One beanbag per player.

Procedures: One player is "it" and tries to touch another player. All players have a beanbag or other suitable object balanced on the head. A player who is tagged becomes "it" and calls out "I'm it." The game continues without interrruption or elimination. It is fun to experiment with balancing the object on different body parts: shoulder, elbow, back, hip, thigh, and foot.

CIRCLE FREEZE TAG

Movement Skills: Dodging, feinting, and axial movements.

Formation: Single circle facing inward with four to six players on the inside.

Equipment: None.

Procedures: One player is "it." Player tries to tag each of the other players. Players who are tagged must freeze in the position in which they were tagged. Play continues until all players are frozen. Last player tagged becomes "it," and four to six children move to the center of the circle. In order to make the game more challenging, require "it" to balance a beanbag while tagging.

MIRROR TOUCH TAG

Movement Skills: Dodging, feinting, and balancing.

Formation: Scatter formation.

Equipment: None.

Procedures: One player is "it" and tries to touch another player. Players are "safe" when one or more of the same body parts are touching. You may try using a variety of body parts during the same game of tag. Permit "it" to call out "safe" body parts (hands, hips, backs, knees, elbows, soles of feet, and so forth).

ANIMAL TAG

Movement Skills: Dodging and feinting.

Formation: Scatter.

Equipment: None.

Procedures: One player is "it" and tries to tag another player. After "it" calls out the name of a familiar animal, all players must imitate that creature while trying to avoid being tagged. When a player is tagged, that player immediately becomes "it" and calls out the name of another animal to be imitated. Some good animals to imitate are prancing horses, bears, elephants, rabbits, and crabs.

AMOEBA TAG

Movement Skills: Dodging and feinting.

Formation: Scatter formation.

Equipment: None.

Procedures: One player is "it" and tries to tag another player. Players who are tagged link one hand, forming a progressively larger amoeba. Only those players on either end of the amoeba may tag, using their free hand.

FLY TRAP

Movement Skills: Axial movements.

Formation: Scatter, with half the players seated cross-legged.

Equipment: None.
Procedures: The players that are seated are the "traps." The remaining players are the "flies." The flies run throughout the traps, being sure to stay in the designated playing area. On the teacher's signal to "Freeze," the flies immediately stop. The traps, from their seated position, stretch out and try to touch the flies. If a fly is touched, he changes places with that trap. The game continues.

OPPOSTIES

Movement Skills: Axial movements.
Formation: Scatter formation facing a leader.
Equipment: None.
Procedures: The teacher serves as the leader. He moves one limb either up or down, forward or backward, or left or right. The class repeats the action, using the *same* limb as the teacher and the *same* direction of movement. This is a more advanced activity than mirroring, requiring transposition of movements.

CIRCLE TUG-OF-WAR

Movement Skills: Dynamic balance and dodging.
Formation: Circle of eight to ten players per circle.
Equipment: One Indian club or potato chip can, placed one foot in front of each player.
Procedures: Players form a single circle facing inward and lock wrists. On the signal "Go" players push and pull one another, trying to cause a person to knock down his or her own club. When a club is knocked down, one point is scored against that player. Players with the fewest points after a designated time are the winners. Score one point for each when two circle players lose their grip. Do not use as an elimination game. Modify the rules as needed in order that everyone continues to play.

SILLY SIMON

Movement Skills: Axial movements.
Formation: Scatter formation facing a leader.

Equipment: None.
Procedures: Leader begins each movement task with the words "Simon says —." Players then do exactly what they were told to do. Sometimes the leader fails to begin a command with the words "Simon says." All players who move are given a letter (*S, I, M, O, N*). Play continues until one or more players spell out the word *Simon*. Then they must do a Silly Simon antic. Play continues. Do not use as an elimination game. Stress a variety of axial movements and static and dynamic balance activities.

CIRCLE-POINT DODGEBALL

Movement Skills: Dodging and feinting.
Formation: Single circle facing in, with half the class inside the circle.
Procedures: The ball is thrown by the players in the circle in an effort to hit one of the players inside the circle. One point is scored for each hit. The number of hits made in a two-minute time limit is recorded as the score. Teams change position. Do not use as an elimination game. Add a second ball only after sufficient skill has developed. Never use a fully inflated ball; foam balls are safest.

TEAM-POINT DODGEBALL

Movement Skills: Dodging, feinting, throwing, and catching.
Formation: Two teams of six to eight players each on either side of a line dividing a 30- × 30-foot area in half.
Equipment: One or more foam balls per game.
Procedures: The balls are thrown back and forth across the line in an effort to hit opposing players on the opposite side. Players have a point scored against their team if they are hit by the ball, or if a player from the opposite team catches a thrown ball. Play continues for a specified time period. Team with the most points is the winner. Do not use as an elimination game; stress inclusion and teamwork. Only use foam balls. Add balls as skill progresses.

ENGINEER AND CABOOSE DODGEBALL

Movement Skills: Dodging, feinting, throwing, catching, and dynamic balance.

Formation: Single circle of eight to ten players facing in, with four more players in the center.

Equipment: One foam ball per circle.

Procedures: Players in the center of the circle hook their arms around the waist of the player in front of them. The first player is the "engineer"; the last, the "caboose." The players in the circle throw the ball, trying to hit the caboose. The engineer calls out directions and tries to maneuver the caboose out of the line of fire. The player hitting the caboose becomes the new engineer, and the caboose moves to the outside circle. Play continues. The engineer is the only player who may use hands to block the ball. Play continues until all have had a chance to be both the engineer and the caboose. It is unsafe to use anything except a foam ball for this game. Players behind the engineer do not have any means of defense other than dodging the ball.

SUGGESTED READING

Hardisty, M. (1972). *Education through the games experience.* Bellingham, WA: Educational Designs and Consultants.

Farina, A. M. (1981). *Developmental games and rhythms for children.* Springfield, IL: Charles C. Thomas.

Fluegelman, A. (1976). *The new-games book.* Garden City, NY: Doubleday.

Latchaw, M. (1976). *A pocket guide of games and rhythms for the elementary school.* Englewood Cliffs, NJ: Prentice-Hall.

Kamer, C., and De Vries, R. (1980). *Group games in early childhood.* Washington, DC: National Education Association.

CHAPTER 32

RELAY ACTIVITIES

Relays are exciting, fun, and are enjoyed by most children if wisely incorporated into the program. Relays are easy to organize and conduct. As used in the developmental approach to teaching physical education, relays are included in the curriculum to *improve* skill and fitness levels, not to *prove* who is the best or the fastest. This important distinction must be remembered; otherwise relays will only be enjoyed by the most skillful.

Relays can be enjoyed by children from the primary grades up. With younger children, relays may be used to reinforce a variety of locomotor, manipulative, and stability abilities. Children at the sport-skill phase of development will benefit from relay activities that make use of various sport skills. In fact, many skill drills can be modified and made into sport-skill relays.

This chapter presents a variety of relay activities for reinforcing basic movement abilities. It should be noted that the introduction of relay activities that emphasize speed before the skill has been adequately developed will generally cause performance to deteriorate. Therefore, emphasis should be on the task being performed, rather than on being "first."

INSTRUCTIONAL PROCEDURES

When including relays in the program, there are several organizational and procedural matters to take into account. Because relays are easy to organize, there is a temptation to overuse them. Care should be taken to use relays as a means of reinforcing and testing movement skills that have been worked on in the instructional portion of the lesson. There is seldom a valid reason for conducting relay races for an entire unit or even an entire lesson.

Organization

When incorporating relays into the lesson, you will find it helpful to follow these organizational guidelines:

1. Use a permanent squad approach as a quick and easy way to get children into groups.
2. Assign squad leaders, but be sure to change leaders at regular intervals during the year.
3. Keep teams small. No more than eight children should be assigned to a squad in order to maximize participation.

4. Be certain that all squads have an equal number of participants. The first person in line for unequal teams should be assigned to go twice (rotate this responsibility).
5. Carefully mark and indicate boundaries, starting lines, and turning lines.
6. Do not permit children to pick their own squads. Divide the class so that squads have equal ability levels.
7. Place poorly skilled individuals in the middle so their lack of skill will not be as obvious to their teammates.
8. Have a predetermined signal to begin the relay.
9. Have a predetermined procedure to indicate when each squad has finished. Sitting in a straight line with legs and arms folded works well.
10. Be certain that the playing area is free from all obstacles.

Presentation

There are a few guidelines to follow when presenting a relay activity. Careful adherence to each will maximize learning and enjoyment.

1. Place the class in the relay formation before explaining the activity.
2. Be certain that all are seated and can see during the explanation.
3. Tell the children the name of the relay and how it is performed, keeping verbalization to a minimum.
4. Demonstrate the relay by having the first one or two children in each squad go through the activity at a slow speed.
5. Use a definite signal to start the relay. A loud voice command or whistle works well.
6. Be certain that the rules are followed by everyone.
7. Assign nonparticipants to act as officials, to insure that players do not start too soon and that they cross the turning line.
8. If speed is the goal, declare winners at the end of each relay.
9. If skill improvement is the goal, declare winners for best use of the skill at the end of each relay.

10. As a rule, do not repeat the same relay more than twice, and do not overuse relays in your program.

Safety Precautions

There are a few precautions that must be taken in order to insure the safety of the children.

1. Modify distances to be covered based on the requirements of the activity. For example, a wheelbarrow or crab-walk relay should cover a shorter distance than a running relay.
2. Never use a wall as a turning line. Turning lines should be at least eight feet away from the wall.
3. Be certain that the playing area is free from obstacles.
4. Be certain that a definite traffic pattern is taught and followed. Passing or turning to the right is a good rule to follow.
5. Be sure that there is ample space between each team in order to avoid collisions.

LOCOMOTOR RELAYS

An endless variety of relays may be devised, using a variety of locomotor skills and formations. Locomotor relays may be classified as *locomotor skill relays, rescue relays, human-obstacle relays, zigzag relays,* and *partner relays.* Examples of each follow.

Objectives

The primary objectives of locomotor relay activities are to:

1. Reinforce and practice fundamental locomotor skills.
2. Reinforce and practice locomotor sport skills.
3. Test one's locomotor performance abilities against others in a controlled, gamelike situation.

4. Improve selected fitness components.
5. Be able to move with speed and control.

Movement Experiences

LOCOMOTOR SKILL RELAYS

Movement Skills: Running, hopping, jumping, skipping, galloping, and so forth.
Formation: Shuttle or circle formation with six to eight players per team.
Equipment: None.
Procedures: On the signal "Go," first player runs (or uses any other predetermined locomotor movement) to the opposite end of the room. If it is a shuttle relay, the player touches the next person and that person runs back. The process is repeated until all have had a turn. If it is a circle or file relay, the player makes one complete circuit, and the next player goes.

RESCUE RELAYS

Movement Skills: Any locomotor skill.
Formation: Split shuttle formation with three or four players at each end.
Equipment: None.
Procedures: Player runs (or uses any other designated locomotor skill) to opposite end, grasps the first player's hand, and returns to the starting line. The player brought back ("rescued") by the first person returns for the second and so forth.
Suggestion: This is an excellent activity to use when changing from a shuttle to a file formation.

HUMAN-OBSTACLE RELAYS

Movement Skills: Any locomotor skill.
Formation: Circle or shuttle formation with each player in a different body posture.
Equipment: None.
Procedures: Players are given a position to assume. Playes may crouch, lie flat, bend forward at the waist, stand straight, stand with legs spread, and so forth. First player must go over, under, around, or through her teammates as designated. When she finished, she goes back to her original position and taps or signals the next player to begin.

ZIGZAG RELAYS

Movement Skills: Any locomotor skill.
Formation: Shuttle formation with cones, or chairs four to six feet apart.
Equipment: Four chairs or cones per group.
Procedures: On the signal "Go," first player weaves in and out of the obstacles, using the designated locomotor skill. The player crosses the turning line and returns to the start, when the next player is tapped.

PARTNER RELAYS

Movement Skills: Any locomotor skill.
Formation: Shuttle formation with the restraining line no farther than 20 feet distant.
Equipment: None.
Procedures: Partner positions are designated, such as wheelbarrow, two-legged, three-legged, back-to-back, or piggyback. On the signal "Go," partners travel to the turning line and back. The next couple begins after being tapped.

MANIPULATIVE RELAYS

Manipulative relays are an excellent way to test fundamental manipulative abilities and sport skills that have been acquired during the skill development portion of the lesson. They should, however, be used only after the basic elements of the skill have been mastered. Remember, control should be achieved prior to speed and accuracy. Manipulative relays may be classified as *manipulative skill relays, zigzag dribble relays, pass-and-catch relays,* and *teacher-ball relays.* Examples of each follow.

Objectives

The primary objectives of manipulative relays are to:

1. To practice and reinforce fundamental manipulative abilities.
2. To practice and reinforce manipulative sport skills.
3. To test one's abilities in selected manipulative skills against others in a controlled, gamelike situation.
4. To improve selected fitness components.
5. To be able to handle a ball with speed, control, and accuracy.

Movement Experiences

MANIPULATIVE SKILL RELAYS

Movement Skills: Throwing, catching, kicking, trapping, dribbling, and so forth.
Formation: A shuttle or circle formation may be used.
Equipment: One appropriate ball for each team.
Procedures: Select the skill to be practiced. Develop an appropriate relay activity that permits practice and utilization of the skill in a controlled setting. Be certain to use basic manipulative relays as a means of reinforcing skills that have previously been practiced in the skill-development portion of the lesson. Skill levels will deteriorate if emphasis is placed on winning before the mechanics have been mastered.

ZIGZAG DRIBBLE RELAYS

Movement Skills: Basketball dribbling or soccer dribbling.
Formation: Shuttle formation with four to six players per team.
Equipment: One soccer ball or basketball per team.
Procedures: Space four road cones or chairs ten feet apart between the starting and turning lines. On the signal "Go," first player dribbles the ball (hand or foot dribble) in and out between the markers to the turning line and back. The process is repeated for all players. As skill develops, move the markers closer together. Vary the activity by dribbling to the turning line and kicking the ball back.

PASS-AND-CATCH RELAYS

Movement Skills: Softball throwing and catching, basketball passing and catching, football passing and catching, soccer passing and trapping, hockey passing and controlling.
Formation: Two parallel lines facing each other with four to eight players per line.
Equipment: One appropriate ball for each team.
Procedures: Team is placed in two parallel lines facing each other. Players are 10 to 30 feet apart (depending upon the skill level of the children and the passing skill being used). The ball begins at one end and is passed to the person directly opposite. This player catches the ball and passes it to the player to right of the starter. The ball continues back and forth in a zigzag fashion.

TEACHER-BALL RELAYS

Movement Skills: Volleying, passing, throwing, kicking, catching, and trapping.
Formation: Circle formation with four to eight players per circle. One player ("teacher") in the center.
Equipment: One ball for each circle.
Procedures: Ball is started by the "teacher," who volleys, throws, or passes it to a player on the circle. The ball is controlled by the player on the circle and immediately volleyed, thrown, or passed back to the teacher. The process continues around the circle. If the ball is dropped or missed, only the player for whom it was intended may retrieve the ball. Keep groups small. Be certain to frequently change the "teacher."

STABILITY RELAYS

There is a variety of fun and exciting stability relays that children enjoy. Many of these relays may also be classified as novelty activities. When incorporating stability relays into the program, emphasis should be placed on movement control. It is important to insist that the rules of the activity be followed not only for their own sake, but also to insure that the full value of the stability experience is realized.

Objectives

The primary objectives of stability relays are:

1. To improve dynamic balance abilities.
2. To enhance rotational balance abilities.
3. To develop movement control and coordination.

Movement Experiences

DIZZ-ISSY

Movement Skills: Rotational balance.
Formation: Shuttle formation with four to eight players per team.
Equipment: One bat per team.
Procedures: First player runs down to the turning line, picks up the bat, and places it in a vertical position on the floor. The player places her palms on the top of the bat and her forehead on the back of her hands. The player walks rapidly around the bat eight times, drops the bat, and returns to the starting line. Each player takes a turn. Require players to *walk* back after spinning.

SHOE BOX RELAY

Movement Skills: Dynamic balance.
Formation: Shuttle formation with four to eight players per group.
Equipment: Two shoe boxes per team.
Procedures: Players place their feet in two shoe boxes and proceed to the turning line and back, one at a time.

COFFEE-CAN STILT RELAY

Movement Skills: Dynamic balance.
Formation: Shuttle formation with four to eight per group.
Equipment: One set of coffee-can stilts per group.
Procedures: Players use the stilts to go from the starting line to the turning line and back. Each player takes a turn. Use number 10 cans for a wider base of support. Tape the bottom of the cans to prevent slipping.

SACK RELAY

Movement Skills: Jumping.
Formation: Shuttle formation with four to eight players per group.
Equipment: One burlap sack per team.
Procedures: Players place both feet in the sack and proceed to the turning line and back, one at a time. This is a good relay for outdoor activities because of less slipping than on a floor and less chance of injury from falls.

THREE-LEGGED RELAY

Movement Skills: Dynamic balance.
Formation: Shuttle formation with six to eight players per group.
Equipment: Short piece of rope or one inner-tube rubber band for each team.
Procedures: Each team forms a double line. With their inside legs tied together, the first couple runs to the turning line and back; then the second couple does the same, then the third, and so forth.

EGG-AND-SPOON RELAY

Movement Skills: Dynamic balance.
Formation: Shuttle formation with four to eight players per group.
Equipment: One table-tennis or tennis ball ("egg") and one spoon per team.
Procedures: The ball is balanced on the spoon. The player walks to the turning line and back. If the ball rolls off, it may be replaced with the player's free hand. The player then returns to the place where the ball rolled off. The relay is more interesting and difficult if the ball is picked up without aid from the free hand.

ERASER RELAY

Movement Skills: Dynamic balance.
Formation: Shuttle formation with four to eight players per team.

Equipment: One eraser or beanbag per team.
Procedures: Players place a beanbag or eraser on the top of their head. First player walks to the turning line and back. Each player takes a turn. If the object falls off, the player must stop, replace it, and then continue.

SUGGESTED READING

Blake, O. W., and Volpe, A. M. (1964). *Lead-up games to team sports.* Englewood Cliffs, NJ: Prentice-Hall.

Roy, M. M. (1977). *Action.* Stevensville, MI: Educational Service Inc.

Bieri, A. P. (1972). *Action games.* Belmont, CA: Fearon Publishers.

CHAPTER 33

LEAD-UP GAME ACTIVITIES

Lead-up games contain two or more elements of the official sport. They are versions of the official sport that have been adapted in terms of the rules, skills, and equipment used. Lead-up activities should be introduced into the lesson *after* children have had an opportunity to practice the skills in controlled drill situations. Remember, a lead-up game is an activity in which developing skills are practiced and applied in a dynamic environment in which the conditions of play are constantly changing. Lead-up games permit introduction of basic rules, strategies, and teamwork. They are an important part of the physical education program, but they should not dominate the lesson.

The lead-up games contained in the chapter are only a sampling of the hundreds available. They have been placed in a progressive sequence from simple to complex. These activities were selected because they are enjoyed by most children, they are easy to organize, and they contribute significantly to learning the official sport. Furthermore, the four sport activities of basketball, soccer, softball, and volleyball were selected for presentation here from among the many possible sports because of their great interest for most North American children.

BASKETBALL

Basketball lead-up games are popular with most children. Care, however, should be taken to match the game to the skill level of your students. Table 33.1, "Suggested Progression for Introducing Basketball Lead-up Games," presents basketball-type games in progression from simple to complex. Modification can be made in the height of the basket and the size of the ball.

Objectives

The objectives of including basketball lead-up games in the program are to:

1. Reinforce the basketball skills of passing and catching, dribbling and pivoting, goal shooting, and guarding.
2. Introduce the basic rules of basketball through modified game activities.
3. Provide opportunities for developing an understanding for, and appreciation of, basic team strategies.

TABLE 33.1   Suggested Progression for Introducing Basketball Lead-Up Games

Basketball Lead-Up Games	Passing and Catching Skills	Dribbling and Pivoting Skills	Goal-Shooting Skills	Guarding Skills	Team Play	Page
Five Passes	X	X				450
Circle Keep Away	X			X		450
Hands Up	X			X		450
Dribble-Pivot-Pass	X	X				451
Base Basketball	X		X			451
Twenty-One			X			451
Around the World			X			451
Six-Hole Basketball			X			452
Nine-Court Basketball	X	X	X	X	X	452
Sideline Basketball	X	X	X			452
Half-Court Basketball	X	X	X	X	X	452
Backline Basketball	X	X	X	X	X	452

4. Encourage a spirit of cooperation and team-work toward a common goal.
5. Permit students to play a modified game of basketball with reasonable skill, and enjoyment.

Movement Experiences

FIVE PASSES

Movement Skills: Passing and dribbling.
Formation: Scatter formation with four to six players per team.
Equipment: One basketball for each group.
Procedures: One team takes the ball and scatters around an area approximately 40' × 40'. The other team assumes a guarding position. The object of the game is for the team with the ball to make five complete passes. If the team guarding intercepts a pass, they attempt to complete five passes. A team is given one point each time they complete five passes. Violations occur: (1) If the ball is passed repeatedly between the same two players, the ball is awarded to the other team. (2) If the team with the ball walks or double dribbles, the ball goes to the other team. (3) If the team with the ball is fouled, it counts as a completed pass.

(4) All "jump balls" are awarded to the team previously in possession of the ball.
Suggestions: Use a junior-model basketball for younger children. Use armbands or pinnies to distinguish teams.

CIRCLE KEEP AWAY

Movement Skills: Passing, catching, and guarding.
Formation: Single circle of eight to ten players facing inward, with one player in the center.
Equipment: One basketball per group.
Procedures: The ball is thrown from one player in the circle to another in any sequence. The center player tries to intercept the ball. If successful, that player trades places with the person who touched the ball last and that person becomes the center player.
Suggestions: Vary the passes used. Score one point for each successful pass. Player with the *lowest* score wins.

HANDS UP

Movement Skills: Passing, catching, and guarding.
Formation: Two teams of six to eight players

each. One team forms a circle; the other is scattered within the circle.

Equipment: One basketball per game.

Procedures: One team makes a circle on the outside of the boundaries while the other team gets into a scatter formation on the inside. The outside players try to pass the ball to each other while the players in the center try to stop the ball by keeping their hands up, to intercept or knock the pass down. The ball may *not* be thrown over the heads of the center players. After two minutes, the teams change positions. One point is scored each time the ball is passed successfully below head level through the opposing team.

DRIBBLE-PIVOT-PASS

Movement Skills: Dribbling, pivoting, and passing.

Formation: File formation with four to eight players per group.

Equipment: One basketball per team.

Procedures: Players in each group line up one behind the other. The first player on each team quickly dribbles the ball to a line 15 feet from the starting line, pivots on the right (work on left also), and passes the ball back to the next player in line for one point. The first team to get 20 points (or any number agreed upon) is the winner.

BASE BASKETBALL

Movement Skills: Passing, catching, and goal shooting.

Formation: Baseball diamond with 30 foot bases drawn on the gymnasium floor with home plate under the basket. Six to ten players per team.

Equipment: Basketball, goal.

Procedures: The players are divided into two teams. Each person is given a number so that a player from one team will have the same number as a player on the opposing team. One team is behind home base, while the other team is in the field.

Number 1 of the batting team passes the ball to a teammate from the home base, using any type basketball pass, then circles the bases without stopping. Meanwhile, the corresponding number sets himself near the basket. His teammates get the ball and must make 2 or 3 chest passes, then pass it to him. The person at the basket must make a goal before the runner circles the bases or the runner is safe and scores a point. If the goal is made before the runner circles the bases, an out is made; three outs constitute a change of sides. One point is scored for each run made.

TWENTY-ONE

Movement Skills: Goal shooting.

Formation: Two to six players scattered around a basket.

Equipment: One basketball and a goal.

Procedures: Players alternate taking long and short shots. Long shots (from behind the foul line) are worth two points if made. Short shots (anywhere in front of the foul line) count one point if made. The first player to get 21 points is the winner. The player shooting baskets continues alternating long and short shots until he misses or reaches 21; then the next player takes his turn.

Suggestions: Score points for hitting the backboard and/or rim for beginners.

AROUND THE WORLD

Movement Skills: Goal shooting.

Formation: Group of four to six players in scatter formation around basket.

Equipment: One basketball and a goal.

Procedures: An area around the basket is marked for one-, ten-, and 15-foot distances on each side of the basket. Each player attempts to make a basket from each of these areas. A player must first make the basket from the distance closer to the basket before progressing to the next distance. A player shoots until he misses (his effort continues where he stopped). The first player to make a basket from each spot wins.

SIX-HOLE BASKETBALL

Movement Skills: Goal shooting.
Formation: Six three-foot circles marked off around the outside of the free-throw shooting area and six to ten players per group.
Equipment: One basketball and one goal for each group.
Procedures: The circles are called holes. Each player in turn tries to make a basket, beginning at circle one. For every basket made, the player advances one hole until he misses. Two holes are marked "safe" (usually two and four). If one player overtakes another and he is not in a hole marked "safe," the first player must return to the first hole and begin again. The first player to get to hole six is the winner.

NINE-COURT BASKETBALL

Movement Skills: Passing, pivoting, goal shooting, guarding, and team play.
Formation: Basketball court divided into nine equal areas, with one player from each team assigned to that area.
Equipment: One basketball, two goals.
Procedures: Played like basketball except each player is assigned an area and must stay within that boundary. Players advance the ball toward their goal by passing and may dribble once. Only forwards may shoot at the goal. The ball is put in play by a center jump. An unguarded free shot, worth one point, is awarded for fouls, such as blocking and holding. The ball is taken out of bounds for infractions such as crossing a line or traveling.

SIDELINE BASKETBALL

Movement Skills: Passing, catching, dribbling, pivoting, and goal shooting.
Formation: Eight to twelve players per team, with half on the sideline and half on the court.
Equipment: One basketball and two goals.
Procedures: Half of the team scatters about the court area and the other half lines up along the sideline. The game begins with a jump ball between any two opponents. The team gaining possession of the ball tries to make a goal (each successful attempt counts two points). The ball is advanced by dribbling and passing. Players on the court may pass the ball to a teammate on sideline, who in turn may pass the ball to a teammate on the court. After each successful goal attempt, stolen ball, or defensive rebound, the ball must be passed to a player on the sideline. Violations are as follows: (1) For touching, double dribble, and foul violations, the other team is awarded the ball. (2) In jump situations, the team in possession is awarded the ball.

HALF-COURT BASKETBALL

Movement Skills: All basic basketball skills.
Formation: Scatter formation with five players per team.
Equipment: One basketball and one goal per game.
Procedures: The rules of basketball govern fouls, penalties, and general playing situations. A throw-in is used to start the game and to restart play after each score. The player making the throw-in must be standing with one foot in the center circle. The player taking the throw-in is unguarded. Out-of-bounds play: On an out-of-bounds play, two completed passes must occur before a goal may be attempted. Violations include: (1) A player may not try for a goal following a free throw missed by a member of the opposing team until the ball has first been passed to the back court and returned. Penalty: The goal, if made, does not score, and the ball is awarded to a member of the opposing team out of bounds at a sideline. (2) A player may not carry or cause the ball to go over the center line. Penalty: The ball is awarded to an opponent out of bounds at a sideline of the neutral zone. Score as in regulation basketball.

BACKLINE BASKETBALL

Movement Skills: All basic basketball skills.
Formation: Standard scatter formation with five players per team.

Equipment: One basketball and one goal per game.

Procedures: The rules and scoring are the same as in Half-Court Basketball. The one difference is that every time a shot is taken, if it is rebounded by the opposition, it must be taken behind the free-throw line before they can take a shot. If the shot is rebounded by the shooting team, it may be shot again.

SOCCER

The following lead-up games to soccer have been selected because they are easy to organize and fun to play. Each incorporates two or more of the basic skills of soccer. Each activity may be played out-of-doors or modified for indoor play. A suggested progression for introducing soccer lead-up games is depicted in Table 33.2.

Objectives

The primary objectives of including soccer lead-up games into the program are to:

1. Reinforce the various soccer skills of kicking, trapping, dribbling, volleying, and tackling and to apply them to gamelike situations.
2. Introduce the basic rules of soccer through modified game activities.
3. Provide opportunities for developing an understanding and application of basic team strategies.
4. Encourage a spirit of cooperation and teamwork toward a common goal.
5. Give students a chance to play a modified game of soccer with reasonable skill and enjoyment.

Movement Experiences

CIRCLE SOCCER

Movement Skills: Kicking and trapping.
Formation: Loose single circle with eight players to each half of the circle.
Equipment: One soccer ball per group.
Procedures: The ball is rolled to one team. Players pass the ball among themselves, then kick to the opposite side of the circle. Opposing players trap or block the ball, trying to prevent it from going outside the circle. A point is scored each time the ball goes out of circle. Three-minute time limit.
Suggestions: Stress passing the ball before kicking. Insist upon trapping and controlling the

TABLE 33.2 Suggested Progression for Introducing Soccer Lead-Up Games

Soccer Lead-Up Games	Kicking Skills	Trapping Skills	Dribbling Skills	Volleying Skills	Tackling Skills	Goal Keeping	Team Play	Page
Circle Soccer	X	X						453
Line Soccer	X	X	X					454
Soccer Keep Away	X	X						454
Sideline Soccer	X	X	X	X				454
Pin Kickball	X	X						454
Soccer Kickball	X	X	X					454
Team Keep Away	X	X	X	X	X			455
Crab Soccer	X		X			X	X	455
Zone Soccer	X	X	X	X		X	X	455
Six-a-Side Soccer	X	X	X	X	X	X	X	456
Regulation Soccer	X	X	X	X	X	X	X	456

ball before the ball is returned do not permit toe kicks. Any ball above the waist may be blocked with the hands or caught without penalty. Do *not* require players to hold hands. Use foam ball or partially deflated ball for beginners.

LINE SOCCER

Movement Skills: Dribbling, kicking, and trapping.
Formation: Two parallel lines of eight players each, 40 to 60 feet apart.
Equipment: One soccer ball per game.
Procedures: Players on each team are given a number. The teacher calls a number and rolls the ball into the center of the playing area. Player who was called attempts to control the ball, dribble it toward the opposing goal line, and score. Goal-line players may trap the ball to prevent a goal. Kicked balls above waist level do not count and may be blocked with the hands or caught. Play continues until a goal is scored. Procedure is repeated.
Suggestions: Emphasize controlling and dribbling the ball prior to kicking. Do not permit toe kicks. As skill increases, call two or three numbers, and stress passing and teamwork. Use foam ball or partially deflated ball until skill develops in trapping and kicking. Avoid long waiting for a turn by keeping size of teams small.

SOCCER KEEP AWAY

Movement Skills: Kicking and trapping.
Formation: Single circle of eight to ten players per group, with one player in the center ("it").
Equipment: One nerf soccer ball per group.
Procedures: Player in the center tries to touch the ball as it is passed from player to player. When "it" touches the ball with his feet, the player who kicked the ball goes to the center.
Suggestions: Stress passing the ball among teammates before kicking across the circle. Do not permit toe kicks. Insist on trapping the ball prior to kicking it back to a teammate.

SIDELINE SOCCER

Movement Skills: Kicking, dribbling, trapping, and volleying.
Formation: 30' by 60' rectangular play area with eight to twelve per team.
Equipment: One soccer ball per group, markings to designate teams in the field.
Procedures: Each team is assigned a goal to defend. Half of each team scatters in its half of the playing area. The other half lines up on one sideline. The game begins with a "face-off" between two opposing players. The object of the game is to kick the ball behind the opposing players standing on the sideline. Players in the field may pass to one another or to teammates on the sideline. Sideline players may pass to players in the field and must use various trapping skills to block the ball. One point is scored for each kick that crosses the opponents' sideline below waist level.

PIN KICKBALL

Movement Skills: Kicking and trapping.
Formation: Two parallel lines of eight to ten players each.
Equipment: Two soccer balls per group, plus eight pins (bowling pins or milk cartons work well).
Procedures: Each team is given a soccer ball. From behind a restraining line, the object is to accurately kick the ball and knock down the pins. One point is scored for each pin knocked over.
Suggestions: Do not let certain players dominate the game. After a point is scored, require the ball to be passed to another player. Add to the number of pins. Add balls. Increase the distance from the pins as accuracy improves.

SOCCER KICKBALL

Movement Skills: Kicking, trapping, and dribbling.
Formation: Six to eight players per team.

Players in the field are informally scattered.

Equipment: One soccer ball per group.

Procedures: The object is to kick the ball from behind the goal and then run to a base about 50 feet away and back before the fielding team can score a goal. Player kicks a stationary ball, runs to the base, and back. Players in the field retrieve the ball without using the hands. They may dribble and pass the ball prior to kicking at the goal area. Players in the field may not stand closer than 15 feet from the base line. If the ball is kicked through the goal before the player crosses the base line, a point is scored for the fielders. If the player crosses the base line, a point is scored for the kickers. Play continues until all have had a turn at kicking the ball.

Suggestions: As kicking skill develops, lengthen the distance of the base from the base line. As skill in the field increases, narrow the goal. Use a foam ball or partially deflated ball when indoors. Stress teamwork in the field and using the instep kick when up to "bat." The game may be modified to include punting.

TEAM KEEP AWAY

Movement Skills: Kicking, dribbling, trapping, tackling, and volleying.

Formation: Team soccer formation with designated boundaries. Six to eight players per team.

Equipment: One soccer ball per group, plus armbands or pinnies to designate team members.

Procedures: The rules are similar to most keep-away games, except that the ball must be kicked or dribbled and not touched with the hands. The object is for a team to maintain control of the ball for as long as possible. Individual players may not control the ball longer than 10 seconds before passing. If a foul occurs, opposing team is awarded the ball.

Suggestions: Use a partially deflated ball or foam ball when playing indoors. Stress playing one's position. Introduce basic elements of tackling. Emphasize ball control while dribbling and accurate passing.

CRAB SOCCER

Movement Skills: Kicking, dribbling, goal keeping, and team play.

Formation: Team soccer formation, with 12 players per team. Indoor playing area at least 40' by 60'.

Equipment: One large foam ball, beachball, or cage ball per group.

Procedures: Players assume a crab-walk position in each of the regular positions of soccer. The ball is put into play with a face-off. Players may advance the ball by kicking to a teammate. Hands must remain in contact with the floor. The object is to kick the ball over the opposing team's goal. The goal keeper may not touch the ball with the hands. Positioning and basic rules of soccer apply.

Suggestions: This is an excellent activity to teach positioning. Stop the game frequently to see that players are in position. Rotate positions after each goal. Remove eyeglasses before playing. Do not permit wild kicking at the ball or mass convergence on the ball.

ZONE SOCCER

Movement Skills: Kicking, trapping, dribbling, volleying, goal keeping, and team play.

Formation: Two teams of twelve players each, divided into three zones (divide gym in thirds).

Equipment: One soccer ball per group.

Procedures: Divide each team into three equal groups. The object is to kick the ball over the opposing team's goal line. The ball is put into play with a regulation kickoff. Players must remain in their own zone and may advance the ball by passing to a teammate in another zone. Goal guards are responsible for defending their goal line. Fullbacks are the last line of defense. Halfbacks receive passes from their fullbacks and relay them to the forwards. Forwards attempt to score goals.

Suggestions: Emphasize playing one's position.

SIX-A-SIDE SOCCER

Movement Skills: All soccer skills.
Formation: Outdoor play area 40 × 80 yards with six players per team.
Equipment: One soccer ball per group.
Procedures: Assign two forwards (strikers), two halfbacks (midfield players), one fullback (defensive player), and a goalie. Follow the basic rules of soccer, modifying as necessary.
Suggestions: Use a foam ball if played indoors. Stress positioning and team play. Permit players to practice at each position. Introduce more complex strategies as skill improves.

REGULATION SOCCER

Movement Skills: All soccer skills.
Formation: Regulation soccer field, 300 to 360 feet long, and 180 to 225 feet wide. Eleven players per side.
Equipment: One soccer ball per group and two goals.
Procedures: Play begins by the center forward of the offensive team kicking the ball to a teammate. The ball must travel its own circumference before being touched by an opposing player, and the opposition may not enter the center circle until after the ball is kicked. Neither team may cross the center line until after the ball is put into play. After that, players may go anywhere on the field. The object is to move the ball down the field and to score a point by putting the ball through the opponents' goal. The ball is moved by kicking, dribbling, or volleying. Defenders may interrupt the ball and reverse the playing action.
Fouls: Fouls are committed when a player other than the goalie handles the ball with any part of the hand or arm. Carrying the ball more than two steps by the goalie is a foul. Pushing an opponent with the hands, arm, or body is also a foul.
Free Kick: A free kick is awarded for any foul committed outside the penalty area. The ball is kicked from the spot of the foul with the opposition at least 10 yards from the ball.
Penalty Kick: A foul committed inside the penalty area by the defensive team results in penalty kick.

The penalty kick is taken from the penalty mark with all players, except the goalie, outside the penalty area.
Corner Kick: A kick from the corner of the field is given the offensive team when the defensive team kicks the ball over its own goal line. The corner kick is taken by the outside forward from the corner nearest the point of exit.
Goalie Kick: A goalie kick is awarded the defensive team when the ball is kicked by the offensive team over the goal line but not through the goal. The opposing team must be at least 10 yards distant. The goalie may pick up the ball with the hands, punt from the goal line, and throw the ball. He may take only two steps with the ball.
Suggestions: Regulation soccer is generally not advised for the elementary physical education class. Various modifications, including six-a-side soccer, are more appropriate for teaching skills and developing the basic concept of cooperative team play.

SOFTBALL

There is a wide variety of softball lead-up games appropriate for elementary school-age children. The games presented here have been selected because of the skills they contribute to, their ease of organization, and because they are fun to play. They are presented in a progression from simple to complex (see Table 33.3). Many of the games may be modified for indoor play by changing the boundaries and the type of ball used.

Objectives

The primary objectives for including softball lead-up games into the lesson are to:

1. Reinforce the various throwing, fielding, batting, and base-running skills of softball.
2. Introduce the basic skills of softball through modified game activities.
3. Provide opportunities for developing an understanding of and appreciation for basic team strategies.

TABLE 33.3 Suggested Progression for Introducing Softball Lead-Up Games

Softball Lead-Up Games	Throwing Skills	Fielding Skills	Batting Skills	Base-Running Skills	Team Play	Page
Team Distance Throw	X					457
Toss-Up	X					457
Circle Overtake	X	X				458
Throw Softball	X	X				458
Around the Bases				X		458
Base-Running Overtake	X	X		X		458
Throw Around	X	X		X		458
Home-Run Derby		X	X			459
Ground-Ball Pursuit		X				459
Line-Ball Pepper		X	X			459
Softball Pop-Up		X				459
500		X	X			459
Three-Pitch Softball	X	X	X	X	X	460
Milk-Carton Softball	X	X	X	X	X	460
Tee Ball	X	X	X	X	X	460
Whiffle Ball	X	X	X	X	X	460

4. Encourage a spirit of cooperation and effort as a team toward a common goal.
5. Have fun and learn to play the game of softball with a reasonable degree of skill.

Movement Experiences

TEAM DISTANCE THROW

Movement Skill: Throwing.
Formation: Columns of four players each in a large outdoor area.
Equipment: Tape measure and one beanbag for each team.
Procedures: After warming up, the first player throws the beanbag as far as possible from behind the restraining line. The entire team advances to the spot where the beanbag lands and lines up behind it. The second player now throws as far as possible. Process is repeated until each child has thrown. The winner is the team with the greatest total distance.
Suggestions: Use different colored beanbags

for each team. Be sure to divide teams evenly. Do not permit long approaches prior to throwing. After the players know how to play the game, work for speed by running to the beanbag.

TOSS-UP

Movement Skills: Fielding.
Formation: Three players per team in a circular formation.
Equipment: One softball per team (a lighter ball may be used for lower skill levels).
Procedures: Player from one team tosses the ball high into the air within the area of the circle. Anyone from the other team may catch the ball. Teams alternate tossing and catching. If the ball is caught, score one point for the catching team. If it is dropped, score one point for the tossing team.
Suggestions: Number players on each team and call a different number each time the ball is tossed. This will insure everyone getting equal opportunity to toss and catch the ball.

CIRCLE OVERTAKE

Movement Skills: Throwing and fielding.
Formation: Large 30′ single circle formed by twelve to sixteen players, with six to eight per team.
Equipment: Two softballs per circle.
Procedures: Number players either "one" or "two." The ones form one team, the twos, another. Each team chooses a captain, who stands in the center of the circle. Both captains have a ball. On the signal "Go," the captains throw the ball from opposite sides of the circle to a member of their team. Teammate returns the ball. The captain and teammates continue to throw back and forth in a clockwise direction until one ball overtakes the other.
Suggestions: Use softer balls for less skilled players. Vary the size of the circle and the type of throw used.

THROW SOFTBALL

Movement Skills: Throwing and fielding.
Formation: Standard softball formation with six to ten players per team.
Equipment: One softball and one set of bases per group.
Procedures: The game is played like regulation softball, except there is no batting. The pitcher throws the ball to the "batter." The batter catches the ball and immediately hits it into the field. The game is then played like regulation softball except that only one throw per time at bat is permitted, and stealing is not allowed. One point is scored for each run.

AROUND THE BASES

Movement Skills: Base running.
Formation: Six players per team. One team lines up behind first base, the other behind third base.
Equipment: Four bases.
Procedures: The object is for a team to be the first to have everyone run the bases. The teams line up on the inside of the diamond at diagonally opposite bases. The first person makes one complete circuit of the bases and then touches off the second player, who does the same thing. The team finishing first is the winner.

BASE-RUNNING OVERTAKE

Movement Skills: Base running, throwing, and fielding.
Formation: Ten players in regulation softball field formation, except one player is designated as the runner.
Equipment: One softball per team.
Procedures: One player is designated as the runner. The others play their position in the field. The runner comes up to home plate and throws the ball in fair territory anywhere in the field. The runner then tries to run around the bases and back to home plate before the ball is fielded and returned to the catcher. Players rotate positions after each try.
Suggestions: Make it a team activity by having one team up to bat and the other in the field.

THROW AROUND

Movement Skills: Base running, throwing, and fielding.
Formation: Six players, consisting of one base runner and all infield positions except the pitcher.
Equipment: Four bases, one softball.
Procedures: The object of the game is for the base runner, starting at home plate, to get all around the base path before the ball can be thrown around the horn (catcher to shortstop to first to second to third and home again). If the runner beats the ball around, he or she goes again and continues until beaten.
Suggestions: If the infielders are beating the base runner easily, have them throw twice around the horn before the runner is out. Adjust the distance between the bases to the ability of the players.

HOME-RUN DERBY

Movement Skills: Batting and fielding.
Formation: Regular softball formation except for pitcher and catcher, who are placed in the field.
Equipment: Batting tee, bat, softball.
Procedures: A restraining line is drawn from first to third base. The four infielders may not go in front of the line. The three outfielders scatter in the field. The object is to hit the ball off the tee into fair territory *beyond* the restraining line on the fly. The team in the field tries to field the ball on the fly. If it catches the ball, no points are scored. If it does not, one point is awarded the team at bat for an infield hit and two points for an outfield hit. Each player gets three swings. Players do not run the bases. Teams trade places after each player has had a turn at bat.
Suggestions: Permit more skillful groups to toss the ball up and hit it (fungo hitting) rather than using a tee stand.

GROUND-BALL PURSUIT

Movement Skills: Fielding ground balls.
Formation: Three players per team, spread along a goal line.
Equipment: One to three softballs per group.
Procedures: Grounders are thrown by one team to the other. Each grounder must bounce at least once before crossing the midfield line. The fielders receiving the ball try to stop it from crossing their goal line. Whoever fields the ball throws it back at the opposing team. Players stay in their own half of the field. One point is scored for each grounder that crosses an opponent's goal line.

LINE-BALL PEPPER

Movement Skills: Batting and fielding.
Formation: One player up to bat with four players in the field.
Equipment: One bat and softball per group.
Procedures: Fielders must stay within a lane

and not go back past the goal line. Fielders throw the ball to the batter, who bunts it or chops it back. If one of the fielders fumbles the ball or lets the ball cross the goal line through his or her lane, that fielder must step back out of line and act as a backstop for the other fielders as they continue. The remaining fielders move in together so that there is not a vacant lane between them and carry on until there is only one fielder left. This fielder then becomes the batter.
Suggestions: Only the fielder can throw the ball to the batter. If one of the players who has been eliminated and is acting as a backstop gets a ball, it must be given to one of the remaining fielders, who then throws it to the batter.

SOFTBALL POP-UP

Movement Skills: Fielding high fly balls.
Formation: Scatter formation within a 50-foot circle. Six players per team.
Equipment: One softball per group.
Procedures: The object is for the fielding team, scattered informally in the center of a large circle, to catch the fly balls thrown by the throwing team, which forms the circle. Each member of the throwing team, in turn, throws the ball as high into the air as possible. The player in the field who has a corresponding number attempts to catch the ball before it touches the ground in the prescribed area. When everyone has thrown, teams exchange roles. One point is scored by the throwing team each time the ball drops in the prescribed area without being caught.

500

Movement Skills: Batting and fielding.
Formation: One batter, four to five fielders.
Equipment: One bat and one softball per team.
Procedures: Batter hits fungos to the fielders. The first person to reach 500 points becomes the batter. Score 200 points for catching a fly ball, 50 points for fielding a grounder, and 100 points for fielding a grounder on the first bounce.
Suggestions: As skill advances, play as just

described, except subtract points as well if the ball is not played cleanly. If a fly ball is dropped, subtract 100 from the total. If a grounder is missed, subtract 50 points. Subtract 75 points for fumbling a ball on the first hop. Instead of hitting fungos, have someone pitch and then play as just described.

THREE-PITCH SOFTBALL

Movement Skills: All basic softball skills.
Formation: Two teams with nine per team. Use a softball diamond and standard player formation.
Equipment: One bat and softball per group, plus one set of bases.
Procedures: The pitcher is a member of the batting team. The batter is out if he or she cannot get a fairly hit ball in three pitches. When three players are out, the side is retired. Since the pitcher is a member of the batter's team, there should be no bunting or base stealing. The batting team may change pitchers at any time. With the exception of these details, all softball rules apply.

MILK-CARTON SOFTBALL

Movement Skills: All basic softball skills.
Formation: Regulation softball formation.
Equipment: One bat, softball, and set of bases, plus four half-gallon milk cartons.
Procedures: The object is for the batter, after hitting a fair ball, to circle the bases before the four cartons can be knocked down in order by the fielders. The game is played like softball, but there is a milk carton on each base. On a fair ball, the batter circles the bases and touches home plate. The fielders retrieve the ball and pass it in order to first, second, third, and to home. As the baseman receives the ball, she knocks down the pin and throws to the next base. The batter is out (1) on a fly ball, (2) if she knocks down a pin, or (3) if the four pins can be knocked down by the fielders before she gets home. Rotate base positions after each inning. After all players on one side have batted,

sides change. One point is scored by the batter if she beats the ball home.
Suggestions: (1) Play by outs; (2) use a batting tee; (3) adjust the number of cartons and base lengths to the ability of players.

TEE BALL

Movement Skills: Batting, fielding, throwing, and base running.
Formation: Standard softball formation.
Equipment: One softball and set of bases per group.
Procedures: Same as for regulation softball, except the ball is batted off a tee.

WHIFFLE BALL

Movement Skills: All softball skills.
Formation: Regulation softball formation with ten players per team.
Equipment: One whiffle ball and bat, plus one set of bases per group.
Procedures: The game is played by the same rules as regulation softball.
Suggestions: Use a larger ball or a large-headed bat if less skilled children are having difficulty hitting the ball.

VOLLEYBALL

The sport of volleyball requires considerable eye–hand coordination and is difficult for many elementary school-age children to master. In order to minimize frustration and to maximize skill learning and enjoyment, it is recommended that modifications be made in the type of ball used for the lead-up activities that follow. Progression from the use of balloons, to beachballs, to foam balls and then to volleyballs generally works best. The lead-up games selected for inclusion here are easy to organize and are challenging and fun. They are presented in a progression from simple to complex in Table 33.4.

TABLE 33.4   Suggested Progression for Introducing Volleyball Lead-Up Games

Volleyball Lead-Up Game	Passing Skills	Set Skills	Bump Skills	Serving Skills	Spiking Skills	Rotating Skills	Team Play	Page
Ten Volleys	X	X						461
Block Volley	X	X						461
Balloon Volleyball	X	X						462
One Bounce						X	X	462
One-Line Volleyball	X			X				462
High Ball		X	X					462
Deck Tennis						X	X	462
Newcomb						X	X	463
Shower Service Ball				X				463
Serve, Pass, and Catch	X			X				463
Bump Game			X					463
Modified Volleyball	X	X		X			X	464
Volleyball	X	X	X	X			X	464

Objective

The primary objectives for including volleyball lead-up games into the lesson are to:

1. Reinforce the various skills of volleyball.
2. Introduce the basic rules of volleyball through modified game activities.
3. Provide opportunities for developing an understanding of, and appreciation for, basic team strategies.
4. Encourage a spirit of cooperation and teamwork.
5. Have fun and learn to play modified volleyball with a reasonable degree of skill.

Movement Experiences

TEN VOLLEYS

Movement Skills: Volleying and setting.
Formation: Circles with four to eight players per circle.
Equipment: One volleyball per circle.
Procedures: At the signal "Go," first player volleys the ball upward and calls out "One." Second player calls out "Two" as she volleys the ball, and so on to "Ten." Players may not contact the ball twice in succession. If the ball contacts the floor, start over. First team to reach ten wins.
Suggestions: Use large plastic balls, beachballs, or foam balls for less skilled groups.

BLOCK VOLLEY

Movement Skills: Volleying, and setting.
Formation: Circle with four to six players.
Equipment: One volleyball per group.
Procedures: Arrange players in a circle, ten feet apart. One player, "it," is at the center of the circle. The plays in the circle volley the ball back and forth to each other across the circle while "it" tries to block the ball from crossing to the other player. The player in the circle becomes "it" if his batted ball is blocked, and the first "it" takes his place in the circle. The object of the game is to try to volley the ball up so that "it" will not be able to block. Team scoring is based upon the number of the times the ball is volleyed before it is blocked.
Suggestions: Use balloons, beachballs, or foam balls for less skilled players.

BALLOON VOLLEYBALL

Movement Skills: Volleying and setting.
Formation: Two teams on either side of a rope stretched six feet off the ground. Three to four players per side in a 15′ × 15′ court.
Equipment: One balloon per group.
Procedures: Players get two attempts to serve the balloon. A serve may be relayed once before going over. The balloon may be hit five times before going over the net. Points are scored the same as in volleyball.
Suggestions: As skill develops, progress to using a beachball, foam ball, and finally a volleyball.

ONE BOUNCE

Movement Skills: Team play.
Formation: Two teams of six players, one team on each side of a net three feet to six feet high.
Equipment: One volleyball and one set per game.
Procedures: Play is begun by throwing the ball over the net. The receiving team must catch the ball on the fly or after one bounce. The ball is then thrown back over to the other side. If the ball hits the floor more than once, the opposite team scores. The first team to reach 15 points wins. Players rotate as in regulation volleyball.
Suggestions: As skill develops, raise the net from three feet to six feet. If skill level is low, allow two bounces.

ONE-LINE VOLLEYBALL

Movement Skills: Passing and serving.
Formation: Regulation volleyball formation with six to nine players per team.
Equipment: One volleyball and one net per game.
Procedures: The ball is served by a player from the right-hand corner position. The ball is volleyed back and forth until it goes out of bounds or fails to be returned, or until a foul (touching net or stepping over line) occurs. The ball may be hit any number of times on a side before it is returned, but not twice in succession by the same player. Players rotate when their team wins the serve. Teams may serve for a specified number of points, then change service.
Suggestions: Teacher may limit the number of times the ball may be hit on each side of the net. The size of the court may be made smaller to take into account the type of ball being used and the skill level of the players.

HIGH BALL

Movement Skills: Set and bump.
Formation: Teams of six to eight players, arranged in a circle with one player in the center.
Equipment: One volleyball per group.
Procedures: The object is to keep the ball in the air by using a set-up or bump pass. The player in the center of the circle volleys to a player in the circle, who volleys it back. Play continues around the circle until one of the balls is missed or handled twice in succession by the same player. When an error is made, the next player of the group puts the ball into play as rapidly as possible. Each time the ball is successfully volleyed from player to player, a score of one point is made. When an error is made, that score is terminated. A new score begins with each renewal of play.
Suggestions: A continuous match may be played by keeping the highest daily score of each group and totaling these scores each week. Use a lighter ball for less skilled groups.

DECK TENNIS

Movement Skills: Rotating skills, and team play
Formation: Two teams of six players on each side of a net three to five feet high.
Equipment: One rubber deck-tennis ring and one net or suspended rope per game.
Procedures: One team begins the game by throwing the deck-tennis ring over the net. If the

opposing team fails to catch the ring, a point is scored for the throwing team. If the thrower fails to get the ring over the net, a point is scored for the other team. A throw that goes outside the boundary lines is a point for the opposite team. A player may not move once he catches the ring. After the ring strikes the floor, the closest player picks it up and starts a new volley for a point by throwing it over the net.

Suggestions: Require the server to call out the score prior to each serve. Use a standard volleyball rotation system. If a deck tennis ring is not available, try a Frisbee disc.

NEWCOMB

Movement Skills: Team play, and rotating skills.
Formation: Two teams of six players each, one team on each side of a net three to seven feet high.
Equipment: One volleyball and one net per game.
Procedures: The ball is served by throwing it from the back right corner. Players on the opposite side try to catch the ball before it touches the ground. If the ball is caught, it may be thrown back over the net or passed to a teammate (two passes are allowed) before it is thrown over the net. Play continues until the ball hits the floor. A player may not change positions after catching a ball. The object is to score 15 points or as many points possible in a set time limit.
Suggestions: Insist on players playing *their* position and not others. Use a lower net or different ball for less skilled players.

SHOWER SERVICE BALL

Movement Skills: Serving.
Formation: Two teams of six to nine players on either side of a suspended net.
Equipment: Several volleyballs and one suspended net for each game.
Procedures: To start the game, the volleyballs are divided between the teams and are handled by players in the serving area. The serving area is between the baseline and the line drawn through the middle of each court. Balls may be served at any time, just so the server is in the serving area of his or her court. Any ball that is served across the net is to be caught by any player near the ball. The person catching or retrieving a ball from the floor moves quickly to his or her serving area and serves. A point is scored for a team whenever a served ball hits the floor in the other court or is dropped by a receiver. Two scorers are needed, one for each side.

Suggestions: As skill develops, add several balls to the game.

SERVE, PASS, AND CATCH

Movement Skills: Serving, and passing.
Formation: Two teams of six players on each side of a six- to seven-foot net.
Equipment: One volleyball and one suspended net per game.
Procedures: Players line up as if they were playing an actual game. When the ball is served, the receiver makes one bump pass to another team member, who catches the ball. A point is scored if the ball is not properly passed or is not caught. Side out is called if the ball is passed correctly and caught. Fifteen points constitute a game.
Suggestions: Limit play to five minutes per game.

BUMP GAME

Movement Skills: Bump pass.
Formation: Two lines of six players each, perpendicular to the net.
Equipment: One volleyball per team.
Procedures: Divide the class up into groups. Team members are lined up behind each other on each side of the net. First player in line runs out to bump a ball that has been tossed out. The ball is bumped over the net, with the first player in the opposite line running out to midcourt to bump it back. Once that player has bumped, the next person in the same line comes out and is ready to bump the next ball that comes over the net. Score is kept. If the ball touches the floor, or if anything

other than a bump pass is used, a point is scored by the opposite team.

Suggestions: Do not require the ball to go over the net. Work for successful forearm passes.

MODIFIED VOLLEYBALL

Movement Skills: Serving and volleying.

Formation: Two teams of six players each, one on each side of a six- to seven-foot net.

Equipment: One volleyball and net per game.

Procedures: A regulation volleyball game is played, with one or more of the following modifications: (1) The server may serve from a position in the center of the court; (2) two or more service trials may be allowed. An assisted serve is permissible; that is, a teammate may relay a ball that has been served in an effort to send it over the net; (3) during the volley, an unlimited number of players may bat the ball before it goes over the net; (4) although position play should be encouraged, it is not a requirement; (5) the ball may not be hit more than three times in succession by the same player; (6) the ball may be played from a bounce or from the air.

VOLLEYBALL

Movement Skills: Set-up, bump, dig, spike, block, net recovery, and serve.

Formation: Two teams of six players each. (May be modified to accommodate nine players on a 30 by 60-foot court.

Equipment: One volleyball and one net suspended 7 feet 6 inches above the floor.

Procedures: The ball is served from the back right corner of the court. The server must stay behind the endline while serving. After the serve, he should move to his position on the court. The serving team scores when the receiving team fails to return the ball to the opponents' court. Only the serving team may score. The receiving team gains the serve when an opponent fails to return the ball over the net. The players may not reach over or touch the net. A player may not play the ball twice in succession. A ball may be played a maximum of three times by any one team before going over the net. A ball touching a boundary line is considered inbounds. A team wins when it scores 15 points and has a two-point advantage. Play continues until the two-point advantage is obtained. Teams exchange courts at the end of each game. The losing team begins a new game. The best three out of five games wins the match.

Suggestions: Modify the regulation game by use of a lighter ball. Permit a maximum of nine players per team. Do *not* divide the class in half for mass volleyball of ten or more per side.

SUGGESTED READING

Blake, O. W., and Volp, A. M. (1964). *Lead-up games to team sports.* Englewood Cliffs, NJ: Prentice-Hall.

Humphrey, H. H., and Humphrey, J. N. (1980). *Sports skills for boys and girls.* Springfield, IL: Charles C Thomas.

CHAPTER 34

GAMES FOR LIMITED SPACES AND SPECIAL PLACES

From time to time it is necessary, because of a variety of factors, to conduct the physical education period in the classroom or in a hallway. Rather than simply cancel the class period, it is recommended that you adapt the program to be conducted in the limited space available. Care will have to be taken to insure the safety of the children, but a variety of fun and worthwhile activities can still be presented. For example, isometric exercises, finger plays, and singing rhythms can be conducted at or next to the children's desks.

This chapter contains a sampling of games suitable for limited spaces and special places. Each is briefly described without use of the format found in the previous game chapters be-

cause the primary purpose of these activities is *not* the improvement of movement skills.

GAMES FOR LIMITED SPACES

Games for limited spaces can be both fun and educational. Although they do not make real use of gross motor movement skills, they do frequently require fine motor coordination and the use of reasoning skills.

Objectives

The primary objectives of using limited-space activities in the physical education program are:

1. To adapt gross motor movement activities for the classroom.
2. To provide a temporary replacement for the regular program of activities, due to unavoidable or unforeseen circumstances.
3. To contribute to socialization skill development.

Movement Experiences

NUT RACE

The players are divided into two teams, both in file formation before a table with a bowl of peanuts on each end. At the starting signal, the first player scoops up as many peanuts as possible on the *back* of his or her hand, walks to the turning line a few feet away, returns, places the peanuts on the table next to the bowl, and touches the next player, who repeats the activity. The team with the most nuts gathered on the table wins the contest.

WORD BREAKDOWN

All players are given pencil and paper, and the group is then given a very long word, such as *antidisestablishmentarianism.* The object of the game is for the players to form as many words as possible from any four or more letters of the main word. A letter cannot be used twice in one new word, unless it appears twice in the main word. The time limit is three minutes. The one who has written the most words is the winner.

QUAKER MEETING

One child stands in front of the room and announces "Quaker meeting has begun; no laughing or talking shall be done." Everything is very quiet while the girl or boy who is "it" goes about the room, trying to make one of the players laugh. "It" may use all kinds of facial expressions. If he or she succeeds, the victim comes to the front of the room and announces that "Quaker meeting" has begun.

OPPOSITE WORDS

The idea is for one child to state a word and for the next to try to give a word with the opposite meaning. There are many opposites known to children: hot–cold, smooth–rough, sweet–sour, small–large, mean–kind, slow–fast, black–white, loud–quiet, left–right, front–back, high–low, sharp–dull, ugly–pretty, and so forth.

DOLLAR, DOLLAR, HOW IT WANDERS

Form a circle standing close together. The hands and arms are extended to the back. One is chosen to get in the center of the circle. The class starts chanting, "Dollar, dollar, how it wanders from one hand into the other; is it fair, is it fair, see poor _____ standing there." (Use the name of the person in the center.) The circle keeps passing carefully behind their backs, a coin or some small object. The player in the center tries to guess who is holding the coin.

WHY AND BECAUSE

Each child takes a piece of paper and writes a question starting with the word *why.* For example: "Why didn't you help your mother with the dishes last night?" The paper is then folded over and passed to any near neighbor. That person does not read the question, but proceeds to write down some answer starting with the word *because.* It might read, "Because I was flying a kite."

FUNNY FACE

Give everyone pencil and paper. Ask everyone to draw, at the top of the paper, the head of a person. The head is folded down and passed to the next child, who adds the torso, and so on until the figure is complete. Then the papers are unfolded and the artistic results are examined. These are often very funny.

HOW MANY CAN YOU REMEMBER?

Place 20 to 30 objects on the table. Everyone looks at them for one to two minutes. Then a cover is placed on them. The winner is the person writing down the greatest number of the objects.

PIG

Players seated around a table are dealt eight cards: fours, fives, sixes, sevens, eights, nines, and so on. On the signal "Go," each one passes one card face down to the player on his left. When anyone can make a book of four cards having the same number, she or he puts the cards down and places one finger to his or her nose while the rest continue playing. The last one to copy the action or to fail to notice that the others have their fingers touching their nose is a P. If the same player is last to do so again, he is a PI; on the next failure, he becomes a PIG. Anyone who answers any question with yes or no also becomes a PIG. Play continues until all are out of the game.

WHAT AM I?

Pin a picture on the back of each player. Players mingle around, trying to find out what the picture is that they are wearing. Players may only ask questions calling for a no or yes answer. When they discover what they represent, they report to the lead, who pins the picture on their lapel. Pictures of animals, cars, famous people, flowers, and so forth may be used.

CHICKEN MARKET

All players are chickens except the two strongest class members. One becomes the buyer; the other, the seller. All players squat down and clasp their hands around their knees and are told not to smile or laugh. The buyer comes to test each chicken by pinching, chin chucking, or tickling. At last the buyer says, "This one is just right." The buyer and the seller take hold of the chicken's arms and swing it, counting "one, two three." As they do so, if the chicken laughs, she is eliminated. If the chicken does not laugh, she is not sold but remains safe.

CANDY FACTORY

Each player has a small paper cup, a straw, and 25 or 30 small red candy hearts. The hearts are placed on a napkin beside the paper cup. Each person tries to fill his or her cup with the candy hearts, picking them up on the end of a straw by sucking in on the straw. Players may not use their hands. The first one to finish is the winner.

HOT AND COLD

One player leaves the room while someone in the room hides an object in plain sight to the children in the room. The one who left the room returns and hunts for the hidden object. When "it" is far away from the object, the children clap very softly (cold). As "it" gets nearer the object, the children clap louder (hot), thus helping the player to find the object. When the player finds the object, he chooses someone to take his place.

PASS IT QUICKLY

One player stands with her eyes closed and with her back to the group. A player in the group has an object—for example, a key or box—that he passes quickly to another player, who in turn passes it quickly on. When the player who has been hiding her eyes claps her hands, the passing of the object stops. "It" turns around, looks at the players, and tries, in three guesses, to guess who has the object. The other players all act as though they have it. If the player guesses successfully, she may choose a person to take her place.

SUITCASE RELAY

The equipment for each team consists of an umbrella and a suitcase containing a number of articles of wearing apparel, such as a hat, coat, scarf, skirt, or slacks. Teams line up in the usual relay formation. At the starting signal, the first person on each team picks up the suitcase and umbrella and runs to a line about thirty feet away. There she opens the suitcase, puts on the clothing, opens the umbrella, picks up the suitcase again, and returns to the starting point. The second person assists the first in removing the clothing and placing it back in the suitcase. Then he picks up the suitcase and repeats the performance.

PAPER-BAG RELAY

The first player on each team runs forward to a chair or a circle on the floor. Here he picks up a paper bag from a pile, which has been placed there before the game starts. Each player blows up the bag, breaks it—he must make sure that it is broken before starting back—and returns to the starting line.

BEAN PASSING

Players on each team line up in files but stand side by side. Each player has a cup and a soda straw. In the first player's cup ten beans are placed. The beans are transferred from player to player by means of the straws, that is, a player inhales through the straw to pick up a bean and then he blows it or drops it into his neighbor's cup. The last player transfers the beans he receives to a cup places on a chair at the end of the line. The team that gets all ten beans in the last cup first wins.

FIND THE LEADER

Players are seated in a circle. Select an "it" and have "it" leave the room. The players then select a leader. When "it" is called into the center of the circle, the leader slyly starts some motion, such as waving his hand, making a face, or wriggling his fingers. All immediately imitate the leader, who changes the motions frequently. "It" tries to see who is starting them. When she discovers the leader, the person who was responsible for giving away the leader's identity takes her place.

GAMES FOR SPECIAL PLACES

Frequently children are confined in the limited space of an automobile or school bus for long periods of time. Time will pass more rapidly and there will be fewer behavior problems if the children have something to keep them occupied. The activities that follow are useful when movement is extremely limited. Each may be played by two or more people, and each is easy to get started.

Objectives

The primary objectives for games for special places are:

1.   To engage children in a quiet activity.
2.   To involve children in the productive use of their time.
3.   To enhance socialization skills.
4.   To help children to have fun and remain productively occupied.

Movement Experiences

ALPHABET TRAVEL

The first player thinks of a country, city, or continent beginning with *A* and says, "I'm taking a trip to Africa. What shall I do there?"

The second player must answer with a verb *and* a noun that both begin with *A*. For example, "Answer advertisements" or "Adopt alligators." The game then continues to the third player, or (if there are only two) back to the first: "I'm taking a trip to Boston. What shall I do there?"

The next player can say, "Buy boats. I'm taking a trip to California. What shall I do there?" and so on, as far as one can go through the alphabet.

AUNT JANE'S TRUNK

This is a word game for two or more players. Imagine you are packing Aunt Jane's trunk for a long trip. You can put anything you want into her trunk. The first player says, for example, "I packed Aunt Jane's trunk with a calico dress." The next player repeats this and adds something new: "I packed Aunt Jane's trunk with a calico dress and a hair brush." The third player (or the first now, if there are only two) may say; "I packed Aunt Jane's trunk with a calico dress and a hairbrush and a hat."

Whoever fails to repeat the whole list and add a new item is out of the game. The winner is the one who can stay in the game the longest.

NEW WORDS

You will need pencils and paper to play the game. Write down a word that has something to do with a car, train, or plane. Examples: *driver, carburetor, conductor, whistle,* or *propeller.* See how many new words each player can make out of the letters in the word you choose. The word *driver* contains *red, rid, ride, river,* and some other words. You can't use a letter twice in a new word unless it appears twice in the original word. Proper names (like *Edward* or *China*) or abbreviations (like *etc.*) don't count.

The winner is the one who writes down the longest list of new words in a given time.

THIS IS MY EYEBROW

Put your finger on your ear and say, "This is my eyebrow; one, two, three, four, five, six, seven, eight, nine, ten." Before you reach ten, the other player must put a finger on his or her eyebrow and say, "This is my ear! One, two, . . . ten." But before this player reaches ten, you must repeat what you did at first—and so on.

The loser is the one who gets mixed up first. The winner has the right to start a new game, naming other parts of the body. (For instance, touch your chin and say, "This is my elbow.")

THE PREACHER'S CAT

Each player must in turn describe the minister's cat with an adjective beginning with *A.* Number one: "The preacher's cat is an amiable cat." Number two: "The preacher's cat is an acrobatic cat."

The player who can keep this up the longest then starts the whole thing over with *B.* "The preacher's cat is a brave cat," and so on. Anyone who can't think of an adjective beginning with the appropriate letter is out of the game.

WORDS, WORDS, WORDS

Take turns making up sentences in which all the main words begin with the same letter. The funnier they are, the better! Begin with *A* and go through the alphabet as far as you can. Each sentence must have at least five words that begin with its letter, or you can agree on a larger number. You probably will have to omit *X.* Here are some samples:

Agnes ate amazing apples at Aunt Annie's apple tree.

Bill brought broken bottles into the back yard.

Cousin Carol cooked cold cabbage.

Zany Zed zeroed zealously into the Zanzibar Zoo.

CHAIN SPELLING

The first player selects a classification—cities, countries, first names of people, animals, foods, and so on—and spells a word belongng to that class. Each player in turn must spell a new word that begins with the final letter of the last word. For example:

SouP		RoberT
PeaS		TheodorE
SpinacH	or	ElleN
HominY		NaomI
YaM . . .		IvaN . . .

If a player mispells a word or fails to think of a new word during the time it takes the last speller to count to ten, he is out. The game ends when there is only one player left.

NO GRINS

Partners play this game. The object is to make your partner grin or laugh without using any sounds or words. First player has one minute, followed by one minute for the partner.

SILENT CONVERSATION

With a partner, carry out a conversation without using any sounds or words. This is an excellent activity for a driver who is at wits' end.

PROGRESSIVE STORY TELLING

In a group of four or more, one player starts a story. The next player carries on and so forth. This goes on until each has had a turn.

SUGGESTED READING

Brandreth, G. (1976). *Games for rains, planes, and trains.* Battleboro, VT: Stephen Greene Press.

Cub scout songbook. (1969). North Brunswick, NJ: Boy Scouts of America.

Fandek, R. W. (1971). *Classroom capers: Movement education in the classroom.* Bellingham, WA: Educational Designs and Consultants.

Fifty games for travel time. (1971). Pleasantville, NY: Reader's Digest Association.

Fleming, J. (1979). *Games (and more) for backpackers.* Portland, OR: Victoria House.

Saunderlin, S. (1967). *Bits and pieces: Imaginative uses for children's learning.* Washington, D.C.: Association For Childhood Education International.

PART VII

RHYTHMS

CHAPTER 35

TEACHING RHYTHMICS

Rhythm plays an important role in the daily lives of children. Responding to rhythm is one of the strongest and most basic urges of childhood. It is basic to the life process itself, as evidenced by the rhythmical functions of the body, as in breathing, the heartbeat, and the performance of any movement in a coordinated manner. Rhythm, therefore, is the measured release of energy made up of repeated units of time.

Children begin developing their rhythmic abilities during infancy, as seen in the infant's cooing response to the soft, rhythmical sounds of a lullabye, and by the infant's repeated attempts to make pleasurable rhythmic sights, sounds, and sensations last. As children develop, they continue to explore their environment. An internalized time structure is established and refined. This ability to respond rhythmically is developed through practice and experience. As a result, rhythmic activities play an important role in the life of children.

One important avenue by which rhythmic abilities may be developed and refined is movement. Rhythm is a basic component of all coordinated movement, and the two may be effectively combined to enhance both of these interdependent areas.

TYPES OF RHYTHMICS

All coordinated movement involves an element of rhythm. Dance is an extension of rhythmical movement into creative, expressive, interpretative, and joyful activity. It is important that children be exposed to a wide variety of rhythmical experiences. The rhythm and dance offering in the elementary school must be presented in a meaningful and purposeful manner in order to meet the individual developmental needs of all the children. Rhythmic activities may be classified into five general and sometimes overlapping areas: fundamental rhythms; auditory rhythms; creative rhythms; folk and square dance; and social dance.

Fundamental Rhythms

Rhythmic fundamentals are the first and most basic form of understanding and interpreting rhythmic movement. Rhythmic fundamentals involve developing an awareness of the various elements of rhythm and being able to express these elements through movement. The following *elements of rhythm* are of concern to the teacher trying to develop fundamental rhythmic abilities.

1. *Underlying beat*—the steady, continuous sound of any rhythmical sequence.
2. *Tempo*—the speed of the movement, music, or accompaniment.
3. *Accent*—the emphasis given to any one beat (usually the first beat of every measure).
4. *Intensity*—the loudness or softness of the movement or music.
5. *Rhythmic pattern*—a group of beats related to the underlying beat.

Each of the elements of rhythm may be expressed through movement that varies in effort, space, and relationships. Hence, an endless variety of movement activities may be devised to develop an increased awareness of both the elements of rhythm and the qualities of movement. A thorough knowledge of the fundamentals of rhythm is prerequisite to adequate performance in any form of rhythmical endeavor, whether it be dance, instrumental music, or vocal music. The child should be able to "feel" the elements of rhythm and be able to express them through coordinated (rhythmic) movement. Chapter 36 will help get you started with a variety of practical fundamental rhythmic activities.

Remember, participation in locomotor, manipulative, and stability activities that stress the elements of rhythm also serves as a means of improving performance in a variety of fundamental movement skills *while* learning about the elements of rhythm. For example, practice with running, jumping, and skipping to different tempos, intensities, and accents serves as a means of enhancing knowledge of the fundamental elements of rhythm as well as promoting increased skill development in the movements themselves.

Singing Rhythms

Singing rhythms are another form of rhythmic expression. They provide children with an opportunity to develop a better understanding of phrasing. Performing the movements required of a particular activity plus singing the words to the rhythm helps children to develop a keener sense of rhythmic movement in a variety of gross motor and fine motor activities. Singing rhythms include rhymes and poems, finger plays, and singing dances. Each may progress from the very simple to the complex. The activities selected will depend upon the ability level, maturity, and interests of your students. Singing rhythms are appealing to children because they (1) tell a story, (2) develop an idea, (3) have a pleasing rhythmic pattern, (4) stimulate use of one's imagination, or (5) have dramatic possibilities. Singing plays an important role in the life of children. They love repetition and will sing the songs they know over and over again. Children like to respond to songs through movement. When responding to active songs, they will usually join in the singing. This singing is important because it helps to internalize the rhythm of the song itself. When simple songs are utilized, children are given a variety of opportunities for repetition of movement and a chance to be creative and express themselves dramatically. Chapter 37, "Singing Rhythmic Activities," contains a variety of rhymes and poems, finger plays, and singing dances.

Creative Rhythms

Creative rhythmics are a second form of expressing rhythm through movement. Creative rhythmics are generally considered to be an extension of rhythmic fundamentals. They should be included in the elementary school curriculum after the children have a basic grasp of the fundamentals of rhythm. Creativity is a major objective of modern education; therefore, creative rhythmics can and should be included in the elementary school physical education curriculum. Creative rhythmic movement allows one to express ideas, emotions, feelings, and interpretations. Creative movement may be expressed in a variety of forms, including exploration, improvisation, rhythmic problem solving, and simple compositions. We only need to look at the inhibited, stereotypical movements to music of the average fourth or fifth grader to realize that we have not adequately fostered creative expression in most children. Chapter 38, "Creative Rhythmic Activities," contains a variety of appropriate activities for elementary school children.

Folk and Square Dance

Folk and square dance are a fourth form of expressing rhythm through movement. Folk dances are structural dances characteristically performed in many countries throughout the world. In fact, one purpose for including folk dance in the elementary school curriculum is often to enhance children's understanding of other cultures. Furthermore, folk and square dances encourage social interaction within the peer group and provide opportunities for combining patterns of movement into an integrated whole with the benefit of musical accompaniment.

Square dances are peculiarly North American and reflect the culture of the early settlers in the West. Both square and folk dances are composed of a wide variety of movements that range from the very simple to the highly complex. Many folk and square dances can be successfully taught in the elementary school. Several are described in Chapter 39.

Social Dance

Social dance is a fifth medium through which rhythm may be expressed by movement. The very nature of social dance is constantly changing as our culture changes. For example, as this text is being written, break dancing is very popular. A few years ago, it was disco dancng and before that, the twist, and before that, the jitterbug. Often, when preparing to include social dance in the curriculum, we fail to recognize and include these nontraditional forms of social dance. As adults we frequently assume that social dance automatically implies waltzes, foxtrots, tangos, and other more traditional forms of social dance. Careful consideration should be given to the need for including *traditional* social dance in the elementary curriculum. For most schools and communities, it is recommended that traditional social dances *not* be included in the curriculum until the children are ready socially. The resistance and immaturity of many fourth, fifth, and sixth graders frequently make it exceedingly difficult to teach traditional social dances. It is, however, suggested that more modern or *nontraditional* forms of social dance be considered as a part of the curriculum because children often have an expressed interest in learning these dance forms.

SELECTING APPROPRIATE RHYTHMIC ACTIVITIES

The inclusion of rhythmic activities in the elementary school physical education program usually begins at the kindergarten level, with the inclusion of fundamental rhythmic activities along with a variety of singing rhythms and finger plays. After mastering the fundamentals of rhythm, children in the first and second grades generally enjoy expressing their rhythmic abilities through a variety of imitative activities, creative rhythmic expression, and simple folk dances. At the third and fourth grade level, children enjoy creative activities that permit interpreting ideas, moods, holidays, and sporting events through movement. They benefit from more complex folk dances and a few simple square dances. Fifth and sixth graders generally benefit from creative activities that permit rhythmic problem solving and from basic dance compositions. They enjoy more complex square dances and an introduction to certain forms of social dance. Children in the seventh and eighth grade enjoy learning the basic elements of more traditional forms of social dance, as well as more complex folk and square dances and creative rhythmic activities.

Determining Objectives

Rhythmic activities are fun. They add an exciting dimension to the developmental physical education program. However, rather than lumping the rhythmic experiences for the school year into one three- or four-week unit, it is suggested that rhythmic activities be viewed as a means to an end and not just an end in themselves. Therefore, it is recommended that rhythmic activities be an aspect of the program throughout the school year, used as a means for enhancing one or more of the following objectives.

1. Movement skill development
    a. To reinforce development of fundamental movement skills (locomotor, manipulative, and stability abilities).
    b. To internalize a "feel" for harmonious movement through music (synchrony, rhythm, and sequence).
    c. To enhance competence in recreational dance activities (folk, square, and nontraditional social dance).
2. Fitness development
    a. To promote improved aerobic endurance (aerobic dance activities).
    b. To promote improved motor abilities (coordination, agility, balance).
3. Social–emotional development
    a. To promote positive social interaction (peer interaction, group cooperation).
    b. To promote positive self-growth (creativity, self-expression, fun).
4. Cognitive development
    a. To foster understanding and application of the elements of rhythm through movement (accent, tempo, intensity, rhythmic pattern).
    b. To reinforce selected cognitive concepts (social studies, mathematics).

Determining Ability Levels

Once you have settled on your objectives for including rhythmic activities into the lesson, you must then determine the level of rhythmic abilities of the class. You will need to have a general idea of their level of competence in being able to listen and respond to various forms of musical accompaniment, ranging from the sound of a drum or the clap of your hands to piano music or a symphonic recording.

You will need to be keenly aware of the social maturity of the class. These factors greatly influence children's ability and willingness to comply with the requirements of the rhythmic activities selected. Remember to focus on the *skill* element involved in dance prior to the *social* element. Introducing dances with partners will be of limited success if the children are not yet sufficiently skillful or are socially immature.

Rhythm, Music, and Movement

Rhythm is a distinctive and essential quality inherent in all coordinated movement. For motion, sound, or design to be rhythmic, there must be a presentation of a formed pattern. Rhythm, music, and/or dance must possess three qualities in order to be rhythmic. First, there must be a regulated flow of energy that is organized in both duration and intensity. Second, the time succession of events must result in balance and harmony. Third, there must be sufficient repetition of regular groupings.

A close parallel of rhythmics exists between music and movement. Rhythmic structure in music is allied with rhythmic structure in movement and, with rare exceptions, children love both. They enjoy the melodic, rhythmic succession of beats characteristic of music and the opportunity to express this through movement.

As children listen to music, they respond to its rhythm in a variety of ways. They kick and laugh, jump and clap. They wiggle and giggle, twirl and skip. Sometimes they listen and relax or simply burst into song and dance. They begin, in their own crude way, to make their own music. They hum, sing, and play a variety of improvised instruments. The formation of a rhythm band utilizing a variety of homemade pieces of rhythmic equipment is an important first opportunity for children to organize their efforts into an expressive whole. All children have music as a part of their being, and it is the teacher's job to help them bring out their interests and explore their potential. Rhythmical music and movement should be a vital part of the school program. You may not feel particularly adept at singing or playing a piano, but you can (1) play chords on a guitar, (2) use a tape recorder, (3) use records, (4) use a small xylophone, (5) use a set of simple bells, (6) use a drum.

PRACTICAL SUGGESTIONS

Steps in Teaching a Structured Dance

The following is a list of suggested steps to follow when teaching structured dance forms:

1. Teach the new material first. This may be a new step, formation, or position that will be used in the dance.
2. Name the dance, its origin, and other interesting facts. This may be a good opportunity to integrate the particular nationality of the dance with material that is being learned in a social studies unit.
3. Listen to the music. The teacher may wish to "talk the dance through."
4. Demonstrate the dance (or its parts) using a partner or a small group of children.
5. Permit the entire class to try the whole dance or parts of it (depending on its complexity), first without the music, and then with music.
6. Unify the parts into the whole dance using the music.
7. Work on problem areas and then practice and refine the movements.

Selecting Partners

One difficulty often expressed by teachers working in the area of rhythmics is that they find it very difficult for the children to select partners. This is particularly true beginning around the third grade and continuing through the sixth grade. The following suggestions may make it easier to arrange the class when partners are necessary:

1. Have a prearranged system that does not permit random choosing of partners.
2. Switch partners often.
3. Modify activities that require boys and girls to assume a closed dance position or skater's waltz position. An elbow turn or hand clasp will do.
4. Do not require boys to take girls' parts or girls to take boys' parts.
5. If the class is all one gender, avoid using terms such as "the girls' part" or "the boys' part." Instead, designate roles by nondescriptive words and term the positions as the "lead" and the "follow" positions.

Teaching Creative Rhythms

Creative rhythmics can be an exciting and fun addition to any program. Start small, gain confidence, and gradually expand your efforts in the area. Here are some practical suggestions:

1. Keep activities relatively simple during the primary grades.
2. Stress rhythmic fundamentals first.
3. Focus on initiative rhythms at the primary level.
4. Emphasize creative rhythmics during the middle grades.
5. Remember, the middle grades are a fertile age for fostering creativity because the child is less self-centered than in the primary grades or the upper grades.
6. For the upper grades, use plenty of vigorous activities, and work in small groups.
7. Be positive and accepting.
8. Be certain to get involved with the children. This will help remove many apprehensions.
9. Use more interpretive activities and less imitative activities with older children.
10. Be sensitive to what children's interests are (sports, space, contemporary music).
11. Develop lesson themes around the children's interests as well as their needs.
12. Include plenty of rhythmic problem solving in the upper grades.
13. Permit children to devise simple group compositions.

Teaching Folk and Square Dances

The following is a list of suggestions for teaching folk and square dance in the elementary school:

1. Proceed from generalized concepts to specific movements (that is, progress from allowing children to utilize any movement form to allowing only select movements).
2. Progress from children working alone to working with partners to working in small groups.
3. Rhythm forms that are unstructured should provide an opportunity for children to develop their creative movement abilities.
4. Folk dances may be taught in conjunction with a unit in social studies or history.
5. Several short units using rhythmics as a focus for the lesson are often more beneficial than one long unit.
6. Remember, the steps used in structured dance are only combinations and variations of fundamental movements.
7. Do not get caught up in the social element of structured dance. Be more concerned with the skill element.
8. Select activities that promote skill development prior to emphasizing social development.
9. Focus on dances without partners prior to dances with partners.
10. Avoid activities that compromise one's gender identification.
11. Focus on vigorous activities, particularly during the early stages of learning folk and square dances.

SUGGESTED READING

Furst, C., and Rockefeller, M. (1981). *The effective dance program in physical education.* West Nyack, NY: Parker Publishing.

Joyce, M. (1984). *Dance technique for children.* Palo Alto, CA: Mayfield.

Joyce, M. (1980). *First steps in teaching creative dance to children.* Palo Alto, CA: Mayfield.

Minton, Sandra (Ed.) (1986, May/June) Educating for the Dance of Life. *Journal of Physical Education, Recreation and Dance* 57:24–55.

Murray, R. L. (1975). *Dance in elementary education.* New York: Harper & Row.

Peck, J. (1979). *Leap to the sun: Learning through dynamic play.* Englewood Cliffs, NJ: Prentice-Hall.

Shreeves, R. (1979). *Movement and educational dance for children.* Boston: Plays Inc.

Winters, S. (1975). *Creative rhythmic movement.* Dubuque, IA: Wm. C. Brown.

CHAPTER 36

FUNDAMENTAL RHYTHMIC ACTIVITIES

An understanding and feel for the elements of rhythm, namely underlying beat, tempo, accent, intensity, and rhythmic pattern, may be achieved effectively through movement. When teaching children about the elements of rhythm, you may use a drum, tambourine, two sticks, record palyer, or piano to supply the musical phrasing. In fact, the children may provide the musical accompaniment themselves through sounds, body percussion, or homemade rhythm instruments.

Using movement as a means of developing the elements of rhythm reinforces fundamental movement skill development and fosters an understanding and feel for rhythm. This is an important point because all coordinated, purposeful movement requires an element of rhythm, and practice in rhythmic fundamentals will reinforce the development of coordinated movement abilities. Through practice with certain fundamental movements, children begin to gain an understanding of the structural elements of rhythm and to be able to express this understanding through coordinated, purposeful movement.

This chapter contains a variety of activity ideas for developing a basic understanding of the elements of rhythm through vigorous, expressive movement. It also contains sections on helping children discover and apply rhythm.

UNDERSTANDING THE ELEMENTS OF RHYTHM

When teaching the elements of rhythm, a drum, two sticks, or any percussive instrument may be used by the teacher while the children perform. The children may even provide the rhythmic accompaniment themselves, or a record may be used. Jumping rope to music or bouncing balls to the beat of the music often aids in developing an understanding of the elements of rhythm.

Underlying Beat

Underlying beat is the steady, continuous sound in any rhythmical sequence. Listening and responding to the underlying beat can be promoted by:

1. The children responding to the beat of a drum or tambourine with appropriate locomotor or axial movements.
2. The children providing their own beat and moving to it.
3. Marching to recordings by John Philip Sousa, the Marine Band, and other march records.
4. Jumping rope to the beat of the music.
5. Bouncing balls to the beat of the music.
6. Keeping time with the beat of the music with a homemade rhythm instrument.

Rhythmic Pattern

Rhythmic pattern is a group of beats related to the underlying beat. The underlying beat may be even or uneven. Children may develop and express an understanding of rhythmic pattern by:

1. Walking, running, hopping, and jumping to an even beat.
2. Skipping, sliding, or galloping to an uneven beat.
3. Clapping rhymes.
4. Playing "echo." (page 482)
5. Playing "names in rhythm." (page 482)
6. Using wooden sticks.
7. Tinikling (page 515)

Tempo

Tempo refers to the speed of the movement, music, or rhythmic accompaniment. Children may increase their understanding of tempo by:

1. Responding to speed changes in the beat of a drum with various locomotor and stability movements.
2. Performing animal walks at various speeds.

3. Bouncing a ball at various speeds.
4. Jumping rope to different tempos.

Accent

Accent is the emphasis that is given to any one beat. The accented note is usually the first beat of every measure. Children may develop a keener awareness of accent by:

1. Listening to the music and clapping on the accented beat.
2. Moving about the room with the appropriate rhythmic pattern and changing direction or level on each accented beat.
3. Clapping on every beat except the accented one.
4. Varying the response to the accented beat with a specific locomotor, stability, or manipulative movement.

Intensity

Intensity is the quality of the music in terms of its loudness or softness. Children can develop an understanding of intensity by:

1. Altering their movements for various intensities.
2. Changing their level for different intensities.
3. Changing the amount of force they use to move for different intensities.
4. Bouncing a ball with appropriate amounts of force.
5. Dribbling a ball as softly as possible, then as loudly as possible.

DISCOVERING RHYTHM

The following compilation of fundamental rhythmic activities is designed to aid children in discovering rhythm. Most of the activities may be used from grade one through grade six, depending on the rhythmic sophistication of the group.

Objectives

Practice in activities that permit children to discover rhythm will aid them in:

1. Developing an understanding of the elements of rhythm.
2. Expressing the elements of rhythm through movement.
3. "Feeling" the beat of a musical composition.
4. Translating the beat of a musical composition into action.

Movement Experiences

IN BEAT

Formation: Any number of children seated in a semicircle, facing the teacher.

Equipment: A record player and a well-known song such as "Clap, Clap, Clap Your Hands" (primary) or "He's Got the Whole World in His Hands" (upper level). If a record is not available, the class may sing the song. A chalkboard or large piece of writing paper and either chalk or magic marker.

Procedures: Lead in with a discussion of rhythm around us and what has a steady beat (heartbeat, a clock, and so on). Then sing or listen to the song, following up by asking the children to keep the steady beat of the song by slapping their thighs. Discover the length of the song by putting a chalk mark on the board for each time the beat occurs in the song. Use a different body instrument every time the song is sung (clap, slap stomach, tap feet). Discover new body sounds (elbow, jaw). Combine these body percussion instruments into a particular sequence such as

Feet — Thighs — Clap — Snap (repeat)
  1   2   3   4

Suggestions: Use a currently popular song and let the children make up their own patterns of body percussion as well as varying the old patterns. Younger children may start with only clapping and thigh slapping until they can add the others without difficulty.

BODY TALK

Formation: Group seated in a semicircle, facing the teacher.

Equipment: A list of several easy poems or nursery rhymes, written either on a chalkboard or on a large piece of paper.

Procedures: Have children listen to the poem, song, or nursery rhyme to feel the rhythm of the composition. Decide upon appropriate body instruments to be used and what pattern or sequence they should follow. Say the poem or rhyme, letting the children put their body instruments to work.

Suggestions: The children culd make up their own short compositions and create new patterns or sequences of body percussion. Simple melodies could be used to enhance the composition. Some appropriate rhymes or sayings:

1. "April Showers Bring May Flowers."
2. "Birds of a Feather Flock Together."
3. "A Bird in the Hand is Worth Two in the Bush."
4. "All is not Gold that Glitters."
5. "The Early Bird Catches the Worm."
6. "An Apple a Day Keeps the Doctor Away."
7. "Rain, Rain Go Away, Little Johnny Wants to Play."
8. "A Stitch in Time Saves Nine."
9. "Early to Bed, Early to Rise, Makes a Man Healthy, Wealthy, and Wise."
10. "If at First You Don't Succeed, Try, Try Again."

COPYCAT

Formation: Group seated in a circle, square, or arc formation.

Equipment: A good recording suitable for the age of the children involved. Older children might enjoy a currently popular record with a lot of percussion sound; younger children might enjoy more descriptive or program music, such as a selection from Mussorgsky's *Pictures at an Exhibition.*

Procedures: One child is chosen to stand in the center and do an assortment of axial movements called for by the music. The other children "copycat," doing exactly what the leader does.

Suggestions: Older children can be encouraged to give the movement separate form or pattern, such as a basic round form (A,B,A,C,A,D,A . . . ,with A for bending, B for stretching, A for bending, C for twisting, and so on).

THE ACCENT

Formation: Class seated in a semicircle.

Equipment: A chalkboard or large piece of paper on which to write several series of numbers.

Procedures: Put the following number pattern on the board:

<u>1</u> 2 <u>3</u> 4 <u>5</u> 6 <u>7</u> 8
<u>1</u> 2 3 <u>4</u> 5 6 <u>7</u> 8
<u>1</u> 2 <u>3</u> 4 <u>5</u> 6 7 8
<u>1</u> 2 3 <u>4</u> 5 6 7 8
<u>1</u> <u>2</u> 3 4 <u>5</u> <u>6</u> 7 8
1 2 <u>3</u> 4 5 <u>6</u> 7 8

Clap only on the underlined numbers. Clap as a round in two parts, three parts, up to six parts. Use rhythm instruments (tambourine, cymbols, shakers, and so on) instead of clapping.

Suggestions: Let the children make up their own patterns. Use different body parts for each different section. Change the meter from fours to sixes.

ECHO

Formation: Groups seated in a semicircle.

Equipment: A set of rhythm instruments for each group of six to eight.

Procedures: The teacher beats out a certain rhythmic pattern, such as:

∏ = slow   a. | ∏ | |
           1   2   3   4

| = quick   b. ∏   ∏ | | ∏   ∏ | |
              1   2   3   4   5   6   7   8

The children try to duplicate the pattern by clapping their hands or with other body instruments. The teacher sings a pattern. The children respond, either with their voices or a body instrument. Rhythm instruments may be substituted.

Suggestions: Let each child have a turn to be "teacher." The silent beat could be discovered by conducting the preceding activity with imaginary beats instead of audible ones.

NAMES IN RHYTHM

Formation: Groups seated in a semicircle.

Procedure: Each child is led to discover the rhythm of his or her name by saying it and clapping it aloud. They can learn to notate this by using ∏ for long sounds and | for short sounds. Thus, *Suzie Smith* would look like this: ∏ | ∏ and *Bobby Taylor* would look like this: ∏ | ∏ ∏

Suggestions: A song could be used to enhance the name patterns. The class could sing "What Is Your Name?" and the children would have to sing back their answer by using the same tune. Several of the names can be put together and organized into a chant or a song.

CONVERSATIONS

Formation: Small groups in a circle.

Procedures: One person begins with a rhythmic pattern and tells it to the next person by using body language. The next person repeats what the first person did and adds his or her own rhythmic phrase. This can continue until each child has had a turn.

Suggestions: This is a good activity for memory, but it probably should be saved for the upper grades.

APPLYING RHYTHM

The following rhythmic activities are designed to help children apply their knowledge of rhythmic fundamentals to a variety of fun and challenging activities. Each of these activities is appropriate throughout the elementary grades, depending more on the rhythmic sophistication of the children than on their movement abilities.

Objectives

Practice in applying rhythms will aid children in the development of:

1. An understanding of the elements of rhythm.
2. The ability to express rhythm through controlled, measured movement.
3. Listening skills.
4. Fine motor control.

Movement Experiences

SOUND COMPOSITIONS

Formation: Groups of six to eight in a scatter formation.
Equipment: Rhythm instruments such as wood block, symbal with mallet, drum, rachet, and xylophone.
Procedures: Have the children decide upon the movements to use and the rhythm instruments to play for each movement, such as:

1. neutral position . . . . drum
2. lift arms . . . . xylophone (ascending)
3. lower arms . . . . xylophone (descending)
4. twisting . . . . cymbal with mallet
5. nodding head . . . . wood block

Choose children to play the various instruments and give them time to decide in what order they will play. Have the children play their instruments one at a time, and allow the class to re-

spond in the decided fashion. Now try the activity without looking at the instrument players.
Suggestions: When the activity has been mastered, have the children write their composition so it can be saved and used later. Read the symbols and perform the movements without the instruments. Create sound montages and have the children perform them. Make the sounds indicated in Figure 36.1.

TAMPERING WITH THE ELEMENTS

Formation: Class in a scatter formation.
Equipment: A large sheet of paper or chalkboard containing the words of the army wake up song, "Reveille," and an accompaniment instrument (drum, piano, and so on).
Song: I can't get 'em up, I can't get 'em up,
I can't get 'em up in the morning (repeat).
The corp'ral's worse than privates;
The sergeant's worse than corp'rals;
Lieutenant's worse than sergeants;
And the captain's worst of all!
Procedures: Chant the words in rhythm. Then sing the words with accompaniment. Once the words are learned, begin experimenting with the expressive qualities. Remember, though, to keep the beat steady.

1. Go from quiet to loud and back to quiet again.
2. Go from loud to quiet to loud again.
3. Begin slowly and accelerate to the end.
4. Begin fast and get slower.
5. For color and mood, sing in the major key (the normal way); then sing it in the minor key (variation).

Suggestions: So the children can visualize what is actually taking place, have them move their bodies to their expressions.

1. Extend arms very far apart and bring them together when the music becomes softer.
2. Place the hands together, then extend them to show a crescendo (increasing loudness).
3. Bend down in a crouching position as the song gets louder, extending upward to a standing position. Reverse the procedure when the music gets softer.

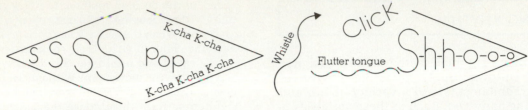

FIGURE 36.1   A sound montage.

CONDUCTING THE BEATS

Formation: Six to eight per group, seated in a semicircle.

Equipment: A conductor's baton if available, or a pencil will be fine for substitution. Record player and recording with a selection of strong, steady beat patterns (such as "Stars and Stripes Forever" $\left(\frac{2}{4}\right)$ and "Dixie $\left(\frac{4}{4}\right)$. Chalkboard with chalk or a large piece of paper and a magic marker.

Procedures: Discover the meter (how the song is counted), whether it is in groups of 2s, 3s, 4s, or 6s. Don't use unusual groups such as 5s, 7s, or 11s at first. Diagram on a chalkboard or piece of paper the conductor's beat patterns (Figure 36.2). Let the children take their preferred hand and trace the patterns in the air. Then use the nonpreferred hand to do the same. After both hands have traced the patterns, do the same exercise with a conductor's baton. Play a recording and let the children conduct with the recording.

Suggestions: Let the children conduct each other in singing and let them see the importance of keeping the beat constant. Use a variety of meters as well as a variety of songs.

PERCUSSION INSTRUMENT STORIES

Formation: Eight to ten per group in a circle formation.

Equipment: The following story, either written on a chalkboard or on a large piece of paper where the children can easily read it. Or have the story duplicated on individual sheets so each child may have a copy; rhythm instruments.

Story: One day I went for a walk. As I walked along on the sidewalk, I could hear my footsteps going . . . walk, walk, walk. Some other people came by there and their fotosteps went . . . walk, walk, walk, walk. I passed a new house. The men were fixing the roof. I could hear their hammers going . . . tap, tap, tap, tap. I heard a train coming, so I ran to the corner to watch it. My feet went . . . run, run, run. Oh, it was a big, long train. The wheels were going 'round and 'round, 'round and 'round while they went . . . clickety-clack, clickety-clack. Then I heard some bells . . . tinkle, tinkle, tinkle. Where were they coming from? I turned around, and there, coming down the street, was an ice-cream man. He was ringing the bells . . . tinkle, tinkle, tinkle. He didn't have a truck. He was riding in a wagon being pulled by a horse. The horse's hoofs went . . . clip-clop, clip-clop. The bell and the horse and the train all together sure made a lot of noise . . . clip-clop, tinkle, tinkle, and clickety-slack. It was getting very late. My watch said . . . tick, tick, tick. It was very late for my dinner. I ran all the way home. My feet went . . . run, run, run. I came to my house and knocked on the door . . . knock, knock, knock. My mother opened the door and slammed it shut . . . slam. I washed my hands and sat down to eat. Everyone was talking . . . yak, yak, yak, yak. It sounded like a broken television . . . noise!"

Procedures: Let the children choose instruments (rhythm and body) to imitate the sounds mentioned in the story (such as a triangle for the tinkling sound of the ice-cream man's wagon). Let them have fun exploring with the different sounds. They might even want to bring some sound instruments from home. Have someone read or tell the story. As a particular sound is mentioned, let that sound be heard the number

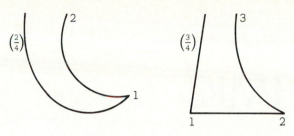

FIGURE 36.2 Diagram of conductor's beat pattern.

of times indicated. At the end, all the instruments can make the noise.

Suggestions: Have the children make up their own story. Older children particularly enjoy this. Let some of the children go through the motions of what is being sounded.

ORCHESTRATION

Formation: Entire class seated in a circle formation. Later break into smaller groups.

Equipment: Rhythm instruments, a recording of a song.

Procedures: Sing the selected simple song for the children, or have everybody listen to a song on a recording. Let them sing or chant along and learn the words and the tune. Practice all rhythms to be played before passing out the instruments. Use body instruments first, then transfer to others.

1. Drum.
2. Maracas (rattlers).
3. Balls.
4. Sand blocks.

Pass out instruments to only a few children who seem to have the idea. Let these children have "understudies" who will concentrate only on that part and will eventually get to have a turn when they catch on. Let the drum begin as an introduction. When the child has established the proper beat, gradually add the other instruments, one after the other. After the instrument players are settled in their parts, add the singers. End the composition in reverse order: singers, the last instrument to the first, and finally the drum. Let the drumbeat fade out gradually.

Suggestions: Have singers work out a body percussion ensemble to join in with the rhythm instrument ensemble. Vary the rhythm patterns as well as the instruments. Make up a dance to go along with the chant or song.

ADDITIONAL RESOURCES

Classroom Rhythms. Educational Record Sales, 157 Chambers Street, New York, NY 10007 (B1037).

Exploring the Rhythm Instruments. Educational Record Sales, 157 Chambers Street, New York, NY 10007 (B1032).

Interpretive Rhythms. Educational Record Sales, 157 Chambers Street, New York, NY 10007 (B1050).

Introducing the Rhythm Instruments. Educational Record Sales, 157 Chambers Street, New York, NY 10007 (B1020).

Kindergarten Sing-A-Long. Educational Record Sales, 157 Chambers Street, New York, NY 10007 (B1146).

Marches. Educational Activities, Box 392, Freeport, NY, 11520 (Hyp-B11).

Our First Rhythm Band, vols. 1 and 2. Educational Record Sales, 157 Chambers Street, New York, NY 10007 (B1066, B1075).

Rhythm from the Land of Make-Believe. Educational Record Sales, 157 Chambers Street, New York, NY 10007 (B1055).

CHAPTER 37

SINGING RHYTHMIC ACTIVITIES

Children need and enjoy singing rhythms. Singing rhythms are made up of actions that the children do as they sing or chant a particular song or repeat a particular rhyme. There may be a great deal of variation in the action patterns used in singing rhythms. It will depend on how the children follow and interpret the actions suggested by the auditory cues, their willingness to express themselves freely, and the teaching cues used.

The incorporation of action patterns with various singing rhythms will do much to enhance auditory rhythmic abilities. Developing and reinforcing an internal sensitivity to tempo, accent, intensity, and rhythmic pattern will be byproducts of successful participation in singing rhythmic activities requiring a movement response.

The importance of developing the ability to express internally perceived rhythm motorically cannot be overemphasized. It is through the development of temporal awareness that children establish a meaningful and effective time structure. To see why the ability to interpret auditory rhythmic patterns is important, we need only look at how children first learn the alphabet or a new song. The sing-song rhythmic cadence used to recite the alphabet or song seems to make it easier to recall and retain. As adults, we find it much easier to recall the words to an old, longfogotten song than those uttered by your instructor just yesterday. For example, listening to the melody of an old Beatles tune ("She Loves You," "I Want to Hold Your Hand") will often trigger recollection of the words that accompany the tune. This would be considerably more difficult if our auditory rhythmic abilities were not adequately developed and refined. Hence, children's practice of and participation in auditory rhythmic activities are important. Incorporation of movement serves as a means of making these experiences more enjoyable and increasing the number of sensory modalities involved.

The following pages present numerous examples of *finger plays, rhymes and poems,* and *singing dances* that may be effectively used with children. Finger plays are generally most appropriate for preschool and primary-grade children, along with most nursery rhymes. Singing dances are generally effective from kindergarten through the second grade.

FINGER PLAYS

Finger plays are generally the first verses committed to memory by children. They are usually short and easy to learn. Many of them have been handed down from generation to generation. The small muscles of the hands and fingers are less well developed in children than their other muscles, so practice in finger plays does much to aid in increasing finger dexterity. They also provide children with an opportunity to begin using movement to interpret specified rhythmical verses. Table 37.1 lists the finger plays contained in this chapter in a recommended progression from simple to more complex.

Objectives

Practice in finger rhythms will contribute to children's:

1. Auditory rhythmic abilities.
2. Fine motor dexterity.
3. Auditory memory abilities.

TABLE 37.1   Selected Finger Plays

Recommended Progression for Children at Beginning Level	Page
Here Is the Beehive	487
This Little Clown	487
I'm a Little Teapot	487
Over the Hills	488
Row, Row, Row	488
Dig a Little Hole	488
Ten Fingers	488
Little Fish	488
Bunny	488
If I Were a Bird—1	488
If I Were a Bird—2	489
Two Little	489
Flowers	489
Left and Right	489

4. Ability to combine rhythmical, auditory, and movement sequences into a coordinated whole.
5. Ability to utilize movement to interpret specified rhythmical sequences.

Movement Experiences

HERE IS THE BEEHIVE

Here is the beehive.
(fold hands)*
But where are the bees?
(puzzled look)
Hiding inside, where nobody sees.
(peek inside)
They're coming out now. They're all alive.
(show surprise)
One, two, three, four, five.
(raise fingers one at a time)
Bzzzzzzzzzzzzzzzzzzzz.

THIS LITTLE CLOWN

This little clown is fat and gay.
(hold up thumb)
This little clown does tricks all day.
(hold up forefinger)
This little clown is tall and strong.
(hold up middle finger)
This little clown sings a funny song.
(hold up ring finger)
This little clown is wee and small.
(hold up little finger)
But he can do anything at all.

I'M A LITTLE TEAPOT

I'm a little teapot, short and stout.
Here is my handle.
(place hand on waist, forming handle)
Here is my spout.
(form spout with the other arm)

*The words in parentheses indicate the suggested action pattern.

When I get all steamed up, then I shout:
(hiss)
Tip me over and pour me out.
(pour the "tea" out the "spout")

OVER THE HILLS

Over the hills and far away
(pounding motion of hands)
We skip and run and laugh and play.
(clap hands)
Smell the flowers and fish the streams,
(sniff a flower—cast a line)
Lie in the sunshine and dream sweet dreams.
(sleep, cheek on hand)

ROW, ROW, ROW

Row, row, row your boat
(rowing motion with both hands)
Gently down the stream.
(forward waving motion, one hand)
Merrily, merrily, merrily, merrily,
(clap hands in rhythm)
Life is but a dream.
(sleep)

DIG A LITTLE HOLE

Dig a little hole, (dig)
Plant a little seed,
(drop seed)
Pour a little water,
(pour)
Pull a little weed.
(pull up and throw away)
Chase a little bug,
(chasing motion with hands)
Heigh-ho, there he goes!
(shade eyes)
Give a little sunshine,
(cup hands, lift to the sun)
Grow a little rose.
(small flower, eyes closed, smiling)

TEN FINGERS

I have ten little fingers;
(extend the ten fingers)
They all belong to me.
I can make them do things;
Would you like to see?
I can open them up wide,
(spread fingers apart)
Shut them up tight,
(clench fists)
Put them out of sight,
(place hands behind back)
Jump them up high,
(raise hands)
Jump them down low,
(lower hands)
Fold them quietly, and sit
(fold them in lap)
Just so!

LITTLE FISH

I hold my fingers like a fish,
(hold hands back-to-back with fingers spread, wave hands to the side as in swimming, continue to and fro)
and wave them as I go,
Through the water with a swish,
So gaily to and fro.

BUNNY

Hippity, hoppety, hop, hop, hop,
(raise hands to side of head)
Here comes a little bunny,
(children hop on both feet)
One ear is down, one ear is up,
(press fingers of one hand against head)
Oh, doesn't he look funny?

IF I WERE A BIRD—1

If I were a bird, I'd sing a song
(entwine the two thumbs, so that palms of the hands are facing inward)

And fly about the whole day long,
(flutter the hands)
And when the night came, go to rest
(fold hands and go to sleep)
Up in my cozy little nest.

IF I WERE A BIRD—2

If I were a bird, I'd sing a song,
(raise both arms, waving them as a bird flying)
And fly about the whole day long.
And when the night came, go to rest,
(place both hands together on one side of face, like sleeping)
Up in my cozy little nest.
Oh, look and see out—airplanes
(raise both arms in horizontal positions, as an airplane)
Away up in the sky.
Watch us gliding through the air,
(fly about, as an airplane)
This is how we fly.

TWO LITTLE

Two little eyes that open and close,
(children point to parts of the body indicated by the verses)
Two little ears and one little nose,
Two little lips and one little chin,
Two little cheeks with the rose shut in,
Two little elbows so dimpled and sweet,
Two little shoes on two little feet.
Two little shoulders so chubby and strong,
Two little legs, running all day long.

FLOWERS

See the blue and yellow blossoms,
(hold both hands above the head with fingers touching)
In the flower bed.
The daisy spreads its petals wide,
(spread hands apart)
The tulip bows its head.
(drop one hand)

LEFT AND RIGHT

This is my right hand, raise it up high,
(raise right hand high)
This is my left hand, I'll touch the sky.
(raise left hand high)
Right hand, left hand, whirl them 'round.
(whirl hands before you)
Left hand, right hand, pound, pound, pound.
(pound left fist with right)
This is my right foot, tap, tap, tap.
(tap right foot three times)
This is my left foot, pat, pat, pat,
(tap left foot three times)
Right foot, left foot, run, run, run,
(run in place)
Right foot, left foot, jump for fun.
(lift right foot, and down; lift left foot, and down; jump up and down)

RHYMES AND POEMS

There are numrous rhymes and poems that have been passed from generation to generation, with which we are all familiar. The following rhymes and poems may be less familiar, but they are equally suitable for adding action sequences. Rhymes are particularly enjoyed by preschool and primary-grade children. Table 37.2 lists a suggested progression of activities from simple to more complex.

Objectives

Practice in rhymes and poems that incorporate action sequences will contribute to children's:

1. Auditory rhythmic abilities.
2. Listening skills.
3. Auditory memory abilities.
4. Ability to combine rhythmical auditory sequences effectively with coordinated action patterns.
5. Ability to utilize movement to interpret specific rhythmical sequence.

TABLE 37.2 Selected Rhymes and Poems

| Rhymes or Poems | Recommended Progression for Children | | Page |
	Beginning Level	Intermediate Level	
My Hands	X		490
The Noble Duke of York	X		490
Choo-Choo	X		490
Windy Weather	X		490
Funny Clown	X		490
My Little Puppy	X		491
How Creatures Move	X		491
Jack-in-the-Box	X		491
Stormy Days	X		491
Follow-the-Leader Rhymes		X	491
Drawing Numerals in Space		X	491
Head, Shoulders, Baby		X	492

Movement Experiences

MY HANDS

I raise my hands up high,
Now on the floor they lie.
Now high, now low,
Now reach up to the sky.
I spread my hands out wide,
Now behind my back they hide.
Now wide, now hide,
Now I put them at my side.
I give my head a shake, shake, shake,
Now not a move I make.
Now shake, shake, shake,
Not a move I make.
Now my whole self I shake.

THE NOBLE DUKE OF YORK

The noble Duke of York,
He had ten thousand men.
He marched them up a hill,
And marched them down again.
So when you're up, you're up,
And when you're down, you're down.

And when you're only halfway up,
You're neither up nor down,
   (children stand and sit in reponse to the words up *and* down*)*

CHOO-CHOO

"Choo-choo" we hear the train.
"Choo-choo" it goes again.
It pulls a heavy load all day.
   (pull self while sliding; use arm and foot movements)

WINDY WEATHER

Like a leaf or a feather
In the windy, windy weather,
We will whirl around
And twirl around
And all sink down together.

FUNNY CLOWN

I am a funny clown.
I move like a funny clown.
I jump, I skip and run.
I stop and have a lot of fun.

MY LITTLE PUPPY

My little puppy's name is Rags,
He eats so much that his tummy sags.
His ears flip-flop, his tail wig-wags,
And when he walks, he zigs and zags.

HOW CREATURES MOVE

The lion walks on padded paws,
The squirrel leaps from limb to limb,
While flies can crawl straight up a wall,
And seals can dive and swim.
The worm, he wiggles all around,
The monkey swings by his tail,
And birds may hop upon the ground
Or spread their wings and sail.
But boys and girls have much more fun;
They leap and dance and walk and run.

JACK-IN-THE-BOX

Jack-in-the-box,
All shut up tight,
Not a breath of air,
Not a peep of light,
How tired he must be,
All in a heap.
I'll open the box
And up he'll leap.

STORMY DAYS

On stormy days
When the wind is high
Tall trees are brooms
Sweeping the sky.

They swish their branches
In buckets of rain
And swish and sweep it
Blue again.

FOLLOW-THE-LEADER RHYMES

Who feels happy? Who feels gay?
All who do clap your hands this way.
Who feels happy? Who feels gay?
All who do tap your feet this way.
Who feels happy? Who feels gay?
All who do skip around this way.
    (Add other activities as desired.)
I'll touch my hair, my eyes,
I'll sit up straight, then I'll rise,
I'll touch my ears, my nose, my chin,
Then quietly I'll sit down again.
The elephant walks just so,
Swaying to and fro—
He lifts up his trunk to the trees,
Then slowly gets down on his knees
Tip-toe, tip-toe, little feet,
Tip-toe, tip-toe, little feet,
Now fast, now slow,
Now very softly—
Tip-toe, tip-toe, little feet.
Tip-toe, tip-toe, little feet.
    (Add other activities as desired.)
Shall we go for a walk today?
A walk today, a walk today?
    (Repeat, using "pick flowers, smell flowers":
    Shall we pick flowers today, etc.
    Shall we smell flowers today, etc.)
    (Use any other ideas to incorporate bending, jump-
    ing, and so on into the above verses.)

DRAWING NUMERALS IN SPACE

A line straight down and that is all
    (repeat twice)
To make the numeral 1.
Around and down and to the right
    (repeat twice)
To make the numeral 2.
Curve around and curve again. (3)
Down, across, than all the way down. (4)
Down, curve around, a line at the top. (5)
Curve down and all the way around. (6)
A line across and then slant down. (7)
Curve around and then back up. (8)
Curve around and then straight down. (9)
A straight line down and circle around. (10)
    (Have the children sit or stand and perform the ac-
    tions of the words as they are sung through.)

HEAD, SHOULDERS, BABY

Head, shoulders, baby, 1, 2, 3.
  (repeat)
Head, shoulders, head, shoulders, head, shoulders,
baby, 1, 2, 3.
Chest, stomach, baby, 1, 2, 3.
  (repeat)
Chest, stomach, chest, stomach, chest, stomach,
baby, 1, 2, 3.
  (Repeat, using: Knees, ankles. Ankles, knees. Stomach, chest. Shoulders, head.)

SINGING DANCES

A singing dance is one in which the children sing verses to a song that provides them cues on how to move. The children will first need to learn the words to the song. If musical accompaniment is used, they should listen to it until they have a general grasp of the words. The action phase of the activity should be added last. Table 37.3 lists a suggested progression of activities from simple to more complex.

Movement Experiences

TABLE 37.3 Selected Singing Dances

Recommended Progression for Children at Beginning Level	Page
Mulberry Bush	492
Ten Little Jingle Bells	493
Lobby Loo	493
Blue Bird	494
Ten Little Indians	494
Farmer in the Dell	494
How Do You Do, My Partner?	495
Round and Round the Village	495
I See You	496
A-Hunting We Will Go	496
Did You Ever See a Lassie?	496
Jolly Is the Miller	497

Objectives

Practice in singing dance activities will aid children in the development of:

1. Auditory memory skills.
2. Listening skills.
3. Auditory rhythmic abilities.
4. Fundamental movement abilities.

MULBERRY BUSH

Formation: Single circle facing in with one child at the center of the circle. Any number may participate.
Song: Here we go round the mulberry bush, the mulberry bush, the mulberry bush,
Here we go round the mulberry bush so early in the morning.
This is the way we wash our clothes, we wash our clothes, we wash our clothes,
This is the way we wash our clothes, so early in the morning.
  (Continue with:)
This is the way we hang our clothes.
This is the way we iron our clothes.
This is the way we fold our clothes.
This is the way we rake the leaves.
This is the way we sweep the floor.
Procedures: Children may form a circle; one child, designated as the mulberry bush, stands in the center. Let them skip around the circle holding hands as they sing the chorus and stopping to perform the action of the verses.
Suggestions: Make up other words to the songs, such as when doing a circus unit. (The words might be ''This is the way the elephant walks,'' ''This is the way the seals clap,'' and so on.)

TEN LITTLE JINGLE BELLS

Formation: Double row of 10 children each row behind the leader
               (horse).
Song: Ten little jingle bells hung in a row,
               Ten little jingle bells helped the horse go.
               Merrily, merrily over the snow,
               Merrily, merrily sleighing we go.

               One little jingle bell fell in the snow
               Nine little jingle bells helped the horse go.
               Merrily, merrily over the snow,
               Merrily, merrily sleighing we go.

                  (Continue subtracting bells until one is left.)
               One little jingle bell fell in the snow.
                  (sing slowly)
               No little jingle bells help the horse go.
               Slowly, so slowly the bells are all gone.
               We'll get some new ones and put them right on.
Procedures: One child may be the horse and 10 children the jingle bells in a double row behind the horse.
               One jingle bell drops off during each verse until only the horse is left. They should carry
               sleigh or jingle bells and ring them as they move to the rhythm.
Suggestions: Have two or three teams of horses so that full participation of all class members is going on.

LOBBY LOO

Formation: Single circle, all facing center with hands joined. Any number may participate.
Song: Here we dance lobby loo,
               Here we dance lobby light,
               Here we dance looby loo,
               All on a Saturday night.

               1. I put my right hand in,
                  I take my right hand out,
                  I give my right hand a shake, shake, shake,
                  And turn myself about.
               2. I put my left hand in, etc. . . .
               3. I put my right foot in, etc. . . .
               4. I put my left foot in, etc. . . .
               5. I put my head way in, etc. . . .
               6. I put my whole self in, etc. . . .

Procedures: On the verse part of the dance, the children stand still, facing the center, and follow the
               directions of the words. On the words *and turn myself about,* they make a complete turn in
               place and get ready to skip around the circle. On the last verse, the children jump forward
               and then backward, shaking themselves vigorously, and then turning about.
Suggestions: This is an excellent activity to help children with left–right concepts. Be sure to use it as
               such.

BLUE BIRD

Formation: Single circle facing inward, with 8 to 10 per circle.
Song: Blue bird, blue bird, in and out my windows,
                Blue bird, blue bird, in and out my windows,
                Oh! Johnny, I am tired.
                Take a boy (girl) and tap him (her) on the shoulders.
                   (Repeat two more times.)
Procedures: The boys and girls form a circle facing inward, with hands joined and raised to form arches. One child (the blue bird) stands outside the circle. Sing the words of the song as the bird goes in and out of the arches. The child who has been tapped becomes the new bluebird, while the former one takes the vacant place in the circle. Repeat until everyone has been the blue bird.
                   (You may need more than one circle.)
Suggestions: Let the children form a chain of blue birds until all of the children become birds and there are no windows left.

TEN LITTLE INDIANS

Formation: Single circle facing inward, with 8 to 10 per group.
Song: First verse: 1 little, 2 little, 3 little Indians,
                            4 little, 5 little, 6 little Indians,
                            7 little, 8 little, 9 little Indians,
                            10 little Indian boys (girls).
               Second verse: 10 little, 9 little, 8 little Indians,
                            7 little, 6 little, 5 little Indians,
                            4 little, 3 little, 2 little Indians,
                            1 little Indian boy (girl).
Procedures: The children stand in a circle facing the center. Each child is given a number from 1 to 10. As the first verse is sung, the children squat when their number is called. During the second verse, they stand when their number is called. The song is repeated with the children hopping and whopping, Indian fashion, counterclockwise during the first verse and clockwise during the second verse.

FARMER IN THE DELL

Formation: Single circle facing inward, with 8 per circle.
Song: First verse: The farmer in the dell,
                            The farmer in the dell,
                            Heigh-ho the dairy, oh,
                            The farmer in the dell.
               Second verse: The farmer takes a wife—
                            (Repeat first verse except for The farmer in the dell.*)*
               Third verse: The wife takes a child—
               Fourth verse: The child takes a nurse—
               Fifth verse: The nurse takes a cat—

Sixth verse: The cat takes a mouse—
Seventh verse: The mouse takes the cheese—
Eighth verse: The cheese stands alone—

Procedures: The children form a circle holding hands, with one child (the farmer) in the center of the circle. The children walk or skip counterclockwise as they sing the song. As they sing the second verse, the farmer chooses somebody to be his wife, and during the singing of the third verse, the wife chooses somebody to be her child. Each time a new verse is sung, a child is chosen to play the role of the character about whom they are singing. The last child selected always chooses the next child. When the children finish the last verse, the "cheese" chases the children about the room. The child tagged becomes the farmer for the next time the dance is performed.

HOW DO YOU DO, MY PARTNER?

Formation: Single circle facing inward. Any number may participate.
Song: How do you do, my partner?
                 How do you do today?
                 Will you dance in a circle?
                 I will show you the way.

                 Chorus: Tra-la-la-la-la-la.
Record: Educational Record Sales (ERS), "Folk Dance Fundamentals." (See page 523 for address.)
Procedures: One child is stationed in the middle of the circle. He faces a member of the circle and shakes hands while the children sing the song. As the song ends, the two skip around the circle as everyone sings, "Tra-la-la-la-la-la." When the chorus ends, the two face new partners and the song begins again. Continue this procedure until all children are dancing.

ROUND AND ROUND THE VILLAGE

Formation: Single circle facing inward with one child on the outside. Ten children per circle.
Song: Chorus: Go round and round the village,
                         Go round and round the village,
                         Go round and round the village,
                         As we have done before.

                 First verse: Go in and out the windows—

                 Second verse: Now stand and face your partner—

                 Third verse: Now follow me to London—
Record: ERS, "Folk Dance Fundamentals." (See page 523 for address.)
Procedures: The children stand in a circle with hands joined, and one child stands outside the circle. The children walk counterclockwise, singing the chorus (the child outside the circle skips clockwise). After the chorus, the children stop and raise their arms to make "windows" while singing the first verse. The child on the outside of the circle goes in and out of the windows. As the circle sings the second verse, the child selects a partner. The partners skip around on the outside of the circle while the other children sing the third verse. Repeat this procedure until all children have a partner.

I SEE YOU

Formation: Double circles facing inward, one behind the other. Any number may participate.

Song: First verse: I see you, I see you,
  Tra-la, la-la, la.
  I see you, I see you,
  Tra-la, la-la, la.

  Second verse: You see me and I'll see you,
  You swing me and I'll swing you,
  You see me and I'll see you,
  You swing me and I'll swing you.

Record: ERS, "Fold Dance Fundamentals." (See page 523 for address.)

Procedures: The children form a circle with the girls standing behind the boys with their hands on the boys' shoulders. They then proceed to play "peek-a-boo" over the boys' shoulders on the first verse in tempo with the verse on each "see" and each "tra-la," "la-la," and "la." On the second verse, the boys face their partners, hook elbows, and skip around in a circle. The boys then change places with their partners and play "peek-a-boo" as the song begins again.

A-HUNTING WE WILL GO

Formation: Two parallel lines facing one another. Six to eight per line.

Song: A-hunting we will go,
A-hunting we will go,
We'll catch a fox and put him in a box
And then we'll let him go.

Procedures: The head couple holds hands and slides down the line with eight fast steps and back again as the song is sung the first time. As the song is repeated, they lead a "parade" of all of the couples skipping in a circular pattern to the foot of the set. The head couple then forms an arch while the other children take the hand of the person across from them and walk through the arch and back to their places. The entire verse is sung while doing this. The dance is repeated until all have had an opportunity to be the head couple.

DID YOU EVER SEE A LASSIE?

Formation: Single circle facing inward, with eight to ten per circle.

Song: Chorus: Did you ever see a Lassie, a Lassie, a Lassie,
  Did you ever see a Lassie go this way and that?
  Go this way and that way, go this way and that way;
  Did you ever see a Lassie go this way and that?

Procedures: The children join hands and form a circle. One child is placed in the center of the circel and is designated to be a Lassie (or Laddie). The other children are also given character names such as farmer, soldier, fireman, cowboy, and so on. When the verse is sung, the child in the center performs various movements to the rhythm of the song and the children in the circle try to imitate these movements. Each time the verse is sung, another name is substituted for Lassie and the procedure is repeated.

JOLLY IS THE MILLER

Formation: Double circle facing counterclockwise. Any number may participate.
Song: Oh, jolly is the miller who lives by the mill.
The wheel turns round with a right good will.
One hand in the hopper and the other in the sack,
The girl steps forward and the boy steps back.
Procedures: The children form a double circle facing counterclockwise and hold their partner's hand. One child is placed in the center of the inner circle (the miller). The children move counterclockwise as they sing the song. They change partners on the words *the girl steps forward* ... At this time the "miller" attempts to get a partner and the child left without a partner becomes the "miller."

ADDITIONAL RESOURCES

Action Songs and Sounds. Bridges, 310 W. Jefferson, Dallas, TX 75208 (HYP508)

Finger Play. Educational Record Sales, 157 Chambers Street, New York, NY 10007 (B1043, B1046).

Fun Dances for Children. Kimbo Records, Box 477, Long Branch, NJ 07740 (KEA1134).

Holiday Songs and Rhythms. Educational Activities, Inc., Box 392, Freeport, NY 11520 (AR538).

Let's Sing and Act Together. Educational Record Sales, 157 Chambers Street, New York, NY 10007 (B1057).

Nursery Rhymes for Dramatic Play. Educational Record Sales, 157 Chambers Street, New York, NY 10007 (B1051).

Primary Musical Games. Education Activities, Inc., Box 392, Freeport, NY 11520.

Rhythmic Activity Songs for Primary Grades. Bridges, 310 W. Jefferson, Dallas, TX 75208 (LP1055, LP1066, LP1077, LP1088).

Simplified Folk Songs. Educational Activities, Inc., Box 392, Freeport, NY 11520 (AR518).

Singing Action Games. Bridges, 310 W. Jefferson, Dallas, TX 75208 (HYP507).

Singing Games Through Folk Dancing. Educational Record Sales (ERS), 157 Chambers Street, New York, NY 10007.

We Move to Poetry. Bridges, 310 W. Jefferson, Dallas, TX 75208.

Won't You Be My Friend. Bridges, 310 W. Jefferson, Dallas, TX 75208 (AR544).

CHAPTER 38

CREATIVE RHYTHMIC ACTIVITIES

Creativity is often talked about, but what is it? When one creates something external, symbols or objects are manipulated in order to produce *unusual* events *uncommon* to the individual and/or environment. To create means to bring into existence, to make something out of a word or an idea for the first time, or to produce along new or unconventional lines. Generally speaking, we have not been trained to use our imagination to apply knowledge we already have and to extend it into creative behavior. Creativity hinges on the need for freedom to explore and experiment. It relies on a flexible schedule that permits time to explore, stand back and evaluate the results, and then continue on with the idea or project. Rhythm and dance constitute one avenue for enhancing creative expression.

Creative rhythmic activities require flexibility on the part of the teacher and classroom techniques oriented toward creativity. The teacher must not leave creativity to chance, but must (1) encourage curiosity, (2) ask questions that require thought, (3) reorganize original creative behavior, (4) be respectful of questions and unusual ideas (show children that their ideas have value), (5) provide opportunities for learning in creative ways, and (6) show a genuine interest in each child's efforts.

As humans, we have the unique capacity to think and act creatively—an ability that makes it possible to reach out for the unknown. All persons have the potential capacity to create, although some seem to have more innate ability than others. Highly creative individuals tend to possess characteristics such as openness to new experiences, aesthetic sensitivity, and imagination. However, all children should be encouraged to develop their creative abilities to the fullest. In order to develop, they must have opportunities to be creative and thus expand their insight, skill, and confidence.

Dance as an art form is concerned with creativity. Even the beginner should be encouraged to make imaginative responses and to self-direct activity. Creative responses can be attained through the process of exploration and improvisation, as well as through dance-making opportunities that encourage children to think, feel, imagine, and create. Creative growth depends on experience and needs time to develop. Children must have the opportunity to progress from the simple to the complex, and the demands of each creative rhythmic endeavor must be related to the developmental level of the individual.

Children are born with a natural drive for movement. They gradually expand their horizons through the cultivation of their inner impulses and urges for movement. They learn to think, act, and create as they move. Creative rhythm is one avenue through which these desirable abilities can be developed and expanded in children. Music and movement ideas that are used in creative rhythms must relate to the child's world in order to initiate spontaneity. The teacher serves as an essential catalyst in helping children develop and expand their powers of creativity and self-expression. You will need to take the time to carefully plan and execute lessons that foster creativity.

CREATIVE RHYTHMIC EXPRESSION

Creative rhythmic expression is a form of movement that permits one to express ideas, feelings, and moods through some form of accompaniment. It is a creative extension of rhythmic fundamentals into new and individually unique ways of expressing oneself rhythmically. Dances may be created from *ideas, songs, words,* and *music.* With children in the regular physical education program, creative rhythmics generally take three forms: *dance making; imitative rhythms,* in which various animate and inanimate objects are imitated; or *interpretive rhythms* that permit acting out of an idea or an event. Table 38.1 provides a list of all three types and a recommended progression of activities.

Ideas and Creative Rhythms

Children in the primary grades enjoy making up dances "about" something. They project themselves into both animate and inanimate things with little difficulty. They respond readily to "Let's pretend," or "Let's be . . . " or "Let's move like . . . "

In selecting simple ideas, you may have the children move like "a new toy," "the snow that fell this morning," and so on. The children will have many ideas. It is important to challenge their imaginations. You may point out contrasts in movement, high and low, big and little, forward and backward.

Children in the upper elementary grades, unlike those in the primary grades, who may pretend to be the objects themselves, relate to objects in one way or another. For example, younger children are the balls that bounce; older children manipulate the ball.

Accompaniment for dances approached from ideas may be improvised. The piano used as a percussion instrument or homemade rhythmic instruments are also suitable.

Songs and Creative Rhythms

Dances made from songs are probably the easiest. "Movement" songs, those in which one or two movements express an idea, are suitable for primary children, while some songs for primary children can be interpreted in more than one way. Older children enjoy using folk songs, rounds, and currently popular songs for creative rhythmic dance making.

Words, Music, and Creative Rhythms

Children like to make up dances using nursery rhymes, nonsense words, chants, and poems. When poetry is used, it is generally best to begin with narrative poetry and then progress to lyric poetry, in which feelings are expressed. Children like to use names of classmates for simple dance making, clapping out the rhythm and then fitting appropriate movement to the rhythmic pattern. The procedure used for including music

TABLE 38.1   Selected Creative Rhythmic Activities

Creative Rhythmic Activity	Suggested Progression for Children			
	Beginning Level	Intermediate Level	Advanced Level	Page
Imitative Rhythms				500
Imitating Living Creatures	X			501
Imitating Things in Nature	X			501
Imitating Objects	X			502
Imitating Events	X			502
Interpretive Rhythms				502
Interpreting Action Words		X		503
Interpreting Feelings and Moods		X		503
Interpreting Art		X		503
Interpreting Action Sequences		X		503
Interpreting Pendular Movements		X		504
Interpreting Special Holidays		X		504
Dance Making				504
Name Dances			X	505
Rhyme Dances			X	505
Slogan Dances			X	505
Menu Dances			X	505

involves selecting the piece of music; listening carefully to determine the quality of movement, tempo, and accent; improvising and experimenting with movement; and listening to the music more critically for its structure. Creative rhythmic expression to words and to music is fun and should be made progressively more challenging as the children become more skilled.

Children like to make dances by combining locomotor and nonlocomotor movements until a pleasing form is obtained. For younger children, this exploration usually results in "being" something. The child dances what the music "tells" him to dance. Older children enjoy movement experimentation. They respond wholeheartedly to a problem in movement where they can invent movements or manipulative objects to achieve a goal.

IMITATIVE RHYTHMS

Through imitative rhythms the children express themselves by trying to "be something." The teacher should, however, be careful to see to it that the children realize the movement potential of their own bodies before they are introduced to imagery as a part of the lesson. In their own minds the children take on the identity of what they are imitating. They act out this identity with expressive movements. They are encouraged to explore and express themselves in various original movements. There are three general approaches to imitative rhythms. In the first, the teacher begins with a rhythm and lets the children decide what each one would like to be, based on the characteristics of the rhythm. This approach is one of "What does this rhythm make you think of?"

In the second method, the teacher selects a piece of music and has the children make a choice of what they would select to imitate. All of the children initiate the same thing. Each child creates the selection as he or she wishes. If the choice were a giant, each child would interpret her own individual concept of a giant.

The third approach begins with a selection for imitation and then choosing an appropriate rhythm for movement. Listening to the musical accompaniment is important in all three approaches, as the children must "feel" the character of the music. The music (ranging from clapping or a drumbeat to piano music or a recording) must be appropriate for the identity to be assumed in order to be effective; otherwise, the movement becomes artificial. The movements of the children should be in time with the music and should reflect a basic understanding of the elements of rhythm.

Objectives

Practice in creative imitative rhythmic activities with children will contribute to their ability:

1. To think of and act out creative movement sequences in response to rhythmic accompaniment.
2. To imitate the function of animate and inanimate objects through creative rhythmical movement.
3. To move efficiently through space in a controlled, rhythmical manner.
4. To think and act creatively.

Movement Experiences

IMITATING LIVING CREATURES

There are many living creatures that children enjoy imitating. These imitations may be done to the beat of a drum, piano, record, or without any form of accompaniment.

Animals:

Elephant	Snake	Fish
Giraffe	Rabbit	Bird
Bear	Kangaroo	Kitten
Lion	Puppy	
Seal	Duck	

People:

Firefighter	Soldier	Cowpoke
Letter carrier	Airplane pilot	Carpenter
Doctor	Mountain climber	
Sailor	Ballet dancer	

Imaginary people and animals:

Martian	Giant	Troll
Goblin	Fairy	Monster
Elf	Pixie	
Dwarf	Dragon	

IMITATING THINGS IN NATURE

Young children are rapidly expanding their knowledge and understanding of the world of nature. There are numerous things in nature that they will enjoy imitating, and through these experiences, they will increase their knowledge and nature vocabulary.

Weather conditions:

Wind	Hail	Storm
Rain	Hurricane	Sun
Snow	Tornado	
Sleet	Clouds	

Climatic conditions:

Hot	Cool	Autumn
Cold	Sunny	Winter
Warm	Summer	Spring

Miscellaneous:

Smoke	Sun	Mineral
Fire	Star	Soil
Wave	Flower	
Moon	Water	

IMITATING OBJECTS

There are several play objects and machines that children enjoy imitating.

Play objects:

Swing	Ball	"Slinky"
Slide	Pull toy	Silly putty
Seesaw	Yo-yo	
Merry-go-round	Frisbee	

Modes of transportation:

Rowboat	Car	Bicycle
Snowmobile	Canoe	Motorcycle
Truck	Rocket	Train

Machines:

Elevator	Crane	Pneumatic drill
Tractor	Cement mixer	Lawn mower
Bulldozer	Old-fashioned coffee grinder	Record player

IMITATING EVENTS

As children's world expands, so does their exposure to special events outside the home. The following is a list of suggested activities and events that may be imitated at strategic times during the year.

The circus:

Clown	High-wire walker	Barker
Acrobat	Trapeze artist	Ringmaster
Juggler	Lion tamer	
Trained animal	Marching band member	

Sporting events (in slow motion, imitate the movements found in the following athletic events):

Soccer	Volleyball	Tennis
Football	Track and field events	Bowling
Baseball	Swimming and diving	Ice hockey
Basketball	Fencing	

INTERPRETATIVE RHYTHMS

Interpretative rhythms are the second form of creative dance. In interpretative rhythms, the children act out an idea, a familiar event, or an ordinary procedure. They may also express feelings, emotions, and moods through movement. The quality and direction of the interpretative movements depend on the mood, intelligence, and personal feelings of the children. In interpretative movement, the teacher creates the atmosphere for the children to express themselves. There are three general approaches. In the first, the teacher begins with an idea, or a story. As the story progresses, suitable rhythmic background is used. A recording, piano selection, percussion instrument, or even a rhythm band can be used. The teacher often provides the verbal background and directions for the drama, but the story can unfold without this.

The second approach begins with a piece of music, generally a recording, and develops an idea to fit the music. The piece of music selected should have sufficient changes in tempo and pattern to provide different kinds and qualities of background. A general idea or plan of action can be selected and fitted to the music. An idea such as "going to the fair" may be selected and an adaptable recording chosen.

In the third approach, the children express moods or feelings. A piece of music may be played and the children may act out how the music makes them feel. An alternative method is simply to give cue words that denote specific moods (happy, sad, and so on) and have the children express these words through movement.

Objectives

Practice in creative interpretative rhythmic activities with children will contribute to their ability

1. To think through and act out creative movement sequences in response to rhythmic accompaniment.
2. To interpret moods, feelings, and ideas and to express them through creative, rhythmic moves.
3. To solve rhythmic problems creatively through expressive movement.
4. To move efficiently through space in a coordinated rhythm.
5. To think and act creatively.
6. To "feel" auditory and visual symbols and to be able to express these feelings through movement.

Movement Experiences

INTERPRETING ACTION WORDS

Numerous verbs provide opportunities for creative movement. Try several during the first few minutes of the lesson. The following represent only a few of the numerous possibilities:

Bang	Blow	Dart
Crack	Bump	Zoom
Spin	Tingle	Bop
Pop	Grab	Zip
Twinkle	Grumble	Boom
Glow	Punch	Pluck
Bubble	Float	

INTERPRETING FEELINGS AND MOODS

Children experience many feelings and moods during the course of their day. They will enjoy openly expressing them through movement. Musical accompaniment may be used in order to enhance the experience.

Happiness	Love	Bravery
Sadness	Hate	Shyness
Confusion	Friendship	Boredom
Pride	Jealousy	Interest
Disappointment	Fear	Laughter
Gladness	Hurt	Tears
Gaiety	Surprise	

INTERPRETING ART

Art is an experience that may, through guided discovery, be successfully interpreted in movement. Various lines, forms, colors, and textures may be expressed this way. Remember that the children should be encouraged to express how these things make them feel. Guessing games may be played, with one group trying to guess what the other is imitating. Discuss the various art forms with the children before they show you their interpretation.

Line:

Straight	Dotted
Curved	Dashed
Zig-zagged	Broken

Form:

Circle	Rectangle
Square	Hexagon
Triangle	

Color:

Red	Blue	Purple	Orange
White	Yellow	Pink	
Green	Black	Brown	

Texture:

Smooth	Hard	Scratchy
Slippery	Soft	Slick
Bumpy	Furry	
Rough	Silky	

INTERPRETING ACTION SEQUENCES

There is an unlimited number of action sequences that children enjoy interpreting. The following is a list of only a few of the possibilities that may be explored.

Move through molasses
Shoo the flies away
Float in water
Hit the punching bag
Grow like a flower
Sway like a tree in the breeze
Build a house

Fight a fire
Rocket to the moon
Ride a bumpy road

INTERPRETING PENDULAR MOVEMENTS

Have the children think of objects that swing (clock, golf club, baseball bat, swing, and so on). Let them move like each one. Use an object that has a pendular motion so they can keep time. Encourage them to swing with their eyes closed and then open to see if they are still in time with the beat. Encourage the children to also swing individual parts of their body one at a time.

INTERPRETING SPECIAL HOLIDAYS

Discuss the meaning of various special holidays with the children, encouraging them to share their experiences with the class.

Christmas/Hanukkah	Flag Day
Passover	Thanksgiving
Halloween	Independence Day
Easter	Summer vacation
Valentine's Day	Snow days

DANCE MAKING

Older children and children with a firm grasp of rhythmic fundamentals enjoy the challenging experience of making their own dances. These dances involve goal-directed creative rhythmic expression. Dance making permits children the freedom to make their own forms of expression and communication. Children need an opportunity to tell the world who they are, what they feel, and what their world means to them. Dance making permits this and encourages children to work together cooperatively toward a common goal. It permits them to attach meaning and dimension to music through the use of their bodies in an expressive form of movement.

The role of the teacher in the process of dance making is to establish an environment conducive to expression, one that is accepting of the children's creative efforts. The teacher's job is to set the stage and act as a catalyst in guiding the creative process. Attempts at creative dance making are likely to meet with only limited success if the children do not have a background in rhythmic fundamentals or if they feel inhibited in expressing themselves through movement. Therefore, it is recommended that, prior to introducing children to dance making, fundamental rhythmic activities, such as those presented in the preceding chapter, be introduced, followed by imitative and interpretative rhythms, such as those discussed earlier in this chapter. The following sequence is suggested for successful experiences in dance making:

1. Divide the class into small groups of four to six per group. Permit each group to decide on what is to be danced (an idea, words, a song, music).
2. Discuss the selection. What does it feel like? What are its characteristics? How can you move to it?
3. Encourage the children to experiment with movements based on their discussion.
4. Encourage further discussion and experimentation.
5. Plan the sequence of the dance, adding the parts best suited to it and discarding others.
6. Decide what accompaniment is to be used. Body instruments or rhythm are appropriate if children are dancing to words or an idea.
7. Try out the entire sequence with the accompaniment. Make modifications as necessary, adding elements or deleting elements from the dance.
8. Practice the dance two or three times.
9. Perform the dance for another group or for the entire class.

Dances are based on the elements of movement (effort, space, relationships). Dances may be made up from songs, instrumental music, words, or ideas. With older children, dance making from songs that they are familiar with is the easiest and most popular. There are, however, a few things to guard against. First, avoid songs that are too abstract or overly sentimental. Second, avoid too literal an interpretation of the words. Choose songs that children can understand and that involve something concrete. Permit the children to listen to the song and to become familiar with the words or instrumentation. After the words have been learned, encourage each group to discuss their meaning and how they can best be danced.

When making dances from an instrumental music selection, children will respond best to music that is familiar and popular. The dance should reproduce the music in terms of accent, tempo, intensity, and rhythmic pattern. Movement phrases should parallel changes in the melody, in the quality of the music, and variations in the accompaniment. The children should be permitted to listen to the structure of the music in order to determine of phrases are repeated. The teacher should help the children become sensitive to the quality of the sound by encouraging them to describe what they hear, such as high–low, fast–slow, light–heavy, soft–loud. Experimentation with movements to interpret the structure of the music is the next step, followed by practice and presentation to the class or another group.

Using words and ideas as the stimulus for dance making is somewhat more abstract and should be practiced by children only after they have had experiences with making dances based on songs and music. Age-appropriate rhymes, poems, and brief stories may be used as a basis for a dance. Children should first listen to the rhythm of the words and then to the idea conveyed. Dances may be devised that express either. First-time experiences with dance making to words or ideas will need to be relatively simple and in tune with the children's interests. As skill develops in dance making to words and ideas, they may become increasingly more abstract.

Objectives

Practice in dance making fosters:

1. Creativity.
2. Freedom of expression.

3. An understanding of the meaning and dimension of music through movement.
4. Cooperative group problem solving.

Movement Experiences

NAME DANCES

Working in small groups, select one of the children's names. Clap out the rhythm of the name, then add expressive movements. As skill progresses, add combinations of first and last names in the group to form a complete phrase.

RHYME DANCES

Working in small groups, select an appropriate rhyme (geared to the maturity level of the group). Develop a dance based around the rhyme or short poem.

SLOGAN DANCES

The teacher selects and combines popular sayings or slogans into a musical phrase. Small groups develop a dance based on the words and the idea conveyed. For example, try:

"Give a hoot, don't pollute"
because
When it's sugar and spice, everything's nice."
or
"Only you can prevent forest fires"
"With a stitch in time that saves nine."

MENU DANCES

Working in small groups, each group selects a menu for either breakfast, lunch, dinner, or a snack. Combine the sounds, movements, and rhythms of the foods chosen. For example, try:

Breakfast:
boiled eggs (roll like a ball)
bacon (sizzle and shrink)

pancakes (flip over)
syrup (act sticky and runny)
toast (pops out of the toaster)
Dinner:
Spaghetti (be real stiff, then limp)
Salad (mix and toss)
Bread (long, loaf)
Snack:
Ice cream (melt)
Popcorn (snap and pop)
Pretzels (twist)

ADDITIONAL RESOURCES

And the Beat Goes on for Physical Education. Folk Rock. Kimbo Educational Record Company, P.O. Box 477, Long Branch, NJ 07740 (KEA 5020-C).

Balloons. Educational Department, RCA Victor Records, 155 E. 24th Street, New York, NY 10010.

Creative Rhythm Album. (A visit to a farm, park, and circus). 622 Rooter Drive, Glendale, CA 91201.

Creative Rhythms for Children. Phoebe James Products, Box 134, Pacific Palisades, CA 90272.

Clap, Snap and Tap. Kimbo Educational Record Company, Box 477, Long Branch, NJ 07740 (EA48-C).

Dance Me a Story. Educational Department, RCA Victor Records, 155 E. 24th Street, New York, NY 10010.

Dances Without Partners. Educational Activities, Inc., Box 392, Freeport, NY 11520.

Flappy and Floppy. Educational Department, RCA Victor Records, 155 E. 24th Street, New York, NY 10010.

Keep on Steppin. Educational Activities, Box 392, Freeport, NY 11520.

Little Duck. Educational Department, RCA Victor Records, 155 E. 24th Street, New York, NY 10010.

Living with Rhythms Series. *Basic Rhythms for Primary Grades; Animal Rhythms; Rhythms and Meter Appreciation.* David McKay Company, 119 W. 40th Street, New York, NY 10010.

Machine Rhythm. Educational Record Sales, 157 Chambers Street, New York, NY 10007 (B1077).

The Magic Mountain. Educational Department, RCA Victor Records, 155 E. 24th Street, New York, NY 10010.

Make Believe in Movement. Kimbo Educational Record Company, Box 477, Long Branch, NJ 07740 (KIM0500-C).

Modern Jazz Movements. Kimbo Educational Record Company, Box 477, Long Branch, NJ 07740 (KIM3030-C).

Move Along Alphabet. Kimbo Educational Record Company, Box 477, Long Branch, NJ 07740 (KIM0510-C).

To Move Is to Be. Educational Activities, Box 392, Freeport, NY 11520.

Music for Creative Movement. Bridges, 310 W. Jefferson, Dallas, TX 75208.

Music for Modern Dance. Kimbo Educational Record Company, Box 477, Long Branch, NJ 07740 (KIM6090-C).

Noah's Ark. Educational Department, RCA Victor Records, 155 E. 24th Street, New York, NY 10010.

Rhythms for the World, Birds, Beasts, Bugs, and Little Fishes. Folkways, 117 W. 46th Street, New York, NY 10010.

CHAPTER 39

FOLK AND SQUARE DANCE ACTIVITIES

Folk dances are the oldest form of dance. They have been used for hundreds of years in ceremonies, rituals, and as an expression of everyday experiences. Folk dance is deeply imbedded in the culture of most countries. The specific dances of the culture have been passed from generation to generation and are enjoyed by both children and adults today.

Square dance is uniquely North American. A square dance is a form of folk dance, but it generally utilizes a square formation rather than the traditional circle and line formations of folk dance. The terminology used in square dancing is also different from that used in folk dance. Both folk and square dancing are concerned primarily with the use of locomotor movements to music. Because folk and square dances are closely related to fundamental locomotor movements, they serve as an excellent means for practicing and reinforcing these skills. Both folk and square dance serve as excellent media for developing basic social skills and improving one's confidence when placed in a social setting with members of the opposite gender.

Folk and square dances are enjoyable and easy to incorporate into the curriculum. Emphasis, however, on the social element at the expense of the skill element is not recommended. This chapter focuses on preparing to teach folk and square dances, basic steps, terms, and formations used. Several folk and square dances are then presented. Each describes the movement skills and desired outcomes of the activity as well as how the dance is performed. A record resource is given for each dance. Complete addresses for obtaining these records are provided at the end of the chapter. A listing of other recommended folk and square dance recordings is also given.

PREPARING TO TEACH A DANCE

Advance preparation is the key to success in teaching folk and square dances. The following are practical suggestions for getting ready and presenting a dance.

Getting Ready

It is of utmost importance that you know your students and what they are capable of prior to selecting a dance. The dances are presented in a progressive order of difficulty according to the skill requirements and the complexity of the dance pattern. Selecting a dance that is beyond the present level of ability of your students will only result in frustration and failure. Conversely, selection of an activity that is below the level of social maturity of your students will lead to unnecessary and unwanted difficulties. Therefore, the first requirement in getting ready to teach a dance is to select one that is appropriate both in terms of the skill requirements and the social requirements. Once you have selected the dances to be taught, it is important to review the music and the steps involved. When purchasing folk and square dance records or tapes, be sure that an instruction sheet accompanies the music. In fact, it is a good idea to make a duplicate of the instruction sheet and store it in a safe place.

When reviewing the music, listen for the introduction and for the point when the dance begins. Be sure to know the phrases of the music and how they fit the steps or figures of the dance. Be certain to note rhythmic changes in the music and where transitions occur.

After you are familiar with the music, practice the steps, first without the music and then with the music. Become comfortable with putting the steps to the music by practicing several times. Talk through the dance while practicing in the same manner in which you will talk to your students. Be certain to count out the beats in each measure and to use the correct name for each step. Practice cueing the start and finish of steps and figures.

Presenting the Dance

After you have practiced the dance yourself, you will be ready to present it to the class. The following sequence of presentation is recommended:

1. Tell the class the name of the dance, its origin, and a little about the country that it comes from.
2. When possible, try to relate the dance to other experiences children might be familiar with.
3. Let the children listen to the music. Then briefly discuss the rhythm, tempo, and other qualities of the music.
4. Teach the basic steps of the dance.
5. Teach difficult steps and figures separately.
6. Use a walk-through, talk-through approach without the music. Begin slowly; gradually work up to actual speed.
7. Practice with the music. If the speed of the music can be slowed, do so at first.
8. For dances that have several different figures, teach one figure at a time, first without the music, then with it.
9. Progressively combine the figures of the dance and work up to the normal tempo.
10. Repeat the dance two or three times so that the students learn it well and have an opportunity to enjoy the activity.

Helpful Hints

1. Progress from simple to complex when teaching a dance. The progression you use will be an important factor in the ease with which the dance is learned.
2. With the music, move from a slower tempo to the normal tempo.
3. With the steps, move from familiar steps to unfamiliar ones.
4. Get the basic idea of the dance across. Don't be overly concerned with form.
5. Set reasonable standards for achievement for the children. Standards that are too high will limit enjoyment.
6. Break the dance down into parts and pro-

gressively teach each one, building skill upon skill.

7. Be certain to have the children in the formation required by the dance when they are listening to the music and you are teaching the steps. This will help the children visualize the activity.

8. Be liberal in your use of praise and positive encouragement.

9. Modify dance positions that require partners if children are not ready for close contact with members of the opposite gender. For example, an elbow turn will work just as well as a more advanced waltz turn.

10. Do not ololoververbalize. Demonstration and the use of key words works best.

11. Keep the lesson informal and stress a wholesome social environment. Folk and square dances are fun, and the children should be encouraged to feel the energy and excitement that they generate.

BASICS OF FOLK AND SQUARE DANCE

Folk and square dances utilize a variety of steps, terms, and formations. It is important to be familiar with them in order to understand and be able to perform the dances. The following is a brief description of steps, terms, and formations commonly used in folk and square dance.

Steps

The following is a list of ten steps common to most folk and square dances.

Bleking Step. The bleking step is done to an even rhythm. Hop left; at the same time, place the right heel forward with the right leg straight. Jump up and reverse position with the left heel forward and the left leg straight. The action is rhythmically repeated.

Buzz Step. The buzz step is used for turning a partner. The partners are in a waltz position.

The right foot of the person in the lead is forward, with the weight on the front of the feet. The right foot remains stationary while the left foot pushes off, turning in a clockwise direction. The action is just the opposite for the person in the follow position.

Grapevine Step. The grapevine step is done by stepping right, crossing the left foot in front, then stepping right again and crossing the left foot behind. The process is rhythmically repeated, alternating crossing in front and behind the stepping leg.

Polka Step. The polka step is done to an uneven rhythm with an upbeat tempo. From a position with the feet together and the weight on the left foot, hop left and raise the right knee slightly and step right forward, Close the left foot to the right, taking some weight off the left, and step forward with the right. The process is repeated starting with a hop on the right foot.

Schottische Step. The schottische is done to an even rhythm and a moderate tempo. Step forward on the right foot, step forward left, step forward right, hop right (step, step, step, hop).

Step–Close. The step–close is done to an even rhythm and a slow tempo. Step sideways to the right while at the same time pointing the left toe to the left side with the left heel raised and the leg straight. Then slowly draw the left foot to the right, taking the weight on to the right foot (step–draw–close). The process is repeated with the same foot leading or reversed to the opposite side.

Slip Step. The slip step is done to an uneven beat and a fast tempo. It is a sideward slide. Slide the right foot to the side, slide the left foot to close to the right. Repeat.

Step–Hop. The step–hop is done to an even rhythm and a moderate tempo. Step forward on the right foot and hop on the right, then step forward on the left foot and hop on the left. Repeat.

Two-Step.   The two-step is done to an uneven beat (quick, quick, slow) and a moderately fast tempo. Step forward with the left foot on count one, then bring the right foot up to the left on count two. Now step forward on the left again. Use key words: step–close–step–hold.

Waltz Run.   The waltz run step is done to an even rhythm and either a slow or fast tempo. From a waltz position, the step consists of a continuous run, forward or backward. The first beat of each measure is accented with a slight stamp. There are three runs to each measure.

Terms

The following is a list of words commonly used in folk and square dance terminology:

Allemande Left.   The boy places his left hand in the left hand of his corner. They turn counterclockwise and back to place.

Circle Eight Hands Around.   Couples join hands and walk clockwise around the set.

Corner.   Person to left of the boy and to the right of the girl in a set.

Do-Si-Do.   Partners face each other, walk forward, pass right shoulders, go around each other, and walk backward to place.

Elbow Swing.   Partners join right elbows, swing around once, and return to place.

Forward and Back.   Three steps to the center of the set and back to place.

Grand Right and Left.   Partners face and clasp right hands in a handshake; they walk in the direction in which they are facing, alternating right- and left-hand clasps with each dancer they meet.

Honor Your Partner or Corner.   The boy bows and the girl curtsies to the person named in the call.

Ladies Chain.   The girls walk forward and clasp right hands, pass right shoulders with girl of opposite couple, give left hand to opposite boy as he turns counterclockwise once around to face center of the set again.

Partner.   The person with whom you are dancing. Girls stand to the boy's right.

Promenade.   Couples assume a skating position (right hand to right hand and left hand to left hand) and walk around the set.

Right-Hand Star.   Four people walk to center of the set, turn right sides to center and join right hands, walk clockwise once around. Reverse the movement for a left-hand star.

Right and Left Through.   Two couples face, walk forward, and pass right shoulders with the opposite dancer. Each boy then takes the girl's left hand with his left hand, places his right hand around the girl's waist, turns her around, repeats the first movement, and returns to the original position.

Sets.   Square dances are done in sets of four couples. The head couple (couple 1) is the couple nearest the caller or the music. The side couples (couples 2 and 4) are opposite one another; the foot couple (couple 3) is opposite the head couple.

Varsovienne Position.   Boy stands behind and to the left of the girl. His right hand is placed in her right hand at shoulder level. Boy's left hand is in girl's left hand at waist level.

Formations

A variety of formations are used in folk dancing. Most use a circle or line formation. Most square dances use a square formation with four couples forming a set. Figure 39.1 provides a diagram of common folk and square dance formations.

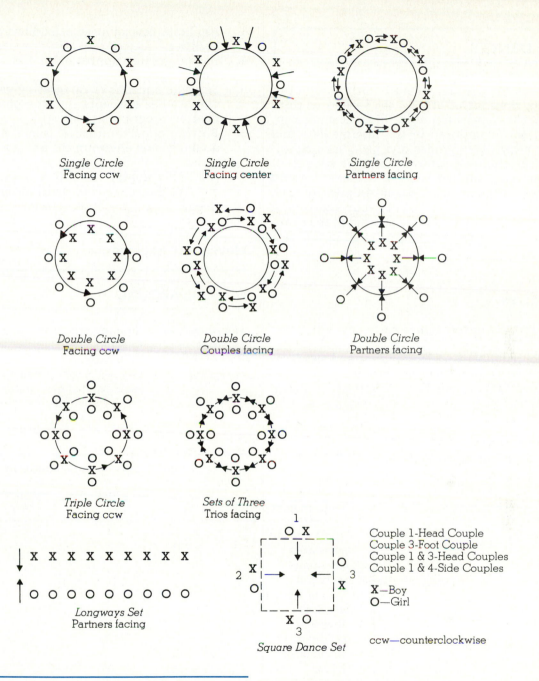

Single Circle
Facing ccw

Single Circle
Facing center

Single Circle
Partners facing

Double Circle
Facing ccw

Double Circle
Couples facing

Double Circle
Partners facing

Triple Circle
Facing ccw

Sets of Three
Trios facing

Longways Set
Partners facing

Square Dance Set

Couple 1-Head Couple
Couple 3-Foot Couple
Couple 1 & 3-Head Couples
Couple 1 & 4-Side Couples

X—Boy
O—Girl

ccw—counterclockwise

FIGURE 39.1 Common folk and square dance formations.

FOLK DANCES

True folk dances are generally introduced after singing rhythms or around the second or third grade. The dances found in this section are appropriate for children in the intermediate and upper elementary grades and have been classified as beginning-, intermediate-, or advanced-level activities in Table 39.1. It will be necessary to listen to the musical accompaniment to each dance prior to presenting it to your students. A record source is provided at the end of the chapter for each of the folk dances found in this section.

Objectives

Participation in folk dance activities will:

1. Contribute to understanding and expressing rhythm through movement.
2. Develop and reinforce a variety of dance steps.
3. Facilitate development of auditory rhythmic abilities.
4. Foster greater appreciation for other cultures.
5. Serve as a means of integrating various social studies concepts into the physical education program.
6. Provide opportunities for social contact in a wholesome environment among boys and girls.
7. Aid in developing the ability to utilize various folk dance steps to rhythmic accompaniment.

Movement Experiences

TURN ME AROUND

Movement Skills: Running, elbow swing, pivoting.
Origin: England.
Record: RCA LPM-1624.
Formation: Double circle, partners facing each other, boys on the inside. Any number may participate.

TABLE 39.1   Selected Folk Dances

| | Suggested Progression for Children | | | |
Folk Dances	Beginning Level	Intermediate Level	Advanced Level	Page
Turn Me Around	X			512
Greensleeves	X			512
Seven Jumps	X			512
Glow Worm	X			512
Chimes of Dunkirk	X			512
Finger Polka	X			513
La Raspa		X		514
Ace of Diamonds		X		514
Oh Susanna		X		515
Girls' Jig		X		515
Patty-Cake Polka		X		515
Tinikling		X		515
Mexican Clap Dance			X	516
Hora			X	516
Virginia Reel			X	517

Procedures: Partners hook right elbows and take seven slow running steps around. They release on the eighth beat, hook left elbows, and run slowly in the opposite direction. Partners join right hands, holding them high. The girl turns in place with four steps followed by the boy. The entire dance is then repeated from the beginning.

GREENSLEEVES

Movement Skills: Skipping, elbow swing, promenade.
Origin: England.
Record: RCA EPA 4141, ERS "Folk Dances for Beginners."
Formation: Double lines with partners facing. Six couples per line.
Procedures: Right and left across—In each set of six couples, the boys take their partner's right hand in their right hand and skip eight steps clockwise. Then they drop right hands, join left hands, and skip eight steps counterclockwise back to their original positions.

Through the arch—Couples join inside hands and the head couple skips four steps backward under the joined hands of couple number two. Couple number two skips forward four steps. Repeat with couple number two skipping backward. Repeat through-the-arch movement.

Promenade the file—Head couple joins inside hands and skips to the bottom of the line while the other five couples clap their hands.

New head couple—All partners, with both hands joined, turn each other around while moving up one place in file formation with the new head couple.

SEVEN JUMPS

Movement Skills: Slide, skip, or step–hop balancing.
Origin: Denmark.
Record: RCA EPA 4138, Folkcraft 1163, ERS "Folk Dances from Near and Far."
Formation: Single circle facing inward. Any number may participate.

Procedures: All the children join hands and take seven sliding, skipping, or step–hop steps to the left and return seven steps to the right during the chorus. On the first sustained note, they raise one leg off the ground and hold it there until the second sustained note sounds, when they lower the leg and stand at attention (position 1). The chorus then begins again and seven slides (skips or step–hops) are taken to the left, then to the right. The following positions are added on succeeding sets of sustained notes:

Position 2—Repeat position 1 and lift the opposite leg.

Position 3—Repeat positions 1 and 2 and add a kneel on one leg.

Position 4—Repeat positions 1, 2, and 3, and add a kneel on the opposite leg.

Position 5—Repeat positions 1, 2, 3, and 4, and place one elbow on the floor.

Position 6—Repeat positions 1, 2, 3, 4, and 5, and place the other elbow on the floor.

Position 7—Repeat positions 1, 2, 3, 4, 5, and 6, and place the head on the floor.

GLOW WORM

Movement Skills: Walking forward and backward to the beat of the music.
Origin: U.S.A.
Record: RCA LPM-1623, ERS "Folk Dances from Near and Far."
Formation: Double circle of couples, boys on the inside. Any number may participate.
Procedures: Facing counterclockwise, all take four walking steps forward, followed by four walking steps backward. Partners then face each other. Girls take four walking steps forward, returning to their original position, while the boys take four walking steps diagonally left and forward to their new partner. The dance is repeated several times.

CHIMES OF DUNKIRK

Movement Skills: Stamping, clapping, and turning to the beat of the music.
Origin: France.

Record: RCA LPM-1624, ERS "Folk Dances from Near and Far."

Formation: Double circle with partners facing each other, boys on the inside. Any number may participate.

Procedures: Everyone stamps their feet (right, left, right), then they all clap their hands three times. Next, partners join both hands and turn clockwise in eight steps back to place. Then they join right hands and step forward on their right foot, back on their left, and repeat. Now they join both hands and walk clockwise around each other in eight counts, with the boys advancing forward to a new partner. The dance is repeated several times.

FINGER POLKA

Movement Skills: Skipping, elbow swing.
Origin: Sweden.
Record: Folkraft F-1419, "Folk Dance Fundamentals."
Formation: Double circle of couples, partners' inside hands joined, facing counterclockwise, boys on the inside. Any number of couples may participate.

Procedures: Partners skip sixteen steps counterclockwise around the circle. Partners face each other with hands on their hips and stamp their feet three times. They then clap their own hands three times and shake their right forefinger at their partner three times. Then they shake their left forefinger at their partner three times. Partners join right elbows and turn once around clockwise. The boy then moves counterclockwise around the circle to the first girl on his left and she becomes his new partner. The entire dance is repeated several times.

LA RASPA

Movement Skills: Bleking step.
Origin: Mexico.

Record: RCA EPA-4139, Folkraft F-1119A, ERS "Folk Dances from Near and Far."

Formation: Double circle of couples, partners facing each other, the boys on the inside. Any number of couples may participate.

Procedures: Bleking step and clap—Hop to the left and put the right foot forward, hop to the right and put the left foot forward, hop to the left and put the right foot forward, pause and clap hands together twice. Repeat. Start each set of bleking steps by reversing the initial foot movement.

Elbow swing and clap—Join left elbows and swing counterclockwise, using eight skipping steps. Partners finish the swing facing each other and clapping their own hands once. Repeat this procedure, swinging clockwise. The boys move counterclockwise around the circle to a new partner and the dance is repeated.

ACE OF DIAMONDS

Movement Skills: Complex hopping patterns, elbow swing, sliding.
Origin: Denmark.
Record: RCA LPM-1622.
Formation: Double circle of couples, partners facing each other, boys on the inside. Any number of couples may participate.

Procedures: Children face their partner, clap their own hands, and place their right heel forward on the floor. They then hook right elbows and walk around each other with six walking steps. The same procedure is repeated, extending the left foot and hooking the left elbow.

The children then hop slowly on their left foot, placing the right heel forward and repeat, hopping on the right foot and placing the left heel forward. The same pattern is repeated four more times but quickly, starting with the right foot. The entire pattern is then repeated, first slowly, then fast, from the beginning.

The children now join hands to form a single circle and slide sixteen steps counterclockwise.

OH SUSANNA

Movement Skills: Grand right and left, promenade.
Origin: U.S.A.
Record: RCA 45-6178, ERS "Folk Dances from Near and Far."
Formation: Single circle with partners facing the center, girls to the right of the boys, 18 to 24 per circle.
Procedures: Ladies to the center—Four steps to the center of the circle, curtsey, and back to place.

Gents to the center—Same as above, except boys bow.

The above calls are repeated.

Grand right and left—Partners face, join right hands, step past partner to person behind him, join left hands and repeat the procedure, stopping with the last person, who becomes the new partner. (When holding right hands, right shoulders should pass. When holding left hands, left shoulders should pass.)

Promenade—Boys put their new partner on their right, join right hand to right and left hand to left, face counterclockwise, and skip 16 steps around the circle.

The entire dance is repeated several times.

GIRLS' JIG

Movement Skills: Slide, skip, and hop.
Origin: Ireland.
Record: RCA LPM 1623.
Formation: Double line with partners facing (girls in one line, boys in the other). Any number may participate.
Procedures: Partners stand facing with their hands on their hips, take four skip steps forward and four skip steps back. Repeat this movement. Hop on left foot while tapping right toe four times, then take four slide steps to the right. Repeat this movement starting with the right foot. Repeat the whole movement pattern in its entirety.

Partners take four skip steps forward and back. Repeat this movement. Partners hop on their left foot, tap right toe and heel two times, then take

four slide steps to the right. Repeat this movement, starting with the right foot. The dance is repeated.

PATTY-CAKE POLKA

Movement Skills: Hopping, heel—toe—point, coordinated clapping.
Origin: Poland.
Record: Columbia 52007.
Formation: Double circle of couples facing each other, boys on the inside, hands joined. Any number may participate.
Procedures: Partners join hands. The boys hop on their right foot and place their left heel to the side. They hop again on their right foot and place their left toe behind their right heel (girls perform the same steps, hopping on their left foot and stepping with their right foot). Couples then slide four steps counterclockwise around the circle. Repeat this procedure using the opposite footwork and slide clockwise.

Clap three times with partner, using right hands, clap left hands three times, clap both hands three times, clap own hands three times. Repeat.

Hook right elbows and swing around clockwise one time. Boys now move counterclockwise around the circle and take a new partner. The entire dance is now repeated.

TINIKLING

Movement Skills: Rhythmical hopping and jumping.
Origin: Philippines.
Record: Kimbo KEA 8095-C and KEAAA 9015-C, ERS, "Folk Dances for People Who Love Folk Dances."
Equipment: Two poles about ten feet long and two 2-foot X 4-foot wood blades three feet long. No record is necessary, but any record with a distinct 3/4 rhythm will do nicely (such as "Alley Cat," ATCA 45-6226).
Formation: Single file at each set of poles

with a beater at the end of each set.

Procedures: The two beaters at each end of the poles strike them together once and then strike them apart twice on the 2X4s. This same beating pattern is repeated throughout the entire dance.

There are several steps that may be performed:

1. Side step—The children stand with their hands on hips outside a set of imaginary poles. Side step to right (over first pole) with right foot, bring left alongside. With right foot, take one more step to the right (over the second pole). The children are now standing on the right foot. The same pattern is repeated, this time having the children start with the left foot. The rhythm pattern is

   Right—step, together, step
   Left—step, together, step
   Right—step, together, step, and so on.

   After the side step has been mastered over the imaginary poles, use the real pole in the 3/4 rhythmical pattern.

2. Forward and back—Children stand facing the pole with hands on hips. They step forward with left foot, following same rhythm pattern as side step:

   Forward—step, together, step
   Back—step, together, step
   Forward—step, together, step

3. Straddle step—Children stand between imaginary poles with hands on hips and feet together. On first beat, straddle jump to slide, and then bring feet together and bounce twice.

MEXICAN CLAP DANCE

Movement Skills: Step–swing, balance step.
Origin: Mexico.
Record: Folkraft 1093, ERS ''Folk Dances for People Who Love Folk Dancing.''
Formation: Double circle of couples, boys on the inside. Any number of couples may participate.
Procedures: Step, swing opposite leg over, and clap—The boy steps to his left with his left foot and swings his right leg across his left leg. He then steps right and swings his left leg across his right

leg. He again steps to his left, swings his right leg across his left, and holds this position while clapping his hands twice. The girl performs the same movement, only starting with a step to the right and swinging her left leg across. The procedure is repeated, but with the footwork reversed.

Balance and clap—The boy, keeping hands joined with his partner, steps away from his partner with his left foot, steps back toward her with his left foot, and again steps away from her with his left foot and holds that position, clapping his hands twice. The girl performs the same movement, except that she steps with the right foot. Repeat this procedure, stepping forward on the first step.

Walk and turn—Partners join inside hands and face counterclockwise around the circle. As they walk around the circle, the girl turns counterclockwise under the boy's arm, using two walking steps. The boy now performs the same movement. Next, they both perform the same movement together. Everybody claps their hands twice and the boy moves counterclockwise to the next girl. She becomes his new partner and the dance is repeated.

HORA

Movement Skills: Modified grapevine step.
Origin: Israel.
Record: Folkraft 1106, RCA EPA-4140, ERS ''Folk Dances from Near and Far.''
Formation: Single circle, hands joined. Any number may participate.
Procedures: The modified grapevine step must first be learned. It consists of a step sideways on the left foot, followed by crossing the right foot behind the left, stepping left again, and hopping at the same time on the same foot while swinging the right foot in front of the left. The same procedure is repeated to the right.

First practice the step in a line formation without the music. Stand with your back to the children while demonstrating. As the step is mastered, increase the tempo and have good performers help others individually. After the children have mastered the step, form a circle and try it to the music. It is composed entirely of grapevine steps to the left and to the right.

VIRGINIA REEL

Movement Skills: Hands around, do-si-do, grand right and left.
Origin: U.S.A.
Record: Folkraft, RCA EPA LPM-1623, RCA 45-6180.
Formation: Two lines of couples facing each other, boys in one line, girls in the other. Four to eight couples per set.
Procedures: Forward and back—The two lines walk forward three steps and bow, then back four steps to place.

Right hand around—The two lines walk forward, grasp right hands, and walk around each other and back to place.

Left hand around—Repeat as above, but with the left hand.

Both hands around—Repeat as above, but with both hands.

Do-si-do with right shoulder—The two lines walk forward and do-si-do, passing right shoulders first, then moving back to place.

Do-si-do with left shoulder—Repeat as above, but with left shoulders passing first.

Head couple down the set—Head couple joins hands and slides eight short steps down the center to the foot of the line and back again with eight more steps.

Reel—The head boy then proceeds to do a grand right and left (see page 000 for a concise explanation) down the girls' line while the head girl does the same down the boys' line. They meet, join hands, and slide back up the set to their places.

Peel off—The boys' and girls' lines take a quarter turn left and right, respectively, and follow the head couple down the outside of the set to the foot.

Form an arch—At the foot of the set, the head couple forms an arch while the other couples join hands and pass through. Couple one now stays at the foot of the set and couple two becomes the head couple.

The dance is repeated so that all couples have an opportunity to be the head couple.

SQUARE DANCES

Square dances are uniquely North American in origin. They are a popular form of folk dancing, and they generally use a square (or "set") as their basic formation. The square dance activities contained in this section and listed in Table 39.2 are appropriate for most children in the upper elementary grades and beyond. Square dancing should be introduced after a variety of other folk dances has been mastered. The basic steps in teaching dance that were discussed earlier should be carefully followed when teaching a square dance. Several have a number of different formations that will require practice separately and without the music prior to putting it all together.

Objectives

Practice in square dance activities will contribute to:

1. The development of improved auditory rhythmic abilities.
2. The ability to combine skillful movement with music.
3. The ability to listen to directions and respond in an appropriate manner.
4. The ability to work cooperatively with a partner and a small group in a common endeavor.
5. An appreciation for the pioneer cultures of the United States and Canada.
6. Wholesome opportunities for social contact among groups of boys and girls.

Movement Experiences

OH JOHNNY

Movement Skills: Elbow swing, allemande left, do-si-do, promenade.
Record: RCA LE 3000.
Formation: Four-couple square.

TABLE 39.2 Selected
Square Dances

	Suggested Progression for Children			
Square Dance	Beginning Level	Intermediate Level	Advanced Level	Page
Oh Johnny	X			517
Red River Valley	X			518
Take a Little Peek	X			518
Birdie in the Cage	X			519
Duck for the Oyster	X			519
Pop Goes the Weasel		X		519
Texas Star		X		520
Ladies Chain		X		520
Corner of the World		X		520
Farmer's Daughter		X		521
Heads and Sides			X	521
Snake Chain			X	521
Inside Out and Outside In			X	521
Grand Square			X	522

Procedures: All join hands and circle the ring—All join hands and circle right.

Stop where you are and give your honey a swing—Boys elbow swing with their partners twice around.

Swing that gal behind you—Boys elbow swing their corner twice around.

Go back home and swing your own—Boys elbow swing their partner twice around.

Allemande left with the corner gal—Left hand to left and walk counterclockwise twice around.

Do-si-do your own—Boys do-si-do their own partner.

All promenade your corner maid—Everyone promenades his corner and sings "Oh Johnny, Oh Johnny, Oh." Repeat the dance with a new partner.

RED RIVER VALLEY

Movement Skills: Elbow swing, do-si-do, right-hand star.
Record: RCA LE 3000, Folkraft 1056.
Formation: Four-couple square with eight per set.
Procedures: All join hands in the valley and circle to the left and to the right—The children all hold hands and circle left four steps and then right four steps.

Swing the girl in the valley—Boys elbow swing with their corner around twice.

Now swing that Red River gal—Boys elbow swing with their own partner around twice.

And you circle to the left and to the right—All couples walk left four steps and then right four steps.

Ladies star in the valley—Girls perform a right-hand star and walk around once clockwise.

Now swing with that Red River gal—Boys elbow swing with their own partner around twice.

Same couples to the left down the valley—Couples one and three walk to their left and join hands with the couples two and four.

And you circle to the left and to the right—All couples walk left four steps and then right four steps

Now gents star in the valley—Boys perform a right-hand star, walking around once clockwise

And you swing that Red River gal—Boys elbow swing with their partner around twice.

Repeat the entire dance.

TAKE A LITTLE PEEK

Movement Skills: Walk and swing.
Record: "Honor Your Partner" (Album 1), ERS "Basic Square Dances."

Formation: Four-couple set.
Procedures: Square the sets.

First couple to the right of the ring—Couple number one moves to face couple number two

Around that couple, take a little peek—Couple number one separates and moves to the outside of the person they are facing, looking at each other behind couple number two.

Back to the center and swing your sweet—Couple number one walks backward to the center of the set and does an elbow swing.

Around that couple and swing once more—Couple number one again peeks around couple number two.

Back to the center and circle up four—Couple number one walks backward to the center of the set and joins hands with couple number two.

Swing your own round and round, Bounce that pretty girl off the ground as you whirl her round the town—Couple number one swings, with the boy whirling the girl in the air and setting her down in front of couple number three. Repeat action with couples three and four.

Couples two, three, and four repeat the entire dance.

BIRDIE IN THE CAGE

Movement Skills: Balance, swing, and do-si-do.
Record: Any good square dance music.
Formation: Four-couple set.
Procedures: First couple balance, first couple swing—First couple balances and swings.

Lead right out to the right of the ring with four hands around—Couple number one moves to couple number two, forms a circle, and moves around clockwise.

Cage the bird with three hands around—Girl number one moves into the circle made by other three dancers.

Bird hops out, crow hops in—Girl number one rejoins circle and boy number one moves to the center of the circle.

Ring up three and you're gone again—Boy number one rejoins the circle between two girls, forming a right hand star moving clockwise.

Back to the left at any cost—Form a left-hand star and circle counterclockwise.

Do-si-do the gent you know—Do-si-do the partner, passing left shoulder.

Ladies go si, and gents go do—Do-si-do, partners passing right shoulders

Take your honey and away you go—Couple number one moves to couple number three and repeats dance. Repeat dance with couple number four. Other couples repeat entire dance.

DUCK FOR THE OYSTER

Movement Skills: Duck through arches, circle four, swing.
Record: "Honor Your Partner" (Album 2), ERS "Basic Square Dances."
Formation: Four-couple set.
Procedures: Honor your partner—Boys bow, girls curtsey.

Swing your corner—Boys perform an elbow swing with girl on the left.

First couple to the right of the ring—Couple number one moves to face couple number two.

With four hands around—Both couples join hands and circle one and one-half times around, with couple one ending up on the outside of the set.

Duck for the oyster—Couple number one goes through the arch formed by couple two and back. Do not drop hands.

Dive for the clam—Couple number two performs the preceding movement while couple number one forms the arch.

Dive for the sardine and take a full can—Couple number one goes through the arch formed by couple two and moves on to face couple number three. Repeat the dance with couples three and four. Allow each couple to repeat the entire dance.

POP GOES THE WEASEL

Movement Skills: Allemande, grand right and left, promenade.
Record: RCA LPM 1623.
Formation: Four-couple set.
Procedures: Head couple moves to couple number two, joins hands and circles left. The head couple "pops" under the arch made by couple two,

and moves on to couples three and four, repeating the movement. This is followed by an allemande left to original positions. Couples then perform a two-hand swing. Couples two, three, and four repeat the procedure. The dance is concluded with a grand right and left and a promenade back to the original positions.

TEXAS STAR

Movement Skills: Right-hand star, left-hand star, swing, promenade.

Record: "Honor Your Partner" (Album 3), ERS "Advanced Beginning Square Dances."

Formation: Four-couple set.

Procedure: Ladies to the center and back—The ladies walk to the center, curtsey, and return to their positions.

Gents to the center and form a star—Boys do a right-hand star clockwise around the center of the set.

Back to the left and don't get lost—Boys stop and perform a left-hand star counterclockwise around the center of the set.

Meet your honey and pass her by—Boys pass partners.

Catch the next girl on the fly—Boys place right arm around waist of the first girl past their partner.

Gents swing out and ladies swing in to form that Texas star again—Boys back around, keeping arm around girls' waist. Girls grasp opposite right hands, moving clockwise.

Ladies swing out and right back in, to form that Texas star again—Boys and girls circle a whole turn to the left. The boys pivot and do a rirght-hand star.

Swing your partner up and down—Boys swing present partner with an elbow swing.

Promenade home and around the town—Boys promenade present partner to his original position. Repeat entire dance.

LADIES CHAIN

Movement Skills: Chain through, swing, turn, do-si-do.

Record: "Honor Your Partner," (Album 2).

Formation: Four-couple set.

Procedures: First couple to the right of the ring—Couple number one moves to face couple number two.

With right hand star you step and sing—All join hands and circle once around to original position.

Ladies chain across the hall—Boys drop hands; girls retain right-hand grasp, turning one-half turn to face the opposite boy and placing their right hand on their right hip. The boy places his right hand on the girl's waist and backs around as the girl moves forward one complete turn.

Chain back through with a hi you all—Repeat previous movement with boys turning girls.

Circle four and away you go—All join hands and circle once.

On to the next with a do-si-do—Couple number one moves to couple number three and couples two and four repeat the dance. Allow each couple to repeat the entire dance.

CORNER OF THE WORLD

Movement Skills: Balance and swing, right-hand star, allemande left, grand right and left.

Record: "Honor Your Partner," (Album 1) or any good square dance music.

Formation: Four-couple set.

Procedures: One and three balance and swing—Couples one and three balance and do a right elbow swing.

Star by the right in the center of the ring—Couples one and three perform a right-hand star in the center of the set, turning once around the set.

Side couples whirl to the corner of the world—Boys turn left and girls turn right one turn, taking large steps.

Heads cross trail through, don't hesitate—Couples one and three move forward to face each other and pass right shoulder to right shoulder.

Left to the corner and don't be late—Face your partner, pass partner, and give your left hand to the person you are facing.

Swing your own for heaven's sake—Everyone swings their own partners.

Star by the right in the center once more—Couples one and three perform a right-hand star in the center of the set.

Side couples whirl as you did before—The boys turn right and girls turn left.

Heads cross trail through across the land—Couples one and three return to original positions.

Left allemande and a right-and-left grand—Turn your corner partner with an allemande left and do a grand right and left, starting with your partner, right hand to right hand.

Meet your honey and promenade home—When you meet your partner, promenade to original position. Repeat dance with couples two and four going to the center of the set.

FARMER'S DAUGHTER

Movement Skills: Swing, promenade, allemande left, grand right and left, do-si-do.

Record: RCA LE 3000 (or any acceptable square dance music).

Formation: Four-couple sets.

Procedures: First gent leads out to the right—Boy of couple number one walks to couple number two.

Shake hands with the farmer—Shake hands with boy number two.

Shake hands with the daughter—Shake hands with girl number two.

Swing the daughter—Boy one and girl two perform an elbow swing.

Now run home and swing your own and everbody swing. Repeat.

HEADS AND SIDES

Movement Skills: Swing, do-si-do, promenade.

Record: "Honor Your Partner," (Album 1).

Formation: Four-couple set.

Procedures: First gent lead out to the right—Boy of couple number one walks to couple number two.

Shake hands with the farmer—Shake hands with boy number two.

Shake hands with the daughter—Shake hands with girl number two.

Swing the daughter—Boy one and girl two perform an elbow swing.

Now run home and swing your own and everybody swing your daughter—Boy number one returns to his original position and everybody swings their partners. Repeat the movement with boy one moving to couples three and four.

"Honor your partner—Boys bow and girls curtsey

Honor your corner—Same movement except with corner partners.

Allemande left your corner—Allemande left with the corner partners.

And a grand right and left—All do a grand right and left.

Meet your partner and do-si-do—When partners meet, do a do-si-do.

Step right up and swing her high and low—Everybody swings their partner.

And promenade home—All promenade partners to original positions. Remaining couples repeat entire dance.

SNAKE CHAIN

Movement Skills: Arches, circles, swing.

Record: RCA CE 3000 (or any acceptable square dance music).

Formation: Any number of couples form a single line.

Procedures: Single line of couples holding hands and standing side by side with the girl on the right. The head couple leads the rest of the dancers through a series of square dance movements. They can create circles within circles (in serpentine fashion), move through arches formed by the other dancers, swing partners, do-si-do partners, and so forth. Be sure to select a head couple that is imaginative. Allow other couples to be the head couple. Work in small groups of four to six people.

INSIDE OUT AND OUTSIDE IN

Movement Skills: Dishrag turn and shuffle step, allemande left, grand right and left.

Record: Any good square dance music.

Formation: Four-couple set.

Procedures: Couples one and three, forward and back—Couples one and three move forward three steps. Ladies curtsey and men bow. All move back four steps.

Forward again on the same old track—Repeat movement.

One dive in for an inside out and an outside in—Couple number three forms an arch and couple number one ducks through the arch. Couple number one forms an arch and couple number three backs through the arch.

Bow your back and do it again—Repeat previous movement.

Forward up and take your opposite girl—Couples one and three move forward facing each other.

Turn to the side with a dishrag whirl—Take both hands of the person you are facing (boy one and girl two; boy three and girl one), turn under your arms toward the outside of the set and face side couples two and four.

Inside out and outside in—Inside couple, boy three and girl one, duck through arch of couple two. Boy one and girl three duck through arch of couple number four. Repeat this movement with couples munber two and four backing through arches to original positions.

Bow your back and do it again—Repeat previous movement.

Allemande left with your left hand—Boys give their left hand to lady in front of them (their original corner).

Right to your honey and a right and left grand—Extend left hand to next person met after passing partners. Proceed around set, alternating hands.

Meet your honey and promenade—Meet your partner and move to gent's home position. Repeat dance.

GRAND SQUARE

Movement Skills: Grand square, ladies chain, half-promenade, right and left through.

Record: Any good square dance music.

Formation: Four-couple set.

Procedures: Grand square couples one and three walk four steps forward; partners face and walk four steps back away from each other; face opposites and walk four steps back; face each other and walk four steps forward to original positions.

At the same time, couples two and four face partners and walk four steps back away from each other; face opposites and walk four steps in; face center and walk four steps to their partner; face opposite and walk four steps back to original positions.

Reverse grand square—Couples one and three repeat action of couples two and four; couples two and four repeat actions of one and three.

Right and left through—Couples one and three walk across set, passing right shoulders; boy takes partner and turns her in place; couples repeat steps, back to place. Couples two and four repeat this movement. Head couples walk to the couple on their right and perform a right and left through and back to place. Side couples walk to their right and perform a right and left through and return to position. All dancers repeat the grand square and reverse grand square.

Ladies chain—Head girl extends right hand to opposite girl and left hand to opposite boy, turn around in place. Side girls repeat their movement. Repeat with head couples turning to the right. Repeat with side couples turning right. Repeat grand square and reverse grand square.

Half-promenade—Couples one and three walk across set and boys pass left shoulders (girls to outside) and turn in place; return to original position with a right and left through. Side couples repeat this movement. Head couples walk to the right; half-promenade and back with a right and left through. Side couples repeat this movement. Repeat grand square and reverse grand square. Bow to partner.

SELECTED RECORD SOURCES

The following companies were cited as record sources for the dance activities on the preceding pages. They will send a complete catalog of their folk and square dance records and tapes and place you on their mailing list upon request.

1. Bowman Records, 622 Radier Drive, Glendale, CA 91201.
2. Columbia Records, Educational Department, 1473 Barnum Ave., Bridgeport, CO 06601.
3. Educational Activities, Box 392, Freeport, NY 11520.
4. Folkraft Record Company, 1159 Broad Street, Newark, NJ 07714.
5. Kimbo Educational Records, P.O. Box 477, Long Beach, NJ 07740.
6. Radio Corporation of America, RCA Victor Educational Records, 155 East 24th Street, New York, NY 10010.
7. Educational Record Sales, 157 Chambers Street, New York, NY 10007. "Young People's Folk Dances," excellent set of LP records: (1) "Folk Dance Fundamentals," (2) "Folk Dance for Beginners," (3) "Folk Dances from Near and Far," (4) "Folk Dances for Everyone," (5) "Holiday Folk Dances," (6) "Joyful Folk Dances," (7) "Folk Dances for People Who Love Folk Dancing."
8. Educational Record Sales, 157 Chambers Street, New York, NY 10007. "Everyone's Square Dances," excellent set of five LP records: (1) "Basic Square Dances," (2) "Beginners Square Dances," (3) "More Beginning Square Dances," (4) "Advanced Beginning Square Dances," (5) "Intermediate Square Dances."

ADDITIONAL RESOURCES

Folk Dance

All-American Dance Winners. Educational Activities, Inc., Box 392, Freeport, NY 11520.

American Folk Dances. Imperial Records, 137 North Western Ave., Los Angeles, CA 90053.

And the Beat Goes on for Physical Education. Kimbo Educational Record Company, P.O. Box 477, Long Branch, NJ 07740 (KEA 5020-C).

Ball Gymnastics. Kimbo Educational Record Company, Box 477, Long Branch, NJ 07740 (KIM 4031-C).

Baltic Dances. Imperial Records, 137 North Western Ave., Los Angeles, CA 90053.

Contemporary Tinikling Activities. Kimbo Educational Activities Record Company, P.O. Box 477, Long Branch, NJ 07740 (KEA 8095-C).

First Folk Dances. Michael Herman, RCA Victor, 124 East 24th Street, New York, NY 10010.

Folk Dance Funfest. Educational Dance, David McKay Company, 119 W. 40th Street, New York, NY 10010 (FD-1, FD-2, FD-3, FD-4).

Holiday Time Album. No. 302, Bowmar Records, 622 Rodier Drive, Glendale, CA 91201.

Jewish Folk Dances, Vols. I and II. Ultra Records, New York, NY. Also available from Michael Herman, Box 201, Flushing, NY 11352.

Keep on Steppin'. Educational Activities, Inc., Box 392, Freeport, NY 11520.

Library of International Dances. Folkraft Record Company, 1159 Broad Street, Newark, NJ 07714.

Russian Folk Dances. Imperial Records, 137 North Western Avenue, Los Angeles, CA 90053.

Scandinavian Folk Dance Album. Michael Herman, Box 201, Flushing, NY 11352.

Tinikling. Kimbo Educational Record Company, Box 477, Long Branch, NJ 07740 (KEA 9015-C).

Square Dance

Bedford, L. *Square Dances* (with calls). Imperial Records, 137 North Western Ave., Los Angeles, CA 90053.

Capon, J., and Hallum, R. *Get Ready to Square Dance.* Educational Activities, Inc., Box 392, Freeport, NY 11520 (AR68).

Clossum, J. *Square Dances* (without calls). Imperial Records, 137 North Western Ave., Los Angeles, CA 90053.

Durlacher, D. *Honor Your Partner.* Square Dance Associates, 102 N. Columbus Avenue, Freeport, NY 11520.

Durlacher, D. *Up-Beat Square Dances.* Educational Activities, Inc., Box 392, Freeport, NY 11520 (AR32, AR33, AR46).

Texas Square Dance Music (without calls). Henlee Record Company, 2402 Harris, Austin, TX 78767.

PART VIII

SELF-TESTING

CHAPTER 40

TEACHING SELF-TESTING ACTIVITIES

Self-testing activities are just what the term implies: movement activities that permit the participant to perform as an individual and to establish personal standards of achievement. Self-testing activities may be performed alone or with a group. They do, however, focus on personal goals and individual achievement rather than on the efforts of the group. Self-testing activities are an especially important part of the elementary school physical education program because children often find it difficult to work cooperatively toward group goals. Self-testing activities are beneficial for older children and adults because they permit one to learn new skills and take part in vigorous physical activity without having to rely on a team as a prerequisite for participation. Activities such as jogging, archery, golf, swimming, and cycling are all self-testing because of the stress placed on individual performance and personal standards of achievement.

TYPES OF SELF-TESTING ACTIVITIES

Self-testing activities may be classified in a variety of ways, depending on their nature and purpose. In the developmental approach to physical education, self-testing activities are viewed as a tool for enhancing a variety of movement, fitness, and perceptual–motor skills. Therefore, the self-testing content area may be classified into *individualized movement challenges, perceptual-motor activities, apparatus activities*, and *fitness activities*.

Individualized Movement Challenges

Throughout this text we have focused on the importance of fundamental movement and sport-skill development. A fundamental movement is an organized series of basic movements, such as running, jumping, throwing, catching, twisting, and turning. A sport skill is a fundamental skill that has been combined with other skills, refined, and applied to a variety of sport-related tasks. Both fundamental and sport-skill abilities can be further developed and refined through the use of movement challenges. Prefacing a challenge with words such as "Who can—," "Let's try—," or "See if you can—" are frequently employed by the teacher who is using individual movement challenges to develop and refine movement skills. The skill theme chapters that focused on fundamental skill development (Chapters 20 through 23) provide an abundance of movement challenge activities.

Perceptual–Motor Activities

Perceptual–motor activities may be gross or fine motor movements. They are intended to contribute to the development and refinement of specific perceptual–motor abilities and selected perceptual skills. The perceptual–motor skills most influenced by quality movement programs are body awareness, spatial awareness, directional awareness, and temporal awareness. Likewise, the perceptual skills most susceptible to influence through movement activities are visual perception (depth, form, and figure–ground perception), auditory perception (listening skills, auditory discrimination, and auditory memory), and tactile/kinesthetic perception (tactile/kinesthetic discrimination and tactile/kinesthetic memory).

All voluntary movement involves an element of perception. From the standpoint of perception, movement differs only in the type and amount of sensory and motor interpretation required. Therefore, by definition, all voluntary movement is actually perceptual–motor in nature. Hence, from the standpoint of teaching, the difference between a motor activity and a perceptual–motor activity lies in the primary objective of the movement task itself. If the primary objective is skill or fitness development, the activity is not classified as a perceptual–motor expereince. If, on the other hand, the primary objective is perceptual enhancement, the activity is classified as perceptual–motor. The activities contained in Chapter 41, "Perceptual–Motor Activities," have been selected because of their contribution to specific perceptual–motor abilities. Remember, however, that these same activities may also serve equally well to improve a variety of movement skill and fitness abilities.

Apparatus Activities

Many elementary schools are not equipped with large apparatus because of the expense and storage problems. This is not the case with small or hand-held apparatus. Equipment such as hoops, wands, beanbags, balls, balance boards, homemade rackets, coffee-can stilts, and so forth can all be effectively put to use in the elementary physical education program. The primary concept behind small-apparatus activities is that there should be sufficient equipment for every child to take part without waiting for a turn. Individualized equipment not only maximizes participation, it also heightens learning and enjoyment. A further benefit tends to be the reduction of boredom and discipline problems. Chapter 42, "Hand Apparatus Activities," provides ideas for a variety of a small apparatus, progressing from simple to complex activities for each piece of equipment.

Fitness Activities

Activities designed with the objective of enhancing specific components of fitness are frequently considered to be self-testing. Although many games, sports, and rhythmic activities may contribute to one's level of fitness, the *primary* objective of fitness activities is to improve one's level of fitness. Fitness activities focus on improved aerobic capacity, greater muscular strength and endurance, increased body flexibility, and improved motor abilities. Therefore, activities such as calisthenics, combatives, weight training, jogging, rope jumping, and distance swimming are all considered to be fitness development activities. Chapter 43, "Fitness Activities," contains several fitness development activities suitable for children.

SELECTING APPROPRIATE SELF-TESTING ACTIVITIES

The self-testing activities selected for inclusion in the program will depend on the specific objectives of the lesson and the ability level of the students. It is important to remember that this content area, like that of games and rhythmics, contains movement activities that may serve a variety of objectives and may be appropriate for varying levels of ability.

Determining Objectives

Self-testing activities permit children to test and improve their abilities without undue concern for group goals or teamwork. By virtue of being self-testing, individualized movement activities permit one to concentrate on the movement task itself. Therefore, the objectives of self-testing activities center around movement skill, perceptual–motor development and fitness development. Individualized movement activities are included in the developmental physical education lesson primarily for one or more of the following reasons:

1. Movement skill development
   a. To enhance fundamental movement abilities (basic locomotor, manipulative, and stability skills).
   b. To enhance sport-skill abilities for participation in individualized activities at a recreational or competitive level.
2. Perceptual–motor development
   a. To enhance perceptual–motor abilities (body, spatial, directional, temporal awareness).
   b. To enhance selected perceptual abilities (visual, auditory, and tactile/kinesthetic).
3. Fitness development
   a. To improve the health-related components of fitness (muscular strength and endurance, aerobic endurance, flexibility).
   b. To improve the performance-related components of fitness (balance, speed, agility, coordination, power).

Determining Ability Levels

The very nature of self-testing activities is *self-improvement*. Therefore, there should be ample room for individual differences, and the lesson should be personalized to fit the often diverse needs of the group. If the objectives of the lesson center around the use of self-testing activities to promote movement skill development, it is important to know where the group is in terms of the skills on which you intend to focus. Similarly, if the objectives of the lesson center around perceptual–motor or fitness activities, you will need to assess the students' present level of ability in each of these areas. The key to success with self-testing activities is to challenge *each* child at whatever his or her present level of ability may be.

PRACTICAL SUGGESTIONS

The following is a compilation of practical suggestions for including self-testing activities into the lesson.

1. Stress total participation.
2. Stress individual standards of achievement.
3. Stress the importance of each child's individuality.
4. Encourage children to learn from one another.
5. View yourself as a facilitator of learning.
6. Emphasize the positive aspects of each child's performance.
7. Encourage alternate solutions to movement challenges.
8. Provide a relaxed atmosphere for learning (that is, deemphasize competition).
9. Utilize informal group organizational techniques (avoid line and circle formations).
10. Present activities that offer challenges for all children.
11. Emphasize combining skills after reasonable mastery of each one alone.
12. Practice skills under static conditions prior to dynamic conditions.

13. Build skill upon skill.
14. Help children understand the "why" of their movement as well as the "how."
15. Stress basic mechanical concepts of weight transference, static and dynamic balance, giving and receiving force.
16. Encourage an awareness of individual capabilities and limitations.
17. Do not force children to attempt activities beyond their capabilities.
18. Emphasize safety at all times.
19. Require responsible use of the equipment.
20. Permit children to demonstrate.
21. Encourage a variety of solutions to movement challenges or tasks.
22. Encourage the children to attempt progressively more challenging activities.
23. Focus on exploration and guided-discovery experiences during the beginning level of skill learning.
24. Focus on combining movement skills and skill application at the intermediate level of skill learning.

SUGGESTED READING

Fowler, J. S. (1981). *Movement education*. Philadelphia: W. B. Saunders.

Gensemer, R. E. (1979). *Movement education*. Washington, DC: National Education Association.

Morrison, R. (1969). *A movement approach to educational gymnastics*. London: J. M. Dent and Sons Limited.

Riggs, M. L. (1980). *Jump to joy*. Englewood Cliffs, NJ: Prentice-Hall.

Staniford, D. J. (1982). *Natural movement for children*. Dubuque, IA: Kendall/Hunt.

Sullivan, M. (1982). *Movement exploration for young children*. Washington, DC: National Association for the Education of Young Children.

Wall, J. (1981). *Beginnings: Movement education for kindergarten and primary children*. Montreal: McGill University Printing Services.

Williams, J. (1979). *Themes for educational gymnastics*. London: Lepus.

CHAPTER 41

PERCEPTUAL–MOTOR ACTIVITIES

We are all constantly being bombarded with stimuli from our environment. The ability to recognize these stimuli, absorb them into the flow of mental processes, and store them for future use is called perception. Being able to absorb, assimilate, and react to the incoming data falls into the area of perceptual–motor ability. Because the very essence of physical education is movement, perceptual–motor skills can easily be introduced, practiced, and refined in a well-organized and sensitive program. Indeed, the physical education program is not the sole place where this type of learning can occur. Programs of this type can and should be carried out by the classroom teacher as well. Perceptual–motor learning is important, and it should be viewed as an essential part of the curriculum of every child.

The physical education curriculum affords a natural teaching base for perceptual–motor skills because in reality all voluntary movement is perceptual–motor. Interaction with our environment is a perceptual as well as a motor process. There is a dependency of voluntary motor processes on perceptual information. Conversely, the perceptual stimuli received by the organism rely on the development of one's voluntary movement abilities.

What we have, then, is a process of stimulation and reaction that is essential to human life. This characteristic must be learned, and the best time for this learning to occur is when children are *young*. During the early years, children are open to a wide variety of new and different situations that can enhance their perceptual–motor abilities.

Perceptual–motor activities help children achieve a *general* stage of readiness that helps prepare them for academic work. These activities provide a foundation for future perceptually and conceptually based learnings. Through a program of perceptual–motor skill development, children can develop and refine their movement abilities as well as their perceptual–motor abilities. Programs that stress the development of fundamental locomotor, manipulative, and stability abilities have a direct effect on enhancing the perceptual–motor components of (1) body awareness, (2) spatial awareness, (3) directional awareness, and (4) temporal awareness. Refer to Chapter 6, "Perceptual–Motor Development," for a complete discussion of these components.

BODY AWARENESS ACTIVITIES

Children are continually exploring the movement potential of their bodies. They are in the process of gaining increased information about the body parts, what the body parts can do, and how to make them do it. Teachers can assist in this exploratory process by structuring informal learning experiences that maximize children's opportunities for using a variety of body parts in a multitude of activities. The following is a compilation of some activities that will be helpful in enhancing body awareness. Table 41.1 provides a suggested progression of body awareness activities for children at the beginning level and intermediate level of perceptual–motor skill development.

Objectives

Through participation in body awareness activities, children will learn:

1. The location of the various parts of the body.
2. The names of these parts.
3. The relationship of one body part to another.
4. The importance of a single body part in leading movement.
5. How to move the body more efficiently.
6. To be aware of the body and its parts at all times.
7. To be able to contract and relax specific muscles.

Movement Experiences

LOCATING THE LARGE BODY PARTS

1. Have the children find the location of their large body parts. Have them see how quickly and accurately they can touch each part as you name it. See how quickly they can touch their

TABLE 41.1 Selected Body Awareness Activities

| Body Awareness Activities | Suggested Progression for Children | | |
	Beginning Level	Intermediate Level	Page
Locating the Large Body Parts	X		532
Locating the Small Body Parts	X		533
Move and Listen	X		533
Partner Practice	X		533
Body-Part Differentiations	X		534
Where Can You Bend?	X		534
Paired Parts	X		535
Put-Together People		X	535
Mirror Activities		X	535

Head
Neck
Chest
Waist
Stomach
Hips
Legs
Elbows
Shoulders
Back
Spine
Front

2. Repeat the activity, this time reversing the procedure. That is, point to the body parts and have the children name them. The body parts may be as general or as specific as you wish, depending on the children's abilities.
3. Have the children find out how large their body parts are. For example:

   • Move your hand down the length of your arm. Where does it start, and where does it stop?
   • Place two hands around your waist. . . . How big is it? . . . How can you move at the waist? Try bending forward, backward, and sideways. . . . Can you twist at the waist?

4. Help the children discover all about the sides of their bodies. For example, you may request that they

   • Move one hand down the sides of their bodies
   • Find the side of the head . . . shoulder . . . chest . . . waist . . . hip . . . knee . . . ankle . . . foot
   • Repeat the same procedure on the opposite side of the body.

LOCATING THE SMALL BODY PARTS

1. While the children are standing, the teacher may have the children
   Put their elbows together.
   Put their feet apart.
   Touch one elbow.
   Put their knees together.

Touch their noses.
Touch their toes with their arms crossed.
Touch one knee and one foot.
Place their palms together.
Touch their heels.
Touch their eyelashes, eyebrows.

2. Use other body parts in place of or in addition to those just mentioned.

MOVE AND LISTEN

1. Have the children perform a locomotor task, but have them stop and position themselves on your command. For example, you may have them moving about the room and tell them to stop on
   One foot
   Both feet
   One hand
   Seat and both feet
   Feet and fingers
   Head, hands, and feet
   Hands and knees
   Back
   One foot and one hand
   One foot, two hands, and head

2. Permit the children to choose their own way of stopping and positioning themselves on your command of "Freeze."

PARTNER PRACTICE

1. Have the children move around the floor to a different person each time and touch the following body parts on that person, as directed by the teacher:

Spine	Arms	Toes	Back
Ears	Elbows	Hands	Knees
Neck	Legs	Fingers	Hips
Chin	Ankles	Chest	Feet
Shoulders	Wrists	Stomach	Heels

2. Repeat the first activity with the children using the body parts you named, instead of the hands, to touch the corresponding body part of another child.

BODY-PART DIFFERENTIATION

1. Hip movement with bending at the knee:
   Draw the knees up to the chest, then thrust them out straight while on the back.
   Do the same thing, but with continuous circular thrusting movements.
   While lying on the stomach, draw both knees up under the stomach and then extend them both outward.
   While on the stomach, bend one knee and draw it up alongside the body, on the floor, until it is in line with the hip.
2. While they are lying on their backs, have the children:
   Lift one leg and lower it.
   Move the leg out to the side along the floor, then return it to the midposition beside the other leg.
   Swing the leg out to the side and back.
   Rotate the leg back and forth on the heel.
   Lift one leg and cross it over the other leg and touch floor if possible.
   Swing one leg over the other.
   Lift the leg and rotate it at the hip, making circles in the air with the foot.
   Hold tightly an object placed between his knees.
3. Repeat the preceding activities while on the stomach.
4. While they are standing, have the children perform the following shoulder movements:
   Move a hand up alongside the body, extend it over the head, and lower it in the same way.
   Extend an arm out at the side, then lower it.
   Extend an arm over the head, then lower it.
   Extend an arm out in front, then lower it.
   Extend an arm out in front, then move it from the center out to the side and back again.
   Hunch the shoulders up and down with the arms at the sides, then swing them forward and backward.
   Swing the arms in a circle in front of the body.
   Swing the arms in a full circle at the side.
   Extend the arms out at the sides and swing them in circles of various sizes.
   Move just the shoulders forward and backward.
   Move the shoulders in a circle.
5. While they are seated, have the children perform the following hand and finger movements:
   Make a fist.
   Spread the fingers apart, then move them back together.
   Bring the tip of the thumb and all of the fingers together.
   Bring the tip of the thumb and the "pointer" finger (forefinger) together.
   Extend the fingers and thumb to maximum and then relax.
   Move the thumb across the four fingers and back.
   Touch each fingertip with the tip of the thumb.
   Begin with the "pointer" finter and move to the little finger, then back.
   Grasp a ball in one hand, then lift one finger at a time.
   Close the hand to a fist, and then release one finger at a time.
   Extend the hands, then lower one finger at a time to form a fist.

WHERE CAN YOU BEND?

1. Permit the children to experiment with a still dowel and with a jointed Barbie doll to see where the body parts bend. If possible, a paper skeleton or a real one and a dentist's jaw could be used to graphically portray the body parts that bend.
2. Encourage the children to move the following joints in as many ways as possible:
   Jaw
   Neck
   Shoulders
   Elbow
   Wrist
   Fingers
   Waist
   Hip
   Knee
   Ankle
   Toes
3. Experiment with what movement is like *without* one of the preceding joints, one at a time.

PAIRED PARTS

1. Have the children touch one body part to another. The following is a list of examples:
   Touch your ear to a shoulder.
   Touch your shoulder to a knee.
   Touch your nose to a knee.
   Touch your elbow to a thigh.
   Touch your thigh to a knee.
   Touch your knee to an ankle.
   Touch your toe to a knee.
   Touch your toe to the chin.
2. There are numerous other possibilities for touching paired parts. Have the children explore them.

PUT-TOGETHER PEOPLE

1. Have the children make a life-sized figure by crushing single pieces of newspaper and stuffing them into long underwear. After the underwear is completely stuffed, dress the figure and have the children each draw a head and features on a paper bag. The hands and feet may be made with gloves and an old pair of shoes. The stuffed figure may be representative of a particular time of the year or theme.
2. Cut out the body parts of a "person" using construction paper or poster board. Have the children assemble the legs, arms, head, and torso of the figures. Hook the pieces together with brads, or tape the pieces together to complete the figure.
3. Cut out the body party parts of two or more "people." Give each child in the group one body part. See if they can assemble the figure. The same activity may be repeated as a relay.
4. Using a doll with movable joints, have the children bend it into various positions and then see if they can reproduce these positions with their bodies.
5. Giants: The children sit in a circle around two giant paper cut-out parts of two bodies, one a boy, the other a girl. Two children are chosen to compete in putting the parts together; the one completing the giant figure first is the winner.

MIRROR ACTIVITIES

1. One child stands in front of a full-length mirror. The other children give directions to locate his body parts. The child can only look at his reflection in the mirror when touching the designated part. If he makes a mistake, the child giving the last instruction takes the mirror position.
2. Repeat the preceding activity, but have the mirror child use both hands to touch his body.
3. Repeat the preceding activities, but indicate the right or left parts of the body in the mirror reflection.
4. The teacher serves as the mirror. The children imitate the movements of the "mirror."

SPATIAL AWARENESS ACTIVITIES

Body awareness involves two primary factors: *egocentric localization* and *objective localization*. Egocentric localization involves development of a subjective space structure in which objects in the environment are located by the child relative to his or her own position in space. Objective localization is more advanced and involves development of an objective structure in which objects are located independent of one's own position in space.

Objectives

Through practice in spatial awareness activities, the children will:

1. Learn how much space their bodies occupy.
2. Be able to project their bodies into external space.
3. Be able to locate objects in space from a personal frame of reference (egocentric localization).
4. Be able to locate objects in space independent of one another (objective localization).

TABLE 41.2   Suggested Spatial Awareness Activities

Spatial Awareness Activities	Suggested Progression for Children		Page
	Beginning Level	Intermediate Level	
Big and Small	X		536
Maze Walk	X		536
Rope Walking	X		536
Back Space	X		536
Obstacle Course	X		537
Body Space		X	537
Near and Far		X	537
Map Activities		X	537
Miscellaneous Activities	X	X	538

5. Improve their fundamental movement abilities.
6. Enhance their efficiency of movement.

Movement Experiences

BIG AND SMALL

1. Have the children find a place on the area where they are free from contact with others. Ask them to make themselves as small as possible. Point out that as small ''balls,'' each child takes up very little room and so does not bother his neighbor.
2. Now have the children make themselves as big as possible. Now point out that as they get bigger, so do their neighbors. This means that each needs more room for himself and to keep from bumping someone else. The children become familiar with their spatial relationships to others.
3 The children can be asked to assume different shapes such as a tree, rock, or telephone pole. Have the children assume the new positions at varying rates of speed. Assuming the shapes of letters and numbers may also be performed.

MAZE WALK

1. Children walk through a maze of chairs and tables without touching.

Walk between objects
Step over objects
Crawl under objects
Walk around objects
Step on objects
2. Perform the maze activities using a variety of locomotor activities.
   Jumping
   Hopping
   Skipping
   Crawling

ROPE WALKING

1. Place ropes in various patterns and geometric shapes on the floor. Have the children walk the rope forward.
   Wavy lines
   Circle
   Square
   Triangle
   Step over and through objects
2. Repeat the activities, but do them while blindfolded. Have children tell you about the shape of the line they are walking on.

BACK SPACE

1. Walk a rope placed on the floor going backward. Place the rope in various patterns.

2. Throw objects backward to a visualized goal.
3. Sit down on an object without visually monitoring it.
   - Chair
   - Beanbag chair
   - Innertube
   - Trampoline
4. Walk backward through a simple obstacle course that the child has had an opportunity to visually memorize.
5. Count the number of steps to a point on the floor while walking forward. Repeat while walking backward and see how close the children come to the predetermined point.

OBSTACLE COURSE

1. Use tasks such as
   - "Footsteps" placed on the floor
   - Carpet squares on the floor
   - Climbing and sliding ropes
   - Crawling over and under and through objects
   - Stepping into shoe boxes
2. Map
   - Follow yarn line through the obstacle course.

BODY SPACE

1. Outline the children's bodies on a sheet of newsprint while they are lying on their backs. Have the children:
   - Cut out their bodies
   - Color their bodies
   - Dress their bodies
   - Hang their bodies up
   - Compare sizes
2. Gross motor activities:
   - Have the children roll over and see how much space they occupied.
   - Have the children spread out and see how much space they can occupy.
   - Have the children see how little space they can occupy.
   - Have them crawl under a table and other objects of different heights and see how well they fit without touching.

Count steps, jumps, and so on taken to go from one point to another.

OTHER SPACE

Using empty milk cartons:
   - Compare different-sized milk cartons (half pint to gallon containers).
   - Compare the water-holding capacity of the containers. Compare size by pouring from carton to carton.
   - Fill different-sized containers with sand. Compare the weights of the containers. Compare the volumes of sand held by each container.

NEAR AND FAR

1. Egocentric localization:
   - Have the children estimate the distance from where they are standing to a specific point by the number of steps that it will take to get there.
   - Measure the distance in steps. Compare estimates.
2. Objective localization:
   - Have the children estimate the distance between two independent points, for example, the doll house and the carpentry bench.
   - Step off the distance and compare.

MAP ACTIVITIES

1. Map reading:
   - Place a large map of the classroom, school, community, or state on the floor. Give them a route to follow, indicating specific points that they must visit before proceeding to the next point.
   - Give each child a map with clues to the "treasure." Indicate in precise terms where they should go and the procedures to be followed.

MISCELLANEOUS SPATIAL AWARENESS ACTIVITIES

1. Locomotor movements:
   Crawling
   Leaping
   Jumping
2. Axial movements:
   Bending
   Rising
   Stretching
   Reaching
   Twisting
   Falling
3. Following objects:
   Following colors
   Following arrows
   Following words
   Tunnel crawling
4. Exploring space:
   Self-space
   Common space
   Moving at different levels
   Moving in different floor patterns

DIRECTIONAL AWARENESS ACTIVITIES

Directional awareness is of considerable concern to the classroom teacher and to children who are beginning formal instruction in reading. Directional awareness involves both an internal and external sensitivity for sidedness. Activities designed to enhance directional awareness may have an influence on perceptual readiness for reading. See Table 41.3 for a recommended progression of directional awareness activities.

Objectives

Practice in movement activities that emphasize the directional aspect of the task may:

1. Contribute to the development of laterality (internal awareness of direction).
2. Contribute to the development of directionality (external projection of laterality).
3. Aid in establishing readiness for reading.
4. Contribute to the development of fundamental movement abilities.
5. Enhance one's ability to move efficiently through space.

TABLE 41.3 Selected Directional Awareness Activities

Directional Awareness Activities	Suggested Progression for Children		
	Beginning Level	Intermediate Level	Page
Clock Games	X		539
Swinging-Ball Activities	X		539
Directional Commands	X		539
Over, Under, and Around	X		539
Walking-Board Activities	X		540
Unilateral, Bilateral, and Cross-Lateral Activities	X	X	540
Throwing Activities		X	540
Chalkboard Activities	X		540
Ladder Activities		X	540
Twist-Board Activities		X	541
Creeping and Walking Activities		X	541
Ball Activities		X	541

Movement Experiences

CLOCK GAMES

1. Make a clock on a chalkboard about 18 inches in diameter. Instruct the children to place their right hand on one of the numbers and their left hand on a second number, holding a piece of chalk in each hand. Ask them to move their left hand to a different number and their right hand to a different number on your command. Both hands should move at the same time and arrive at their goals at the same time.
2. Variations:
   Toward the center: Place hands on the circumference of circle and bring both to center (0). Place hands on 1 and 5 and bring to 0, then 6 and 2 to 0.
   Away from center: Begin with both hands on 0 and move out to specified numbers.
   Parallel movements: Put the left hand on 7 and right hand on 0, then move the left hand to 0 and right hand to 3. Change directions.
   Crossed midline movements. Place the left hand on 7 and right hand on 1, then move both hands to 0. Change directions.
   Left to right: Place the left hand at 7 and right hand at 0, then move the left hand to 0 and right hand to 1.

SWINGING-BALL ACTIVITIES

1. Attach a ball to a string. Move it in different directions and in different orientations to the child.
   Tap it, then catch it.
   Swing it with one hand, then the other, then both.
2. Swinging activities:
   Swing ball to the left and to the right.
   Swing ball forward and backward.
   Swing ball in circles around the child.
   Swing ball in circles in front of the child.
   Swing ball in different planes above the child as he lies on his back.
   While he is on his back, swing ball from left to right, then from head to toe.

3. Striking activities: repeat the preceding activities but using striking motions.

DIRECTIONAL COMMANDS

The following are some examples of patterns in which children may move in order to enhance directional awareness. The number of possibilities is limitless. Use your imagination.

Run forward ten steps and walk backward five steps.
Put your feet together and jump to one side.
Hop forward three times on one foot, then backward three times on the other foot.
Move sideways across the room.
Have the child move close to you and then move far away.
Move from the front of room to the rear of room, going over one object and under another object.
Stand near the desk.
Stand far away from the pencil sharpener.
Point to the wall nearest you and walk to that wall.
Place the closest chair between the desk and the wall.
One child sits and another stands. Have the standing child move in front of, to the side of (etc.) the sitting child.

OVER, UNDER, AND AROUND

1. Long jumping rope:
   Two people hold a jump rope and place the rope on the floor. The child runs and jumps over it. The rope is raised slightly for each succeeding jump. Game ends when the child hits the rope.
   Go under a high rope, which is then lowered slightly each try.
   Walk over instead of running and jumping.
2. Place several objects around the gym, such as jump ropes, walking boards, mats, chairs, tires, ladder, or any large equipment. Children follow the leader and imitate as he moves around the obstacles.
   Could be played in the classroom as leader moves around room.

Place objects on the floor and permit each child to go around the objects in his or her own direction and name the direction in which he went.

Give verbal commands for the direction of each obstacle.

3. Blindfold the children. Have them work with a "seeing" partner who gives directional commands (no tactile clues) on how to get to the object.

WALKING-BOARD ACTIVITIES

1. Walk forward.
2. Walk backward—discourage looking back.
3. Walk sideways—slide one foot over, then bring the other one to meet it.
4. Turn on the board:
   Walk forward, turn, and walk sideways.
   Walk forward, turn, and return, walking forward.
   Walk backward, turn, and return, walking backward.
   Vary combinations.
5. Step over and under objects placed on the board.
6. Walk across the board carrying heavy objects.

UNILATERAL, BILATERAL, AND CROSS-LATERAL ACTIVITIES

1. Bilateral movements:
   Lie flat on the floor on your back with your arms at your sides and your feet together.
   Move feet apart as far as you can, keeping the knees stiff.
   Move the arms along the floor until the hands come together above the head, keeping elbows stiff.
   Move the arms and legs at the same time.
2. Unilateral and cross-lateral movements:
   Lie flat on the floor on your back with your arms at your sides and your feet together.
   Move the right leg only to an extended position and return it.
   Repeat, with the left leg only, right arm only, and left arm only.
   Move the right leg and right arm together.

Move the left arm and leg together.
Move the right arm and the left together.
Move the left arm and the right leg.

THROWING ACTIVITIES

1. Use beanbag and a wastebasket:
   Set a basket in front of the child and have him throw at it.
   Vary the basket's orientation to the right or left and have child throw at it.
2. Use a ball to roll at a bowling pin.
   Vary the location of the bowling pin or the child.
   Vary the distance of the roll.
3. From a prone position or a supine position, have the child throw a beanbag:
   Upward
   Forward
   Backward
   To each side

CHALKBOARD ACTIVITIES

1. Dot-to-dot. Teacher makes two dots, child connects, teacher makes a third dot and child connects, and so on.
   (Do not cross child's midline here.)
2. Dot-to-dot, but cross child's midline.
3. Draw double circles and change directions after completion and/or in the middle of drawing.
4. Draw "lazy-eight" figures. With one hand, then the other; one direction, then reverse.
5. Draw vertical lines, up–down, down–up.
6. Draw horizontal lines, left–right, right–left.
7. Draw horizontal lines and vertical lines simultaneously.
8. Draw a square, then alter size, direction, and starting point.

LADDER ACTIVITIES

1. *Walking:* Looking straight ahead, the child walks the length of the ladder.
   Walk forward in the spaces.
   Walk backward in the spaces.

Walk sideways in the spaces. Walking side-ways may be done by

    Leading with the left foot

    Leading with the right foot

    Continually crossing the lead foot in front

    Continually crossing the lead foot in back

    Walk the rungs (forward, backward, side-ways).

2. Crawling: The ladder is turned on its side, and to secure it, the teacher sits on the top side. The children crawl in and out of the spaces.

    Crawl forward.

    Crawl backward.

    Do not touch the rungs if possible.

TWIST-BOARD ACTIVITIES

1. The child places his feet about shoulder width apart on the board and bends his knees slightly. He may twist by

    Moving both of his arms to one side and then to the other side.

    Swinging one arm forward and up, and swing-ing the other arm backward and down.

2. The child puts his left arm behind his back and uses his right arm to simulate a one-arm breast stroke. This will cause the child to turn com-pletely around.

3. Repeat step 2, and change arm positions (right arm behind back, left arm moving).

4. While twisting, the child

    Crosses his arm in front of his chest.

    Extends his arms (hands clasped):

        In front of his body

        Behind his body

        Over his head

CREEPING AND WALKING ACTIVITIES

1. Creeping:

    Creep in a homolateral pattern (left hand with left knee, right hand with right knee) while looking at target placed at eye level.

    Creep in a cross-lateral pattern (left hand with right knee, right hand with left knee), looking first at eye-level target, then at the forward hand.

    Creep in a homolateral pattern while looking at the hand that goes out in front.

    Creep forward, backward, and to the side us-ing the preceding patterns.

2. Walking:

    Walk in a homolateral pattern (left hand points to left toes while right arm is stretched behind the child, then right hand points to right toes).

    Cross-lateral walking.

    Midair change—begin with the left arm for-ward and the left foot forward, with the weight evenly distributed on both feet. Right arm should be straight out in back. On command "Change," each child jumps up in the air, re-versing the position of arms and legs. The eyes should fixate on a target at all times and the child should land on the takeoff spot.

    Midair change—cross-lateral movement (left arm and right leg forward).

BALL ACTIVITIES

1. Use one hand, then repeat the skills with the other hand.

    Tap a swinging ball.

    Bounce and catch a ball with one hand.

    Dribble a ball with one hand.

    Bounce and catch with alternating hands.

    Throw in various directions.

    Catch from different directions.

2. Use one foot, then repeat the skills with the other foot.

    Kick a ball with alternate feet, using the toe.

    Kick a ball with alternate feet, using the in-step.

    Trap a ball with one foot, then the other.

    Trap a ball with one knee, then the other.

TEMPORAL AWARENESS ACTIVITIES

Temporal awareness involves the development of a time structure within the body. Eye—hand coordination and eye—foot coordination refer to the child's ability to coordinate movements and are the end result of a fully established time structure within the child. This "clock mechanism" helps children to better coordinate the movements of their bodies with the various sensory systems. Refer to Table 41.4 for a recommended progression of activities.

Objectives

Through temporal awareness movement activities, children will learn:

1. *Synchrony,* which is the ability to get the body parts to work together smoothly.
2. *Rhythm,* which is the process of performing many synchronous acts in a harmonious pattern or succession.
3. *Sequence,* which is the proper order of actions required to perform a skill.
4. *Eye–hand coordination* and *eye–foot coordination,* which are the end results of synchrony, rhythm, and sequence being efficiently integrated.

Movement Experiences

BALL ACTIVITIES

1. Stationary ball:
   Contact it with an open hand.
   Contact it with an implement.
   Kick at it.
   Contact it with various body parts.
2. Swinging ball:
   Contact it with an open hand as a fist.
   Alternate left and right hands.
   Contact it with various body parts.
   Contact it with various implements, moving from shorter to longer levers (spoon, table-tennis paddle, tennis racket, squash racket, baseball bat).
   Catch the swinging ball with both hands.
   Catch the swinging ball with one hand.
   Visually track the ball as it swings, without moving the head.
   Visually track the ball and point at it as it swings.

RHYTHMIC MOVEMENT

1. On the signal, have children find their own "personal space." Have them make a low, balanced shape, keeping one hand free to tap on the floor along with the beat of the drum. When the drum changes beat and pattern, the children must do the same.
2. Have the children, remaining balanced, tap with a foot, elbow, and heel. Have a body part move in the air, following the drum. Use different

TABLE 41.4 Selected Temporal Awareness Activities

Temporal Awareness Activities	Suggested Progression for Children		
	Beginning Level	Intermediate Level	Page
Ball Activities	X		542
Rhythmic Movement	X		542
My Beat	X		543
Free Flow	X		543
Moving-Target Toss	X	X	543
Balloon-Volleying Activities	X	X	543
Miscellaneous Large-Motor Temporal Activities	X	X	543
Miscellaneous Fine-Motor Temporal Activities	X	X	543

tempos in each a position. Keep the tempo even. Don't accelerate or decelerate.

MY BEAT

This activity enables the children to make and follow their own tempo and sequence.

1. Each child makes his or her own accompaniment and sets his or her own beat. They can make noises with their mouths or slap a hand against their bodies. Once they have established even beats, have them explore their personal space (the area around them) while moving to the beat.
2. Have each child explore around the room while moving to the beat. Let them move to a different tempo.

FREE FLOW

1. Ask the children to perform a relaxed, smooth, swinging motion with their bodies. The motion can take them anywhere around the play area. (Stress spatial awareness to avoid collisions.) Have them perform a controlled swing so that it can be stopped on command. Make sure that when they stop a movement, they are in complete balance and control.
2. Introduce physical obstacles that the children must successfully negotiate in order to improve body control and movement.

MOVING-TARGET TOSS

1. Have the children line up facing the target. Use an inflatable toy punching clown that will right itself after being pushed down. Use a barrel, waste basket, or pot and attempt to toss an object at it while it is moving from a reclining position to its normal upright position.
2. Suspend a hoop from a rope. Start it swinging in a pendular motion. Have children throw beanbags through the swinging hoop.
3. Roll a hoop or tire along the floor. Toss objects through it.

BALLOON-VOLLEYING ACTIVITIES

Keep a balloon up in the air by
Using a volleying motion.
Hitting it underhand.
Hitting it above the head.
Hiting it below the waist.
Using various body parts to hit it.
Weighting the balloon slightly and repeating the preceding activities.

MISCELLANEOUS LARGE-MOTOR TEMPORAL ACTIVITIES

1. Move in different ways to a beat.
2. Jump rope to a beat.
3. Bounce a ball to a beat.
4. Pass a ball rhythmically.
5. Partners make their own beat and move to it.
6. Perform movements in sequence.
7. Accelerate and decelerate movement.
8. Create and absorb force.
9. Perform tossing and catching activities.
10. Perform kicking and trapping activities.
11. Perform dodging activities.

MISCELLANEOUS FINE-MOTOR TEMPORAL ACTIVITIES

1. Bead stringing.
2. Jacks.
3. Pick-up sticks.
4. Lacing and sewing cards.
5. Clay modeling.
6. Cutting.
7. Coloring and pasting.
8. Finger painting.
9. Nuts and bolts.
10. Sewing.
11. Weaving.
12. Zipping, snapping, and buttoning.
13. Carpentry activities.
14. Puppetry.
15. Chalkboard activities.

16. Tracing.
17. Pouring skills.

2. To increase the ability to utilize external clues in determining depth, distance, and size.
3. To enhance the ability to move efficiently in three-dimensional space.
4. To enhance fundamental movement abilities.

VISUAL PERCEPTION ACTIVITIES

The visual apparatus is complete and functional at birth. Visual abilities develop rapidly during the early years of life and are crucial to effective functioning in a world that is visually oriented. The processes of maturation and gaining experience both contribute to the development of highly sophisticated visual perception abilities. It has been estimated that up to 80 percent of all information we take in and utilize comes from the visual modality. As a result, it becomes abundantly clear that the development and refinement of accurate visual perception are extremely important. The following pages contain a variety of movement experiences that have been found helpful in developing three aspects of visual perception crucial to effective functioning in school and the world, namely depth perception, form perception, and figure–ground perception. Refer to Table 41.5 for a recommended progression of activities for children at the beginning and intermediate level of visual perception skill development.

Depth Perception

Depth perception is the ability to judge relative distances in three-dimensional space. Teachers working with depth-perception activities need to consciously plan many and varied spatial and dimensional cues to serve as reference points for judgment of distance.

Objectives
Depth-perception enhancement activities are designed:

1. To enhance the ability to accurately judge distances and depth.

Movement Experiences

BOWLING

When rolling a ball toward an object, line the lane moving toward the target with Indian clubs or markers of some type.

TARGETS

Use a box within which balls land in various lengths and depths. It can be used as a target for throwing, striking, and kicking a light ball. Target throwing with all types of objects and at various distances is helpful.

HOOPS

Crawling through hula hoops arranged in three-dimensional formations, plywood boxes with shapes cut out of the sides, pipes, and logs is good for tactile realization of depth.

JUMPING

Jumping from heights, over objects, and from one object to another develops perception of depth and distance. Use jumping from various heights on an angled balance beam or steps to the floor.

BALANCE BEAM

Place a balance beam diagonally toward the wall. Have the children find the point where they can

TABLE 41.5   Selected Visual Perception Activities

Visual Perception Activities	Suggested Progression for Children		Page
	Beginning Level	Intermediate Level	
Depth-Perception Activities			
Bowling	X		544
Targets	X		544
Hoops	X		544
Jumping		X	544
Balance Beam		X	544
Boxes		X	546
Form-Perception Activities			
Shape Walking	X		546
Tracing	X		546
Making Things	X		546
Body Shapes	X		547
Shape Tag	X		547
Stepping Shapes	X		547
Matching Shapes	X		547
Beanbag Toss		X	547
Shadow Pantomime		X	547
Figure—Ground Perception Activities			
Discrimination	X		547
Sorting	X		548
Attention	X		548
Ladder Maze	X		548
Target Toss	X		548
Eggshell Walk	X		548
Rope Walk	X		548
Paddle Balance		X	548
Rope Maze		X	548
Candyland		X	548
Hidden Objects		X	548
Finger Fixation		X	548
Pencil—Wall Fixation		X	548
Paper-Punch Pictures		X	548

reach and touch the wall while walking on the beam. Tape several points onto the balance beam. Show the children one piece of tape; remove it and have the children walk and stop where they think the tape was.

BOXES

Place boxes of various heights in the center of a room. Attach objects at various heights to the wall. Instruct the children to select the box that will best assist them in retrieving the object they want.

Form Perception

Form perception, or the ability to recognize shapes, forms, and symbols, is necessary for academic success. Children may be able to identify shapes correctly, but because of distortions of their visual memory, are often unable to reproduce them. Perception of shape constancy becomes crucial to children's ability to recognoze shapes. They must learn that two- and three-dimensional forms belong to certain categories of shapes, regardless of size, color, texture, mode of representation, or the angle seen by the perceiver. Recognition of similarities and differences is the first step in identifying shapes and forms. Object discrimination is the second.

Three- and four-year-olds rely on shape or form rather than color for identification of objects. At five years of age, color is generally a more important tool than form for identification of an object. At ages six to seven, color and form are both important.

Objectives
Form perception activities are used to help children:

1. Recognize and reproduce basic shapes.
2. Perceive differences in shapes and pieces of a puzzle.
3. Match similar symbols.
4. Recognize and reproduce basic forms and use them in generalized situations (for example, to be able to see that a square and a triangle can form a house).
5. Draw forms that exist in the environment and that can be seen in isolation of one another.

Movement Experiences

SHAPE WALKING

Walk simple geometric shapes placed on the floor.

1. Have the children walk a rope that is placed in various geometric shapes. Walking barefoot will enhance the tactile clues.
2. Walk a masking-tape line and "feel" the shape with your toes.
3. Present a simple geometric shape to the children. Permit them to visually monitor it while they attempt to walk out the shape on the floor. They should strive to arrive back at the starting point when they complete the shape.
4. Repeat the preceding activity, but do not permit visual monitoring of the displayed form.
5. Name a shape and have the children walk it out, returning to the starting point when they have completed the shapes.

TRACING

Trace around geometric shapes with the fingers.

1. Use three-dimensional shapes.
2. Use templates.
3. Trace shapes drawn on a sheet of paper.
4. Reproduce the shapes by tracing over them.
5. Have the children complete incomplete geometric shapes drawn for them.

MAKING THINGS

Make a variety of things utilizing various shapes.

1. Make a collage of geometric shapes.
2. Use various-shaped blocks to build a familiar object.

3. Draw a picture of a person composed entirely of different geometric shapes.
4. Make shapes using toothpicks, straws, or tongue depressors.

BODY SHAPES

Have the children use their bodies to make a variety of shapes.

1. Have the children form various shapes, letters, and numerals with their bodies.
2. Have the children form part of a shape with their bodies. Ask one to help complete the shape he or she thinks the others are forming.

SHAPE TAG

Play tag using selected shapes as free places.

STEPPING SHAPES

Spread various shapes on the floor around the room. Have the children step only on certain shapes. Make and play a game of twister, using shapes as the focal point.

MATCHING SHAPES

Play matching games using various shapes and sizes. Sort objects according to shape.

BEANBAG TOSS

Throw beanbags on targets with different-shaped holes cut out. Points are scored for throwing through the various shapes.

SHADOW PANTOMIME

Hang a sheet with a light in front of it in a closet with the door open. Have child imitate physical activities while the others guess what they think is being done.

Figure—Ground Perception

Visual figure—ground perception is the ability to select a limited number of stimuli from a mass. These particular stimuli (auditory, tactile, olfactory, kinesthetic, visual, and/or gustatory) form the figure. The others form a dim field. This figure is the center of attention. When the attention shifts, the former figure fades into the background. We can only perceive something in its relation to its field.

In teaching children who have not fully developed their figure—ground perception, attempt to limit the number of stimuli in the background and progress by adding gradually. For example, practice dribbling the "red" ball *not* on the red-and-black tiled floor, but on a posterboard (white or light solid color) or sheet to simplify contrasting the figure of attention and the background. Do not place the children in a milieu of posters, streamers, and other attention-grabbers.

Objectives
Visual figure—ground activities help children:

1. Focus attention on the object of regard.
2. Move efficiently through the visual field.
3. Locate objects located in the field of vision.
4. Improve eye—hand and eye—foot coordination.

Movement Experiences

DISCRIMINATION

Discriminate between various objects in a room. Find objects that are difficult to locate.

SORTING

Sort according to size, shape, color, texture, number, thickness, and length.

ATTENTION

Practice shifting attention by selecting designated objects from a box or bag.

LADDER MAZE

Place a ladder on a floor of a solid design, on one with a diagonal design, and on one with various other designs. Have the children step between the rungs without touching them.

TARGET TOSS

Use targets to focus attention. Throw beanbags at selected parts of the target. For example, you may use a large human picture and throw at various body parts.

EGGSHELL WALK

Place a path of eggshell halves on the floor. Cross that path with other paths of various materials, such as rope, tape, and paper. Have the children step on anything except the eggshells.

ROPE WALK

Walk on a rope winding through a myriad of objects.

PADDLE BALANCE

Have the children balance a ball on a paddle or board.

ROPE MAZE

Form a maze of rope paths on the floor. Have identical clues at each end of the same rope. Send the children to find the match of the clue they are given.

CANDYLAND

Play a life-sized version of "Candyland" (by Parker Brothers) where the children spin for colors and take their places on the appropriate color on the "board."

HIDDEN OBJECTS

Use *Highlights* magazine for pictures with concealed objects that the children can find.

FINGER FIXATION

Have the children hold their right and left forefingers about a foot apart and a foot from their eyes. They then look quickly from one finger to the other. They must be sure to "land" each time. If they have difficulty, they can be helped by having another person move her own finger in the same way the eyes are to move.

PENCIL–WALL FIXATION

The children hold a pencil erect about 10 to 12 inches in front of their nose. They then look from pencil to numbers on a calendar (or picture on the wall) and back again for several "round trips." They must move their eyes quickly and fixate on each object.

PAPER-PUNCH PICTURES

Punch holes in a picture until the childrren are no longer able to obtain meaning from the pictures.

Pictures of many objects are harder to perceive than pictures of only one subject.

AUDITORY PERCEPTION ACTIVITIES

The development of auditory perceptual abilities has not received the attention by authors and practitioners that the visual modality has. Auditory perception, however, is important, particularly with young children. Their inability to read makes their formal education primarily one of (1) listening to auditory clues, (2) discriminating between sounds, and (3) applying meaning to them.

Auditory perception is enhanced when children attend to verbal directions, translate music into movement, and interpret the "feel" of various sounds through movement. The use of musical instruments aids in developing the auditory abilities. The following pages contain numerous activities for developing and reinforcing listening skills, auditory discrimination, and auditory memory abilities. Refer to Table 41.6 for a recommended progression of activities.

Listening Skills

It is important for children to hear and remember what is said, but it is also crucial that they first *listen* to what is being said. Learning to listen is basic to auditory perception. Many children have been conditioned to "tune out" certain auditory clues. Take, for example, the child engrossed in a television program who somehow manages not to hear the pleas of mother or father to come to dinner. We are all familiar with children who "never listen." Learning to listen to auditory clues can be developed through a variety of activities. Games that involve an awareness and identification of sound sources enhance listening abilities. Activities that require the following of simple directions are also helpful, as well as activities that require a motoric response to a verbal command.

Objectives

Auditory perception activities to develop listening skills contribute to children's ability:

1. To develop an awareness of sound sources.
2. To identify various familiar sounds.
3. To listen to auditory clues in the immediate environment.
4. To respond appropriately to auditory commands.
5. To respond efficiently, through movement, to auditory clues.
6. To discriminate between various auditory clues.

Movement Experiences

TRADITIONAL GAMES

Many traditional games that children have played down through the years involve a considerable amount of listening skills:

1. Simon Says
2. Mother May I
3. Red Rover
4. Red Light

HOT AND COLD

Hide an object somewhere in the room while "it" is not looking. "It" attempts to find the object by moving around the room and listening to the loudness or softness of the class's clapping. As he or she approaches the object, the clapping becomes louder. As he or she moves away from it, the clapping becomes softer.

CLAP CLAP

The class is spread out around the room. One child is told to clap her hands twice when "it" says "Clap clap." "It" points to the person who she thought did the clapping.

TABLE 41.6   Selected Auditory Perception Activities

| Auditory Perception Activities | Suggested Progression for Children | | Page |
	Beginning Level	Intermediate Level	
Listening Skills			549
Traditional Games	X		549
Hot and Cold	X		549
Clap Clap	X		549
Poems	X		551
Music	X		551
Bounce Bounce	X		551
Active Animals	X		551
Hands	X		551
Echo	X		551
Listening Walk	X		551
It Is I		X	551
Tape-Recorder Sounds		X	551
Voice Recording		X	552
Freeze and Melt		X	552
Marching		X	552
Auditory Discrimination			552
Close Your Eyes	X		553
Musical Instruments	X		553
What Does It Sound Like?	X		553
What Is It?	X		553
Where Is the Bell?	X		553
Keep Off		X	553
Sound Targets		X	553
Bounce Off		X	553
Match the Cans		X	553
Auditory Memory			553
A Trip to the Zoo	X		554
Story Telling	X		554
Action Rhymes	X		554
Instrument Playing	X		554
Silly Hat		X	554
Horse Race		X	554
The Winner Is ...		X	554
Lost and Found		X	554

POEMS

Read a poem to the class, requesting them to fill in the rhyming words.

MUSIC

Listen to music that has a variety of fast and slow sections. Request that they move about the room in time to the music. If space does not permit active movement, simply have the children raise their hands when they hear the fast part or the slow part.

BOUNCE BOUNCE

Have a small group of children sit down with their backs toward you. Drop a utility ball from waist height and let it bounce. Children should count the number of bounces that the ball makes.

ACTIVE ANIMALS

Use a variety of rhythm instruments to depict the sounds of moving animals while telling a story containing the names of several animals. Whenever the animal's name is mentioned, the child with the corresponding instrument makes its sound. For example:

1. Drum for a lumbering elephant.
2. Sandpaper blocks for a slithering snake.
3. Triangle for birds.
4. Xylophone for caterpillar.
5. Rhythmic sticks for galloping horses.

HANDS

One child is blindfolded and must guess what another child is doing with her hands. She may, for example, be clapping, snapping, rubbing, scratching the desk, or tapping the chalkboard.

ECHO

The teacher claps out a simple rhythmic pattern, using slow or fast beats, even or uneven beats, and the children respond by moving around the room to the appropriate beat.

LISTENING WALK

The children and teacher take a walk around the playground for the purpose of listening to and identifying different sounds. Sounds may be categorized as

1. Human sounds (walking, talking, etc.).
2. Animal sounds (running and cries of cats, dogs, birds, etc.).
3. Machinery sounds (noise of cars, buses, power mowers, trucks, etc.).
4. Nature sounds (wind, rustling of trees, leaves, etc.).

IT IS I

Play this game when the children know one another fairly well. One child sits in a chair with his back to the class. Another child comes up behind the seated child and knocks three times on the back of the chair. The seated child asks, "Who is knocking at my door?" and the other child replies, "It is I." The seated child tries to guess who is knocking by identifying the child's voice. The teacher sets the number of guesses permitted.

TAPE-RECORDER SOUNDS

Use a tape recorder to record many familiar and easily distinguished sounds, such as a car horn, paper tearing, breathing, crying, clock ticking, sneezing, and so forth. Make a list of the sounds in their proper order so that you know what they are. Have the children try to identify the sounds.

VOICE RECORDING

Record several children's voices on the tape recorder and have them attempt to identify their classmates' voices and their own.

FREEZE AND MELT

The teacher or a student says the word *freeze* while the class is moving about the room. They immediatly stop what they are doing and cease all movement (of the body and the mouth). When the word *melt* is called out, they resume moving around the room. This is an effective activity for the teacher to introduce as a game and to incorporate later into the classroom routine as a means of getting the immediate attention of the class.

MARCHING

Performing a variety of marching activities in which the children must respond to verbal commands is excellent for helping older children learn to listen. Marching is also helpful in developing directional awareness.

Auditory Discrimination

Auditory discrimination is similar to visual figure–ground perception. It is the ability to detect one specific tonal quality and frequency within a whole complexity of sound stimuli. Individuals tend to initiate movement toward the direction from which the sound cue emerges (directional awareness). Auditory rhythm is an aspect of discrimination and is the ability to identify a regulated series of sounds interspersed by regulated moments of silence in repeated patterns.

The following is a list of general teaching hints for children experiencing difficulty in auditory discrimination.

1. Speak slowly, distinctly, and on the child's level.
2. Speak in natural volume. Extra volume can confuse the child's ability to discriminate what you say.
3. Speak so that the child can see your lips (for severe disabilities).
4. Maintain eye-to-eye contact.
5. Deliver brief, simple directions.
6. Control the environment.
7. Use situations with verbal responses, physical responses, and both responses.
8. Avoid repeating directions whenever possible.
9. Use a blindfold for emphasis on developing auditory sensations.

Objectives

Auditory discrimination activities enable children:

1. To respond to sounds or verbal commands.
2. To react independently to verbal commands without visually monitoring others.
3. To listen to a command and then carry it out without verbal repetition.
4. To enhance fundamental rhythmic abilities.
5. To distinguish between similar sounds.
6. To distinguish between dissimilar sounds.

Movement Experiences

CLOSE YOUR EYES

Ask the children to close their eyes as you clap your hands several times. Ask the children to "clap just as I did." Vary this procedure by clapping in different rhythms.

1. You may also use two drums, having children imitate drum beats.
2. Repeat the activity with stamping, clapping, and snapping fingers.
3. Begin with even beats and progress to syncopated rhythm.

MUSICAL INSTRUMENTS

Select several rhythm-producing instruments such as a drum, a triangle, a sand block, or a wooden block. Children watch as you make a sound on each. Ask the children to close their eyes and listen carefully. Strike a sound on one of the instruments and have the children open their eyes and tell you which instrument you played. Next have the children close their eyes as the teacher plays two instruments. Have the children tell you which instrument was played first, and which one was played last.

WHAT DOES IT SOUND LIKE?

Using familiar noises, have the children differentiate between loud and soft, fast and slow, first and last, high and low.

WHAT IS IT?

Place a number of objects on a table. Tap these objects in order to familiarize the children with the sound produced. Have the children put their heads down. Tap an object and ask, ''What is it?'' After the children have become familiar with the objects, tap several of them and ask which you tapped first, second, and so on.

WHERE IS THE BELL?

Seat the children in a circle. Have one child leave the room. Give one of the children in the room a bell small enough to hide in his hand. Ask the child who left the room to come back in. When the child has returned, have all of the children stand and shake their fists above their heads. You may use more than one bell when the children become accustomed to the game.

KEEP OFF

A stretched canvas piece is strung taut in a rectangular frame, about 3½ feet off the floor. The child is beneath. The teacher tosses a beanbag onto the canvas. By the sound of its landing, the child can hear where to bump it to hit it off the canvas.

SOUND TARGETS

Throwing blindfolded, the children listen to hear their beanbag hit a target made out of resounding material.

BOUNCE OFF

Various textures and materials are situated as targets around the gym. They are used as rebound targets for the children throwing balls to hear the difference in sounds the bounces make.

MATCH THE CANS

Take ten cans. Fill five with five different materials and duplicate these with the last five cans. Mix up the order and ask the child to match the cans by sound.

Auditory Memory

Auditory memory is the ability to retain auditory clues. Since much of the child's world involves the auditory modality, a great deal of information must be stored and retained. The following activities are designed to encourage retention of auditory clues.

Objectives
Auditory memory activities are designed:

1. To enhance the ability to remember auditory clues.
2. To enhance the ability to readily remember directions.
3. To develop listening skills.
4. To enhance comprehension of what is heard.

5. To increase the ability to move efficiently to a series of auditory clues.

Movement Experiences

A TRIP TO THE ZOO

Begin a story about a trip to the zoo and all the animals that you will see. Give each child the name of an animal to imitate. When you name that animal in the story, the child with the name of that animal acts out his or her interpretation. Perform the same activity, having the children repeat the actions of the animal mentioned along with those that preceded it.

STORY TELLING

Tell a familiar story (such as *"Green Eggs and Ham,"* *"Cat in the Hat,"* or *"Jack in the Beanstalk"*), having the children supply the repetitive phrases at the proper place in the story.

ACTION RHYMES

Sing a familiar "action" rhyme such as *"Head, Shoulders, Knees, and Toes."* Omit a word from the song, such as *head*, and have the children touch that body part instead of naming it.

INSTRUMENT PLAYING

Using the same idea as in previous exercise, play a simple pattern of notes on a xylophone several times. After the pattern is well known, omit a note and have the children fill it in.

SILLY HAT

Using an old hat (a beanbag will do), give the children a series of silly things to do. Start with two directions and gradually increase the number and complexity of the instructions.

HORSE RACE

Using children as the "horses," conduct a horse race. Put a number on each child. Begin the race using only two or three "horses." Have them race (gallop) to a designated point and declare a winner, indicating the number of the "horse" and its place (i.e., "number three came in first, and number eight came in second"). Have the remainder of the group tell you the order of the finish, using the horse numbers only. Increase the number of horses to four or more after practice with having the children recall the first three, four, or five "horses" to cross the finish line.

THE WINNER IS . . . .

Repeat the preceding activity, but declare the ribbon winners. For example, "The horse that came in first wins the blue ribbon. Which number was it? The horse that came in second wins the red ribbon. Which number was it?" and so forth. You may then want to continue with "What color ribbon did number four win?" and so forth.

LOST AND FOUND

Pretend that several children in class lost an article of clothing. Have the children recall the names of those missing something.

TACTILE/KINESTHETIC PERCEPTION ACTIVITIES

The development of the sense of touch serves as a means of enhancing children's knowledge of the world about them. It is the modality by which they come into actual physical contact with their world. As with the visual and auditory channels, the tactile modality is developed through experience with objects in the environment. Tactile discrimination is the first and most basic aspect of tactile perception and involves the development of an awareness of the "feel" of things. Tactile memory involves the ability to associate tactile impressions with known objects.

The tactile modality is often neglected in the education of young children and is assumed to develop "naturally." It has been the experience of the author, however, that touch plays an important role in developing a more accurate sense of body awareness. Children should learn to direct their tactile movements in such activities as climbing a ladder, crawling through a tunnel, tracing a maze blindfolded, or walking on a slippery surface. See Table 41.7 for a suggested teaching progression for tactile perception.

Tactile Discrimination and Matching

Tactile discrimination is the earliest form of tactile development and involves developing an awareness of things through touch. Young chil-

dren developing their tactile discrimination abilities are also in the process of developing a corresponding vocabulary of words such as *hard, soft, spongy, rough, smooth, bumpy, coarse, slick,* and *sticky.* The ability to distinguish form through tactile clues also begins to develop. Differentiating between circles, squares, and triangles as well as large and small objects develops, along with the ability to sort and match objects by tactile means.

Objectives
Tactile perception activities are designed:

1. To develop an awareness of tactile sensations.
2. To aid in discriminating between tactile clues.
3. To develop the ability to sort objects according to tactile characteristics.
4. To develop the ability to match objects according to feel.

TABLE 41.7 Suggested Tactile Perception Activities

Tactile/Kinesthetic Perception Activities	Suggested Progression for Children		
	Beginning Level	Intermediate Level	Page
Tactile Discrimination and Matching			555
Collections	X		556
Textural Paintings	X		556
Collages	X		556
Creative Movement	X		556
Mystery Bag	X		556
Tag an Object	X		556
Geometric Shapes	X		556
Shape Trace		X	556
Heavy and Light		X	557
Sandpaper Sort		X	557
Touch Tag		X	557
Search		X	557
Tactile/Kinesthetic Memory			557
Where Is It?	X		557
Guess Who?	X		557
Put in Order	X		557
Memory Ball		X	557
Sandpaper Numbers and Letters		X	558

Movement Experiences

COLLECTIONS

Make collections of several types of objects and describe how they feel.

1. Cloth (nylon, cotton, velvet, fur, burlap, dotted swiss, leather, wool, corduroy, etc.).
2. Balls (ping-pong, rubber, cork, styrofoam, steel, fringe balls, beachballs, golf balls, bowling balls, etc.).
3. Seeds (from pine cones, black walnuts, chestnuts, buckeyes, acorns, coconuts, sumas, beans, pods, etc.).
4. Minerals (shale, sandstone, gypsum, granite, marble, limestone, etc.).
5. Sandpaper (assorted grades of sandpaper, ranging from coarse to very fine).
6. Food wrap (aluminum foil, waxed paper, plastic wrap, butcher paper, cellophane, brown paper bags, etc.).
7. Household staples (salt, sugar, flour, peppercorns, rice, macaroni, etc.).
8. Kitchen items (blunt scissors, butter spreader, various-sized spoons, fork, spatula, rubber scraper, cookie cutter, etc.).
9. Miscellaneous (plastic, metal, aluminum, steel, glass, tin, etc.).

TEXTURED PAINTINGS

Make textured paintings, using glue to secure such things as rice, sawdust, tissue paper, small stones, seeds and pods, popcorn, and sand.

COLLAGES

Make collages using a wide variety of textures.

CREATIVE MOVEMENT

Discriminate between various textures through movement. Have the children feel a texture such as silk and interpret it by moving the way it feels.

Use a variety of textures that exhibit characteristics, such as

1. Bumpy.
2. Smooth.
3. Coarse.
4. Prickly.

MYSTERY BAG

Place familiar but similar objects in a sack, such as a toy car, boats, and trucks. Have a child reach in the bag, without looking, and describe to the class how one object feels. Children guess what object is being held. Repeat the preceding activity, but have the child who is reaching in guess what the object is after describing it to the class.

TAG AN OBJECT

Place several different objects on the floor (use as many different objects as there are children). Blindfold each child (four to eight at a time works well) and whisper the name of the object they are to locate. On the signal "Go," send them around the area trying to locate their object. They may remove their blindfolds when they think they have located the proper object. Repeat the same activity using several geometric shapes.

GEOMETRIC SHAPES

Blindfold a child. Hand the child one geometric shape at a time. Have him tell all about it and name the shape.

SHAPE TRACE

Using your finger, trace a geometric shape on the child's back. The child then tells about the shape and names it if possible.

HEAVY AND LIGHT

Sort a variety of objects into two categories of heavy and light. The same may be done with rough–smooth, soft–hard.

SANDPAPER SORT

Using different grades of sandpaper, sort them blindfolded according to texture. Repeat the same activity, but sort according to size, shape, and texture. Perform first while visually monitoring, then with a blindfold.

TOUCH TAG

Play a game of tag in which you tell the children to touch something soft, hard, smooth, wide, sharp, and so forth. The last child touching that type of object sits in the "mush pot" for one turn (avoid excluding children in games of this nature).

SEARCH

Place several different objects in a large cloth bag. Have the children reach in without looking and find, by touch, the correct object described, such as

1. "Find something you eat with."
2. "Find something you wear."
3. "Find something you write with."

Tactile/Kinesthetic Memory

Tactile/kinesthetic memory activities are similar to discrimination activities, but they involve a greater degree of sophistication. Memory activities require the child to discriminate nonvisually between familiar and unfamiliar objects and to apply verbal labels to these tactile clues.

Objectives

Tactile memory activities help children:

1. To remember what objects feel like.
2. To identify unfamiliar objects by touch.
3. To identify familiar objects by touch.

Movement Experiences

WHERE IS IT?

Using a textured drawing of a familiar figure (kitten, donkey, Santa Claus), have the children locate its various body parts while blindfolded.

GUESS WHO?

Have the children form a circle. "It" is blindfolded, turned around twice, and placed in the center of the circle. He then steps forward until he touches another child and attempts to determine who it is. He feels the child's clothing, hair, face, and so forth. Three guesses are permitted, then a new child is "it."

PUT IN ORDER

Scatter several objects on the floor. Blindfold the children and tell them the type of object they must locate. Begin with three types. Have them locate the objects and place them in order. For example, tell them to find something round, then something hard, then something smooth.

MEMORY BALL

Use several different types of balls from the gymnasium (football, basketball, baseball, softball, soccerball, volleyball, kick ball, tennis ball, and whiffle ball). Place the balls on the floor and have the children, blindfolded, locate and name the various balls and tell what they are used for.

SANDPAPER NUMBERS AND LETTERS

Blindfold the children and have them distinguish between various numbers and letters by touch. Older children can solve simple addition or subtraction problems using the numbers, or they can spell words using the letters.

ADDITIONAL RESOURCES

Perceptual–Motor

Brazelton, Ambrose. *Clap, Snap and Tap.* Kimbo Records, Box 246, Deal, NJ 07723 (EA48).

Capon, J. (1975). *Perceptual–motor lesson plans.* Alameda, CA: Front Row Experience.

Capon, Jack, and Hallum, Rosemary. *Perceptual–Motor Rhythm Games,* Educational Activities, Inc., Box 392, Freeport, NY 11520 (AR50, AC50).

Cratty, Bryant, J. *Physical Development for Children.* Kimbo Records, Box 246, Deal, NJ 07723 (EA-PD).

Glass, Henry "Buzz," *Learning by Doing, Dancing, and Discovering.* Educational Activities, Inc., Box 392, Freeport, NY 11520 (AR76).

Hallum, Rosemary, and Glass, Henry Buzz. *Individualization in Movement and Music.* Educational Activities, Inc., Box 392, Freeport, NY 11520 (AR49, AC49).

Hissam, Harold. *Coordination Skills.* Educational Activities, Inc., and Kimbo Educational Records, P.O. Box 392, Freeport, NY 11520 (KEA 6050).

Lee, Karol. *Music for Movement Exploration.* Educational Activities, Inc., Box 392, Freeport, NY 11520 (KEA 5090).

Lewandowski, Diane, Iversen, Ken, Baldassarre, Herman, and Marciante, Robert. *Limb Learning.* Educational Activities, Inc., Box 392, Freeport, NY 11520 (KEA 1145).

Palmer, Hap. *Creative Movement and Rhythmic Exploration.* Educational Activities, Inc., Box 392, Freeport, NY 11520 (AR/AC 533).

Palmer, Hap. *Easy Does It.* Educational Activities, Inc., Box 392, Freeport, NY 11520 (AR/AC 581).

Palmer, Hap. *Homemade Band.* Educational Activities, Inc., Box 392, Freeport, NY 11520 (AR/AC 545).

Palmer, Hap. *Mod Marches.* Educational Activities, Inc., Box 392, Freeport, NY 11520 (AR/AC 527).

Palmer, Hap. *Getting to Know Myself.* Educational Activities, Inc., Box 392, Freeport, NY 11520.

Riccione, Georgiana. *Developmental Motor Skills for Self-awareness.* Kimbo Records, Box 246, Deal, NJ 07723 (KIM 9075).

Visual–Auditory–Tactile

Berman, Marcia, Zeitlin, Patty, and Barlin, Ann. *Rainy Day Dances, Rainy Day Songs.* Educational Activities, Box 392, Freeport, NY 11520 (AR 570).

Berman, Marcia, Zeitlin, Patty, and Barlin, Ann. *Body Jive.* Educational Activities, Inc., Box 392, Freeport, NY 11520 (AR 96, AC 96).

Berman, Marcia, Zeitlin, Patty, and Barlin, Ann. *Clap, Snap, and Tap.* Educational Activities, Box 392, Freeport, NY 11520 (AR 48).

Berman, Marcia, Zeitlin, Patty, and Barlin, Ann. *Get Fit While You Sit.* Educational Activities, Inc., Box 392, Freeport, NY 11520 (AR 516).

Berman, Marcia, Zeitlin, Patty, and Barlin, Ann. *Only Just Begun.* Educational Activities, Box 392, Freeport, NY 11520 (KEA 5025).

Finger Games. Bridges, 310 W. Jefferson, Dallas, TX 75208 (HYP506).

Gallina, Jill, and Gallina, Michael. *Hand Jivin'.* Educational Activities, Box 392, Freeport, NY 11520 (AR 95, AC 95).

Glass, Henry "Buzz." *It's Action Time—Let's Move!* Educational Activities, Box 392, Freeport, NY 11520 (AR 79).

Glass, Henry "Buzz," and Hallum, Rosemary. *Rhythm Stick Activities.* Educational Activities, Box 392, Freeport, NY 11520 (AR 55).

Hallum, Rosemary. *Fingerplay Fun.* Educational Activities, Box 392, Freeport, NY 11520 (AR 529).

Johnson, Laura. *Simplified Lummi Stick Activities.* Educational Activities, Box 392, Freeport, NY 11520 (K 2015).

Kaplin, Dorothy. *Perceptual Development Through Paper Folding.* Bridges, 310 W. Jefferson, Dallas, TX 75208 (LP9010).

Lummi Stick Fun. Kimbo Records, Box 246, Deal, NJ 07723 (KIM2000).

Riccione, Georgiana. *Fun Activities for Fine Motor Skills.* Kimbo Records, Box 246, Deal, NJ 07723 (KIM9076).

Smith, Les, and DeSantis, Gabe. *Roomnastics.* Educational Activities, Box 392, Freeport, NY 11520 (KEA 1131).

Williams, Linda, and Wemple, Donna. *Sensorimotor Training in the Classroom,* Volume I. Educational Activities, Box 392, Freeport, NY 11520 (AR 532).

Williams, Linda, and Wemple, Donna. *Sensorimotor Training in the Classroom,* Volume II. Educational Activities, Box 392, Freeport, NY 11520 (AR 566).

CHAPTER 42

HAND APPARATUS ACTIVITIES

Small apparatus, or hand apparatus, as it is frequently called, is a must in every elementary physical education program. Hand apparatus such as balls, hoops, wands, and beanbags may be commercially purchased or homemade. It is important, whenever possible, for each child to have his or her own piece of equipment for use. Such a policy promotes maximum activity on the part of all and will do much to reduce discipline problems that frequently erupt while children are waiting for a turn. The hand apparatus activities in this chapter are only a sampling of the endless variety possible. When selecting activities for inclusion in the lesson, care should be taken to first identify the objectives of the lesson and the ability level of your students. Then it is a relatively simple matter to determine appropriate activities.

Activity ideas are included in this chapter for *balance boards and stilts, balloons, balls, beanbags, hoops, jump ropes, parachutes, stretch ropes*, and *wands*. The objectives for use of each piece of equipment are included, along with a recommended progression of movement experiences, ranging from simple to more complex activities (see Table 42.1). You may find it helpful

TABLE 42.1   Selected Hand
Apparatus Activities

Hand Apparatus Activities	Suggested Progression for Children			Page
	Beginning Level	Intermediate Level	Advanced Level	
Balance-Board Activities	X	X	X	560
Low Stilts Activities	X	X		561
Balloon Activities	X	X		561
Ball Challenge Activities	X	X	X	562
Beanbag-Balancing Activities	X	X	X	562
Beanbag-Tossing Activities	X	X		563
Individual Hoop Activities	X	X	X	563
Partner Hoop Activities		X		564
Hoop-Twirling Activities		X	X	564
Short Jump Rope Activities	X	X	X	564
Long Jump Rope Activities	X	X		565
Parachute Activities	X	X		566
Stretch Rope Activities	X	X		567
Chinese Jump Rope Activities		X	X	568
Wand Activities	X	X	X	568

to refer to Chapter 21, "Fundamental Manipulative Skills," for additional information.

BALANCE BOARDS AND STILTS

Balance boards are easily constructed and offer a variety of challenging activities. A mat should be placed under the balance board to avoid slipping. Coffee-can stilts are easily made from metal coffee containers and a length of rope. They offer a new dimension to stability because the center of gravity is raised, thus making balancing more difficult.

Objectives

Practice with balance boards and stilts will:

1. Improve static balance activities.
2. Enhance dynamic balance abilities.
3. Enhance body and spatial awareness.
4. Promote improved coordination and agility.

Movement Experiences

While on a balance board, try to:

• Balance on the board any way possible.
• Balance with the feet apart.

- Balance with the feet together.
- Balance with the arms out from the sides.
- Balance with the arms down at the sides.
- Balance with the eyes closed.
- Squat down and balance.
- Squat halfway down and balance.
- Touch various body parts while balancing.
- Balance with a beanbag or eraser on the head.
- Balance and catch a ball.
- Toss a ball while balancing.
- Throw at a target while balancing.
- Balance on one foot.
- Bounce a ball while balancing.
- Balance with a partner on another board while holding hands.
- Toss and catch a ball while balancing.
- Turn around on the board while balancing.

With a set of coffee-can stilts—

- Walk in various directions (forward, sideways, and backward).
- Step over a low object.
- Step under objects.
- Walk at various levels (high, low, and medium).
- Walk at various speeds.
- Hop on one foot.
- Jump forward.
- Have races.
- Move a disc forward while walking on the stilts.
- Go through an obstacle course.

BALLOONS

Round balloons offer an excellent means for children to practice striking and volleying skills. Because of their lightness, balloons are easier to contact than a regulation volleyball or playground ball. They are inexpensive enough for each child to have one and may be used over and over if rubber bands are used to secure inflated balloons instead of a knot.

Objectives

Balloon striking and volleying activities are designed:

1. To enhance fundamental striking skills.
2. To develop basic volleying abilities.
3. To promote improved spatial awareness.
4. To promote improved body awareness.
5. Improve eye–hand coordination.

Movement Experiences

Toss the balloon and catch it in the following ways:

- Toss it to different heights and catch.
- Toss it from various body positions and catch.
- Toss it up and catch it with different body parts.
- Toss it back and forth to a partner.
- Toss two balloons back and forth with a partner.
- Strike the balloon with the hands.
- Strike the balloon at different levels.
- Strike the balloon with various body parts.
- Keep the balloon in the air as long as possible.
- Stay in one spot while hitting the balloon repeatedly into the air.
- Move to the other side of the room while keeping the balloon in the air.
- Walk in a circle while hitting the balloon.
- Make a full turn each time the balloon is hit.
- Use a table-tennis paddle, tennis racquet, or bat to hit the balloon repeatedly.
- Hit the balloon as hard or as softly as possible.
- Hit the balloon using different swinging motions: sidearm, overarm, underhand.
- Volley the balloon with a partner.

- Volley the balloon with a partner, both of you using an implement.

BALLS

Balls come in a variety of sizes, shapes, colors, and textures. In the elementary physical education program, it is important that each child have a ball when taking part in activities. Playground balls, soccer balls, volleyballs, tennis balls, foam balls, or beachballs can all be used for the activity ideas that follow. These activities represent only a sampling of a progression of challenge activities that can be included in the lesson.

Objectives

Practice in ball handling activities helps children:

1. To develop the ability to manipulate balls in a variety of ways.
2. To be able to use a variety of different types of balls with control.
3. To become familiar with balls in a variety of movement situations.
4. To improve eye–hand and eye–foot coordination.
5. To enhance body awareness and directional awareness.

Movement Experiences

Individual ball challenges:

- See how many ways you can toss the ball to yourself.
- Find how many directions you can use to throw the ball to yourself.
- Find different ways to throw the ball without using your hands.
- Throw your ball up and catch it. Find different ways to move and still catch the ball.
- Use different levels to toss the ball and catch it.

- Toss the ball up, take three steps, and catch it on the fly.
- Find different ways that you can get the ball from where you are to the wall.
- Make the ball move forward without throwing it.
- Find different ways to make the ball go around you.
- See what you can do with your ball using only one hand.
- Find different levels to bounce the ball.
- See how many different ways you can move while dribbling the ball.
- See how many different parts of your body you can use to bounce the ball.
- Make a full turn after you bounce the ball, then catch it.
- Dribble the ball straight ahead on a line.
- Dribble the ball while moving in different directions.
- Bounce up and down as the ball bounces up and down.
- Dribble the ball as fast as you can.
- Dribble the ball around markers on the floor.
- Dribble the ball focusing straight ahead.
- Dribble the ball so a partner can't take it away.
- Throw at targets on the wall using overhead and underhand throws.
- From a square or circle drawn on the floor, throw the ball up high on the wall and catch it while remaining in the figure.
- With two squares drawn on the floor about 10 feet apart and parallel to the wall, throw the ball at the wall from the first square and catch it on the rebound in the second square. Repeat.
- Hit the ball against the wall with a paddle or racket as often as possible.

BEANBAGS

Beanbags are easy and inexpensive to make. They are an excellent implement for practicing throwing, catching, and balancing skills. Whenever possible, each child should have his or her own beanbag.

Objectives

The beanbag activities contained here are intended:

1. To enhance the fundamental manipulative abilities of throwing and catching.
2. To enhance fundamental dynamic and static balance abilities.
3. To improve body awareness abilities.
4. To contribute to improved coordination.

Movement Experiences

Balancing a beanbag:

- See how many body parts can balance the beanbag.
- Balance the beanbag on parts of the body above the waist.
- Balance it on parts below the waist.
- Balance it on parts of the body that are on the right side.
- Balance it on parts to the left.
- Balance it on parts above the waist and on the right side.
- Balance it on a part below the waist and on the left side.
- Balance it on parts that cannot be seen.
- Move at different levels while balancing on various parts.
- Move in different directions while balancing on various parts.
- Move at different speeds while balancing on various parts.
- Balance it on body parts above the waist and move it to body parts below the waist without using the hands.
- Balance it on body parts below the waist on one side of the body and move to body parts above the waist on the other side without using the hands.

- Balance it on parts that can be seen and transfer it to parts that can't be seen without using the hands.
- Balance it on parts that can't be seen and transfer it to other parts that can't be seen without using the hands.
- Repeat all of the preceding activities with a partner.
- Toss it to a partner, who catches the beanbag with designated body parts other than the hands.

Tossing and catching a beanbag:

- Toss the beanbag up low with both hands and catch it with both hands.
- Toss it up low with both hands and catch it with one.
- Toss it up low with one hand and catch it with the same hand.
- Toss it up low with one hand and catch with the opposite hand.
- Repeat all of the preceding exercises with higher and higher tosses.
- Toss the beanbag up and catch it with a variety of implements (scoops, boxes, towels).
- Throw it in different directions.
- Throw at various speeds.
- Play toss and catch for distance with a partner.
- Throw at a wall target.
- Throw at a suspended tire or hoop.
- Throw through a swinging tire or hoop.
- Play pitch-catcher.

HOOPS

Hoops are great pieces of small apparatus for use wiht a variety of movement activities. Hoops may be purchased, but they can be easily made from surgical tubing or black plastic water pipe. Homemade hoops are generally less expensive and more sturdy than the commercially purchased variety.

Objectives

Hoop activities contribute:

1. To improved fundamental locomotor abilities.
2. To improved basic body and object manipulation skills.
3. To reinforcing spatial and body awareness abilities.
4. To enhancing coordination and agility.

Movement Experiences

Using a hoop by yourself:

- See how many ways there are to move with the hoop.
- Move around the hoop while keeping it stationary.
- Move around the hoop while it is moving.
- Support the body in and out of the hoop.
- Roll the hoop so it comes back to you.
- Roll the hoop in a straight line.
- Roll the hoop in a circle.
- Roll the hoop using a wand.
- Roll the hoop and then move faster than the hoop.
- Roll the hoop and go through it while it is moving.
- "Jump rope" with the hoop.
- While you are on the floor, roll the hoop on a balance beam.
- While you are on the beam, roll a hoop on the floor.
- Jump through a self-turned hoop while you are on the beam.

With a partner:

- With a partner holding the hoop, go in and out of the hoop.
- Go under a hoop held by a partner.

- Jump through a hoop held by a partner.
- Without touching them, step over and under a line of hoops that are held by partners.
- While your partner rolls the hoop, you run through it.
- While your partner rolls the hoop, both of you go through it before it stops moving. Then reverse roles.

Twirl a hoop:

- Around your wrist.
- Around your forearm.
- Around your waist.
- Around your neck.
- Around your foot.
- Around your foot and jump through with the other foot.
- Around your waist.
- Around a body part and transfer it, while twirling, to another body part.

Tossing and catching the hoop:

- Toss the hoop high and catch it.
- Toss the hoop with one hand and catch it with the same hand.
- Toss the hoop with one hand and catch it with the opposite hand.
- Toss the hoop to a partner.
- Toss the hoop to a partner while he or she tosses another to you.
- Toss and catch two hoops at the same time.

JUMP ROPES

Jump ropes provide a challenging and inexpensive piece of equipment for each child. They can be used effectively in the program for children of all ages and ability levels. The activities that follow progress from simple to complex.

Objectives

Rope jumping activities are great for:

1. Improving aerobic endurance.
2. Improving eye–hand and eye–foot coordination.
3. Reinforcing fundamental jumping, hopping, and skipping skills.
4. Promoting increased muscular endurance in the legs.

Movement Experiences

Using a single jump rope:

- Move the rope back and forth, jumping over it each time.
- Move the rope around the body with one hand. Now try it with the other hand, over the head, to the left side, and to the right side.
- Move the rope under the feet using just one hand.
- Make a circle with the rope and move into the center and out again.
- Turn the rope and jump over it one time. Repeat rhythmically.
- Turn the rope, jump over it, and move around the floor.
- Skip (stand on right foot, hop on right foot, and pass the rope under. Stand on the left foot, hop on left foot, and pass the rope under).
- Run (run in place with no hop between steps).
- Douple jump (with both feet together, jump the rope with an intervening step).
- Single jump (with both feet together, jump the rope without an intervening step).
- One-leg hop (hold one leg off the floor and hop on the other with an intervening step).
- Distance hop (hold one leg off the floor and hop forward on the other without an intervening step).
- Rocking step (place one foot in front of the other. Jump on alternate feet with an intervening step).

- Skip step (place one foot in front of the other. Jump and alternate the lead foot).
- Backward skipping, hopping, and jumping (with the rope hold in front from a starting position, any of the preceding may be used).
- Stiff-leg kick forward (same as preceding except the raised leg is thrown back on each step).
- Spread eagle (alternate between a closed step with an intervening step and a straddle step with an intervening step).
- Double jump with arms crossed (execute a double jump, cross the arms as the rope is on the downswing, and jump through it. Then uncross the arms as the rope nears completion of upswing). Can be done forward and backward.
- Double turn (turn the rope under the feet two times while body is in the air).
- Crossed and uncrossed legs (jump once with the legs uncrossed, then cross the legs and jump again. Use an intervening step).
- Toe tap (skip on one foot, touch toe to the floor to the rear with the other foot).

With a long stationary rope:

- Jump from one foot and land on both.
- Hop from one foot, land on the same foot.
- Jump from one foot, land on the opposite foot.
- Jump from one foot, land on the same foot.
- Jump from both feet, land on both feet.
- Repeat the preceding activities with a pendulum-swinging rope.

Using a long, pendulum-swinging rope, try to follow the same progression as just described.
With a long, turning rope:

- Run through the rope.
- Run in, take one jump, and run out the same side.
- Run in, take one jump, and run out the opposite side.
- Run in, take one jump with a half turn, and run out backward.

- Do "front door" (the rope is turned away from the jumper after hitting the floor).
- Do "back door" (the rope is turned toward the jumper after hitting the floor).

PARACHUTE

The parachute is a piece of equipment enjoyed by both young and older children. Parachutes may be commercially purchased from physical education supply companies, or they may be secured through a local airbase or Army–Navy surplus store. Parachutes make for excellent introductory and organizational activities. Successful parachute activities require group cooperation and teamwork. The following is a compilation of several game-type activities that can be played with the parachute.

Objectives

Parachute activities contribute:

1. To learning how to cooperate and work together.
2. To the development of listening skills.
3. To the reinforcment of basic movement abilities.

Movement Experiences

Number Chase.   Have students stretch out the parachute and space themselves as evenly as possible. Help students count off by fours (or other appropriate number). Have students raise the parachute to an umbrella position. When the parachute reaches its highest position, the teacher calls out a number (such as 2). All (2s) run in a counterclockwise (or clockwise) direction, trying to tap the person in front of them before they reach their original position around the parachute.

Smash-A-Chute.   Divide class into two teams. Number off so each person has a different number but matches a number of a player on the opposite team. Give each team a color as a team name. Place two marked foam balls opposite each other with the team and color of ball also opposite, so one team's ball is nearer the other team. With the class holding the parachute, have them raise the chute to an umbrella position. When chute reaches its highest position call out a number (such as 5). The two number 5s run under the parachute and pick up the ball with the same color as their team color and try to hit their opponent below the waist by throwing the ball at him or her before the opponent hits them. The first person to hit the opponent scores one point for their team. If no one is hit before the chute falls, no point is scored for either team.

Parachute Soccer.   Divide players into two teams, lined up opposite each other around the parachute. Use basic soccer skills, already previously practiced. Have the students pass and kick the ball back and forth, trying to get the ball to go between two players on the opposite team. One point is scored for each ball that passes between two players outside the parachute area.

Chute the Bacon.   Place the object to be used as the bacon under the parachute in the middle. Divide the class into two teams. Number off so each person has a different number, one that matches the number of a player on the oposite team. With the students holding the parachute, have them raise the parachute to an umbrella position. Call out a number (such as 6). Both 6s release the parachute and run to the middle of the chute. Sixes try to pick up and take a ball back to their team, while a second player tries to tag that player with the bacon. If the "stealer" is successful, that team receives one point. If the tagger is successful in tagging the first player, then a point is scored for that team. If the chute falls before a point is scored, both players return to their original positions with no point scored for either team.

Big Top.   Use the chute as a "circus Big Top" with mats for performing stunts under it.

Pass the Ball.   Players hold the edge of a parachute lowered over one player in the middle, who holds a basketball. On signal, the players lift the chute, and before they can bring it down again, the player in the center must pass the ball to a player on the perimeter and exchange places with him before the chute touches either player.

Steal the Ball.   Players hold the edge of chute

and each of them is given a number. A basketball is placed on the floor in the center under the chute. At the teacher's command, the chute is lifted overhead and at the same time the teacher calls a number. The player whose number it is must run to the ball, pick it up, dribble once around the circle, place the ball back on the floor in the center, and return to his place on the perimeter before the chute falls and touches the player.

Chute Dribble.   Each player holds the outside edge of chute with one hand while holding a basketball in the other hand. At the teacher's command, the players begin to walk or run in a circle while continuing to hold the edge of the chute in one hand and dribbling the ball with the other hand.

Simon Says.   Simple parachute routines can be made more exciting by using commands from the game "Simon Says." Such activities as raising and lowering the parachute, sitting, kneeling, and standing can be included in these drills. Moving in one direction with the parachute, changing directions, running, stopping, and jumping are also challenging.

Team Popcorn.   With two teams and six light balls (two colors), shake the chute and try to get all of one team's balls off the chute first. The first team to shake off all of the opposing team's balls wins.

Roll Through.   Children hold the chute at waist level. Two balls are put on the chute. As a group, the children try to roll the balls through the center of the chute.

Poison Parachute.   Inflate the chute, take three steps forward, release the chute, and drop to the floor in a front lying position. If the chute falls on any part of children's bodies, those children are "poisoned" and must sit on the sidelines until a new person(s) gets poisoned.

Colors.   Inflate the chute; call out a color. Children wearing that color move to a new position before the parachute comes down. As a variation, have the children do various locomotor activities while changing places.

Mousetrap.   Number off by three's; call a number, and those with that number are the mice. They run in and out of the parachute while it is lifted in the air. On command, the parachute is pulled down, trying to catch the mice.

Huddle.   Number off in three's. Raise the parachute on a signal and then call one of the numbers. Those people form a "huddle" in the middle and see how long they can remain there without getting touched by the chute. They try to get out at the very last moment. Repeat, using the other numbers.

Jacks.   The parachute is raised and lowered at an even tempo. While this is being done, one student at a time goes under and collects a number of beanbags. The first person collects one; the next, two; and so on. A person is out if caught under the parachute while trying to collect the beanbags. Then the next student resumes at one beanbag. The student who is out continues to help raise and lower the parachute.

Parachute Golf.   With two teams and eight yarn balls (two colors), and using slow movements, try to get the balls through the center hole. If the blue balls go through the center hole first, the blue team wins; likewise for the red. Balls falling off the sides do not count.

Heads in the Basket.   Students raise the chute overhead, forming a mushroom. On command, they lie in a prone position on the floor, pulling the chute down and around their necks. Only the heads are inside the parachute. This is a fun culminating activity with the chute.

STRETCH ROPES

Stretch ropes are inexpensive to purchase and offer practice in a variety of challenging locomotor activities. Stretch ropes may be easily made by purchasing several yards of elastic cord, cutting it to eight-foot lengths, and tying ends together.

Objectives

Stretch rope activities contribute:

1.   To improved eye–foot coordination.
2.   To enhancing dynamic balance abilities.
3.   To reinforcing fundamental jumping and hopping skills.
4.   To improving aerobic endurance.

Movement Experiences

With a single strand of stretch rope:

- Walk along the rope.
- Run and step over the rope (vary the level).
- Run and jump over the rope.
- Skip and crawl under the rope.
- Hop over the rope.
- Leap over the rope.
- Go over the rope on four parts of the body.
- Do a balance over the rope. Change balance points.

With a double strand of stretch rope:

- Step over the first rope and bend under the second rope.
- Jump oner the first rope and go under the second rope.
- Go over both ropes (make contact between the ropes).
- Go over the ropes with two body parts.
- Go over the ropes with only one body part.
- Go over the first rope and go under the second rope.
- Jump over both ropes.
- Jump over the first rope and roll under the second rope.
- Jump and roll alternately across the ropes from one end to the other.

Chinese Jump Rope. Tie the rope together at the ends and hook it around the ankles of two partners. A performer is in the middle. A stationary object may be used in place of one person if a third person is not available. The basic routine follows. After each successful completion of a routine, the rope is moved higher. The height progression goes from: ankles, lower calf, midcalf, upper calf, knees, lower thigh, mid-thigh, upper thigh, buttocks, waist.

1. Plainies.
   a. Big In (performer begins with legs straddled outside the rope, takes off with both feet, and lands with feet together inside the rope).
   b. Big Out (performer straddles the rope again).
   c. Side by Side (performer straddles rope with one foot in and the other on the outside and repeats to the other side).
   d. Ons (performer now jumps and lands on the stretch rope).
   e. Little In (performer jumps and lands with both feet inside the rope).
   f. Little Out (performer jumps and lands with both feet outside the rope).
2. Snappies (the same routine as previous one is repeated while snapping the fingers in rhythm to the jumps).
3. Clappies (repeat the routine, clapping to the rhythm of the routine).
4. Clickies (repeat the routine, clicking the heels on each jump).
5. Twirlies (repeat the routine with a half turn on each jump).
6. Name Game—Facing the rope, hook the rope under on foot and cross over the opposite rope to opposite side. Put the free foot in between the ropes and push out, forming a diamond shape. Performer now spells his name, making a quarter turn for each letter. Step to one side with the top rope and jump over the other rope.
7. Scissors—Begin in straddle position with both feet outside the ropes. Now slide the feet together and cross them.
   a. Jump and land with both feet inside the ropes.
   b. Jump and land with both feet in a straddle position outside the ropes.
   c. Jump and land with one foot inside and one outside the rope.
   d. Jump and repeat to the opposite side.
   e. Jump and land on the ropes.

WANDS

Wands can be easily made from 3/4-inch dowling cut to three-foot lengths. Plastic golf tubes may also be used. A variety of balance principles may be illustrated with wands as well as numerous challenging activities.

Objectives

Wand activities can contribute:

1. To enhancing static and dynamic balance abilities.
2. To improving fine motor control.

Movement Experiences

Try to:

- Balance the wand on the floor horizontally, then vertically. Which is easier or harder? Why?
- Balance a wand vertically, clap hands, and grab it before it falls to the ground.
- Run around the wand while it is balancing and catch it before it falls to the ground.
- Balance the wand horizontally on two fingers.
- Balance the wand horizontally on one finger.
- Balance the wand horizontally on different body parts.
- Find the middle and balance the wand any way possible horizontally.
- Balance the wand horizontally *without* the balance point being in the middle (use a couterbalance such as canary jar lid).
- Balance the wand vertically on a variety of body parts.
- Find out what the eyes do when balancing the wand vertically. Where do they look? Try looking at different parts of the wand while it is balancing vertically.

- Move about the room while balancing the wand vertically.
- Balance the wand vertically while moving from a standing to a sitting position.
- Balance the wand vertically as long as possible.
- Balance the wand vertically and transfer it from one part of the hand to another.
- Balance the wand vertically and transfer it from one finger to the corresponding finger on the opposite hand.
- Change balance points while balancing the wand vertically.
- Lead a partner around the room while balancing the wand horizontally, vertically.
- Walk around a partner while balancing the wand.
- Go under a partner's outstretched arms while balancing the wand.
- Balance the wand somewhere on a partner's body.
- Pass the wand to a partner, keeping it in balance.
- Find two ways to pass the wand to your partner, keeping it in balance with only one balance point.

SUGGESTED READING

Capon, J. (1975). *Ball, rope, hoop activities*. Belmont, CA: Fearon Pitman Publishers.

Erans, D. (1972). *Parachute activities for fun and fitness*. Sioux Falls, SD: Raven Industries.

French, R., and Horvat, M. (1983). *Parachute movement activities*. Byron, CA: Front Row Experience.

CHAPTER 43

FITNESS ACTIVITIES

Fitness activites are included in the physical education program for the specific purpose of contributing to the heatlh-related aspects of physical development. Aerobic endurance, muscular endurance, muscular strength, and flexibility are the primary components of physical fitness. Virtually all of the activities presented in the preceding chapters contribute in some measure to the development or maintenance of fitness. These activities, however, focused on skill development as their primary objective, with fitness benefits being a byproduct. The low level of physical fitness that has been repeatedly demonstrated among the youth of America makes it vitally important that physical fitness activities be included into the instructional program for their own sake.

A *portion* of the physical education lesson should be devoted to instruction in fitness as well as skill development. Ideally, an in-school, home, or community-based daily fitness program should be available to every child. Unfortunately, this is not so. Therefore, the physical education program has the responsibility of:

1. Increasing children's knowledge base and developing positive attitudes toward the importance of fitness.
2. Motivating children to take part in regular vigorous physical activity.
3. Teaching children how to exercise and what to do to improve their personal level of fitness.
4. Providing opportunities for children to enhance their physical fitness.

Physical education is *not* physical fitness, but this important aspect of the child's development can be included in the instructional program if these four guidelines are adhered to. Fitness activities should be a "thread" running through the entire physical education curriculum. *Rather than focusing on fitness as a theme for a single unit of instruction, it is highly recommended that instruction in fitness be included as a part of lessons throughout the entire school year.* Fitness is not an isolated part of the physical education program. It is continually fostered through a vigorous developmental program of movement skill acquisition.

This chapter contains several practical suggestions for motivating children toward fitness. A variety of aerobic endurance, muscular strength and endurance, and flexibility activities is included. The activities are listed in progression from simple to more complex in terms of the requirements placed on the child to perform them and the complexity of the activities themselves. A personal fitness profile suitable for use with children is included at the end. You may find it helpful to refer back to Chapter 3, ''Fitness Development,'' and the end of the sport-skill chapters (Chapters 25 through 29) for additional information.

MOTIVATIONAL IDEAS

Children frequently quit before a training effect can be achieved. They often say ''It isn't fun,'' or ''It hurts.'' The following motivational ideas will help overcome this problem.

1. Work out with a partner.
2. Work out to music.
3. Chart laps and repetitions.
4. Vary distances, number of repetitions, or time.
5. Develop fitness bulletin boards.
6. Publish information on fitness in the school newspaper.
7. Develop graphs and charts of individual performance scores (Figure 43.1).
8. Incorporate obstacle courses into the program.
9. Use timed circuits, varying the circuit regularly.
10. Try treasure hunts and orienteering skills.
11. Develop a run-a-thon, or join the Jump Rope for Heart program sponsored by the AAHPERD.
12. Hold a cross-country meet.
13. Develop a jump-rope, cross-country, aerobics, or fitness club.
14. Provide for small awards such as buttons, pins, ribbons, or certificates for individual improvement.
15. Exercise with the children.

AEROBIC ACTIVITIES

Aerobic endurance is the ability of the heart, lungs, and vascular systems to function efficiently during the stress of exercise. Experts consider aerobic endurance to be the most important component of total fitness. Any activity resulting in a sustained elevated heart rate is considered to be aerobic in nature. The keys to developing increased aerobic capacity are *intensity*, *duration*, *frequency*, and *variety*.

In order for children to receive the most benefits from vigorous exercise, it must be of sufficient intensity to elevate the heart rate to about 150 beats per minute or more. The average daily routine of most North American children provides few occasions for the heart rate to reach such levels.

The duration that the heart rate is elevated is the second key to aerobic endurance. Experts agree that it isn't enough to simply achieve an elevated heart rate, but that it must be sustained for 10 minutes or longer in order to achieve a positive training effect. Again, the normal daily routine of most children does not provide for situations where high heart rates are sustained for a sufficient duration to achieve an aerobic benefit.

Frequency is the third key to increased aerobic capacity. In addition to elevating one's heart rate for a sustained period of time, aerobic exercise must be engaged in no less than three times per week for a positive training effect. In fact, most experts recommend five times per week as the ideal. A daily fitness program in the schools (see Chapter 17) is the only place where we can guarantee that every child will have the frequency of exercise needed.

The fourth, and probably most important key, to increasing aerobic endurance is variety. Children respond favorably if there is variety in the

FIGURE 43.1 Sample personalized fitness profile.

Personal Fitness Profile

Name _____ Grade _____

Body Build Profile

	Trial 1	Trial 2	Trial 3	Trial 4
Date				
Age				
Height				
Weight				
Frame Size				

Aerobic Fitness Profile

	Trial 1	Trial 2	Trial 3	Trial 4
Distance Run				
Resting heart rate				
Exercise heart rate				
1-minute recovery rate				
5-minute recovery rate				

Physical and Motor Fitness Profile

	Trial 1	Trial 2	Trial 3	Trial 4
Arm endurance: pushups				
Abdominal endurance: situps				
Leg power: standing long jump				
Arm power: softball throw				
Flexibility: sit and reach				
Speed: 50-yard dash				
Agility: shuttle run				
Coordination: cable jump				
Balance: one-foot stand				

Summary

I am: ____ overweight, ____ about right, ____ underweight

I have: ____ too much fat, ____ about right, ____ too little fat

My aerobic condition is: ____ excellent, ____ good, ____ fair, ____ poor

My general fitness is: ____ excellent, ____ good, ____ fair, ____ poor

Comments:

aerobics training program. For children, the activity must be fun. If it isn't, many will soon tire of the activity and quit. Aerobic activities are presented here with the concepts of variety and progression in mind (see Table 43.1).

Objectives

1. To gain an understanding of the four keys to improved aerobic endurance: intensity; duration; frequency; and variety.
2. To be able to identify vigorous physical activities that contribute to aerobic endurance.
3. To select one or more aerobic activities and take part in it on a regular basis.
4. To improve one's level of aerobic endurance.

Movement Experiences

Partner Tag. One player chases another until tagged; then they reverse.

Monster Tag. The entire group runs, trying to escape the "monster." The monster tries to tag someone. When tagged, that person immediately becomes the monster. Keep groups small, and do not permit "tag backs."

Shadow. One player attempts to get away from another by running, dodging, and feinting. The partner attempts to be a "shadow" by staying directly behind.

Shipwreck. The play area is marked off as the bow, stern, port, and starboard of a ship. The leader calls out a part of the ship, and the children run to that area. If desired, score may be kept by awarding a point to the first one there.

TABLE 43.1 Selected Aerobic Activities

Aerobic Activities	Suggested Progression for Children			
	Beginning Level	Intermediate Level	Advanced Level	Page
Partner Tag	X			573
Monster Tag	X			573
Shadow	X			573
Shipwreck	X			573
Rabbit and Turtle	X			573
Freeze and Melt	X			574
Red, White, Blue	X			574
Circle Chase		X		574
Circle Change		X		574
Beanbag Drop		X		574
Line Touch		X		574
Rhythmical Running		X		574
Rhythmical Rope Jumping		X		574
Aerobic Rhythm Exercise		X		574
Hit the Deck			X	574
Capture the Flag			X	574
Take the Point			X	574
Run for Distance			X	574
Run for Time			X	574

Rabbit and Turtle. Leader tells a story about the rabbit and the turtle. Every time the word *rabbit* is mentioned, the players run in place as fast as they can. Every time *turtle* is mentioned, they run slowly in place.

Freeze and Melt. Players run around the perimeter of the gymnasium or the play area. Each time the leader says "Freeze," they stop in their tracks and hold a motionless position until they hear the leader say "Melt."

Red, White, Blue. From a large circle formation, children are counted off into the colors red, white, and blue. All sit down except one color. All the children who are this color take two giant steps back and face in one direction. On the signal "Go," runners try to get around the circle as many times as they can in a designated time. Repeat with each color.

Circle Chase. From a large circle formation, count off by three's. All groups sit except one. They run around the circle, trying to tag the person in front of them. If they get tagged, they keep running and trying to tag the next person in front. Repeat with all members.

Circle Change. From a large circle formation, count off by three's. All groups are seated except one. They run around the circle as fast as they can, changing direction each time the leader says "Change." Allow one to two minutes for each group.

Beanbag Drop. Hoops arranged in a large circle around the gym or play area. One partner sits in the hoop; the other serves as the runner. Runners run around the area as fast as possible, picking up a beanbag (or other suitable object) from a central location. They continue around the circle and drop it in their hoop. Leader calls "Halt" after one to two minutes or when all the beanbag have been taken. The group with the most beanbags in their hoop is the winner. The activity is repeated in the opposite manner with the second person returning beanbags to the central location.

Line Touch. Five or more parallel lines are drawn five meters apart, with the players lined up on the first line. On the signal "Go," they run and touch line 2 and return to line 1, then up to line 3, back to line 1, then up to line 4 and back to line 1, and so forth. Repeat the opposite way.

Rhythmical Running. Players run around the gymnasium or play area. The leader calls out "Fast," "Medium," or "Slow." Runners change speeds on each command.

Rhythmical Rope Jumping. Each child has an individual jump rope. Players jump rope for increasing lengths of time. Musical accompaniment serves as a great motivator. Develop jump-rope routines. Jump with a partner. Vary the routines.

Aerobic Rhythm Exercise. Perform a variety of stretching, and in-place running activities to music. Gradually increase the tempo of the music and the length of the exercise session.

Hit the Deck. Players face the leader, running in place. Leader calls out the following commands and the players perform: (1) "Run in slow motion" (in place), (2) "Double time," (3) "Hit the deck" (down on the floor on the stomach), (4) "On your back," (5) "Back to your feet," (6) "Slap your thighs" (high knee running with hands slapping the thighs). Repeat several times.

Capture the Flag. The class is divided into two teams. All children have a flag tucked loosely into their belt or waist. Flags may be made from strips of cloth. The object of the game is to steal flags from the opposing team. When a flag is stolen, it is placed at one end of the gymnasium and the person losing it becomes a prisoner. To get the flag back, the player must do a specified activity (such as 20 jumping jacks or a seal crawl the length of the room). Once the Flag is retrieved, the person can again try to capture other flags.

Take the Point. Children are in a group of four to six, jogging single file around the gymnasium or play area. On the teacher's signal, the end runner must overtake the lead runner and become the "point" person. Jogging continues until each have had a chance to run the point position.

Run for Distance. Using a running course set up in the gymnasium or on the play field, children run around the course as often as possible in a specified time. Gradually increase the time as endurance increases.

Run for Time. The children run a specified distance in as short a time as possible. Gradually increase the distance as endurance increases.

MUSCULAR STRENGTH/ENDURANCE ACTIVITIES

Muscular strength is the maximum force that a muscle can exert in one effort. Muscular endurance refers to the ability to sustain effort over time against a submaximal load. Both muscular strength and muscular endurance are important aspects of the fitness training program. They are closely related and are improved in elementary school-age children primarily through *conditioning exercises* and *combative activities*.

Conditioning exercises are familiar to most people. They are repetitive exercises such as situps, pushups, and jumping jacks. They can be performed without equipment and either alone or with a group. Mass conditioning has received renewed interest among many with the surge of popularity in exercising to music. This concept should be kept in mind when using conditioning exercises with children. Introduction of a rhythmic component plus the fast-paced change from exercise to exercise tends to heighten interest and encourage participation. Also, the use of a timed-circuit or station approach to conditioning exercises is recommended. Movement from station to station and achievement of specific *individual* goals for each exercise frequently heightens interest in conditioning activities. Table 43.2 provides several exercises that can be engaged in by children at the beginning, intermediate, and advanced levels of developing their muscular strength and endurance.

Combatives are a second form of muscular strength and endurance training enjoyed by elementary school children. They pit one child against another of similar size and ability in a contest of strength or endurance. Combative contests may be used at the beginning or at the end of a class period and need not occupy more than five to ten minutes. Figure about one contest for every two minutes. A single contest may be used throughout the combative session with frequent partner changes, or several contests may be performed. The key to success in combative contests is action. Keep the contests going with as little wasted time as possible. Stress participation and giving your best effort. Do not overemphasize winning or determine a class champion. Table 43.3 lists several combative activities appropriate for children.

Objectives

1. To become knowledgeable about the differences between strength and endurance and how each is developed.
2. To know the major muscle groups of the body and how to exercise each.
3. To be able to determine one's level of strength and endurance and to make individual improvement.
4. To develop an appreciation for and desire to be involved in vigorous physical activity.

Conditioning Experiences

Seal Crawl (arms and shoulders.)   From a pushup position with the arms extended and toes pointed, drag the body forward, using only the arms.

Coffee Grinder (arms and shoulders).   From a side-support lying position with the support arm extended, walk around the support arm several times. Repeat with the opposite arm.

Spread-Eagle Walk (arms and shoulders).   From a pushup position with the arms extended and wide apart and the legs wide apart, walk forward, then back.

Bent-Knee Pushups (arms and shoulders).   From a pushup position with the knees bent and the arms extended, do pushups, bringing the nose to the surface in *front* of the hands.

Pushups (arms and shoulders).   From a pushup position, do repeated pushups, keeping the back flat and touching the chest back to the floor.

Shoulder Curl (abdominals).   From a bent-knee situp position with the arms folded across the chest, raise the head and shoulders off the surface and hold for three counts. Return and repeat several times.

Half Curl (abdominals).   Same as the shoulder curl except the upper back is raised entirely off

TABLE 43.2 Selected Conditioning Activities for Muscular Strength and Endurance

Strength/Endurance Activities	Suggested Progression for Children			
	Beginning Level	Intermediate Level	Advanced Level	Page
Arm and Shoulder Exercises				
Seal Crawl	X			575
Coffee Grinder	X			575
Spread-Eagle Walk	X			575
Bent-Knee Pushups		X	*	575
Pushups		X	*	575
Abdominal Exercises				
Shoulder Curl	X			575
Half Curl	X			575
Half V-Sits	X			576
Bent-Knee Situps		X	*	576
Alternate-Knee-Touch Situps		X	*	576
V-Sits		X	*	576
Lower Back Exercises				
Alternate Leg Lifts	X			577
Double Leg Lifts		X	*	577
Back Arch		X	*	577
Rocking Horse		X	*	577
Leg Exercises				
Rabbit Hop	X			577
Blast Off	X			577
Sprinter	X			577
Heel Lifts	X			577
Heel Drops		X	*	577
Pogo Jumps		X	*	577
Squat Thrusts		X	*	577

*These exercises may be upgraded to the advanced level by increasing repetitions and/or resistance.

the surface. Be certain that the lower back remains in solid contact with the surface. Repeat several times.

Half V-Sits (abdominals). From a sitting position on the floor with the legs straight and together and the hands supporting the hips, raise one leg and hold for three counts and return. Repeat with the opposite leg. Repeat several times.

Bent-Knee Situps (abdominals). From a bent-knee back lying position with the feet flat on the surface and the arms crossed in front of the chest or behind the head (more difficult), perform repeated sit-ups.

Alternate-Knee-Touch Situps (abdominals). From a back lying bent-knee situp position with the hands behind the head, situp and twist to one side, touching the elbow to the opposite knee.

V-Sits (abdominals). Same as the half V except both legs are raised at the same time. Repeat.

TABLE 43.3 Selected Combative Activities for Muscular Strength and Endurance

| Combative Activities | Suggested Progression for Children | | | Page |
	Beginning Level	Intermediate Level	Advanced Level	
One-Person Pull		X		578
One-Person Push		X		578
Rooster Fight		X		578
Hand Push		X		578
Hand Wrestle		X		578
Back-to-Back Tug		X		578
Knee Slap		X		578
Club Knock		X		578
Indian Wrestle			X	578
Breaking Arms			X	578
Drake Fight			X	578
Elbow Struggle			X	578
Back-to-Back Lift			X	579
Back-to-Back Push			X	579
Stepping on Toes			X	579
All-Fours Ankle Drag			X	579
Ball Wrestle			X	579
American Wrestle			X	579

Alternate Leg Lifts (lower back). From a back lying position with the legs straight and hands at the side, raise one leg at a time to a vertical position and return. Repeat several times.

Double Leg Lifts (lower back). From a back lying position, bend both knees up to the chest. Straighten overhead and slowly lower. Stress keeping the lower back flat on the floor. Repeat.

Back Arch (lower back). From a front lying position with the arms extended overhead, raise the head and legs off the ground, hold, and return. Repeat.

Rocking Horse (lower back). Same as the back arch, except the body is rocked back and forth from the arched position.

Rabbit Hop (legs). From a squat position, reach forward with the hands; kick the heels up and forward to reach the hands. Repeat the action several times.

Blast Off (legs). From a stand with the arms extended overhead and touching, count down "5,4,3,2,1," as the children gradually assume a *half* squat position. On the signal "Blast off," they spring high into the air. Repeat several times.

Sprinter (legs). From a squat position with one leg extended back and the hands placed on the surface outside the knees, alternate bringing one leg forward and then the other. Repeat rhythmically several times.

Heel Lifts (legs). From a stand, raise up on the toes as high as possible and return. Repeat several times.

Heel Drops (legs). From a standing position on the edge of a stair, block of wood, or book, drop the heels as low as possible, hold, and then slowly pushup onto the toes. Repeat several times.

Pogo Jumps (legs). From a stand with the hands laced behind the head, alternate jumping with a *half* squat, placing one foot forward and then the other.

Squat Thrusts (legs). From a standing position, squat down with the weight placed on the hands, extend the legs straight back, return to a squat, and stand. Repeat rapidly several times.

Combative Experiences

One-Person Pull (arms, shoulders).   Two contestants face each other at a distance of three feet. Establish a line ten feet in back of each contestant—that is the contestant's base line. Each contestant grasp the opponent's wrists. At the signal, each attempts to pull the opponent back across his base line.

One-Person Push (arms, shoulders).   Two contestants face each other at a distance of three feet. Establish a line ten feet in back of each contestant as his base line. Each contestant places his hands on the shoulder of the opponent. At the signal, each contestant attempts to push his opponent back across the base line. Only straight pushing is permitted.

Rooster Fight (legs).   Two contestants stand facing each other at a distance of five feet. Each stands on the right foot, clasps the left foot with the left hand, and places the right arm across the front of the body, clasping the left arm. At the signal, each contestant hops forward and attempts by, bucking or sidestepping, to overthrow the opponent or cause him to release his grasp on foot.

Hand Push (arms).   Two contestants stand toe to toe, facing each other with feet spread. They raise both hands and place them against the opponent's palms at shoulder level. At the signal, each contestant pushes against the hands of the opponent, attempting to make her step back.

Hand Wrestle (arms and legs).   Two contestants stand with their feet firmly spread in a stride position; each contestant with the right foot forward, touching the outside of the opponent's foot. Contestants grasp right hands at the signal, and each attempts, by pulling, pushing, turning, and twisting of hands, to overbalance the opponent or cause her to move either foot from its original position. Repeat with the left hand.

Back-to-Back Tug (legs and back).   Two contestants stand back to back with both arms linked at the elbows. Establish a line ten feet in front of each opponent. At a signal, each contestant attempts to drag the opponent over her base line.

Lifting and carrying of the opponent are permitted. Contestants must maintain their original position with arms linked. The contestant pulled across the opponent's base line loses.

Knee Slap (arms and legs)   (intermediate–middle school): Place two contestants in an upright "referee's position" as in wrestling. At the signal, each attempts to slap one of the opponent's knees with the right hand. The left hand remains behind the opponent's head. Keeping legs back and bending forward at the hips are the important points.

Club Knock (legs, arms).   Set an Indian club or potato-chip can on end. Two contestants face each other on opposite sides of the club, each holding the other by both shoulders. At the signal, each attempts to force the other to knock over the club. Pulling, pushing, twisting, and turning may be used. Hands must remain on the opponent's shoulders at all times.

Indian Wrestle (legs).   Two contestants lie side by side on their backs with their heads in opposite directions (each contestant's head is resting at a point just opposite the opponent's buttocks). Contestants place inside arms straight down by their side on the opponent's shoulder. Opponents place outside hands on their hips. At the count of three, each contestant lifts the inside leg, with the leg stiff, to a point just above the vertical, 'hooks ankles with the opponent,' and attempts to roll the opponent over backward. Repeat with the other leg.

Breaking Arms (arms and shoulders).   Two contestants face each other on their knees on a mat at a distance of three feet. Each contestant makes a circle with her arms, each clasping her own hands within the circle created by the opponent (the arms link together like the links of a chain). At a signal, each attempts to break the opponent's linked arms. Twisting, jerking, pulling, turning, and other tactics that do not involve bodily har, are permissible.

Drake Fight (legs).   Two contestants face each other at a distance of four feet. Each leans forward and grasps one of his own ankles with both hands. At a signal, each moves forward and, by butting, shouldering, and sidestepping, attempts to cause the other person to release one or both hands.

Elbow Struggle (arms).   Two contestants lie on

their stomachs, facing each other. They place right elbows on the mat surface so that the points of the elbow touch and clasp hands. On a signal, each contestant attempts to force his opponent's hand to the side. The elbow must keep contact with the surface in their original position throughout the contest. The person forced to touch the back of her hand on the floor loses. Repeat with opposite arms.

Back-to-Back Lift (lower back). Place two contestants standing back to back with elbows linked. At a signal, each one, by pulling and bending forward, attempts to lift the other off the floor. The contestant lifted off the floor loses the bout. Do not permit students to pull each other over their shoulders.

Back-to-Back Push (legs and back). Two contestants stand back to back with elbows linked. Establish a line ten feet in front of each contestant. At a signal, each, by pushing backward, attempts to push the other over the line.

Stepping on Toes (legs). Two contestants face each other at a distance of four feet. At the signal, each attempts, through quick stepping and jumping, to step on the toes of the opponent's feet. The hands should be clasped behind the back throughout the contest and not used.

All-Fours Ankle Drag (arms, abdominals, legs). Two contestants face in opposite directions in a hands-and-knees position on a mat. Their bodies should be side by side with the right sides touching. Each grasps the right ankle of the opponent. At the signal, each contestant attempts to drag the opponent over the line ten feet in front. Contestants must remain on all fours throughout the contest.

Ball Wrestle (arms, abdominals). Two contestants face each other at a distance of three feet in a kneeling position on a mat. They wrap both arms around a playground ball. At the signal, each attempts to take the ball away from the other. In attempting to secure the ball, no part of the body may touch the ball.

American Wrestle (legs, arms). Contestants stand facing each other on a mat with their chests touching. Each places his left arm over the opponent's shoulder and his right arm about the opponent's waist, clasping his two hands behind the opponent's back. At a signal, the contestants attempt to get in back of their opponent

with the arms encircling the opponent's waist. After the signal has been given, the original hold may be broken. The contestant who secures the opponent around the waist from behind, whether standing, sitting, lying, or kneeling, wins.

FLEXIBILITY ACTIVITIES

Flexibility refers to the range of motion of a joint. Although children are generally thought to be flexible, research clearly indicates that flexiibility is related to the type and amount of physical activity engaged in by the individual. Joint flexibility diminishes without sufficient stretching and suppling activities. The activities that follow are designed to maintain and improve flexibility in the back and trunk, the upper arms and shoulders, and the lower limbs. These activities should be performed in a static manner; that is, passive stretch should be placed on the muscles rather than the ballistic action of dynamic stretching. Table 43.4 lists a recommended progression of stretching experiences for children at the beginning, intermediate, and advanced levels of joint flexibility. Each activity will contribute to improved flexibility if properly and regularly performed.

Objectives

1. To become knowledgeable about the importance of flexibility.
2. To know how to maintain and improve flexibility at a joint.
3. To take part in a variety of static stretching activities.
4. To improve flexibility in the back and trunk, upper arms and shoulders, and upper and lower leg.

Movement Experiences

Side Stretch (back and trunk). Standing with the feet spread, bend at the waist slowly to one side and hold. Repeat to the opposite side. Hold-

TABLES 43.4 Selected Activities for Improving Flexibility

Flexibility Activities	Suggested Progression for Children			
	Beginning Level	Intermediate Level	Advanced Level	Page
Back and Trunk Stretching				
Side Stretch	X			579
Windshield Wiper	X			580
Trunk Circles	X			580
Knee Lifts		X		580
Ankle Pull		X		580
Bicycle		X		580
Knee Arch			X	580
Drawbridge			X	580
Willow Bend			X	580
Arm and Shoulder Stretching				
Arm Circles	X			581
Star Burst	X			581
Giraffe		X		581
Chicken Hawk		X		581
Greet Yourself			X	581
Towel Stretch			X	581
Towel Dislocate			X	581
Leg Stretching				
Toe-Toucher	X			581
Straddle Stretch		X		581
Center Stretch			X	581
Fencer's Lunge		X		581
Heel Drop			X	581
Heel Stretch		X		581
Angle Circles			X	581

ing a hoop, rope, or wand overhead aids in performance. Repeat.

Windshield Wiper (back and trunk). From a standing position with the feet spread and arms out from the side, twist first in one direction *slowly* as far as possible without moving the feet, then twist in the opposite direction. Repeat.

Trunk Circles (back and trunk). From a stand with hands on the hips, bend forward, sideways, and backward at the waist in a circular motion.

Knee Lifts (back and trunk). From a stand, bring one knee up and pull to the chest with both arms; stretch and hold. Repeat with the other leg.

Ankle Pull (back and trunk). From a stand with

the feet together, bend forward at the waist as far as possible while keeping the legs straight and grasping the ankles. Hold for four counts and return slowly to an upright position. Repeat several times.

Bicycle (back and trunk). From a back lying position, extend the hips upward and pretend to peddle a bicycle with the legs.

Knee Arch (back and trunk). From a kneeling position on a mat, arch back and hold. Repeat.

Drawbridge (back and trunk). From a kneeling position on a mat arch back and hold. Repeat.

Willow Bend (back and trunk). From a kneeling position on one knee with the other extended to the side, bend to the extended side at the waist and hold. Repeat to the other side.

Arm Circles (arms and shoulders). From a standing position with the arms out from the sides, make small circular motions, first in one direction, then in the other.

Star Burst (arms and shoulders). From a stand with the hands clasped, keep the arms and body straight and raise the arms. Slowly release and push them back past the head.

Giraffe (arms and shoulders). From a stand with the hands clasped behind the back, bend forward at the waist while raising the arms to a vertical postition and hold.

Chicken Hawk (arms and shoulders). From a stand or seat with the hands clasped behind the neck, press the elbows back and hold. Repeat.

Greet Yourself (arms and shoulders). From a stand, try to clasp hands behind the back by putting one arm over the shoulder and bending the opposite behind the back. Stretch and hold.

Towel Stretch (arms and shoulders). From a stand with the arms grasping a towel or rope overhead about shoulder width apart, pull out ward on the towel and stretch the arms back. Hold and repeat.

Towel Dislocate (arms and shoulders). From a stand with the arms greater than shoulder width apart, and grasping a towel or rope overhead, try to bring the towel down behind you without bending the elbows. The wider the grip, the easier the exercise. Repeat.

Toe-Toucher (upper leg). From a stand with the feet crossed, bend forward slowly at the waist and try to touch the toes. Bend as low as possible without bending at the knees. Hold.

Straddle Stretch (upper leg). From a sitting position with the legs spread and the toes facing skyward, bend forward at the waist, grasp one leg, and try to pull the chin to one knee. Hold for several seconds. Repeat to the other leg.

Center Stretch (upper leg). Same position as the straddle stretch except that the pull is toward the center while grasping both ankles at the same time. Bend, stretch, and hold.

Fencer's Lunge (upper leg). From a fencer's on-guard position, lunge forward, stretch, and hold. Repeat in the opposite direction.

Heel Drop (lower leg). Stand on the edge of a step or object four to six inches high. Drop the heels over the edge and hold.

Heel Stretch (lower leg). From a feet-together standing position about three feet from a wall, lean forward to a bent-arm position against the wall, stretching the lower calf and ankles.

Ankle Circles (lower leg). From a sitting position, grasp one ankle and slowly rotate it, first in one direction, then in the other.

SUGGESTED READING

Cook, B., and Stewart, G. W. (1981). *Get strong.* Santa Barbara, CA: 3S Fitness Group.

Corbin, C. B., and Lindsey, R. (1983). *Fitness for life.* Glenview, IL: Scott, Foresman.

Jackson, D. (1981). *Stretching for athletics.* West Point, NY: Leisure Press.

Kuntzleman, C. T. (1979). *Fitness for children.* Spring Arbor, MI: Arbor Press.

Kuntzleman, C. T., et al. (1982). *Aerobics with fun.* Spring Arbor, MI: Arbor Press.

Main, S., Stewart, G. W., and Bradshaw, R. (1984). *Fit all over.* Santa Barbara, CA: 3S Fitness Group.

Petray, Claryr K., and Blazer, Sandra L. (1986). *Health related physical fitness: Concepts and activities for elementary school children,* Edna, MN: Bellwether Press.

Priest, L. (1981). *Teach for fitness: A manual of teaching fitness concepts for K–12 physical education.* Washington, DC: ERIC Clearinghouse on Teacher Education.

Stewart, G. W., and Faulkner, R. A. (1984). *Bend and stretch.* Santa Barbara, CA: 3S Fitness Group.

Stillwell, J. L. and Stockard, J. R. (1983). *Fitness exercises for children.* West Point, NY: Leisure Press.

Westcott, W. L. (1983). *Strength fitness.* Boston: Allyn and Bacon.

APPENDIXES

APPENDIX A: SUGGESTED GYMNASIUM LAYOUT*

The purpose of this gymnasium design is to provide a space that is useful for elementary age students in which the instructor can quickly and easily organize skills and activities. The areas should be brightly colored, attractive, and stimulate children's interest. Suggestions follow:

1. Divide the gymnasium into 32 (or more) equal areas with brightly colored lines and spots in the middle of each area. Assign each student an area ("self space") at the beginning of the year. This enables the instructor to learn names easier and faster and lets you know quickly who is or isn't in class. The individual spaces also enable you to quickly organize the class into groups in many different ways, or to work on individual skills in one's self-space.

2. Make the circle in the middle of the floor larger than the normal basketball jump circle in order to enable you to accommodate more students in circle activities or movement skills in which a large circle is needed.

3. Make the basketball free throw lines 3 feet shorter than normal. Place baskets at the ends of the gymnasium and on the side walls.

4. Paint bowling pin spots on the floor for easy and quick set up.

5. Paint baselines for an easily recognizable softball teaching station. Also, paint double lines under the basket as soccer goal markings.

*Courtesy of Bob Johnson, Independent School District 181, Brainerd, MN.

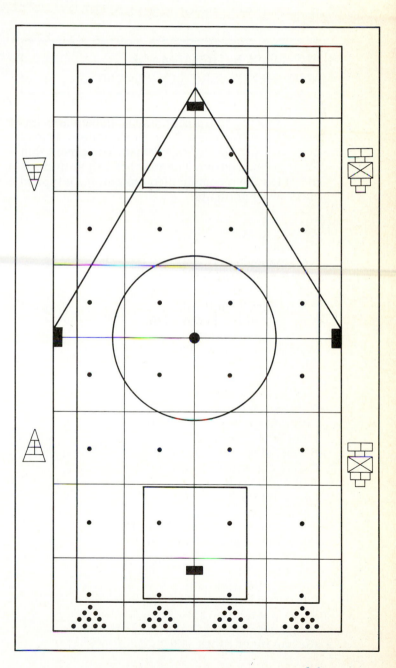

6. Volleyball spaces can easily set up with spaces of their own for play.
7. Paint shuffle board and hop-scotch diagrams on the sides of gymnasium.
8. Paint creatures on the basketball backboards with their eyes becoming the target for basket shooting.
9. Locate brightly colored targets on the side walls.
10. Place bulletin boards and wall charts close to entrances and exits.

APPENDIX B: HOMEMADE AND INEXPENSIVE EQUIPMENT

The following equipment may be homemade, improvised, or purchased for a few dollars. It may be effectively used to *supplement* equipment that must be purchased. The number in parenthesis indicates the recommended amount for a typical class of 30 students.

Beanbags   (30)
Yarn balls   (30)
Newspaper balls   (30)
Coat hanger paddles   (30)
Balloons   (30)
Broomstick wands   (30)
Surgical tubing hoops   (30)
Carpet squares   (30)
Plastic jug scoops   (30)
Rhythm sticks   (60)
Balance blocks   (30)
Streamers   (30)
Rhythm instruments   (30)
Individual jump ropes   (30)
Long jump ropes   (5)
Elastic stretch ropes   (10)
Coffee can stilts   (5 sets)
Balance boards   (4)
Low balance beam   (1)
Traffic cones   (8)
Jump and crawl standards   (4 sets)
High jump standards   (3 sets)
Low hurdles   (1 set of 6)
Scooters   (8)
Automobile tires   (8)
Large truck inner tubes   (6)
Large parachute   (1)
Cargo net   (1)
Bicycle inner tubes   (8)
Jump and reach board   (1)
Tinikling poles   (6 sets)

Selected Resources for Making Homemade Equipment

Canada Mortgage and Housing Corporation. (1981). *Children's environments advisory service (CEAS) list of resource material*

Christian, Quentin, A. (1983) *The beanbag curriculum.* Byron, CA: Front Row Experiences.

Frost, Joe, L., and Klein, Barry, L. (1979). *Children's play and playgrounds.* Boston: Allyn and Bacon.

Frost, Joe, L., and Sunderlin, Sylvia. (1986). *When children play.* Wheaton, MD. Association For Childhood International.

Gallahue, David, L. (1975). *Developmental play equipment for home and school.* New York: Wiley.

Grayson, John. (1976). *Environments of musical sculpture you can build.* Vancouver: The Aesthetic Research Centre of Canada.

Hall, Tom. (1981). *Classroom made movement materials.* Byron, CA: Front Row Experiences.

Herkowitz, Jacqueline. (1984). *Developmentally engineered equipment and playgrounds in motor development during childhood and adolescence.* Jerry R. Thomas (Ed.). Minneapolis: Burgess.

Herkowitz, Jacqueline. (1986). *Playground safety.* A paper presented at the National Convention of the AAHPERD, Cincinnati, Ohio.

Hogan, Paul. (1982). *The nuts and bolts of playground construction.* West Point, NY: Leisure Press.

Mason, John. (1982). *The environment of play.* West Point, NY: Leisure Press.

Miller, Peggy L. (1972). *Creative outdoor play areas.* Englewood Cliffs, NJ: Prentice-Hall.

Moyer, Joan. (1986). *Selecting educational equipment and material for school and home.* Wheaton, MD:

Association For Childhood Education International.

Noren-Bjorn, Eva. (1982). *The impossible playground.* West Point, NY: Leisure Press.

U.S. Consumers Product Safety Commission. (1982). *A handbook for public playground safety. Volume I: General guidelines for new and existing playgrounds.* Washington, D.C.: Superintendent of Documents, U.S. Government Printing Office.

U.S. Consumers Product Safety Commission. (1982). *A handbook for public playground safety. Volume II: Technical guidelines for equipment and surfacing.* Washington, D.C.: Superintendent of Documents, U.S. Government Printing Office.

Werner, P.H., and Simmons, R.A. (1976). *Inexpensive physical education equipment for children.* Minneapolis: Burgess.

APPENDIX C: EQUIPMENT TO BE PURCHASED

The number in parentheses represents the recommended amount of equipment for a typical class of 30 students. Refer to Appendix D for a list of vendors.

I. Manipulative Equipment

Playground/utility balls   (15)
Soccer balls   (8)
Youth footballs   (8)
Volleyballs   (8)
Softballs   (8)
Super soft softballs   (8)
Nerf type balls: utility, soccer, and footballs (8 each)
Tennis balls   (15)
Whiffle balls   (8)
Beachballs   (8)
Balloons   (30)
Yarn/fluff balls   (30)
Softball bats   (4)
Plastic bats   (8)
Plastic hockey equipment   (2 sets)
Shorty tennis rackets   (15)
Paddles   (15)
Frisbee-type discs   (15)
Beanbags   (30)
Single jump ropes   (30)
Long jump ropes   (5)
Plastic hoops   (30)
Wands   (30)
Rubber horseshoes   (2 sets)
Plastic bowling pins   (24)
Plastic bowling balls   (4)
Rhythm sticks   (30 pairs)

II. Large Apparatus

Indoor climbing equipment   (1 set)
Climbing ropes   (4)
Turning bar   (1)
Chinning bar   (1)
Vaulting box   (1)
Vaulting benches   (4)
Parallel bars   (1)
Low balance beam   (1)
Walking boards   (4)
Tumbling mats   (8)

III. Miscellaneous

Parachute   (1)
Cage ball   (1)
Low stilts   (4 sets)
Catchers mit   (2)
Catchers mask   (2)
Air pump   (1)
Pressure gauge   (1)
Stop watches   (4)
Pinnies   (4 sets)
Ball bags   (6)
Floor tape   (6 rolls)
Chalkboard   (1)
Bulletin boards   (2)

Record/cassette player   (1)   Tinikling poles   (6 sets)
Rhythm records/cassettes   Ball repair kit   (1)
Road cones   (8)   100-foot Measuring Tape   (1)
Tambourine   (1)   Ball cart   (1)

APPENDIX D: VENDORS

I. Gymnasium and Playground Equipment

Cosom Equipment Corp.   Plastic and foam equipment
P.O. Box 1426
Minneapolis, MN 55440
(612) 540-0511

Flaghouse   General equipment sales
18 W. 18th Street
New York, NY 10011
(212) 989-9700

GSC Athletic Equipment   General equipment sales
600 N. Pacific Avenue
San Pedro, CA 90733
(213) 831-0131

J.E. Gregory, Inc.   General equipment sales
P.O. Box 3483
Spokane, WA 92220
(509) 838-8333

Kenko Sports Inc.   Indoor balls
242 E. Route 109
Farmingdale, NY 11735
(516) 293-2277

Laurentian Gymnastic Industries, Ltd. Indoor climbing equipment
15 Melanie Drive
Brampton, Ontario L6T 4K8 Canada
(416) 791-5757

Nissen Corp.   Gymnastic equipment, mats
930 27th Avenue, SW
Cedar Rapids, IA 52406
(319) 365-7561

Passon's Sports   General equipment sales
1017 Arch Street
Philadelphia, PA 19107
(215) 925-7557

Porter Athletic Equipment   Gymnastic equipment
9555 Irving Park Road
Schiller Park, IL 60176
(312) 671-0110

R. W. Whittle, Ltd.   Indoor climbing equipment
P. V. Works
Monton, Eccles
Manchester, England

Shield Manufacturing   Plastic and foam equipment
425 Fillmore Avenue
Tonawanda, NY 14150
(800) 828-7669

Sportime   General equipment sales
2905 Amwiler Road
Atlanta, GA 30360
(404) 449-5700

Tachikara   Balls
Arch Billmire Co.
P.O. Box 1650
Sparks, NV 89431
(702) 359-1800

Things From Bell, Inc.   General equipment sales
4 Lincoln Avenue
P.O. Box 706
Cortland, NY 13045
(607) 753-8291

UCS Incorporated   Mats and developmental equipment
155 State Street
Hackensack, NJ 07601
(201) 343-6550

Voit Rubber Corporation   Balls
3801 S. Harbor Blvd.
Santa Ana, CA 92704

Wolverine Sports   General equipment sales
745 Circle
Box 1941
Ann Arbor, MI 48106
(313) 761-5690

II. Playground Equipment

Game Time
P.O. Box 21
Fort Payne, AL 35967
(205) 845-5610

Metal and wood

Miracle Recreation Equipment Co.
P.O. Box 275
Grinnell, IA 50112
(515) 236-7536

Metal and wood

Big Toys
2601 South Hood St.
Tacoma, WA 98409
1-800-426-9788

Wood

Recreation Equipment Co.
724 West Eighth St.
P.O. Box 2188, Dept. #38
Anderson, IN 46018-2188
(317) 643-5315

Metal

Delmer Harris Co.
P.O. Box 288, Dept. J
Concordia, KS 66901
(913) 243-3321

Metal

Playworld Systems
P.O. Box 227
New Berlin, PA 17855
(717) 966-1015

Metal and wood

Iron Mountain Forge
P.O. Box 897
One Landrum Circle
Farmington, MO 63640
(314) 756-4591

Metal with wood

Interplay
c/o Columbia Cascade Timber Co.
1975 S. W. Fifth Avenue
Portland, OR 97201
(503) 223-1157

Wood

Creative Play Systems
4320 E. 63rd Drive, RR 24
Terre Haute, IN 47802
(812) 299-4341

Wood

The Wooden Works
P.O. Box 20574
Indianapolis, IN 46220
(317) 923-1600

Wood

III. Preschool Equipment

Lakeshore Curriculum Materials Co.
2695 E. Dominguez St.
P.O. Box 6261
Carson, CA 90749
(213) 537-8600

Fine and gross motor equipment

Mosier Materials, Inc.
61328 Yakwahtin Court
Benin, OR 97702
(503) 388-4494

Gross and fine motor equipment

Growing Child
22 North Second Street
P.O. Box 620
Lafayette, IN 47902
(317) 423-2627

Fine motor toys

Front Row Experiences
540 Discovery Bay Blvd.
Byron, CA 94514
(415) 634-5710

Gross motor and educational play equipment, fine
motor puzzles and games

Discovery Toys
400 Ellinwood Way, Suite 300
Pleasant Hill, CA 94523
(415) 680-8697

Fine and gross motor toys

Beckley Cardy
229 S. Alex Road
Dayton, OH 45449
(513) 866-0761

Plastic portable playground equipment

North American Learning and Leisure
P.O. Box 430
F. H. Station
New Haven, CT 66513
(203) 787-9430

Fine and gross motor equipment

The Judy Company
4325 Hiawatha Avenue, South
Minneapolis, MN 55406
(612) 721-5761

Fine motor puzzles and games

Angeles Toys, Inc.   Riding toys
8106 Allport Avenue
Santa Fe Springs, CA 90670
(213) 693-8510

APPENDIX E: FREE AND INEXPENSIVE MATERIALS

Creative Critters   Puppets
Box 448
Eureka Springs, AR 72632
(501) 253-8053

Marine Corps League   Children's physical fitness test, ages 8-18 (free)
"Physical Fitness Program"
939 N. Kenmore Street
Arlington, VA 22201
(703) 524-1137

Kellog Company   Spirit masters, puzzles, games, and nutritional
"Project Nutrition"   unit plans
P.O. Box 9113
St. Paul, MN 55191

Kellog Company   Activities, teacher's guide, transparancies, and
"Kellog's Fitness Focus"   spirit masters for grades 5–9
P.O. Box 5012
Kalamazoo, MI 49003

Kellogg Company   Lesson plans, spirit masters, games, posters for
"Kellog's Energize at Sunrise"   Grades K–3
P.O. Box 5012
Kalamazoo, MI 49003

Nabisco Brands, Inc.   Spirit masters, activities for family and com-
"Family in Training Leader's Guide"   munity fitness programs
AAU House
3400 West 86th Street
Indianapolis, IN 46268

Amateur Athletic Union   Children's fitness test, ages 6–17 (free)
"AAU Physical Fitness Program"
160 HPER Building
Bloomington, IN 47405
(812) 335-2059

National Dairy Council
6820 Hawthorn Park Drive
Indianapolis, IN
(317) 842-3060

Booklets, resource guides, teaching materials, and posters

American Cancer Society
"ABC's Health Network" (grades 4–6) and
"Your Body and You" (grades K–3)
2421 Willowbrook Parkway
Indianapolis, IN
(317) 257-7121

Educational kits with activities, filmstrips, and planning guides

AAHPERD
American Alliance Publications
P.O. Box 704
Waldorf, MD 20601

Outstanding source of several publications and current resources: the AAHPERD Youth Fitness Test and the AAHPERD Health-related Physical Fitness Test

Eric Clearinghouse on Teacher Education
"Teach for Fitness: A Manual for Teaching Fitness Concepts for Physical Education"
Publication Sales
One Dupont Circle, Suite 610
Washington, DC 20036

Activities covering specified fitness concepts

U.S. Government Printing Office
"Promoting Health/Preventing Disease: Objectives for the Nation"
Superintendent of Documents
Washington, DC 20402

Books
Stock # - 017-001-004359

Shawnee Mission Public Schools
"Sunflower Project"
Mohawk Instructional Center
6649 Lamar
Shawnee Mission, KS 66202

Educational materials

Chicago Heart Health Curriculum Program
Chicago Heart Association
20 North Wacker Drive
Chicago, IL 60606

Fitness literature

American Health Foundation
"Know Your Body"
320 East 43rd Street
New York, NY 10017

Fitness literature

The President's Council on Physical Fitness and Sports
450 Fifth Street, NW
Room 7103
Washington, DC 20001

Fitness literature

"Participation"
80 Richmond Street, NW
Suite 805
Vanier, Ontario K1L 8B9, Canada
(613) 746-7740

Literature on the Canadian movement for personal fitness

Canadian Public Health Association
1335 Carling Avenue
Suite 210
Ottawa, Ontario K1Z 8N8, Canada
(613) 725-3769

Health and fitness literature

Canada Fitness Survey
506-294 Albert Street
Ottawa, Ontario K1P 6E6, Canada

Report on fitness and lifestyle in Canada

Special Educators Press
P.O. Box 24240
Los Angeles, CA 90024
(213) 474-5175

Key resources for the handicapped

Campbell Soup Co.
Campbell's Institute For Health & Fitness
Campbell Place
Camden, NJ 08101-2499

Publisher
Turnaround Times
Fitnessgram®
free individual computer fitness report
the AAHPERD Youth Fitness Test (free)

3S Fitness Group
P.O. Box 705
Santa Barbara, CA 93102
(805) 969-4004

Wall charts and posters

McDonald's Corporation
Consumer Affairs Dept.
McDonald's Plaza
Oakbrook, IL 60521
(312) 887-6198

"Action Packet"™ and films

National Geographic
Educational Services
Dept. 86
Washington, DC 20036
(301) 921-1330

Maps, charts, posters, books

American Red Cross
Audio-Visual Loan Library
5816 Seminary Road
Falls Church, VA 22041
(703) 379-8160

Videos on first aid, CPR, blood education, and self growth

AAHPERD
Fitting In
1900 Association Drive
Reston, VA 22091
(703) 476-3432

Children's fitness newsletter for 5th and 6th Grades

AAHPERD
"Jump Rope for Heart"
1900 Association Drive
Reston, VA 22091
(703) 476-3488

Educational and fund raising programs

APPENDIX F: PROGRAM APPRAISAL CHECKLIST FOR ELEMENTARY SCHOOL PHYSICAL EDUCATION PROGRAMS*

A Project of:

- Council On Physical Education for Children (COPEC)
- National Association for Sport and Physical Education (NASPE)
- American Alliance for Health, Physical Education, Recreation and Dance (AAHPERD)

Program Appraisal Checklist for Elementary School Physical Education Programs

Physical education is an integral part of the total educational process. It makes unique contributions to the growth and motor development of children. To become skillful movers, children need a variety of opportunities for practice, positive encouragement, and quality instruction. In order to help achieve this important objective, the essential characteristics of a quality elementary physical education program must be identified. The Program Appraisal Checklist provides such a measuring device, and may be used on the AAHPERD position paper entitled, "Essentials of a Quality Elementary School Physical Education Program," and is composed of 98 items divided into seven categories.

How to Administer
Evaluative criteria are presented in the form of positive statements describing attributes that are considered highly desirable. The evaluator should carefully read each statement and determine as objectively as possible the extent to which he/she believes that the statement describes the school's program. This extent is indicated by circling:

A—Excellent
B—Adequate
C—Undecided
D—Disagree
E—No basis for evaluation

- A rating of "A" for an item suggests that the stated attribute of the school's program is in *consistent agreement* with what actually is present in the physical education program.
- A rating of "B" indicates that the item is *generally in agreement* but that there may be need for improvement in this area.
- A rating of "C" indicates that the evaluator is *undecided* whether the item describes the program or not.

*Used with permission.

- A rating of "D" indicates that the evaluator *definitely disagrees* that the item describes what actually is present in the physical education program and there is a definite need for improvement in this area.
- A rating of "E" indicates that the evaluator has *no basis for evaluation.*

How to Use

The completed checklist may be used to identify specific areas of the program that need improvement, and for the on-going assessment and improvement of the total physical education program. More specifically it may be effectively used as:

1. An informal self-assessment guide by the instructor.
2. An informal program assessment guide by the school principal.
3. A conference guide between the teacher and principal.

I. The Teacher

The Teacher Is the Key Element in any Successful Educational Endeavor. The Teacher In Charge of the Physical Education Program:

1. works effectively with children.	A	B	C	D	E
2. is an involved contributing member of the school.	A	B	C	D	E
3. works effectively with other teachers, administrators, and parents.	A	B	C	D	E
4. establishes and maintains positive pupil–teacher relationships.	A	B	C	D	E
5. makes a consistent effort to interpret the program to the public.	A	B	C	D	E
6. motivates students by her/his own enthusiasm.	A	B	C	D	E
7. sets a positive example of personal fitness and health habits.	A	B	C	D	E
8. integrates knowledge of human movement, child development, and current learning theories.	A	B	C	D	E
9. is knowledgeable in the area of child growth and motor development.	A	B	C	D	E
10. is knowledgeable about the structure and function of human movement.	A	B	C	D	E
11. is competent in the observation and assessment of children's movement.	A	B	C	D	E
12. is knowledgeable about learning processes, teaching strategies, and factors that affect movement skill learning.	A	B	C	D	E
13. participates in curricular development.	A	B	C	D	E
14. plans effectively for daily instruction.	A	B	C	D	E
15. has clearly stated objectives.	A	B	C	D	E
16. plans adequately for inclement weather.	A	B	C	D	E
17. is capable of assessing and working with children who have special needs.	A	B	C	D	E
18. is skilled in meeting the needs and interests of children as individuals.	A	B	C	D	E
19. takes adequate safety precautions.	A	B	C	D	E
20. is able to modify lesson content as needed.	A	B	C	D	E
21. provides maximum opportunities for active learning time by all.	A	B	C	D	E

22. effectively utilizes a variety of teaching strategies and methods.   A   B   C   D   E
23. maintains an environment in which children are consistently challenged to become skillful movers.   A   B   C   D   E

II. Staff Development

The Continual Development of Staff Is Crucial to Maintaining Up-To-Date Dynamic Educational Programs. The Teacher In Charge of the Physical Education Program:

24. is specifically trained to teach in the area of elementary school physical education.   A   B   C   D   E
25. takes advantage of staff development opportunities offered through inservice training, professional workshops, conferences, and university courses.   A   B   C   D   E
26. participates in professional organizations at the local, state, and national level.   A   B   C   D   E
27. utilizes up-to-date resource materials to enhance knowledge and aid in program planning.   A   B   C   D   E
29. is given release time for attending professional meetings.   A   B   C   D   E
30. has a local supervisor or other resource person regularly available as a consultant.   A   B   C   D   E

III. The Instructional Program

All Educational Programs Should Be Designed to Help Each Child Become a More Self-Directed, Self-Reliant, and Fully Functioning Individual. The Physical Education Program:

31. is an integral part of, and consistent with, the total educational philosophy of the school.   A   B   C   D   E
32. serves the divergent needs of all children whether gifted, average, slow learners, or handicapped.   A   B   C   D   E
33. is based on an established written curriculum.   A   B   C   D   E
34. is of sufficient breadth and depth to be challenging to all.   A   B   C   D   E
35. is developmentally based and progressively sequenced from year to year.   A   B   C   D   E
36. is regularly updated and revised.   A   B   C   D   E
37. has well-defined objectives for progressive learning.   A   B   C   D   E
38. is built around the development of efficient, effective, and expressive movement abilities.   A   B   C   D   E
39. provides opportunities for the development of fundamental movement patterns and specific movement skills.   A   B   C   D   E
40. encourages children in the development of physical fitness.   A   B   C   D   E
41. provides opportunities for children to enhance their *abilities* in games/sports, dance, and gymnastics.   A   B   C   D   E
42. provides opportunities for children to enhance their *knowledge and understanding* of games/sports, dance, and gymnastics.   A   B   C   D   E

43. instills a positive regard for safety.   A   B   C   D   E
44. fosters creativity.   A   B   C   D   E
45. promotes self-understanding and acceptance.   A   B   C   D   E
46. promotes positive social interaction and self-control.   A   B   C   D   E
47. recognizes and provides for learning enjoyment (fun).   A   B   C   D   E
48. strives for a healthy balance between cooperation and competition.   A   B   C   D   E

IV. Program Evaluation

Evaluation Is a Key Aspect of the Teaching/Learning/Assessment Triad. The Teacher In Charge of the Physical Education Program:

49. utilizes assessment as a continuous aspect of the program.   A   B   C   D   E
50. assesses individual student progress toward achieving program objectives. A   B   C   D   E
51. utilizes assessment as a means of improving teaching.   A   B   C   D   E
52. utilizes assessment as one means of describing the program to parents. A   B   C   D   E
53. uses assessment as a means of motivating children to self-improvement. A   B   C   D   E
54. refrains from being overly concerned about the child's rank in relation to others and national norms. A   B   C   D   E
55. objectively assesses children's movement and skill development.   A   B   C   D   E
56. objectively assesses children's physical fitness.   A   B   C   D   E
57. makes provisions for periodic evaluation of the total physical education program by other teachers, administrators, and children. A   B   C   D   E

V. Organization/Administration

Proper Organization and Administration Is Crucial to the Success of Any Educational Endeavor. The Physical Education Program:

58. provides for a minimum of 120 minutes per week of instructional time in addition to time allotted for supervised play and recess. A   B   C   D   E
59. provides at least 30 minute class periods for all grade levels.   A   B   C   D   E
60. provides for the time allocated to instruction to be exclusive of time used for dressing, showering, recess, and noon-hour activities. A   B   C   D   E
61. groups children coeducationally for instruction.   A   B   C   D   E
62. groups children for instruction to reflect special needs.   A   B   C   D   E
63. provides the physical education specialist with a daily planning period if all teachers have one. A   B   C   D   E
64. provides adequate time for travel and planning for teachers who must travel between schools. A   B   C   D   E
65. schedules primary and intermediate grade classes in teaching blocks in order to maximize teacher efficiency. A   B   C   D   E

66. requires teachers and students to be appropriately dressed for the types of activities being conducted.   A   B   C   D   E

67. has a standardized procedure for filling out and filing accident report forms.   A   B   C   D   E

68. has first aid supplies readily available.   A   B   C   D   E

69. has a qualified person readily available to administer first aid in case of injury.   A   B   C   D   E

70. requires a medical statement for students to be excused from class for an extended period of time, or to be readmitted following serious illness or injury.   A   B   C   D   E

71. provides for scheduling extra class sessions for children with special needs.   A   B   C   D   E

72. documents all quiz and testing data.   A   B   C   D   E

73. has a standard procedure for notifying teachers of a severe weather warning or other emergency situation.   A   B   C   D   E

VI. Equipment and Facilities

The Equipment and Facilities Made Available Establish the Boundries of What Can Be Accomplished in Any Education Program. In Physical Education:

74. equipment is purchased and maintained through the regular school budget.   A   B   C   D   E

75. supplies and equipment are purchased with the aid of established standards.   A   B   C   D   E

76. equipment is in ample supply for optimal learning to take place.   A   B   C   D   E

77. the teacher makes effective use of available facilities and equipment.   A   B   C   D   E

78. indoor facilities are sufficient for optimal learning to take place.   A   B   C   D   E

79. outdoor facilities are sufficient for optimal learning to take place.   A   B   C   D   E

80. all facilities are adequately maintained and promote a safe and healthful environment.   A   B   C   D   E

81. indoor and outdoor apparatus are selected for developmental values.   A   B   C   D   E

82. "All weather" outdoor surface areas are provided, properly marked, and maintained.   A   B   C   D   E

83. outdoor apparatus has appropriate landing areas in case of falls by students.   A   B   C   D   E

84. natural grassy outdoor play areas are provided and maintained.   A   B   C   D   E

85. facility planning is done in cooperation with teachers, principals, and other resource persons.   A   B   C   D   E

86. available community facilities are effectively utilized (i.e., recreation centers, parks, bowling alleys, YMCA/YWCA, etc.).   A   B   C   D   E

87. there is an established policy for the regular inspection, and repair of defective equipment and facilities.   A   B   C   D   E

88. is provided a budget for the regular purchase and maintenance of   A   B   C   D   E
equipment.

89. there is an established policy for taking inventory and ordering   A   B   C   D   E
supplies and equipment.

90. bulletin boards, charts, and other visual aids are made available   A   B   C   D   E
and used on a regular basis.

91. an office or other appropriate facility is made available to the teacher.   A   B   C   D   E

92. proper, adequate, and safe storage space is provided for all equip-   A   B   C   D   E
ment.

93. parent/teacher organizations or other groups assist in the purchase   A   B   C   D   E
of equipment from their funds.

VII. School-Related Programs

School-Related Programs Provide Enrichment Opportunities for All Students as an Extension of Physical Education. The School-Related Program:

94. provides enrichment (before school, during the noon hour, or after   A   B   C   D   E
school) for intermediate, and upper grade children who choose to
participate.

95. provides for all levels of skill within the enrichment program.   A   B   C   D   E

96. provides for variety in content and organization.   A   B   C   D   E

97. provides an intramural program during the upper elementary grades   A   B   C   D   E
for all who choose to participate.

98. provides opportunities for parents and interested community mem-   A   B   C   D   E
bers to attend an annual gym show or public demonstration.

APPENDIX G: BIBLIOGRAPHY

Motor Development

Clark, J., and Humphrey, J. (1985). *Motor development: Current selected research.* Volume I, Princeton, New Jersey: Princeton Book Company.

Corbin, C. (1980). *A textbook of motor development.* Second Edition. Dubuque, IA: Wm. C. Brown Company.

Cratty, B. (1986). *Perceptual and motor development in infants and children.* Englewood Cliffs, New Jersey: Prentice-Hall.

Espenschade, A., and Eckert, H. (1980). *Motor development.* Columbus: Charles E. Merrill.

Gallahue, D. (1982). *Understanding motor development in children.* New York: Wiley.

Haywood, K.M. (1986). *Life span motor development.* Champaign, IL: Human Kinetics.

Haywood, K., Loughrey, T., Imergoot, M., and Wilson, K. (1981). *Motor development: Basic stuff series 1.* Reston, VA: AAHPERD.

Holle, B. (1976). *Motor development in children: Normal and retarded.* Denmark: Villadsen and Christensen.

Kelso, J., and Clarke, J. (1982). *The development of movement control and coordination.* New York: Wiley.

Keough, J., and Sugden, D. (1985). *Movement skill development.* New York: Macmillan.

Malina, R. (1975). *Growth and development: The first twenty years in man.* Minneapolis, Burgess.

Morley, D., and Woodland, M. (1979). *See how they grow.* New York: Oxford University Press.

Rarick, G. (1973). *Physical activity: Human growth and development.* New York: Academic Press.

Roberton, M., and Halverson, L. (1984). *Developing children—their changing movement.* Philadelphia: Lea and Febiger.

Skinner, L. (1979). *Motor development in the preschool years.* Springfield, IL: Charles C. Thomas.

Thomas, J. (1984). *Motor development during childhood and adolescence.* Minneapolis: Burgess.

Wickstrom, R. (1983). *Fundamental motor patterns.* Philadelphia: Lea and Febiger.

Williams, H. (1983). *Perceptual and motor development.* Englewood Cliffs, N.J.: Prentice-Hall.

Zaichkowsky, L., Zaichkowsky, L., and Martinek, T. (1980). *Growth and development: The child and physical activity.* St. Louis: C.V. Mosby.

Youth Sport

Corbin, C. (1977). *The athletic snowball.* Champaign, IL: Human Kinetics.

Magill, R., Ash, M., and Smoll, F. (1982). *Children in sport.* Champaign, IL: Human Kinetics.

Martens, R. (1978). *Joy and sadness in children's sports.* Champaign, IL: Human Kinetics.

Martens, R., Christina, R., Harvey, J., and Sharkey, B. (1981). *Coaching young athletes.* Champaign, IL: Human Kinetics.

Martens, R., and Seefeldt, V. (1979). *Guidelines for children's sports.* Washington, D.C.: AAHPERD.

Paulson, W. (1980). *Coaching cooperative youth sports: A values education approach.* LaGrange, IL: Youth Sports Press.

Thomas, J. (1978). *What parents and coaches should know about youth sports.* Washington, D.C.: AAHPER.

Young Winners—Basketball. (1980). LaGrange, IL: Youth Sports Press.

Young Winners—Flag Football. (1980). LaGrange, IL: Youth Sports Press.

Young Winners—Soccer. (1980). LaGrange, IL: Youth Sports Press.

Young Winners—Softball. (1980). LaGrange, IL: Youth Sports Press.

Elementary Methods

Arnheim, D., and Pestolesi, R. (1978). *Elementary physical education.* St. Louis: C.V. Mosby.

Bucher, C., and Thaxton, N. (1979). *Physical education for children.* New York: Macmillan.

Burton, E. (1977). *The new physical education for elementary school children.* Boston: Houghton Mifflin.

Corbin, C. (1976). *Becoming physically educated in the elementary school.* Philadelphia: Lea and Febiger.

Dauer, V., and Pangrazi, R. (1986). *Dynamic physical education for elementary school children.* Minneapolis: Burgess.

Davis, R. (1979). *Elementary physical education: A systematic approach.* Winston-Salem, NC: Hunter Publishing.

Essentials of a quality elementary school physical education program. (1981). Washington, DC: AAHPERD.

Gallahue, D. (1982). *Developmental movement experiences for children.* New York: Wiley.

Gallahue, D., and Meadors, W. (1979). *Let's move.* Dubuque, IA: Kendall/Hunt.

Gallahue, D.L., Werner, P.H., and Luedke, G.C. (1975). *A conceptual approach to moving and learning.* New York: Wiley.

Graham, G., Holt, H., and Parker, M. (1987). *Children moving.* Palo Alto, CA: Mayfield.

Hall, J., Sweeny, N., and Esser, J. (1980). *Physical education in the elementary school.* Santa Monica, CA: Goodyear Publishing.

Hall, J., Sweeny, N., and Esser, J. (1979). *Until the whistle blows.* Santa Monica, CA: Goodyear Publishing.

Hoffman, H., Young, J., and Klesius, S. (1985). *Meaningful movement for children.* Dubuque, IA: Kendall/Hunt.

Kirchner, G. (1985). *Physical education for elementary school children.* Dubuque, IA: Wm. C. Brown.

Logsdon, B., Barrett, K., Broer, M., McGee, R., Ammons, M., Halverson, L., and Roberton, M. (1984). *Physical education for children: A focus on the teaching process.* Philadelphia: Lea and Febiger.

Morris, G. (1980). *Elementary physical education: Toward inclusion.* Salt Lake City: Brighton Publishing.

Nichols, B. (1986). *Moving and learning.* St. Louis: Mosby.

Schurr, E. (1980). *Movement experiences for children.* Englewood Cliffs, NJ: Prentice-Hall.

Siedentop, D., Herkowitz, J., and Rink, J. (1984). *Elementary physical education methods.* Englewood Cliffs, NJ: Prentice-Hall.

Movement Education

Barrett, K. (1965). *Exploration: A method for teaching movement.* Madison, Wisconsin: College Printing and Typing Co.

Fowler, J. (1981). *Movement education.* Philadelphia: Saunders College Publishing.

Frostig, M. (1970). *Movement education: Theory and practice.* Chicago: Follett.

Gensemer, R. (1979). *Movement education,* Washington, DC: National Education Association.

Gilliom, B. (1970). *Basic movement education for children,* Reading, MA: Addison-Wesley.

Glass, H. (1966). *Exploring movement.* New York: Educational Activities.

Hackett, L., and Jenson, R. (1966). *A guide to movement exploration.* Palo Alto, CA: Peek Publishing.

Kirchner, G., Cunningham, J., and Warrell, E. (1970). *Introduction to movement education.* Dubuque, IA: Wm. C. Brown.

Kruger, H., and Kruger J. (1977). *Movement education in physical education.* Dubuque, IA: Wm. C. Brown.

Metheny, E. (1968). *Movement and meaning.* New York: McGraw-Hill.

Morison, R. (1969). *A movement approach to educational gymnastics.* London: J.M. Dent and Sons Ltd.

Rizzitiello, T. (1977). *An annotated bibliography on movement education.* Washington, DC: AAHPER.

Stanley, S. (1969). *Physical education: A movement orientation.* Toronto: McGraw-Hill.

Sullivan, M. (1982). *Feeling strong, feeling free: Movement exploration for young children.* Washington, DC: National Association for the Education of Young Children.

Sweeney, R. (1970). *Selected readings in movement education.* Reading, MA: Addison-Wesley.

Wall, J. (1981). *Beginnings.* Toronto: McGill University Printing Service.

Williams, J. (1979). *Themes for educational gymnastics.* London: Lepus Books.

Witkin, K. (1977). *To move, to learn.* New York: Schocken Books.

Preschool Movement

Bailey, R., and Burton, E. (1982). *The dynamic self.* St. Louis: C.V. Mosby.

Block, S. (1977). *Me I'm great: Physical education for children three through eight.* Minneapolis: Burgess.

Cohen, M. (1976). *Growing free,* Washington, DC: Association for Childhood Education International.

Croft, D., and Hess, R. (1972). *An activities handbook for teachers of young children.* Boston: Houghton Mifflin.

Curtis, S. (1982). *The joy of movement in early childhood.* New York: Teachers College, Columbia University.

Dalley, M. *Moving and growing,* Ontario: The Canadian Institute of Child Health.

Fontana, D. (1978). *The education of the young child.* London: Open Books Publishing Limited.

Gallahue, D.L. (1976). *Motor development and movement experiences for young children.* New York: Wiley.

Gernsemer, R. (1979). *Movement education.* Washington, DC: National Education Association.

Gerhardt, L. (1973). *Moving and knowing.* Englewood Cliffs, NJ: Prentice-Hall.

Hagstrom, J. (1981). *More games babies play.* New York: A & W Visual Library.

Hagstrom, J., and Morrill, J. (1979). *Games babies play.* New York: A & W Visual Library.

Johnson, R. (1985). *Sticky icky movement activities.* Byron, CA: Front Row Experience.

Levy, J. (1975). *The baby exercise book.* New York: Pantheon Books.

Luke, M., and Warrell, E. (1985). *Physical Education in Early Childhood.* Vancouver: University of British Columbia.

Peck, J. (1979). *Leap to the sun.* Englewood Cliffs, NJ: Prentice-Hall.

Riggs, M. (1980). *Jump to joy.* Englewood Cliffs, NJ: Prentice-Hall.

Shank, C. (1983). *A child's way to water play.* New York: Leisure Press.

Staniford, D. (1982) *Natural movement for children,* Dubuque, IA: Kendall/Hunt.

Torbert, M. (1980). *Follow me.* Englewood Cliffs, NJ: Prentice-Hall.

Movement Activities

Brandreth, G. (1974). *Games for rains, planes and trains,* Brattleboro, VT: Stephen Greene Press.

Capon, J. (1975). *Perceptual motor development—Book 1, Book 2, Book 3, and Book 4.* Belmont, CA: Fearon-Pitman Publishers.

Capon, J. (1975). *Perceptual motor lesson plans.* Byron, CA: Front Row Experience.

Capon, J. (1981). *Successful movement challenges: Movement activities for the developing child.* Byron, CA: Front Row Experience.

Davis, R., and Isaacs, L. (1983). *Elementary physical education.* NC: Hunter Textbooks.

Farina, A. (1981). *Developmental games and rhythms for children.* Springfield, IL: Charles C Thomas.

Fleming, J. (1979). *Games (and more!) for backpackers.* Portland, OR: Victoria House.

French, R., and Horvat, M. (1983). *Parachute movement activities.* Byron, CA: Front Row Experiences.

Furst, C., and Rockefeller, M. (1981). *The effective dance program in physical education.* Nayak, NY: Parker Publishing.

Hardisty, M. (1972). *Education through the games experience.* Bellingham, Washington: Educational Designs and Consultants.

Hill, K., Lee, A., Turner, M., and Johnson, M. (1977). *Movement plus.* Dubuque, IA: Kendall/Hunt Publishing.

Humphrey, J. (1980). *Sports skills for boys and girls.* Springfield, IL: Charles C Thomas.

Joyce, M. (1980). *First steps in teaching creative dance to children.* Palo Alto, CA: Mayfield.

Joyce, M. (1984). *Dance technique for children.* Palo Alto, CA: Mayfield.

Kamii, C., and DeVries, R. (1980). *Group games in early education.* Washington, DC: The National Association for the Education of Young Children.

Lawrence, C., and Hackett, L. (1975). *Water Learning.* Palo Alto, CA: Peek Publications.

Neilson, N., Bestmann, L., and Davis, R. (1977). *Balance bend jump and hop.* San Diego: Grossmont Press.

Poley, M. (1981). *Dance aerobics.* Mountain View, CA: Anderson World.

Roddick, D. (1980). *Frisbee disc basics.* Englewood Cliffs, NJ: Prentice-Hall.

Movement Activities, Cooperative

Fluegelman, A. (1981). *More new games!.* NY: Dolphin Books/Doubleday.

Fluegelman, A. (1986). *The new games book.* NY: Dolphin Books/Doubleday.

Honig, A. (1982). *Playtime learning games for young children.* New York: Syracuse University Press.

Mauldon, E., and Redfern, H. (1981). *Games teaching.* London: MacDonald and Evans Ltd.

Michaelis, B. (1977). *Learning through non-competitive activities and play.* Palo Alto, CA: Learning Handbooks.

Morris, G. (1980). *How to change the games children play.* Minneapolis, MN: Burgess.

Orlick, T. (1978). *The cooperative sports and games book.* NY: Patheon.

Orlick, T. (1978). *Winning through cooperation.* Washington, DC: Acropolis Books.

Orlick, T., and Botterill, C. (1975). *Every kid can win.* Chicago: Nelson-Hall.

Ravielli, A. (1981). *Street games.* NY: Atheneum Publishing.

Tutko, T., and Bruns, W. (1976). *Winning is everything and other American myths.* NY: Macmillan.

Werner, P. (1979). *A movement approach to games for children.* St. Louis: Mosby.

Wood, D., and Gillis, J. (1979). *Adventure Education,* Washington DC: National Education Association.

ACTIVITIES INDEX

SKILLS INDEX

SUBJECT INDEX